The Individual in the Changing Working Life

Working life has been the subject of great change in recent years, with contemporary conditions generally providing increased opportunities and autonomy for individuals. But these benefits can coincide with greater demands and responsibilities, increasing the pressure to work outside of traditional working hours and so creating conflict between work and family life. This book contributes towards our understanding of contemporary working life, considering how recent changes have affected the work climates, attitudes, and well-being of individuals. Combining traditional theoretical frameworks with innovative new research, it discusses both the positive and negative effects contemporary working life has on organizations and employees. International experts in the fields of work and organizational psychology present strategies to prevent negative working conditions and help individuals achieve a healthy work–life balance.

KATHARINA NÄSWALL is Associate Professor of Psychology in the Department of Psychology at Stockholm University.

JOHNNY HELLGREN is Associate Professor of Psychology and Director of the undergraduate program in the Department of Psychology at Stockholm University.

MAGNUS SVERKE is Professor and Head of the Division of Work and Organizational Psychology in the Department of Psychology at Stockholm University.

The Individual in the Changing Working Life

Edited by

Katharina Näswall,

Johnny Hellgren

and

Magnus Sverke

CAMBRIDGE
UNIVERSITY PRESS

CAMBRIDGE UNIVERSITY PRESS
Cambridge, New York, Melbourne, Madrid, Cape Town, Singapore,
São Paulo, Delhi, Dubai, Tokyo, Mexico City

Cambridge University Press
The Edinburgh Building, Cambridge CB2 8RU, UK

Published in the United States of America by Cambridge University Press, New York

www.cambridge.org
Information on this title: www.cambridge.org/9780521182904

First published 2008
First paperback edition 2010

A catalogue record for this publication is available from the British Library

ISBN 978-0-521-87946-0 Hardback
ISBN 978-0-521-18290-4 Paperback

Contents

Figures

Tables

Cases

Contributors

MICHAEL ALLVIN, National Institute for Working Life, Sweden

JULIAN BARLING, Queen's University, Canada

ROLAND W. B. BLONK, TNO Work and Employment, the Netherlands

JENNIFER CARSON, Queen's University, Canada

NIK CHMIEL, Queen's University Belfast, UK

SARAH J. COTTON, University of South Australia, Australia

CHRISTOPHER J. L. CUNNINGHAM, University of Tennessee at
  Chattanooga, USA

ARLA DAY, St Mary's University, Canada

NELE DE CUYPER, K. U. Leuven, Belgium

GABRIEL M. DE LA ROSA, Bowling Green State University, USA

HANS DE WITTE, K. U. Leuven, Belgium

MAUREEN F. DOLLARD, University of South Australia, Australia

CHRISTIAN DORMANN, Johannes Gutenberg University, Germany

DANIEL G. GALLAGHER, James Madison University, USA

SABINE A. E. GEURTS, University of Nijmegen, the Netherlands

JOHNNY HELLGREN, Stockholm University, Sweden

JOSEPH J. HURRELL JR., St Mary's University, Canada

STEVE M. JEX, Bowling Green State University, USA

JAN DE JONGE, Eindhoven University of Technology, the Netherlands

E. KEVIN KELLOWAY, CN Centre for Occupational Health and Safety,
  St Mary's University, Canada

ULLA KINNUNEN, University of Tampere, Finland

MICHIEL A. J. KOMPIER, University of Nijmegen, the Netherlands

SUZANNE LAGERVELD, TNO Work and Employment, the Netherlands

PASCALE M. LE BLANC, Utrecht University and Research Institute for Psychology and Health, the Netherlands

SAIJA MAUNO, University of Jyväskylä, Finland

TUIJA MUHONEN, National Institute for Working Life, Sweden

KATHARINA NÄSWALL, Stockholm University, Sweden

WIDO G. M. OERLEMANS, Utrecht University, the Netherlands

MARIA C. W. PEETERS, Utrecht University, the Netherlands

JOSÉ M. PEIRÓ, University of Valencia and Instituto Valenciano de Investigaciones Economicas, Spain

JACO PIENAAR, North-West University, South Africa

MARISA SALANOVA, Universitat Jaume I, Spain

WILMAR B. SCHAUFELI, Utrecht University, the Netherlands

MAGNUS SVERKE, Stockholm University, Sweden

TOON W. TARIS, University of Nijmegen, the Netherlands

LOIS E. TETRICK, George Mason University, USA

MARIEKE VAN DEN TOOREN, Eindhoven University of Technology, the Netherlands

EVA TORKELSON, Lund University, Sweden

LEA WATERS, University of Melbourne, Australia

Acknowledgements

The work on this book was conducted with the financial support of grants from Alecta, from the Swedish National Institute for Working Life (NIWL) through the Joint Programme for Working Life Research in Europe (SALTSA), and from the Swedish Council for Working Life and Social Research. We also would like to thank specifically those who played important parts in the preparation and completion of the manuscript. First of all, this includes the contributors, who provided the interesting and important chapters, and Andrew Peart at Cambridge University Press who facilitated the editorial work and was accessible throughout the project. We would also like to thank David Speeckaert for his valuable contributions as language editor for much of this book.

1   The individual in the changing working life: introduction

Katharina Näswall, Johnny Hellgren, and Magnus Sverke

Working life has undergone changes since the 1990s that have entailed both threats and challenges for employees. While these transformations have resulted in advances and benefits for some employees, they have been experienced less positively by others. When examining these changes, it is therefore essential not only to focus on what has actually taken place, but also to take the perceptions of individuals into account. By expanding the knowledge of both the negative and positive aspects of working life from the individual's perspective, we can gain a better understanding of the nature of the changing working life. Such knowledge would help provide insight into individuals' reactions and also aid in determining how different aspects of working life can be dealt with in the most positive way. The purpose of this book is to provide a step in this direction by focusing on how individuals react to the salient phenomena of contemporary working life, and how organizations can provide the most beneficial environment for their employees.

Working life in transition

Observers describing the emerging working life indicate that recent decades have been marked by a number of transitions (e.g. Burke and Nelson, 1998; Tetrick and Quick, 2003). These changes include technological advances that minimize the need for manual labor, improvements in information technology that maximize the accessibility and ease of communication, and expanding globalization that has made it possible for employees from different parts of the world to call each other colleagues. The new conditions employees face have been both dreaded and welcomed, and the reactions to these circumstances are varied as well as contradictory. For example, the new technology has been hailed for its power to facilitate work and speed up work processes, as well as for its role in putting people in touch regardless of distances or location. However,

1

this ease of communication has often brought with it an increase in interruptions throughout the workday, making individuals too accessible, and making it more difficult to disengage from work when needed.

Another development is that heavy manufacturing jobs are now made easier with the help of new technology. The labor markets of industrialized countries can be characterized by a moving away from manufacturing jobs, with an increased number of jobs not being directly related to manufacturing a product, but rather to providing a service (ILO, 2006; Tetrick and Quick, 2003). At the same time, as technological advances have made jobs less labor-intensive, many employees have been made redundant, contributing to the loss of employment for large groups of people (Pfeffer, 1997). This also involves an increase in the portion of the labor force that is engaged in white-collar or professional work, as opposed to manual types of jobs. The changes in the type of work that is carried out are also reflected in the general increase in the proportion of the population acquiring higher education in the industrialized countries. Education and training throughout the career has become more common (Eurostat, 2005), making the workforces of many countries the most educated yet, and increasing the potential for employees to continuously develop and further their own competencies. This improves the employability of individuals by providing more alternatives in the labor market and also potentially increasing individuals' leverage in negotiations (Fugate, Kinicki, and Ashforth, 2004). Besides serving as a personal resource, the development of skills and knowledge, and the accompanying generally higher education level among employees, contributes to a more competitive labor market, as a greater number of people are qualified for each available job.

The transition from manufacturing to service jobs implies that a larger proportion of workers enjoy less physically strenuous jobs and less exposure to physical health risks. Moreover, as a consequence of the gradual shift from production to service, employees have been given greater independence and self-direction. However, these types of jobs bring about new types of demands. Since the performance outcomes rely less on the tangible products of traditional manufacturing jobs, work goals and tasks have become less concrete (Tetrick and Quick, 2003). This has resulted in employees being given more responsibility in deciding when work goals have been reached or when a task can be considered completed or adequately carried out, which may be difficult when goals and tasks are vague. Such vague tasks may be stressful for employees, rather than empowering, especially given the ever-increasing pace at work. Statistics show that the output per person has increased by 15% during the last decade (ILO, 2004), indicating that employee productivity is higher than ever. The greater demands on employees to be independent and effective, along with the increased pace at which work is expected to be carried out, may result in a generally more demanding work situation for employees.

Influence over decision-making and work processes, as well as a sense of empowerment, have traditionally been regarded as positive aspects of work, contributing to positive work outcomes (e.g. Hackman and Oldham, 1976). The idea that independence and influence over work augment satisfaction and well-being in the workplace has been applied to job design and work organization, and an increasing number of employees in many occupations have experienced decentralization and self-direction (Theorell, 2003). Such discretion can be positive for employees, in the sense that it lends a feeling of control, which is often suggested to lessen the negative impact of demands (Karasek and Theorell, 1990). However, the question of whether self-direction always constitutes something beneficial for the employee has become an important issue in contemporary working life (Allvin, Aronsson, Hagström, Johansson, and Lundberg, 2006). If self-direction is not accompanied by clearly delineated tasks and demands, there is a risk that independence becomes a burden for employees, who may experience accountability without the necessary authority. The presence of resources is crucial for whether a situation is interpreted as a threat or a challenge (Lazarus and Folkman, 1984). This issue is important in the context of the relation between demands and resources, and illustrates how something generally beneficial, such as self-direction, which is positive in combination with adequate resources, may become a burden when the necessary resources are not present (e.g. Demerouti, Nachreiner, Bakker, and Schaufeli, 2001; Karasek and Theorell, 1990).

The business climate has generally become more competitive, and organizations have had to cut costs and increase their flexibility in order to be able to respond to changes in market demands. One way of achieving numerical flexibility is by hiring a larger proportion of employees on fixed-term contracts, and, indeed, the number of employees in different types of so-called flexible or contingent employment has grown over the past decades (Aronsson, 1999; Connelly and Gallagher, 2004). Part-time employment has increased slightly since 1990 (OECD, 2005a), and can be associated with part-time unemployment and the underutilization of employees. The growing utilization of non-standard types of employment indicates that a smaller proportion of employees are now formally attached to an organization via full-time, permanent contracts, and has resulted in employees being categorized as either part of the core or part of the periphery of the organization (Aronsson, Gustafsson, and Dallner, 2002). A less formal organizational attachment has been associated with stronger experiences of uncertainty among employees (Isaksson, De Cuyper, and De Witte, 2005), but also with a greater flexibility for both organizations and individuals (Reilly, 1998). A less permanent attachment between individual and organization has the potential of being both an asset and a threat to the individual. While less static employment relations provide the individual with a certain amount of flexibility, these types of contracts expose the individual to a great deal of unpredictability, and this development has been related to increased feelings of uncertainty, more negative attitudes, and perhaps even stress on the job. However, studies investigating the psychological impact of temporary status have not been able to unanimously conclude whether temporary employees fare worse or better in terms of well-being and work attitudes, compared to their colleagues holding permanent contracts (McLean Parks, Kidder, and Gallagher, 1998).

In relation to this, another recent development reveals that in spite of the reduction in the total rate of unemployment during the last few years, the proportion of employees who have been unemployed at some point of their career has increased. Employees in many different types of jobs have experienced unemployment at some point in time, and during the 1990s it became evident that even highly educated persons were at risk of losing their jobs. Unemployment is therefore no longer primarily something that happens to workers during plant closures or downsizings; rather, the movement in and out of work has become more frequent (Kanfer, Wanberg, and Kantrowitz, 2001). A person's career is no longer necessarily continuous, but is likely to be broken up by different types of jobs and periods of unemployment (Super, 1992). These new types of employment and career patterns point to a development where traditional theories, which assume that work is full time, permanent, and performed at a particular place intended for work, are put into question (Connelly and Gallagher, 2004).

In the wake of increased technological advances and new types of work tasks, work has become less dependent on the place where it is carried out, and it is increasingly common for work to be performed in places and at times which traditionally have been reserved for leisure time. The boundaries between work and non-work are at risk of becoming more blurred for many groups of employees (Arthur, Inkson, and Pringle, 1999). Moreover, the larger proportion of women in the workforce, as well as of dual-earner couples and working parents, has increased the number of roles that employees have to distribute their time between (Hakim, 2000). This has led to more frequent interference between work and the part of life which is supposed to be devoted to activities other than paid work (Byron, 2005). Less distinct boundaries have been associated with an increased flexibility for the individual, since employees to a greater extent may choose when and where work should be carried out, but this flexibility also brings with it the risk of work intruding on life outside of work and causing an imbalance between work and non-work roles (Allvin *et al.*, 2006). Such an imbalance not only entails that individuals will be less able to regard time at home as time away from work, as they find it more difficult to fulfill the requirements of the different roles, but also has been associated with negative consequences for individuals, such as wanting to leave the organization or mental distress (Frone, 2003).

The importance of social relations in the work context has increased. Traditional human service occupations, such as those within health care, have always involved a high degree of social interaction, but in addition to these, the growth of service production has expanded the need for people to interact in a variety of other types of occupations. Another aspect of social relations is that between co-workers, and changes in employment relations also bring about changes in the types of social relations that develop in the work context. The increased heterogeneity of workers, in regard to both gender and ethnicity, should also be mentioned in the context of relations associated with the work situation. The proportion of women in the workforce has steadily grown during the twentieth century, and in many countries women constitute approximately half of the employees (OECD, 2005b). Also, with the increased migration between countries, employees originate from different cultures and ethnicities to a greater extent than before. It has been suggested that a heterogeneous workforce promotes creativity and the exchange of different ideas, and prevents stagnation, when individuals with different backgrounds and frames of reference jointly solve work tasks (Jackson, 1992). However, heterogeneity can present problems not previously encountered for the same reasons that it contributes to creativity. Individuals who do not have similar frames of reference run a greater risk of misunderstanding each other and, perhaps, ending up in conflicts, which does not enhance productivity or creativity.

An individual perspective

Working life has the potential to affect the individual both positively and negatively. A positive work situation is often associated with demands that are not too difficult for the individual to handle. The perception of demands is affected by the extent to which an individual perceives herself as having control of or access to adequate resources for dealing with the demands (Demerouti *et al.*, 2001; Karasek and Theorell, 1990).

The subjective interpretation of objective phenomena is central for how individuals react in a working context. A particular situation may be interpreted as a challenge instead of a threat if the employee perceives that she has resources and opportunities to deal with the situation in a satisfactory way (Lazarus and Folkman, 1984). Such perceptions of resources and opportunities are dependent on individual characteristics, but also on the context in which the individual works (Katz and Kahn, 1978). Thus, an individual's reaction to a certain phenomenon has to be viewed with respect to both individual and situational characteristics, since both are central to the individual's interpretation of the situation (James and Sells, 1981).

As reports of new demands and challenges for employees are put forth, an increased research interest in how individuals and organizations are affected by these developments has emerged. Investigations have shown that individual reactions may be grouped into three very general categories: attitudinal, behavioral, and health related (Jex and Beehr, 1991). Attitudinal reactions, such as job satisfaction or commitment to the organization, influence how the individual will approach her work tasks (Allen and Meyer, 1990; Locke, 1976). The work situation can also give rise to behavioral reactions, such as performance, turnover behavior, or compliance with safety regulations (Probst and Brubaker, 2001; Steel and Ovalle, 1984). Health-related reactions, such as mental health complaints and somatic symptoms, are also often associated with stressful conditions at work (Spector, 2000). Reactions to working conditions may be both positive and negative. For example, a positively perceived work climate may give rise to job satisfaction and organizational commitment, inspire good performance, and enhance well-being. On the other hand, a negatively perceived work environment has been consistently associated with detrimental reactions such as negative attitudes toward the organization, lowered performance, and health complaints.

Individuals exposed to demands attempt to handle these in ways that minimize their negative impact. Naturally, organizations and management are also affected by employee reactions and coping behaviors (cf. Greenhalgh and Rosenblatt, 1984). For instance, employee work attitudes, turnover behaviors, and performance affect the productivity of the organization, and employees on sick-leave present costs for both rehabilitation and loss of work input (Matteson and Ivancevich, 1990). Thus, how individuals handle their work situation becomes a concern for the organization as well. Moreover, organizations constitute an important part of the equation, which produces reactions among employees since the context in which the individual works is central to perceptions of stress and reactions to demands (cf. Katz and Kahn, 1978).

Organizations thereby play a vital role in providing resources for employees to deal with the demands organizations put on their employees (Theorell, 2003). It is important that organizations realize what measures they may take to affect working conditions in order for tasks to be perceived as challenges rather than threats by the employees.

In this context, the prevention of ill-health and negative attitudes, as well as the promotion of health and well-being at work, have become increasingly important (Quick, Quick, Nelson, and Hurrell, 1997). This includes organizational interventions and strategies to minimize the negative impact of work on employees, and also strategies to maximize positive factors to motivate employees and promote employee well-being. Such prevention and promotion programs benefit both employees and organizations, and organizations are well advised to be proactive in helping their employees to handle demands that arise in the course of work (Quick *et al.*, 1997).

Aim of the book

This volume aims to increase the understanding of the different emerging aspects of working life from the perspective of the individual experiencing these phenomena. This involves highlighting the research and theoretical developments that have occurred in recent years and discussing how traditional theoretical models can be used to understand the evolving working life. In doing so, one objective of the volume is to identify factors that individuals face in working life by focusing on how individuals are affected by them. This includes, for example, exploring what the threats and challenges are that employees currently face – as well as examining what the consequences of these factors are. No less important is the question of how well-being and behaviors at work are affected by current working life. Another objective of this volume is to reveal how employees deal with various aspects of contemporary working life and to provide direction for how individuals and organizations may better handle the negative aspects and take advantage of the positive aspects. It is important to know how individuals deal with the conditions they are facing and to look into how the associated threats and challenges can be handled so that individuals are not harmed. Not least of all, it is also important to explore what measures an organization can take in order to create working conditions that are beneficial for the both the vitality of the organization and the well-being of the employees.

In relation to this, research on working life has gone through changes to reflect the developments it studies. Such changes are gradual and perhaps difficult to notice, and therefore need to be explicitly discussed.

A discussion of the models that have been developed to help explain the more recent phenomena of contemporary working life is at present an important ambition. Traditional theories have been sufficient in some instances, but, in others, the transformations have brought about an emerging need for new theoretical frameworks – or at least amendments to existing theories. Additionally, in studies on work stress, it has become important for the researcher not only to assess whether there are problems in an organization or work group, but also to be able to suggest solutions and improvements, and to evaluate the effectiveness of these. This makes it necessary to reexamine the theories used as frameworks for understanding working conditions, and to reevaluate which methods are appropriate for studying contemporary working life.

In order to address the objectives presented above, the following chapters have been arranged in three parts. The chapters in the first part primarily focus on the identification of different factors in modern working life and their consequences for individuals. In the second part, the chapters describe different approaches that individuals take in handling aspects of working life and the consequences these approaches have. The third part contains chapters presenting what strategies organizations and research may employ in order to prevent negative outcomes for individuals and promote a positive working life.

Part I   Threats and challenges

The first part of this book focuses on the threats and challenges that individuals face in working life and the impact of these factors. The chapters explore the emerging phenomena in working life that affect employees and organizations in both positive and negative ways. These chapters also present theoretical models used to understand and describe contemporary working life.

The recent changes in working life have brought about a blurring of the various types of boundaries at work. Demands, for example, are often less clearly delineated, and the boundary between working life and life outside of work has also become less distinct. In chapter 2, Michael Allvin provides a theoretical discussion of the boundaryless working life, and presents an empirical study of employees dealing with less distinct boundaries.

In chapter 3, Johnny Hellgren, Magnus Sverke, and Katharina Näswall illustrate a number of factors present in contemporary working life and how they affect individuals. The chapter discusses new types of threats and challenges that have emerged during recent decades and contrasts these to traditional work stressors. The chapter also provides an empirical illustration of the emerging constructs and their relation to employee reactions.

The transitions occurring in working life have brought about a need for up-to-date theoretical models that take new types of stressors into account. Traditional models have been criticized for their inability to accommodate today's emerging working conditions. As a reaction to this, in chapter 4, Jan de Jonge, Christian Dormann, and Marieke van den Tooren present a recently developed model of the stressor–strain relationship, which suggests that there needs to be a match between stressors, strain, and type of resource. The authors also discuss empirical evidence regarding the applicability of the model in working life.

One of the major recent changes has been the increasing move from permanent employment toward the use of more short-term, temporary employment, and other atypical forms of employment such as self-employment and independent contracting. These temporary workers may have different work experiences and be exposed to different health risks compared to permanent employees (Kochan, Smith, Wells, and Rebitzer, 1994). Less is known about whether the traditional models used in working life research can be applied to these types of employees, who have yet to receive the same amount of research attention as individuals employed under traditional arrangements. Several chapters in this volume focus on different types of non-traditional contracts in various ways. In chapter 5, Nele De Cuyper and Hans De Witte discuss the experiencing of job insecurity among temporary workers, investigate how employability may figure in this context, and offer an explanatory framework for understanding the various psychological effects of temporary and permanent contracts.

There has been little research on how other types of non-traditional workers, such as independent contractors, are affected in terms of health and well-being. In chapter 6, Daniel G. Gallagher identifies and discusses the work-related pressures and challenges that may affect individuals employed as independent contractors. The chapter also focuses on the effort to identify and model the types of factors associated with the independent contractor status that may influence individuals' levels of satisfaction with their employment status as well as their overall well-being.

As mentioned, it has been observed that the new flexible employment conditions contribute to less distinct boundaries between work and non-work, with the increased pace of work in many occupations making it more difficult to limit work to traditional work hours. As a consequence of this, the concept of work–family conflict has recently become even more critical than before, especially with the increasing rate of dual-earner couples alongside less strictly defined workplaces and work hours

(Allen, Herst, Bruck, and Sutton, 2000). The concept of work–family conflict can be contrasted to family–work conflict, a related but separate construct involving life outside of work interfering with work. Ulla Kinnunen and Saija Mauno devote chapter 7 to a literature review of research on the antecedents and consequences of work–family interference, and examine how this phenomenon can be related to contemporary working life. The chapter also discusses family–work conflict and how it differs from work–family conflict.

The proportion of workers who are self-employed was estimated to be approximately 8% in the European Union in 2002 (Eurostat, 2002), which points to the need for research on the situation of this particular category of workers. Many of these workers carry out their work in their own home, which increases the risk of interference between work and family life. In chapter 8, Toon W. Taris, Sabine A. E. Geurts, Michiel A. J. Kompier, Suzanne Lagerveld, and Roland W. B. Blonk discuss to what extent self-employed experience interference between work and family life compared to other employees. The chapter also presents an empirical investigation of how the interaction between work and home affects the attitudes and well-being of the self-employed.

The increased output per person indicates that the pace of work has become increasingly high. A high work pace and a pressure to perform at a rapid rate have increased the risk of incidents that jeopardize worker safety (Probst and Brubaker, 2001). Nevertheless, the specific working conditions that increase the risk of employee injury and that decrease safety may have changed with the transformation of working life. In chapter 9, Nik Chmiel provides a review of how research on safety at work has evolved since the 1990s and how management practices and views on safety are changing.

The impact of social relations at work has gained some empirical attention, yet little is known about how romantic relationships at work can be accepted without detriment to the work environment or output. Positive relationships in the workplace are likely to relate to positive attitudes and well-being, which makes the way romantic relationships are accepted and managed an important issue in today's working life. In chapter 10, Jennifer Carson and Julian Barling give an overview of the nature, development, and potential outcomes of romantic relationships at work, and show how these relationships are influenced by management policies. The authors also provide a novel view of romantic relationships as an occurrence that cannot be prevented, and postulate that such relationships may actually benefit employee well-being.

Diversity amongst the personnel places demands on employees and managers to handle new and perhaps unknown attributes in their co-workers, and policies to manage diversity have been put forth in many organizations. However, research on the impact of ethnic diversity in the workplace has been inconclusive as to how diversity affects factors such as effectiveness and work climate, and more studies need to be conducted on this important aspect of working life. In chapter 11, Wido G. M. Oerlemans, Maria C. W. Peeters, and Wilmar B. Schaufeli discuss what constitutes ethnic diversity and what impact it may be expected to have on performance and attitudes, based on two theoretical frameworks and with the support of empirical studies.

Part II   Individual attempts at restoring the balance

The second part of this book has a general focus on the different strategies that individuals use to restore the balance that has been disrupted by new demands. The purpose of this part is to describe how individuals deal with factors in modern working life, and how different strategies for dealing with demands and challenges affect the reactions to the different factors individuals are facing.

Research interest on the subject of how individuals cope, and how coping can be facilitated, has followed on reports of a demanding working life. Knowledge concerning how different coping strategies facilitate individuals' dealing with stress has become more important for both individuals and organizations. Previous studies have recognized that certain coping strategies may be more effective than others (Callan, 1993), which suggests that more effective strategies should be encouraged and facilitated. In this volume, several chapters, with different perspectives, are explicitly devoted to the discussion of coping. In chapter 12, Jaco Pienaar reviews research on coping and presents a systematic overview of various findings on this important phenomenon. The chapter also presents a general model for coping strategies, and discusses the mechanisms by which coping is expected to alleviate stress reactions.

The issue of individual differences is important in the context of work stress, especially when stress perceptions are considered to result from the individual's interpretation of the situation. Since this interpretation is filtered through the individual's disposition, dispositional characteristics become important in the understanding of individual reactions to work stress. In chapter 13, Christopher J. L. Cunningham, Gabriel M. De La Rosa, and Steve M. Jex provide a literature review of the impact of disposition on the relation between work stress and reactions.

Previous research has focused largely on presenting results that may be generalized to other contexts, and less on context specific factors that can affect coping strategies and their outcomes. Thus, studies investigating the role of situational context in conjunction with individual factors in determining coping behaviors are becoming more important. In chapter 14, José M. Peiró describes a different approach to research on stress and coping, which takes context and positive aspects into account to a greater degree than previous research, and actually allows for the investigation of how contextual aspects influence coping strategies and their effectiveness.

Another area that has received less attention in previous research on coping is gender, and how men and women may differ in their use of more or less effective strategies. It is likely that women and men utilize different coping resources and strategies, which may influence their abilities to cope. In chapter 15, Eva Torkelson and Tuija Muhonen present an empirical investigation on how gender differences relate to differences in coping with work stress. The authors also discuss the implications of these gender-related differences on health and well-being.

One factor facing employees in the labor market is unemployment, and for employees to experience periods of unemployment during their careers is becoming more common today. Unemployment is no longer something that only affects certain groups of employees, or employees in certain types of jobs. This highlights the importance of bringing people who are currently outside the labor market back into employment, and thereby avoiding the trap of long-term unemployment, which has been shown to predict symptoms of negative well-being (Leana and Feldman, 1992). In chapter 16, Lea Waters discusses the impact of protean career attitudes on individual well-being during periods of unemployment, and how such attitudes can affect reentry into employment.

Part III   Intervention and promotion on the organizational level

In addition to investigating how individuals handle the threats and challenges they are faced with, it is important to focus on what can be done to help individuals cope with their situations, and to try to prevent stressors from arising in the first place. Accordingly, the last part of this book concentrates on strategies for both prevention and intervention, as well as promotion of well-being at work.

Research has an important function in the improvement of working conditions of employees. In many cases, suggestions for improvement are proposed after the completion of a research study. In chapter 17, however, Maureen F. Dollard, Pascale Le Blanc, and Sarah J. Cotton discuss how one particular method, participatory action research, can be used both as a method of assessment, and as a method of organizational intervention and employee health promotion. This method postulates that the success of organizational interventions is contingent on the participation and engagement of both researchers and the employees under study. The authors describe case studies based on action research, and propose how this method can be utilized in other situations to improve working conditions for employees.

The focus of stress prevention does not only have to be the prevention of stressors, as it may also focus on the enhancing of work's positive aspects. In chapter 18, Wilmar B. Schaufeli and Marisa Salanova suggest that current working conditions require organizations to aim at having not only healthy employees, but engaged employees as well. This calls for more than just having an absence of negative stressors, and the authors propose various strategies for achieving engagement through human resource management practices. Their recommendations are based on an overview of research investigating antecedents and consequences of work engagement.

In a similar vein, in chapter 19, Lois E. Tetrick provides an integration of two related strategies, concerning health protection and health promotion. These two strategies have been utilized in organizations, but have been approached from different research traditions. In this chapter, the two are integrated into a common framework in order to gain the most from the knowledge that exists in the two traditions, and also to understand what strategies are most effective and useful.

The last chapter of this book focuses on organizational strategies for dealing with stress prevention. In chapter 20, E. Kevin Kelloway, Arla Day, and Joseph J. Hurrell Jr. discuss organizational interventions. The authors describe organizational strategies that can prevent or diminish stressors and facilitate stress coping among employees.

References

Allen, N. J. and Meyer, J. P. (1990). The measurement and antecedents of affective, continuance and normative commitment to the organization. *Journal of Occupational Psychology* 63: 1–18.

Allen, T. D., Herst, D. E. L., Bruck, C. S., and Sutton, M. (2000). Consequences associated with work-to-family conflict: a review and agenda for future research. *Journal of Occupational Health Psychology* 5: 278–308.

Allvin, M., Aronsson, G., Hagström, T., Johansson, G., and Lundberg, U. (2006). *Gränslöst arbete: socialpsykologiska perspektiv på det nya arbetslivet* [Boundaryless work: the new working life from a social psychological perspective]. Malmö: Liber.

Aronsson, G. (1999). Contingent workers and health and safety. *Work, Employment, and Society* 13: 439–59.

Aronsson, G., Gustafsson, K., and Dallner, M. (2002). Work environment and health in different types of temporary jobs. *European Journal of Work and Organizational Psychology* 11: 151–76.

Arthur, M. B., Inkson, K., and Pringle, J. K. (1999). *The new careers: individual action and economic change.* London: Sage.

Burke, R. J. and Nelson, D. (1998). Mergers and acquisitions, downsizing, and privatization: a North American perspective. In M. K. Gowing, J. D. Kraft, and J. C. Quick (eds.), *The new organizational reality: downsizing, restructuring, and revitalization* (pp. 21–54). Washington, DC: American Psychological Association.

Byron, K. (2005). A meta-analytic review of work–family conflict and its antecedents. *Journal of Vocational behavior* 67: 169–98.

Callan, V. J. (1993). Individual and organizational strategies for coping with organizational change. *Work and Stress* 1: 63–75.

Connelly, C. E. and Gallagher, D. G. (2004). Emerging trends in contingent work research. *Journal of Management* 30: 959–83.

Demerouti, E., Nachreiner, R., Bakker, A. B., and Schaufeli, W. B. (2001). The Job Demands–Resources model of burnout. *Journal of Applied Psychology* 86: 499–512.

Eurostat (2002). The entrepreneurial gap between women and men. *Statistics in Focus 11/2002.* Luxemburg: Eurostat.

    (2005). Labour market latest trends. *Statistics in Focus 16/2005.* Luxemburg: Eurostat.

Frone, M. R. (2003). Work–family balance. In J. C. Quick and L. E. Tetrick (eds.), *Handbook of occupational health psychology* (pp. 143–62). Washington, DC: American Psychological Association.

Fugate, M., Kinicki, A. J., and Ashforth, B. E. (2004). Employability: a psychosocial construct, its dimensions, and applications. *Journal of Vocational behavior* 65: 14–38.

Greenhalgh, L. and Rosenblatt, Z. (1984). Job insecurity: toward conceptual clarity. *Academy of Management Review* 9: 438–48.

Hackman, J. R. and Oldham, G. R. (1976). Motivation through the design of work: test of a theory. *Organizational Behavior and Human Performance* 16: 250–79.

Hakim, C. (2000). *Work–lifestyle choices in the 21st century: preference theory.* Oxford: Oxford University Press.

ILO (2004). *World employment report 2004–05: employment, productivity and poverty reduction.* Geneva: ILO.

    (2006). *Global employment trends brief, January 2006.* Geneva: ILO.

Isaksson, K., De Cuyper, N., and De Witte, H. (2005). Employment contracts and well-being among European workers: Introduction. In N. De Cuyper, H. De Witte, and K. Isaksson (eds.), *Employment contracts and well-being among European workers* (pp. 1–14). Aldershot: Ashgate.

Jackson, S. E. (1992). Team composition in organizational settings: issues in managing an increasingly diverse workforce. In S. Worchel, W. Wood, and J. A. Simpson (eds.), *Group process and productivity* (pp. 138–73). Newbury Park, MA: Sage.

James, L. R. and Sells, S. B. (1981). Psychological climate: theoretical perspectives and empirical research. In D. Magnusson (ed.), *Toward a psychology of situations: an interactional perspective* (pp. 275–95). Hillsdale, NJ: Erlbaum.

Jex, S. M. and Beehr, T. A. (1991). Emerging theoretical and methodological issues in the study of work-related stress. In K. Rowland and G. Ferries (eds.), *Research in personnel and human resources management* (vol. 9, pp. 311–65). Greenwich, CT: JAI Press.

Kanfer, R., Wanberg, C., and Kantrowitz, T. (2001). Job search and employment: a personality-motivational analysis and meta-analytic review. *Journal of Applied Psychology* 86: 837–55.

Karasek, R. A. and Theorell, T. (1990). *Healthy work: stress, productivity, and the reconstruction of working life*. New York: Basic Books.

Katz, D. and Kahn, R. L. (1978). *The social psychology of organizations* (2nd edn). New York: Wiley.

Kochan, T. A., Smith, M., Wells, J. C., and Rebitzer, J. B. (1994). Human resource strategies and contingent workers: the case of safety and health in the petrochemical industry. *Human Resource Management* 33: 55–77.

Lazarus, R. S. and Folkman, S. (1984). *Stress, appraisal, and coping*. New York: Springer.

Leana, C. R. and Feldman, D. C. (1992). *Individual responses to job loss: how individuals, organizations and communities respond to layoffs*. New York: Lexington.

Locke, E. A. (1976). The nature and causes of job satisfaction. In M. Dunnette (ed.), *Handbook of industrial and organizational psychology* (pp. 1297–349). Chicago: Rand McNally.

Matteson, M. T. and Ivancevich, J. M. (1990). Merger and acquisition stress: fear and uncertainty at mid-career. *Prevention in Human Services* 8: 139–58.

McLean Parks, J., Kidder, D. L., and Gallagher, D. G. (1998). Fitting square pegs into round holes: mapping the domain of contingent work arrangements onto the psychological contract. *Journal of Organizational behavior* 19: 697–730.

OECD (2005a). *Employment outlook*. Paris: Office for Economic Cooperation and Development.

    (2005b). *Labor force statistics 1984–2004*. Paris: Office for Economic Cooperation and Development.

Pfeffer, J. (1997). *New directions for organization theory*. New York: Oxford University Press.

Probst, T. M. and Brubaker, T. L. (2001). The effects of job insecurity on employee safety outcomes: cross-sectional and longitudinal explorations. *Journal of Occupational Health Psychology* 6: 139–59.

Quick, J. C., Quick, J. D., Nelson, D. L., and Hurrell, J. J. (eds.) (1997). *Preventive stress management in organizations*. Washington, DC: American Psychological Association.

Reilly, P. (1998). Balancing flexibility – meeting the interests of employer and employee. *European Journal of Work and Organizational Psychology* 7: 7–22.

Spector, P. E. (2000). A control theory of the job stress process. In C. L. Cooper (ed.), *Theories of organizational stress* (pp. 153–69). Oxford: Oxford University Press.

Steel, R. P. and Ovalle, N. K. (1984). A review and meta-analysis of research on the relationship between behavioral intentions and employee turnover. *Journal of Applied Psychology* 69: 673–86.

Super, D. E. (1992). Toward a comprehensive theory of career development. In D. H. Montross and C. J. Shinkman (eds.), *Career development: theory and practice* (pp. 35–64). Springfield, IL: Charles C. Thomas.

Tetrick, L. E. and Quick, J. C. (2003). Prevention at work: public health in occupational settings. In J. C. Quick and L. E. Tetrick (eds.), *Handbook of occupational health psychology* (pp. 3–17). Washington, DC: American Psychological Association.

Theorell, T. (2003). To be able to exert control over one's own situation: a necessary condition for coping with stressors. In J. C. Quick and L. E. Tetrick (eds.), *Handbook of occupational health psychology* (pp. 201–19). Washington, DC: American Psychological Association.

Part I

Threats and challenges

2 New rules of work: exploring the boundaryless job

Michael Allvin

> Profit arises out of the inherent, absolute unpredictability of things, out
> of the sheer brute fact that the results of human activity cannot be
> anticipated and then only in so far as even a probability calculation in
> regard to them is impossible and meaningless. (Knight, 1921: 311)

In 1921, Frank H. Knight made a classic distinction between "risk" and
"uncertainty" in economic endeavors, claiming that while risk can be
calculated, uncertainty cannot. Since then, a variety of methods for
assessing and reducing risk have been developed and used, while essentially ignoring uncertainty. In the 1970s, however, in the face of increasing international competition, oil crisis, floating currencies, political
unrest, and the idiosyncratic demands of lifestyle consumption, turning
a blind eye toward the uncertainties of enterprising was no longer a
feasible option. Rather, uncertainty had to be recognized as a fundamental precondition of modern corporations. Out of Japan came the realization that planning and organizing for it, and not just against it, could
provide a competitive advantage (Ouchi, 1981; Porter, 1990). The general strategy for coping with uncertainty, introduced by the Japanese, was
to increase the *flexibility* of production (Piore and Sabel, 1984). The
principles of flexibility have since been introduced into almost every
aspect of corporate life.

Corporate flexibility may be described in many different ways: as
customer-oriented operations (D'Aveni, 1994; Harrison, 1994); as compressed, time-based, even instantaneous productions (Clark and Fujimoto,
1991; Hutchins, 1988; Peters and Waterman, 1982); or as project organizations, network organizations, or just decentralized organizations.
A common denominator in all of these descriptions, however, is a heightened awareness of time. To be sure, time has always been an essential
standard of machine and labor utilization. But, unlike before, when
time was considered a constant, delimited by technology and human
capacity – and identified as such by planning division engineers – the
flexible corporation recognizes no such restrictions. In the flexible corporation, time is constantly challenged. Consequently, time is no longer a

constraint to be approached scientifically; it is a possibility to be exploited (Stalk and Hout, 1990).

Perhaps the most obvious consequence of organizational flexibility is the extensive dismantling of the permanent structures securing the internal continuity of a corporation (Ashkenas, 1995). These structures do not only regulate the corporation as such. They also regulate and define the work performed within that corporation, thereby providing it with a stable, integrated, and clearly defined form. In a fluid and uncertain environment, however, these structures have the characteristics of a ready-made model. They become too tight when business goes up and too loose when it goes down. In order to "squeeze the air out of the system" and make the enterprise more pliable, its organization is deregulated. As a consequence, the work within that organization is also deregulated.

A deregulation of work may manifest itself in various ways and on various levels. The different shapes and forms of flexibility have evolved and multiplied since the early 1980s. They have, however, usually appeared as separate trends with their individual label or brand name, like flexiwork, flexitime, telework, telecommuting, tele-cottages, mobile work, team work, project work, consulting, Management by Objectives, and networking (cf. Avery and Zabel, 2001). The extensive selection of forms and conditions for flexibility has made the world of work increasingly more heterogeneous and disorganized. We may even say that when work is fitted to meet with an unpredictable reality, it will become more unpredictable itself. It will, to put it metaphorically, become *boundaryless*.

This poses a series of problems, both theoretical and practical. The general theoretical problem is of course how to define and delimit work. If the common standard for work becomes less common, then how do we envisage and theorize work? If the conditions of work vary, how do we determine, compare, and generalize their consequences? How can we even assume an independent relation between the conditions and their consequences?

Consider, for instance, the example of "burnout." In 1974, Herbert Freudenberger observed a gradual energy depletion and depression among young idealistic volunteers working at a "Free Clinic" for drug addicts in New York. Almost simultaneously, Christina Maslach observed the same emotional exhaustion among health care workers in California. They both, independently of each other, called the syndrome "burnout" and described it as a loss of motivation (Shaufeli and Enzmann, 1998). Unlike being overworked or worn out, which follows from working too hard for too long, burnout presupposes a personal commitment. You don't just work a lot; you try to achieve something that is important to you. It is symptomatic that the phenomenon was first observed among human service professionals. A personal commitment to the relationship with the patient or client is an intrinsic part of the job. It is, however, also symptomatic that the phenomenon has since been spreading among the many newly created jobs of the so-called New Economy. Many of these jobs have very flexible working conditions and rely heavily on the personal abilities and commitment of the individual worker. The question, then, is whether the burnout syndrome may be considered a consequence of work. Being overworked probably could be, since the independent cause most likely can be established in terms of the assigned or expected work quota. This is, however, not necessarily the case with burnout. Since the burnout syndrome presupposes a personal commitment, there is no independent cause to the problem. Burnout therefore cannot readily be identified as a consequence of work, nor can it be limited to the field of work.

The case of burnout also addresses an underlying practical problem. If we cannot define and delimit the work, then how can we identify the conditions and environment for work? And, if we cannot identify these, how can we establish the responsibilities involved? Who, for example, is responsible for a person being burned out, and whose responsibility is it to make sure it doesn't happen to others? Furthermore, if jobs are being deregulated, how can the problems of these jobs be fitted and addressed within the common set of rules and regulations established by society, such as current laws, general agreements, and public conventions (Allvin and Aronsson, 2003)?

Of course, these questions cannot be resolved here. I'm not even sure it is possible to answer them as posed. In any case, the answers would presuppose an understanding of flexible or deregulated work. The purpose of this chapter is, therefore, to explore jobs that are deregulated, and to offer a framework through which they may be conceptualized and investigated. The chapter is based on two interview studies of people working under more or less boundaryless conditions. The studies are exploratory in the sense that they aim to capture the phenomenon as such, rather than to verify the existence or propagation of an operational definition. In doing so, they seek to *explain* the phenomenon, not by identifying its causes, but by uncovering its logic of action, or rationality. Furthermore, the studies focus on the individual level and are concerned with the institutional setting, or set of expectations, facing the individual. Our purpose, in other words, is to uncover *the new rules of work*.

In the first part of this chapter, a general framework with regard to social rules is established. In the second part, this framework is formulated more concretely into an operational approach, which focuses on the rules of work. In the third part, we see this approach applied to two interview studies, thereby revealing not only the working conditions as such but the implicit arrangement of work, as well as some general consequences following from it. The chapter ends with a short discussion considering further implications of the studies.

Theorizing the boundaryless job

In any study, it is essential to maintain focus and control over the process of knowledge formation by establishing some kind of theoretical framework. However, since this study is meant to be exploratory, it is important not to restrain the process by setting up any unnecessary conceptual limitations through the use of a particular theory. Therefore, the theoretical framework may well be devised on a fairly abstract level, although it must, of course, address the appropriate level of investigation, in this case the institutional setting of the individual.

By institutional setting, I am referring to the rules and regulations that individuals face at work. Here, rules will be understood in a very broad sense, as the distillate of all systematic expectations placed on the individual by other people, by the surrounding environment, as well as by herself (Giddens, 1984). Thus, most expectations facing the individual are not directly experienced as "rules." Instead, the expectations are implicit, informal, unspoken, or taken for granted and, subsequently, merely experienced as "the order of things."

In social organizations, rules are used to regulate individual activities in a systematic way, thereby reproducing the organization as a whole. The organization's ability to reproduce itself is, therefore, directly proportional to its ability to regulate the actions at its disposal (Burns and Flam, 1987). Furthermore, the different actions can only be said to be a part of (or contribute to) the organization to the extent that they are regulated by the organization. Hence, a social organization can be analyzed by examining the different actions through which it is reproduced, and the individual action can be analyzed by examining the regulations through which it contributes to the reproduction of the social organization as a whole (Mills and Murgatroyd, 1991).

Now, in most, if not all, tasks, the actions of an individual are regulated in two different ways (Beck, 1975). A given task can be performed by acting from *routine*, from a prescription or out of habit. The individual will in this case perform the task in a more or less automatic fashion, requiring no thought to do so. At some point, however, and for some reason, the routine is inevitably broken. The individual is then forced to become aware of what she is doing and why. She is thrown back onto herself and must resort to her own interpretation of the task. In this instance, she will act, not through an established routine, but from an *idea*. Although her actions will still be regulated, they will be so in a different manner than before. To put it another way: she will no longer be performing her task in accordance with the same *kind* of rules.

We can here make a distinction between what John Searle (1969) has called "constitutive" and "regulative" rules. *Constitutive rules* are rules that *define* the actions performed in accordance with them, thereby constituting the actions as part of a given rule system. The traditional examples are rules of games – like chess or football. A chess move *is* a move performed in accordance with the rules that constitute the game of chess. Any move *not* performed in accordance with these rules is, by definition, not a part of the game. Conversely, the game of chess manifests itself only through the moves that are made in accordance with its rules. The game does not exist, except in a figurative sense, if it is not played, and, one might add, played by the rules. Constitutive rules, therefore, cannot be understood apart from the actions performed in accordance with them. *Regulative rules*, on the other hand, are rules that *direct* actions. Traditional examples are norms, traffic rules, and rules of thumb. Regulative rules are "followed," and can therefore be understood independently of the actions performed in accordance with them (Searle, 1969).

The difference between constitutive and regulative rules, then, lies not in the regularities of the rules themselves, but in the actor's relation to these regularities – more specifically, in whether she is aware of them or not. Constitutive rules define, or constitute, the actions, to the actor as well as to others, as part of a given rule system. Acting in accordance with such rules is just something that one does while being part of this type of rule system. Regulative rules, on the other hand, are rules that the actor deliberately chooses to follow, being well aware of the fact that they are part of a given rule system. Consequently, regulative rules, unlike constitutive rules, presuppose a willful act.

Within the framework of a functional organization, to act in accordance with constitutive rules is to act in accordance with what the organization defines as being functional (cf. Luhmann, 1995). The actor herself does not have to be aware of whether her actions are functional or not. All she has to care about is getting them right. To act in accordance with regulative rules, on the other hand, requires that the actor see herself as a functional part of the organization. It requires, to put it differently, a functional interpretation of the organization as a guiding principle for action. Accordingly, a distinction must then be made between, on the one hand, acting *automatically*, from habit or a routine that has proven functional, and, on the other hand, acting *willfully*, from a predicted, and reasoned, functionality. In both cases, the acting is done in accordance with rules that are functional for the organization. However, in the first case, it is the rules that define the actions as being functional, while in the second case it is the actor that defines the rules as being functional. Constitutive rules, then, presuppose actions which are part of the organization, while regulative rules presuppose an actor who is taking part in the organization, while being independent of the organization. Or, to use an old psychedelic metaphor, constitutive rules presuppose an actor that is inside the system looking out, while regulative rules presuppose an actor that is outside the system looking in.

The Danish engineer Jens Rasmussen (1986) has given a description of how the act of decision-making can be conceptualized in such a way. According to Rasmussen, decision-making can be broken down into three successive information-processing phases: diagnosis, interpretation, and planning. He goes on to show that, in practice, decision-making seldom involves any interpretation. Instead, the act proceeds with the actor going directly from the diagnostic to the planning phase, acting only on routine. By analyzing the diagnostic and the planning phases even further, through examining their different information-processing events, he is able to demonstrate that, *as a rule*, a given event in the planning phase follows upon certain information in the diagnostic phase. *If* certain diagnostic information is present, *then* a certain course of action is implied. An act performed in accordance with such a rule is performed automatically and does not require any interpretation. Such an act is, in Rasmussen's own terminology, "rule-based," or "skill-based" if it proceeds in a purely reflexive manner (see also Hacker, 1978, 1986).

Let us illustrate this type of action with the case of a physician who is confronting a well-known symptom. Being "well-known," the symptom requires no interpretation with regard to any theoretical model. Instead, the symptom itself implies a certain course of action. The step from "diagnosing the symptom" to "planning the treatment" is taken without the physician being aware of it. The decision for a certain treatment is, so to speak, already inherent in the diagnosis. Thus, when the physician identifies the symptom and prescribes a treatment, she is not acting "on her own." She is only performing in accordance with the rules constituting the medical task before her.

If, on the other hand, such a routine performance is not possible, the actor will have to form a model of functionality and act in accordance with it. Such a model is not formed individually or arbitrarily; it is, rather, mediated and supplied by the profession or organization. The model may, for instance, be presented on the surface of a system, as an interface between man and machine. The interface reduces the complexity of a system by raising the level of abstraction and integrating the information, thereby making the system *appear* as both comprehensible and manageable. Jens Rasmussen has, along with Mark Pejtersen, designed an interface which makes it possible to run (or maybe "ride" is a better word) an entire nuclear power plant single-handedly (Rasmussen and Vicente, 1990). By depicting the dynamic relations between a few essential parameters in the form of an abstract but simple shape, the nuclear process can actually be monitored and steered from a single terminal. The interface thus furnishes the operator with a practical model of the system. Actions guided by such a "mental model" are, in the terminology of Rasmussen (1986), labeled as "knowledge-based."

Another example of such a furnished model is a calculated and premeditated corporate culture. A corporate culture may be described as a collective notion of a common history, shared ambitions, conditions, problems, conflicts, and above all a common language (Alvesson and Berg, 1992; Kunda, 1992). As such, it forms a common frame of reference through which a particular experience can be made comprehensible. Even though a corporate culture, like any other social culture, is communicated and maintained symbolically, it is at the same time an artifact, in that it is designed specifically for the purpose of making social action functional, or systemic. For this very purpose, it employs different managerial techniques, such as the forging of a corporate image, narratives, or brand names. Other techniques are individual career plans, internal marketing, and customer orientation (Czarniawska, 1997; du Gay and Salaman, 1992; Hendry, 1995).

In both of these examples, actions are not regulated directly. Instead, the regulations operate by justifying and framing the situation in a way that only recognizes certain actions as feasible. The important thing to notice in both of these examples, however, is that the individual's actions are systematically regulated, in this case, through professional and organizational knowledge, while still being intentionally and willfully performed.

The point that I have been trying to make so far is that human action can be functionally regulated, while being both automatically and willfully performed. Now, to use the terminology thereby established, I would like to double back to my initial question and claim that flexibility within a social system presupposes willfully performed actions. Consequently, a turn toward a more flexible approach in production systems implies a *shift* from actions regulated by constitutive rules toward actions regulated by regulative rules. As suggested by the latter term, this does not necessarily mean that human actions are less regulated than before. They are only regulated in a different way.

There are, of course, several implications of such reasoning. I will, however, restrict myself in specifying three general consequences readily deduced from the conceptual framework.

1. Since constitutive rules define and reproduce a social system, or organization, as an absolute form, a shift away from these rules should render the organization, as a formal structure, superfluous. Regardless of whether the organizational transformation requires an actual change of rules or merely a change of rule status, the suspension of hitherto established rules will be perceived as a process of deregulation and, hence, a dissolution of the absolute organization.

2. A shift from constitutive to regulative rules of work should dissolve *work* as a positively delineated activity. Being constitutive, the rules of work do not only regulate the day-to-day performance of work; they also constitute work as such, in the sense that they determine what should count as "work." But, by establishing what work is, they also establish the opposite – that which should *not* count as work. Consequently, the rules regulating the performance of work do not only manage the workforce by specifying their performance, they also establish a clear and unambiguous distinction between work and non-work. Hence, a shift away from these (constitutive) rules should *invalidate* the traditionally clear and unambiguous distinction between work and non-work.

3. Another consequence of our conceptual framework is the disconnection of the individual. Since regulative rules, as opposed to constitutive rules, presuppose an actor that is herself independent of the system, in the sense that her actions are willfully regulated, a shift toward these rules should lead to the individual acting more *independently* vis-à-vis the system as a whole. To put it differently, the relationship between the individual and the system would be based on choice rather than identity.

These consequences follow logically from the conceptual framework. We may therefore view them as propositions to be investigated and given a practical form. As such, they should be able to guide the exploration of boundaryless jobs to which we now turn.

Method: approaching the boundaryless job

In order to investigate the forms of regulation following a shift from a constitutive to a regulative regulation of work, a total of twenty-four persons, working under more or less flexible conditions, were interviewed in two separate studies (Allvin *et al.*, 1998; Allvin, Wiklund, Härenstam, and Aronsson, 1999). Both studies were of an exploratory kind and involved the use of open and semi-structured interviews. The results of these interviews were subsequently structured, categorized, and analyzed using conventional methods for qualitative data analysis (Glaser, 1978; Glaser and Strauss, 1967; Miles and Huberman, 1994a, 1994b; Strauss and Corbin, 1990).

The respondents were selected from a body of more than a hundred other persons also interviewed; the criteria being that their jobs were deregulated in one or more of the traditional dimensions regulating work (see below). The respondents came from different jobs, varying from high-status jobs with extremely flexible conditions (consultants, salespersons, and positions within media production [television], as well as organization and software development) to low-status jobs that were only partly flexible (switchboard operators and temporary office aids; see table below). The attitudes of the respondents also varied, from those who praised and actively sought the professional and personal freedom of their flexible working conditions to those who were more reluctant and had been forced into these conditions by rationalizations or organizational changes beyond their control. As a consequence, not all of the respondents, much less all of their statements, were used to substantiate *all* of the aspects of deregulation and flexibility. On the contrary, no single job or person represents the whole phenomenon, but all of them represent at least one aspect each.

The rules regulating the performance of work were tentatively outlined in five different dimensions:

> *Time.* Rules specifying the extent and placement of the time for work, during the working day, for twenty-four hours, a week, a year or for the life span as a whole.
>
> *Space.* Rules specifying the extent and placement of the space for work, as applies to different tasks, the assignment as a whole, and the workplace as a whole.
>
> *Horizontal organization.* Rules specifying the performance in relation to a certain goal (technical rules); that is, rules making up the labor process as such.
>
> *Vertical organization.* Rules specifying the performance in relation to other assignments (administrative rules); that is, rules establishing an organizational structure.
>
> *Employment.* Rules specifying the terms of employment, either formalized in a contract between the employer and employee or codified in laws and decrees.

Together, the different dimensions constitute the screen through which work traditionally has been studied, measured, and regulated, both practically and theoretically (Allvin, 2004). Regulating work in time and space, for instance, was the precondition and focal point of the first industrial revolution back in the eighteenth century. The horizontal and vertical regulation of work developed as a consequence of the increasingly larger organizations emerging during the later nineteenth century, establishing the practical and theoretical agenda of both industrial engineering and organizational management, and conceptualized in the classical writings of, among others, Frederick W. Taylor (1911) and Henri Fayol (1916/1988).

By examining work in its different dimensions, I wish to draw attention to the fact that work is both de- and re-regulated in various degrees and ways. A job may be regulated in a regulative, or flexible, manner in any one, or several, of the dimensions, and thus be partially flexible, or it may be regulated in a regulative manner in all of the dimensions and be entirely flexible, or boundaryless. The regulatory variation among the interviewed subjects may be systematically illustrated in a matrix form as in the Table 2.1.

The table is meant to be illustrative by showing the job descriptions of the interviewed subjects as well as the regulatory requirements of their jobs distributed over the different dimensions. As can be seen, all of the combinations do not appear in the interviews. There are, for instance, no jobs that are solely unregulated in time or the horizontal organization. However, this issue was not a concern when selecting the subjects. Rather, the final selection was determined by "saturation," i.e. when a new subject did not present any further information (Glaser, 1978; Glaser and Strauss, 1967).

Results: exploring the boundaryless job

When examining the work described by the respondents using the five-dimensional schema explained above, the most characteristic feature was the almost complete absence of invariable and objective conditions. It proved almost impossible to find out when and where the respondents performed their work – the reason for this being, of course, that they worked, as one respondent said, "always and everywhere." This claim should not be understood in the sense that they did nothing but work. Rather, it suggests that a clear and unambiguous distinction between work and non-work cannot be made. Work, or work-related activities, was performed at all possible times and in all possible places. The same can be said about the process of work. There were no pre-structured lines

Table 2.1 *The jobs of the interviewed subjects and their corresponding regulatory variations*

Subject/job	Time	Space	Horizontal organization	Vertical organization	Employment
Tele-working telephone operator	C	R	C	C	C
Tele-working telephone operator	C	R	C	C	C
Temporary office worker	C	C	C	C	R
Computer technician in a small enterprise	C	C	C	R	C
Computer technician in a small enterprise	C	C	C	R	C
Computer teacher in e-education	R	R	R	C	C
Systems developer	R	R	R	C	C
Systems maintenance	R	R	R	C	C
Systems consultant	R	R	R	R	C
Systems consultant	R	R	R	R	C
Script girl (TV)	R	R	R	C	R
Developer in a large tele-company	R	R	R	R	C
Sales manager	R	R	R	R	C
Organization developer	R	R	R	R	C
Self-employed props manager (TV)	R	R	R	R	R
Part-owner in a small enterprise	R	R	R	R	R
Part-owner in a small enterprise	R	R	R	R	R
Self-employed in marketing	R	R	R	R	R
Marketing manager	R	R	R	R	R
Management consultant	R	R	R	R	R
Self-employed in marketing	R	R	R	R	R
Part-owner in a small enterprise	R	R	R	R	R
Part-owner in a small enterprise	R	R	R	R	R
Systems consultant	R	R	R	R	R

Note: "C" stands for being regulated in a constitutive manner and "R" in a regulative manner. The cells displaying an R are shaded to highlight regulatory differences among the selected respondents. In the column "Employment," anybody not having a tenured employment, full or part time, is considered as having their employment relation regulated in a regulative manner.

of action, manuals, techniques, structured tasks, or clearly specified results. Most respondents did not even have a clearly defined objective guiding their performance. On the contrary, there was nothing in their assignment stating what to do or how it should be done. Consequently, there was nothing stating what was part of the assignment and what was not. The assignments as such did not include, or exclude, anything. They operated, however, within the general context of an industry, a large organization or enterprise. This means that their performance was guided by the general requirements of a specific trade, professional field, customer, or market. These requirements were generally so vague, though, that they demanded a careful and recurrent process of interpretation.

We're more guided by a purpose than oriented toward a goal. We try to achieve something and then it's up to us what to do with it. We are accountable to a committee, though. And that keeps us in line. We meet with them about once a month and show them what we've done. They serve as discussants or mentors, and they give us constructive criticism. So, that's how our work is managed. (*Developer of communication systems*)

Most of those interviewed were employed, and serving within a larger organization. The hierarchical or functional division of labor of that organization nevertheless appeared to have very little bearing on their performance. Many did not have any formal titles, ranks, or positions. Some of the respondents even had difficulties identifying their immediate supervisor, and their performance did not appear to be directed by any explicit management or feedback. Even though they associated with their fellow workers, they had no fixed colleagues with whom they collaborated. Nor did their performance seem to rely on any other function within the organization. Furthermore, their assignments did not appear to involve too many activities that served to reproduce the organization, such as repeated participation in ritually conducted meetings and committees; the writing and reading of periodic letters, memos, notes, or accounts; and having recurrent breaks, lunches, or informal meetings with colleagues. All of these activities, be they large or small, provide a social organization with continuity, unity, and structural coherency, and thus furnish the work performed within that organization with a certain regularity and predictability. Also noteworthy is the fact that their working day did not seem to involve too many social commitments, such as coffee talk, chit-chat, and local gossip, whose main purpose is to reinforce a communal bond. Several respondents even pointed out that the absence of such recurrent activities was one of the big advantages with the way they worked.

I don't need all this domestic bullshit and struggle to maintain one's prestige, existing in most places. I don't have to go to any meetings or committees. Think of all the papers that I don't have to read. Instead I can concentrate on what's productive. (*Self-employed in marketing*)

That's what I like about this role. I don't have to drink coffee at quarter past three with everybody else. Well, maybe I do miss a few things, but I'm sure I can miss most of it. (*Systems consultant*)

Although the respondents differed as to whether they held steady employment or not, their attitudes toward the employment relation were found to be quite similar. Very few expressed any deeper commitment toward the company employing them, or voiced any particular advantage with being employed. One formerly employed respondent even expressed concern over the insecurity of having a steady employment: "There is no control whatsoever, even if you are an executive manager." The implication being that the only way to be in control is to be self-employed. Furthermore, most respondents declared that their earnings were very important to them. But it was not the regularity of their income they were referring to. It was the personal bonus, reward, and feedback for a job well done that was important to them.

To sum up, many respondents described their work as presupposing few invariable regulations, that is, regulations independent of a particular individual or context. Some respondents even described their job as being without any fixed boundaries whatsoever. Thus, the most characteristic feature of their job was the absence of constitutive rules.

The new rules of work

When the respondents described their working conditions as having no fixed boundaries, it did not mean, however, that their performance was in any way unstructured or unsystematic; it was, in fact, quite the opposite. With the absence of objective regulations, another, more subjective kind of regulation emerged, a regulation that was both individually and contextually contingent. A representation of such a subjective regulation can be further elaborated using the five dimensions described above.

Time and space

Even if the respondents could not determine exactly when and where they did or did not perform their work, they were all very well aware of when and where they performed their *best*, and when and where they *preferred* to do their work. They could invariably state when, during the day, they were most productive or, inversely, when they could not get anything done. Furthermore, they could clearly state which period of the day, the week, or the season was most suitable for the performance of a particular task and give their reasons for why that was. The same was true for the spatial dimension. The respondents were able to clearly point out the places that were most suitable for the performance of certain tasks and explain why.

The respondents also seemed to have structured their work, as well as their lives, along these lines. This was evident in the fact that they all stressed how important it was to plan, structure, and discipline their work in order to prevent it from drifting out of control, and they all had their different strategies for doing so. For example, those who were working at home, but also had a formal workplace, chose to work at least one day a week at that workplace in order to meet with management and fellow workers. Even the work at home seemed to follow a definite schedule. They turned off their mobile phone at certain times, did not read e-mail before or after a certain time, etc. The respondents also adjusted their timetables to fit the demands of particular customers or markets, global time differences, family needs, as well as their own personal preferences. These principles were the same for the spatial dimension. Almost all of the respondents had a separate working space in their home. It was generally well furnished with office as well as communication technology. All had mobile phones and most had portable computers to assure maximum accessibility and spatial flexibility.

Another widespread method that respondents used to structure their lives and delimit their work involved actively and deliberately distinguishing, in both temporal and spatial terms, relaxation from work, which generally took the form of physical activities, such as hockey, sailing, gardening, meditation, etc.

Horizontal organization

The most salient criterion for the structuring of respondents' performance in time and space was the work objective. In this context, the work objective should not be understood to exist in the form of an official or written prescription, but, rather, as the respondents' perceptions of the purpose of their work. The work of the respondents, as well as their performance in general, was characterized by awareness and concentration, and they invariably stressed the importance of efficiency and focus. They were more or less constantly seeking and exchanging applicable information. Social contacts, professional as well as private, were assessed in functional or strategic terms. For some, this was even a commercial concept:

> My *niche* is to show people how to use their personal network to achieve their objectives, or to be successful in their professional life. I call this "active networking." I use it as a framework in my job, but all it really means is how to form favorable relations with other people, how to increase the flow of opportunities in your life by having relationships with other people. (*Self-employed in marketing*)

An acute demand for ample performance, under very unrestrained conditions, seemed to accentuate the importance of being purpose-oriented. This sense of purpose may be characterized in two ways. First, it can be characterized as a constant demand for *initiatives*. Throughout, the respondents were talking about the importance of continually setting new goals for themselves, "keeping up" with developments, being "on the edge," and pushing the "frontline," as well as marketing themselves, making sure they're attractive to the market, driving the evolution and not letting themselves be driven by it, etc.

> You can't sit still and wait for information. If you're not active, you're kicked out. It is cruel, but that's how it is. If you don't seize the opportunities, and advance you're own qualifications and career, you'll be side-stepped and eventually kicked out. (*Organization developer*)

Secondly, the purpose described by the respondents can be characterized as an increased demand for *personal responsibility*. According to the respondents, it is not enough just to initiate their own work; they must also plan, structure, and discipline it. It is not enough just to pursue new information; they must also process, sort, and digest that information in order to make it useful. It is not enough just to start a project; they must also complete it. Nor is it enough simply to make contact with other people; they must also contribute, keep track of their contacts, and cultivate them. Consequently, the initiatives and creativity that are so necessary for flexible jobs have to be backed up by organization and discipline. This presupposes a constant demand for tidiness with regard to agendas, address lists, appointments, deadlines, budgets, invoices, etc. Thus, this purpose to be found in work can be conceptualized in the form of *projects* that are more or less structured and more or less formalized.

Vertical organization

Almost all of the respondents characterized their work as independent, but at the same time described it as being largely about establishing, maintaining, advancing, and exploiting social relationships. This reads almost as a paradox. The individual is increasingly left to herself, while at the same time being more socially committed than ever. This "paradox" can be explained by the disintegration of the formal organization – the hierarchy – which has given way to a more informal organization – *the network*. The term "social network" is used here to refer to a set of relationships that are not independent of the persons taking part in them. It is within this network that the practicalities of work are carried out.

To me the line organization is dead. It just serves as an organizational residence, a kind of social security. The real organization is the network, and it's alive. (*Organization developer*)

In comparison with the definite properties of the formal organization, this type of network appears transitory, almost amoeba-like. Nevertheless, none of the respondents seemed to have any problems defining their network. Most of them were active in several networks, both professional and private. But even though these networks seemed to be well separated in regard to both their structure and their personnel, they did not seem to be *functionally* distinguishable from each other. Both the professional and the private networks of the respondents were continually and more or less systematically tapped into for information that could be of use in the performance of work.

The whole life is a network, that's how it works today. There are no boundaries in our organizations anymore . . . I'm part of two networks at the moment. (*Sales manager*)

There are two parts to this. On the one hand there is the social network, and that's all my relationships, and with me in the middle. They are a couple of hundred persons, with a core of maybe fifty that constitute my personal network. On the other hand there is what I call, the "network groups." They are formed around a common interest. A tennis club could be such a network. (*Self-employed in marketing*)

The traditional distinction made between professional and private networks, that is, between work and private matters, seems to be without significance in this context. Instead, a much more adequate distinction is made between the technical and the social interactions within the different networks. Interactions concerning technical topics were described as more formal, condensed, detached, and preferably communicated through e-mail, while the mutual trust building, so indispensable to social networks, was described as being almost painstakingly social and informal.

The job as such, the work process, and the meetings, can equally well be carried out through e-mail. So, when you finally meet with each other, it's under more informal circumstances, over a beer and a discussion that's not necessarily job-related. Everything to build these essential bonds. (*Part-owner in a small enterprise*)

Employment

Even though most of the respondents were employed, it was not the advancement in professional skills, career, and titles that seemed to hold the most sway for them. The advancement pursued was not associated with a certain context, task, or organization. Their working conditions required more general and individualized qualifications in order for them to master a number of techniques and designs, to quickly get acquainted with and evaluate a situation, and to undertake responsibilities and develop their self-reliance.

To many respondents, the measure of work success was grounded in their own "personal development."

My career . . . it's more about developing myself and learning new things. That's what's important to me. (*Developer in a large tele-company*)

Consequently, the individually set salary was emphasized as constituting both an important means of feedback and an objective measure of personal performance.

It's the confirmation that what I'm doing is valuable to the company, and that it is appreciated. (*Developer in a large tele-company*)

Still, despite the rhetoric about the importance of pursuing "well-being," "happiness," and "communal respect," the respondents invariably described their experiences and progress in a highly instrumental manner. More than anything, they seemed to desire useful abilities that would make them more attractive to the labor market. Thus, it was their *employability*, rather than their self-realization, which they were referring to when talking about their personal development.

It's important to reach a higher market value, to see yourself as a kind of trademark that you develop and that you can take with you and promote in some other line of business or company. (*Part-owner in a small enterprise*)

What is illustrated here is that boundaryless jobs are just as regulated as traditional jobs, although in a different way. They are *not* regulated through a functionally structured division of labor independent of the individual performing the job. Instead, they are regulated by the individual's purpose-oriented interpretation of her circumstances. This means that the boundaryless job will assume a different and more individualized form of regulation than with traditional jobs, although it may still be regulated along the same dimensions as traditional jobs. Thus, a more individualized form of regulation, which complements or replaces the horizontal organization of work, is to be found in the goal-directed "project." Likewise, it is the social "network" that complements or replaces the vertical organization, and the unilateral commitment toward one's own "employability" that complements or replaces the mutual commitment found in regular employment, etc.

Some expected consequences of the conceptual framework

In the first part of this chapter, a conceptual framework suitable for the study of decidedly flexible jobs was outlined. Based on this framework, some general consequences were drawn and formulated as three propositions. A shift from constitutive to regulative rules would tend (1) to dissolve the formal organization, (2) to dissolve the work/non-work distinction, and (3) to disconnect the individual. In the following, I will use these propositions in structuring and interpreting the interviews.

1.   *Dissolution of the formal organization*

As I have argued, a turn toward flexibility implies a shift from constitutive to regulative rules. Since constitutive rules, as opposed to regulative rules, define, make up, and reproduce the systemic features of an organization, a shift away from these rules should render the organization, as a formal structure, superfluous. The consequences of such dissolution can be observed in the horizontal as well as the vertical dimensions of an organization.

The first thing to be noted about the horizontal organization, as described by the respondents, is its lack of permanence. Since the procedure of work follows on the specific circumstances and objectives of the assignment or task currently being performed, the structure of the labor process is bound to be temporary. As we have already noted, the horizontal organization thereby takes on the appearance of a series of more or less divergent projects. But the structure is also temporary in the sense that it is largely unpredictable. The task unfolds as they go along. In the interviews, this was particularly noticeable when the production involved the gathering, processing, transforming, and packaging of information. Here, the production could not be described as a delimited process of construction, as when a raw material becomes a manufactured product. Rather, it is better characterized as a compounding of symbols to other symbols. As such, it is a continuous process of transformation with no clear beginning or end. The transformation itself occurs in the confrontation between the persons involved, or, more specifically, between their different expectations and conceptions. Consequently, the sequential structure of the production process, as well as the clear distinction between it and the individuals involved in furthering it, has to a large extent vanished.

Another feature of this kind of organization concerns the end user, who has been pulled into the production process. Since the process does not include the construction of a predefined product, but an interpretation of the customer's needs and anticipations, the process of production could also be described as a process of communication – a process whose aim is to produce an adequate interpretation. Whether the interpretation was adequate or not is ultimately a question of agreement between the different parties concerned.

The question is whether it is a customer who is mature or whether it is a customer that does not have a clue about anything. If the customer is immature, but doesn't know it, they will have a definite opinion about how it all will be done. Then nothing will come of it. But with a mature customer, who has a lot of knowledge, we may not make as much money on consulting and such, but the deal will run easily and smoothly. So, it's all a question of whether they're humble or not. (*Systems consultant*)

As indicated here, it was not just the customer who was pulled into the process of production, the producer's responsibility also stretched beyond the process of production and into the reality of the customer.

It's a lot about trying to interpret what they're saying, and trying to translate it to something more general. You have to lay low in the beginning and listen. What names and concepts do they use? After a while you learn, and you start using their language instead. (*Part-owner in a small enterprise*)

This mutual understanding and participation in the transformation process blurs the traditionally clear distinction between customer and producer, and thereby the *external* boundaries of the organization.

When the production process becomes a series of transactions and the relationship between the different parties involved becomes a question of agreement, the boundaries between different assignments also become obscured. The unpredictability of the process forces the individual to be continuously aware of the process as a whole. This means that the individual is supposed to master a much wider domain than is specified by her particular task. Since individual competencies will naturally overlap to a large extent, the borders between the different functions of the transforming process may be controversial, and, consequently, subject to continuous negotiation. Such a continuous negotiation of the relations between the different tasks and assignments will, in turn, blur the *internal* boundaries of the organization.

The insignificance of the organization as a formal structure also implies that the performance of an individual is not defined and justified by her

position in a functional division of labor. Rather, the individual's participation is justified by whether or not she possesses the qualifications
necessary to perform a specific task. In the continuation of such a development lies, of course, the prospect of the totally disconnected individual, the employee who is available as a set of qualifications when the need
arises, or, to put it differently, the individual who is perpetually "just in
time" or "just the one."

I call this the "virtual team." For each assignment, and at each moment, you
should ask yourself: "Who is the best right now to solve this?" And that is the one
to use. Let's say you have certain profile, and are available on a market, and a
corporation is in need of your competence, well, then you're just plugged in to that
corporation, through the Internet. (*Organization developer*)

2.   Dissolution of the work/non-work distinction

The interfusion of work and leisure was a recurring theme throughout the
interviews. The many manifestations of such an interfusion can schemati-
cally be characterized either by work spilling over into non-work, or vice
versa. Perhaps the most common theme with the respondents was the
invasion of work into their private life. They worked too much, too often,
and everywhere. They were, as one respondent phrased it, "reachable all
the way into the bedroom." They complained, or more often their families complained, about their inability to relax.

I often bring along my laptop when watching television with the family. I can
write programming or something, and now and again, I look at the TV. (*Systems
consultant*)

A much less obvious theme, though, concerned the private life or
personality of the respondents spilling over into their work. Their personal interests, values, and needs influenced their work as well as the
social relations of work. Although this is fundamental to creativity, it also
increases the scope of capricious and idiosyncratic strategies.

Another theme concerned what we might refer to as "symbolic spillover." As work becomes more unstructured and the enterprise, as a
consequence, loses much of its corporeal presence, the *image* of the
enterprise will become a much more important feature in terms of its
external communication as well as its internal integration. As the foremost and sometimes sole manifestation of the enterprise, its personnel are
burdened with a heavy symbolic responsibility that is imposed on their
personal character. Several respondents even testified to the fact that the
credibility of their company depended on the personal credibility of its
personnel. Conversely, the image of their company also reflected upon

themselves, in accordance with the simple rules of transferred identity: if you work with a successful company, you are assumed to be successful yourself. Or: it is important to abandon a failing enterprise, so as not to be associated with its failure.

3.   *Disconnection of the individual*

A condition that was often referred to by the respondents was the *informal* division of labor, describing the fact that assignments were formed around certain individuals rather than from a general principle of functionality. The distribution of responsibility and authority, however, was not always, maybe not even primarily, determined by individual competence. More often, it was determined by individual choice. According to our respondents, it was not uncommon for the individual to define her own assignment. This was not necessarily done via a formal request or application, followed by an explicit choice. Rather, it was more a case of individuals doing what they had to do in order to get the job done, a process which involved "seizing opportunities," "assuming responsibility," and "receiving authority." The assignment then grew according to the principle: the more one can handle, the more one is burdened with. Thus, the distribution of responsibility could be administered very spontaneously and matter-of-factly.

It's not like you walk into the boss's office saying "I need this and that in order to run the project properly." No, all of a sudden you're just responsible for the whole thing. *[laughter]* ... "If you say it, you get it." (*Part-owner in a small enterprise*)

Responsibility could also be taken through bold initiatives.

It's very informal. If we believe something is worth fighting for, we just do it. (*Part-owner in a small enterprise*)

But, of course, it could also be allocated on more irrational grounds, like personality or gender, or it could be allocated through "non-decisions," which was often the case with left-over responsibilities that nobody wanted but somebody nevertheless ended up with. People were also incidentally, and some people even continually, excluded from the decision-making process.

If you are not there, around the coffee table, when the decision is made, you will not know what was decided or why, and you will not be part of the decision. (*Part-owner in a small enterprise*)

As we can see, the informality of the boundaryless organization does not inspire the individual to take charge and to look out for herself; it *forces* her to it. It would therefore be more accurate to say that a lack of boundaries *abandons* the worker rather than liberates her. It is very clear, though, that this abandonment should not primarily be interpreted as a general arbitrariness, following the lack of a more formal division of labor. Rather, it is an intentional abandonment, where the enterprise is surrendered to individual initiatives in the hope of gaining flexibility and momentum. As a consequence, such a strategy allows the individual a lot of room to pursue her own plans, while at the same time relying heavily on her commitment to the enterprise as a whole. This means that the relationship between the individual and the organization is essentially problematic, vacillating between self-reliance and commitment. Furthermore, the problem is always present since the relationship is continuously open to reinterpretation.

I have seen a lot of negative consequences from this [tele-working] these last two years, and the thing is: it corrodes loyalty. I wouldn't normally do anything against the company. But, before, when I was offered a job, I turned it down without giving it a thought. Now, I go over there and talk about it. I haven't taken the final step yet, but ... (*Systems consultant*)

According to the respondents, the commitment they felt toward their organization or company was primarily carried by the particular project they were working on. Their plans, for their job as well as their life, were usually realized within a project, or even *as* a project. The project served as a link-up between the individual and the organization, framing and joining both interests. The project form, thus, is not just a way to organize production; it is also a temporary contract between the individual and the organization specifying their mutual commitments. It is important to understand, however, that the bond between the individual and the organization that is realized in the project form is a result not of having the same interests, but of having *compatible* interests. The respondents generally described themselves as being independent of the organization as such. The organization was presented as an environment offering them certain possibilities, while the individual was portrayed as a satellite – in orbit around the organization, but alone in its mission.

This company is good for me. They give me the freedom of action I need, and I get my salary. But, I would probably have done the same thing if it had been another company employing me. So, the company itself is not a motive for me. They have given me the opportunity to advance, but other companies could have done that. (*Systems developer*)

Hence, the mutuality achieved through the project form is better described as a *mutual exploitation*. The respondents outlined their work as going beyond their organization. They readily admitted, for example, that their career plans went beyond their current employment. The success of a project was primarily a personal achievement and a merit for future assignments. Furthermore, they more often received their personal acknowledgement from a professional network stretching beyond the organization. Loyalty was given to those within that network, not to those who merely "existed" within the same organization.

The organization, then, was primarily seen as a more or less convenient setting for the realization of certain plans. While these plans may have been executed within the context of an organization, they were conceived in reference to the labor market as a whole. For most respondents, the main concern was not with their current employment, but with their future employability. Thus, the main *social arena* for work was not their organization, but the labor market as a whole.

Discussion

In this chapter, I have called attention to the flexible, even boundaryless, conditions of work. I have tried to show that these conditions imply a deregulation as compared to the traditional regulations of work. I have, furthermore, demonstrated that such a deregulation can manifest itself in various degrees and ways. It can, more specifically, involve when, where, how, and with whom work is to be performed, as well as the kind of assignment or employment that links the individual to her job. The flexibility arises from the individual subjecting herself to any or all of the working conditions out of *choice* rather than routine, even if the choice only involves a choice between two evils. This changes the relation between the individual and her working conditions in the sense that the obligations of work are lifted from the authoritative rules and regulations of the organization and placed in the hands of the individual worker. The deregulation, consequently, entails that the individual assume increased responsibility for herself as a worker and for the work that she does.

It is important to note, however, that the jobs are not deregulated in the strict sense of the word. They are not unregulated. Instead, it would be more accurate to say that they are re-regulated. These new rules may even be described, structured, and analyzed along the same dimensions as the "old" rules, that is, time, space, horizontal and vertical organization. Characteristic of these new rules is that they are embedded within the knowledge about the context and conditions of work, a context and conditions that also involve the working individual. Furthermore, the behavioral outcome of these rules appears to be intentional and reasoned, rather than spontaneous or habitual. In other words, the rules seem to take the active self-awareness of the worker for granted.

There are several implications of such a de- or re-regulation. From a theoretical perspective, a rule-sensitive framework would be expected to put the spotlight on the various forms of monitoring and control indigenous to work. On the one hand, the employment of intentional and reasoned rule-following requires managerial technologies that presuppose human volition; technologies that are embedded in knowledge, reason and subjectivity, as described by Michel Foucault (1978/2002, 1980, 1982; see also Rose, 1999). On the other hand, it emphasizes the worker's ability to cope with her work and fellow workers. Special attention would then be given to the *strategies* of the individual. By strategies I am referring to the ways an individual chooses to tackle the conditions of work. Strategies may, of course, be restricted by the actual circumstances of work, but they can never be reduced to them. As long as there is a choice involved, the strategies of the individual will be a possible and perhaps significant ground for explanation. In the attempt to deal with her work, the individual may, for instance, use strategies that are hazardous to her health. In some cases, this may be done unconsciously, or out of ignorance, and in other cases as the only feasible option. Confronting the issues and problems of work, then, is not necessarily limited to an alteration of the circumstances for work. It may also involve an improvement of the individual's repertoire of actions, or, as Amartya Sen (1999) would say, her capability set.

From a methodological standpoint, the boundarylessness of re-regulation requires taking the individual into the equation. Individual variables such as competence, attitude, reasoning, and way of thinking become factors of increasing importance regarding performance at work. In-depth inquiry into the individual's frame of mind, her calculations, intentions, and aspirations becomes a necessary complement to more traditional surveys and experiments. Also, background analyses of the context, and the historical and structural situation in which the individual is embedded, are necessary to make sense of the information received. One cannot understand the actions of an individual without understanding the situation in which her actions are meant to have an impact. As a result, variables like career, the labor market, and the life situation are becoming more important. Such a multi-methodological approach should be the rule rather than the exception when approaching more fluid conditions of work.

Finally, the new rules of work will, of course, also have practical implications. Work-related problems, for instance, have traditionally been treated as work environment issues, that is, as caused by factors independent of and beyond the control of the individual. The deregulation of many jobs should make it increasingly difficult to take such a detachment for granted. This means that the problems of working life will only to a limited extent be identified as work environment issues. When they are, it will mainly be within the domains of the labor market retaining more traditional conditions of work. At the same time, and this pertains to the labor market as a whole, the person-related issues will be increasing.

References

Allvin, M. (2004). The individualisation of labour. In C. Garsten and K. Jacobsson (eds.), *Learning to be employable* (pp. 23–41). Houndsmills: Palgrave Macmillan.

Allvin, M. and Aronsson, G. (2003). The future of work environment reforms: does the concept of work environment apply within the new economy? *International Journal of Health Services* 33: 99–111.

Allvin, M., Aronsson, G., Hagström, T., Johansson, G., Lundberg, U., and Skärstrand, E. (1998). *Gränslöst arbete eller arbetets nya gränser: delstudie 1* (Arbete och Hälsa 1998:21). Stockholm: Arbetslivsinstitutet.

Allvin, M., Wiklund, P., Härenstam, A., and Aronsson, G. (1999). *Frikopplad eller frånkopplad: om innebörder och konsekvenser av gränslösa arbeten* (Arbete och Hälsa 1999:2). Stockholm: Arbetslivsinstitutet.

Alvesson, M. and Berg, P. -O. (1992). *Corporate culture and organizational symbolism*. Berlin: de Gruyter.

Ashkenas, R. (1995). *The boundaryless organization: breaking the chains of organizational structure*. San Francisco: Jossey-Bass.

Avery, C. and Zabel, D. (2001). *The flexible workplace: a sourcebook of information and research*. Westport, CT: Quorum Books.

Beck, L. W. (1975). *The actor and the spectator*. New Haven: Yale University Press.

Burns, T. R. and Flam, H. (1987). *The shaping of social organization: social rule system theory with applications*. London: Sage.

Clark, B. K. and Fujimoto, T. (1991). *Product development performance: strategy, organization, and management in the world auto industry*. Boston, MA: Harvard Business School Press.

Czarniawska, B. (1997). *Narrating the organization: dramas of institutional identity*. Chicago: University of Chicago Press.

D'Aveni, A. R. (1994). *Hypercompetition: managing the dynamics of strategic maneuvering*. New York: The Free Press.

du Gay, P. and Salaman, G. (1992). The cult(ure) of the customer. *Journal of Management Studies* 29: 615–33.

Fayol, H. (1916/1988). *General and industrial management*. London: Pitman.

Foucault, M. (1978/2002). Governmentality. In J. D. Faubion (ed.), *Essential works of Foucault 1954–1984, vol. 3: Power* (pp. 201–22). London: Penguin.

(1980). *Power/knowledge: selected interviews and other writings 1972–1977 by Michel Foucault.* London: Harvester Wheatsheaf.

(1982). The subject and power. In H. L. Dreyfus and P. Rabinow (eds.), *Michel Foucault: beyond structuralism and hermeneutics* (pp. 208–28). London: Harvester Wheatsheaf.

Giddens, A. (1984). *The constitution of society: outline of the theory of structuration.* Cambridge: Polity Press.

Glaser, B. G. (1978). *Theoretical sensitivity: advances in the methodology of grounded theory.* Mill Valley, CA: The Sociology Press.

Glaser, B. G. and Strauss, A. L. (1967). *The discovery of grounded theory: strategies for qualitative research.* Chicago: Aldine.

Hacker, W. (1978). *Allgemeine Arbeits- und Ingenieurpsychologie.* Stuttgart: Verlag Hans Huber.

(1986). *Arbeitspsychologie* (vol. 41). Stuttgart: Verlag Hans Huber.

Harrison, B. (1994). *Lean and mean: the changing landscape of corporate power in the age of flexibility.* New York: Basic Books.

Hendry, C. (1995). *Human resource management: a strategic approach to employment.* Oxford: Butterworth-Heinemann.

Hutchins, D. (1988). *Just in time.* Aldershot: Gower.

Knight, F. H. (1921). *Risk, uncertainty and profit.* Boston: Houghton Mifflin.

Kunda, G. (1992). *Engineering culture: control and commitment in a high-tech corporation.* Philadelphia: Temple University Press.

Luhmann, N. (1995). *Social systems.* Stanford, CA: Stanford University Press.

Miles, M. B. and Huberman, A. M. (1994a). Data management and analysis methods. In N. K. Denzin and Y. Lincoln (eds.), *Handbook of qualitative research* (pp. 428–44). Thousand Oaks, CA: Sage.

(1994b). *Qualitative data analysis.* Thousand Oaks, CA: Sage.

Mills, A. J. and Murgatroyd, S. J. (1991). *Organizational rules: a framework for understanding organizational action.* Buckingham: Open University Press.

Ouchi, W. G. (1981). *Theory Z: how American business can meet the Japanese challenge.* Reading, MA: Addison Wesley.

Peters, T. J. and Waterman, R. H. J. (1982). *In search of excellence: lessons from America's best-run companies.* New York: Harper and Row.

Piore, M. J. and Sabel, C. F. (1984). *The second industrial divide.* New York: Basic Books.

Porter, E. M. (1990). *The competitive advantage of nations.* New York: The Free Press.

Rasmussen, J. (1986). *Information processing and human–machine interaction: an approach to cognitive engineering* (vol. 12). Amsterdam: North-Holland.

Rasmussen, J. and Vicente, K. J. (1990). Ecological interfaces: a technological imperative in high tech systems? *International Journal of Human Computer Interaction* 2: 93ff.

Rose, N. (1999). *Powers of freedom: reframing political thought.* Cambridge: Cambridge University Press.

Schaufeli, W. and Enzmann, D. (1998). *The burnout companion to study and practice: a critical analysis.* London: Taylor and Francis.

Searle, J. R. (1969). *Speech acts.* Cambridge: Cambridge University Press.

Sen, A. (1999). *Development as freedom.* New York: Random House.

Stalk, G. Jr. and Hout, T. M. (1990). *Competing against time: how time-based competition is reshaping global markets*. London: Macmillan.

Strauss, A. and Corbin, J. (1990). *Basics of qualitative research*. Newbury Park, CA: Sage.

Taylor, F. W. (1911). *The principles of scientific management*. New York: Harper and Brother.

3   Changing work roles: new demands and challenges

Johnny Hellgren, Magnus Sverke, and Katharina Näswall

Working life has gone through numerous changes in recent decades, as has been observed and commented on by a number of researchers and practitioners (e.g. Burke and Cooper, 2000; Gowing, Kraft, and Quick, 1997; Gallie, White, Cheng, and Tomlinson, 1998; Howard, 1995; Pfeffer, 1997). Some of the changes often described in the literature relate to the increased occurrence of reorganizations, happening not only through changes in ownership but also in connection with downsizing (Burke and Nelson, 1998; Pfeffer, 1997), which have been found to bring about both a diminished degree of predictability and an increased experiencing of job insecurity for individuals (Ferrie, Shipley, Marmot, Stanfeld, and Smith, 1998; Sverke, Hellgren, and Näswall, 2002). However, it is not only organizational and structural changes that define the new working life, as it has been argued that the work itself, as well as its conditions, has also changed (Howard, 1995; Burchell, Ladipo, and Wilkinson, 2002).

One of the more prominent changes has been the gradual transition from a product industry to a service industry (Tetrick and Quick, 2003). The demands placed on the individual have accordingly become more mental than physical in nature, as the object of work has had less to do with the manufacturing of finished products. What characterizes service-oriented work, rather, is the process of communication, in which the concern is to identify the needs and wishes of the customer. The rising demands for increased individual responsibility and flexibility in regard to work put an increased demand on employees to be goal-oriented and self-directed, and implies a shift from a traditional, more objective regulation of work, to a more subjective one (Gallie *et al.*, 1998). However, when it comes to self-direction and autonomy, it may be problematic if the employee lacks sufficient resources for handling such conditions, especially if they are combined with tasks and expectations that are vaguely defined.

Literature on this subject has argued that having the possibility of exercising control both in and over the work situation is vital in order for individuals to experience their work situation as satisfactory (Ganster and Fusilier, 1989; Theorell, 2003; Warr, 1987). When it comes to control and the providing of self-direction and autonomy at work, however, the situation becomes more complicated, since an increased degree of these two latter conditions may instead lead to uncertainty and a *lack* of control, along with the risk that individuals may react with negative experiences rather than positive (cf. Warr's Vitamin model, 1987). If an employee is unsure about what she is expected to do, and unclear about what goals she should strive toward, it is reasonable to question whether the increased autonomy is of benefit to her – and also whether she has in fact gained increased control at all (Gallie *et al.*, 1998). Too high a degree of autonomy at work in combination with unclear goals may furthermore lead to frustration and tension, which, in the long run, may lead to the development of stress symptoms.

Given these changes, it is important to investigate how today's employees experience their work situation regarding the demands and individual control they encounter in the new working life, and also to examine whether these factors act as stressors rather than contributing to an increase in individuals' sense of control over their work. This would further allow us to explore and identify those factors of the modern working life that affect individuals' health and well-being. To shed some light on this, we have investigated these new potential challenges and demands, whose importance for workers' motivation, performance, and well-being extends beyond the more traditional role stressors (role overload, role conflict, and role ambiguity). More specifically, this chapter investigates the relative importance of both traditional and newer work stressors for employees' mental health and their experiencing of work motivation (job satisfaction, organizational commitment, and perceived performance). To approach this research question, a pilot study using group interviews was first conducted in order to provide some insight into how the employees experienced their daily work situation and what they considered to be problematic at work. Based on these results, a questionnaire was then developed for the purpose of capturing the critical aspects of the work situation, and to relate them to the outcome factors.

Stress models

Most often, stress is described as a process in which the individual interacts with her environment and where the experiencing of stress is seen as emerging through a series of factors that begin in the actual surroundings and end in the individual's reactions. The individual interprets the objective situation through her subjective perception of the situation, and uses this interpretation to determine the significance of the situation, thereby deciding whether it is positive or negative (Katz and Kahn, 1978; Lazarus and Folkman, 1984). This appraisal is then followed by more direct reactions. Accordingly, different individuals may be likely to form different interpretations of the very same environment and, in turn, react in different ways to the same situation (Beehr, 2000).

The stress models commonly presented in the literature tend to be based on a perspective that emphasizes balance, according to which there should be an even distribution between, for example, demand and control factors (Karasek and Theorell, 1990) or between an individual's efforts and rewards (Siegrist, 1996). In these models, stress is seen as a function of an imbalance between the resources and supplies that an individual believes she possesses and the threats or demands which that individual interprets and experiences to be connected with the given situation (Cooper, 2000; Kahn and Byosiere, 1992).

One of the most common models for identifying and explaining stress experiences, within the area of working life, is known as the Job Demand–Control model (Karasek, 1979; Karasek and Theorell, 1990). The basic reasoning behind this model is based on the presumption that stress is a function of two underlying work attributes, namely, work demands and influence/control at work. Psychological work demands are usually defined as the occurrence of psychologically stressful factors in the work environment, such as workload, degree of task difficulty, and time pressure. The dimension of control, on the other hand, relates to an individual's opportunity to exert influence and control over the work situation (Karasek and Theorell, 1990). This model holds that stress experiences arise when high demands are combined with low control, and that a high degree of control can reduce the possible negative consequences of high demands.

Most stress models and various work environment inventories focus on various physical work demands such as load and time pressure, as well as on unclear work objectives, and interpersonal factors such as conflict and leadership in their attempts to identify stress factors in the work situation (e.g. Brown and Leigh, 1996; Hackman and Oldham, 1975; James and Sells, 1981; Karasek and Theorell, 1990). In response to the changes occurring in the work environment, traditional stress models have had to undergo modifications in order to take into account other work demands, such as emotional demands in order to reflect the difficulties found in the relations with customers, clients, and patients (see e.g. the Demands–Resources model; Demerouti, Bakker, Nachreiner, and Schaufeli, 2001; Marshall, Barnett, and Sayer, 1997; Söderfeldt *et al.*, 1997). This, coupled with working life becoming increasingly more marked by demands for self-initiative and autonomy, with more diffuse work demands and objectives, and, moreover, with individuals to a greater extent being expected to take responsibility for aspects of work that perhaps would have previously fallen to the supervisor (Gallie *et al.*, 1998; Howard, 1995), has made it necessary to look again at previously accepted stress and work climate models with the purpose of reexamining in what specific ways they need to be complemented in order to adequately capture and elucidate the stress situations prevalent today. Indeed, current stress models and work environment inventories may need to be expanded and supplemented to include factors that more clearly focus on the work roles that characterize today's working life.

The pilot study

The pilot study was carried out at the main office of a private organization, centered in Stockholm, whose business concerned information technology. The study was conducted with the help of focus groups, made up of four or five persons, whom the researchers met and spoke with. These conversations did not take the form of traditional interviews, but were carried out in such a way that would stimulate relaxed and open group discussions. The researchers, nevertheless, adhered to their agenda and, to a certain degree, guided the discussions in the desired direction. This approach makes it easier to reach shared conclusions in a group and to bring forth an account that is told in its context (Patton, 1987; Steyaert and Bouwen, 1994).

One discussion was with the employees at the organization, while another was with the union representatives who were also employed there. In addition, a private interview was also held with the organization's personnel supervisor. These two discussion groups and the private interview were used with the purpose of obtaining as broad a sample as possible, thus allowing employees, union representatives, and organizational management to all have a say. Willing participation was received from all persons who were asked to take part in these interview discussions. The interviews went on until a so-called saturation effect was reached and no further new information could be ascertained from the discussions (Miles and Huberman, 1994; Strauss and Corbin, 1990), which took approximately two hours in both cases. The interview with the personnel supervisor lasted about an hour. The objective of this pilot study was to look into that which characterizes professional employees' work, and also to examine what has happened to their work situation and how the work may have changed.

After the recorded discussions had been transcribed, the content was grouped according to a number of different themes that were identified in the material. To increase validity, the grouping was first carried out by two persons, independent of each other, before the two were combined into a general grouping of the themes (Cassell and Symon, 1994). After further groupings and categorizations, three distinct themes emerged that could be said to describe the employees' experiences of new stressors in their work situation. In order to validate these results, the topics of the three themes were revisited with the focus groups in a discussion about their relevance. Not only could the personnel supervisor identify with the themes, but both focus groups were of the opinion that the three topics fittingly reflected their experiencing of work as it had been discussed at the interviews (for a more thorough description of the pilot study, see van der Vliet and Hellgren, 2002).

The first of the three themes concerns the experiencing of a shifting from an objective regulating of work to a more subjective one. The work was considered to be less clearly defined and delimited, in both time and space, and in regard to the work's structure and content. It was also found that, to a greater extent, it was left up to the individuals themselves to see that their competencies were in line with those needed to carry out their work tasks. Those interviewed experienced, for example, that there was a constant demand for renewing their competencies – that their knowledge and abilities constantly needed to be developed and updated in order to be able to do the work and ensure their gradual career advancement within the organization. A frustration was also expressed over not knowing specifically which competencies would come to be in demand for subsequent work tasks. Always to be prepared for the eventuality that one's knowledge would be lacking and would need to be complemented in order to complete the assigned work was seen as a demand in itself.

The second theme to be identified concerns difficulties in judging when an assignment/service is completed. The interviewees felt this to be especially problematic when it came to independent work where the individual does not have the opportunity to check with a colleague on whether the work should be considered finished. It was thought that this could lead to the experiencing of stress, particularly when the individual feels that she always could have done a little more but instead chose to consider the work finished. It was also expressed that the work often lacked a well-defined completion point that could clearly be recognized and related to, as well as that it is not always the case that colleagues come to the same judgement in respect to when the work is finished, which can lead to differences of opinion. The same applies to the relationship with the customer (in those cases where there is a customer), in that differences can exist between the interviewee's and the customer's mental images of what constitutes the finished product, which may bring about a lack of accord and an uncertainty that is experienced as stressful and unpleasant.

In connection with this, the third theme to emerge concerned the demand for individuals to personally appraise the quality of their work, as individuals themselves were often expected to be able to judge whether their work results were of high enough quality. Similar to the problems associated with the delimiting of work, this was also thought to be especially the case when an individual worked independently and was personally responsible for the work's quality. If an individual lacks a definitive measure for comparison or someone to consult with about how well the work is being carried out, a sense of uncertainty arises which can lead to the experiencing of stress.

To a large degree, the results of the interview study confirm the general trends of today's changing working life that have been previously described in the literature (e.g. Howard, 1995; Tetrick and Quick, 2003), including the gradual increase in the exercise of self-direction and autonomy at work, and the element of having more diffuse work assignments, objectives, and limits (see also chapter 2 of this book). There is a possibility that the experiencing of the demands and uncertainties that were mentioned by those interviewed could lead to the experiencing of stress, particularly when the individual feels a constant pressure to continuously refresh her knowledge and abilities, for example when a bulk of new information must be attained in order to complete an assignment. It is also quite conceivable that, although the results of this pilot study suggest that the content of the work demands has partially changed (as has been found previously, see Gallie et al., 1998; Howard, 1995), these demands are also experienced as stressful and carry with them consequences similar to those which characterize traditional demands (see e.g. Karasek and Theorell, 1990).

The interviews also indicated that the employees experienced a higher degree of autonomy along with the increased demand to make their own determinations in regard to both their own work and decisions involving their customers and clients. This was combined with the fact that one had to be goal-oriented and self-initiating, when it came to both the organization's objectives and the objectives of one's own work. Those interviewed considered these changes to be a function of a trend toward more independent work, in which the supervisor is less and less involved in the daily work, and where it is the final product, often in the form of a service rather than a physical product, that is evaluated.

Previously, the demands of work have tended to concern the experiencing of overload, where the individual not only felt that she had too much to do, but also experienced conflicts that could be related both to the objectives of the work and to the receiving of conflicting work demands and directives (e.g. Karasek and Theorell, 1990; Katz and Kahn, 1978). The "new" stress factors, however, according to those interviewed, were more related to the uncertainty they felt about the work and their own competencies. It was also expressed that the work today tends to be less clearly defined in respect to knowing which work tasks are to be carried out by the individual, and when these work tasks should be completed by. A number of respondents felt that certain tasks could easily end up in a no-man's-land where it is unclear whose responsibility they are. There was also a feeling among some respondents that, at times, they might have been able to perform a little better, a little more, or a little quicker – especially when the work did not involve another person who could give input on whether the work was sufficiently completed.

In sum, the results of the pilot study show that a demand can be experienced when the individual feels that her competencies are not adequate, and that she has to continually complement and develop herself in order to complete the work assignments. Increased difficulties in being able to judge the amount of work necessitated for a task, as well as the level of one's performance in the work, were also reported, which may likely lead to the individual experiencing an uncertain and stressful work situation and, in the long run, reacting with diminished satisfaction, commitment, and motivation in regard to both the work and the organization. As has been noted in previous research (see, for example, Brown and Leigh, 1996; Karasek and Theorell, 1990; Levi, 2000; Quick and Tetrick, 2003), such circumstances may also be expected to carry with them a risk for the development of mental and physical health problems in the long run as well.

As mentioned above, the common stress models and work environment inventories typically focus on physical demands and interpersonal problems, rather than on the experiencing of mental and emotional demands, as causes of individuals' stress experiences. The question is whether the three themes identified in the pilot study – the demands for continual competency development, difficulties in judging whether the work is completed, and difficulties in judging how well the work is carried out – can serve to complement and expand the previous stress models.

The questionnaire study

The next step in the investigation was to construct a set of measures for these new potential stressors to see if they could be measured and empirically differentiated from previously recognized and measured stress factors, and to look into whether these new stressors could be related to outcome variables such as attitudes, performance, and mental health. The three themes that emerged in the pilot study were operationalized as competency demands, task completion ambiguity, and task quality ambiguity.

The data on which the study is based were collected with the help of questionnaires that were distributed among all of the employees of two similarly sized organizations in Sweden, one of which was an accounting firm and the other a municipality. Out of the 1,153 questionnaires sent out, 916 were returned, which yielded a response rate of 79%. Women constituted 64% of the sample, and the mean age was 46 (SD = 11). After adjusting for internal attrition, the analyses in this study finally came to be based on a pool of 905 individuals who had complete data for all of the study's variables.

In order to capture each of the three factors (competency demands, task completion ambiguity, task quality ambiguity), items were constructed with the purpose of measuring the extent of demand and uncertainty individuals experienced in their work situation. Specifically, three items were constructed for capturing competency demands, four items for task completion ambiguity, and four items for task quality ambiguity. To validate the new measures and see whether they could be differentiated from previous common measures, three classic work stressors were also included, namely role overload (3 items; Beehr, Walsh, and Taber, 1976), role conflict (5 items; Rizzo, House, and Lirtzman, 1970), and role ambiguity (4 items; Rizzo et al., 1970). The item wordings for the new as well as the classic stressors, which all utilized five-point response scales (1 = strongly disagree, 5 = strongly agree), are presented in Table 3.1.

Dimensionality

Two factor analyses were conducted in order to test whether the new scales, as measured with the constructed items, were adequately distinct from the classic work stressors, and to check whether the new and the established items could be used as desired. The material was first divided into two subsamples based on organizational affiliation. The items were first subjected to exploratory factor analyses (EFA) using the municipality employees (n = 408), followed by confirmatory factor analyses (CFA) among the accountants (n = 508). This was done in order to check whether the factor structure found from the exploratory analysis could be replicated in an independent sample using a confirmatory analysis,

Table 3.1 *Factor loadings for the classic stressors and the "new" stressors from both exploratory (EFA) and confirmatory (CFA) factor analyses*

Item	Factor loadings (EFA)	Factor loadings (CFA)
Role overload (Beehr et al., 1976)		
1. I am given enough time to do what is expected of me in my job (r)	.87	.77
2. It fairly often happens that I have to work under a heavy time pressure	.58	.77
3. I often have too much to do in my job	.77	.66
Role conflict (Rizzo et al., 1970)		
1. I receive incompatible requests from two or more people	.65	.82
2. I have things to do that should be done differently	.38	.59
3. I have to buck a rule or policy in order to carry out an assignment	.58	.54
4. I do things that are apt to be accepted by one person and not accepted by others	.39	.59
5. I receive an assignment without adequate resources and materials to execute it	.79	.84
Role ambiguity (Rizzo et al., 1970)		
1. I know exactly what is expected of me (r)	.77	.75
2. Explanation is clear of what has to be done (r)	.78	.92
3. I know what my responsibilities are (r)	.58	.88
4. There exist no clear, planned goals and objectives for my job	.47	.69
Competency demands		
1. I am expected to develop my competence	.88	.82
2. The nature of my work means that I continually have to develop myself and learn to think in new ways	.71	.72
3. I feel pressure to continually learn in order to manage my work task	.53	.71
Task completion ambiguity		
1. I can determine when my work assignments are completed (r)	.76	.88
2. I know when a task is completed (r)	.46	.87
3. I can decide if my work task is finished or not (r)	.77	.79
4. It is up to me to assess when my work assignment is completed (r)	.73	.78
Task quality ambiguity		
1. I know when I have done good work (r)	.88	.94
2. I can sense when I have carried out a job well (r)	.90	.99
3. I can judge the quality of my work (r)	.39	.64
4. When my work is carried out well, I can feel it (r)	.68	.91

(r) = reverse coded. EFA factor loadings generated from principal axis factoring with oblimin rotation (only loadings on the hypothesized factors shown). CFA factor loadings are from the completely standardized solution.

which would also help prevent us from making any hasty conclusions concerning the dimensionality of the data. The factor loadings for the individual items are presented in Table 3.1. The exploratory factor analysis was conducted using principal axis factoring with oblimin rotation, in which the criteria of eigenvalues above 1 and factor loadings above .40 were used in identifying the factors. For each item, only the factor loadings on the proposed factors that were generated in the exploratory factor analysis are presented. The confirmatory factor analysis was conducted using the robust maximum likelihood estimation procedures in Lisrel 8.71 (Jöreskog and Sörbom, 1996).

The results of the exploratory factor analysis showed that there were six underlying factors with an eigenvalue above 1. These factors correspond to the three new potential stressors and the three classic stressors. The results also showed that all items loaded on their expected factors, and that there were no double loadings, that is, any items with loadings above .40 on more than one factor. Two items from the classic stress measures loaded below .40: items two and four in the scale measuring *role conflict*, which loaded .38 and .39, respectively, in factor 2. This indicates that these items may give rise to problems of reliability as well as validity, but since the loadings were very close to .40 and there were no cross-loadings with other factors, the risk appears low. One of the newly constructed items loaded below .40 as well (item three in the scale measuring *task quality ambiguity* loaded at .39). As in the case of role conflict, we consider this less of a problem since the loading is close to .40 and no cross-loadings or other problems were detected in the analysis. This indicates that the development of this item should be continued in order to improve the measurement characteristics of the scale. Based on the generally positive results, there were no changes made to any of the scales after the exploratory factor analysis, and the exact same model was subjected to confirmatory factor analysis using the subsample of accountants.

Table 3.2 presents the chi-square values, degrees of freedom, and the different goodness of fit measures for the models tested. The Root Mean Square Error of Approximation (RMSEA) ranges between 0 and 1, and a value close to 0 represents a good fit of the model to the data. Browne and Cudeck (1993) suggest that RMSEA levels of .08 and below indicate a reasonable error of approximation in relation to the degrees of freedom, and that levels of .05 or below indicate a close fit of the model to the data. The Comparative Fit Index (CFI) indicator varies between 0 and 1, where higher levels indicate a better fit of the model to the data (Bentler, 1990).

The results of the confirmatory factor analysis show that a six-factor solution, where each item is related to its proposed factor, was the model which best represented the data. This model was compared to a

Table 3.2 *Model comparisons between the various confirmatory factor models*

Model	df	χ^2	RMSEA	CFI	Model Comparison	Δdf	$\Delta\chi^2$
0. Null model	253	13808.64*	0.34	0.20	—	—	—
1. 1-Factor	230	3292.45*	0.16	0.82	1vs0	23	10516.19*
2. 2-factor	229	2190.93*	0.13	0.88	2vs1	1	1101.52*
3. 6-factor	215	653.39*	0.06	0.97	3vs2	14	1537.5*

$^* = p < .05.$

two-factor model, where the new and the classic stressors were proposed to reflect two underlying factors. The six-factor model was also compared to a one-factor model, where all items represented one latent factor, and a null model, where no associations between items were specified.

The correlations between the factors obtained in the confirmatory factor analysis were moderate (.03–.69), with the strongest association being between role conflict and role ambiguity. The results also showed that among the new stressors, competency demand was almost unrelated to the two other new stressors (.01 and −.03, respectively). On the other hand, there was a correlation of .67 between task completion ambiguity and task quality ambiguity. The results of the two factor analyses indicate that it is reasonable to conclude that there are six underlying factors in the material, and that these factors to a certain degree represent separate experiences of stress in the work environment. The results also indicate that the scales for the new stressors measure something distinct from those of the classical measures of work stressors, and that the new factors also capture three distinct phenomena of the work environment of the respondents. Subsequent reliability analyses also show that the internal consistencies of the new measures were satisfactory, with Cronbach's alpha ranging from .76 to .89.

Predicting attitudes, performance, and mental health

In order to answer the question of what impact the new stressors have on different individual outcomes, regression analyses were conducted on the entire sample (n = 916). The outcomes measured in the questionnaire were job satisfaction, organizational commitment, performance, and health. Job satisfaction was measured with three items (e.g. I enjoy being at my job; Hellgren, Sverke, and Isaksson, 1999). Organizational commitment was measured using four items developed by Allen and

Meyer (1990; e.g. I enjoy discussing my organization with people outside it). Self-reported performance was measured with five questions developed by Hall and Hall (1976; e.g. I manage most of the situations that arise in my work). Mental health was measured with Goldberg's (1979) General health questionnaire (the twelve-item version; e.g. Have you in the past two weeks been able to concentrate on whatever you're doing?). All items were measured on a scale between 1 (strongly disagree) and 5 (strongly agree), except mental health, which was measured on a scale from 0 (never) to 3 (always). Year of birth and sex (0 = female, 1 = male) were measured with one question each. Demographics were included in the study in order to control for any effects of age and sex on the outcomes. These variables have been shown to have impact on outcomes such as attitudes, behavior, and health, especially when these are measured by self-reports (e.g. Diener, Suh, Lucas, and Smith, 1999; Mohr, 2000). Descriptive statistics, correlations, and reliabilities (Cronbach's alpha) for all variables are shown in Table 3.3.

Four multiple regression analyses were used to investigate the relative impact of the background variables (age and sex), classic stressors (role overload, role conflict, and role ambiguity), and new stressors (competency demands, task completion ambiguity, and task quality ambiguity) on the outcomes (job satisfaction, organizational commitment, perceived performance, and mental health). The analyses were conducted in two steps. Demographics and the classical stressors were entered in the first step, while the new stressors were entered in the second. This made it possible to investigate how much of the variance explained in the outcomes could be attributed to the new stressors, after demographics and the classical stressors had been taken into account. The results of the four regression analyses are presented in Table 3.4. The table only presents the last step of the analysis.

Job satisfaction was predicted by age, as the older employees tended to be more satisfied at work than their younger counterparts. Of the classic work stressors, role conflict and role ambiguity had negative effects, which indicates that increased degrees of role conflict and role ambiguity are associated with a decreased degree of job satisfaction. In total, the demographic variables and the classic stressors explained 26% of the variation in job satisfaction. When it came to the new stressors, higher degrees of task completion ambiguity and task quality ambiguity were found to be related to a lower degree of experienced job satisfaction. The predictors explained a total of 30% of the variation in job satisfaction. The three new stressors accounted for 4% of the individual variation in job satisfaction beyond that which was explained by the demographic variables and the classic stressors.

Table 3.3 *Intercorrelations and descriptive statistics for all study variables*

Variable	1	2	3	4	5	6	7	8	9	10	11	12	Mean	SD	α
1. Age	1.0												46.01	10.87	—
2. Sex (male)	.12	1.0											0.36	—	—
3. Role overload	-.05	-.09	1.0										3.37	0.96	.80
4. Role conflict	-.04	.00	.37	1.0									2.10	0.78	.77
5. Role ambiguity	-.16	-.07	.16	.52	1.0								3.86	0.83	.85
6. Competency demands	.14	.07	.34	.22	.04	1.0							3.44	0.93	.76
7. Task completion ambiguity	-.28	-.09	.14	.32	.41	.09	1.0						4.14	0.75	.85
8. Task quality ambiguity	-.21	-.13	.03	.18	.38	.02	.57	1.0					3.99	0.75	.89
9. Job satisfaction	.24	.05	-.03	-.32	-.49	-.00	-.39	-.37	1.0				3.86	0.92	.89
10. Organizational commitment	.15	.14	.11	-.06	-.23	.14	-.17	-.12	.47	1.0			2.96	0.74	.63
11. Perceived performance	.18	.00	.06	-.10	-.29	.03	-.44	-.48	.43	.23	1.0		4.32	0.46	.69
12. Mental health	-.02	-.04	-.21	-.28	-.28	-.06	-.26	-.23	.38	.16	.27	1.0	0.74	0.40	.75

—= not applicable, correlations >.09 significant at the .05 level.

Table 3.4 *Results of multiple hierarchical regression (standardized regression coefficients) analyses predicting job satisfaction, perceived performance, and mental health*

Predictor	Job satisfaction	Organizational commitment	Perceived performance	Mental health
Age	.13***	.11*	.05	.07
Sex (male)	−.01	.12*	−.08	.01
Role overload	−.09	.13*	.09	−.13**
Role conflict	−.13**	−.01	.07	−.11*
Role ambiguity	−.32***	−.21***	−.12*	−.12*
Competency demands	−.03	.13*	.02	−.01
Task completion ambiguity	−.12**	−.09	−.25***	−.12*
Task quality ambiguity	−.13**	−.05	−.30***	−.11*
R^2	.30***	.10***	.29***	.13***
ΔR^2 (new stressors)	.04***	.01*	.18***	.03**

$^*p < .05,\ ^{**}p < .01,\ ^{***}p < .001.$

Organizational commitment was predicted by both sex and age, as the older and male employees reported greater unity with the organization compared to those who were younger and female. Of the classic stressors, a higher degree of role overload was related to a higher degree of commitment, indicating that those who experience a higher workload identify with the organization to a greater extent than those who experience less of a workload. In contrast to this, those who experienced a higher degree of role ambiguity reported a lower degree of organizational commitment as compared to those who experienced having fewer unclear objectives in their work. In all, the background factors and the classic stressors together explained 9% of the variation in organizational commitment. In respect to the new stressors, the results show that only that of competency demands was associated with organizational commitment. This association was positive, indicating that those experiencing higher competency demands also report a stronger commitment to the organization than those reporting fewer competency demands. All in all, the model explained 10% of the variance in organizational commitment, and the new stressors added 1% to the explained variance.

Self-reported work performance was predicted only by role ambiguity in the first step. This relation was negative, which indicates that the experiencing of role ambiguity tends to be associated with a decreased degree of performance at work. The background factors and classic stressors accounted for a total of 11% of the variation in performance. In regard to the new stressors, work performance was predicted by task completion ambiguity and task quality ambiguity, with the relation being negative in both cases, which suggests that an increased degree of uncertainty over whether the job is completed and over its quality, respectively, are associated with a lower degree of self-reported work performance. A total of 29% of the variation in performance was explained by the model, and, in the last step of the regression, the new stressors explained another 18%.

Mental health was explained by all three of the classic stressors and two of the new: task completion ambiguity and task quality ambiguity. In all cases, the relation was found to be negative, implying that an increased experiencing of these stressors is associated with decreased mental well-being. Altogether, the predictors explained 11% of the variation in mental health. The demographic variables and the classic stressors could together account for 8% of the variation in mental health, with another 3% being explained by the new stressors in the final step of the regression.

In all, the results show that the classic stress factors are important for the outcome variables, but it can also be said that the new stress factors accounted for a significant and substantial amount of the explained variance in all cases. The factor of competency demands was only related to identification with the organization and was unrelated to the other outcomes. In the end, the results showed that the demographic variables had only a marginal association with the various outcome variables.

Discussion

The new working life has shown itself to be characterized by a higher degree of independence and responsibility in connection with a diffusion of the boundaries surrounding work and its performance, with today's work results being more difficult to define and evaluate. Against such a background, the purpose of this chapter has been to investigate how the work situation may have changed and whether any of these possible changes can be related to employees' work attitudes, performance, and well-being.

The results of our pilot study indicate that working life is still in a process of change, as it is becoming to a greater degree more characterized by mental rather than physical demands. Consequently, the classic models on stress and the work climate (e.g. James and Sells, 1981; Karasek and Theorell, 1990), which have been commonly used as bases for reasoning in these areas, are perhaps now in need of modification and expansion in order to capture relevant aspects of the new working life. This suggests that these previous models need to be expanded in order to comprehend more thoroughly the areas and factors that are most pertinent to the problems encountered by today's employees. Similar observations have previously been made by other researchers who have argued that the traditional stress and work environment inventories should be complemented with those aspects that more clearly relate to the problems that can be associated with modern working life (e.g. Demerouti *et al.*, 2001; Gallie *et al.*, 1998; Marshall, Barnett, and Sayer, 1997; Söderfeldt *et al.*, 1997).

The three themes identified in the pilot study – the demands for continual competency development, difficulties in judging whether the work is completed, and difficulties in judging how well the work has been carried out – can contribute to enriching and developing the existing stress and work environment models. All of those interviewed could relate to the three themes as were described to them, which attests to the finding that they are relevant to the new working life and that they essentially differ from the more classic stress factors. Above all, the results of the pilot study show that it can be worthwhile to focus also on phenomena concerning the demand for continual learning in order to do the job, the uncertainty regarding when work is completed, and the question of the level of quality in the completed work.

The next question concerned whether it was empirically possible to measure these three aspects. The results of the factor analyses demonstrate that the so-called new stressors that emerged in the investigation are relevant and measurable concepts. The fact that both the exploratory and the confirmatory factor analyses lent support for the postulated model indicates that the new stressors capture something distinctive from the classic stressors, and that the three new stressors can be utilized to shed some light on the three new and distinct aspects of the work situation. This also indicates that it could be appropriate to expand the concept of stress by including the new phenomena and measures, especially if our ambition is to keep pace with the changing working life in our attempts to understand and explain the new phenomena that arise, and even add to existing models. It almost need not be said that although there can also exist a number of other aspects in the new working life as well as other new work conditions that may be relevant in this context, this study nevertheless constitutes one step along the road to increasing our understanding of what has been transpiring in recent years.

The third aim of the present study was to investigate whether the new stressors could add something to the explanations of outcomes beyond that which we have already garnered from the classic factors. Earlier stress and work climate models have identified negative relations between stress experiences and outcomes such as attitudes, behavior, and well-being (e.g. Brown and Leigh, 1996; Hackman and Oldham, 1975; James and Sells, 1981; Karasek and Theorell, 1990).

Among the new stressors, both task completion ambiguity and task quality ambiguity were related to job satisfaction, performance, and mental health, while competency demands were only associated with organizational commitment. It thus appears that the difficulties in determining whether the work is completed and in knowing what quality it holds are important aspects for job satisfaction and mental health – and even more important for self-reported performance – seeing as these factors were the ones that most strongly related to performance. Individuals who experience less uncertainty in regard to the delimiting and carrying out of work as well as in regard to its quality reported a higher degree of satisfaction and well-being in comparison to those who experienced a higher degree of uncertainty in respect to these factors. These results are in accordance with previous research on stress experiences and their negative relations to attitudes and health (Cooper, 2000; Theorell, 2003). Accordingly, these findings point to the new stressors having consequences that are similar to those displayed by the earlier stressors. The results also indicate that those individuals who reported a high degree of uncertainty in respect to whether the work was completed or not, and who were also unsure of its quality, simply felt that they performed worse than those who experienced a lesser degree of this uncertainty did. This implies that these types of uncertainties, in the long run, can impede an individual's work performance, which should call attention to the importance of having some instrument for providing support, feedback, and information that could keep a check on and, if needed, serve to militate against or even eliminate uncertainty. Similar arguments have been made in regard to other types of stressors and uncertainty factors (e.g. Karasek and Theorell, 1990; Sverke *et al.*, 2002; Warr, 1987).

Competency demands in the work situation were not related to job satisfaction, performance, or health, which can be interpreted as indicating that this aspect does not affect individuals' feelings toward the work itself or toward their own performance or well-being. Another interesting and rather surprising result is that competency demands were positively related to organizational commitment, implying that the experiencing of the organization's demand to continually learn new things in order to complete given assignments increases commitment to the organization. A similarly counter-intuitive result was obtained in the case of overload, which was found to be positively related to organizational commitment, which at first glace may seem remarkable, since it indicates that those who feel they had too much to do at work responded with a stronger sense of identification and unity with the organization. A possible explanation for these results is that the causal relations go in the other direction; in other words, those who already have a strong sense of commitment to the organization are those who work a lot and need to update their competencies, and who in turn report a higher degree of workload and competency demands.

From the results, it is also apparent that the classic stressors, as expected, related to the various outcomes, which indicates that these stressors are still important and should not be overlooked. Furthermore, in many cases, the classic stressors were most strongly related to the outcomes in terms of regression coefficients and the proportion of explained variance in the outcome variables. This, however, does not mean that the new stressors are unimportant. On the contrary, the results show that these new potential stress factors significantly relate to all of the outcome variables. It should also be pointed out that these stressors were entered last in the analysis, after the demographic variables and the classic stressors had been taken into account, which made it a relatively conservative testing. If we were to have instead inserted them first, a higher proportion of the explained variance in the outcomes could probably have been assigned to these new stress factors. A test of this shows that if the demographic variables and the new stress factors were inserted in the first step, these variables would explain 19% of the variation in job satisfaction, 7% of the variation in organizational commitment and mental health, and 28% of the variation in performance. In spite of this, we chose to go with the more conservative testing approach in order to avoid overestimating the importance of the new factors, and subject them to a relatively robust testing.

There are, as is often the case, a number of limitations in this study that need to be addressed. For one thing, it is very possible that the pilot study did not cover all relevant aspects and that there are additional significant aspects to working life that should also be taken into account in the future. It is also possible that somewhat different results would have been produced if other focus groups were to have been used. One of the strengths of the study, however, is that the pilot study and the survey were based on two completely independent samples, and two different methods, which substantiates that the results, to a certain degree, can be seen as generalizable. In regard to the survey study itself, it was only a cross-sectional study and, therefore, no conclusions can be drawn from it regarding the direction of the relationships between either the new or the classic stressors and the outcomes. The new stress measures should, of course, also be validated over time in order that the stability in the factor structure as well as in the predictive strength can be controlled over time. It would also be beneficial to validate the new measures' relation to the various outcomes by using additional data collection methods for the outcome measures, especially to avoid possible mono-method bias as much as possible (e.g. physiological measures of stress and ill-health, and registry data on sick-absence). The new items also need to be tested and validated in further samples to ensure that they are valid and reliable for other situations and contexts. This is of particular importance in respect to the item wordings that may need to be reformulated and further developed, and which were brought to our attention in the factor analysis where one of the items demonstrated a factor loading under .40.

Despite these limitations, we are confident that the new stressors, as the classic stressors, are important to take into account when attitudes, motivation, performance, and well-being in the new working life are to be considered and investigated. By so doing, our understanding of these stress factors will improve, and strategies for counteracting them will undoubtedly develop and find use. To feel good at work, it is important for individuals to feel that they are adequately competent and also able to judge the amount of work that is necessary, when tasks are completed, and how well they have performed. In order to achieve this, organizations and companies must work toward understanding and lessening the problems that today's employees experience in their work.

References

Allen, N. J. and Meyer, J. P. (1990). The measurement and antecedents of affective, continuance and normative commitment to the organization. *Journal of Occupational Psychology* 63: 1–18.

Beehr, T. (2000). An organizational psychology meta-model of occupational stress. In C. L. Cooper (ed.), *Theories of organizational stress* (pp. 6–27). Oxford: Oxford University Press.

Beehr, T. A., Walsh, J. T., and Taber, T. D. (1976). Relationship of stress to individually and organizationally valued states: higher order needs as a moderator. *Journal of Applied Psychology* 61: 41–7.

Bentler, P. M. (1990). Comparative fit indexes in structural models. *Psychological Bulletin* 107: 238–46.

Brown, S. P. and Leigh, T. W. (1996). A new look at psychological climate and its relationships to job involvement, effort, and performance. *Journal of Applied Psychology* 81: 358–68.

Browne, M. W. and Cudeck, R. (1993). Alternative ways of assessing model fit. In K. A. Bollen and J. S. Long (eds.), *Testing structural equation models* (pp. 136–62). Newbury Park, CA: Sage.

Burchell, B., Ladipo, D., and Wilkingson, F. (eds.) (2002). *Job insecurity and work intensification*. London: Routledge.

Burke, R. J. and Cooper, C. L. (2000). *The organization in crisis: downsizing, restructuring, and privatization*. Oxford: Blackwell.

Burke, R. J. and Nelson, D. (1998). Mergers and acquisitions, downsizing, and privatization: a North American perspective. In M. K. Gowing, J. D. Kraft, and J. C. Quick (eds.), *The new organizational reality: downsizing, restructuring, and revitalization* (pp. 21–54). Washington, DC: American Psychological Association.

Cooper, C. L. (2000). *Theories of organizational stress*. Oxford: Oxford University Press.

Demerouti, E., Bakker, A. B., Nachreiner, F., and Schaufeli, W. B. (2001). The Job Demands–Resources model of burnout. *Journal of Applied Psychology* 86: 499–512.

Diener, E., Suh, E. M., Lucas, R. E., and Smith, H. L. (1999). Subjective well-being: three decades of progress. *Psychological Bulletin* 25: 276–302.

Ferrie, J. E., Shipley, M. J., Marmot, M. G., Stansfeld, S. A., and Smith, G. S. (1998). An uncertain future: the health effects of threats to employment security in white-collar men and women. *American Journal of Public Health* 7: 1030–6.

Gallie, D., White, M., Cheng, Y., and Tomlinson, M. (1998). *Restructuring the employment relationship*. Oxford: Clarendon Press.

Ganster, D. C. and Fusilier, M. R. (1989). Control in the workplace. In C. L. Cooper and I. Robertson (eds.), *International review of industrial and organizational psychology* (pp. 235–80). London: Wiley.

Goldberg, D. (1979). *Manual of the general health questionnaire*. London: NFER Nelson.

Gowing, M. K., Kraft, J. D., and Quick, J. C. (eds.) (1997). *The new organizational reality: downsizing, restructuring, and revitalization*. Washington, DC: American Psychological Association.

Hackman, J. R. and Oldham, G. R. (1975). Development of the job diagnostic survey. *Journal of Applied Psychology* 60: 159–70.

Hall, D. T. and Hall, F. S. (1976). The relationship between goals, performance, self-image, and involvement under different organizational climates. *Journal of Vocational Behavior* 9: 267–78.

Hellgren, J., Sverke, M., and Isaksson, K. (1999). A two-dimensional approach to job insecurity: consequences for employee attitudes and well-being. *European Journal of Work and Organizational Psychology* 8: 179–95.

Howard, A. (1995). *The changing nature of work*. San Francisco, CA: Jossey-Bass.

James, L. R. and Sells, S. B. (1981). Psychological climate: theoretical perspectives and empirical research. In D. Magnusson (ed.), *Toward a psychology of situations: an interactional perspective* (pp. 275–95). Hillsdale, NJ: Lawrence Erlbaum.

Jöreskog, K. G. and Sörbom, D. (1996). *Lisrel 8: user's reference guide*. Chicago: Scientific Software.

Kahn, R. and Byosiere, P. (eds.) (1992). *Stress in organizations*. Palo Alto, CA: Consulting Psychologist Press.

Karasek, R. A. (1979). Job demands, job decision latitude, and mental strain: implications for job redesign. *Administrative Science Quarterly* 24: 285–307.

Karasek, R. and Theorell, T. (1990). *Healthy work: stress, productivity, and the reconstruction of working life*. New York: Basic Books.

Katz, D. and Kahn, R. L. (1978). *The social psychology of organizations* (2nd edn). New York: Wiley.

Lazarus, R. S. and Folkman, S. (1984). *Stress appraisal and coping*. New York: Springer.

Levi, L. (2000). Preface: stress in organizations – theoretical and empirical approaches. In C. L. Cooper (ed.), *Theories of organizational stress* (pp. 5–12). Oxford: Oxford University Press.

Marshall, N. L., Barnett, R. C., and Sayer, A. (1997). The changing workforce, job stress, and psychological distress. *Journal of Occupational Health Psychology* 2: 99–107.

Miles, M. B. and Huberman, M. A. (1994). *Qualitative data analysis* (2nd edn). Newbury Park, CA: Sage.

Mohr, G. B. (2000). The changing significance of different stressors after the announcement of bankruptcy: a longitudinal investigation with special emphasis on job insecurity. *Journal of Organizational Behavior* 21: 337–59.

Patton, M. Q. (1987). *How to use qualitative methods in evaluation*. Newbury Park, CA: Sage.

Pfeffer, J. (1997). *New directions for organization theory: problems and prospects*. New York: Oxford University Press.

Quick, J. C. and Tetrick, L. E. (eds.) (2003). *Handbook of occupational health psychology*. Washington, DC: American Psychological Association.

Rizzo, J. R., House, R. J., and Lirtzman, S. I. (1970). Role conflict and ambiguity in complex organizations. *Administrative Sciences Quarterly* 15: 150–63.

Siegrist, J. (1996). Adverse health effects of high-effort/low-reward conditions. *Journal of Occupational Health Psychology* 1: 27–41.

Söderfeldt, B., Söderfeldt, M., Jones, K., O'Campo, P., Ohlson, C. G., and Warg, L. E. (1997). Does organization matter? A multilevel analysis of the demand-control model applied to human services. *Social Science and Medicine* 44: 527–34.

Steyaert, C. and Bouwen, R. (1994). Group methods of organizational analysis. In C. Cassell and G. Symon (eds.), *Qualitative methods in organizational research: a practical guide*. London: Sage.

Strauss, A. and Corbin, J. (1990). *Basics of qualitative research: grounded theory procedures and techniques*. Newbury Park, CA: Sage.

Sverke, M., Hellgren, J., and Näswall, K. (2002). No security: a meta-analysis and review of job insecurity and its consequences. *Journal of Occupational Health Psychology* 7: 242–64.

Tetrick, L. E. and Campbell Quick, J. (2003). Prevention at work: public health in occupational settings. In J. Campbell Quick and L. E. Tetrick (eds.), *Handbook of occupational health psychology* (pp. 3–17). Washington, DC: American Psychological Association.

Theorell, T. (2003). To be able to exert control over one's own situation: a necessary condition for coping with stressors. In J. Campbell Quick and L. E. Tetrick (eds.), *Handbook of occupational health psychology* (pp. 201–19). Washington, DC: American Psychological Association.

van der Vliet, C. and Hellgren, J. (2002). *The modern working life: its impact on employee attitudes, performance and health*. SALTSA report no 4: 2002. Stockholm: National Institute for Working Life and SALTSA.

Warr, P. (1987). *Work, unemployment and mental health*. Oxford: Clarendon Press.

4 The Demand-Induced Strain Compensation model: renewed theoretical considerations and empirical evidence

Jan de Jonge, Christian Dormann, and Marieke van den Tooren

> Consider a researcher who uses three measures of stressors, three measures of strains, and three measures of support. If a subset of the 27 interactions were significant, the question becomes whether the significant terms were due to Type I error? In several cases, researchers seemed to provide post hoc explanations as to why the significant terms occurred. Future research should endeavor to refine theoretical models that guide how different sources of support can be matched to particular stressors and strains. (Viswesvaran, Sanchez, and Fisher, 1999: 328)

This chapter presents a recently developed theoretical model on job-related stress and performance, the so-called Demand-Induced Strain Compensation (DISC) model. The DISC model predicts in general that adverse health effects of high job demands can best be compensated for by matching job resources to the high demands. Furthermore, the model predicts that a well-balanced mixture of specific job demands and corresponding job resources will stimulate employee learning, growth, and performance. Not restricting ourselves to social support, which is mentioned in the quote above and which indeed represents one important resource in job stress (cf. Viswesvaran *et al.*, 1999), we present some refined theoretical predictions on emotional, cognitive, and physical processes that guide how different kinds of job resources can be matched to particular job demands and job-related strains. The aim of this chapter is thus twofold: (1) to present a new job stress theory, and (2) to show recent empirical evidence for its basic assumptions by means of a narrative review.

Research in job stress has concentrated on identifying demands at work as they relate to job strain. Under the heading of "job resources" (i.e. cognitive-energetic reservoirs in the work environment that can be tapped), research has tried to identify work characteristics that buffer against the adverse effects of job demands. Because job demands cannot often be reduced, the idea of increasing job resources instead of combating strain is appealing for current working life. As a consequence, several theoretical frameworks have been advanced to explain the role of job resources in the job stress process (cf. Cooper, 1998; Kahn and Byosiere, 1992). Most of these frameworks focus on the additive and interactive effects of job demands and job resources in the prediction of job strain, which represents the core elements of most theories on job stress (Cooper, Dewe, and O'Driscoll, 2001). Additive effect models assume that demands and resources independently impact strains, whereas interactive effect models propose that resources moderate the relation between demands and strains. Prominent examples of interactive effect models are Karasek's (1979) Demand–Control (DC) model, the buffering model of social support (Viswesvaran et al., 1999), and Siegrist's (1996) Effort–Reward Imbalance (ERI) model.

While there seems to be little debate about the additive effects of job demands and job resources on health, the evidence concerning synergistic effects being mirrored in moderating or interaction effects has received mixed support at best (Cooper et al., 2001; van der Doef and Maes, 1999; van Vegchel, de Jonge, Bosma, and Schaufeli, 2005; Viswesvaran et al., 1999). There is at least one important reason why so many studies failed to find moderating effects. Early job stress research tended to treat job demands and job resources as global and unidimensional constructs, which obscured the differential impact of specific components (e.g. Karasek, 1979; Viswesvaran et al., 1999).

Subsequently, some researchers have argued that the associations between demands, resources, and strains depend on the respective types of demands, resources, and strains (e.g. Cohen and Wills, 1985; Cutrona and Russell, 1990; de Jonge, Dollard, Dormann, Le Blanc, and Houtman, 2000; Sargent and Terry, 1998; Viswesvaran et al., 1999; Wall, Jackson, Mullarkey, and Parker, 1996). More specifically, it has been proposed that specific demands and specific resources should *match* in order to show moderating effects in the prediction of strain. This line of thinking is referred to as the *matching hypothesis*, which posits that if the types of available job resources correspond to existing job demands, the resources should then mitigate the effects of those demands, thereby resulting in less strain (see Viswesvaran et al., 1999). For instance, emotional support by colleagues is most likely to buffer the effect of emotional demands (e.g. irate customers) on emotional exhaustion.

To summarize, the discovery of optimal demand–resource combinations could help improve our understanding of how specific job demands threaten employees and how specific job resources protect employees from developing strain or even enhance their well-being and performance (see Cutrona and Russell, 1990). For this very reason, de Jonge and Dormann (2003, 2006) developed the Demand-Induced Strain Compensation (DISC) model.

The Demand-Induced Strain Compensation model

The Demand-Induced Strain Compensation (DISC) model tries to unify principles that are common to current job stress models, and claims to be a more cohesive theoretical model of job stress. As the theoretical basis of the DISC model, we propose homeostatic regulation processes (see also de Jonge and Dormann, 2006). To survive, a living organism must maintain certain critical parameters within a bounded range. For instance, the human body must regulate its temperature, amount of fluids, and energy level. Maintaining each critical parameter requires that the body come into contact with the corresponding satiatory stimulus (i.e. clothes, water, and food) at the right time. The process by which these critical parameters are maintained (i.e. to keep something regular) is generally referred to as *homeostatic regulation*. For instance, in the area of immune functioning, homeostatic regulation processes are known to cause an activation of internal resources (e.g. hormones, neurotransmitters, and cytokines) when particular demands occur (Lekander, 2002). Through evolutionary processes, the release of functional, matching internal resources is more likely than the release of dysfunctional, non-matching immune parameters (Lekander, 2002). Similar homeostatic regulation processes can be found in the nervous system as well, which in fact has much in common with the immune system. For example, homeostatic regulation processes engage the fine-scale organization and operation of volumes of neural tissue to provide powerful and functional resources for neural signal integration and stable long-term storage of information (Montague, 1996).

The idea of functional homeostatic regulation can be transferred to organizational settings (e.g. Vancouver, 2000). Functional homeostatic regulation at work involves self-regulation processes whose function is to cope with states of psychological imbalance induced by job demands (Pomaki and Maes, 2002). Thus, similar to homeostatic regulation in the immune system and nervous system, we propose that individuals activate *functional*, corresponding job-related resources to mitigate the effects of specific job demands. Basically, a match exists if an external resource provides a function similar to that of an internal resource when combating stress. For example, when emotional problems with customers arise (e.g. insolent customers), an emotional self-regulation capability is likely to be quite helpful. When individuals lack this internal resource, emotionally supportive colleagues may do an almost similarly effective job. Even if supportive colleagues are unavailable, other job resources can be useful to some extent, such as information provided by a supervisor about how to handle a certain troublesome customer, for example. We propose that demands are first dealt with by attempting to turn to easily available internal resources. If these resources are depleted, a demand for matching external resources is created, which may be of similar use (cf. Hobfoll, 1989, 2002). If such matching external resources are not available or if they are depleted, individuals search for other resources. They will then use even those resources that do not closely correspond to the demand (cf. Vohs, Baumeister, and Ciarocco, 2005). Accordingly, it is internal, matching resources which are most powerful in combating demands (when present), followed by corresponding external resources, and then non-matching external resources.

The DISC model is premised on four key principles. First, de Jonge and Dormann (2003, 2006) emphasize the need to recognize the multidimensionality of the stress concepts used. They propose that job demands, job resources, and job-related strains each contain cognitive, emotional, and physical elements. As far as job demands are concerned, three types can be distinguished: (1) cognitive demands that impinge primarily on the brain processes involved in information processing (Hockey, 2000); (2) emotional demands, mainly concerning the effort needed to deal with organizationally desired emotions during interpersonal transactions (Morris and Feldman, 1996); and (3) physical demands that are primarily associated with the musculo-skeletal system (i.e. sensorymotor and physical aspects of behavior; Hockey, 2000). Similarly, job resources may have a cognitive-informational component (e.g. colleagues providing information), an emotional component (e.g. colleagues providing sympathy and affection), and a physical component such as instrumental help of colleagues or ergonomic aids (Cohen and Wills, 1985; Cutrona and Russell, 1990). Finally, in a similar vein to demands and resources, strains may also comprise cognitive, emotional, and physical dimensions (Koslowski, 1998; Le Blanc, de Jonge, and Schaufeli, in press). For instance, employee creativity and active learning represent cognitively laden outcomes (e.g. Amabile, 1996; Taris and Kompier, 2005), emotional exhaustion ("burnout") represents an emotionally laden strain variable (e.g. Maslach and Jackson, 1986), and physical health complaints can be reasonably assumed mainly to reflect bodily sensations.

Secondly, a key principle regarding the so-called *triple-matching* of concepts (i.e. matching demands and resources and strains) was developed (de Jonge and Dormann, 2006). The idea of there being matches between job demands and job resources was first mentioned in industrial and organizational psychology by Cohen and McKay (1984; see also Cohen and Wills, 1985). They proposed that interaction effects were greatest when there was a match between specific kinds of job demands and certain forms of social support (as a job resource). For instance, instrumental aid from colleagues ("resource") may help reduce strain caused by heavy lifting ("demand"). We call this correspondence between a demand and a resource a *double-match of common kind*, because (1) the first two out of three constructs (i.e. demand, resource, strain) match, and (2) this kind of match between independent variables has been commonly proposed by several scholars in the field (e.g. Cohen and Wills, 1985; Sargent and Terry, 1998; Wall *et al.*, 1996). The double-match of common kind hypothesis has received some support (e.g. Terry and Jimmieson, 1999; Terry, Nielsen, and Perchard, 1993), but the overall evidence is mixed. In the late nineties, this match notion was extended by Frese (1999). He argued that the third component of the demand–resource–strain triad, that is, the strain component, should be considered as a source of match or non-match as well. More specifically, Frese proposed that this match occurs between job resources on the one hand, and strain on the other, which, in accordance with Frese's suggestion, we label *double-match of extended kind*. In other words, the match is extended to the dependent variables, but is still a double-match (between two out of three constructs: resource and strain). For instance, social types of resources (e.g. support from colleagues) are supposed to function more regularly as a buffer in relation to social types of strain (such as social anxiety and irritation) than in relation to less social areas of strain (like physical symptoms; see also Dormann and Zapf, 1999).

When such a double-match of extended kind is investigated, it is still a theoretical challenge to predict which type of job resource will mitigate the relation between job demands and job strain (e.g. Viswesvaran *et al.*, 1999). However, based upon the above-mentioned ideas regarding double-match of common kind, double-match of extended kind, and the multidimensionality of constructs, the *triple-match principle* (TMP) was developed (de Jonge and Dormann, 2003, 2006). The TMP, as depicted in Figure 4.1, proposes that the strongest interactive effects of job demands and job resources are observed when demands *and* resources *and* strains are based on qualitatively identical dimensions. For instance, according to the TMP, emotional support by colleagues is highly likely to moderate (i.e. mitigate) the relations between emotional demands (e.g. insolent customers) and emotional exhaustion. So, the TMP suggests not only that demands and resources should match (i.e. double-match of common kind; cf. Cohen and Wills, 1985), and that resources

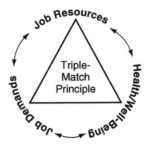

Figure 4.1 The triple-match principle of the DISC model

should match strains (i.e. double-match of extended kind; cf. Frese, 1999), but also that demands should match strains. For instance, insolent customers are more likely to cause emotional disorders than deficits in active learning or physical complaints. In other words, the TMP applies to two different levels: (1) the match between job demands and job resources; and (2) the match between job demands/resources and job strain outcomes. In regression analysis, the effect of the match between job demands and job resources is statistically modeled by means of a multiplicative interaction term ("demands * resources"; de Jonge and Dormann, 2003, p. 61). Figure 4.2 illustrates an example of a triple-match interaction between emotional demands and emotional support from colleagues and supervisors in the prediction of the burnout component, "emotional exhaustion." As depicted in Figure 4.2, the combination of high emotional demands and low emotional support (dotted line) was associated with higher feelings of emotional exhaustion. In addition, Figure 4.2 also shows that with high levels of emotional support ($+1$ SD), the impact of emotional demands on emotional exhaustion became substantially mitigated.

The first two principles of the DISC model lead to two further corollaries pertaining to compensation and balance mechanisms. The *compensation principle* suggests that the negative effects of job demands can be counteracted through the availability and activation of job resources. It also predicts that job resources from within the same domain as the job demands (i.e. cognitive, emotional, or physical) will produce a greater likelihood of counteracting the negative job demands. The *balance principle* of the DISC model holds that the optimal conditions for active learning, growth, creativity, and performance exist where a balanced mixture of (high) job demands and corresponding job resources occurs. For instance, employee creativity may occur if an employee has a lot of cognitive control when facing high mental demands (see also Amabile, 1996). To recapitulate both principles, compensation has to do with

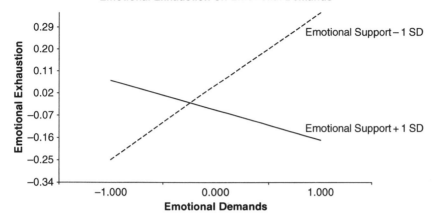

Figure 4.2 Illustration of a triple-match interaction between emotional demands and emotional support in the prediction of emotional exhaustion

"survival": taxing job demands need complementary job resources with a minimum loss of energy to reduce adverse health/well-being (Hobfoll, 2001). Balance, on the other hand, is about avoiding energy depletion and personal growth. In order to learn and grow, an employee needs both challenging job demands and usable, matching job resources, which has to do with "investment" (de Jonge and Dormann, 2003).

The main difference between the two principles can be further explained by Higgins' (1997, 2000) regulatory focus theory. In short, regulatory focus theory assumes that employees' self-regulation operates differently when serving two fundamentally different needs, i.e. (1) survival needs and (2) nurturance needs. Survival needs, such as security and protection, usually involve a prevention focus – a regulatory state concerned with the absence or presence of negative outcomes. Nurturance needs ("investment"), like nourishment, learning, and aspirations, usually involve a promotion focus – a regulatory state concerned with the presence or absence of positive outcomes. Applied to the DISC propositions, if the situation calls for preventing or diminishing poor health, poor well-being, and/or poor performance ("prevention focus"), the employee is likely to be in a survival mode and therefore s/he will try to use (limited) job resources to combat high job demands. However, if the situation involves promoting health, well-being, and/or performance ("promotion focus"), the employee is likely to be in an investment mode and, consequently, will try to use job resources to balance job demands (Spiegel et al., 2004). More specifically, because a prevention focus involves a

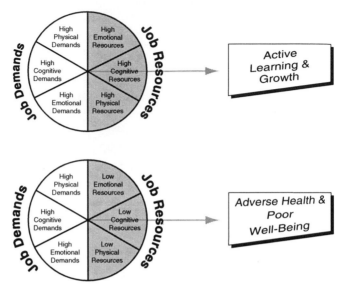

Figure 4.3 The Demand-Induced Strain Compensation (DISC) model

sensitivity to negative outcomes, an inclination to avoid mismatches between demands and resources seems to be a natural strategy for prevention-oriented self-regulation. In contrast, because a promotion focus involves a sensitivity to positive outcomes, an inclination to approach matches between demands and resources seems to be a natural strategy for promotion-oriented self-regulation (Higgins, 1997). So, the effective use of job resources to combat strain or to promote well-being could depend on the regulatory focus concerned (Higgins, 1997, 2000).

Figure 4.3 shows a graphical representation of the core propositions of the DISC model. The three kinds of job demands (i.e. cognitive, emotional, and physical) and the three kinds of job resources (i.e. cognitive, emotional, and physical) are situated on a sixfold disc, with matching demands and resources diametrically opposed to each other. The upper disc represents the balance principle (i.e. high demands versus high resources in the prediction of learning and growth), whereas the lower disc represents the compensation principle (i.e. high demands versus low resources in the prediction of adverse health and poor well-being).

Empirical evidence for the DISC model

First of all, to measure job demands and job resources, a new instrument called the DISQ ("Q" for questionnaire) was developed, which is now available in four different languages, namely Dutch, English, German, and Japanese (see www.jandejonge.nl/disq.html). The DISQ has shown promising psychometric properties thus far. The proposed three-dimensional structure of both job demands and job resources has been confirmed quite well in all countries mentioned, and internal consistencies as well as test-retest coefficients are satisfactory (cf. de Jonge et al., forthcoming).

De Jonge and Dormann (2004) presented an overview of the evidence for the assumptions in the DISC model, which has been updated in this chapter (see Table 4.1).

Studies conducted to test the principles of the DISC model show that results in general have been supportive. More specifically, eight out of the eleven DISC studies reported in Table 4.1 showed some evidence in support of the triple-match principle. It should be noted that in order to identify a triple-match in a regression analysis, the interaction term between similar demands and resources in the prediction of an identical outcome should be significant (see also Figure 4.2). Furthermore, seven cross-sectional studies support the DISC model (i.e. de Hoon, van Riet, and Schippers, 2005; de Jonge, Dormann, and von Nordheim, 2006; de Jonge, Dormann, and van Vegchel, 2004; Haeslich, Streit, Richter, de Jonge, and Merkel, 2003; Hoek and van Walsem-Reedeker, 2004; Langen, Aaij, and Nelson, 2005; Plasschaert, 2004). Six out of these seven cross-sectional studies reported a significant triple-match interaction of emotional kind. In a study among 830 Belgian health care workers, for example, Plasschaert (2004) found a significant triple-match interaction between (high) emotional demands and (low) emotional resources (i.e. supervisor and co-worker support) in the prediction of emotional exhaustion. Furthermore, five out of six cross-sectional studies reported a significant triple-match interaction of cognitive kind. For instance, Haeslich and colleagues (2003) found a significant triple-match interaction between (high) cognitive demands and (high) cognitive resources (i.e. job control) in the prediction of active learning in a sample of medical doctors. The same cognitive triple-match interaction was replicated by de Jonge et al. (2004). Interestingly, Langen and colleagues (2005) detected a significant triple-match interaction between (high) cognitive demands and (low) cognitive resources in the prediction of an adverse health outcome, that is, mental fatigue. This effect reflects the compensation principle within a cognitive context. Only two out of seven cross-sectional studies reported a significant physical triple-match interaction. For instance, in successive studies among 471 and 405 nursing home employees, de Jonge and his team (2004) detected a significant triple-match interaction between (high) physical demands and (low) physical resources in the prediction of physical health complaints.

Table 4.1 *Overview of empirical evidence for the DISC model*

Country	Author(s)	Population	Design	Outcomes	Triple Match Interaction?
Australia	Davis (2003)	135 employees	Cross-sectional study	Personal accompl.	No
				Emot. exhaustion	No
				Phys. complaints	No
Australia	Halik (2003)	102 call center workers	Cross-sectional study	Job satisfaction	No
				Emot. exhaustion	No
Belgium	Plasschaert (2004)	830 health care workers	Cross-sectional study	Personal accompl.	No
				Job satisfaction	Yes (cognitive)
				Emot. exhaustion	Yes (emotional)
				Depersonalization	Yes (emotional)
Germany	Haeslich *et al.* (2003)	313 doctors and nurses (general hospital)	Baseline (from a 2-wave panel study)	Active learning	Yes (cognitive)
				Emot. exhaustion	Yes (emotional)
				Phys. complaints	Yes (physical)
Netherlands	de Graauw (2003)	698 psychiatric nurses	Cross-sectional study	Job satisfaction	No
				Emot. exhaustion	No
Netherlands	de Jonge *et al.* (2004)	471 and 405 nursing home workers	Cross-sectional (two studies)	Active learning	Yes (cognitive)
				Emot. exhaustion	Yes (emotional)
				Phys. complaints	Yes (physical)
Netherlands	Hoek and van Walsem–Reedeker (2004)	347 retail trade workers	Cross-sectional study	Active learning	No
				Emot. exhaustion	Yes (emotional)
				Phys. complaints	No
Netherlands	de Hoon *et al.* (2005)	51 nursing home workers	Cross-sectional study	Creativity	Yes (cognitive)
				Emot. exhaustion	Yes (emotional)
				Phys. complaints	No

Country	Author	Sample	Design	Outcome	Result
Netherlands	Langen *et al.* (2005)	78 employees working in the service sector	Cross-sectional study	Creativity	No
				Active learning	No
				Mental fatigue	Yes (cognitive)
				Emot. exhaustion	No
				Phys. complaints	No
Netherlands	de Jonge, Dormann, and von Nordheim (2006)	49 health care workers for disabled people	Cross-sectional study	Active learning	No
				Emot. exhaustion	Yes (emotional)
				Phys. complaints	No
Netherlands	de Jonge and Dormann (2006)	280 and 267 nursing home workers	Two 2-wave panel studies	Active learning	No
				Emot. exhaustion	Yes (emotional)
				Phys. complaints	Yes (physical)

Three cross-sectional studies were not supportive at all regarding triple-match interactions (i.e. Davis, 2003; de Graauw, 2003; Halik, 2003). For example, a convenience sampling survey among 135 employees with different jobs from Adelaide (South Australia) showed only a main effect of cognitive demands and cognitive resources in the prediction of personal accomplishment (Davis, 2003). No significant matching interaction effects were reported.

In regard to longitudinal studies, the only one yet published in this area has found support for the model's assumptions. Two two-wave panel studies among 280 and 267 health care workers, conducted by de Jonge and Dormann (2006), showed a significant interaction between baseline (high) physical demands and (low) physical resources in predicting physical health complaints two years later. In addition, they also detected a significant interaction between baseline (high) emotional demands and (low) emotional resources in predicting emotional exhaustion two years later. Remarkably, the likelihood of finding interaction effects was linearly related to the degree of match, with 33.3% of all tested interactions becoming significant when there was a triple-match, 16.7% significant interactions when testing for double-matches (common kind as well as extended kind), and 0.0% significant interactions when there was no match.

To conclude, results of Belgian, German, and Dutch studies show in general that particular combinations of specific job demands and matching job resources have the highest predictive validity with regard to cognitive, emotional, and physical outcomes, which is in line with the core propositions of the DISC model. More specifically, eight out of eleven DISC studies reported here showed evidence in support of the triple-match principle.

Discussion and conclusions

The purpose of this chapter has been to present a new integrative theoretical framework, along with related empirical evidence, which is designed to solve inconsistencies in demonstrating interaction effects between job demands and job resources in the prediction of employee health and performance. The Demand-Induced Strain Compensation (DISC) model addresses the question of *matching* job demands, job resources, and outcomes: how do specific job resources foster compensation for specific job strain due to specific high job demands, and how do specific job resources balance specific job demands to increase specific positive outcomes such as learning, growth, and performance? Based upon homeostatic regulation processes in the immune and nervous systems, it was argued that interactions between job demands and job resources predominantly occur if demands, resources, and job-related strains address similar domains of human functioning. This key proposition of the DISC model is expressed in the so-called triple-match principle (TMP), which suggests not only that job demands and job resources should match, but also that both demands and resources should match job strains. More specifically, cognitive demands and cognitive resources are more likely to affect cognitive outcomes; emotional demands and emotional resources are more likely to affect emotional outcomes; and physical demands and physical resources are more likely to affect physical outcomes.

The evidence of the studies presented in Table 4.1 supported the DISC model's key proposition. Most convincing is the study of de Jonge and Dormann (2006), which shows that the valid percentage of significant interaction effects found (i.e. interactions with a shape that confirms the model's key proposition) is a perfect linear function of the degree of match. In general, findings were most consistent if there was an emotional match. This conclusion not only confirms the triple-match principle, but also adds to the literature on burnout (cf. Halbesleben and Buckley, 2004). Research on professional burnout has shown that emotional demands may lead to emotional exhaustion (e.g. Schaufeli and Enzmann, 1998; Zapf et al., 2001). Although research on emotional demands has been growing recently, how best to combat their negative impact on employees remains an open question. So, based upon our results, burnout (in terms of its key variable: emotional exhaustion) seems to be a response to emotionally demanding tasks, which will be reinforced if a particular kind of emotional resource (such as attention, affect, and esteem from colleagues and supervisor) is absent. In addition, the present findings underscore the importance of emotional resources in human service work. Dollard and colleagues (2003) have noted that the stress literature on human service work has so far added little to our knowledge of the *specific* job resources that are useful in combating work stress. In particular, empirical evidence of the moderating effect of specific service-related job resources is wanting. All in all, the current findings show that emotional resources are indeed important as stress buffers for human service employees.

Furthermore, a number of DISC studies reported a significant triple-match interaction of cognitive kind. All but one of these triple-match interactions showed evidence for the balance principle: the combination of high cognitive demands and high cognitive resources was associated with high active learning and creativity. Previous models like Karasek's (1998) Demand–Control model also suggested that active learning and growth will occur in the presence of high job demands coupled with high job resources (e.g. job decision latitude). We do not believe that this is entirely true without further qualification of what particular kinds of resources are important. According to the DISC model, active learning and/or creativity occur only through actual utilization of *matching* (i.e. cognitive) job resources.

With regard to the triple-match interactions of physical kind, only three studies showed convergent evidence in line with the model's key proposition. Risk factors for physical health complaints such as neck and low back pain can generally be divided into three groups: (1) physical risk factors, (2) psychosocial risk factors, and (3) individual risk factors. Systematic reviews showed that physical demands constituted risk factors for physical health complaints more consistently, and thus more strongly, than psychosocial risk factors such as cognitive demands (Ariëns, van Mechelen, Bongers, Bouter, and van der Wal, 2001; Hoogendoorn, van Poppel, Bongers, Koes, and Bouter, 2000). The current findings therefore support the idea that the moderating role of physical resources (e.g. instrumental support or ergonomic aids) is more likely in cases involving physical demands and physical health outcomes, which is in line with the triple-match principle.

In the area of job stress, the importance of matching external resources should not be underestimated. Hockey (2000) noted that in studies on stress and performance, decreases in performance are typically observed in the laboratory but *not* in real-life work situations. Our explanation is that in real-life work situations, individuals frequently have internal and external resources to utilize in order to prevent a decline in performance, whereas in controlled laboratory settings they lack such resources. Rather, demands imposed on individuals in the laboratory drain individuals' internal resources ("spare capacity" in Hockey's terms) until they are depleted. When the laboratory experiment is demanding enough, decreases in performance are thus highly likely.

Suggestions for future research

The question of whether a particular job demand and a particular job resource will match or not match is not so easy to answer. It usually depends on the context. However, this applies to every theory because every theory represents an abstraction from reality. The triple-match principle reflects such an abstraction as well, but the current empirical evidence proves this abstraction to be very promising. As Higgins (2006: 550) noted, "to understand a theory and use it effectively, it is essential to learn its boundary conditions – where it makes predictions and where it is simply *silent.*" Furthermore, to learn more about the theoretical mechanisms and processes, researchers should listen to the data. With this in mind, a suggestion for future research is to conduct more longitudinal multi-wave studies with different time-lags in order to test the DISC model's key assumptions and regulatory processes (cf. Dormann and Zapf, 2002). As de Lange and colleagues (2004) have noted, there is little information available about the "right" length of time-lags in occupational health research. Ideally, the time-lag of a research study encompasses the potential true change in the organization. Another suggestion is to measure directly the compensation and balance principles; that is, to measure causal attributions (e.g. employees' beliefs) relating to which job resources help under which demanding work conditions (cf. de Jonge *et al.*, 2006; Langen *et al.*, 2005). The reason for this is that, when using only survey techniques, the issue of match is merely determined by the statistical program, in which employees merely report on whether job resources are available or not. However, employees could also decide by themselves whether job resources are *relevant* for combating job demands and whether they are *used* for this purpose. This arguing is in line with Hobfoll's (1989) Conservation of Resources theory, which postulates that people approach resources with the underlying thought to obtain, retain, and protect them. Such studies should therefore explore (1) what kind of job resources are perceived as relevant in particular types of demanding work situations, (2) whether or not various types of job resources are perceived as available, even if they are not viewed as relevant, and (3) whether or not job resources will be used anyway. Preliminary evidence thus far shows that the relevance of (matching) job resources is just as important as the availability of (matching) job resources in corresponding types of demanding work situations (de Jonge *et al.*, 2006; Langen *et al.*, 2005). If future research yields similar findings, it might be useful to design survey studies in which respondents are asked to indicate the relevance and actual use of job resources along with their availability.

As there is a fairly small body of well-performed research on job stress interventions (Kompier and Taris, 2004), a final suggestion for future research is to apply DISC propositions to real practice. We expect that interventions targeted primarily at *specific* kinds of job demands and corresponding job resources will reduce detrimental effects and enhance beneficial effects. Moreover, research should explore whether regulatory focus concerns will strengthen the effective use of (limited or non-limited) job resources. Collaboration with other disciplines (e.g. economists and industrial engineers) will strengthen the evaluation of potential "hard" outcome measures such as reliability rates, accident rates, client satisfaction, and financial effects.

Physical exercise as a metaphor for cognitive and emotional regulatory processes?

The combination of high physical demands with high physical resources resembles physical exercise in which certain limits are not exceeded. One can speculate on whether the combination of cognitive and emotional demands with appropriate job resources is fitting to apply to this exercise metaphor, as well. Theories on self-control strength support this (Baumeister, Bratslavsky, Muraven, and Tice, 1998; Muraven and Baumeister, 2000). These authors argue that any kind of self-regulatory activity (behavior that is not shown by default, and which requires some sort of will-action) will deplete self-regulation strength in the short run. However, like training a muscle, self-regulation strength will increase in the long run. In a similar vein, one can speculate that dealing with emotional demands such as being confronted with death and dying may deplete emotional self-regulation capabilities in the short run. However, if there are emotional buffers which prevent the demands for emotional self-regulation from becoming too high (e.g. emotional support by colleagues), the long-term result might actually be low levels of emotional exhaustion. A similar argument can be made for cognitive regulation, since self-regulation strength theory is not limited to emotional processing but applicable to any kind of self-regulation activity. For instance, active learning means that the self engages in changing the way it usually thinks, feels, or behaves, which perfectly corresponds to common definitions of self-regulation. The right combination of high cognitive demands combined with high cognitive resources should, thus, finally lead to an increase in self-control strength. Muraven and Baumeister (2000) suggested that each self-regulation activity rests on a single source of self-control strength; there is nothing specific about cognitive, emotional, or behavioral self-regulation strength. On the contrary, research findings show that creativity, active learning, lack of emotional exhaustion, and lack of physical symptoms cannot be substituted with each other when the effects of cognitive, emotional, and physical demands and resources are investigated. There may actually be different processes involved. Even though the triple-match principle was not supported in all studies, we feel it represents an important step forward, leaving the other all too simple models that are open to arbitrary substitutions of job demands, job resources, and outcomes clearly behind.

Final remarks

... a theory, like a child, must be allowed to develop through contact with the world – both the world as found in theory-related research data and the world as found within those scientists who are the theory's parents and extended family. The purpose of such world contact is to learn what a theory is and what it is not. (Higgins, 2006: 549)

In applying this recent metaphor by Higgins (2006) to the DISC model's developing contact with the scientific arena, it is hoped that future research on the model will provide an impetus to examine more critically the impact of job demands and job resources on employee health, well-being, and performance. Employee mental health ("mental capital") is becoming more and more important for economic performance (e.g. Weehuizen, 2003). Today's work is "using up" the mental (and also emotional and physical) capital of employees as never before, accompanied by substantial, sometimes hidden costs (e.g. burnout, sickness absence, work disability, lost productivity, counterproductive work behavior, and loss of experienced utility). The DISC model is intended to contribute to "healthy work," particularly in human service work. Future job stress research may benefit from the idea that job demands and job resources do not interact randomly in the prediction of health, well-being, and performance outcomes. Rather, it is the notion of the *common match* (i.e. job demands and job resources should match) and the *extended match* (job demands and job resources should also match job-related outcomes), both reflected in the *triple-match principle*, that merits attention in future job stress research.

From a practical view, empirical evidence on the DISC model has shown that job-related interventions should ideally focus on *specific* types of job resources in order to reduce detrimental effects and enhance beneficial effects of *specific* types of job demands. The ultimate goal is to find a good balance between cognitive, emotional, and physical regulation processes in employees' working life. Further development of the DISC model could pave the way for a more effective approach to combating job-related health, well-being, and performance problems, which could be beneficial for interventions in today's working life.

References

Amabile, T. M. (1996). *Creativity in context: update to the social psychology of creativity*. Boulder, CO: Westview Press.

Ariëns, G. A. M., van Mechelen, W., Bongers, P. M., Bouter, L. M., and van der Wal, G.(2001). Psychosocial risk factors for neck pain: a systematic review. *American Journal of Industrial Medicine* 39: 180–93.

Baumeister, R. F., Bratslavsky, E., Muraven, M., and Tice, D. M. (1998). Ego-depletion: is the active self a limited resource? *Journal of Personality and Social Psychology* 74: 1252–65.

Cohen, S. and McKay, G. (1984). Social support, stress and the buffering hypothesis: a theoretical analysis. In A. Baum, S. E. Taylor, and J. E. Singer (eds.), *Handbook of psychology and health* (pp. 253–67). Hillsdale, NJ: Erlbaum.

Cohen, S. and Wills, T. A. (1985). Stress, social support, and the buffering hypothesis. *Psychological Bulletin* 98: 310–57.

Cooper, C. L. (1998). *Theories of organizational stress.* New York: Oxford University Press.

Cooper, C. L., Dewe, P. J., and O'Driscoll, M. P. (2001). *Organizational stress: a review and critique of theory, research, and applications.* Thousand Oaks, CA: Sage.

Cutrona, C. E. and Russell, D. W. (1990). Type of social support and specific stress: toward a theory of optimal matching. In B. R. Sarason, I. G. Sarason, and G. R. Pierce (eds.), *Social support: an interactional view* (pp. 319–66). New York: Wiley.

Davis, N. (2003). Demand-induced strain compensation: a new model of occupational stress and the effects of sense of coherence. Honours thesis, University of South Australia, School of Psychology.

de Graauw, R. (2003). Werkstress . . . of juist tevreden? Een toetsing van het Demand-Induced Strain Compensation model [Work stress, or just satisfied? A test of the Demand-Induced Strain Compensation model]. Masters thesis, Utrecht University.

de Hoon, D., van Riet, M., and Schippers, M. (2005). De invloed van coping op het DISC-model [The influence of coping on the DISC-model]. Bachelors thesis, Utrecht University.

de Jonge, J., Dollard, M. F., Dormann, C., Le Blanc, P. M., and Houtman, I. L. D. (2000). The Demand–Control model: specific demands, specific control, and well-defined groups. *International Journal of Stress Management* 7: 269–87.

de Jonge, J. and Dormann, C. (2003). The DISC model: Demand-Induced Strain Compensation mechanisms in job stress. In M. F. Dollard, A. H. Winefield, and H. R. Winefield (eds.), *Occupational stress in the service professions* (pp. 43–74). London: Taylor and Francis.

    (2004). Matching demands, resources, and strains: a test of the Demand-Induced Strain Compensation model in three different countries. *International Journal of Behavioral Medicine* 11: Supplement, 187.

    (2006). Stressors, resources, and strain at work: a longitudinal test of the Triple Match Principle. *Journal of Applied Psychology* 91: 1359–74.

de Jonge, J., Dormann, C., and von Nordheim, T. (2006). Matching job demands and job resources: a vignette study. Paper presented at the APA-NIOSH Work, Stress, and Health Conference 2006, Miami.

de Jonge, J. Dormann, C., and van Vegchel, N. (2004). Taakeisen, hulpbronnen en psychische gezondheid: het Demand-Induced Strain Compensation (DISC)-model [Job demands, job resources, and mental health: the Demand-Induced Strain Compensation model]. *Gedrag en Organisatie* 17: 59–79.

de Jonge, J., van den Tooren, M., Dormann, C., Dollard, M. F., Vlerick, P., Tsutsumi, A., and Shimazu, A. (forthcoming). DISQ: a new instrument for

measuring job demands and job resources. Manuscript submitted for publication.
de Lange, A. H., Taris, T. W., Kompier, M. A. J., Houtman, I. L. D., and Bongers, P. M. (2004). The relationships between work characteristics and mental health: examining normal, reversed and reciprocal relationships in a 4-wave study. *Work and Stress* 18: 149–66.
Dollard, M. F., Dormann, C., Boyd, C. M., Winefield, H. R., and Winefield, A. H. (2003). Unique aspects of stress in human service work. *Australian Psychologist* 38: 84–91.
Dormann, C. and Zapf, D. (1999). Social support, social stressors at work and depression: testing for main and moderating effects with structural equations in a 3-wave longitudinal study. *Journal of Applied Psychology* 84: 874–84.
(2002). Social stressors at work, irritation, and depressive symptoms: accounting for unmeasured third variables in a multi-wave study. *Journal of Occupational and Organizational Psychology* 75: 33–58.
Frese, M. (1999). Social support as a moderator of the relationship between work stressors and psychological dysfunctioning: a longitudinal study with objective measures. *Journal of Occupational Health Psychology* 4: 179–92.
Haeslich, G., Streit, B., Richter, P., de Jonge, J., and Merkel, S. (2003). Testing the Demand-Induced Strain Compensation model in health care work. Paper presented at the 8th ENOP Conference, Vienna.
Halbesleben, J. R. B. and Buckley, M. R. (2004). Burnout in organizational life. *Journal of Management* 30: 859–79.
Halik, A. N. (2003). The effects of emotional labour on call-centre workers: a test of the Demand-Induced Strain Compensation model. Honours thesis, University of South Australia, School of Psychology.
Higgins, E. T. (1997). Beyond pleasure and pain. *American Psychologist* 52: 1280–1300.
(2000). Making a good decision: value from fit. *American Psychologist* 55: 1217–30.
(2006). Theory development as a family affair. *Journal of Experimental Social Psychology* 42: 549–52.
Hobfoll, S. E. (1989). Conservation of resources: a new attempt at conceptualizing stress. *American Psychologist* 44: 513–24.
(2001). The influence of culture, community, and the nested-self in the stress process: advancing Conservation of Resources theory. *Applied Psychology: An International Review* 50: 337–70.
(2002). Social and psychological resources and adaptation. *Review of General Psychology* 6: 307–24.
Hockey, G. R. J. (2000). Work environments and performance. In N. Chmiel (ed.), *Introduction to work and organisational psychology: a European perspective* (pp. 206–30). Oxford: Blackwell.
Hoek, A. A. and van Walsem-Reedeker, M. (2004). Taakeisen, hulpbronnen en psychische gezondheid in de tabaksdetailhandel [Job demands, job resources, and mental health in the tobacco retail trade]. Masters thesis, Utrecht University.

Hoogendoorn, W. E., van Poppel, M. N. M., Bongers, P. M., Koes, B. W., and Bouter, L. M. (2000). Systematic review of psychosocial factors at work and private life as risk factors for back pain. *Spine* 25: 2114–25.

Kahn, R. L. and Byosiere, P. (1992). Stress in organizations. In M. D. Dunnette and L. M. Hough (eds.), *Handbook of industrial and organizational psychology* (vol. 3, 2nd edn, pp. 571–650). Palo Alto, CA: Consulting Psychologists Press.

Karasek, R. A. Jr. (1979). Job demands, job decision latitude, and mental strain: implications for job redesign. *Administrative Science Quarterly* 24: 285–308.

    (1998). Demand/Control model: a social, emotional, and physiological approach to stress risk and active behaviour development. In J. M. Stellman (ed.), *Encyclopaedia of occupational health and safety* (pp. 34.6–34.14). Geneva: ILO.

Kompier, M. and Taris, T. (2004). Assessing methodological quality and biological plausibility in occupational health psychology. *Scandinavian Journal of Work, Environment and Health* 30: 81–3.

Koslowski, M. (1998). *Modeling the stress–strain relationship in work settings.* London: Routledge.

Langen, J., Aaij, S., and Nelson, P. (2005). Het Demand-Induced Strain Compensation (DISC)-model: cognitieve gezondheidsklachten, creatief werkgedrag, actief leergedrag and gebruik van hulpbronnen [The Demand-Induced Strain Compensation (DISC)-model: cognitive health complaints, creative work behavior, active learning behavior and use of job resources]. Bachelors thesis, Utrecht University.

Le Blanc, P. M., de Jonge, J., and Schaufeli, W. B. (in press). Job stress and occupational health. In N. Chmiel (ed.), *An introduction to work and organizational psychology: a European perspective* (2nd edn). Oxford: Blackwell.

Lekander, M. (2002). Ecological immunology: the role of the immune system in psychology and neuroscience. *European Psychologist* 7: 98–115.

Maslach, C. and Jackson, S. E. (1986). *Maslach Burnout Inventory: manual* (2nd edn). Palo Alto, CA: Consulting Psychologists Press.

Montague, P. R., (1996). The resource consumption principle: attention and memory in volumes of neural tissue. *Proceedings of the National Academy of Sciences of the United States of America* 93: 3619–23.

Morris, J. A. and Feldman, D. C. (1996). The dimensions, antecedents, and consequences of emotional labor. *Academy of Management Review* 21: 986–1010.

Muraven, M. and Baumeister, R. F. (2000). Self-regulation and depletion of limited resources: does self-control resemble a muscle? *Psychological Bulletin* 126: 147–259.

Plasschaert, M. (2004). Burnout en jobsatisfactie in ROB/RVT: een onderzoek naar de rol van emotionele belasting [Burnout and job satisfaction in ROB/ RVT: an investigation into the role of emotional demands]. Masters thesis, University of Ghent.

Pomaki, G. and Maes, S. (2002). Predicting quality of work life: from work conditions to self-regulation. In E. Gullone and R. A. Cummins (eds.), *The universality of subjective well-being indicators* (pp. 151–73). Dordrecht: Kluwer Academic.

Sargent, L. D. and Terry, D. J. (1998). The effects of work control and job demands on employee adjustment and work performance. *Journal of Occupational and Organizational Psychology* 71: 219–36.

Schaufeli, W. B. and Enzmann, D. (1998). *The burnout companion to study and practice: a critical analysis.* London: Taylor and Francis.

Siegrist, J. (1996). Adverse health effects of high-effort/low-reward conditions. *Journal of Occupational Health Psychology* 1: 27–41.

Spiegel, S., Grant-Pillow, H., and Higgins, E. T. (2004). How regulatory fit enhances motivational strength during goal pursuit. *European Journal of Social Psychology* 34: 39–54.

Taris, T. W. and Kompier, M. A. J. (2005). Job demands, job control, strain and learning behavior: review and research agenda. In A. Stamatios Antoniou and C. L. Cooper (eds.), *Research companion to organizational health psychology* (pp. 132–50). London: Edward Elgar.

Terry, D. J. and Jimmieson, N. L. (1999). Work control and employee well-being: a decade review. In C. L. Cooper and I. T. Robertson (eds.), *International review of industrial and organizational psychology* (vol. 14, pp. 95–148). Chichester: Wiley.

Terry, D. J., Nielsen, M., and Perchard, L. (1993). The effects of work stress on psychological well-being and job satisfaction: the stress buffering role of social support. *Australian Journal of Psychology* 45: 168–75.

Vancouver, J. B. (2000). Self-regulation in organizational settings: a tale of two paradigms. In M. Boekaerts, P. R. Pintrich, and M. Zeidner (eds.), *Handbook of self-regulation* (pp. 303–41). San Diego, CA: Academic Press.

van der Doef, M. and Maes, S. (1999). The Job Demand–Control (-support) model and psychological well-being: a review of 20 years of empirical research. *Work and Stress* 13: 87–114.

Van Vegchel, N., de Jonge, J., Bosma, H., and Schaufeli, W.B. (2005). Reviewing the Effort–Reward Imbalance model: drawing up the balance of 45 empirical studies. *Social Science and Medicine* 60: 1117–31.

van Vegchel, N., de Jonge, J., and Landsbergis, P. A. (2005). Occupational stress in (inter)action: the interplay between job demands and job resources. *Journal of Organizational Behavior* 26: 535–60.

Viswesvaran, C., Sanchez, J. I., and Fisher, J. (1999). The role of social support in the process of work stress: a meta-analysis. *Journal of Vocational behavior* 54: 314–34.

Vohs, K. D., Baumeister, R. F., and Ciarocco, N. J. (2005). Self-regulation and self-presentation: regulatory resource depletion impairs impression management and effortful self-presentation depletes regulatory resources. *Journal of Personality and Social Psychology* 88: 632–57.

Wall, T. D., Jackson, P. R., Mullarkey, S., and Parker, S. K. (1996). The Demands-Control model of job strain: a more specific test. *Journal of Occupational and Organizational Psychology* 69: 153–66.

Weehuizen, R. (2003). *Mental capital: position paper Ministry of Economic Affairs of the Netherlands.* Maastricht: MERIT.

Zapf, D., Seifert, C., Schmutte, B., Mertini, H., and Holz, M. (2001). Emotion work and job stressors and their effects on burnout. *Psychology and Health* 16: 527–45.

5 Job insecurity and employability among temporary workers: a theoretical approach based on the psychological contract

Nele De Cuyper and Hans De Witte

Socio-economic studies have been reporting on the rapid growth of temporary employment and on its problematic nature in terms of low pay, limited access to fringe benefits, and limited union protection (Kalleberg, Reskin, and Hudson, 2000; Korpi and Levin, 2001). Temporary employment refers to dependent jobs of limited duration, with fixed-term employment contracts and temporary agency work being the most common contract types in Europe (OECD, 2002). With this evolution in the foreground, a major theme among work and organizational psychologists concerns the impact of temporary employment arrangements on employees' well-being, attitudes, and behavior. The possible benevolent or detrimental consequences of temporary employment as compared to permanent employment are still hotly debated. Results until now have been inconclusive (Connelly and Gallagher, 2004; De Cuyper, De Witte, and Isaksson, 2005; Guest, 2004). While this has encouraged studies to explore the differences between permanent and temporary workers, the mixed evidence has resulted in a lack of theoretically informed studies (Davis-Blake and Uzzi, 1993). Hence, our understanding of the psychological impact of temporary employment and its underlying processes remains limited.

In this chapter, we formulate a theory that may respond to this lacuna. We draw upon psychological contract literature to interpret the inconsistent findings of contract type as found in previous research. Furthermore, we illustrate the possible implications of this theory for the experience and impact of job insecurity and employability. Both may be crucial in analyses on temporary employment; job insecurity has often been suggested as a critical factor in the understanding of temporary workers' work experiences (De Witte and Näswall, 2003), while employability may offer an alternative form of security that is especially relevant for these workers (Forrier and Sels, 2003a). In this study, we also show how the heterogeneity of temporary workers in terms of contract preference, contract duration, and employee prospects fits a psychological contract perspective. We start by summarizing earlier attempts at understanding the psychological experiences of temporary workers, and discuss why these may not be fully adequate for interpreting empirical results.

Previous research on temporary employment

Initially, researchers tried to understand the psychological impact of temporary employment by retesting theoretical models that proved valuable in predicting outcomes among permanent employees (Connelly and Gallagher, 2004). These authors foremost argued in favor of a mediational framework; drawing on job characteristic theories, they suggested that the outcomes of temporary employment heavily depend on its effects on employees' work characteristics (De Gilder, 2003; De Witte and Näswall, 2003; Sverke, Gallagher, and Hellgren, 2000). Their ideas correspond with the Flexible Firm model of Atkinson (1984), in which temporary workers constitute the organization's periphery, which is associated with unfavorable job characteristics and poor working conditions. Beard and Edwards (1995), for example, define five key features (job insecurity, control, predictability, social comparison, and the psychological contract) in which temporary workers are disadvantaged as compared to permanent workers. The authors conclude that, in turn, the likely effects will be negative for temporary workers. Similarly, the Second as well as the Third European Survey on Working and Living Conditions (Goudswaard and Andries, 2002) point out the generally worse job characteristics of temporaries, which highlights their potential precariousness in terms of well-being. Empirical evidence, however, does not support this assumption. Studies on the psychological consequences of being temporarily employed have yielded inconsistent and often contradictory results. For example, Connelly and Gallagher (2004) summarize studies that point to there being equal, lower, or higher levels of job satisfaction and organizational commitment among temporary as compared to permanent workers. Similar conclusions are drawn by Virtanen and colleagues (2005) in their review on temporary employment and health. The European literature review by De Cuyper et al. (2005), including both published and unpublished studies, suggests that non-significant differences or poorer results for permanents are mainly found with multiple outcomes, such as job satisfaction, health, psychological distress, and sick leave.

Researchers have initiated more complex studies to determine the possible reasons for these inconsistencies. Parker, Griffin, Sprigg, and Wall (2002) as well as Saloniemi, Virtanen, and Vahtera (2004) suggest that researchers' focus upon negative aspects of temporary employment may have masked its potential benefits, such as lower job demands. Parker and colleagues (Parker *et al.*, 2002) furthermore argue that the positive impact of temporary employment on role demands outweighs the negative effects of reduced job security and participative decision-making. While this study highlights the potential limitations of earlier theoretical considerations, it has some shortcomings. First, the study fails to address research evidence that temporaries are more likely than permanents to experience low job control or low decision latitude (Aronsson, Gustafsson, and Dallner, 2002). Combined with low workload, this may hint at a large share of temporaries being in passive rather than low-strain jobs (Karasek, 1979). This is supported by in-depth interviews with temporary workers (Rogers, 1995). Temporaries may experience work underload, which may be as harmful as work overload (Warr, 1994). Second, temporaries and permanents may have quite similar job characteristics when performing exactly the same job (Beard and Edwards, 1995; Sverke *et al.*, 2000). This may apply to a significant share of temporary workers; for example, those employed in manufacturing or those hired to replace permanent workers. Altogether, a stream of evidence suggests that studies exclusively relying on explanations in terms of job characteristics may not succeed in predicting responses of temporaries.

Another major thesis in the literature suggests that the mixed observations regarding the effects of contract type stem from the heterogeneity of temporary workers. A growing number of studies focus on the attitudinal and behavioral differences between those preferring and those not preferring temporary employment (e.g. Ellingson, Gruys, and Sackett, 1998; Feldman, Doerpinghaus, and Turnley, 1994; Krausz, 2000; Krausz, Brandwein, and Fox, 1995). These studies largely confirm the favorable impact of having control over one's working life. However, they may be less pertinent in explaining inconsistent findings in labor markets where such choice is limited (Parker *et al.*, 2002). Optimistic reports suggest that only about one employee out of three prefers his or her temporary employment arrangement to permanent employment (Cohany, 1996, 1998; Dinatale, 2001; Morris and Vekker, 2001; Polivka, 1996).

Other authors have sought the heterogeneity of temporary employment in other dimensions. For example, Guest, Mackenzie Davey, and Patch (2003) as well as Guest and Conway (2000) report more favorable attitudinal outcomes among fixed-term contract workers as compared to agency workers. These results may be caused by increased employment stability (e.g. in terms of contract duration) among fixed-term contract workers (Virtanen *et al.*, 2005; Bernhard-Oettel, Sverke, and De Witte, 2005). Similarly, different results are observed when comparing on-call workers, fixed-term contract workers, and independent contractors, with the latter being highest on job satisfaction, general health, and organizational commitment (Feldman, 1990). Goudswaard, Kraan, and Dhondt (2000) identified employees' prospects of future employment as an important factor in shaping employees' responses. Employees who assess their chances of receiving a permanent contract or a renewed contract as being high, rather than low, report higher levels of job satisfaction. While the heterogeneity of the temporary workforce may be crucial, it does not however explain the underlying processes that may affect temporaries. Furthermore, there may be other potentially useful dimensions with which to describe the variety of temporary workers (e.g. Bernhard and Sverke, 2003), suggesting that theoretical frameworks based on this heterogeneity are not that parsimonious.

More recently, Gallagher and colleagues (Gallagher and McLean Parks, 2001; Gallagher and Sverke, 2005; McLean Parks, Kidder, and Gallagher, 1998) questioned the relevance of well-established theories explaining temporaries' well-being, attitudes, and behaviors. More specifically, they argue that most theories falsely take the dominant paradigm of permanent employment for granted, which is illustrated primarily by theories on organizational commitment. Other researchers have formulated similar concerns. Guest and Clinton (2005), for example, doubt whether questions on turnover intention carry the same meaning for temporaries as they do for permanents. Indeed, for temporary workers, turnover is expected and agreed upon – and therefore not a good criterion for showing dissatisfaction with the job.

By and large, the mixed evidence in this area calls into question the use of traditional psychological explanations for predicting overall impaired well-being as well as less desirable attitudes and behaviors among temporaries. Furthermore, the inconsistencies hamper the development of new theoretical approaches. As Isaksson and Bellaagh (2002) point out, alternative stress models for temporary workers are needed, and these models should ideally include factors describing the interaction between the employee and the organization.

A psychological contract perspective on temporary employment

The psychological contract refers to "the idiosyncratic set of reciprocal expectations held by employees concerning their obligations (what they will do for the employer) and their entitlements (what they expect to receive in return)" (McLean Parks et al., 1998: 698). Contract type is suggested to be a decisive factor in distinguishing the content of the psychological contract along a transactional–relational dimension

(Coyle-Shapiro and Kessler, 2000; McDonald and Makin, 2000; McLean Parks *et al.*, 1998; Rousseau, 1995; Rousseau and Schalk, 2000). Transactional and relational psychological contracts are however not mutually exclusive; for example, relational elements may be added to psychological contracts that were initially transactional in nature (Rousseau, 1995). In their most prototypical way, transactional psychological contracts are based upon economic- and performance-based considerations (e.g. pay for attendance). The exchange relationship between the parties evolves over a specific period of time, as in the case of temporary workers. The relational psychological contract, in contrast, evolves under the condition of open-ended employment, characteristic for permanent workers. Entitlements typically include job security and a focus on advancement in the internal labor market, and these are exchanged for employees' loyalty (Rousseau, 1995). Empirical studies support the hypothesis forwarding the close relationship between employment contracts and psychological contracts; Millward and colleagues (Millward and Brewerton, 2000; Millward and Hopkins, 1998) established that relational elements dominate amongst permanent workers, while transactional elements are dominant for temporaries.

Unlike many previous studies (Beard and Edwards, 1995; Chambel and Castanheira, in press; McDonald and Makin, 2000; Millward and Hopkins, 1998; Van Dyne and Ang, 1998), but in accordance with Rousseau (1995) and Herriot and Pemberton (1995), we do not interpret transactional psychological contracts as being less favorable in terms of expected outcomes, or even less desirable, than relational psychological contracts. This will be argued below, based (1) on empirical evidence that psychological contract content might be less predictive for employees' responses than psychological contract breach and justice perceptions, and (2) on theoretical arguments that the transactional psychological contract may define alternative though equally constructive exchanges. Both these issues imply that temporary employment is different from, rather than inferior to, permanent employment.

First, we suggest that the key construct behind predicting employees' attitudes and behaviors is psychological contract breach and not so much the contents of the contract (Coyle-Shapiro and Kessler, 2002; Conway and Briner, 2002; Johnson and O'Leary-Kelly, 2003). Psychological contract breach refers to the perception that an obligation within the contract terms has not been met (Shore and Tetrick, 1994). In this respect, Lambert, Edwards, and Cable (2003) provide firm evidence that satisfaction is related to the delivery of the deal rather than to the specific nature of promises. In fact, their data show that employees who perceive that they receive less than they were promised feel betrayed and may display poorer well-being, and unfavorable attitudes and behaviors. Guest and colleagues (Guest, 2004; Guest *et al.*, 2003) furthermore suggest that transactional psychological contracts might be easier to monitor, and hence, might effect less breach. Literature on justice perceptions provides a somewhat similar reasoning, where Barringer and Sturman (1998) suggest that treating employees well is perceived as an organization's commitment toward its employees, creating an obligation in return. Fair treatment is derived from distributive justice for those holding transactional psychological contracts, while procedural justice is decisive in the case of relational contracting (McLean Parks *et al.*, 1998; Robinson and Morrison, 1995). Taken together, since temporaries and permanents have different psychological contracts, their respective unmet expectations and justice considerations shape their well-being, attitudes, and behavior. Basically, this implies that temporary and permanent employees have different standards of what constitutes good employment. This may explain the absence of clear-cut effects of contract type on psychological outcomes. Moreover, to the extent that transactional psychological contracts are easier to fulfill, temporaries may in fact report more positive attitudes, and they may show more constructive behavior.

It could be argued that, when fulfilled, relational psychological contract content is more satisfying than transactional psychological contract content. However, this argument is based on a fairly restrictive interpretation of transactional and relational psychological contracts. In this respect, leading authors in the field of work psychology and management have stressed the emergence of a new psychological contract (e.g. Anderson and Schalk, 1998; Coyle-Shapiro and Kessler, 2000; Hall and Moss, 1998; Herriot and Pemberton, 1995; Hiltrop, 1995; Millward and Brewerton, 2000; Rousseau, 1995). This evolution is described by analogy as a shift from "paternalism," and a career controlled by the employer, to partnership and a career controlled by both the employee and the employer (Hall and Chandler, 2005; Hall and Moss, 1998; Mirvis and Hall, 1994). In this new deal, employability and flexibility rather than job security and loyalty are foremost. While these last two aspects are indicative of the old deal as present in the relational psychological contract, the new deal seems rather to relate to the transactional psychological contract. Transactional psychological contracts, then, may have different commodities for exchange that are as constructive for employees' responses. These exchanges may include training (Gallagher and McLean Parks, 2001; Koh and Yer, 2000), opportunities to increase marketability (Matusik and Hill, 1998), or opportunities to improve the work–life balance. Also, the explicit and objective nature of transactional inducements may evoke satisfaction for many workers in today's rapidly changing environment (Millward and Brewerton, 1999).

We realize that this new deal discussion has primarily speculative roots (Guest, 2004). First, the extent to which employees have adopted this new psychological contract is unclear (Guest and Clinton, 2005; Kluytmans and Ott, 1999). Findings reported by Forrier and Sels (2003a) and by Delsen (1998), however, suggest that temporaries as compared to permanents may have accepted this new deal to a greater extent; temporaries take greater responsibility in training matters, indicating self-control and employability awareness. Their investment in training is mostly focused upon reinforcing their labor market position, while permanents mainly aim at personal development. Similarly, temporaries scored significantly higher on the item of career development in the study by McDonald and Makin (2000). If confirmed by further research, their acceptance of new psychological contract terms suggests that temporaries may have engaged in a high-quality relationship with their employer.

Second, factor structures including items on the new psychological contract are unstable. For example, while training has been judged to be distinctly transactional (Robinson and Rousseau, 1994; Rousseau, 1990), it has also been found to carry a relational factor loading (Robinson, Kraatz, and Rousseau, 1994). More recently, three factors were identified (e.g. Coyle-Shapiro and Kessler, 2000; De Witte, De Cuyper, Bernhard-Oettel, and Isaksson, 2005) that reflect transactional, relational and new psychological contract content. These different observations invite researchers to further explore psychological contract types, how they are related, and how they might change over time. As for now, however, we define transactional psychological contracts as those in which transactional content, including aspects of the new deal, dominates, and relational psychological contracts as those with a clear socioemotional focus.

In sum, we have argued that the psychological contracts of temporary and permanent workers differ along the transactional–relational dimension. In itself, psychological contract content, however, does not generate differences between permanents and temporaries in regard to various outcomes. Rather, it implies that temporaries and permanents use different though equally constructive standards for evaluating the employment relationship. It has previously been found that, in this evaluation, the aspects of met and unmet expectations, as well as justice considerations, are crucial in shaping employees' well-being, attitudes, and behaviors. Accordingly, it is quite possible that the inconsistent findings on the effects of contract type may originate from employees' differing frames of reference.

Job insecurity and employability among temporary workers

Job insecurity refers to an overall concern about the continued existence of the job in the future (Sverke, Hellgren, and Näswall, 2002). A large body of literature has documented the adverse effects of job insecurity on various psychological outcomes (e.g. De Witte, 1999; Sverke and Hellgren, 2002; Sverke *et al.*, 2002). Adapting from Forrier and Sels (2003b: 106), we define employability as "an individual's chance of a job in the external labor market," with perceived ease of movement as a crucial dimension. Most authors stress the role of the employer in providing the employee with chances and opportunities to strengthen one's employability (De Grip, Van Loo, and Sanders, 2004; Forrier and Sels, 2003a; McQuaid and Lindsay, 2005). This would suggest that employability is a shared responsibility between employer and employee. Few studies have investigated the impact of employability for employees (for an exception, see Berntson and Marklund, 2006). Employability is, however, likely to enhance employees' well-being and to further favorable attitudes and constructive behavior; it is considered to be the new protection mechanism in the current labor market, gradually replacing job security (Forrier and Sels, 2003b; Worth, 2002). This alternative form of security, or the feeling of being in control of one's career, may positively affect employees' experience of work (Fugate, Kinicki, and Ashforth, 2003; Marler, Barringer, and Milkovich, 2002). Furthermore, the favorable effect of employability-enhancing activities, such as training, on workers' satisfaction and motivation has been illustrated (Virtanen, Kivimäki, Virtanen, Elovianio, and Vahtera, 2003).

As outlined earlier, job security is the key element in defining the relational psychological contract (Millward and Brewerton, 2000). Accordingly, job insecurity represents a major breach of the relational psychological contract. This may imply that the harmful effects of job insecurity are related to an unwelcome change in the relational psychological contract (King, 2000; Pearce, 1998; Rousseau, 1995). This concurs with the perspective advanced by Pearce (1998) that betrayals should be distinguished from job insecurity. Furthermore, job insecurity should be unrelated to transactional psychological contract breach; transactional psychological contracts do not include job security as a basic promise, and are thereby not breached when employees feel insecure about their job. Similarly, employability is considered crucial to successfully engage in transactional psychological contracting. Low employability, then, may evoke perceptions of psychological contract breach among those holding transactional psychological contracts. Any possible adverse effects of perceived low employability may be explained by transactional psychological contract breach. Employability, however, is not an issue for those holding relational psychological contracts. On the contrary, relational psychological contract holders establish a long-term employment relationship with the same employer, which is at variance with putting a strong focus on the external labor market. Research on these assumptions is limited. De Cuyper and De Witte (2006) show that job insecurity no longer predicts reduced job satisfaction, organizational commitment, life satisfaction, and performance when relational psychological contract breach is introduced as a predictor. No such mediation was found for transactional psychological contract violation. In fact, transactional psychological contract breach was found to be unrelated to job insecurity.

This interpretation of job insecurity and employability challenges common assumptions about their impact. Most studies have turned to the established harmful effects of job insecurity as found among samples largely dominated by permanents as a starting point. These studies predict similar effects among temporaries (Beard and Edwards, 1995; Parker *et al.*, 2002; Pearce, 1998; Virtanen, Vahtera, Kivimäki, Pentti, and Ferrie, 2002). Similarly, the level of employability is often hypothesized to positively affect the well-being, attitudes, and behaviors of both temporaries and permanents to the same extent. Psychological contract theory, in contrast, predicts differential effects for temporaries and permanents.

Following the psychological contract framework, job insecurity may be especially detrimental in terms of outcomes for permanents as compared to temporaries. Permanents are likely to hold a relational psychological contract, which includes job security as a basic promise, while job security is not promised to temporaries. Rather, job insecurity is part of temporaries' expectations (Cavanaugh and Noe, 1999), as well as their work experience (Kinnunen and Nätti, 1994; Näswall and De Witte, 2003; Sverke *et al.*, 2000). When the negative effects of job insecurity are manifested only through psychological contract breach, as hypothesized, permanents may suffer more from feeling insecure than temporaries. Similarly, employability may be more predictive in terms of outcomes among temporaries as compared to permanents (Kluytmans and Ott, 1999). Temporaries probably include employability-promoting activities in their psychological contract, while permanents' expectations may not focus as much on external labor market issues. Low employability is therefore likely to represent psychological contract breach for temporaries, but not for permanents. This, in turn, may result in unfavorable outcomes among temporaries who feel less employable as compared to those who feel highly employable. No such employability effects are predicted for

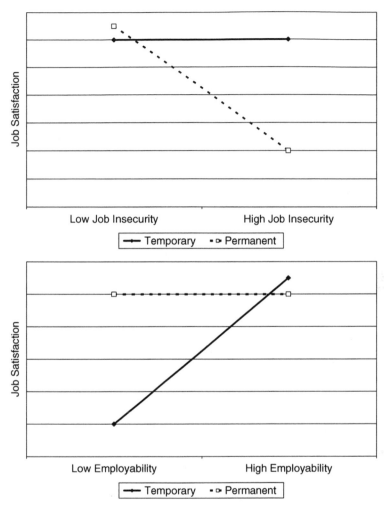

Figure 5.1 The impact of (a) job insecurity and (b) employability on job satisfaction among temporary and permanent employees, in accordance with psychological contract theory (hypothetical examples)

permanents. Figure 5.1a summarizes our assumptions on the impact of job insecurity. Figure 5.1b shows our theoretical assumptions on the impact of employability.

Evidence, until now, has largely supported the psychological contract perspective. Job insecurity has been found to be problematic for permanents, but not for temporaries, when it comes to job satisfaction and organizational commitment, in the studies by Guest and Conway (2000),

Mauno, Kinnunen, Mäkikangas, and Nätti (2005), and De Cuyper and De Witte (2005, 2006). De Witte and Näswall (2003) found similar interaction effects, albeit in only two out of the four country samples. Also, the interaction term between job insecurity and contract type added significantly in predicting other work-related outcomes, such as engagement, positive work–home interference, trust, and turnover intention (De Cuyper and De Witte, 2005). Up until now, three studies have been able to replicate this interaction effect in predicting psychological distress and health (Bernhard-Oettel *et al.*, 2005; Sverke *et al.*, 2000; Virtanen *et al.*, 2002), while two others did not (De Cuyper and De Witte, 2005, 2006). We are not aware of any studies on the possible differential impact of employability for temporaries and permanents. This remains an important area for future research.

In sum, psychological contract theory implies that temporary and permanent workers differ in their reactions to possible stressors, such as job insecurity and low employability. More specifically, temporaries may suffer more from feeling low employability as compared to permanents, while job insecurity may be especially harmful for permanents. These hypotheses follow from two assumptions: (1) temporaries and permanents are likely to hold transactional and relational psychological contracts respectively, and (2) job insecurity violates the relational psychological contract, while low employability violates the transactional psychological contract.

The heterogeneity of temporary workers

As outlined earlier, a developing body of research has pointed to the heterogeneity of the temporary workforce, most notably in terms of contract preference, contract duration, and employees' prospects of future employment. These dimensions may affect the psychological contracts of temporaries. For example, Freese and Schalk (1996) suggest that employees will actively seek information on highly valued job and career aspects. This implies that employees' preferences may at least partly affect psychological contract development. In this respect, those preferring permanent to temporary employment may aim at a relational psychological contract (Beard and Edwards, 1995), while voluntary temporaries may seek out transactional exchanges (Millward and Brewerton, 2000; Van Dyne and Ang, 1998). Direct hires who were high on preference established a more economic and less socio-economic relationship in the study by Chambel and Castanheira (in press). Similarly, Rousseau (1995; Rousseau and Wade-Benzoni, 1995) suggests that contract duration is a governing principle in the formulation of relational promises. She states that relational elements could be added to psychological contracts that were originally purely transactional in nature, as might be the case for renewed fixed-term contracts. Finally, employees who assess their chances of receiving a permanent contract or a renewed contract as being high, compared to low, might anticipate a relational psychological contract (Connelly and Gallagher, 2004; Gallagher and McLean Parks, 2001).

This suggests that temporaries may differ in the extent to which they engage in transactional and relational contracting. More specifically, involuntary temporaries, those on long-term temporary assignments, and those with the prospect of continued employment may be somewhat more relationally focused, and somewhat less transactionally focused. Similarly, transactional psychological contract content may be foremost for those preferring temporary employment, for those on short-term contracts, and for those with limited prospects. Accordingly, job insecurity and employability may have different effects on different types of temporaries. For example, we expect job insecurity to have more adverse consequences for those on long-term temporary arrangements, involuntary temporaries, and those with high prospects as compared to their counterparts. Similarly, weak employability perceptions may be especially harmful to voluntary temporaries, those on short-term temporary assignments, and those who perceive their chances of continued employment in their current job to be unfavorable.

Concluding remarks

In this chapter, we have aimed to advance the general understanding of the consequences of being temporarily versus permanently employed from a theoretical perspective. We have highlighted the importance of contract type for the constructing of expectations as formulated in employees' psychological contract. The evaluation of the psychological contract in terms of met and unmet expectations is crucial in shaping employees' well-being, attitudes, and behavior. This suggests that temporaries and permanents have different standards for evaluating their employment relationships, and it is this evaluation that shapes employees' responses. The inconsistent findings reported in earlier studies possibly reflect these different frames of reference, as the impact of temporary employment cannot be assessed using the dominant standard of permanent employment. In addition, we have argued that job insecurity and employability may affect temporaries and permanents differently. The impact of these factors may only be felt when they constitute a breach of one's psychological contract. This may be the case when permanents feel insecure, or when temporaries perceive their chances in the external labor market to be slim. Finally, with the psychological contract framework taking into account the diversity of temporary workers, and their possible differences in psychological contract orientation, this approach implies that temporaries may differ amongst themselves in how strongly they react to stressors. We hope to encourage researchers to further develop this approach, first by providing empirical evidence on the assumptions and implications of this theory, and second, by critically reconsidering research on various forms of atypical employment.

Implications for research

This psychological contract based framework has implications for future research in the domain of work and organizational psychology. First, it is critical of studies that implicitly use the standard of permanent employment to evaluate other employment situations. Kluytmans and Ott (1999: 262) refer to this research tradition as "the psychology of lifetime employment." In this respect, psychological contract theory may be useful for understanding other forms of flexible employment. For example, an article by Conway and Briner (2002) on the psychological experiences of part-time workers points to some interesting parallels, finding that part-time employees are treated unfavorably at the organizational level (e.g. in terms of pay). These workers, however, may have had different career orientations, leading the authors to suggest that they may have knowingly made trade-offs as a form of compensation (e.g. improved work–life balance in exchange for lower pay). Their psychological contract may moreover be transactionally rather than relationally focused, suggesting a reduced risk of breach.

Second, the psychological contract based framework highlights the limitations of studies that generalize the effects of stressors to all employees. It challenges researchers to critically reconsider the effects of variables that proved predictive among permanent employees. For example, psychological contract theory could account for the observation by De Gilder (2003) that trust is relevant in predicting organizational citizenship behavior for permanents but not for temporaries. Trust might indeed reflect a socio-emotional, i.e. relational, aspect.

Implications for practice

If empirically validated, this perspective may also have important practical implications. First, it suggests that even organizations that do not provide lifelong employment may still be able to establish mutually satisfactory employment relationships (Baruch and Hind, 1999).

Likewise, temporary employment may not need to be problematic if temporaries are provided with inducements that match their expectations. This argues for the critical importance of a transparent communication strategy, and, to the extent that these are part of temporaries' psychological contract, for employers to pay attention to employability-promoting activities. This focus upon employability, however, may exemplify the difficulties in establishing valuable transactional psychological contracts among temporaries. Human capital theory hypothesizes that employers want to recoup their investments in training (Davis-Blake and Uzzi, 1993; OECD, 2005). This return on investments, however, is limited in the case of temporary employees because of their high exit probability. Various empirical studies support the hypothesis that temporary contracts are at odds with employers' willingness to invest in training (Aronsson *et al.*, 2002; Delsen, 1998; Forrier and Sels, 2003a; Hoque and Kirkpatrick, 2003; Virtanen *et al.*, 2003). Another potential drawback in the study of temporary employment arrangements is that we do not yet know about the long-term effects of transactional contracting. This aspect may end up being important, given Millward and Brewerton's (1999) claim that transactional psychological contracting is becoming increasingly important for all employees.

References

Anderson, N. and Schalk, R. (1998). The psychological contract in retrospect and prospect. *Journal of Organizational Behavior* 19: 637–47.

Aronsson, G., Gustafsson, K., and Dallner, M. (2002). Work environment and health in different types of temporary jobs. *European Journal of Work and Organizational Psychology* 11: 151–75.

Atkinson, J. (1984). Manpower strategies for flexible organizations. *Personnel Management* August: 28–31.

Barringer, M. W. and Sturman, M. C. (1998). The effects of variable work arrangements on the organizational commitment of contingent workers. Working paper, Cornell University.

Baruch, Y. and Hind, P. (1999). Perpetual motion in organizations: effective management and the impact of the new psychological contract on "survivor syndrome." *European Journal of Work and Organizational Psychology* 8: 295–306.

Beard, K. M. and Edwards, J. R. (1995). Employees at risk: contingent work and the psychological experience of contingent workers. In C. I. Cooper and D. M. Rousseau (eds.), *Trends in organizational behavior* (vol. 2, pp. 109–26). Oxford: Wiley.

Bernhard, C. and Sverke, M. (2003). Work attitudes, role stress and health among different types of temporary workers in the Swedish health care sector. *Research and Practice in Human Resource Management* 11: 1–16.

Bernhard-Oettel, C., Sverke, M., and De Witte, H. (2005). Comparing three alternative types of employment with permanent full-time work: how do employment contract and perceived job conditions relate to health complaints? *Work and Stress* 19: 301–18.

Berntson, E. and Marklund, S. (2006). The relationship between employability and subsequent health. Paper presented at the Sixth Conference on Psychology and Health, 8–10 May, Kerkrade, The Netherlands.

Cavanaugh, M. A. and Noe, R. A. (1999). Antecedents and consequences of relational components of the new psychological contract. *Journal of Organizational Behavior* 20: 323–40.

Chambel, M. J. and Castanheira, F. (in press). They don't want to be temporaries: similarities between temps and core workers. *Journal of Organizational Behavior*.

Cohany, S. R. (1996). Workers in alternative employment arrangements. *Monthly Labor Review* 119: 31–45.

— (1998). Workers in alternative employment arrangements. A second look. *Monthly Labor Review* 121: 3–21.

Connelly, C. E. and Gallagher, D. G. (2004). Emerging trends in contingent work research. *Journal of Management* 30: 959–83.

Conway, N. and Briner, R. B. (2002). Full-time versus part-time employees: understanding the link between work status, the psychological contract and attitudes. *Journal of Vocational Behavior* 61: 279–301.

Coyle-Shapiro, J. A. M. and Kessler, I. (2000). Consequences of the psychological contract for the employment relationship: a large scale survey. *Journal of Management Studies* 37: 903–29.

— (2002). Contingent and non-contingent working in local government: contrasting psychological contracts. *Public Administration* 80: 77–101.

Davis-Blake, A. and Uzzi, B. (1993). Determinants of employment externalization: a study of temporary workers and independent contractors. *Administrative Science Quarterly* 38: 195–223.

De Cuyper, N. and De Witte, H. (2005). Job insecurity: mediator or moderator of the relationship between type of contract and various outcomes? *South-African Journal of Industrial Psychology (special issue)* 31: 79–86.

— (2006). The impact of job insecurity and contract type on attitudes, well-being and behavioural reports: a psychological contract perspective. *Journal of Occupational and Organizational Psychology* 79: 395–409.

De Cuyper, N., De Witte, H., and Isaksson, K. (2005). Temporary employment in Europe: conclusions. In N. De Cuyper, K. Isaksson, and H. De Witte (eds.), *Employment contracts and well-being among European workers* (pp. 225–43). Aldershot: Ashgate.

de Gilder, D. (2003). Commitment, trust and work behavior. The case of contingent workers. *Personnel Review* 32: 588–604.

De Grip, A., van Loo, J., and Sanders, J. (2004). The industry employability index: taking account of supply and demand characteristics. *International Labour Review* 143: 211–33.

Delsen, L. (1998). Zijn externe flexibiliteit en employability strijdig? [Do external flexibility and employability conflict?]. *Tijdschrift voor HRM* 1: 27–45.

De Witte, H. (1999). Job insecurity and psychological well-being: review of the literature and exploration of some unresolved issues. *European Journal of Work and Organizational Psychology* 8: 155–77.

De Witte, H., De Cuyper, N., Bernhard-Oettel, C., and Isaksson, K. (2005). The psychological contract of temporary workers. Paper presented at the 12th European Congress of Work and Organizational Psychology, Istanbul.

De Witte, H. and Näswall, K. (2003). Objective versus subjective job insecurity: consequences of temporary work for job satisfaction and organizational commitment in four European countries. *Economic and Industrial Democracy* 24: 149–88.

DiNatale, M. (2001). Characteristics of and preference for alternative work arrangements. *Monthly Labor Review* 124: 28–49.

Ellingson, J. E., Gruys, M. L., and Sackett, P. R. (1998). Factors related to the satisfaction and performance of temporary employees. *Journal of Applied Psychology* 83: 913–21.

Feldman, D. C. (1990). Reconceptualizing the nature and consequences of part-time work. *Academy of Management Review* 15: 103–12.

Feldman, D. C., Doerpinghaus, H. I., and Turnley, W. H. (1994). Managing temporary workers: a permanent HRM challenge. *Organizational Dynamics* 23: 49–63.

Forrier, A. and Sels, L. (2003a). Temporary employment and employability: training opportunities and efforts of temporary and permanent employees in Belgium. *Work, Employment and Society* 17: 641–66.

    (2003b). The concept employability: a complex mosaic. *International Journal of Human Resource Development and Management* 3: 103–24.

Freese, C. and Schalk, R. (1996). Implications of differences in psychological contracts for human resource management. *European Journal of Work and Organizational Psychology* 5: 501–9.

Fugate, M., Kinicki, A. J., and Ashforth, B. E. (2003). Employability: a psychosocial construct, its dimensions, and applications. *Journal of Vocational Behavior* 65: 14–38.

Gallagher, D. G. and McLean Parks, J. (2001). I pledge thee my troth . . . contingently: commitment and the contingent work relationship. *Human Resource Management Review* 11: 181–208.

Gallagher, D. G. and Sverke, M. (2005). Contingent employment contracts: are existing employment theories still relevant? *Economic and Industrial Democracy* 26: 181–203.

Goudswaard, A. and Andries, F. (2002). *Employment status and working conditions.* Luxemburg: European Foundation for the Improvement of Living and Working Conditions, Office for Official Publications of the European Communities.

Goudswaard, A., Kraan, K. O., and Dhondt, S. (2000). *Flexibiliteit in balans: flexibilisering en de gevolgen voor werkgever én werknemer* [Flexibility in balance: flexibility of labor and the consequences for employer and employee]. Hoofddorp: TNO Arbeid.

Guest, D. (2004). Flexible employment contracts, the psychological contract and employee outcomes: an analysis and review of the evidence. *International Journal of Management Review* 5/6: 1–19.

Guest, D. and Clinton M. (2005). Contracting in the UK: current research evidence on the impact of flexible employment and the nature of psychological contracts. In N. De Cuyper, K. Isaksson, and H. De Witte (eds.), *Employment contracts and well-being among European workers* (pp. 201–24). Aldershot: Ashgate.

Guest, D. and Conway, N. (2000). *The psychological contract in the public sector.* London: CIPD.

Guest, D., Mackenzie Davey, K., and Patch, A. (2003). The psychological contracts, attitudes and behaviour of workers on temporary and permanent contracts. Management Centre Working Paper 19. London: King's College.

Hall, D. T. and Chandler, D. E. (2005). Psychological success: when the career is a calling. *Journal of Organizational Behavior* 26: 155–76.

Hall, D. T. and Moss, J. E. (1998). The new protean career contract: helping organizations and employees adapt. *Organizational Dynamics* 26: 22–37.

Herriot, P. and Pemberton, C. (1995). *New deals: the revolution in managerial careers.* Chichester: Wiley.

Hiltrop, J. M. (1995). The changing psychological contract: the human resource challenge of the 1990s. *European Management Journal* 13: 286–94.

Hoque, K. and Kirkpatrick, I. (2003). Non-standard employment in the management and the professional workforce: training, consultation, and gender implications. *Work, Employment and Society* 17: 667–89.

Isaksson, K. S. and Bellaagh, K. (2002). Health problems and quitting among female "temps." *European Journal of Work and Organizational Psychology* 11: 27–45.

Johnson, J. L. and O'Leary-Kelly, A. M. (2003). The effects of psychological contract breach and organizational cynicism: not all social exchange violations are created equal. *Journal of Organizational Behavior* 24: 627–47.

Kalleberg, A. L., Reskin, B. F., and Hudson, K. (2000). Bad jobs in America: standard and nonstandard employment relations and job quality in the United States. *American Sociological Review* 65: 256–78.

Karasek, R. A. (1979). Job demands, job decision latitude, and mental strain: implications for job redesign. *Administrative Science Quarterly* 24: 285–308.

King, J. E. (2000). White collar reactions to job insecurity and the role of the psychological contract: implications of human resource management. *Human Resource Management* 39: 79–92.

Kinnunen, U. and Nätti, J. (1994). Job insecurity in Finland: antecedents and consequences. *European Journal of Work and Organizational Psychology* 4: 297–321.

Kluytmans, F. and Ott, M. (1999). Management of employability in the Netherlands. *European Journal of Work and Organizational Psychology* 8: 261–72.

Koh, W. L. and Yer, L. K. (2000). The impact of employee–organization relationship on temporary employees' performance and attitudes: testing a Singaporean sample. *International Journal of Human Resource Management* 11: 366–87.

Korpi, T. and Levin, H. (2001). Precarious footing: temporary employment as a stepping stone out of unemployment in Sweden. *Work, Employment and Society* 15: 127–48.

Krausz, M. (2000). Effects of short- and long-term preference for temporary work upon psychological outcomes. *International Journal of Manpower* 21: 635–47.

Krausz, M., Brandwein, T., and Fox, S. (1995). Work attitudes and emotional responses of permanent, voluntary, and involuntary temporary-help employees: an exploratory study. *Applied Psychology: An International Review* 44: 217–32.

Lambert, L., Edwards, J. R., and Cable, D. M. (2003). Breach and fulfillment of the psychological contract: a comparison of traditional and expanded views. *Personnel Psychology* 56: 895–934.

Marler, J. H., Barringer, M. W., and Milkovich, G. T. (2002). Boundaryless and traditional contingent employees: worlds apart. *Journal of Organizational Behavior* 23: 425–53.

Matusik, S. F. and Hill, C. W. (1998). The utilization of contingent work, knowledge creation, and competitive advantage. *Academy of Management Review* 23: 680–97.

Mauno, S., Kinnunen, U., Mäkikangas, A., and Nätti, J. (2005). Psychological consequences of fixed-term employment and perceived job insecurity among health care staff. *European Journal of Work and Organizational Psychology* 14: 209–38.

McDonald, D. J. and Makin, P. J. (2000). The psychological contract, organizational commitment and job satisfaction of temporary staff. *Leadership and Organizational Development Journal* 21: 84–91.

McLean Parks, J., Kidder, D. L., and Gallagher, D. G. (1998). Fitting square pegs into round holes: mapping the domain of contingent work arrangements onto the psychological contract. *Journal of Organizational Behavior* 19: 697–730.

McQuaid, R. W. and Lindsay, C. (2005). The concept of employability. *Urban Studies* 42: 179–219.

Millward, L. J. and Brewerton, P. M. (1999). Contractors and their psychological contract. *British Journal of Management* 10: 253–74.
    (2000). Psychological contracts: employee relations for the twenty-first century? In C. L. Cooper and I. T. Robertson (eds.), *International review of industrial and organizational psychology* (vol. 15, pp. 1–61). Chichester: Wiley.

Millward, L. J. and Hopkins, L. (1998). Psychological contracts, organizational and job commitment. *Journal of Applied Social Psychology* 28: 1530–56.

Mirvis, P. H. and Hall, D. T. (1994). Psychological success and the boundaryless career. *Journal of Organizational Behavior* 15: 365–80.

Morris, M. D. S. and Vekker, A. (2001). An alternative look at temporary workers, their choices, and the growth in temporary employment. *Journal of Labor Research* 22: 373–90.

Näswall, K. and De Witte, H. (2003). Who feels insecure in Europe? Predicting job insecurity from background variables. *Economic and Industrial Democracy* 24: 189–215.

OECD (2005). *Employment outlook*. Paris: Organization for Economic Co-operation and Development.

Parker, S. K., Griffin, M. A., Sprigg, C. A., and Wall, T. A. (2002). Effect of temporary contracts on perceived work characteristics and job strain: a longitudinal study. *Personnel Psychology* 55: 689–717.

Pearce, J. L. (1998). Job insecurity is important, but not for the reasons you might think: the example of contingent workers. In C. L. Cooper and D. M. Rousseau (eds.), *Trends in organization behavior* (Vol. 5, pp. 31–46). New York: Wiley.

Polivka, A. E. (1996). Into contingent and alternative employment: by choice? *Monthly Labor Review* 119: 55–74.

Robinson, S. L., Kraatz, M. S., and Rousseau, D. M. (1994). Changing obligations and the psychological contract: a longitudinal study. *Academy of Management Journal* 37: 137–52.

Robinson, S. L. and Morrison, E. W. (1995). Psychological contracts and OCB: the effect of unfulfilled obligations on civic virtue behavior. *Journal of Organizational Behavior* 16: 289–98.

Robinson, S. L. and Rousseau, D. M. (1994). Violating the psychological contract: not the exception but the norm. *Journal of Organizational Behavior* 15: 245–59.

Rogers, J. K. (1995). Just a temp. Experience and structure of alienation in temporary clerical employment. *Work and Occupations* 22: 137–66.

Rousseau, D. M. (1990). New hire perceptions of their own and their employer's obligations: a study of psychological contracts. *Journal of Organizational Behavior* 11: 389–400.

(1995). *Psychological contracts in organizations: understanding written and unwritten agreements*. Thousand Oaks, CA: Sage.

Rousseau, D. M. and Schalk, R. (2000). *Psychological contracts in employment: cross cultural perspectives*. Thousand Oaks, CA: Sage.

Rousseau, D. M. and Wade-Benzoni, K. A. (1995). Changing individual–organization attachments. A two-way street. In A. Howard (ed.), *The changing nature of work* (pp. 290–322). The Jossey-Bass Social and Behavioral Science Series. San Francisco: Jossey-Bass/Pfeiffer.

Saloniemi, A., Virtanen, P., and Vahtera, J. (2004). The work environment in fixed-term jobs: are poor psychosocial conditions inevitable? *Work, Employment and Society* 18: 193–208.

Shore, L. M. and Tetrick, L. E. (1994). The psychological contract as an explanatory framework in the employment relationship. In C. L. Cooper and D. M. Rousseau (eds.), *Trends in organizational behavior* (pp. 91–109). New York: Wiley.

Sverke, M., Gallagher, D. G., and Hellgren, J. (2000). Alternative work arrangements: job stress, well-being, and work attitudes among employees with different employment contracts. In K. Isaksson, L. Hogstedt, C. Eriksson, and T. Theorell (eds.), *Health effects of the new labour market* (pp. 85–101). New York: Plenum.

Sverke, M. and Hellgren, J. (2002). The nature of job insecurity: understanding employment uncertainty on the brink of a new millennium. *Applied Psychology: An International Review* 51: 23–42.

Sverke, M., Hellgren, J., and Näswall, K. (2002). No security: a meta-analysis and review of job insecurity and its consequences. *Journal of Occupational Health Psychology* 7: 242–64.

Van Dyne, L. and Ang, S. (1998), Organizational citizenship behavior of contingent workers in Singapore. *Academy of Management Journal* 41: 692–703.

Virtanen, M., Kivimäki, M., Joensuu, M., Virtanen, P., Elovainio, M., and Vahtera, J. (2005). Temporary employment and health: a review. *International Journal of Epidemiology* 34: 610–22.

Virtanen, M., Kivimäki, M., Virtanen, P., Elovainio, M., and Vahtera, J. (2003). Disparity in occupational training and career planning between contingent and permanent employees. *European Journal of Work and Organizational Psychology* 12: 19–36.

Virtanen, P., Vahtera, J., Kivimäki, M., Pentti, J., and Ferrie, J. F. (2002). Employment security and health. *Journal of Epidemiological Community Health* 56: 569–74.

Warr, P. (1994). A conceptual framework for the study of work and mental health. *Work and Stress* 8: 84–97.

Worth, S. (2002). Education and employability: school leavers' attitudes to the prospect of non-standard work. *Journal of Education and Work* 15: 163–79.

6   Independent contracting: finding a balance between flexibility and individual well-being

Daniel G. Gallagher

In recent years there has been a well-documented international trend involving the gradual restructuring of employment contracts away from the standard or traditional ongoing employer–employee relationship and more toward increasing organizational reliance on contractual work arrangements which are more contingent, precarious, or fixed-term in nature (Connelly and Gallagher, 2004; Kalleberg, Reynolds, and Marsden, 2003; Mauno, Kinnunen, Mäkikangas, and Nätti, 2005; Quinlan and Bohle, 2004; Silla, Gracia, and Peiró, 2005). This is not to suggest that the "standard" employment deal of the twentieth century is in immediate danger of extinction. However, there does appear to be a growing strategic interest by contemporary organizations in hiring workers on a contingent basis as a means of making labor itself more of a "variable" rather than a relatively "fixed" operating cost. Such an interest in fixed-term contracts also appears to fit well in the context of rising organizational focus on flexibility in the production of goods and services within many post-industrial nations (Handy, 1989; Piore and Sabel, 1984; Reilly, 1998).

For many people, contingent or fixed-term contracts are often seen as being synonymous with organizational reliance upon the services of temporary-help staffing firms (e.g. Adecco, Manpower, Randstad, etc.) to provide workers on an "ad hoc" basis. Traditionally the temporary-help staffing industry in Europe and North America has served as an efficient market mechanism for providing employers with clerical and manual laborers to serve the purpose of replacing absent permanent staff (e.g. holiday coverage, illness, etc.) or to staff the organization for short-term projects or seasonal demands. Today, staffing firms not only meet the temporary replacement needs of employer organizations, but more frequently operate as a mechanism by which organizations are able to quickly, and with minimal non-direct wage cost, expand and contract the size of their workforce to meet cyclical or incidental demand for labor.

What has become especially remarkable about the hiring of workers on short or fixed-term contracts has been the accelerating growth of contingent workers who are employed as "independent contractors" or "free agents" (Ang and Slaughter, 2001; Barley and Kunda, 2004; Ho, Ang, and Straub, 2003; Marler, Barringer, and Milkovich, 2002; Pink, 2001). Although a precise definition may be elusive, independent contractors can broadly be characterized as individuals who sell their services or skills to a "client" organization for a specified number of hours or on a project basis (Gallagher, 2002). Once the project or task is completed, the contractual relationship between the contractor and the client is terminated unless a decision is made by both parties to enter into a subsequent contract. A further defining characteristic of independent contractor status rests in the fact that independent contractors, or free-agents, are not technically employees of the client organization nor are they directly employed by an intermediary organization (e.g. professional consulting firm). Also characteristic of true independent contractor status is the ability of the contractor or free-agent to have extensive control over how (and often when) the work is performed. Within many countries, a legal distinction between independent contractor and temporary employee status takes into consideration the ability of the worker (contractor) to earn a profit, but also suffer financial loss, the absence of dependence on the client organization for training, and the contractor's ability to work for multiple clients at a single time (Connelly and Gallagher, 2006).

As noted by a number of writers in both the academic and the popular press, the growing presence and visibility of independent contractors as part of the contemporary workforce has been strongly influenced by both demand and supply-side forces. From the perspective of employer organizations, the ability to remain competitive or efficient has been associated with the aforementioned principle of being able to become increasingly flexible. As noted by Reilly (1998), flexibility from a human resource or staffing perspective is limited not simply to the ability to more readily expand and contract the size of the workforce, but also to the ability of the organization to quickly access the particular types of worker skills for which there is an immediate need. Although the hiring of workers on an independent contractor or free-agent basis has long been a staple of the pre-industrial economies (Cappelli, 1999), it has ironically been the accelerating rate of technological change that has spurred the growth of workers being employed on an individual and fixed-term contract basis. Most notable and universally visible has been the growth of computer-based information technology changes which manifested itself in an increased need for professional and technical expertise. As noted by Poppo and Zenger (1998) and Matusik and Hill (1998), the level of technological change as well as the specificity of professional staffing needs has led many contemporary organizations to evaluate the relative benefits of securing technical and professional human resources on a fixed-term or project basis rather than following the more traditional industrial-era practice of ongoing employment contracts. For many organizations, the hiring of professional and technical workers on a fixed-term, independent contractor basis represents a means not only for gaining access to "up-to-date skill sets" but also for escaping or minimizing the procedural and monetary costs often associated with the downsizing of more traditional or "permanent" employees (Greene, 2000).

In comparison to other segments of the broader contingent workforce, individual contractors or free-agents have been increasingly viewed as holding an "elite" status (Barley and Kunda, 2006). This elite status in many ways is reflective of the fact that, owing to the professional or technical nature of their skills, independent contractors are disproportionately older, more experienced, highly educated, and better paid compared to most other workers employed under other types of contingent contracts (Nollen, 1999). Also, evidence exists to indicate that the majority of workers who pursue careers as independent contractors are most likely to do so on a voluntary basis (Silla *et al.*, 2005).

It is not uncommon in both the popular and the scholarly press to view independent contractors or free-agents as a new breed of entrepreneur who has sought to escape the coercive, remunerative, and normative controls associated with organizationally based employment (Evans, Kunda, and Barley, 2004). In an ethnographic study of highly skilled technical contractors Kunda and colleagues found that the decision to become independent contractors was often reflective of "a mix of structural and economic factors, as well as a set of motives rooted in a professional ideology of work" (Kunda, Barley, and Evans, 2002: 247). The frequently cited motivations for undertaking independent contracting careers include the allure of higher compensation, increased autonomy, distain for organizational politics, and incompetent management (Kunda *et al.*, 2002). As noted by Daniel Pink (2001) in his popular book *Free Agent Nation*, free-agency has been facilitated by increasing personal access to many of the technological tools of production (computers, internet access, photocopiers, etc.) which allow workers low cost of entry into independent contractor careers.

Despite the positive image that has been associated with independent contracting or the "boundaryless career" (Marler *et al.*, 2002), it has been increasingly recognized that independent contracting may also have a dark side which could be a potential detriment both to individual well-being and to the work–family relationship. In particular, Kunda *et al.* (2002) have found that despite the economic advantage associated with independent contracting in the technical skill area, many independent contractors reported feelings of anxiety and estrangement.

Barley and Kunda (2004) note that independent contracting creates a paradigm where workers redefine job insecurity as an issue of employability and that the quest for continued employability has consequences upon how independent contractors manage their professional and personal lives. Furthermore, the factors contributing to these negative experiences may be reflective of a broad range of organizational, market, and individual considerations.

The primary objectives of this chapter will be to further explore the issues of job insecurity and employability in the context of the contemporary world of independent contractors. Particular emphasis will be directed toward an attempt to identify salient sources of stress which may be associated with independent contracting and potentially impact worker well-being and the work–family relationship. Drawing upon existing research in the area of work stress and well-being, the study will seek to identify organizational, market, and individual factors which may intervene in the stressor and well-being relationship among independent contractors. Attention will be drawn to aspects of independent contracting which are outside of many existing theoretical frameworks found in the employee well-being literature. The chapter will conclude with some suggestions for both practical applications and future empirical research.

Sources of stress for independent contractors

Insecurity

By definition, all contingent work contracts, and more specifically independent contracting, can be viewed as an "objectively" insecure form of employment (Cappelli and Neumark, 2004; De Witte and Näswall, 2003; Mauno et al., 2005). Furthermore, and not unexpectedly, there exists reasonable empirical evidence to suggest that contingent workers subjectively perceive more job insecurity than workers performing similar types of work on a more permanent basis (De Witte and Näswall, 2003; Klein Hesselink and van Vuurren, 1999; Parker, Griffin, Sprigg, and Wall, 2002). As such, in the context of an extensive body of literature establishing a linkage between job security and worker well-being (see Sverke, Hellgren, and Näswall, 2002), one would expect to find a strong negative linkage between contingent employment and well-being as measured by indicators of psychological and physiological well-being. However, as recently noted by Mauno et al. (2005) and Silla et al. (2005), emerging empirical research on fixed-term and temporary employment has led to mixed and inconclusive findings between non-permanent work status and individual well-being. These findings are also supportive of the viewpoint that temporary work cannot be studied as a unitary construct, but rather that research on insecurity and associated well-being needs to pay particular attention to the nature of the temporary contract and the extent to which temporary workers prefer non-standard working arrangements (e.g. Isaksson and Bellagh, 2002; Silla *et al.*, 2005).

As previously noted, as a breed of contingent workers, independent contractors are distinguishable from other temporary workers by virtue of the fact that they are likely to prefer to maintain a non-permanent work status and that they are, by definition, self-employed and thus technically are their own employers (Gallagher and McLean Parks, 2001). In addition, in their study of technical contractors, Evans *et al.* (2004) suggest that "job security" with a particular client organization may be of less salience for independent contractors than is the broader market-based issue of "employability." In many respects, for skilled independent contractors, concern over the termination of the "job" is of less concern than the ability to maintain a skill set that is competitively marketable. From a theoretical perspective, it can be hypothesized that perceived employability directly impacts individualized perceptions of employment security, which in turn may influence the psychological and physiological well-being of the individual contractor. Such a hypothesized mediated relationship has the basis of some support in Silla *et al.*'s (2005) study of temporary workers in Spain, which found perceived employability to be related to job insecurity and, in turn, that job insecurity was associated with lower levels of well-being. Given the apparent greater importance which employability may hold for independent contractors (Evans *et al.*, 2004), it might further be suggested that this possible mediated relationship between employability and well-being may in fact be more pronounced among independent contractors who operate in markets with rapid rates of skill obsolescence and relatively low barriers of entry for competitive contractors.

Role related

Within the occupational stress and well-being literature, there has been a long-standing recognition of the manner and degree to which "role related" variables contribute to safety and health (Danna and Griffin, 1999; Frone, Russell, and Cooper, 1995; Kelloway and Barling, 1991; Quinlan and Bohle, 2004). In the context of contingent work, but more specifically independent contracting, the concept of "role" could be more complex. Since much of the existing work on stress and well-being has been developed in the realm of the traditional ongoing employer–employee relationship, role has primarily been conceptualized as expectations and behaviors associated with a particular job which is imbedded within an employer organization (Cartwright and Cooper, 1997; Jex, 1998; Karasek, 1979). For independent contractors, role and associated aspects such as ambiguity and scope (overload and underload) and role conflict may also be recognizable sources of potential stress which deserve consideration. However, the fact that independent contracting is based on a series of fixed-term client–contractor relationships may potentially create somewhat different sources of role-related stressors which are not as common in ongoing employment relationships.

Two particular role related variables which have the potential for being salient sources of stress are the issues of role ambiguity and role overload. With regard to role ambiguity, on the surface it would normally appear as part of the contractual agreement between the client and independent contractor, that the duties and responsibilities would be clearly articulated. Even from the perspective of a psychological contract, the basis of the client–contractor relationship would be expected to be relatively "transactional" in nature. However, as noted by Barling, Inness, and Gallagher (2002), Evans et al. (2004), and Gallagher (2005), independent contractors may find themselves hired to work on a specific fixed-term project by reason of their expertise and hours of labor which they bring to complete the task, but without any clearly defined process related expectations. Role-related ambiguity may become a particularly salient issue when the independent contractor loses a degree of "independence" by being included as part of a broader functional unit with other contractors or more permanent organizational members. In more traditional work relationships, role ambiguity is often most prevalent when workers first join an organization or in instances where they experience a change in job-related duties. Job-related ambiguity is usually dissipated over time through increased familiarity with the job. However, in the case of independent contractors, the nature of the career often requires them to move readily between different clients. As either the number of clients increases or the duration of the contracts becomes shorter, it would appear that the potential increases for independent contractors to be exposed to work-related roles which may be ambiguous in nature. Furthermore, the fixed-term nature of the contract and possible non-familiarity with managers and co-workers may hinder the speed and process by which ambiguity associated with the assignment is reduced. Conversely, one would expect that the likelihood of job or role ambiguity as a work-related stressor for independent contractors would be substantially reduced in circumstances where the terms of contractual duties and responsibility are clearly articulated.

Workload

As noted above, a further role-related stressor of greater importance to the understanding of well-being among independent contractors is the issue of workload in the form of role or job scope. In contrast to role ambiguity, role or job scope addresses the level of expectations or demands placed upon the individual contractor by the client organization. Once again, these expectations may be clearly articulated in the contractual agreement between the client and the contractor. In an ethnographic study of technical contractors in the US, Evans *et al.* (2004) reported that even under conditions of clearly defined transitional contracts, client organizations often ask contractors to engage in more responsibilities or expend more time than initially stipulated. As noted by Evans *et al.* (2004), the ability of the client organization to add on to the scope of contractor responsibilities and time commitment, without additional compensation, rests in the aforementioned fact that the ability of independent contractors to secure future projects or assignments is a function of their "reputation." Since many independent contractors are heavily reliant on referrals, client requests to expand the scope of the responsibilities are often reluctantly accepted by contractors as a means of protecting their future employability. As analogous to the notion of the psychological contract, the client–contractor relationship may be both more relational and fungible than one might expect (McLean Parks, Kidder, and Gallagher, 1998). But such flexibility may at times result in "shades of coercive control" (Evans *et al.*, 2004: 6) and the potential for increased stress on the contractors by way of increased tasks and longer uncompensated hours of project work. It is also important to note that many independent contractors have multiple client relationships. As a result, contractors may find the potential stress of addressing the above noted client demands to be magnified by the extent to which multiple clients simultaneously place pressure on the contractor to engage in behaviors which exceed the scope of a simple transactional contract.

Hours of work

As well documented in the stress and well-being literature, excessive work hours can have negative consequences for an individual's health and safety (Breslow and Buell, 1960; Cartwright and Cooper, 1997). For independent contractors, time or working hour demands can be more complex and broadly defined than may be the case of workers in more traditional, ongoing employment relationships.

First, for many independent contractors, the self-employed nature of independent contracting often results in the existence of "professionally engaged hours of work" which can well extend beyond hours of direct payroll or project time with a client organization (Evans *et al.*, 2004). In particular, hours of professional engagement may also include time associated with the search for prospective clients as well as the preparation, submission, and negotiation of project proposals. Since such search costs are normally non-compensated, there would be an inherent pressure on contractors to minimize such time, but ironically as less paid work is contracted, the pressure to increase the level of search time increases. For many independent contractors, work time demands may be an ongoing process involving a mix of both paid and unpaid activities. For independent contractors in areas of rapid technological change or shifting customer preferences, part of the engaged work hours may be associated with the task of keeping their skill set current. Such skill updating may be accomplished through a variety of formal and informal methods, but regardless of the approach, the fact remains that such skill updating does require a further expenditure of non-compensated time which adds to the total number of hours associated with the maintenance of their independent contractor status. From a related perspective, the number of professionally engaged hours of work represent time which is reallocated away from family interaction. Such reallocation of time may have the effect of diminishing the frequency and quality of the work–family relationship.

Another time-related stressor associated with independent contracting careers is the scheduling and intensity of work hours. Despite the popular suggestion that free-agency or independent contracting allows individuals a great deal of control over their work lives, it may well be the case that scheduling of work hours is driven by client needs rather than contractor preferences. Within some professional fields, independent contractors are often hired by client organizations at short notice to resolve emergency situations or supplement existing staff in the task of meeting impending deadlines. The challenge of meeting deadlines or solving an urgent problem may itself be stress for an independent contractor: such events may cause the schedules of independent contractors to become rather hazardous, involving long periods of work activity and variable hours, followed by inactivity. This absence of a clearly defined work schedule not only may be a further source of stress but can substantially contribute to work–family conflict (Parasuraman and Simmers, 2001) by disrupting or preventing a predictable schedule of interaction among family members. Further, in the presence of irregular working hours and schedules, the ability of family members to share household and family responsibilities becomes more problematic and a further potential source of intra-family conflict.

Third, recent work by Evans *et al.* (2004) suggests that even among independent contractors who are extremely successful in securing and performing fixed-term contract work, this can create the situation where the opportunity for rest and relaxation may itself be a source of stress. More specifically, for some independent contractors "downtime" (scheduled or unscheduled), even when spent with friends and family, may translate into a source of stress when contractors begin to equate time with money. For salaried income workers, time off is normally not associated with a resulting decrease in income. However, given the project-based or hourly compensation context in which independent contractors evaluate their time, some contractors may view non-work time as a loss of income which outweighs the potential benefit of non-work activities.

Profit and loss

A final potential source of stress that may be more of an issue for independent contractors than for workers in ongoing employment relationships, as well as other forms of contingent employment, is the fact that pure independent contracting (a form of self-employment) includes not only the potential to make an income, but also the potential for incurring financial loss. In many respects, independent contractors are self-employed entrepreneurs. Depending on the nature of their work, they may carry capital and administrative overhead costs. In addition, they are responsible for their own insurance and benefit packages. Although standard workers may find themselves in a precarious economic position in the event of job loss, market conditions (competition, service demand, and quality) may also threaten to negatively affect the economic security of the independent contractor (Probst, 2005). In effect, not only is employability an ongoing issue, so is the profitability of the self-contracting enterprise.

Intervening factors

Within the broad range of theoretical frameworks which have been utilized to the antecedents and outcomes of work-related stress, considerable attention is often given to the consideration of environmental, organizational, and individual level factors which may mediate causal relationships between the principal variables of interest (Barling, Kelloway, and Frone, 2005; Jex, 1998). The importance of intervening or mediating variables has also been recognized in emerging research which has begun to study well-being in the context of contingent workers (e.g. De Cuyper, Isaksson, and De Witte, 2005; Isaksson and Bellagh, 2002; Silla *et al.*, 2005). In the context of independent contracting, attention can be directed to a number of specific factors which may impact how individuals respond to work-related stressors.

Volition

Within the area of research on the topic of contingent work, it has become a well-established finding that worker attitudes and responses to contingent work are strongly influenced by the extent to which the individual worker voluntarily chooses to pursue work under contingent contracts or engage in such work due to a lack of more permanent alternatives (Ellingson, Gruys, and Sackett, 1998; Krausz, 2000). As previously noted, as a category of contingent work, independent contracting tends to be comprised of a high percentage of individuals who have voluntarily chosen such careers. However, there does exist a subset of independent contractors whose motivation for becoming an independent contractor is not of their own volition. Most notably, some workers move to independent contractor status as a result of job loss and the inability to find comparable employment on a permanent basis. In addition, as part of organizationally based schemes to enhance flexibility, some workers may have been terminated from ongoing employment with an organization and subsequently rehired with the status of an "independent" contractor.

In many respects it is reasonable to assume that all workers who take the leap into careers as independent contractors are likely to be confronted initially with many of the aforementioned stressors which are often absent or buffeted in the context of more permanent employer–employee relationships. However, it may be fair to hypothesize that individual contractor responses to such stressors can be influenced by the extent to which the decision to enter into independent contracting was deliberately chosen by the individual worker. It might also be suggested that the possible effect of involuntary choice can itself be moderated by the length of time over which a worker transitioned from traditional employment to independent contracting work.

Dependence

Although workers may hold the title of independent contractor, free-worker, or free-agent, a number of writers have questioned the actual level of "independence" or "freedom" associated with such work (Greene, 2000; Connelly and Gallagher, 2006). Most salient is the question of the extent to which independent contractors are over-reliant upon a single or small set of client organizations. Dependence may possibly increase the intensity of contractor responses to organizational and role related stressors. In contrast, true "independent" contractors with a long portfolio of clients (Pink, 2001) may be more willing and able to have the luxury of avoiding or walking away from more stressful client organizations. As such, both the magnitude of client-based stressors and the stressor–well-being relationship may be moderated by the contractor's perceived level of dependency on the client organization(s).

Control

Very closely related to the issue of dependency is the question of the extent to which individual contractors actually have control over how the work is performed. Once again, the issue turns upon the extent to which the contractor has independence. From a theoretical perspective, demand–control-based models of stress and well-being would suggest that workers who have greater control over how the work is performed are more able to minimize the negative impact which may be inherent in various types of role-related and organizational demands (e.g. Parker *et al.*, 2002). Such a moderating relationship would appear to be equally applicable in the context of contingent work and more specifically independent contracting. For such reasons, contractors who are brought into a client organization and subject to close management or permanent co-worker direction and supervision may be less likely to minimize the magnitude of the source of stress or implement strategies to minimize the negative impact. Alternatively, the truer the level of independence or control, the greater the ability of the individual contractor to reduce stress and stress-related consequences.

Social support networks

Social exclusion within the workplace has long been identified as a source of worker anxiety and stress (Baumeister and Leary, 1995; Ganster, Fusilier, and Mayes, 1986). Internal social exclusion has been found to be prevalent among workers performing contingent employment under a variety of contractual arrangements (Galup, Saunders, Nelson, and Cerveny, 1997; Sias, Kramer, and Jenkins, 1997). For independent contractors who regularly move from one client organization to another, the absence of opportunity to be part of an intra-client social network may possibly increase their exposure to a stressor–negative well-being relationship. Ironically however, among contractors who have a high level of dependence upon a single client organization or have moved from permanent to independent contractor status within the same organization, there may be greater familiarity and history of social support with other members of the client organization. Hence, what they may lose in independence is partially offset through greater internal social support systems.

From another perspective, for true independent contractors who readily move from one client organization to the next, external or professionally based support organizations may assume greater importance than support systems within an organization. As noted by Castaneda (1999) and Evans et al. (2004), the concerns and stresses of independent contracting can be greatly reduced among individual contractors who are formally or informally associated with a network of other contractors within similar professional fields who can provide not only social support, but also access to occupational knowledge which will enhance their ability to deal with project-related challenges. Depending upon the primacy of social versus technical needs, independents may choose to structure their support networks differently in terms of the scope and tightness of those extra-organizational contacts (Castaneda, 1999).

Personality

Either inherently or explicitly, most studies of work stress and well-being have emphasized the importance of individual personality as a factor in determining how workers perceive and handle work-related stress (Barling et al., 2002; Galais and Moser, 2005). To date, personality-based considerations have not received a great deal of attention in the context of how contingent workers deal with the stressor–well-being relationship. However, recent findings by Galais and Moser (2005), in a study of temporary workers in Germany, found a strong correlation between the extent to which individuals possessed self-monitoring skills and self-reported well-being. Drawing upon De Witte and Näswall (2003), it may also be noted that personality factors may influence how contingent workers interpret and react to work-related stressors. Among independent contractors, it might well be hypothesized that such personality factors as "tolerance for ambiguity" and an "internal locus of control" may be particularly important factors which influence how such contractors respond to stress and *uncertainty* (Hellgren and Sverke, 2003). However, it is also possible that these same personality characteristics may distinguish those who seek out careers as independent contractors rather than remaining in the relative security of a standard employment agreement.

Practical implications and future research directions

Based upon the preceding discussion of the nature of independent contracting and associated stressors which may impact worker well-being, a few concluding comments are offered concerning both practical application and a much needed call for future research directions.

Practical implications

For individuals undertaking careers as independent contractors, there is an inescapable realization that their work experiences and associated responses are more dependent upon market-based factors than the internal policies and practices of a single employer organization. In many respects independent contractors may be escaping the standard employment environment of coercive and remunerative employer control only to find themselves subject to an alternative set of demands and controls which, if not well managed, may represent sources of potential stress which may negatively impact their well-being.

For independent contractors, practical advice rests less upon organizationally based theories of behavior but more upon individualized career management considerations. As suggested, one prominent issue which should be of concern to individual contractors is their ability to remain "employable." Employability can be enhanced by a number of means, but perhaps the most fundamental is the ability of the individual contractor to constantly upgrade their skills to such a level that they remain an attractive asset for prospective client organizations. The ability of a contractor to upgrade their skills may be in part a function of access to more formalized and structured classroom training, but it is also in large part a function of on-the-job experiences. Most notably, contractors who are able to secure project contracts with innovative client organizations are also able to gain exposure to new techniques and technologies which will ultimately improve their employability or market value. In many respects, for independent contractors, the issues of practical concern should be not only of securing contracts, but also of securing contracts with client organizations where the contractor can gain access to knowledge and experiences which will subsequently be marketable to other organizations. Such a strategy also suggests that contractor dependence on one or a few client organizations for employment may actually have the short-range benefits of security and familiarity, but be potentially detrimental in terms of the individual contractor's exposure to broader trends and innovations which exist in the marketplace. In many respects, the notion of seeking to contract with clients who have the most up-to-date technologies and highly complex challenges might best serve an individual contractor's longer-term market value.

A second and important practical consideration for independent contractors in the contemporary workforce is the ability to develop and maintain effective social or professional networking arrangements which will provide them with efficient access to both professional knowledge and future employment options. As noted by Evans *et al.* (2004) and Castaneda (1999), although networking is also an important issue for employees in more standard ongoing employment arrangements, the ability to access a network of professional colleagues for professional and psychological support is of particular importance. Again, from a practical perspective, individual contractors need to consider how to combine the technical goals of project completion with the more social challenges of network building. In many respects, social and professional network building call upon a different set of interpersonal skills which are not necessarily similar to the skill sets which are job or task focused.

Finally, it might be simple but reasonable to suggest that in the same way that client organizations have outsourced organizational tasks to independent contractors, contractors themselves may need to consider the feasibility and potential benefits of securing the services of intermediary organizations to manage many of the administrative responsibilities which are associated with self-employment. Although such a suggestion requires contractors to assume an increased final cost of operation, such third party administrative support may reduce the scope and magnitude of administrative burdens which may be potential sources of stress for independent contractors.

Future research

In recent years there has been an emergence of empirical research examining the individual and, to a lesser degree, the organizational consequences associated with contingent work arrangements (see Gallagher and Connelly, 2004). However, among these studies, relatively few have given specific attention to the issue of well-being among contingent workers (e.g. De Cuyper *et al.*, 2005; Mauno *et al.*, 2005; Silla *et al.*, 2005) and fewer examine well-being in the context of potentially more stress in the contingent work subcategory of independent contracting (Evans *et al.*, 2004). In many respects it would appear that, from a research perspective, the door is wide open for future empirical research dealing with issues pertaining to independent contracting and health-related outcomes. It might also be suggested that there needs to be a better understanding of what, if any, consequences contingent work in general, and independent contracting specifically, have on the work–family relationship. And how such potential work–family impacts may fit into the broader scheme of worker well-being.

It is strongly recommended that, before researchers journey too far down the path of empirically investigating the relationship between independent contracting and both personal and family well-being, greater attention should also be given to consideration of the extent to which existing models of individual stress and well-being are applicable to the experiences of independent contracting. This caveat is raised for the reason that many of our existing theoretical frameworks or models of workplace behaviors and outcomes have been principally developed in the context of the industrial era's emphasis on an identifiable employer organization and an ongoing employer–employee relationship (Beard and Edwards, 1995). As indicated earlier in this chapter, independent contracting or free-agency is an approach to work which exists outside traditional organizational roles and involves greater exposure to direct market forces. This is to suggest not that existing models of well-being are not fundamentally applicable to understanding stress and well-being among independent contractors, but rather the possibility that the sources of stress and viable response mechanisms may vary from what is known about ongoing employment relationships.

Finally, although easy to suggest but difficult to implement, it is recommended that future empirical research on the topic of independent contracting give consideration to the development of longitudinal research designs. Longitudinal designs have the obvious benefit of allowing research to draw more definitive conclusions concerning causality. However, in the case of independent contractors who readily move between client organizations, it might be particularly important to understand how work-related stress may vary from one client relationship to another. Furthermore, a longitudinal design would enable researchers to better understand the adaptive mechanisms which are developed by independent contractors to stressful situations, but could also provide valuable clues in the understanding how volition, control, social networks, personality, and other intermediary variables have the effect of moderating or mediating the link between stresses and well-being.

References

Ang, S. and Slaughter, S. A. (2001). Work outcomes and job design for contract versus permanent information systems professionals on software development teams. *MIS Quarterly* 25: 321–50.

Barley, S. R. and Kunda, G. (2004). *Gurus, hired guns, and warm bodies: itinerant experts in the knowledge economy*. Princeton, NJ: Princeton University Press.

(2006). Contracting: a new form of professional practice. *Academy of Management Perspectives* 20: 45–66.

Barling, J., Inness, M., and Gallagher, D. G. (2002). Alternative work arrangements and employee well being. In P. Perrewé and D. Ganster (eds.),

Historical and current perspectives on stress and well being (vol. 2, pp. 183–216). Oxford: Elsevier.

Barling, J., Kelloway, E. K., and Frone, M. R. (eds.) (2005). *Handbook of work stress*. Thousand Oaks, CA: Sage.

Baumeister, R. F. and Leary, M. R. (1995). The need to belong: desire for interpersonal attachments as a fundamental human motivation. *Psychological Bulletin* 117: 497–529.

Beard, K. M. and Edwards, J. R. (1995). Employees at risk: contingent work and the experience of contingent workers. In C. L. Cooper and D. M. Rousseau (eds.), *Trends in organizational behavior* (vol. 2, pp. 109–26). Chichester: Wiley.

Breslow, L. and Buell, P. (1960). Mortality from coronary heart disease and physical activity of work in California. *Journal of Chronic Diseases* 11: 615–25.

Cappelli, P. (1999). *The new deal at work*. Boston, MA: Harvard Business School Press.

Cappelli, P. and Neumark, D. (2004). External churning and internal flexibility: evidence on the functional flexibility and core periphery hypotheses. *Industrial Relations* 43: 148–82.

Cartwright, S. and Cooper, C. L. (1997). *Managing workplace stress*. Thousand Oaks, CA: Sage.

Castaneda, L. W. (1999). Social networks in the open labor market: an exploration of independent contractors' careers. Paper presented at Academy of Management meeting in Chicago.

Connelly, C. E. and Gallagher, D. G. (2004). Emerging trends in contingent work research. *Journal of Management* 30: 959–83.

(2006). Independent and dependent contracting: meaning and implications. *Human Resource Management Review* 16: 95–106.

Danna, K. and Griffin, R. W. (1999). Health and well-being in the workplace: a review and synthesis of the literature. *Journal of Management* 25: 357–84.

De Cuyper, N., Isaksson, K., and De Witte, H. (eds.) (2005). *Employment contracts and well-being among European workers*. Aldershot: Ashgate.

De Witte, H. and Näswall, K. (2003). "Objective" vs. "subjective" job insecurity: consequences of temporary work for job satisfaction and organizational commitment in four European countries. *Economic and Industrial Democracy* 24: 149–88.

Ellingson, J. E., Gruys, M. L., and Sackett, P. R. (1998). Factors related to the satisfaction and performance of temporary employees. *Journal of Applied Psychology* 83: 913–21.

Evans, J. A., Kunda, G., and Barley, S. R. (2004). Beach time, bridge time, and billable hours: the temporal structure of technical contracting. *Administrative Science Quarterly* 49: 1–38.

Frone, M. R., Russell, M., and Cooper, M. L. (1995). Job stress, job involvement, and employee health: a test of identity theory. *Journal of Occupational and Organizational Psychology* 68: 1–11.

Galais, N. and Moser, K. (2005). Temporary agency work as a stepping stone? Individual determinants of transition into a permanent job and effects of failure on well being. Paper presented at Academy of Management meeting in Honolulu, Hawaii.

Gallagher, D. G. (2002). Contingent work contracts: practice and theory. In C. L. Cooper and R. J. Burke (eds.), *The new world of work* (pp. 115–36). Oxford: Blackwell.

—— (2005). Part-time and contingent employment. In J. Barling, E. K. Kelloway, and M. R. Frone (eds.), *Handbook of work stress* (pp. 517–41). Thousand Oaks, CA: Sage.

Gallagher, D. G. and McLean Parks, J. (2001). I pledge thee my troth … contingently: commitment and the contingent work relationship. *Human Resource Management Review* 11: 181–208.

Galup, S., Saunders, C., Nelson, R. E., and Cerveny, R. (1997). The use of temporary staff and managers in a local government environment. *Communication Research* 24: 698–730.

Ganster, D. C., Fusilier, M. R., and Mayes, B. T. (1986). Role of social support in the experience of stress at work. *Journal of Applied Psychology* 71: 102–10.

Greene, B. (2000). Independent contractors: an attractive option? *New Zealand Journal of Industrial Relations* 25: 183–204.

Handy, C. (1989). *The age of unreason*. Boston, MA: Harvard University Press.

Hellgren, J. and Sverke, M. (2003). Does job insecurity lead to impaired well-being or vice versa? Estimation of cross-lagged effects using latent variable modeling. *Journal of Organizational Behavior* 24: 215–36.

Ho, V. T., Ang, S., and Straub, D. (2003). When subordinates become IT contractors: persistent managerial expectations in IT outsourcing. *Information Systems Research* 14: 66–86.

Isaksson, K. and Bellagh, K. (2002). Health problems and quitting among female "temps." *European Journal of Work and Organizational Psychology* 11: 27–45.

Jex, S. M. (1998). *Stress and job performance*. Thousand Oaks, CA: Sage.

Kalleberg, A. L., Reynolds, J., and Marsden, P. V. (2003). Externalizing employment: flexible staffing arrangements in US organizations. *Social Science Research* 32: 525–52.

Karasek, R. A. (1979). Job demands, job decision latitude, and mental strain: implications for job redesign. *Administrative Science Quarterly* 24: 285–308.

Kelloway, E. K. and Barling, J. (1991). Job characteristics, role stress and mental health. *Journal of Occupational Psychology* 64: 291–304.

Klein Hesselink, D. J. and van Vuuren, T. (1999). Job flexibility and job insecurity: the Dutch case. *European Journal of Work and Organizational Psychology* 8: 273–94.

Krausz, M. (2000). Effects of short- and long-term preference for temporary work upon psychological outcomes. *International Journal of Manpower* 21: 635–47.

Kunda, G., Barley, S. R., and Evans, J. (2002). Why do contractors contract? The experience of highly skilled technical professionals in a contingent labor market. *Industrial and Labor Relations* 55: 234–60.

Marler, J. H., Barringer, M. W., and Milkovich, G. T. (2002). Boundaryless and traditional contingent employees: worlds apart. *Journal of Organizational Behavior* 23: 425–52.

Matusik, S. F. and Hill, C. W. (1998). The utilization of contingent work, knowledge creation, and competitive advantage. *Academy of Management Review* 23: 690–7.

Mauno, S., Kinnunen, U., Mäkikangas, A., and Nätti, J. (2005). Psychological consequences of fixed-term employment and perceived job insecurity among health care staff. *European Journal of Work and Organizational Psychology* 14: 209–37.

McLean Parks, J., Kidder, D. L., and Gallagher, D. G. (1998). Fitting square pegs into round holes: mapping the domain of contingent work arrangements onto the psychological contract. *Journal of Organizational Behavior* 19: 697–730.

Nollen, S. (1999). Flexible working arrangements: an overview of developments in the United States. In I. U. Zeytinoglu (ed.), *Changing work relationships in industrialized economies* (pp. 21–39). Amsterdam: John Benjamins.

Parker, S. K., Griffin, M. A., Sprigg, C. A., and Wall, T. D. (2002). Effect of temporary contracts on perceived work characteristics and job strain: a longitudinal study. *Personnel Psychology* 55: 689–719.

Parasuraman, S. and Simmers, C. A. (2001). Type of employment, work–family conflict and well-being: a comparative study. *Journal of Organizational Behavior* 22: 551–68.

Pink, D. H. (2001). *Free agent nation*. New York: Time Warner.

Piore, M. J. and Sabel, C. F. (1984). *The second industrial divide: possibilities for prosperity*. New York: Basic Books.

Poppo, L. and Zenger, T. (1998). Testing alternative theories of the firm: A transaction cost, knowledge based, and measurement explanations for make-or-buy decisions in information services. *Strategic Management Journal* 19: 853–77.

Probst, T. (2005). Economic stressors. In J. Barling, E. K. Kelloway, and M. R. Frone (eds.), *Handbook of work stress* (pp. 267–98). Thousand Oaks, CA: Sage.

Quinlan, M. and Bohle, P. (2004). Contingent work and occupational safety. In J. Barling and M. R. Frone (eds.), *The psychology of workplace safety* (pp. 81–105). Washington, DC: American Psychological Association.

Reilly, P. A. (1998). Balancing flexibility, meeting the interests of employer and employee. *European Journal of Work and Organizational Psychology* 7: 7–22.

Sias, P. M., Kramer, M. W., and Jenkins, E. (1997). A comparison of the communication behaviors of temporary employees and new hires. *Communication Research* 24: 731–54.

Silla, I., Gracia, F. J., and Peiró, J. M. (2005). Job insecurity and health-related outcomes among different types of temporary workers. *Economic and Industrial Democracy* 26: 89–117.

Sverke, M., Hellgren, J., and Näswall, K. (2002). No security: a meta-analysis and review of job insecurity and its consequences. *Journal of Occupational Health Psychology* 7: 242–64.

7 Work–family conflict in individuals' lives: prevalence, antecedents, and outcomes

Ulla Kinnunen and Saija Mauno

The topic of how to balance the demands of work and family life continues to be an increasing problem in today's western society. This is due in part to the changing roles of men and women both in the workplace and at home. Not only are women now more likely to work outside the home, but it is also now more common for men to fulfill more responsibilities within the home. Thus, the increasing participation of women in the workforce as well as the greater number of working single parents and dual-earner families are just a few examples of trends providing employees with challenges in juggling work and family life today. Although this development may produce distinct advantages, such as increased gender equality, enhanced role performance, and generally higher family incomes, it has also increased the likelihood that employees will face difficulties in combining work and family responsibilities.

Working life has also experienced rapid changes since the beginning of the 1990s. The 1990s and the beginning of the twenty-first century are described as a time of major technological and economic change, and these changes are making a lasting impression on the work–family interface. For example, technological advances in communication have made it possible to work almost anywhere: at home or even while traveling. This also means that traditional office work hours are giving way as a twenty-four hour work society emerges – one that is always ready to respond to the global movements of people, goods, and information across time zones and national borders. This has resulted in an increase in non-standard work schedules (i.e. evening, night and weekend work) among the workforce. At the same time, instability in working life has increased, and temporary employment (e.g. fixed-term job contracts) and perceived job insecurity (i.e. the threat of unemployment) make it difficult for individuals and families to plan their future. Owing to these changes in family and working life, it is not surprising that the competing demands of work and family roles often result in conflict for both working men and women.

The aim of this chapter is to shed light on the issue of work–family conflict in individuals' lives. This topic is important not only for the sake of individual employees and families, but also for the sake of employers and work organizations. It has been clearly shown that work–family conflict is associated with various negative individual (e.g. strain symptoms), family (e.g. family stress) and organization level (e.g. decreased organizational commitment) outcomes (see Allen, Herst, Bruck, and Sutton, 2000, for a review). Thus, preventing work–family conflict in individuals' lives contributes to enhanced well-being and functions in both families and organizations.

We begin our chapter with a theoretical discussion concerning the construct of work–family conflict, and continue with an empirical review of the prevalence, antecedents, and outcomes related to work–family conflict. In this empirical section, we provide a literature review, with an emphasis on recent studies. The literature review, however, is not systematic, as the enormous amount of research in this area is impossible to review in one chapter. Our literature review focuses on reviews and meta-analyses recently made available on the topic. In the last part of this empirical review, we discuss the role of moderators in the relationship between antecedents and work–family conflict, and between work–family conflict and its outcomes. Not only can moderators provide us with information on the conditions that may prevent work–family conflict or its negative outcomes, they can also reveal those conditions through which these relationships are strengthened. We focus on two potential moderators – gender and social support – because they have thus far received the most research attention. Finally, we also present suggestions for future research and practice.

The concept of work–family conflict

The work–family interface has classically been studied from the perspective of the role stress theory, which posits that the management of multiple roles (e.g. spouse, parent, employee) is difficult and inevitably creates strain and conflicts between the demands of work and family (Greenhaus and Beutell, 1985). The argument is that because people possess fixed and limited amounts of resources, the fulfillment of multiple roles is likely to result in the depletion of these scarce resources and ultimately result in stress (see e.g. Rothbard, 2001).

Greenhaus and Beutell (1985: 77) defined work–family conflict as "a form of inter-role conflict in which the role pressures from the work and family domains are mutually incompatible in some respect. That is, participation in the work (family) role is made more difficult by virtue of participation in the family (work) role." Thus, work–family conflict entails a perception of insufficient time and/or energy for successfully performing both work and family roles. Furthermore, expectations regarding behavior (e.g. the degree of emotionality and nurturance) in work and family roles can be incompatible. This definition prompted researchers to examine the work–family conflict from a bi-directional perspective, taking into account the fact that the conflict may originate either from the demands of work (work-to-family conflict) or family (family-to-work conflict). These two types of conflicts are also described as work interference with family and family interference with work (e.g. Frone, Russell, and Cooper, 1992a; Gutek, Searle, and Klepa, 1991).

Early research, however, employed work–family conflict as a uni-dimensional concept that did not distinguish the direction of conflict (e.g. Kopelman, Greenhaus, and Conolly, 1983). Support for distin-guishing the two types of conflicts comes from several sources: both recent theory and research on work–family conflict suggests that these concepts may have different causes and outcomes. For example, Byron's (2005) meta-analytic review of more than sixty studies showed, in line with theoretical expectations (e.g. Frone, 2003), that work-related ante-cedents related more strongly to work-to-family conflict, and some non-work-related antecedents were more strongly related to family-to-work conflict. In addition, Mesmer-Magnus and Viswesvaran's (2005) meta-analytic study supports discriminant validity between these concepts. From their meta-analysis of twenty-five studies, they found that job stressors correlated more highly with work-to-family conflict and that non-work stressors correlated highly with family-to-work conflict. When it comes to the outcomes of work–family conflict, the results have not always supported the discriminant validity between the conflicts. For example, organizational withdrawal behaviors (e.g. turnover intentions) and job satisfaction were equally related to work-to-family and family-to-work conflict, although theoretically (e.g. Frone, 2003) these out-comes should correlate more strongly with family-to-work conflict than work-to-family conflict (Mesmer-Magnus and Viswesvaran, 2005).

From these meta-analyses it has been concluded that, despite some overlap, the two concepts have sufficient unique variance to warrant independent examinations. Thus, work–family conflict is increasingly recognized as consisting of two distinct, though related, concepts. In both meta-analyses mentioned above, the reliability-corrected cor-relation between work-to-family and family-to-work conflict was .48. To some extent, an overlap is expected; each individual has fixed amounts of physical and psychological resources (e.g. time, mental energy), so that conflict in one direction is likely to be coupled with expressions of conflict in the other direction (Mesmer-Magnus and Viswesvaran, 2005).

In addition, both work-to-family and family-to-work conflict have been seen to consist of three sub-types of conflict (Greenhaus and Beutell, 1985). Time-based conflict (from work to family or from family to work) is experienced when time pressures associated with one role prevent one from fulfilling the expectations of the other role, for example, when long working hours prevent the performance of duties at home or a child's illness prevents attendance at work. Strain-based conflict is experienced when strain in one role affects performance in the other. For example, when work (or family life) is so demanding that it produces strain symptoms, such as tension, fatigue, and irritability, it may prevent the individual from contributing to family life (or work). Behavior-based conflict occurs when specific behaviors required in one role are incompatible with the expected behaviors of another role. For example, if a manager is expected to behave in a demanding way at work, but at home is expected to show more nurturance and support rather than to be demanding, he or she is likely to experience behavior-based conflict between work and home roles.

Although there is some evidence showing that the six sub-types of work–family conflict may each to some degree feature a unique set of antecedents and outcomes (e.g. Carlson, Kacmar, and Williams, 2000), evidence that would fully confirm the discriminant and predictive validity of the six sub-types is limited. For example, when it comes to antecedents, high work role conflict was only associated with high strain-based work-to-family conflict, whereas high work involvement contributed to high levels of all three (time-, strain-, and behavior-based) sub-types of work-to-family conflict. Instead, high family role conflict contributed to high levels of all three (time-, strain-, and behavior-based) sub-types of family-to-work conflict, and high family involvement only to high behavior-based family-to-work conflict. It is, however, quite reasonable to expect a considerable overlap between the antecedents and outcomes of the sub-types of work-to-family and family-to-work conflict. If an employee, for instance, experiences time-based conflict (i.e. lack of time), it may contribute to strain-based conflict (i.e. strain symptoms), which may make it difficult to keep their outcomes and antecedents separated upon evaluation.

The prevalence of work-to-family and family-to-work conflict among men and women

Previous studies have consistently shown that work-to-family conflict is reported to occur more frequently than family-to-work conflict for both sexes (see Frone, 2003; Geurts and Demerouti, 2003, for reviews).

For example, among Finnish male and female employees, some 40% experienced work-to-family conflict at least some of the time, whereas less than 10% experienced family-to-work conflict equally frequently (Kinnunen and Mauno, 1998). This may be due to the fact that work demands are easier to quantify (Gutek *et al.*, 1991). Moreover, family boundaries may be more permeable to work demands than work boundaries are to family demands (Frone, Russell, and Cooper, 1992b). Not only is it easier to reduce the number of hours spent on family responsibilities, but family responsibilities also tend to be more flexible than work responsibilities (McElwain, Korabik, and Rosin, 2005). It is also likely that employees' evaluations are colored by their notions of what is expected of an ideal worker. According to Lewis (1997, 2000), the male model of work (e.g. full-time job, preferring work to family, overwork) is still prevalent in working life and serves as the criterion for the ideal worker. Therefore, it is natural that as long as the male model of work remains the norm, one might expect that family-to-work conflict will be seldom reported.

It is often argued that work–family conflict should be found to be more prevalent in women's than in men's lives because of women's double workload. Even nowadays, although men's share in family responsibilities has increased, women continue to bear the main responsibility of domestic duties. Especially for those women working full-time, this often involves performing double shifts – one shift at work and another at home. Findings have even indicated that when there are heavy responsibilities in both work and family domains, it is more likely for work–family conflict to arise (McElwain *et al.*, 2005). However, other recent research evidence does not support this view. Across twenty-seven studies (Byron, 2005), male employees tended to have slightly more work-to-family conflict and female employees tended to have more family-to-work conflict. Gender was, however, such a weak contributor that the author concluded that, overall, men and women have similar levels of both types of conflict. Other reviews also point to a similar conclusion (e.g. Frone, 2003; Geurts and Demerouti, 2003).

Gender comparisons, such as described above, often ignore the fact that male and female employees are very likely to differ on various background factors, such as occupational level or family situation. Accordingly, the experiences of men and women who, for example, work at similar occupational levels or have similar family situations have not been compared. In many cases where gender comparisons were performed within specific occupational groups, other differences (e.g. differences in age or working hours) between the male and female employees were often ignored.

We have analyzed gender differences by taking into account a number of relevant background factors. Our analysis (Kinnunen, Geurts, and Mauno, 2004), among Finnish men ($n = 218$) and women ($n = 208$) at two time-points with a one-year time-lag, showed that there were no significant differences between the men and the women in regard to work-to-family conflict, at both measurement occasions, and after background factors (age, living with partner, number of children, socioeconomic status, weekly working hours, working schedule) were controlled for. In addition, when testing more thoroughly the roles of the background factors for men's and women's work-to-family conflict, we found that the perceptions differed for both genders only according to the occupational level; higher-level white-collar women (i.e. women employed as teachers, lawyers, or managers, etc.) had a higher level of work-to-family conflict than higher-level white-collar men, after adjusting for relevant background variables. Thus, the combination of having a family and a highly demanding job (a higher-level white-collar occupation) was more challenging for women than men in terms of their work–family balance.

In another analysis, however, based on an ongoing survey (Kinnunen, Mauno, and Feldt, in preparation) of a single demanding occupational group, managers, we were not able to fully confirm the obtained gender difference among white-collar workers. In this study, we measured both time- and strain-based work-to-family and family-to-work conflict on the basis of twelve items (three items per scale), as developed by Carlson *et al.* (2000). The 2 (gender) × 3 (managerial level) covariance analysis, controlling for significant background factors in which male and female managers differed, showed that there were no differences either in time-based work-to-family or family-to-work conflict between Finnish male and female managers ($n = 1,188$) employed at different levels of management (lower, middle, and top management). Instead, in both strain-based work-to-family and family-to-work conflicts, there were gender differences (see Figure 7.1). Female managers at every managerial level reported more strain-based work-to-family conflict than male managers did ($p < .001$), whereas strain-based family-to-work conflict was slightly higher among male managers compared to female managers ($p < .05$). The experience of work–family conflict did not vary according to the managerial level. Strain-based work-to-family conflict was again more prevalent than family-to-work conflict (see Figure 7.1); this was also true in the case of time-based work–family conflict.

These gender differences may be interpreted with the help of the sex-role hypothesis (e.g. Voydanoff, 2002), which suggests that female managers are prone to feelings of guilt that may arise out of social expectations. Since women are expected to be good spouses and mothers, and

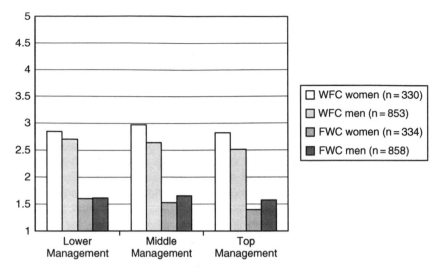

Figure 7.1 Finnish managers' perceived strain-based work-to-family conflict (WFC) and family-to-work conflict (FWC) according to gender and managerial level (1 = strongly disagree, 5 = strongly agree) (Kinnunen *et al.*, in preparation). Women: lower management n = 193, middle n = 76, top n = 63; men: lower management n = 290, middle n = 241, top n = 325

devote their energy to the family, they feel the interfering influences that work brings to their family life. Male managers, in turn, seem to experience the situation in a quite opposite way; they may feel that family interferes with their work life, as they are expected to be good employees and devote their energy to working. Thus, we believe that the prevailing social expectations regarding appropriate roles for men and women can give rise to these experiences.

The antecedents of work–family conflict

According to Byron (2005), the previously researched antecedents of work–family conflict can be classified into three categories: (1) work domain variables, (2) non-work domain variables, and (3) individual and demographic variables (see also Eby, Casper, Lockwood, Bordeaux, and Brinley, 2005). As already stated, *antecedents related to an individual's job* (work domain variables) are expected to be more related to work-to-family than to family-to-work conflict. This was also verified by Byron's (2005) meta-analysis of more than sixty studies, where it was found that employees who had higher job involvement or job stress, or who spent more time at work, had more work-to-family than family-to-work conflict, and employees who had less supportive co-workers or supervisors, or less flexible schedules, had more work-to-family than family-to-work conflict. Among these work variables, high job stress (.48) and low schedule flexibility (−.30) were the strongest predictors of high work-to-family conflict (Byron, 2005).

In Voydanoff's (2004) study, which was not included in the meta-analysis conducted by Byron (2005), work-related antecedents were classified into three categories – job demands, job resources, and boundary-spanning resources. Of these, it was job demands that best explained work-to-family conflict. All four work demands (paid work hours, extra work, job insecurity, and time pressure) were positively related to conflict; that is, the higher the levels of working hours per week, job insecurity, and time pressures at work, the higher the level of work-to-family conflict. Following this, boundary-spanning resources, which address the interface between work and family domains, explained next best the presence of work-to-family conflict. All four of the resources of this type (parental leave, time off for family, supportive work–family culture, and supervisor work–family support) showed negative associations with work-to-family conflict. Thus, those who thought that it was easy to use parental leave or time off for family and those who perceived that organizational culture and managers were supportive in regard to family matters reported work-to-family conflict less frequently. In addition to this, job resources (high levels of autonomy and respect, meaningful work) showed significant negative relationships to work-to-family conflict, but when all variables were included in the model it was only meaningful work that contributed significantly to work-to-family conflict. Accordingly, the higher the meaningfulness of the work reported, the lower the resulting work-to-family conflict.

Other studies also show that it is not the availability of family support policies at the workplace but rather the informal work–family supportiveness that is related to work-family conflict. For example, Behson (2005) found that informal means of work–family support (e.g. job control, manager support, and career impact concerns) explained a greater share of variance in employee outcomes, including work-to-family conflict, than did formal mechanisms (e.g. schedule flexibility, available work–family benefits). This informal organizational support is also termed by researchers as supportive work–family culture (e.g. Mauno, Kinnunen, and Pyykkö, 2005; Thompson, Beauvais, and Lyness, 1999; see Kinnunen, Mauno, Geurts, and Dikkers, 2005, for a review). According to Thompson et al. (1999), it consists of three components: (1) managerial support in which managers show social support for and sensitivity to employees' family responsibilities; (2) career consequences, which refers to the perception of negative career development opportunities as a consequence of utilizing work–family benefits or spending time in family-related activities; and (3) organizational time demands that refer to expectations that employees prioritize working time above family time.

There is still additional evidence that work–family policy implementation alone will probably fail to generate enough of an effect for either employees or organizations. Allen (2001) and Thompson *et al.* (1999), for example, provide strong evidence that employee perceptions of informal work–family supportiveness are more strongly related to important outcomes such as work-to-family conflict than the availability of work–family benefits. Thus, a supportive work–family culture seems to increase – either directly or through the use of work–family policies – favorable employee effects, such as better work–family balance (see Kinnunen *et al.*, 2005, for a review).

According to the findings of Byron's (2005) meta-analytic study, the correlations between *antecedents related to non-work domain* (i.e. family domain) and family-to-work conflict were not stronger than their correlations with work-to-family conflict. This was contrary to theoretical expectations, according to which family-related antecedents should be more strongly related to family-to-work conflict (e.g. Frone, 2003). Several of the non-work variables (e.g. low family support, high family conflict, small children in the family) were related to increased conflicts of both types. However, four non-work variables – hours of non-work activities, family stress, number of children, and marital status – demonstrated a pattern that was consistent with expectations. The more hours spent on family-related activities (e.g. household tasks, child care), combined with experiencing increasing levels of family-related stress, the more family-to-work than work-to-family conflict was reported. In addition, employees who had more children or who were single had more family-to-work than work-to-family conflict. Among the non-work variables, high level of family stress (.47) and family conflict (.32) were the strongest predictors of family-to-work conflict (Byron, 2005).

Demographics and individual antecedent variables have alone turned out to be poor predictors of work–family conflict, especially as concerns such demographics as gender and income (see Byron, 2005). For example, as already stated (p. 130 above), gender was such a weak contributor that Byron concluded that, overall, men and women were found to have similar levels of both types of conflict. Appropriate coping style and skills, the only individual variables that were considered in Byron's (2005) meta-analysis, seemed to offer some benefit to employees (across six studies). Those with better time management skills and an active coping style tended to have less work-to-family as well as family-to-work conflict.

Recently, personality characteristics have also been considered in this regard. Findings concerning the Big Five personality factors (e.g. Bruck and Allen, 2003; Rantanen, Pulkkinen, and Kinnunen, 2005; Wayne, Musisca, and Fleeson, 2004) have shown that the link between neuroticism and work–family conflict is the most coherent, with high neuroticism constituting a clear risk factor for greater work-to-family and family-to-work conflict. In addition, it seems that conscientiousness functions as a resource factor, as those employees high in conscientiousness have less of both types of conflicts. These links between personality factors and work–family conflict are partly assumed to occur as a result of individuals' coping strategies. Individuals high in neuroticism have a tendency to experience negative affect and use coping strategies that maintain stress, whereas for those who are conscientious of efficient time use, organizational skills and orderliness may protect them from work–family conflict.

To sum up, the most important predictors of work–family conflict lie in the domains of work and family. The characteristics of work and workplaces (e.g. workload, time pressures, work–family culture) and family life (e.g. overload, family stress, family conflict) are the primary sources of work–family conflict. However, demographic (e.g. being a single parent) and personal factors (e.g. coping strategies and personality) also play a role, although seemingly minor. It should be remembered that these personal factors have been studied less often in the context of the work–family interface. In general, the fact that work and family factors are emphasized among the sources of work–family conflict provides a good starting point for the prevention of work–family conflict, since these factors can be improved more easily than the more permanent personal factors (e.g. personality).

The outcomes of work–family conflict

Recent meta-analyses (e.g. Allen *et al.*, 2000; Kossek and Ozeki, 1998) underscore the potentially negative effects of work-to-family conflict for individuals and their employers. Nonetheless, family-to-work conflict has not been as intensively studied as work-to-family conflict and because of this there is no meta-analysis available which examines its relationship to expected outcomes. According to the theoretical view presented by Frone (2003; Frone, Yardley, and Markel, 1997b), work-to-family and family-to-work conflicts have unique role-related outcomes that reside in the family and work domains, respectively. Frone (2003) emphasizes, however, that because both types of work–family conflicts are positively correlated, studies that merely report zero-order correlations can lead to a biased conclusion regarding the role-related outcomes of work–family conflict. The role-related outcomes that have been examined can be divided into affective (e.g. satisfaction, distress) and behavioral (e.g. absenteeism, role performance) types.

It seems that this theoretical differentiation between the outcomes related to work-to-family or family-to-work conflict is not fully supported by previous research, where evidence both confirms (see e.g. Frone, 2003) and contradicts the view. For example, the strongest correlations of work-to-family conflict in Allen *et al.*'s (2000) meta-analysis concerned work-related stress outcomes, high work-related strain (.41, across fifteen studies) and burnout (.42, across ten studies), and not family-related outcomes, as would be theoretically expected. These figures may, however, be biased since we cannot rule out the possibility that family-to-work conflict, as an unmeasured third variable, is partially behind the perceived relationships. According to Wayne *et al.* (2004), in whose study both conflicts were measured, work–family conflict was associated with affective outcomes (such as dissatisfaction) in the originating role (the domain causing the conflict) and with behavioral outcomes (such as the amount of effort placed on the domain) in the receiving role (the domain where the conflict spills over). For example, high family-to-work conflict was related to family dissatisfaction and low effort being put into one's job. Theoretically, this finding indicates that when one role interferes with the other, it may result in poor performance for the role being interfered with (the receiving role), even though individuals psychologically blame the interference on the source (originating) role. In line with this reasoning, it was found that family-to-work conflict related to marital and parental dissatisfaction especially among women (Kinnunen and Mauno, 1998), that work-to-family conflict related to job dissatisfaction, and that family-to-work conflict related to marital dissatisfaction, but not vice versa (Kinnunen, Feldt, Geurts, and Pulkkinen, 2006).

The findings concerning the overall health-related negative outcomes of work–family conflict consistently show that both work-to-family and family-to-work conflict are similarly related to such indicators as psychological strain, depression, and physical symptoms (e.g. Frone, 2003). These similar outcomes have been explained, for example, on the basis of identity theory (Frone, Russell, and Barnes, 1996). Consequently, because both work and family roles represent core components of adult identity, impediments to work- and family-related identity formation and maintenance are likely to be experienced as stressful. Therefore, both types of work–family conflict are positively related to deleterious health-related outcomes.

The longitudinal evidence of the negative consequences associated with work–family conflict is mixed. Longitudinal studies give support to there being causal (e.g. Frone, Russell, and Cooper, 1997a; Grant-Vallone and Donaldson, 2001; Peeters, de Jonge, Janssen, and van der Linden, 2004), reversed causal (e.g. Kelloway, Gottlieb, and Barham, 1999; Kinnunen *et al.*, 2004) and reciprocal (Demerouti, Bakker, and Bulters, 2004; Leiter and Durup, 1996) relationships between work–family conflict and its outcomes. Of these three relationships, the causal relationship refers to a situation in which work–family conflict predicts negative outcomes (e.g. psychological strain) across time, while the reversed causal relationship means the opposite being true – that high psychological strain leads to high work–family conflict later on. The reciprocal relationship includes both these conditions; thus, high work–family conflict may produce high psychological strain, which in turn leads to high work–family conflict. The mixed longitudinal results may be due to several reasons, such as different follow-up periods, different measures, or different statistical procedures. Theoretically, it is very difficult to define an optimal follow-up period within which, for example, the negative outcomes of work–family conflict should emerge. Since the question has to do with a process that occurs over time, it is also difficult to know when to start measuring the process.

Despite there being some disagreement about whether the effects of work-to-family and family-to-work conflict are differential or not, the evidence, on the whole, indicates that work–family conflict is detrimental to an employee's well-being, satisfaction, and health. The longitudinal evidence is still minor and the findings concerning the temporal ordering of the phenomena (i.e. work–family conflict and its hypothesized outcomes) are mixed. However, among them are findings that show that both types of work–family conflict produce detrimental health effects even over a four-year period (Frone *et al.*, 1997a). Thus, it seems warranted to conclude that work–family conflict produces detrimental outcomes; therefore, the question regarding under what conditions these harmful effects can be avoided becomes the central focus, and this issue is discussed next.

The moderators of work–family conflict

Previous studies have mainly focused on demonstrating the direct relationships between work–family conflict and its antecedents and outcomes. Questions regarding how work–family conflict caused by work and family demands or how the negative outcomes caused by work–family conflict can be avoided have received less attention. Recently, however, an examination of the factors that may function as moderators, first in the relationship between antecedents and conflict and second in the relationship between conflict and outcomes, has been called for. Therefore, in order to try to clarify under what conditions these relationships exist, we focus here on two potential moderators, gender and social support, which have thus far received the most research attention in this regard.

Gender differences have been considered since work–family conflict comprises two areas of life – work and family – that have traditionally been gender-specific. Frone *et al.* (1996) based their reasoning on identity theory and gender-role socialization when they discussed potential gender differences in the relationship between work–family conflict and its detrimental outcomes. First, identity theory suggests that both types of conflicts will be related to similar negative health-related outcomes; this is because the conflicts are stressful and thereby an obstacle to maintaining a positive family- and work-related self-image. Second, since men and women have been socialized to differently value their work- and family-related self-images – the former being more important for men and the latter being more important for women – gender is likely to moderate the relationship between the two types of work–family conflict and health. Specifically, work-to-family conflict should be expected to have a stronger impact on the well-being and health of women, whereas family-to-work conflict should have a stronger impact on the well-being and health of men. In line with this theoretical reasoning, McElwain *et al.* (2005) recently found that family-to-work conflict showed a stronger relationship to job satisfaction among Canadian men as compared to women, but there were no expected gender differences in the relationship between work-to-family conflict and family satisfaction. All in all, research evidence thus far does not support the moderating effect of gender in this regard (see Frone, 2003).

Gender differences in the antecedents–conflict relationship are also expected on the basis of the differences in role demands and salience (Voydanoff, 2002). Because the family role is more demanding and important for women, family demands may show a stronger relationship with family-to-work conflict among women than among men. Correspondingly, work demands might show a stronger relationship with work-to-family conflict among men than among women. In the study by McElwain *et al.* (2005), this first hypothesis received support; family demands were more strongly related to family-to-work conflict among women than among men. The second hypothesis, however, was not confirmed, as work demands were just as strongly related to work-to-family conflict for both genders.

According to Byron's (2005) meta-analysis, family domain antecedents were more positively related to both work-to-family and family-to-work conflict among men than among women, and flexible work schedules provided more of a protective benefit against work-to-family and family-to-work conflict for women than men. This latter finding, however, has been contradicted in a longitudinal study among American dual-earner couples (Hammer, Neal, Newsom, Brockwood, and Colton, 2005). In this study, the use of alternative work arrangements (e.g. flexible work hours, telecommuting) and dependent care support (e.g. unpaid or paid leave) were positively related to family-to-work conflict among women; in other words, those women who used these arrangements ended up experiencing higher levels of family-to-work conflict. The authors conclude that the use of such support may lead to increased family expectations from oneself and from one's partner and family, resulting in higher levels of family-to-work conflict.

To summarize, there is no consistent view on how gender moderates either the antecedents–conflict relationship or the conflict–outcomes relationship. However, it might be concluded that there is more evidence showing that gender may function as a moderator in the former rather than in the latter relationship. Altogether, the findings have provided stronger support for the social role explanation (comparable role involvements have similar effects on men and women) than for the sex role explanation (demands and distress related to the family role have more effect on women, and demands and distress related to the work role have more effect on men) (Voydanoff, 2002). However, quite often the gender perspective has been ignored.

The viewing of *social support* as a potential moderator or buffering factor can be explained through several theoretical viewpoints. First, on the basis of stress theories, and more specifically on the basis of the Job Demand–Control–Support model (Karasek and Theorell, 1990), social support is considered to be a factor that may decrease the negative impact of high job demands and low job control, which are conceptualized as psychosocial job stressors. Second, on the basis of coping theory (e.g. Lazarus and Folkman, 1984), social support can be seen as a coping strategy that may help an individual to maintain his or her psychological, physical, and social well-being in stressful situations. In addition, available social support may even indicate to what extent an individual is likely to experience a given situation as stressful (Viswesvaran, Sanchez, and Fisher, 1999). As work–family conflict may be regarded as a potential stressor, a role stressor, social support may function as a protective process both in antecedents–conflict and conflict–outcomes relationships.

Studies of the moderating role of social support (from partner or family, colleagues and supervisors, and organization) have produced more uniform results than those of gender. Spousal support has been found to diminish the relationship between parental overload and family-to-work conflict, and supervisor support has similarly diminished the relationship between work role stressors and work-to-family conflict (see Poelmans, O'Driscoll, and Beham, 2005, for a review). Organizational support has alleviated the negative effects of work–home interference on cynicism, which is one dimension of burnout (Bakker, Demerouti, and Euwema, 2005). Furthermore, a recent Finnish study showed that one specific form of organizational support – a supportive work–family culture – moderated the negative effects of work-to-family conflict on two outcomes: organizational commitment and physical symptoms (Mauno, Kinnunen, and Ruokolainen, 2006). Thus, employees reported less organizational commitment and more physical symptoms under conditions of high work-to-family conflict and low organizational support, whereas those who assessed the work–family culture as supportive were protected from these negative effects of high work-to-family conflict. However, there are also studies in which such buffering effects of social support (e.g. Carlson and Perrewé, 1999; Haar, 2004; see also Poelmans *et al.*, 2005) have not been confirmed.

There exist other potential moderators, which Voydanoff (2002) has termed as social categories (e.g. race and ethnicity, social class) and to which gender belongs. The other potential moderators belong to the same category as social support. This category has been described as coping resources, and it consists, for example, of individual (e.g. individual strategies and personality traits) and family (e.g. adaptability, cohesion) coping resources (Voydanoff, 2002). Although the research is still limited in this regard, *personality characteristics* have received growing attention. It has been shown that neuroticism and negative affectivity tend to strengthen the link between work-to-family conflict and psychological distress (Kinnunen, Vermulst, Gerris, and Mäkikangas, 2003; Rantanen *et al.*, 2005; Stoeva, Chiu, and Greenhaus, 2002), while agreeableness has attenuated the link between work-to-family conflict and marital dissatisfaction (Kinnunen *et al.*, 2003). Moreover, negative affectivity has been found to strengthen the relationship between family stressors and family-to-work conflict but not the relationship between job stressors and work-to-family conflict (Stoeva *et al.*, 2002).

In sum, the evidence concerning the described moderators is thus far quite limited. As already stated, gender has not shown any consistent moderating role; instead, social support is more promising in this regard. It seems that high social support has the potential to function as a protective factor against high work–family conflict and its negative outcomes. Neuroticism or negative affectivity, on the other hand, has the potential to function the other way around. That is, under conditions of high work–family conflict, the outcomes are more negative for those high in neuroticism than for those low in neuroticism.

Conclusions

As an effect of globalization, development toward a twenty-four-hour society is likely to continue and even intensify in the future. Around-the-clock economies (Strazdins, Korda, Lim, Broom, and D'Souza, 2004) alter the way work is organized, which, in turn, reshapes the work–family interface. At the same time, a more balanced distribution of work and family responsibilities among men and women may be expected to emerge as the family role continues to change. Given this, we expect that work–family conflict is also likely to keep affecting male and female employees in the future.

Despite these prevailing antecedents residing in the development of society and the economy, the situational antecedents of work–family conflict have special practical implications for individuals' lives. These situational factors, which are the primary sources of work–family conflict from the viewpoint of individual employees, include various work and family demands (e.g. amount of time, overload) and resources (e.g. control, support). They are of more practical importance since they can be changed or improved more easily than individual factors (e.g. personality). The present analysis, based on current research findings, suggests a number of things that individual employees might do to reduce both types of work–family conflict. They can seek out and develop appropriate social support networks at work or at home, reduce or reorganize the time devoted to work and family demands, and find ways to reduce or better cope with stressors and distress at work and home. However, research is still limited when it comes to coping strategies and their effectiveness in the context of the work–family interface.

Work–family conflict is not only a problem on the individual level. As the literature review indicated, work–family conflict has both organizational level antecedents and outcomes. The negative organizational level outcomes identified (e.g. decreased organizational commitment, increased turnover intentions) may motivate work organizations to focus more effort on this issue. This may be the case particularly in the future, when the competition for competent and committed employees is expected to become still harder. More studies in which employee behaviors (e.g. absenteeism, job performance) are studied may be needed, however. Further demonstrating the relationship between work–family conflict and employee behavior might help to better legitimize work–family issues in the eyes of organizational decision makers.

The organizational initiatives can be discussed under the general rubric of family-friendly organizational policies and culture. These initiatives fall into several categories that include flexible work arrangements, work leaves, dependent-care assistance, and general resource services. However, a key question seems to be that of how to improve informal family supportiveness of organizations, which is also known as work–family culture. In this regard, the role of managers is important. When managers are able to see that their employees have a life outside of work, it seems to increase the employees' work–family balance and their well-being. Furthermore, the general improvement of the quality of working life remains important. As the study findings have shown, decreasing work demands (e.g. time pressure, job insecurity) and increasing work resources (e.g. job control, social support) are related to better work–family balance.

Finally, given the fact that individuals and employers are always operating within larger sociopolitical cultures or regimes, where the role of the state varies in offering work–family policies, the national context plays an important role. It has been argued (e.g. Lewis, 1997) that family-friendly organizations cannot be created without government intervention, since without state action, the broader social culture within which organizations operate will remain the same. Even in the Nordic countries where the role of the state is active, the key question is how to increase employees' – and especially male employees' – entitlement to use already existing family-friendly arrangements available in organizations. Again, the work–family culture prevailing in organizations comes into central focus.

Recent research on the work–family interface has been dominated by role stress theory. This has involved approaching the work–family interface from a negative perspective, using role conflict as the phenomenon by which the different life domains (work and family) may be connected. However, there are also other linking mechanisms, such as role balance and role enhancement, and therefore having multiple roles may also lead to work–family fit or work–family facilitation (Frone, 2003; Voydanoff, 2002). These concepts refer to the processes by which participation in one role (e.g. employee) is made better or easier by virtue of participation in another role (e.g. spouse or parent). Not until recently has this positive side of the work–family interface begun to gain growing attention, and as a consequence, we still have a long road to travel before a comprehensive map of its underlying processes can be developed. More studies are thereby needed in the future in which to integrate these two realms of the work–family interface, namely, the negative view toward conflict and the positive view toward facilitation.

Although the work–family interface is a dynamic, complex phenomenon, few empirical studies have ventured to examine the processes by which work–family conflict develops. Therefore, there is a clear need for longitudinal studies, especially at a daily level. This entails studies with short-term, repeated-measures designs on a daily basis that can capture the microprocesses by which work- and family-related stress and strain fluctuate in daily life. This kind of intensive research can reveal where the processes that occur between work–family conflict and its antecedents and outcomes begin, and how they evolve and culminate in long-term effects. In addition, more research on the experiences of couples and families (including children) would contribute to our understanding of the process by which work–family conflict is developed and managed in the context of family relationships. As a result, we would be in a better position to create functional prevention and intervention strategies.

References

Allen, T. (2001). Family-supportive work environments: the role of organizational perceptions. *Journal of Vocational Behavior* 58: 414–35.

Allen, T., Herst, D., Bruck, C., and Sutton, M. (2000). Consequences associated with work-to-family conflict: a review and agenda for future research. *Journal of Occupational Health Psychology* 5: 278–308.

Bakker, A., Demerouti, E., and Euwema, M. C. (2005). Job resources buffer the impact of job demands on burnout. *Journal of Occupational Health Psychology* 10: 170–80.

Behson, S. J. (2005). The relative contribution of formal and informal organizational work–family support. *Journal of Vocational Behavior* 66: 487–500.

Bruck, C. S. and Allen, T. D. (2003). The relationship between Big Five personality traits, negative affectivity, type A behavior, and work–family conflict. *Journal of Vocational Behavior* 63: 457–72.

Byron, K. (2005). A meta-analytic review of work–family conflict and its antecedents. *Journal of Vocational Behavior* 67: 169–98.

Carlson, D. S., Kacmar, K. M., and Williams, L. J. (2000). Construction and initial validation of a multidimensional measure of work–family conflict. *Journal of Vocational Behavior* 56: 249–76.

Carlson, D. S. and Perrewe, P. L. (1999). The role of social support in the job stressor–strain relationship: an examination of work–family conflict. *Journal of Management* 25: 513–40.

Demerouti, E., Bakker, A. B., and Bulters, A. J. (2004). The loss spiral of work pressure, work–home interference and exhaustion: reciprocal relations in a three-wave study. *Journal of Vocational Behavior* 64: 131–49.

Eby, L. T., Casper, W. J., Lockwood, A., Bordeaux, C., and Brinley, A. (2005). Work–family research in IO/OB: content analysis and review of the literature (1980–2002). *Journal of Vocational Behavior* 66: 124–97.

Frone, M. R. (2003). Work–family balance. In J. C. Quick and E. Tertic (eds.), *Handbook of occupational health psychology* (pp. 143–62). Washington, DC: American Psychological Association.

Frone, M. R., Russell, M., and Barnes, G. M. (1996). Work–family conflict, gender, and health-related outcomes: a study of employed parents in two community samples. *Journal of Occupational Health Psychology* 1: 57–69.

Frone, M. R., Russell, M., and Cooper, M. L. (1992a). Antecedents and outcomes of work–family conflict: testing a model of the work–family interface. *Journal of Applied Psychology* 77: 65–78.

(1992b). Prevalence of work–family conflict: are work and family boundaries asymmetrically permeable? *Journal of Organizational Behavior* 13: 723–9.

(1997a). Relation of work–family conflict to health outcomes: a four-year longitudinal study of employed parents. *Journal of Occupational and Organizational Psychology* 70: 325–35.

Frone, M. R., Yardley, J. K., and Markel, K. S. (1997b). Developing and testing an integrative model of the work–family interface. *Journal of Vocational Behavior* 50: 145–67.

Geurts, S. A. E. and Demerouti, E. (2003). Work/non-work interface: a review of theories and findings. In M. J. Schabracq, J. A. M. Winnubst, and C. L. Cooper (eds.), *The handbook of work and health psychology* (pp. 279–312). Chichester: Wiley.

Grant-Vallone, E. J. and Donaldson, S. I. (2001). Consequences of work–family conflict on employee well-being over time. *Work and Stress* 15: 214–26.

Greenhaus, J. H. and Beutell, N. J. (1985). Sources of conflict between work and family roles. *Academy of Management Review* 10: 76–88.

Gutek, B. A., Searle, S., and Klepa, L. (1991). Rational versus gender role expectations for work–family conflict. *Journal of Applied Psychology* 76: 560–8.

Haar, S. M. (2004). Work–family conflict and turnover intention: exploring the moderation effects of perceived work–family support. *New Zealand Journal of Psychology* 33: 35–9.

Hammer, L., Neal, M., Newsom, J., Brockwood, K., and Colton, C. (2005). A longitudinal study of the effects of dual-earner couples' utilization of family-friendly workplace supports on work and family outcomes. *Journal of Applied Psychology* 90: 799–810.

Karasek, R. and Theorell, T. (1990). *Healthy work*. New York: Basic Books.

Kelloway, E. K., Gottlieb, B. H., and Barham, L. (1999). The source, nature, and direction of work and family conflict: a longitudinal investigation. *Journal of Occupational Health Psychology* 4: 337–46.

Kinnunen, U., Feldt, T., Geurts, S., and Pulkkinen, L. (2006). Types of work–family interface: well-being correlates of negative and positive spillover between work and family. *Scandinavian Journal of Psychology* 47: 149–62.

Kinnunen, U., Geurts, S., and Mauno, S. (2004). Work-to-family conflict and its relationship with well-being and satisfaction: a one-year longitudinal study on gender differences. *Work and Stress* 18: 1–22.

Kinnunen, U. and Mauno, S. (1998). Antecedents and outcomes of work–family conflict among employed women and men in Finland. *Human Relations* 51: 157–77.

Kinnunen, U., Mauno, S., and Feldt, T. (in preparation). Work–family interface among Finnish managers. Manuscript under preparation.

Kinnunen, U., Mauno, S., Geurts, S., and Dikkers, J. (2005). Work–family culture in organizations: theoretical and empirical approaches. In S. A. Y. Poelmans (ed.), *Work and family: an international research perspective* (pp. 87–120). Mahwah, NJ: Lawrence Erlbaum.

Kinnunen, U., Vermulst, A., Gerris, J., and Mäkikangas, A. (2003). Work–family conflict and its relations to well-being: the role of personality as a moderating factor. *Personality and Individual Differences* 35: 1669–83.

Kopelman, R., Greenhaus, J. H., and Conolly, T. F. (1983). A model of work, family, and interrole conflict: a construct validation study. *Organizational Behavior and Human Performance* 32: 198–215.

Kossek, E. E. and Ozeki, C. (1998). Work–family conflict, policies, and the job–life satisfaction relationship: a review and directions for organizational behavior–human resources research. *Journal of Applied Psychology* 83: 139–49.

Lazarus, R. S. and Folkman, S. (1984). *Psychological stress and the coping process.* New York: Springer.

Leiter, M. P. and Durup, M. J. (1996). Work, home, and in-between: a longitudinal study of spillover. *Journal of Applied Behavioral Science* 32: 29–47.

Lewis, S. (1997). Family friendly employment policies: a route to changing organizational culture or playing about at the margins. *Gender, Work and Organization* 4: 13–23.

(2000). Restructuring workplace cultures: the ultimate work–family challenge? *Women in Management Review* 16: 21–9.

Mauno, S., Kinnunen, U., and Pyykkö, M. (2005). Does work–family conflict mediate the relationship between work–family culture and self-reported distress? Evidence from five Finnish organizations. *Journal of Occupational and Organizational Psychology* 78: 1–23.

Mauno, S., Kinnunen, U., and Ruokolainen, M. (2006). Exploring work- and organization-based resources as moderators between work–family conflict, well-being and job attitudes. *Work and Stress* 20: 210–33.

McElwain, A., Kobarik, K., and Rosin, H. (2005). An examination of gender differences in work–family conflict. *Canadian Journal of Behavioral Science* 37: 283–98.

Mesmer-Magnus, J. R. and Viswesvaran, C. (2005). Convergence between measures of work-to-family and family-to-work conflict: a meta-analytic examination. *Journal of Vocational Behavior* 67: 215–32.

Peeters, M. C. W., de Jonge, J., Janssen, P. P. M., and van der Linden, S. (2004). Work–home interference, job stressors, and employee health in a longitudinal perspective. *International Journal of Stress Management* 4: 305–22.

Poelmans, S., O'Driscoll, M., and Beham, B. (2005). An overview of international research on the work–family interface. In S. A. Y. Poelmans (ed.), *Work and family: an international research perspective* (pp. 3–46). Mahwah, NJ: Lawrence Erlbaum.

Rantanen, J., Pulkkinen, L., and Kinnunen, U. (2005). The Big Five personality dimensions, work–family conflict, and psychological distress. *Journal of Individual Differences* 26: 155–66.

Rothbard, N. P. (2001). Enriching or depleting? The dynamics of engagement in work and family roles. *Administrative Science Quarterly* 46: 655–84.

Stoeva, A. Z., Chiu, R. K., and Greenhaus, J. H. (2002). Negative affectivity, role stress and work–family conflict. *Journal of Vocational Behavior* 60: 1–16.

Strazdins, L., Korda, R., Lim, L., Broom, D., and D'Souza, R. (2004). Around-the-clock: parent work schedules and children's well-being in a 24-h economy. *Social Science and Medicine* 59: 1517–27.

Thompson, C., Beauvais, L., and Lyness, K. (1999). When work–family benefits are not enough: the influence of work–family culture on benefit utilization, organizational attachment, and work–family conflict. *Journal of Vocational Behavior* 54: 329–415.

Viswesvaran, C., Sanchez, J., and Fisher, J. (1999). The role of social support in the process of work stress: a meta analysis. *Journal of Vocational Behavior* 54: 314–34.

Voydanoff, P. (2002). Linkages between the work–family interface and work, family, and individual outcomes. *Journal of Family Issues* 23: 138–64.

(2004). The effects of work demands and resources on work-to-family conflict and facilitation. *Journal of Marriage and Family* 66: 398–412.

Wayne, J. H., Musisca, N., and Fleeson, W. (2004). Considering the role of personality in the work–family experience: relationships of the big five to work–family conflict and facilitation. *Journal of Vocational Behavior* 64: 108–30.

8 My love, my life, my everything: work–home interaction among self-employed

Toon W. Taris, Sabine A. E. Geurts, Michiel A. J. Kompier, Suzanne Lagerveld, and Roland W. B. Blonk

As a result of the increased number of dual-earner families and the widespread availability of information and communication technology, the boundaries between work and non-work have become blurred. Today, work is no longer necessarily spatially, temporally, and socially distinct from home. As a consequence, the amount of research into the work–home interface has increased. For example, statistics from the United States indicate that over 45% of employed parents feel that work interferes with their family life (_negative work–home interaction_; Bond, Thompson, Galinsky, and Prottas, 2003). Even higher percentages (58%) have been reported for the Canadian workforce (Duxbury and Higgins, 2001).

Work may also have positive consequences for functioning at home (Carlson, Kacmar, Wayne, and Grzywacz, 2006; Geurts _et al._, 2005; Greenhaus and Powell, 2006), for example because skills, positive moods, and acquired knowledge spill over to private life, helping workers to "become a better family member" (_positive work–home interaction_, Carlson _et al._, 2006). Similarly, the home situation may also interfere with or enhance functioning at work, for instance because one worries about one's children being ill (_negative home–work interaction_) or because positive moods spill over to the work situation (_positive home–work interaction_). Thus, work–home interaction may be defined as a process in which a worker's functioning in one domain is influenced by (negative or positive) load reactions that have built up in the other domain (Geurts, Kompier, Roxburgh, and Houtman, 2003).

Self-employed versus organizationally employed workers

Previous research has suggested that the work–home interface (and especially negative work–home interaction) may be a key factor in understanding the links between work and home characteristics on the one hand, and health and well-being of workers on the other (Allen, Herst, Bruck, and Sutton, 2000; Eby, Casper, Lockwood, Bordeaux, and Brinley, 2005; Geurts and Demerouti, 2003, for reviews). Interestingly, to date, most research on this issue has been conducted among employees, that is, workers who are employed by contract by an organization. However, as yet it is unclear whether these findings can be generalized to other populations, such as self-employed workers. Here we might find other patterns, since the work situation of *self*-employed differs in many respects from that of employed workers (Eden, 1973, for an early account). Apart from the fact that self-employed workers do not have an employment contract that specifies the number of hours they are obliged to work, the number of days off they can take, and the pay they receive for their work, self-employed men and women work longer and more irregular hours (Chay, 1993; but see Bond *et al.*, 2003, who reported that 38% of their self-employed worked fewer than 35 hours), and have more flexible work schedules (Bond *et al.*, 2003; Loscocco, 1997; Parasuraman and Simmers, 2001). They also report higher levels of perceived job control and job insecurity and lower levels of social support as compared to employed workers (Bond *et al.*, 2003; Loscocco, 1997; Mannheim and Schiffrin, 1984; Parasuraman, Purohit, Godshalk, and Beutell, 1996; Rahim, 1996). Furthermore, the motivation to work may differ for organizationally employed versus self-employed. As one female self-employed landscaper exclaimed: "I'm aching to do more with my business [. . .] I love being with my family, too, but I'm aching to do my soul work" (cited in Loscocco, 1997: 212), suggesting that at least some self-employed actually created their job to be able to do the work they like most.

Given some features of the work of self-employed persons as compared to those of organizationally employed persons, it is an interesting question whether the findings regarding the nature of the work–home interface obtained for employed workers generalize to self-employed as well. From a practical point of view it is important to have some understanding of the prevalence, antecedents, and consequences of various forms of work–home interaction among this occupational group; for example, about 11% of the US labor force (12.2 million people, excluding agricultural self-employed; Fairlie, 2004) is self-employed. Similarly, in the Netherlands 10.3% of the total labor force is self-employed (CBS, 2005). However, from a scientific perspective this group is perhaps even more interesting, in that (1) there is no official upper limit with respect to their working hours, and they often work long hours; (2) in many cases husband and wife operate a business together, rendering a further intertwining of work and non-work; and (3) as they are self-employed, their work autonomy (and thus their opportunities to adjust work and family demands) is presumably high. Thus, it would seem likely that various forms of work–home interaction manifest themselves to their fullest extent in this particular occupational group.

Outline of this chapter

This chapter deals with the nature of the work–home interaction among self-employed workers. We first present a short overview of research on the work–home interface, and possible antecedents and consequences. We then focus on work–home interaction among self-employed workers. Specifically, we present (1) the prevalence and interrelations of four types of work–home interaction among Dutch self-employed; (2) a comparison of these prevalences with those of a reference group of Dutch organizationally employed workers; and (3) an analysis of the relationships among these four types of work–home interaction and various activities at home and work, work characteristics, and well-being.

Antecedents and consequences of work–home interaction

One potentially useful theoretical framework for studying the associations among work and home characteristics, work–home interaction and worker well-being is Meijman and Mulder's (1998) Effort–Recovery theory. This theory proposes that expending effort is associated with short-term psychophysiological reactions (such as accelerated heart rate, increased hormone secretion, and mood changes). In principle, these reactions are adaptive (for example, by providing feedback on the effort that was needed to perform the task to be done) and reversible (when the need to expend effort ceases, the functional systems that were activated will recover within a certain period of time).

However, these originally adaptive responses develop into *negative* reactions to effort expenditure (that is, negative load reactions such as sustained activation, strain, and/or short-term psychosomatic health complaints) when recovery opportunities during the exposure period are insufficient (Geurts *et al.*, 2005). This may occur in job settings that provide workers with insufficient possibilities to regulate demands (for instance, when job demands are too high) and/or to adjust their work strategy (work behavior) when they consider it necessary (for instance, one cannot switch to less demanding tasks when one needs to recuperate). Because of workers' inability to regulate effort investment, effort expenditure will exceed acceptable limits, resulting in negative load reactions that may spill over to the home domain. A similar reasoning can be followed for spillover from home to work; when home demands are too high or cannot be regulated adequately (for instance, when caring for members of one's family requires chronic high effort investment that cannot be delegated to others), *strain* will develop, possibly spilling over to the work domain.

In line with Effort–Recovery theory, negative spillover has detrimental health effects when recovery opportunities between successive periods of high effort expenditure are insufficient in terms of quantity (recovery time is too short, perhaps due to persisting demands) and/or quality (for example, when individuals unwind slowly and remain activated after the exposure period: Ursin, 1980). Under these circumstances, functional systems remain activated or are reactivated before having had the chance to stabilize at a baseline level. The individual, still in a suboptimal state, must then invest additional effort to perform adequately when confronted with (new) task demands, resulting in an increased intensity of the negative load reactions making even higher demands on the recovery process. Consequently, a cumulative process is started that in the long run may seriously affect health and well-being (Sluiter, Frings-Dresen, Van der Beek, and Meijman, 2001; Van Hooff *et al.*, 2005).

However, not only negative but also *positive* reactions (further referred to as positive load reactions) may develop as a function of work or home characteristics (Geurts *et al.*, 2005). For example, in job settings that are characterized by high regulation possibilities in conjunction with high (but not overwhelming) demands, workers can align their work behavior with their current need for recovery. Consequently, effort expenditure remains within acceptable limits and is accompanied by positive load reactions (including skill acquisition, motivation for learning, positive affect, and self-efficacy). Similarly, particular home characteristics may result in positive load effects that spill over to the work domain. Insofar as studies have addressed this reasoning, they show that the availability of regulation possibilities at work is associated with the absence of strain and the presence of learning experiences and personal development (see Taris and Kompier, 2005, for an overview). However, empirical tests of the positive spillover between both life domains are rare. One recent exception is by Rothbard (2001), who showed that work engagement was related to family positive affect. Two other studies revealed that workers reported more positive influence from work on home when they experienced more "job resources" (such as learning opportunities and meaningful work, Voydanoff, 2004; autonomy, performance feedback, and possibilities for professional development, Bakker and Geurts, 2004; and social support at work, Geurts *et al.*, 2005).

Antecedents of work–home and home–work interaction

Based on the above reasoning, the major determinants of various types of work–home interaction are either effort-related concepts (for the work domain, one may think of quantitative, qualitative, and emotional demands; similar constructs may be envisaged for the home domain), or concepts that promote recovery (such as job autonomy). For example, for the work domain, high levels of job control allow workers to regulate their effort expenditure, by taking a break when necessary or alternating demanding with less demanding tasks (Taris *et al.*, 2006). Similarly, being able to organize (instrumental) social support also increases one's possibilities to regulate effort expenditure; many hands make light work. Corresponding concepts can be envisaged for the home domain. For instance, doing the household chores requires effort expenditure, and the ability to regulate this expenditure will help in recovering from these efforts.

Based on Effort–Recovery theory, negative work–home (home–work) interaction may be construed as the result of an imbalance between the effort expenditure required in a particular domain (demands that are too high) and the recovery opportunities (too low regulation opportunities) in that same domain. If effort expenditure prevails over recovery opportunities, negative load reactions may spill over to the other domain. Conversely, positive work–home (home–work) interaction may occur when recovery opportunities outweigh effort expenditure. As regards *negative and positive work–home interaction*, previous research consistently demonstrated that negative work–home interaction was reported more often by workers who were confronted with relatively high job pressure and relatively low levels of job control and job support (Eby *et al.*, 2005; Geurts and Demerouti, 2003; Geurts *et al.*, 2005), supporting the assumption that negative load reactions develop particularly in jobs characterized by high pressure and low levels of control and support. Geurts *et al.* (2005) and Grzywacz and Marks (2000) showed that more job control and job support were associated with more positive work–family spillover. Similar findings have been reported for *negative and positive home–work interaction*. For example, Geurts *et al.* (2005) found that relatively high levels of home demands and low levels of home support were associated with relatively high levels of negative home–work interaction. Somewhat unexpectedly, they also reported that positive home–work interaction was positively associated with *higher* home demands. Evidence on the antecedents of home–work interaction is still scant, however.

Outcomes of work–home and home–work interaction

If various forms of work–home interaction indeed reflect a (positive or negative) imbalance between effort expenditure and recovery opportunities, one would expect work–home interaction to relate to health outcomes as well. Previous research provided evidence for strong (albeit cross-sectional) associations between negative work–home interaction/home–work interaction and fatigue (Allen *et al.*, 2000; Geurts *et al.*, 2003, 2005), as well as for temporal relationships with decreased levels of psychological health across time (Demerouti, Bakker, and Bulters, 2004; Van Hooff *et al.*, 2005). Similarly, Eby *et al.*'s (2005) review revealed that high levels of negative work–home interaction were associated with consequences such as physical complaints, anxiety, and mood disorders (Frone, 2000). Thus, it appears that high levels of negative work–home/home–work interaction are associated with adverse consequences for health and well-being. Conversely, relatively high levels of positive work–home/home–work interaction signify the spillover of positive load reactions. Thus, one would expect positive work–home/home–work interaction to be associated with positive consequences. In line with this reasoning, Cohen (1997) found that employees of a school district who reported positive work–home interaction also reported more organizational commitment. Similar findings were reported by Geurts *et al.* (2005). Thus, albeit research on this issue is as yet scarce, it appears that positive work–home/home–work interaction does indeed have positive consequences for health and well-being.

Work–home interaction among self-employed: a case study

As virtually all research on the interaction between the work and home domains has been conducted among organizationally employed workers, it is unclear whether earlier findings also generalize to self-employed workers. However, since the work situation of self-employed differs dramatically from that of organizationally employed workers, it is important to examine whether current insights on the work–home interface apply to this group as well. To date, few studies have explicitly examined the work–family interface among self-employed, and most of these focused primarily on negative work–home/home–work interaction, that is, the degree to which work and family interfered with each other.

Levels of work–home and home–work interaction: self-employed versus organizationally employed workers

Bond *et al.* (2003) found in their representative sample of 3,500 American workers that self-employed persons without employees reported lower levels of *negative work–home interaction* than the organizationally employed workers and small business owners (that is, self-employed workers with employees), possibly because the first group worked significantly fewer hours than the other groups. This finding is consistent with findings reported by Hundley (2001). Drawing on data from the 1997 National Study of the Changing Work Force (that included 2,489 organizationally employed and 478 self-employed participants), Hundley demonstrated that self-employed women experienced relatively low levels of negative work–home interaction, especially when they had young children in the household. For the men, no such association was observed. These findings support the idea that self-employment offers, especially for women, good opportunities for aligning family obligations with work responsibilities. For example, Berke (2003: 533) cites a self-employed Mary Kay beauty consultant who says, "You can do other things while you work, particularly if you're on the phone. And you have a lot of phone work. I can be loading the dishwasher, or putting a load of clothes in the laundry. Things that other women can't even think about when they're at their job. But I can do that while I'm still concentrating on a phone call."

Interestingly, these positive findings were only partly supported in a study by Parasuraman and Simmers (2001). Using data from a comparatively small sample of 287 organizationally employed and 99 self-employed persons working in many different occupations and branches, they found that self-employed persons reported significantly *higher* levels of negative work–home interaction than organizationally employed persons. Although women reported lower levels of negative work–home interaction than men, the interaction of gender and employment type was not significant. Thus, whereas the two large-N studies by Bond *et al.* (2003) and Hundley (2001) suggest that entrepreneurs (especially the females among them) may experience lower levels of negative work–home interaction than others, Parasuraman and Simmers' findings show that this may not always be the case.

As regards *negative home–work interaction*, Hundley (2001) observed that self-employed women with young children report relatively high levels of negative home–work interaction. In the words of another Mary Kay beauty consultant: "Home can get tiring and the walls close in on you. You've had enough of being here and you need to get out. Kids can be distracting at the same time – mommy do this, mommy do that – and it's hard to make phone calls a lot of time [*sic*] if the kids are needing me or deciding to be ornery or fighting or whatever" (Berke, 2003: 534). Thus, even when work does not severely interfere with family life, having preschool children around may well interfere with one's work obligations.

*Covariates of work–home and home–work interaction
among self-employed workers*

Above, we showed that self-employed and organizationally employed workers may differ in the degree to which they experience various types of
work–home interaction. But what do we know about the correlates of
various types of work–home interaction among self-employed workers?
Parasuraman *et al.* (1996) showed, among a sample of 111 entrepreneurs,
that high levels of *negative work–home interaction* were associated with high
levels of work-role overload (job demands), high parental demands, high
commitment to work, and low commitment to and involvement with one's
family. These findings were largely confirmed by Parasuraman and Simmers
(2001), who reported that high levels of negative work–home interaction
among the self-employed were associated with high time commitment
to work, high parental demands, and low commitment to the family.

Regarding *negative home–work interaction*, Parasuraman *et al.* (1996)
found that high levels of *negative home–work interaction* were associated
with low levels of work autonomy and high levels of job involvement.
Additionally, Parasuraman and Simmers (2001) showed that high levels
of negative work–home interaction were associated with low levels of job
satisfaction and high levels of "life stress" (a state of negative affect in
relation to specific life stressors).

Evaluation of previous research

The findings obtained for self-employed workers, on the one hand, partly
converge with those obtained for employed workers; high demands were
associated with high negative work–home interaction, which in turn was
associated with low levels of well-being (that is, commitment and satisfaction). On the other hand, these findings are partly based on small
samples, are restricted to negative work–home/home–work interaction
only, provide diverging evidence on differences in the levels of work–home
interaction for self-employed versus organizationally employed workers,
and seem primarily data driven. Therefore, the present study was designed
to shed more light on the issue of work–home interaction among self-
employed. Specifically, we address the following three questions:

1. To what degree do self-employed workers experience positive and
   negative work–home and home–work interaction, and how are these
   four types of work–home interaction associated with each other?
2. How do the scores of these self-employed workers on these four types
   of work–home interaction compare to those of organizationally
   employed workers?

3. How are the scores of these self-employed workers associated with various activities at home and work, work characteristics, and well-being?

Method

Participants: The study was conducted among self-employed workers. Our sample was drawn from the files of a Dutch company that provides insurance against work disability; this company is the second largest in this field, having a market share of about 11%. To be included, participants were required to be healthy (that is, not have any claims filed with the company). All participants in the target sample ($N = 1,917$) received a structured questionnaire, addressing topics such as work–home interaction, well-being, job perceptions, etc. After sending two reminders to all persons in the target sample, 491 usable questionnaires had been returned (25.8% response rate). Although this response rate is low, it is within the normal range for this type of occupational group (Baruch, 1999).

Most of the participants in the final sample were male (82%), which is quite characteristic for this type of sample; their average age was 43, $SD = 9$, and 28.7% held a college or university degree. As regards their family circumstances, 83% lived with a partner, either married or unmarried; 74% had children (average number of children was 2.40, $SD = .94$); and 93% of the participants who had children had at least one young child (age < 7 years). As regards their business, most of the participants (64.9%) had no personnel ("one-man bands"), 14.1% had one employee, and 16.9% had multiple employees. On average, the participants had been self-employed for 11.5 years ($SD = 8.8$), and for 91.7% this was the first business of their own. The four most important branches in which the participants were active were agriculture, fishing and minerals (27.4%); professional service industry (such as consultants, 17.4%); trade (16.5%); and the building industry (13.2%). An inspection of the population figures on the distribution of self-employed workers across these branches (CBS, 2005) showed that our sample reflected this distribution adequately (chi-square with 10 $df = 8.4, p > .50$).

Regarding the motivations for why our participants had started a business of their own, "being independent from others" was the most often mentioned reason (70.4% mentioned this reason). Other reasons were considerably less often cited. Relevant to the present study, 15.0% reported that having more flexibility, especially with respect to the combination of home and work, working at home, etc., was a major reason for starting their own company. Further analysis revealed that especially younger and more highly educated participants mentioned this motivation. Interestingly, we found no statistically significant associations with the presence of children or gender.

Measures: Work–home interaction was measured with the Survey Work–Home Interaction – Nijmegen (SWING, Geurts *et al.*, 2005). This instrument captures the positive and negative interaction between work and home, and home and work, respectively. Based on the notion that the absence of negative load reactions does not automatically imply the presence of positive load reactions, Geurts *et al.* developed a four-dimensional scale measuring four types of interaction: (1) negative work–home interaction, that is, negative load reactions developed at work that hamper functioning at home; (2) positive work–home interaction, that is, positive load reactions developed at work that facilitate functioning at home; (3) negative home–work interaction, that is, negative load reactions developed at home that interfere with one's functioning at work; and (4) positive home–work interaction, referring to positive load reactions developed in the home domain that facilitate functioning at work.

Table 8.1 presents sample items for the four scales of the SWING, as well as information on the number of items and reliability of these scales (Cronbach's alpha) as obtained for the present sample of self-employed workers. As correlates of the four forms of work–home interaction, we included scales capturing *job characteristics* (job control and job demands), *well-being* (including psychological complaints, exhaustion, and depersonalization as indicators of negative well-being, and feelings of personal accomplishment as a positive indicator of well-being), and several items capturing forms of *effort expenditure* (the number of hours spent at work, doing household chores, and care giving; an item measuring whether one worked during evenings and/or weekends). Table 8.1 presents some psychometric information on these scales and items.

Results: To what degree do self-employed workers experience positive/ negative work–home/home–work interaction, and how are these four types of work–home interaction associated with each other?

Table 8.2 presents the means and standard deviations of our sample of entrepreneurs for the four work–home interaction dimensions. Based on the participants' responses, given on a scale ranging from 0 ("seldom or never") to 3 ("often/always"), it is evident that they experienced little positive work–home interaction ($M = .21$). Levels of negative work–home

Table 8.1 *Scales used in the study among self-employed (N = 491)*

Sample items and item anchors	# of items (alpha)	M(SD)
Effort expenditure		
• To which degree do you work during evening hours and weekends?[a]	1 (–)	3.27 (.78)
• How many hours a week do you spend on average in your own company, including administration and acquisition?[b]	1 (–)	58.27 (14.15)
• How many hours a week do you on average spend on household chores (shopping, cleaning, gardening, etc.)[b]	1 (–)	6.94 (7.06)
• How many hours a week do you on average spend on caring (including looking after the children, etc.)[b]	1 (–)	5.91 (10.14)
Negative work–home interaction (Geurts et al., 2005)		
• How often does it happen than you are irritable at home because your work is demanding?[c]	8 (.86)	.90 (.50)
Positive work–home interaction (Geurts et al., 2005)		
• How often does it happen that you fulfill your domestic obligations better because of the things you have learned on your job?[c]	4 (.84)	0.21 (.38)
Negative home–work interaction (Geurts et al., 2005)		
• How often does it happen that you do not fully enjoy your work because you worry about your home situation?[c]	5 (.82)	1.24 (.59)
Positive home–work interaction (Geurts et al., 2005)		
• How often does it happen that you have greater self-confidence at work because you have your home life well organized?[c]	5 (.90)	1.16 (.74)
Job demands (Van Veldhoven and Meijman, 1994)		
• My work requires that I work very fast[d]	4 (.78)	2.80 (.47)
Job control (Van Veldhoven and Meijman, 1994)		
• My job offers me the opportunity do decide many things on my own[d]	3 (.62)	3.36 (.46)
Exhaustion (Schaufeli, Leiter, Maslach, and Jackson, 1996)		
• Working all day is really a strain to me[e]	5 (.80)	1.45 (1.08)
Cynicism (Schaufeli et al., 1996)		
• I have become more cynical about the effects of my work[e]	4 (.76)	.91 (.92)
Personal accomplishment (Schaufeli et al., 1996)		
• I have accomplished many worthwhile things in this job[e]	6 (.78)	4.61 (.96)
Psychological complaints (Dirken, 1969)		
• Do you often suffer from headaches?[f]	13 (.79)	1.20 (.19)

[a] Answer categories ranged from 1 (never) to 4 (often).
[b] This was an open question.
[c] Answer categories ranged from 0 (seldom/never) to 3 (often/always).
[d] Answer categories ranged from 1 (completely disagree) to 4 (completely agree).
[e] Answer categories ranged from 0 (never) to 6 (every day).
[f] Answer categories were 1 (no) and 2 (yes).

Table 8.2 *Comparison of the scores of self-employed to those of employees on the four dimensions of the Survey Work–Home Interaction Nijmegen*

Work–Home Dimensions	Self-employed (N = 491)		Employees[a] (N = 1,857)		
	M	SD	M	SD	T[b]
Negative work–home interaction	.90	.50	.86 (.64 – .96)	.48 (.42 – .96)	1.59
Negative home–work interaction	1.24	.59	.47 (.36 – .56)	.41 (.37 – .45)	27.23*
Positive work–home interaction	.21	.38	.83 (.56 – .94)	.57 (.51 – .65)	28.63*
Positive home–work interaction	1.16	.74	1.15 (.97–1.27)	.74 (.65 – .79)	.27

[a] Based on five separate samples. The range of the means and standard deviations for these samples is presented in brackets.
[b] T-value after correction for heterogeneous variances.
* = $p < .001$.

and positive home–work interaction are moderate, *M*s are .90 and 1.16, respectively. The average score on negative home–work interaction is comparatively high ($M = 1.24$); thus, it appears that a substantial proportion of our self-employed feel that the home domain interferes with their work.

An inspection of the correlations among the four types of work–home interaction revealed two significant associations. Negative work–home interaction and negative home–work interaction were correlated, $r = .36$, $p < .001$; the same applied to positive work–home and positive home–work interaction, $r = .69$, $p < 001$. Thus, those who experience positive (or negative) work–home interaction tend to report both forms of positive (or negative) work–home interaction together (Geurts *et al.*, 2005, for similar results). Further analysis revealed that these associations were not due to the effects of personal dispositions such as the tendency to see things either in a positive or in a negative light; after partialling out negative and positive affect, the pattern of correlations among the four work–home interaction scales remained virtually unchanged. It should also be noted that the low correlations among positive and negative forms of work–home interaction imply that self-employed workers may very well experience negative and positive forms of work–home interaction simultaneously.

How do the work–home interaction scores of self-employed workers compare to those of organizationally employed workers? Table 8.2 further presents the means and standard deviations of a sample of 1,857 organizationally employed workers. These data were collected in five separate studies, conducted in a manufacturing company in the electronics industry, the Dutch Post Office, a financial consultancy firm, a governmental institute in the service sector, and, finally, seventeen primary schools (Geurts *et al.*, 2005, present further details on the data collection procedures for these samples). The average response rate across these five studies was 46%, and sample sizes varied from 201 (for the schools) to 732 (for the post office). Nonparametric chi-square tests revealed that each sample was similar to its company population with regard to age and gender, with the exception of the post office sample, where younger workers were slightly underrepresented. For the total sample, M_{age} was 42.40 years ($SD = 8.45$); 67% were male; 36% held a college degree or higher; 59% were full-time employed; 22% held a managerial position; and 56% had children living in the household. Although presumably not representative for the total Dutch population of organizationally employed workers, comparison of this group to the present sample of self-employed workers may give a reasonable first impression of the possible differences between self and organizationally employed workers.

Comparison of the average scores of the two groups reveals that the self-employed report significantly lower levels of positive work–home interaction and higher levels of negative home–work interaction (this latter finding is consistent with Hundley, 2001). This is the case not only when comparing the scores of the self-employed sample to those of the overall organizationally employed sample, but also when the mean scores of the five separate samples are considered; the low scores of the self-employed on positive work–home interaction and their high scores on negative home–work interaction differ remarkably from those of the five employee samples. Thus, we may conclude that self-employed generally feel that their work does not enhance their functioning in the home domain, while they think that their home domain interferes *strongly* with their work.

How are the work–home interaction scores of these self-employed workers associated with various activities at home and work, work characteristics, and well-being? Table 8.3 presents the associations among the four dimensions of the work–home interface and various "antecedents" and "consequences." This table shows that *negative work–home interaction* correlates substantially with these antecedents

Table 8.3 *Associations among the four dimensions of the Survey Work–Home Interaction Nijmegen, various work and home activities, work characteristics and well-being indicators (sample size varies from 450 to 487)*

	Work–Home Dimensions			
	Negative work–home interaction	Negative home–work interaction	Positive work–home interaction	Positive home–work interaction
Work and home activities				
Works during evenings/ weekends	.33***	.02	.01	−.04
Number of hours spent with ...				
... work	.30***	.00	−.03	−.08
... household chores	−.09*	.07	.06	.11*
... caring	−.04	.06	.01	.05
Job characteristics				
Job control	−.07	−.13**	.13**	.10*
Job demands	.41***	.05	.08	.07
Well-being				
Psychosomatic complaints	.41***	.36***	.00	−.02
Exhaustion	.49***	.29***	−.05	−.02
Depersonalization	.33***	.39***	−.05	−.04
Personal accomplishment	−.13**	−.21***	.18***	.19***

$^* = p < .05,$
$^{**} = p < .01,$
$^{***} = p < .001.$

and consequences. Self-employed who work during evenings and/or weekends or who spend many hours on their work, more often report that their work interferes with the home domain – findings that speak for themselves. Additionally, they tend to devote somewhat less time to the household chores. Furthermore, high job demands and low job control were found to be associated with high levels of negative work–home interaction, perhaps because such factors tend to be associated with high levels of stress. Consistent with this reasoning, high levels of negative work–home interaction were found to be associated with high levels of physical complaints, exhaustion and cynicism, and low levels of personal accomplishment. These results suggest that high levels of negative work–home interaction could constitute a major risk factor for well-being.

Negative home–work interaction was not associated with any of the four indicators of effort expenditure in Table 8.3, but low levels of control were linked with high levels of negative home–work interaction. Moreover, high negative home–work interaction was associated with high levels of physical complaints, exhaustion and cynicism, and low levels of personal accomplishment. Thus, it appears that experiencing high levels of negative home–work interaction is systematically related to low levels of well-being.

Positive work–home interaction was largely unrelated to the correlates included in the present study, with the exceptions of job control and personal accomplishment. Self-employed workers reporting high levels of positive work–home interaction tended to experience high levels of job control and personal accomplishment.

Finally, *positive home–work interaction* was significantly related to job control, personal accomplishment, and the number of hours spent on doing the household chores. The interpretation of the latter association could run two ways. First, people who feel that their home domain affects their work positively may be willing to spend relatively more time in the home domain. Conversely, those who have to spend a lot of time doing their household chores may judge these more positively (for example, by regarding it as a factor that enhances their functioning at work), if only to justify to themselves that they spend so much time on it.

Discussion of the case study

Our findings show that the average self-employed worker feels that his or her work contributes little to their functioning at home, believing that the home domain interferes strongly with their work. Organizationally employed workers, however, report considerably higher levels of positive work–home interaction and lower levels of negative home–work interaction. The interpretation of these results is not altogether clear. On the one hand, the high scores regarding negative home–work interaction (that is, our participants feel relatively strongly that their home interferes with their work) in combination with the fact that our participants work on average almost sixty hours a week (see Table 8.1) may suggest that many self-employed qualify as workaholics, for whom their business is the central element in life. The landscaper cited above may be an example, feeling that her job was her "soul work" and appearing to feel that her family was holding her back from investing more time and effort in her job. On the other hand, since our participants also report that their work does little to enhance their functioning at home, they cannot easily be qualified as "work enthusiasts" who uncritically feel that their job makes them happy.

Furthermore, our results revealed that negative work–home interaction, in particular, was linked to effort expenditure at work and home, and to adverse well-being. The latter also applied to negative home–work interaction. The lack of associations between both positive forms of work–home interaction and antecedents/consequences may partly be due to the fact that our study did not include home characteristics. However, other research on the positive dimensions of work–home interaction also failed to produce substantial associations between these dimensions and other concepts (including home characteristics, Geurts *et al.*, 2005). Thus, as in other research, the present study underscores the importance of negative work–home and home–work interaction; the problems and stress built up in one domain may affect functioning in the other domain adversely, and this is also visible in terms of the links with other concepts. Conversely, while one may well *feel* that positive experiences gained in one domain generalize to the other, as yet there seems to be little evidence that these experiences spill over, in terms of positive outcomes, to the other domain.

Final remarks

This chapter has addressed the concept of work–home interaction among self-employed workers. First, we presented a general discussion of the concept of work–home interaction, distinguishing between two major dimensions, and questioning whether (1) the interaction between home and work was positive or negative (*valence*), and (2) whether skills, moods, and knowledge spill over from work to home, or vice versa (*direction*). The links among the resulting four dimensions of work–home interaction and their antecedents and consequences were then discussed in the context of Effort–Recovery theory. Basically, when high levels of effort are not matched by an appropriate amount of recovery, negative work–home (home–work) interaction will occur, and in the long run negative outcomes, such as exhaustion and physical complaints, will ensue. Conversely, when effort expenditure is adequately compensated for by recovery opportunities, positive work–home (home–work) interaction may occur, possibly having positive consequences for the individual and his/her organization.

Application of these ideas to the findings of previous research as well as to our own study among self-employed revealed that these notions receive only partial support. Although the links between negative work–home interaction (and, to some degree, negative home–work interaction), effort expenditure, recovery opportunities, and well-being are largely confirmed, this is much less so for the two positive dimensions of the work–home interface. For example, whereas our study among self-employed revealed substantial correlations among the two negative forms of work–home interaction and well-being, the two positive dimensions of work–home interaction were almost unrelated to the other concepts studied here.

Venues for future research

The latter findings – that replicate findings obtained for organizationally employed workers (among others, Geurts *et al.*, 2005) – may raise the question whether the conceptualization of the interface between work and home as four separate dimensions is appropriate. The issue does not seem to be whether it is possible to distinguish among four types of work–home interaction (previous research has demonstrated that all four dimensions can be measured reliably and that they can be distinguished from each other), but rather concerns the value of the theoretical models used to study work–home interaction. In the present study among self-employed as well as in previous research among organizationally employed workers (Bakker and Geurts, 2004; Geurts *et al.*, 2005), we used Effort–Recovery theory to account for various types of work–home interaction. This approach was quite useful with respect to the occurrence of negative work–home interaction, showing that high effort expenditure is related to high levels of negative work–home interaction. Similar findings were obtained by Parasuraman *et al.* (1996) and Parasuraman and Simmers (2001) among entrepreneurs, suggesting that spending more effort at one's work increases the risk of experiencing negative work–home interaction.

Conversely, the value of the Effort–Recovery framework for examining the three other dimensions of work–home interaction was quite limited. This could partly be due to the fact that research into the positive dimensions has only just started to be published, in conjunction with the fact that home characteristics have not frequently been studied as predictors of work–home interaction. There seems no *a priori* reason to expect that effort expended at home would differ in its effects on functioning at work; in that sense, we expect that Effort–Recovery theory will be useful in studying the antecedents of both negative work–home and negative home–work interaction.

However, the Effort–Recovery model may be less appropriate for examining the two positive forms of work–home interaction. Our findings suggest that work characteristics (especially having high levels of job control) may be more important here than effort expenditure (note that Geurts *et al.*, 2005, and Grzywacz and Marks, 2000, reported similar

associations between job control and positive forms of work–family interaction). The question, then, is why having greater job control seems to
facilitate positive spillover from home to work and vice versa. One possibility is that having high job control offers workers good opportunities to
combine work and family obligations. However, while this reasoning
suffices to account for the fact that work (home) does not *interfere* with
home (work), it does not explain why having job control would *enhance*
one's functioning at home (or work).

A different perspective on this issue is proposed by Karasek (1998),
who argued that having high control would increase one's possibilities
for competence development. He argued that these competences could
be applied in other domains as well. An inspection of the content of the
two scales capturing positive spillover (see Table 8.1) suggests that this
reasoning may indeed apply, in that positive spillover is characterized
here in terms of increased confidence and the acquisition of additional
skills. In this sense, a learning perspective on positive work–home and
home–work interaction may be more fruitful than Effort–Recovery
theory. Additional research is needed here, incorporating both work
and home characteristics and employing a clear conceptualization of the
processes that link the various forms of work–home interaction to work
and home characteristics.

There seems little reason to expect that the basic processes that account
for the relations between the various types of work–home interactions and
their antecedents and consequences would differ for self-employed as
compared to organizationally employed workers. However, there are
major differences between these groups in terms of the average levels of
negative home–work interaction (which is considerably higher for self-
employed) and positive work–home interaction (which is considerably
lower for this group). The problem, then, is what specific factors account
for these differences. Unfortunately (as said above), the research published thus far (including the present study) has shed little light on this
issue. This again underscores the need for focused research on the antecedents of various forms of work–home interaction among self-employed
and organizationally employed workers.

Practical implications: work–home interaction among self-employed

The preceding section identifies a number of avenues for future research
on the study of the work–home interaction in general, and among self-
employed workers in particular. These gaps in our knowledge notwith-
standing, it is still possible to discuss some implications of previous as well
as our own research on work–home interaction among self-employed.

Perhaps the most appealing finding of our case study among self-employed concerned the relatively high levels of negative home–work interaction experienced in this group. It appears that a considerable proportion of the participants in our sample feel that the home domain holds them back from performing well at work; in this sense, to many of our participants, their work is indeed *their love, their life,* and perhaps even *their everything.* Our findings revealed that the consequences of this attitude for well-being may not be positive; the self-employed workers who experienced high levels of negative home–work interaction reported low levels of well-being as well. Similarly, we found very substantial associations between negative work–home interaction and well-being. These findings suggest that it may be desirable to alleviate the levels of negative home–work and work–home interaction among this group. Unfortunately, this may be difficult to accomplish. First, the results presented so far offer few handles on how to deal with *negative home–work interaction,* since the possible causes of this phenomenon are largely unknown. Our analyses only revealed that low job control tended to coincide with high negative home–work interaction, but this effect was rather weak and difficult to interpret, especially since the causal direction of this effect is unknown. Thus, we simply do not know what causes high negative home–work interaction, which hinders practical interventions. For *negative work–home interaction* we found positive associations with excessive effort expenditure at work (i.e. working long hours, during evenings and/or weekends, and experiencing high job demands). This suggests that a simple way to reduce negative work–home interaction is to reduce entrepreneurs' effort investments in their work.

However, this leads to a second problem: can self-employed workers be motivated to expend less effort at work? Seeing as these workers set their own working hours, they could, in principle, decide to work fewer hours. However, the self-employed may be reluctant to work fewer hours, even if it were financially possible. For them, there is no natural boundary between work and home domains; indeed, their success in the work domain probably depends substantially on the number of hours they are willing to invest in their own business. The fact that self-employed workers have no supervisors who might coach them on how to combine work and home obligations further compounds this problem. While it may be possible to assist self-employed who actively seek help in combining their work and family obligations (for instance, by instructing them in time-management techniques), it seems likely that many others would continue to experience high levels of negative work–home and home–work interaction, along with the corresponding adverse consequences for their health and well-being. From this viewpoint, it seems likely that the self-employed will continue to constitute a high-risk group for experiencing the negative consequences of negative work–home and home–work interaction.

Acknowledgements

This study was partly supported by grants #580-02-104 and #015.000.027 from the Dutch Organization for Scientific Research to S. Geurts.

References

Allen, T. D., Herst, D. E., Bruck, C. S., and Sutton, M. (2000). Consequences associated with work-to-family conflict: a review and agenda for future research. *Journal of Occupational Health Psychology* 5: 278–308.

Bakker, A. B. and Geurts, S. A. E. (2004). Towards a dual-process model of work–home interference. *Work and Occupations* 31: 345–66.

Baruch, Y. (1999). Response rate in academic studies: a comparative analysis. *Human Relations* 52: 421–38.

Berke, D. L. (2003). Coming home again: the challenges and rewards of home-based self-employment. *Journal of Family Issues* 24: 513–46.

Bond, J. T., Thompson, C., Galinsky, E., and Prottas, D. (2003). *Highlights of the national study of the changing workforce*. New York: Families and Work Institute.

Carlson, D. S., Kacmar, K. M., Wayne, J. H., and Grzywacz, J. G. (2006). Measuring the positive side of the work–family interface: development and validation of a work–family enrichment scale. *Journal of Vocational Behavior* 68: 131–64.

CBS (Central Bureau of Statistics) (2005). *Werkzame personen, banen en arbeidsjaren* (Working persons, jobs, and work years). Retrieved November 1, 2005, from http://statline.cbs.nl.

Chay, Y. W. (1993). Social support, individual differences and well-being: a study of small business entrepreneurs and employees. *Journal of Occupational and Organizational Psychology* 66: 285–302.

Cohen, A. (1977). Personal and organizational responses to work–nonwork interface as related to organizational commitment. *Journal of Applied Social Psychology* 27: 1085–1114.

De Lange, A. H., Taris, T. W., Kompier, M. A. J., Houtman, I. L. D., and Bongers, P. M. (2003). "The very best of the millennium": longitudinal research and the Demand–Control-(support) model. *Journal of Occupational Health Psychology* 8: 282–305.

Demerouti, E., Bakker, A. B., and Bulters, A. J. (2004). The loss spiral of work pressure, work–home interference and exhaustion: reciprocal relations in a three-wave study. *Journal of Vocational Behavior* 64: 131–49.

Dirken, J. M. (1969). *Arbeid en stress* (Work and stress). Groningen: Wolters Noordhoff.

Duxbury, L. and Higgins, L. (2001). *Work–life balance in the new millennium: Where are we? Where do we need to go?* CPRN Discussion Paper No. W/12. Ottawa: CPRN.

Eby, L. T., Casper, W. J., Lockwood, A., Bordeaux, C., and Brinley, A. (2005). Work and family research in IO/OB: content analysis and review of the literature (1980–2002). *Journal of Vocational Behavior* 66: 124–97.

Eden, D. (1973). Self-employed workers: a comparison group for organizational psychology. *Organizational Behavior and Human Performance* 9: 186–214.

Fairlie, R. W. (2004). Self-employed business ownership rates in the United States: 1997–2003. *Small Business Research Summary 243.*

Frone, M. R. (2000). Work–family conflict and employee psychiatric disorders: the National Comorbidity Study. *Journal of Applied Psychology* 85: 888–95.

Geurts, S. A. E. and Demerouti, E. (2003). Work–nonwork interface: a review of theories and findings. In M. Schabracq, J. Winnubst, and C. Cooper (eds.), *Handbook of work and health psychology* (pp. 279–312). Chichester: Wiley.

Geurts, S. A. E., Kompier, M. A. J., Roxburgh, S., and Houtman, I. L. D. (2003). Does work–home interference mediate the relationship between workload and well-being? *Journal of Vocational Behavior* 63: 532–59.

Geurts, S. A. E., Taris, T. W., Kompier, M. A. J., Dikkers, J. S. E., Van Hooff, M. L. M., and Kinnunen, U. M. (2005). Work–home interaction from a work psychological perspective: development and validation of a new questionnaire, the SWING. *Work and Stress* 19: 319–39.

Greenhaus, J. H. and Powell, G. N. (2006). When work and family are allies: a theory of work–family enrichment. *Academy of Management Review* 31: 72–92.

Grzywacz, J. G. and Marks, N. F. (2000). Reconceptualizing the work–family interface: an ecological perspective on the correlates of positive and negative spillover between work and family. *Journal of Occupational Health Psychology* 5: 111–26.

Hundley, G. (2001). Domestic division of labor and self/organizationally employed differences in job attitudes and earnings. *Journal of Family and Economic Issues* 22: 121–39.

Karasek, R. A. (1998). Demand–Control model: a social, emotional, and physiological approach to stress risk and active behavior development. In J. M. Stellman (ed.), *Encyclopaedia of occupational health and safety* (4th edn, pp. 34.6–34.14). Geneva: International Labour Office.

Loscocco, K. A. (1997). Work–family linkages among self-employed women and men. *Journal of Vocational Behavior* 50: 204–26.

Mannheim, B. and Schiffrin, M. (1984). Family structure, job characteristics, rewards and strains as related to work-role centrality of employed and self-employed professional women with children. *Journal of Occupational Behavior* 5: 83–101.

Meijman, T. F. and Mulder, G. (1998). Psychological aspects of workload. In P. J. Drenth, H. Thierry, and C. J. de Wolff (eds.), *Handbook of work and organizational psychology* (2nd edn, pp. 5–33). Hove: Psychology Press.

Parasuraman, S., Purohit, Y. S., Godshalk, V. M., and Beutell, N. J. (1996). Work and family variables, entrepreneurial career success and psychological well-being. *Journal of Vocational Behavior* 48: 275–300.

Parasuraman, S. and Simmers, C. (2001). Type of employment, work–family conflict and well-being: a comparative study. *Journal of Organizational Behavior* 22: 551–68.

Rahim, A. (1996). Stress, strain: a comparison of entrepreneurs and managers. *Journal of Small Business Management* 34: 46–58.

Rothbard, N. P. (2001). Enriching or depleting? The dynamics of engagement in work and family roles. *Administrative Science Quarterly* 46: 655–84.

Schaufeli, W. B., Leiter, M. P., Maslach, C., and Jackson, S. E. (1996). Maslach Burnout Inventory – general survey. In C. Maslach, S. E. Jackson, and M. P. Leiter (eds.), *The Maslach Burnout Inventory: test manual* (3rd edn). Palo Alto, CA: Consulting Psychologists Press.

Sluiter, J. K., Frings-Dresen, M. H. W., Van der Beek, A. J., and Meijman, T. F. (2001). The relation between work-induced neuroendocrine reactivity and recovery, subjective need for recovery, and health status. *Journal of Psychosomatic Research* 50: 29–37.

Taris, T. W., Beckers, D., Verhoeven, L. C., Geurts, S. A. E., Kompier, M. A. J., and Van der Linden, D. (2006). Recovery opportunities, work–home interference, and wellbeing among managers. *European Journal of Work and Organizational Psychology* 15: 139–57.

Taris, T. and Kompier, M. A. J. (2005). Job characteristics and learning behavior: review and psychological mechanisms. In P. L. Perrewé and D. C. Ganster (eds.), *Research in occupational stress and well being, vol. 4: Exploring interpersonal dynamics* (pp. 127–66). Amsterdam: JAI Press.

Ursin, H. (1980). Personality, activation and somatic health: a new psychosomatic theory. In S. Levine and H. Ursin (eds.), *Coping and health* (pp. 259–79). New York: Plenum Press.

Van der Hulst, M. and Geurts, S. A. E. (2001). Associations between overtime and psychological health in high and low reward jobs. *Work and Stress* 15: 227–40.

Van Hooff, M., Geurts, S. A. E., Taris, T. W., Kompier, M. A. J., Dikkers, J. S. E., Houtman, I. L. D., and Van den Heuvel, F. (2005). Disentangling the relationships between work–home interference and employee health: a longitudinal study among Dutch police officers. *Scandinavian Journal of Work, Environment and Health* 31: 15–29.

Van Veldhoven, M. and Meijman, T. F. (1994). *Het meten van psychosociale arbeidsbelasting met een vragenlijst: de vragenlijst beleving en beoordeling van de arbeid* (VBBA) [The measurement of psychosocial strain at work: the questionnaire experience and evaluation of work]. Amsterdam: NIA.

Voydanoff, P. (2004). The effects of work demands and resources on work-to-family conflict and facilitation. *Journal of Marriage and Family* 66: 398–412.

9   Modern work and safety

Nik Chmiel

This chapter is concerned with safety within contemporary work contexts from a work and organizational psychology perspective. The aim of the chapter is to provide a critical appreciation of the contribution of recent questionnaire studies to modern work and safety issues in light of previous work on human error.

Background

The scientific study of safety at work has been characterized by Hale and Hovden (1998) as having three ages. The first age was concerned with "technical measures to guard machinery, stop explosions and prevent structures collapsing" (p. 129) and lasted from the nineteenth century until after 1945. The second age, initiated between the two world wars, witnessed research into prevention measures based on personnel selection, training, and motivation, often referred to as theories of accident proneness. Hale and Hovden indicate that the technical and individual-based approaches merged in the 1960s and 70s with developments in ergonomics and probabilistic risk analysis, and the study of human error as a field of inquiry. They go on to identify the 1980s as characterized by "an increasing dissatisfaction with the idea that health and safety could be captured simply by matching the individual to technology" (p. 130) and that the 1990s were well into the third age of safety.

The third age Hale and Hovden (1998: 130) characterize as focused on management systems, and the literature, to the 1980s at least, as "accumulated common sense and as general management principles applied to the specific field of safety" rather than science. They point out that as recently as 1992 a thorough review of the field of risk, including risk management, by the Royal Society in the UK had no review of research or practice at the level of company management. In a similar vein a number of case studies form the basis of the review by Hofmann, Jacobs, and Landy (1995: 131) outlining possible organizational influences on accident outcomes. Hofmann *et al.* proposed their paper "serve as a starting point for continued consideration of the influences of socio-organizational factors on safety." Thus, a need for more systematic studies of the relationship between organizational influences and safety has been identified, a need that has been addressed within work and organizational psychology largely by questionnaire-based studies. This chapter focuses on those studies produced since 1995 with the aim of weighing their contribution to understanding safety in modern work contexts.

The European Agency for Health and Safety at Work reported on "New trends in accident prevention due to the changing world of work" (de Beeck and van Heuverswyn, 2002). The report was based on the views of experts on the challenges facing the management of organizational safety in Europe, and suggests modern work and its influence on accident prevention involves more free-market, privatization and down-sizing, changes in technology, changes in working hours, work pace, and workload, a growth of sub-contracting, more service work, an increase in part-time jobs, temporary work, more women, an aging workforce, and greater globalization and integration of work. The report mentions in particular that smaller companies often do not have the management structure to develop efficient accident prevention, sub-contracting creates uncertainty about the responsibilities for safety, and new technologies may reduce old risk, but also may create new risks.

The major aspects of de Beeck and van Heuverswyn's (2002) report can be considered to relate respectively to organizational practices and their influence on accidents, to the relationship between how individuals regard their organizations and safety, and to the shift toward mental work as a function of computer-based technology and the implications for cognitive error and accidents. This chapter therefore considers questionnaire-based findings within these three broad categories.

The primary focus of safety at work is the avoidance of accidents that lead to physical harm. For present purposes harm is defined as injury rather than disease. The chapter therefore considers primarily questionnaire-based studies which relate findings to injury outcomes. Surprisingly, given the interest in safety at work, the number of such studies is small. There are studies that focus on "safety performance" that encompass a variety of safety behaviors as outcomes and I consider the validity of these below.

The study of human error, rooted in Hale and Hovden's (1998) terms in the second age of the scientific study of safety, and influential particularly in safety-critical industries such as nuclear power, has largely depended on retrospective analyses of accidents. Therefore, concepts and findings from questionnaire studies are compared, where appropriate, to those from accident analyses that consider psychological antecedents.

Accident investigation and questionnaires

Before considering questionnaire findings in more detail some general points should be made about how psychological aspects of safety can be, and have been, investigated.

Accident reporting schemes

It is an attractive proposition that safety at work should be understood through the very thing that safety measures are designed to avoid. Brown (1990: 755), for example, asserted that "reporting accidents is the only practical way of evaluating system safety under real operating conditions, and of identifying factors which may be contributing to accident causation." Brown proposed further that, to be useful, accident reporting systems at work should highlight primary safety improvements, capture antecedent behavior, avoid subjectivity, avoid apportioning blame, detail task and system demands, collect data on all accidents regardless of their consequences, and detail the nature, severity, and causes of accidental injury.

However, accident reporting systems have come in for some trenchant criticism. Sheehy and Chapman (1987) observed that accident reporting systems had, by and large, grown to meet specific organizational, medical, and legal needs, and contained crude sub-divisions of accidents (e.g. burns, falls, lost time) and categories that gave a false impression of reliability, yet suffered from definitional problems. Thus comparison across headline figures and organizations is difficult. A similar point has been recognized in the European Union in relation to national reporting schemes, with the result being an initiative aimed at accident reporting harmonisation across member states (Jacinto and Aspinwall, 2004).

Sheehy and Chapman (1987: 203) pointed out that schemes failed to elicit ergonomic information and, tellingly, reflected implicit theories of accident causation by only including categories thought to be relevant. Further, and crucially, they pointed out that accident reports "cannot begin to cater for the complexity of emotional responses associated with the occurrence, prevention, and investigation of accidents." Thus, as a means of understanding safety at work within organizations, accident reporting schemes have considerable limitations.

Accident data

The reduction of accidents is a main focus for safety initiatives and policies related to workplace safety. Although vital as the outcome of interest, there are two fundamental practical problems in using accident occurrence in the investigation and understanding of safety.

The first problem is that workplace accidents appear frequently to be underreported to the relevant people, and this may apply much more so to less severe accidents. Individual workplaces will, in practice, vary in how much underreporting goes on. Chmiel (2005) reported that a comparison of recorded and self-reported minor injuries revealed a large discrepancy, a ratio of approximately 1:11, in a study in the chemical processing sector. Weddle (1996) reported that of hospital environmental service workers who recalled having been injured in the previous year 39% had not reported one or more injuries, and that the most frequently cited reason for not reporting was that the injury had seemed too minor, even though roughly 64% of unreported injuries required medical care and 44% resulted in lost work time. The next most common reason involved not wanting a supervisor to think that the worker was careless. Other studies suggest underreporting because of the perceived reaction and negative attitude of managers (Clarke, 1998), the fear of blame and punishment (Reason, 1997), and per-ceived lack of importance to understanding safety (van der Schaaf and Kanse, 2004).

The second practical problem, fortunately, is that accidents happen relatively infrequently. Thus, to obtain adequate outcome measures, data may have to be collected over long periods of time, making it relatively difficult to relate psychological and organizational antecedents to them. This is especially the case with major accidents involving death and major injury. Zohar (2000) has proposed that micro-accidents could provide a solution to this problem. Micro-accidents are on-the-job behavior-dependent minor injuries requiring medical attention but that do not incur any lost workdays. However, micro-accidents are subject to reporting biases too (Chmiel, 2005). Another approach is to use self-reports of injury involvement, and these are discussed in more detail next, since they form the outcome in a number of recent questionnaire studies.

Self-reports and accident outcomes

Thompson, Hilton, and Witt (1998: 21) suggested that

perceptual data (i.e. self reports) might be the preferred criteria for safety research...Members of the workforce out on the shop floor are likely to be sensitive to the type and frequency of accidents that go under-reported. Their perceived sense of workplace safety conditions might, therefore, be a better indicator of safety risk.

Although Thompson *et al.* (1998) used perceptions of safety conditions as an outcome, since they made their comment a number of studies have used self-reported accident involvement. These studies, however, have measured involvement in a variety of ways, with reference to major and minor injuries and a variety of time spans, e.g. three years (Wallace and Vodanovich, 2003), three months (Westaby and Lee, 2003), and nine months (Frone, 1998). An important problem with asking this type of question is that the measure of accident involvement is subject to retrospective recall over a period, and when this is extended in time major accidents are far more likely to be recalled than minor ones given their more dramatic nature and longer-lasting impact (Dejoy, 1985).

Another approach is exemplified by the first study reported by Barling, Loughlin, and Kelloway (2002). Respondents had to rate experience of occupationally relevant minor and major injuries in the previous year on a five-point Likert scale ranging from "never" to "frequently." Studies using this type of general rating scale about accident involvement may increase vulnerability to a number of recall biases and socially desirable responding. It is easier to "guesstimate" with such a scale compared to indicating how many injuries one has received. Barling *et al.* (2002: 494) noted that "where future research makes primary use of self-reported data some control for socially desirable responding is in order."

The two approaches to self-report accident involvement outlined above have not sought to differentiate between various degrees of severity of injury. The point is important because of the likely differential recall of major versus minor accidents already noted, and the possibility that major and minor accidents have different antecedents. Thus, ideally, an accident involvement self-report measure should be more specific rather than more general, and it should be more diagnostic with respect to accident severity than not. A checklist approach is closer to this ideal than rating scale methods (Chmiel, 2005).

Accident figures and accident exposure

Questionnaire studies involve the analysis of accident frequencies and their association with behavioral, psychological, and organizational correlates. Hodge and Richardson (1985) pointed out that comparisons of accident frequency data cannot be made properly without understanding the nature of accident exposure involved in the comparison. Their notion of exposure was drawn from Chapman (1973: 99), who proposed that "exposure is the number of opportunities for accidents of a certain type in a given time in a given area." Accident exposure is rarely addressed in questionnaire studies. Exceptions are Zohar (2000), who used ratings of risk as a control variable in his analyses, and Chmiel (2005), who used job role. The adequacy of these different measures is open to critical review but clearly this is a topic that deserves further investigation since without controls for accident exposure the interpretation of effects related to accident frequencies is problematic.

Safety-related behaviors

Retrospective analyses of accidents suggest most accidents are thought to involve some kind of safety-related human behavior, violations of procedures as well as cognitive error (Reason, 1990; Salminen and Tallberg, 1996; Wagenaar and Groeneweg, 1987); therefore identifying and understanding the nature of such behavior is an important goal for research into safety at work.

Reason (1990) proposed a taxonomy that divided unsafe acts into those that were unintentional, and those that were intended in pursuit of planned goals. Unintended errors (slips and lapses) involved cognitive processes such as momentary inattention. These could be detected readily since they were unintended, and could also be investigated through questionnaire methods. Intended errors included errors of reasoning, judgement, and problem-solving, but Reason (1990) argued that because the actions were intended this class of errors were not easily self-detected prior to their consequences, invalidating the use of questionnaires. Intended violations could include a range of behaviors, for example taking shortcuts rather than following procedures, or non-compliance with self-protective precautions, for example not wearing personal protective equipment (Reason, Parker, and Lawton, 1998). Deliberate violations of safety rules are self-evidently amenable to self-reports. The latter types of behavior have appeared of most immediate interest to work and organizational psychologists in relation to safety.

By and large cognitive errors have not been the focus to date for questionnaire-based studies considering the effect of organizational factors on such errors. However, questionnaire-based measures have been developed and these are discussed below also.

Dimensionality of self-reported safety behaviors

What types of safety behaviors have been studied typically in questionnaire-based approaches? Most attention has been directed at violations or compliance behaviors and another category that could be called safety citizenship behaviors. Some development work has been done on scales measuring cognitive errors. The description of these behavioral measures is discussed next, followed by consideration of their validity.

Safety compliance/violation Using exploratory factor analysis of responses from 889 nurses, DeJoy, Searcy, Murphy, and Gershon (2000) extracted two factors from an eleven-item set they called "compliance with personal protective equipment" (PPE) and "general compliance" (GP). Griffin and Neal (2000) and Neal, Griffin, and Hart (2000) used two scales they called "safety compliance" and "safety participation." The latter falls into the safety citizenship category discussed below. An example item from the former scale was "I use the correct personal protective equipment for the task I am doing."

Chmiel (2005) constructed two scales through exploratory factor analysis that he labeled "working safely" (e.g. "I always use safety equipment, even when it's not easily available") and "bending rules" (e.g. "Occasionally I bend the rules when I know it is safe to do so"). The bending rules scale included two items that were identical to those used by Parker, Axtell, and Turner (2001) in their three-item scale that correlated modestly, but significantly, with team leaders' ratings of safety compliance and safety-related consciousness.

Burke, Sarpy, Tesluk, and Smith-Crowe (2002) attempted to produce a model of general safety performance. Using confirmatory techniques they produced four factors related to "typical coworker" performance as judged by nuclear hazardous waste disposal workers. The factors were described as using personal protective equipment, engaging in work practices to reduce risk, communicating health and safety information, and exercising employee rights and responsibilities. The factors were highly correlated but the four-factor solution was found to fit the data better than a single-factor solution. The first two factors appear similar to other measures of compliance behavior.

Safety citizenship Turner, Chmiel, and Walls (2005) used safety role definitions, and Cheyne, Cox, Oliver, and Tomas (1998) used involvement in safety activities as safety performance measures. Together with the last two factors produced by Burke *et al.* (2002) and the safety participation scale from Griffin and Neal (2000), these measures could be considered safety citizenship, akin to organizational citizenship in concept (Hofmann, Morgeson, and Gerras, 2003). These measures are not, a priori, "safe behaviors" as defined above. Thus this class of behaviors represents a widening of the perspective on safety from a performance standpoint and is a contribution made possible by the questionnaire approach contrasted with that from accident analyses.

Cognitive errors Finally Wallace and Chen (2005) developed a scale measuring work-specific cognitive failures (Workplace Cognitive Failure Scale, WCFS), basing their conceptualization on the more general cognitive failures questionnaire (CFQ) of Broadbent, Cooper, Fitzgerald, and Parkes (1982). Their conceptualization supposed that such failures were those of memory, attention, and action, and were unintended. Their results supported a three-factor solution, as well as their claim that the three factors related to a common second-order factor. The WCFS is contextualized for work settings and is therefore more specific, but nonetheless is similar in nature to the CFQ.

The Short Inventory of Minor Lapses (SIML), too, was based on a similar approach to the CFQ (see e.g. Reason, 1993), and these measures have been found to correlate quite highly. The CFQ has been taken to indicate a predisposition to cognitive failure similar to a trait. If taken this way then the WCFS and SIML are measures not of behavior per se but of a disposition to cognitive error. However, all these scales ask respondents to indicate how frequently they have made cognitive errors within a relatively short prior timeframe (typically six months). In addition, the CFQ has been found not to correlate with other dispositional measures (such as trait measures of personality, intelligence, and obsessive personality), but, rather, to correlate with time-limited obsessive symptoms (Broadbent, Broadbent, and Jones, 1986). It appears plausible, therefore, to consider the CFQ, SIML, and WCFS as self-report scales of error behaviors, similar to those for the violations discussed above. The SIML has been used in this way to examine how changes in mood may affect cognitive errors (Reason, 1993).

Safety behavior and accident outcomes

A key question concerns whether self-reported safety behaviors of the type discussed above are associated with accident outcomes. In other words, are the behaviors that have been measured in recent questionnaire studies valid as predictors of injury outcomes? Surprisingly, there are not very many questionnaire-based studies that include both safety behaviors and accident outcomes.

In a recent meta-analysis Clarke (2006) summarized the situation with respect to the relationships between safety compliance, safety participation, and accidents. She was able to include only nine studies relating safety compliance to accident outcomes, and only three studies relating safety participation to such criteria. Clarke found that, overall, the relationships between safety performance and accidents and injuries were valid and generalizable, but the effect sizes were small, with that for safety participation stronger than for safety compliance.

Clarke's (2006) findings are intriguing because they suggest a limited effect for the relationship between behavior and accidents, contrasting with the perspective gained from accident analyses. At first sight it would appear that the compliance and participation measures used in recent questionnaire studies have limited validity for predicting accident outcome. The behavioral measures chosen may therefore require further refinement, or there may need to be other behaviors, such as cognitive error, included in future meta-analyses. However, there is another consideration when judging effect size, and that is whether the possible effect of unsafe behaviors is moderated by system defenses (see the general accident causation scenario below). In brief, adequate defenses prevent unsafe behaviors turning into accidents. Defenses are not usually measured in questionnaire approaches but could be considered to affect accident exposure and thus deserve future consideration.

The meta-analysis by Clarke (2006) included studies with relationships at the group level of analysis, and severity of accident outcome was not considered. Both these factors may turn out to be important in understanding the relationship of safety-related behaviors to accident involvement even if behavioral measures are further refined: first, because different behaviors may matter more for different severity of outcome, and second, because some types of behavior may have more impact than others on group-level accident outcomes. Two studies illustrate these points. In the study by Chmiel (2005), noted above, only one type of behavior, "bending rules," predicted minor injury involvement whereas "working safely" did not. This result demonstrates that not all behaviors are implicated in accident involvement in any particular situation.

Drawing on accident analyses, Neal and Griffin (2006: 947) argued that safety compliance and participation "may not directly affect the person who fails to carry out these behaviors but can create the conditions that make it more likely that someone else will be injured later on." This suggests that a link between safety behavior and accidents should be observed at a group level, and this effect is likely to be lagged. Neal and Griffin tested this by forming a composite behavioral measure from safety participation and compliance and aggregating it to the group level, and then relating it to group accident data. Their results were consistent with their claim. A further interesting aspect of their findings is that in addition to prior behavior having a lagged negative effect on accidents (better behavior led to fewer accidents later on), earlier accidents had a positive relationship with later behavior. Neal and Griffin used this observation to argue that reverse causality could be ruled out, that is, the negative relationship between behavior and accidents was due to behavior affecting accident outcome, consistent with accident analyses.

The question whether safety participation and compliance have similar effects at the group level is still open. It can be argued that safety compliance will have stronger impact on individual accident involvement than safety participation, since the latter is inherently a social activity whereas the former also involves behavior likely to put the individual directly at risk. Neal and Griffin (2006) showed that a measure of the extent to which individuals viewed safety as an important part of their work life (called safety motivation) had a lagged effect on safety participation but not on safety compliance, which indicates that the two aspects of behavior operate differently.

In sum, we have a situation with more questions than answers at the moment with respect to socially referenced safety behaviors. Are the behavioral measures currently used in questionnaire studies valid? Do they need further differentiation and refinement (see Reason *et al.*, 1998, for a consideration of how this could be done)? Are they appropriate for some accident outcomes but not for others? Should we expect and look for differential lagged effects between compliance, participation, and accidents? Should behaviors be aggregated to the group level, and, if so, what behaviors should have most influence at this level?

In terms of cognitive error behavior, Larson, Alderton, Neideffer, and Underhill (1997) found that CFQ score was associated with what they called "composite mishaps," defined as an accident- or injury-caused hospitalization or serious fall. However, when these were split there were CFQ differences between those involved in a fall or hospitalized, but not for accident involvement. More compelling evidence for a link between CFQ scores and accidents comes from Wallace and Vodanovich (2003), who showed a significant positive association between the CFQ and self-reported involvement in injuries requiring treatment but not time off work. Wallace and Chen (2005) also showed that the common factor from their WCFS scale predicted a similar measure of accident involvement. Neither of these studies was ideal from a validity standpoint, since accident involvement over the previous three years was asked for, whereas the CFQ and WCFS asks for errors over the previous six months. The difference in time spans is less important if the CFQ is used as an indicator of trait-like disposition to error, as assumed by the authors, but becomes more crucial for interpreting the scales as cognitive error measures. The validity of the latter approach therefore is still open, but has interesting possibilities for future research.

Given the analysis of the validity of behavioral measures above, only those questionnaire studies that relate organizational and individual factors to an accident outcome are considered in the present chapter. Studies that have only behavioral or other safety performance outcome measures are not reviewed unless the behaviors have been shown to relate to accidents in other studies.

Organizational practices and accidents

This section considers whether organizational practices affect organizational and work-group accident rates. Wagenaar, Hudson, and Reason (1990: 274) discuss their retrospective analysis of accidents within the framework of "a generalized causation scenario, which describes how all accidents originate." The final event in a scenario is an accident, and is preceded by unsafe acts. Defense mechanisms built into the system prevent most unsafe acts becoming accidents. Unsafe acts have their "immediate origins" in psychological states of mind or patterns of reasoning which the authors called psychological precursors. The latter are elicited by the physical and organizational environment, identified by the authors as General Failure Types (GFTs), that are created by management decisions.

Wagenaar et al. (1990) defined a limited number of General Failure Types (GFTs), based on features of an operation that have been wrong for some time but remain unrecognized as problematic until implicated in an accident, and which promote cognitive precursors to unsafe acts. The types were defined "somewhat arbitrarily, but after reading and analyzing hundreds of accident scenarios" (p. 287). The GFTs were grouped into three broad categories: physical environment (including design failures, missing defenses, hardware defects, negligent housekeeping, and error-enforcing conditions), human behavior (including poor procedures and defective training), and management (including organizational failures, incompatible goals, and lack of communication). For example, error-enforcing conditions were those that "force people to operate in a manner not foreseen by the system designers" (Wagenaar et al., 1990: 289), including working under extreme time pressure or with a lack of qualified personnel. Organizational failure was considered to lead to a lack of planning, inappropriate plans, loss of motivation, and obstruction, and generally to a culture in which safety is no longer an important goal. Wagenaar, Groeneweg, Hudson, and Reason (1994: 2001) refined the types to include failures in maintenance, giving eleven types where the "frequencies of occurrence of failures in the eleven classes are essentially independent."

Salminen, Saari, Saarela, and Räsänen (1993) analyzed interviews with injured workers, foremen, and co-workers involved in serious accidents in southern Finland. Their results suggested that the need to save time, working to tight schedules, and a lack of caution had a greater influence on accidents than the foremen, co-workers, customers, or wage system. In addition, accident risk was significantly greater for subcontractors.

Shannon, Mayr, and Haines (1997) reviewed studies that included at least twenty workplaces and looked for factors in at least two studies that were consistently associated with injury rates (represented by workers' compensation rates, that is, the frequency of claims for injury-related compensation), a measure which ignores injury severity. Ten studies were used in all. Organizational factors associated with injury outcomes could be grouped under management style and culture (including empowerment of the workforce and good relations between management and workforce), organizational philosophy on health and safety (including delegation of safety activities, training, and an active role in health and safety of top management), good housekeeping, and safety controls on machinery. Shannon *et al.* (1997) noted, however, that the strength of their conclusions was limited by the nature of the studies: response rates were modest; several studies had not been published in peer review journals; most studies did not report their power to detect important associations; quantitative pooling of the data was not possible; and different sets of variables were studied, using different questionnaires.

Kaminski (2001: 127) noted that there was "little empirical work to date that examines the relationship between organizational practices and safety across a large number of organizations." She collected data from eighty-six manufacturing firms, mostly from the Midwest of the USA, by questionnaires completed by plant operators, human resource managers or both. All firms included in her analysis had more than fifty employees. Six management practices were investigated: performance-based pay, temporary employees, hours worked per week, amount of formal training per year, whether any employees were in teams, and the percentage of employees who worked on a production line. In her analysis, Kaminski controlled for unionization and, interestingly, for industry injury rate on the basis that some industries are more hazardous than others. Performance-based pay was a positive predictor, and hours per week, training, and team were negative predictors.

Vredenburgh (2002) reported on sixty-two hospitals, ranging in size from fifty-five to six thousand employees, in the US healthcare sector. She examined the relationship between rewards for reporting safety hazards, safety training, selecting those with a good safety record, communication/feedback on incidents and unsafe behaviors, worker participation in safety decisions, and management commitment to safety. The management practices Vredenburgh included in her study were derived from reports on safety culture by practitioners and experts, rather than from research results. The management practices thus identified were measured using a questionnaire sent to a person performing the role of risk management in each hospital. Her outcome measure was a combination of injury frequency over three years weighted by expert-rated severity of outcome. She found that, as a whole, the management practices accounted for 16.5% of the variance in safety outcome in her sample, and that the only practice that predicted the safety outcome was hiring practices related to safety.

Hoonakker *et al.* (2005) looked at the longitudinal effect of safety initiatives on an objective measure of safety performance related to company claims for injuries in the construction industry in the USA. Safety performance was measured at two time points four years apart. Of the 209 companies that responded, most were "small-size" employing fewer than twenty people, with nearly half of them employing fewer than five people. Safety initiatives were measured by a set of questions. (Does your company have written policy on safety? Is there a safety committee in your company? Is there a required safety training program for new employees? Do you have regularly scheduled safety meetings?) The authors found that while larger companies generally had safety initiatives in place, less than 20% of small-size companies had any kind of safety initiatives. These findings support the observations made in the report by de Beeck and van Heuverswyn (2002). Further, companies reporting regularly scheduled safety meetings at time one, compared to those companies that did not, had better safety performance four years later. The results for the other initiatives were non-significant.

Zacharatos, Barling, and Iverson (2005) identified ten practices and defined them collectively as constituting a high-performance work system (HPWS). The practices were employment security, selective hiring, extensive training, self-managed teams and decentralized decision-making, reduced status distinctions, information sharing, compensation contingent on safe performance, transformational leadership, high-quality work, and measurement of management practices. In their study, human resource directors in 138 (of 1,471 who were approached) manufacturing organizations completed questions about the extent to which they thought a practice existed in their organizations, and estimated the percentage of employees to which a high-commitment practice applied. Practices were combined into a single index measuring a HPWS. HR directors further reported the number of lost-time injuries and number of days lost due to eight specific types of injuries ranging from fractures to superficial wounds. The HPWS index predicted an additional 8% of the variance in lost-time injuries after controlling for the nature, size, and age of the organizations.

Zohar (1980) developed a concept of safety climate that has been influential since. His starting point was the view that climate measures be based on "perceptions held by employees about aspects of their organizational environment, summarized over individual employees" (p. 96). Through a literature review with the purpose "to define organizational characteristics that differentiate between high versus low accident-rate companies" (p. 97), he identified companies with good accident records as having several features: management demonstrated a commitment to safety (for example, top management was involved in routine safety activities, safety was given high priority at company meetings and in production scheduling, and safety officers had a higher status); safety training was given importance; open communication and frequent contact between management and workers was higher; there was good housekeeping, for instance through orderly plant operations and use of safety devices; safety promotion was through guidance and counseling rather than enforcement and admonition, and included individual praise or recognition for safe performance; and low accident companies had a stable workforce, with less turnover and older workers.

Zohar (1980) developed a questionnaire to measure these organizational aspects through workforce perceptions. Eight dimensions were identified: importance of safety training programs; management attitudes to safety; effects of safe conduct on promotion; level of risk in the workplace; pace of work demands related to safety; status of the safety officer; the effects of safe conduct on social status; and status of the safety committee. The questionnaire was given to a stratified Israeli sample of production workers in metal fabrication, food processing, chemicals, and textiles factories. Variance in individual scores within factories was found to be significantly smaller than variance between factories, thus supporting the idea that each factory could be considered to have a safety climate representing a fairly homogeneous set of shared perceptions among employees. Four experienced safety inspectors ranked factories according to their safety practices and accident-prevention programs. The textiles and three other factories could not be ranked. However, the agreement between the rankings for the remainder and their safety climate scores was high (metal and chemicals) to moderate (food processing), providing support for the validity of the safety climate questionnaire.

Subsequent research on organizational safety climate has concentrated on the number and nature of the dimensions involved, but has not led to a universal consensus (Brown and Holmes, 1986; Cooper and Philips, 2004; Dedobbeleer and Beland, 1991; Mueller, DaSilva, Townsend and Tetrick, 1999, cited in Wiegmann, Zhang and von Thaden, 2001). A key aspect of safety climate that emerges from these analyses is management's relationship to safety, and in particular the perception that management is committed to safety. This factor is seen as a central component of most safety climate measures (see e.g. Flin, Mearns, O'Connor, and Bryden, 2000), and has been shown to affect more than just safety outcomes (Michael, Evans, Jansen, and Haight, 2005).

Considerable conceptual clarity was brought to this situation by Griffin and Neal (2000), who referenced conceptualizations of both general organizational climate and specific types of climate to provide a basis for defining the key features of safety climate. They proposed that climate is considered as a higher-order factor comprised of more specific first-order factors, and that these reflect perceptions of safety-related policies, procedures, and rewards. The higher-order factor reflects the extent to which employees believe that safety is valued within the organization, which appears akin to management commitment to safety (Zohar and Luria, 2005). In contrast, ratings of risk, affective reactions to safety issues, normative beliefs about safety, and self-reports of safety behavior, they argued, should not be considered to be perceptions of safety climate. Griffin and Neal suggested that in "determining the overall impact of safety climate on safety outcomes, a higher order factor of safety climate will be most appropriate" (2000: 348). Taking a similar view, and using items covering the range of activities outlined in the British Standards Institute's (2000) safety management code to measure safety climate, Zohar and Luria (2005) showed a significant association between organizational safety climate scores and organizational safety as measured through a safety audit procedure carried out by a senior safety inspector and three observers. The audit did not include accident outcomes. However, Probst, Brubaker, and Barsotti (2006) reported on thirty-eight contractor companies working on a large construction project. Their findings showed that companies with a weak safety climate had many more recordable injuries compared to those with a strong climate.

A summary of organizational-level analysis is that a number of organizational aspects could be related to safety outcomes but this is mainly based on expert opinion and experience. Some management practices have been linked empirically with safety outcome, but the results are suggestive rather than conclusive, and indicate they may only explain a very modest amount of the variance in injuries. Safety climate has been associated with expert ratings of safety, and, only recently, injury rate.

Workgroups and accidents

In an extension from organizations to teams within organizations, Hofmann and Stetzer (1996) found that safety climate – as measured using

Dedobbeleer and Beland's (1991) scales, but analyzed using individual perceptions aggregated to the group level – was negatively correlated with group-level major accidents.

Zohar (2000) conceptualized the notion of a group safety climate related to supervisory practices and developed two scales to measure it. The action scale referred to overt supervisory reaction to subordinates' conduct and the initiation of action concerning safety issues. The expectation scale referred to non-commensurate task facets, mostly related to safety versus productivity. The safety outcome was objective records of micro-accidents. Micro-accidents were defined as on-the-job behavior-dependent minor injuries requiring medical attention, but not incurring any lost workdays. Fifty-three workgroups of production workers in a metal-processing plant were studied. To obtain group-level measures Zohar divided the number of micro-accidents per group by the group size. Zohar found that both action and expectation scales added significant prediction to group-level micro-accident rate once risk was controlled for. Wallace, Popp, and Mondore (2006), studying delivery drivers from a large multinational shipping and transportation company, found supervisory safety climate, measured with a combination of expectation and action scales, predicted driving accidents harming equipment or people.

Zohar (2002) used group-level micro-accidents as a dependent variable in an intervention study designed to change supervisory practices in relation to safety. Participants in the study were in thirty-six workgroups in a maintenance center specializing in repair and upgrading of heavy-duty equipment. Eighteen workgroups were assigned to the experimental condition and eighteen groups acted as controls. He found that following the intervention the experimental workgroups had a significantly lower injury rate than the control groups, and that climate scores had also changed in the expected direction for both action and expectancy scores. Zohar and Luria (2003) further showed that interventions at the supervisory level in an oil refinery, a food processing company, and a milk processing company produced improvements in safety-related behaviors, and, in the oil refinery where it was measured, increases in workgroup safety climate scores.

Neal and Griffin (2006) showed in thirty-three groups of employees from a single Australian hospital that group safety climate significantly predicted later safety motivation and safety participation, but not safety compliance. Interestingly, although they found associations between group safety climate and accidents in one of the years they studied, the effect was non-significant in another year. They found that safety climate did not predict later accidents, although they noted that the power to detect effects at the group level in their study was low. Intriguingly, earlier accident rate predicted later accident rate.

In sum, the concept of a workgroup climate for safety appears fruitful for understanding accident outcomes, and it may mediate organizational safety climate (Zohar and Luria, 2005). Supervisors appear to play a major role in workgroup climate. It will be interesting to see in future research whether other organizational players, for example co-workers, are also influential.

Individuals and safety

Research at the group and organizational level strongly implicates safety climate in accidents. Safety climate measures at these levels consist of aggregated individual perceptions. At the individual level the question is whether unaggregated individual perceptions, often called "perceived safety climate," are related to individual accident involvement. This question is one among several that ask whether perceptions of workplace factors such as climate, job characteristics, workload, and the like relate to injury.

Organizational factors and safety outcomes

Safety climate and leadership Griffin and Neal (2000) and Neal and Griffin (2000) used earlier theories of individual work performance to propose a relationship between safety climate and behavior. Their theorizing proposes that there are task and contextual components of safety performance (safety compliance and participation respectively), and that these are preceded by determinants of safety performance, argued to be limited to knowledge, skill, and motivation. The antecedents of safety performance, which can be at the individual or organizational level, are proposed to affect safety performance by acting through the determinants. In this framework safety climate thus is an antecedent. Griffin and Neal (2000) demonstrated that a structural model that had safety climate acting on safety performance through safety motivation and knowledge fitted their data well. It is interesting to note their model is similar in topology to the general accident causation scenario.

Barling et al. (2002), in a study of 164 young Canadian people, mainly in the service sector, showed a direct link between safety climate and self-reported frequency of injury involvement. They also reported significant links between transformational leadership and perceived safety climate, and role overload and safety climate. Kelloway, Mullen, and Francis (2006) extended these findings, showing that safety-specific transformational leadership and passive leadership predicted injuries, and safety climate. In their structural model, leadership styles had effects directly on safety climate, and indirectly through safety consciousness, and safety climate related to injuries through safety events.

Zacharatos *et al.* (2005), in their second study, used data from 189 employees from two Canadian organizations from the petroleum and telecommunications industries. They used a set of high-performance work system (HPWS) items somewhat different from their first study discussed above, that emphasized employees' perceptions of the extent to which HPWS practices had been adopted by their organization, and a measure of some safety climate dimensions amongst other measures. They asked employees to report the incidence of injury requiring first aid during the last six months. The only two significant correlations with first-aid injuries were a composite HPSW index and a trust in management scale. When self-reported injuries were combined with near misses, confirmatory analyses showed safety climate significantly and directly related to safety outcome, and to what the authors called personal safety orientation, which consisted of items relating to safety motivation, knowledge, and behavior. HPWS was directly related to safety climate. In a study of UK chemical production workers, Chmiel (2005) found that perceived safety climate predicted involvement in minor injury outcomes. Thus the evidence points to perceived safety climate as an important element in individual safety.

Job-related factors Barling, Kelloway, and Iverson (2003) used archival data from the Australian 1995 Workplace Industrial Relations Survey. Their sample size was 16,466 employees. They defined high-quality work as measured through extent of training received, task variety, and autonomy. Occupational injuries were measured through responses to whether employees had experienced an injury in the past year. Those who reported an injury were asked about the number of days they had off as a result: 7.2% had experienced an injury requiring no time off work, and 6.3% an injury requiring one or more days away from work. Results showed perceptions of high-quality work predicted occupational injury directly, and through job satisfaction; higher job satisfaction and high-quality work were associated with less injury. Turner *et al.* (2005) found that safety role definitions were related to job demands and job control, where job control had a positive relationship and job demands a negative relationship with safety role definitions. Interestingly the interaction between job control and demands was significant, indicating that low control and high demands were associated with lower safety role definitions. Parker *et al.* (2001) found job autonomy predicted safety compliance behavior and Chmiel (2005) found job control predicted involvement in minor injury; higher control decreased the odds of being involved.

Support from colleagues or supervisors Iverson and Erwin (1997), in a sample of 362 blue-collar production and assembly workers, found that supervisory and co-worker support predicted whether a worker had been injured or not in the twelve months following the survey; more support predicted fewer injuries. Injuries were defined as those resulting in physical incapacitation, absence from work, and compensation paid to the injured worker; 7.5% of their sample fell into this category. Parker *et al.* (2001) found that, in a sample of 161 shop-floor workers, supportive (not safety-related) supervision positively predicted later safe working.

Oliver, Cheyne, Tomas, and Cox (2002), analyzing data from 525 Spanish workers from a wide range of industrial sectors, found support for direct links between organizational involvement in safety and accidents, where a greater involvement predicted fewer accidents. Organizational involvement included indicators of safety management and policy, supervisors' safety support and behavior, and co-workers safety support and behavior. Accident indicators included major and minor accidents and near misses.

New technology and mental work

Chmiel (1998) has categorized the history of technological change at work since the industrial revolution into three phases, namely power provision, automation of function, and information and control of process. The third phase, the change from traditional to computerized technologies, has involved the extensive use of computers to control technology. For example, the 1990 Workplace Industrial Relations Survey in the UK showed that 75% of work establishments had some kind of on-site computing facility compared to 47% in 1984, and that, for workplaces with non-manual employees, 52% had experienced technological change in the previous three years. McLoughlin and Clark (1994) propose that the net effect of recent technological change is that the nature of work has shifted from physical to mental labor. Thus the importance of cognitive errors in safety related to new technology has increased as a result. Case studies also highlight the involvement of organizational conditions in disasters involving technology (Reason, 1990). Modern computer-based systems have become part of organization- and workplace-wide control systems, where one person's error may not affect them directly at all, but may cause a safety problem for someone else. To some extent the effects for accidents will depend on the complexity of the system and how tightly linked the processes and people involved are (Perrow, 1994). Thus, in the round, new technology may lead not only to cognitive error becoming important in more industrial settings, but also to such error having the potential for a large impact at the group, system, or organizational level.

Currently, to the author's knowledge there are no questionnaire-based studies at the individual level reporting on organizational and psychological antecedents to cognitive error similar to those for other behaviors. The direct interaction between people and technologies is well researched and could be understood from a safety perspective by reference to the work on human error. Future questionnaire studies are likely to have greatest impact in investigating how new technologies alter work patterns, communications, allocation of responsibilities for safety, and the formation of functional groups beyond single organizations and formally defined groups within them.

Conclusions

Several things become clear when considering the questionnaire-based approach evident in the work and organizational psychology research literature on safety in light of the work done in the second age of safety on the retrospective analyses of accident scenarios and human error. The first is that the topology of accident causation is remarkably similar in the two approaches, and thus potentially fruitful as a guide to future research and more detailed understanding of the elements involved. The second is that the framework is useful in organizing the contributions of the various questionnaire-based studies done to date. The third is that far more concentration has been given to linking organizational factors to accident outcomes in the questionnaire studies than to the relationships between organizational factors, psychological precursors or states, and the behaviors involved. The fourth is that the types of questionnaire-based behavioral measures used to predict accident outcomes need further consideration with respect to their validity. The fifth is that more work needs to be done on identifying the psychological states that predict the types of behaviors that predict accident involvement. Sixth, it is clear that studies differ in the type of accident outcome predicted. It is possible that the antecedents of minor versus major injury differ, and so these outcomes would be better distinguished in future research. Seventh, different behaviors may be differentially important at different levels of analysis, for example the workgroup versus the individual level. A related point is whether it is appropriate to aggregate individual accidents to a workgroup level when considering how people working together interact to produce an accident that potentially affects them all. In short, the nature of the workgroup outcome criterion deserves further attention. Eighth, the role of accident exposure is a neglected aspect in questionnaire studies but affects the interpretation of accident frequency data and so should be addressed in future studies.

Has progress been made in producing insights into safety in the third age through questionnaire-based approaches? Undoubtedly the answer to this question must be yes – for at least two reasons that should be clear from the review of the studies presented in this chapter. One reason is that safety climate as a measure of perceptions of organizational factors related to safety has emerged as a key explanatory construct, and questionnaires make it possible to consider related variables in a systematic and principled way. A second reason is the important identification and examination of behaviors like safety participation and other aspects of safety citizenship that may turn out to be central to explanations of workgroup functioning and safety.

Finally, are we, as work and organizational psychologists, in a position to provide some advice based on questionnaire studies on the safety issues raised by the experts in connection with modern work (de Beeck and van Heuverswyn, 2002)? Recall that the report suggested modern work and its influence on accident prevention involves greater free-market, privatization and downsizing, changes in technology, changes in working hours, work pace, and workload, a growth of sub-contracting, more service work, an increase in part-time jobs and temporary work, more women, an aging workforce, and greater globalization and integration of work.

In terms of the broad categories outlined at the beginning of the chapter we can say that some organizational practices make a difference, but at the moment the difference does not appear that great. Selection and training practices may have some effect, as may scheduling regular safety meetings and other high-performance work practices. These aspects are better represented in larger companies and may therefore place the management structures of small companies at a disadvantage. However, such companies can take to heart that the effects discovered to date have appeared modest. In contrast, the effect of safety climate has appeared much more important and pervasive for accident involvement, and safety climate reflects management values, commitment, and attitudes to safety as manifest through policies, procedures, rewards, and practices. Thus management commitment to safety can be manifested in a variety of ways and through leadership style and action. Identifying these ways for effective safety in small companies without developed organizational structures would appear to be the way forward.

In similar vein it is likely to be safety climate that holds the key to preserving safety standards through privatization and downsizing initiatives, although other aspects are likely to be important too. One or two studies have shown that job control is a potential factor for safety behavior and accidents. Greater control has been shown to predict increased safety behavior and fewer accidents. Intriguingly, it is plausible that safety in response to increased work pace and workload may be moderated by job control in a way similar to that of work stress. The results from Turner *et al.* (2005), indicating that the interaction of high job demands and low control is associated with lower safety role definitions, is consistent with this perspective. Less clear at present are the effects of an aging workforce on safety, the growth in service work, subcontracting, and temporary work patterns, and what the important organizational and psychological variables will be in these instances.

Lastly it is likely that increasing globalization and integration of work will create an increased likelihood that work systems will become more complex and linked, raising the importance of cognitive error on the one hand, and a need for system-level analysis of accident causality beyond single organizations or workgroups on the other. Accident analyses have been in the forefront of providing understanding of the latter; questionnaire-based approaches have yet to make a significant contribution, but have considerable potential to do so.

References

Barling, J., Kelloway, E. K., and Iverson, R. D. (2003). High-quality work, job satisfaction, and occupational injuries. *Journal of Applied Psychology* 88: 276–83.

Barling, J., Loughlin, C., and Kelloway, E. K. (2002). Development and test of a model linking safety specific transformational leadership and occupational safety. *Journal of Applied Psychology* 87: 488–96.

British Standards Institute (2000). *Occupational Health and Safety Management Systems: Guidelines for the Implementation of OHSAS 18001* (Publication No. BSI-02-2000). London: British Standards Institute.

Broadbent, D. E., Broadbent, M. H. P., and Jones, J. L. (1986). Performance correlates of self-reported cognitive failure and of obsessionality. *British Journal of Clinical Psychology* 25: 285–99.

Broadbent, D. E., Cooper, P. J., Fitzgerald, P. F., and Parkes, K. R. (1982). The Cognitive Failures Questionnaire (CFQ) and its correlates. *British Journal of Clinical Psychology* 21: 1–16.

Brown, I. (1990). Accident reporting and analysis. In J. R. Wilson and E. N. Corlett (eds.), *Evaluation of Human Work* (pp. 969–92). London: Taylor and Francis.

Brown, R. L. and Holmes, H. (1986). The use of a factor-analytic procedure for assessing the validity of an employee safety climate model. *Accident Analysis and Prevention* 18: 445–70.

Burke, M. J., Sarpy, S. A., Tesluk, P. E., and Smith-Crowe, K. (2002). General safety performance: a test of a grounded theoretical model. *Personnel Psychology* 55: 429–57.

Chapman, R. (1973). The concept of exposure. *Accident Analysis and Prevention* 5: 95–110.

Cheyne, A., Cox, S., Oliver, A., and Tomas, J. M. (1998). Modelling safety climate in the prediction of safety activity. *Work and Stress* 12: 255–71.

Chmiel, N. (1998). *Jobs, technology and people*. London: Routledge.

(2005). Promoting healthy work: self-reported minor injuries, work characteristics, and safety behaviour. In C. Korunka and P. Hoffman (eds.), *Change and quality in human service work* (pp. 277–88). Munich and Mering: Rainer Hampp Verlag.

Clarke, S. (1998). Organizational factors affecting the incident reporting of train drivers. *Work and Stress* 12: 6–16.

(2006). The relationship between safety climate and safety performance: a meta-analytic review. *Journal of Occupational Health Psychology* 11: 315–27.

Cooper, M. D. and Phillips, R. A. (2004). Exploratory analysis of the safety climate and safety behavior relationship. *Journal of Safety Research* 35: 497–512.

de Beeck, R. and van Heuverswyn, K. (2002). *European Agency for Safety and Health at Work: new trends in accident prevention due to the changing world of work*. Luxemburg: Office for Official Publications of the European Communities.

Dedobbeleer, N. and Beland, F. (1991). A safety climate measure for construction sites. *Journal of Safety Research* 22: 97–103.

DeJoy, D. M. (1985). Attributional processes and hazard control management in industry. *Journal of Safety Research* 16: 61–71.

DeJoy, D. M., Searcy, C. A., Murphy, L. R., and Gershon, R. R. M. (2000). Behavioral-diagnostic analysis of compliance with universal precautions among nurses. *Journal of Occupational Health Psychology* 5: 127–41.

Flin, R., Mearns, K., O'Connor, P., and Bryden, R. (2000). Measuring safety climate: identifying the common features. *Safety Science* 34: 177–92.

Frone, M. R. (1998). Predictors of work injuries among employed adolescents. *Journal of Applied Psychology* 83: 565–76.

Griffin, M. A. and Neal, N. (2000). Perceptions of safety at work: a framework for linking safety climate to safety performance, knowledge, and motivation. *Journal of Occupational Health Psychology* 5: 347–58.

Hale, A. R. and Hovden, J. (1998). Management and culture: the third age of safety. A review of approaches to organizational aspects of safety, health, and environment. In A.-M. Feyer and A. Williamson (eds.), *Occupational injury: risk, prevention and intervention* (pp. 129–66). London: Taylor and Francis.

Hodge, G. A. and Richardson, A. J. (1985). The role of accident exposure in transport system safety evaluations I: intersection and link site exposure. *Journal of Advanced Transportation* 19: 179–213.

Hofmann, D. A., Jacobs, R., and Landy, F. (1995). High reliability process industries: individual micro, and macro organizational influences on safety performance. *Journal of Safety Research* 26: 131–49.

Hofmann, D. A., Morgeson, F. P., and Gerras, S. J. (2003). Climate as a moderator of the relationship between leader–member exchange and content specific citizenship: safety climate as an exemplar. *Journal of Applied Psychology* 88: 170–8.

Hofmann, D. A. and Stetzer, A. (1996). A cross-level investigation of factors influencing unsafe behaviors and accidents. *Personnel Psychology* 49: 307–39.

Hoonakker, P., Loushine, T., Carayon, P., Kallman, J., Kapp, A., and Smith, M. J. (2005). The effect of safety initiatives on safety performance: a longitudinal study. *Applied Ergonomics* 36: 461–9.

Iverson, R. D. and Erwin, P. J. (1997). Predicting occupational injury: the role of affectivity. *Journal of Occupational and Organizational Psychology* 70: 113–28.

Jacinto, C. and Aspinwall, E. (2004). A survey on occupational accidents' reporting and registration systems in the European Union. *Safety Science* 42: 933–60.

Kaminski, M. (2001). Unintended consequences: organizational practices and their impact on workplace safety and productivity. *Journal of Occupational Health Psychology* 6: 127–38.

Kelloway, E. K., Mullen, J., and Francis, L. (2006). Divergent effects of transformational and passive leadership on employee safety. *Journal of Occupational Health Psychology* 11: 76–86.

Larson, G. E., Alderton, D. L., Neideffer, M., and Underhill, E. (1997). Further evidence on the dimensionality and correlates of the Cognitive Failures Questionnaire. *British Journal of Psychology* 88: 29–38.

McLoughlin, I. and Clark, J. (1994). *Technological change at work* (2nd edn). Buckingham: Open University Press.

Michael, J. H., Evans, D. D., Jansen, K. J., and Haight, J. M. (2005). Management commitment to safety as organizational support: relationships with non-safety outcomes in wood manufacturing employees. *Journal of Safety Research* 36: 171–9.

Mueller, L., DaSilva, N., Townsend, J., and Tetrick, L. (1999). An empirical evaluation of competing safety climate measurement models. Paper presented at the annual meeting of the Society for Industrial and Organizational Psychology, Atlanta, GA.

Neal, A. and Griffin, M. A. (2006). A study of the lagged relationships among safety climate, safety motivation, safety behavior, and accidents at the individual and group levels. *Journal of Applied Psychology* 91: 946–53.

Neal, A., Griffin, M. A., and Hart, P. M. (2000). The impact of organizational climate on safety climate and individual behavior. *Safety Science* 34: 99–109.

Oliver, A., Cheyne, A., Tomas, J. M., and Cox, S. (2002). The effects of organizational and individual factors on occupational accidents. *Journal of Occupational and Organizational Psychology* 75: 473–88.

Parker, S., Axtell, C., and Turner, N. (2001). Designing a safer workplace: importance of job autonomy, communication quality, and supportive supervisors. *Journal of Occupational Health Psychology* 6: 211–28.

Perrow, C. (1994). Accidents in high risk systems. *Technology Studies Offprint* 1: 1–20.

Probst, T. M., Brubaker, T. L., and Barsotti, A. (2006). Organizational injury rate under-reporting: the moderating effect of organizational safety climate.

Paper presented to the Society of Industrial and Organizational Psychology, Dallas, Texas.

Reason, J. T. (1990). *Human error*. Cambridge: Cambridge University Press.

(1993). Self-report questionnaires in cognitive psychology: have they delivered the goods? In A. Baddeley and L. Weiskrantz (eds.), *Attention: selection, awareness, and control – a tribute to Donald Broadbent* (pp. 406–23). Oxford: Oxford University Press.

(1997). *Managing the risks of organizational accidents*. Aldershot: Ashgate.

Reason, J. T., Parker, D., and Lawton, R. (1998). Organizational controls and safety: the varieties of rule-related behaviour. *Journal of Occupational and Organizational Psychology* 71: 289–304.

Salminen, S., Saari, J., Saarela, K. L., and Räsänen, T. (1993). Organizational factors influencing occupational accidents. *Scandinavian Journal of Work Environment and Health* 19: 352–7.

Salminen, S. and Tallberg, T. (1996). Human errors in fatal and serious occupational accidents in Finland. *Ergonomics* 39: 980–8.

Shannon, H. S., Mayr, J., and Haines, T. (1997). Overview of the relationship between organizational and workplace factors and injury rates. *Safety Science* 26: 201–17.

Sheehy, N. and Chapman, A. (1987). Industrial accidents. In C. L. Cooper and I. T. Robertson (eds.), *International review of industrial and organizational psychology*. Oxford: Wiley.

Thompson, R., Hilton, T., and Witt, L. (1998). Where the safety rubber meets the shop floor: a confirmatory model of management influence on workplace safety. *Journal of Safety Research* 29: 15–24.

Turner, N., Chmiel, N., and Walls, M. (2005). Railing for safety: job demands, job control, and safety citizenship role definitions. *Journal of Occupational Health Psychology* 10: 504–12.

van der Schaaf, T. and Kanse, L. (2004). Biases in incident reporting databases: an empirical study in the chemical process industry. *Safety Science* 42: 57–67.

Vredenburgh, A. G. (2002). Organizational safety: which management practices are most effective in reducing employee injury rates? *Journal of Safety Research* 33: 259–76.

Wagenaar, W. A. and Groeneweg, J. (1987). Accidents at sea: multiple causes and impossible consequences. *International Journal of Man-Machine Studies* 27: 587–98.

Wagenaar, W. A., Groeneweg, J., Hudson, P. T. W., and Reason, J. T. (1994). Promoting safety in the oil industry. *Ergonomics* 37: 1999–2013.

Wagenaar, W. A., Hudson, P. T. W., and Reason, J. T. (1990). Cognitive failures and accidents. *Applied Cognitive Psychology* 4: 273–94.

Wallace, J. C. and Chen, G. (2005). Development and validation of a work-specific measure of cognitive failure: implications for occupational safety. *Journal of Occupational and Organizational Psychology* 78: 615–32.

Wallace, J. C., Popp, E., and Mondore, S. (2006). Safety climate as a mediator between foundation climates and occupational accidents: a group-level investigation. *Journal of Applied Psychology* 91: 681–8.

Wallace, J. C. and Vodanovich, S. J. (2003). Workplace safety performance: conscientiousness, cognitive failure, and their interaction. *Journal of Occupational Health Psychology* 8: 316–27.

Weddle, M. G. (1996). Reporting occupational injuries: the first step. *Journal of Safety Research* 27: 217–33.

Westaby, J. D. and Lee, B. C. (2003). Antecedents of injury among youth in agricultural settings: a longitudinal examination of safety consciousness, dangerous risk taking, and safety knowledge. *Journal of Safety Research* 34: 227–40.

Wiegmann, D. A., Zhang, H., and von Thaden, T. (2001). *Defining and assessing safety culture in high reliability systems: an annotated bibliography.* Technical report ARL-01-12/FAA-01-4, Aviation Research Lab, Institute of Aviation, University of Illinois.

Zacharatos, A., Barling, J., and Iverson, R. D. (2005). High-performance work systems and occupational safety. *Journal of Applied Psychology* 90: 77–93.

Zohar, D. (1980). Safety climate in industrial organizations: theoretical and applied implications. *Journal of Applied Psychology* 65: 96–102.

(2000). A group-level model of safety climate: testing the effect of group climate on microaccidents in manufacturing jobs. *Journal of Applied Psychology* 85: 587–96.

(2002). Modifying supervisory practices to improve subunit safety: a leadership-based intervention model. *Journal of Applied Psychology* 87: 156–63.

Zohar, D. and Luria, G. (2003). The use of supervisory practices as leverage to improve safety behavior: a cross-level intervention model. *Journal of Safety Research* 34: 567–77.

(2005). A multilevel model of safety climate: cross-level relationships between organizational and group-level climates. *Journal of Applied Psychology* 90: 616–28.

10 Romantic relationships at work: old issues, new challenges

Jennifer Carson and Julian Barling

> Sex and romance develop in offices because that's where the people are. Men and women ... are likely to get together in ways not mentioned in the corporate policy manual. (Horn and Horn, 1982: 83)

Over the past several decades, increasing numbers of individuals have been meeting their significant others at work. This means that in addition to professional relationships and social friendships in the workplace, romantic relationships are adding another dynamic into workplace interactions. Indeed, conditions in today's workplace are such that romantic relationships may well be inevitable. Given this, managers can take one of two approaches. The first and most frequent approach is to focus on preventing such relationships and their potentially negative consequences. However, a more recent development in the organizational literature provides a new perspective for how organizations view their employees; positive psychology and positive organizational behavior suggest that work experiences can promote mental health (Turner, Barling, and Zacharatos, 2002). Thus, the second approach changes the practitioner's primary focus from the costs of romantic relationships at work to include potential benefits. At a time when organizations are increasingly focusing on employee health, organizations may find ways to promote positive mental health gains (and limit any damage) for their employees through supporting romantic relationships.

Consistent with this new perspective, the purpose of this chapter is twofold. First, we provide an overview of the nature, development, and potential outcomes of romantic relationships at work, and how these outcomes are influenced by the internal relationship dynamics, organizational environment, and the management interventions or responses used in the face of workplace relationships. Second, we offer a way of thinking about romantic relationships at work that is consistent with current organizational and societal realities. Our thinking is guided by two fundamental assumptions: romantic relationships at work (a) are inevitable, and (b) can have positive benefits for well-being.

Development of romantic relationships at work

Sternberg (1986) characterizes love – the cornerstone of a romantic relationship – as consisting of three main components: intimacy, passion, and commitment. Research has identified several factors that are important in the development of love in general, all of which have considerable importance in the organizational context. Specifically, the opportunity to interact, repeated exposure, attitude similarity, and desire to foster a romantic relationship are precursors to romantic relationships (Pierce, Byrne, and Aguinis, 1996). It is not surprising, then, that at least a third of relationships begin in the workplace (Bordwin, 1994), as it is likely that these factors will be present.

Proximity

To begin, the opportunity for interaction is a necessary precursor for a romantic relationship (Horn and Horn, 1982; Paul and Townsend, 1998). Surveying individuals in a New York airport, Quinn (1977) found that three types of proximity create opportunities for interaction in the workplace. This is critical because "without the opportunity for interaction, there can be no opportunity for attraction" (Byrne and Neuman, 1992: 32). The first is ongoing geographic proximity. For example, with employees' workstations being ever closer together, employees are enjoying better opportunities for close interactions. The second proximity criterion involves interrelated work tasks. Working interdependently maximizes opportunities for socialization (e.g. training, teamwork, business trips, meetings). The third type of proximity that facilitates interaction is occasional contact. Encountering other employees (e.g. in elevators, at meetings) provides opportunities for interaction (Pierce *et al.*, 1996). Thus, the increasing proximity that characterizes current workplaces heightens the likelihood of romantic relationships at work.

Repeated exposure

By itself, however, opportunities for interaction may be insufficient. But having this occur repeatedly substantially increases the likelihood of a workplace romance. When people work together and see each other regularly, research shows that it is more likely they will become attracted to one another (Pierce *et al.*, 1996).

Liking

In addition to proximity and repeated exposure, employees must also share similar attitudes, and want to foster and engage in a romantic relationship. Perceived similarity in attitudes can result in liking (Pierce *et al.*, 1996); "liking" is clearly a precursor to romantic relationships when both parties are interested in fostering a relationship. This involves a mutual sexual attraction, and both parties wanting to be in a romantic relationship (Mainiero, 1986).

By its very nature, then, the workplace environment would encourage the development of romantic relationships. In fact, recent changes in the nature of work and workplaces mean that the likelihood of developing romantic relationships at work may be more pronounced today than in the workplace of yesteryear. Today's workplaces are characterized by a blurring of the work–life and work–family balance for many; teamwork, flexitime, overtime, teleworking, shift work, frequent short-term travel, and longer-term overseas postings due to globalization can cause the boundaries of work and personal life to overlap. In addition, North American data show that younger people are focusing more on careers and choosing to stay single for longer (Loughlin and Barling, 2001). Taken together, these factors provide additional opportunities for proximity, repeated exposure, and liking, which strongly support our first assumption: romantic relationships at work are now close to inevitable. But what does this mean for organizations and their members?

Consequences of workplace romantic relationships

The impact of workplace romantic relationships varies considerably across situations and people. In the past, however, attention has focused overwhelmingly on the negative repercussions of office romances. In fact, the outcomes of a workplace relationship need not be negative; they can also be positive, or nonexistent (Quinn, 1977), and can affect not only the individual but also the organization. We now focus our attention on consequences of workplace relationships, and look at productivity, morale, intragroup conflict, and sexual harassment.

Productivity

Productivity is frequently viewed as being hurt by romantic relationships; however, whether the effect is positive or negative remains elusive. In some case studies, romantic relationships resulted in decreases in productivity, presumably because during a relationship participants are cognitively distracted, and are thus more prone to errors and mistakes, are more frequently late, and are more likely to miss meetings (Quinn and Lees, 1984). However, there is also evidence that for some couples, workplace romances increase quantitative and qualitative productivity (Mainiero, 1986). Other studies report no significant effect on productivity as the result of romantic relationship (Pierce and Aguinis, 2003; Pierce *et al.*, 1996).

One possibility is that any effects on productivity are situationally dependent, and future research needs to uncover the situational factors that moderate the link between romantic relationships at work and productivity. At the same time, research should assess whether there are any effects on team performance. Recent research on sexual harassment in North America shows that team performance is hurt when a member of the team is sexually harassed (Raver and Gelfand, 2005), and research should address the effects of workplace romantic relationships on team performance.

Morale

A second area potentially affected by a workplace romance is employee morale (Mainiero, 1989; Pierce *et al.*, 1996; Quinn, 1977). In fact, 34% of women surveyed by Mainiero (1989) found that an office romance was energizing and had a positive impact on morale. Yet other studies suggest that morale is lowered as a result of office relationships (Pierce *et al.*, 1996). Again, the different outcomes are likely a function of situational differences. As one example, it is possible that jealousy on the part of co-workers may influence how they respond to the development of such a relationship.

Intragroup conflict

Teamwork can also be affected by workplace relationships. Although positive effects of romance on the group have been reported (e.g. improved communication, reduced tension; Paul and Townsend, 1998), conflict in workgroups is not uncommon. The most frequently discussed outcomes are reduced productivity (Quinn and Lees, 1984), and gossip among group members (Pierce *et al.*, 1996), which itself might account for some of the reductions in group productivity.

Depending on the positions of the employees relative to each other, intragroup conflict can be exacerbated by role conflict. This occurs when a situation simultaneously requires conflicting or different behavior from one's personal and professional roles (Paul and Townsend 1998). This could affect productivity and turnover if the workplace romantic relationships result in favoritism, or the perception of favoritism (Schaefer and

Tudor, 2001). So, the outcome of romance on teamwork is often negative, but not uniformly so.

Sexual harassment

The last, and most serious, consequence of relationships in the workplace is sexual harassment. Concern has often been expressed that romantic relationships at work open the organization to potential sexual harassment charges (e.g. Bordwin, 1994; Paul and Townsend, 1998; Quinn, 1977). This is a serious concern, because according to the Society of Human Resource Management (1998), 24% of sexual harassment charges emanate from romantic relationships at work. One possibility is that if a relationship 'goes sour', one partner (most commonly the woman) may file a sexual harassment claim (Jones, 1999; Karl and Sutton, 2000). Another possibility is that a dissolved relationship may foster sexually harassing behavior (Pierce and Aguinis, 2004), and this is one of the most common arguments for having strict policies against workplace romantic relationships.

As can be seen, the possible outcomes of romantic relationships at work on productivity, morale, teamwork and sexual harassment are not uniform, and depend instead on the situation. But then what contextual factors make a difference to these outcomes? We suggest that three groups of contextual factors are important to consider. These are (1) the internal dynamics of the relationship, (2) the organizational environment, and (3) management interventions. We now focus on how each of these contextual factors mitigates the effect of a workplace romance on the individuals as well as the organization.

Factors that mitigate romantic relationships at work

Relationship type

The type of the relationship is important in predicting its possible effects in an organizational setting. Quinn and Lees (1984) suggest that there are three general workplace relationship categories. The first is *true love*, a relationship with altruistic motives and a long-term orientation. The second category is a *fling*, which is typified by intense emotions and a short-term orientation. Last is a *utilitarian relationship*, where the relationship is used to obtain extrinsic benefits such as power or status within the organization.

The reason for labeling relationships into one of these categories is not to define the relationship, but to establish how it is perceived by others in the workplace, as other employees will react differently depending on what they perceive to be the motives of the partners (Quinn, 1977). For example, it is more likely that the impact on morale and teamwork will be positive if it is a *true love* relationship, and even more so if it endures. Oppositely, the most negative effects can be predicted for a *utilitarian* relationship (Jones, 1999), because it has the highest potential for favoritism which can negatively affect productivity, morale, and teamwork. Also, where one partner feels exploited by the other, her/his productivity is likely to suffer (Mainiero, 1986). It is possible for a *fling* to have a minimal or non-existent impact since it is often short-lived. However, due to the intense nature of the relationship, it is also more likely to be volatile and end badly for at least one of the partners, which would have a negative impact on productivity and group work. Thus, the type of relationship will influence the impact of the relationship on the organization.

Once the relationship forms, the couple's behavior is important in determining the impact of the relationship on the organization. If the two people are able to act professionally when they are at work, it is less likely that there will be a negative reaction by co-workers (Karl and Sutton, 2000). This professionalism can also be conceptualized as maintaining a balance between the poles of intimacy and distance. Both extreme intimacy and extreme distance can have negative effects on a workgroup (e.g. increased hostility, distorted communication), and reduced productivity, reduced employee morale, and group conflict are likely. However, if the two are able to maintain an appropriate level of separation between their personal and work relationship, dysfunctional effects on their workgroup may be avoided (Paul and Townsend, 1998).

Power distance

Another internal relationship factor that influences the organizational consequences of the romance is the power dynamic within the relationship. There are two main types of relationships that can occur within organizations, namely lateral (peer-to-peer) and hierarchal (supervisor–subordinate) relationships (Karl and Sutton, 2000). Hierarchal relationships are generally of greater concern to the organization since they are seen to be more disruptive than co-worker relationships (Jones, 1999); "most co-workers and peers feel anxious about the impact of an intimate relationship on their own working relationships with the individuals involved" (Powell, 1986: 30). Because of this, 70% of North American companies have formal policies prohibiting such relationships (Schaefer and Tudor, 2001).

There are several factors which render hierarchical relationships more contentious. The first has to do with assumptions co-workers make about the motives of the couple. Even though co-workers are not able to accurately determine the motives of participants (Mainiero, 1986), utilitarian motives are usually perceived to be what underlies hierarchal relationships, especially when the lower-level employee is female (Jones, 1999; Powell, 2001). Because the perception of utilitarian motives increases the likelihood that negative repercussions will occur, this is one reason why a hierarchal relationship is more likely to result in negative organizational consequences.

Another perspective on hierarchical relationships is taken from social exchange theory. The difficulty with a hierarchical relationship is the inherent power imbalance. Relationships are usually based on the exchange of resources between equal partners. These resources can be socio-economic, or personal/sexual in nature. However, when a workplace relationship involves a hierarchical imbalance, workplace resources such as salary, performance evaluations, and work assignments can be affected (Jones, 1999; Pierce et al., 2000). In one study, participants in hierarchal relationships were, in the most extreme cases, found to be favouring their partner (e.g. allotting promotions, flaunting power; Quinn 1977). Even if favors are not offered, the perception remains among co-workers that such preferential treatment could occur. Negative consequences in the organization such as reduced morale and intragroup conflict will be far more likely when co-workers perceive the potential for a relationship to be exploitative (Mainiero, 1986).

Mainiero suggests that thinking of the relationship as a power coalition – a political tool used to accrue power (Pfeffer, 1981) – is another way to conceptualize how a hierarchal relationship would affect the organization. This is relevant to workplace romances because a hierarchal relationship can constitute a power coalition, which provides the opportunity to participate in an exchange of resources from which other employees are excluded (Mainiero, 1986). So, if employees feel that a coalition has been formed from which they are excluded, retaliation and aggression (Twenge, Baumeister, Tice, and Stucke, 2001) and even poorer health (Cohen, 2004) may well result. As Berry and Worthington (2001: 447) note, "Interpersonal relationships can influence physical and mental health . . . social isolation and loneliness increase the risk for morbidity and mortality."

Two additional issues related to power distance need to be considered. First, because the power difference between the partners may affect how others respond to the workplace relationship, it is possible that the partners' gender complicates this effect. Specifically, perceptions of the role of power within the relationship may well differ depending on whether the female partner is at a higher or lower status in the organizational hierarchy.

A second issue must be considered: throughout this chapter, it is assumed that all relationships under discussion are heterosexual in nature. While gay couples may well have more concerns about making their relationships public knowledge, prejudices on the part of co-workers would probably affect their responses to gay romantic relationships in the workplace.

Relationship dissolution

Perhaps the most obvious and most common factor contributing to negative relationship outcomes at work is the dissolution of that relationship. It is possible that many positive outcomes will naturally occur as the result of a relationship, but it is less likely that positive outcomes will naturally occur from the dissolution of that relationship. One study showed that 48% of workplace relationships end in dissolution (Pierce and Aguinis, 2001). As mentioned earlier, the dissolution of a romantic relationship can create difficulties for the employees involved, their teams, and the organization as a whole. However, the potential benefits from maintaining open lines of communication and supporting one's employees when they need it most is not always apparent. Yet, such situations provide a unique opportunity for management to support its employees, and such managerial support will provide vicarious and symbolic leadership during difficult times. As Stanford economist Paul Romer reminds us, "A crisis is a terrible thing to waste."

Thus, characteristics of the romantic relationship mitigate its impact on the organization. However, these characteristics alone cannot explain all the variance in workplace outcomes; aspects of the organizational environment further mitigate the effects of romantic relationships.

Organizational environment

Two components of the organizational environment influence the impact an office romance has on the organization, namely organizational culture and workgroup characteristics.

Organizational culture

Organizational culture, which constitutes the organization's "personality" and encompasses its norms, attitudes, and values (Foley and Powell, 1999), could mitigate any impact of workplace relationships. Organizational culture dictates what is regarded as appropriate behavior within the firm, and influences employee reactions toward relationships (Pierce *et al.*, 1996). Due to both selection and socialization factors, individuals working in a conservative culture will be more likely to exhibit negative attitudes toward workplace relationships than those working in a liberal culture (Foley and Powell, 1999; Pierce et al., 1996).

The effects of organizational culture are also manifest or signaled through managements' attitudes and behaviors (Pierce et al., 1996). Where managers hold negative attitudes toward romantic relationships at work, these attitudes are transmitted to subordinates. Under such conditions, other employees may be less accepting of, and more likely to react negatively to, romantic relationships at work.

Workgroup characteristics

Workgroup characteristics are the second integral part of the organizational environment that may mitigate the outcomes of romantic relationships at work. Quinn (1977) noted that the most important characteristics that can influence relationship outcomes are group climate, closeness of supervision, closeness of interpersonal relationships, and the intensity or importance of the work or mission. Some groups will have strict unwritten rules for becoming involved with a co-worker. Still others will encourage romantic relationships.

Group climate can be conceptualized as comprising the group's informal policies, practices, and procedures. This concept is extended to romantic relationships by Powell (2001), who discussed the importance of group expectations. He found that if the group expected that a relationship would result in work disruption, there was a greater likelihood members would react negatively. Employees' prior experience with workplace romances also creates expectations within the group. Jones (1999) found that individuals who either had been in a romantic relationship at work, and/or who had positive experiences with them in the past, would react more positively to co-workers engaging in a relationship. Workgroup climate can have a strong influence on couple behavior; Quinn (1977) showed that when the climate expressed disapproval, participants experienced pressure to dissolve the relationship, illustrating the power of the workgroup to influence the consequences of the relationship not only for the organization, but also for the couple involved.

Managerial interventions

After considering the internal relationship dynamics and organizational environment, the last major factor that will mitigate the consequences of a romantic relationship is the type of management action used by the organization in response to a romantic relationship. Organizations vary considerably in how management acts or reacts in response to romantic relationships at work. These responses are critical not just in their potential impact on the romantic relationship. Instead, how organizations respond may well have effects beyond the partners in the relationship, as they signal to other employees how management responds to difficult situations in general. Essentially, organizations can choose to respond punitively (e.g. reprimands, transfers, terminations), positively (e.g. counseling employees) or not at all.

Punitive action

Policies constitute one of the simplest ways to deal with workplace romances. Having a strict policy disallowing romantic relationships at work provides managers with guidelines as to how to react to a workplace relationship (e.g. reprimand, relocation, termination), and legitimates any management actions along these lines. Such policies are most common in conservative organizational cultures; whether it is because of the culture and/or the policy, employees may be less willing to become involved in workplace relationships (Foley and Powell, 1999). In a survey of undergraduate and MBA students (Powell, 1986), respondents agreed that managers should dissuade employees from becoming romantically involved. However, just over a decade later, Karl and Sutton (2000) found that 92% of companies have no formal policies that prohibit co-workers from dating one another. It is possible that this is because people have become more tolerant of workplace relationships: in 1987, 39% of employees felt that a workplace relationship was none of the company's business (Karl and Sutton, 2000); by 1994, 70% responded similarly (Jones, 1999).

However, this argument does not necessarily extend to all relationships. Hierarchal relationships are still thought to be potentially disruptive and worth regulating. Many employers, who do not create policies prohibiting romantic relationships, do have a written rule prohibiting supervisor–subordinate relationships (Schaefer and Tudor, 2000). Even participants who had neutral responses to co-workers becoming romantically involved felt that if a supervisor is involved, he/she should be reprimanded (Powell, 1986).

Nonetheless, it may be naïve to think that two employees who enjoy geographical proximity, are sufficiently attracted to each other, and are motivated to initiate a relationship would be willing to disengage because of the existence of company rules or policies,

Managers can create policies and rules promising serious consequences for violation of their dating policies, but it's impossible to prevent people from being attracted to one another and falling in love. Strict rules merely force employees to go underground with their relationship. (Schaefer and Tudor, 2001: 5)

Thus, couples may be more likely to hide than to terminate their relationship, and some organizational policies may thereby have unintended negative consequences.

There are also legal considerations when creating formal policies against dating. Policies that prohibit relationships could be an invasion of employees' privacy, or an act of discrimination (Bordwin 1994; Paul and Townsend, 1998). Consequently, some jurisdictions (e.g. New York State) have passed legislation prohibiting such organizational policies (Jones, 1999). Thus, a formal policy against workplace relationships may not be the most effective form of management reaction to a romantic relationship at work.

Where an organization may not want to institute formal policies, informal policies may exist instead. These "unwritten" rules reflect one way for employers to deter employees from becoming involved in relationships with each other, without explicitly forbidding the relationships. However, the implementation of informal policies is usually inconsistent. Some employees may know and understand these "rules"; others may be unaware. As a result, the informal policy would probably not achieve its objective, and might even set the stage for conflict among team members (Schaefer and Tudor, 2000).

Positive action

Another managerial option is to take positive action. This includes openly discussing the relationship and counseling the couple on what to do (Foley and Powell, 1999). This approach is proactive because it could potentially prevent reductions in productivity and team conflict by articulating the risks involved in a workplace relationship, as well as management's expectations (e.g. continued punctuality, awareness of public displays of affection). In a study of hierarchal relationships, this approach was found, by employees, to be the preferred action for management to take (Powell 2001). A positive and proactive approach recognizes that stopping relationships in the workplace is close to futile. But by maintaining an open dialogue with employees, potentially negative consequences for the organization are much less likely to be a concern.

No action

Finally, if management chooses not to take punitive or positive action, the default position is no action. This may not necessarily constitute laissez-faire leadership, however. Organizations can take the explicit stance that romantic matters are the personal business of the individuals involved, and not the concern of management. According to Foley and Powell (1999), this is the most common response to romantic relationships in the workplace. In practice, organizations generally do not take effective action (Jones, 1999). In fact, even when a relationship has begun to exert negative effects on the organization, the problem is often ignored (Powell, 2001; Quinn, 1977; Quinn and Lees, 1984). Although ignoring the problem is often the path of least resistance for managers, there are situations where ignoring the relationship could actually exacerbate the negative consequences for the organization.

Thus, managers have several options when encountering workplace relationships. They can take punitive action, positive action, or no action. The choices management make will influence how the organization is affected by the romantic relationship both directly and indirectly. Thus, if the action management takes is so significant, what action *should* management take to maximize the positive effects of the relationship and minimize the negative ones?

Like most other issues relating to workplace relationships, determining the "best" action is not an uncomplicated decision. Schaefer and Tudor (2001) assert that in today's complex workplaces, the most appropriate action may be to create specific policies to regulate workplace romances. Some executives believe companies need definitive strategies to guide responses to romantic relationships at work. However, Karl and Sutton (2000) found that half of respondents in a 1994 survey felt that companies should outline expectations for workplace romances, but should not attempt to ban these relationships. Clearly, there is no one right answer for how to manage these delicate situations.

Nonetheless, a common theme in the literature would suggest that *how* management chooses what to do may be as important as the actual decision they make. Essentially, any implementation should maximize employee perceptions of justice. Listening to employees and offering counseling (Karl and Sutton, 2000), and respecting employees' decisions and judgement, would enhance interpersonal justice. Ensuring that there is no favoritism and that outcomes are allocated to employees according to their contribution would enhance distributive justice, while ensuring that employees have input into formal policies relating to romantic relationships at work (Greenberg, 1994) would augment perceptions of procedural fairness. However, what might be perceived as fair is situationally dependent: for example, stricter policies were perceived by employees as fair when it was stated that productivity had declined as a result of the relationship (Karl and Sutton, 2000). If employees are more accepting of workplace relationships, the negative consequences attributed to romantic relationships resulting from increased tension, reduced communication, and favoritism are less apt to appear.

A model proposed by Foley and Powell (1999) suggests that employees develop preferences for management action or inaction in workplace romances, which influence their perception of distributive justice in the organization, which in turn affects their attitudes and behaviors. Further, they propose that because employees tend to retaliate when they perceive injustice, if employees believe the actions taken by management are fair, the organization will experience fewer negative consequences such as decreased morale or productivity.

So, if it is true that the negative consequences of workplace relationships are moderated by whether or not fellow employees believe the actions taken by management are fair, it would be in an organization's best interests to ensure they are creating and implementing policies and following practices that are perceived by employees to be just.

Concluding thoughts

Relationships are the "stuff of life", and this is no less true in organizations. Whether in school, at work, or at play, if the conditions of proximity, repeated exposure, attitude similarity, and attraction are met, romantic relationships are inevitable. In today's diverse and highly interactive workplace, these conditions will almost certainly be present (Pierce *et al.*, 1996; Quinn, 1977). In fact, as found in a study done in the United Kingdom, socialization outside of work is often commonplace and the line between friendships and relationships can itself become blurred (Riach and Wilson, 2006). Historically, organizations have typically been wary of romantic relationships in the workplace – despite their inevitability, and the possibility for some benefits.

Overall, there are several points of consensus in the literature on romantic relationships at work; these concern the precursors and potential for negative consequences of such relationships. However, considering that workplace romances may well be inevitable, there remains insufficient rigorous and current research from which to inform management about a pervasive and significant issue (Jones, 1999). The majority of research in this field is anecdotal or case-based (Powell, 2001) and is cross-sectional (Karl and Sutton, 2000). More experimental and longitudinal designs are needed. Much of the research is dated, having been conducted in the 1970s and 1980s at a time when women were just beginning to become a significant part of the workforce. Therefore, old assumptions and theories should be retested, in today's workplace.

Perhaps most significantly, the very form of the question posed in research needs to change. Research on maternal employment in the 1970s and 1980s consistently showed its negative effects; yet a close examination of this research revealed that research had overwhelmingly focused on negative outcomes (Barling, 1990). Only when the research started to ask about potential beneficial effects of maternal employment did such effects become apparent. A similar situation may well exist with research on romantic relationships at work. Guided by social and managerial stereotypes, most research has focused on potential negative effects emerging from romantic relationships at work. Yet organizational experience, lessons learned from research on maternal employment, and findings from the emerging fields of positive psychology and positive organizational behavior all dictate that research should now ask about the possible benefits of romantic relationships at work, for organizations as well as for their members.

In conclusion, the impacts of relationships vary considerably across situations. The role of the organization can no longer be to dictate how or when romantic relationships can occur. Indeed, it may well be impossible to do so. Instead, organizations should focus on finding ways to support romantic relationships in the workplace. By taking a positive and proactive stance on workplace relationships, organizations may be able to foster and support love, well-being, and productivity.

References

Barling, J. (1990). *Employment, stress and family functioning.* Chichester: Wiley.

Bordwin, M. (1994). Containing Cupid's arrow. *Small Business Reports* 19: 53–8.

Byrne, D. and Neuman, J. H. (1992). The implications of attraction research for organizational issues. In K. Kelly (ed.), *Issues, theory and research in industrial/organizational psychology* (pp. 29–70). Amsterdam: North-Holland.

Cohen, S. (2004). Social relationships and health. *American Psychologist* 59: 676–84.

Foley, S. and Powell, G. N. (1999). Not all is fair in love and work: co-workers' preferences for and responses to managerial interventions regarding workplace romances. *Journal of Organizational Behavior* 20: 1043–56.

Greenberg, J. (1994). Using socially fair treatment to promote acceptance of a work site smoking ban. *Journal of Applied Psychology* 79: 288–97.

Horn, P. D. and Horn, J. (1982). *Sex in the office.* Reading, MA: Addison Wesley.

Jones, G. E. (1999). Hierarchal workplace romance: an experimental examination of team member perceptions. *Journal of Organizational Behavior* 20: 1057–72.

Karl, K. A. and Sutton, C. L. (2000). An examination of the perceived fairness of workplace romance policies. *Journal of Business and Psychology* 14: 429–42.

Loughlin, C. and Barling, J. (2001). Young workers' work values, attitudes, and behaviors. *Journal of Occupational and Organizational Psychology* 74: 543–58.

Mainiero, L. (1986). A review and analysis of power dynamics in organizational romances. *Academy of Management Review* 11: 750–62.

(1989). *Office romance: love, power and sex in the workplace*. New York: Rawson Associates.

Paul, R. J. and Townsend, J. B. (1998). Managing the workplace romance: protecting employee and employer rights. *Review of Business* 19: 25–31.

Pfeffer, J. (1981). *Power in organizations*. Marshfield, MA: Pitman.

Pierce, C. A. and Aguinis, H. (2001). A framework for investigating the link between workplace romance and sexual harassment. *Group and Organizational Management* 26: 206–29.

(2003). Romantic relationships in organizations. *Management Research* 1: 161–9.

(2004). Responding to sexual harassment complaints: effects of a dissolved workplace romance on decision-making standards. *Organizational Behavior and Human Decision Processes* 95: 66–82.

Pierce, C. A., Aguinis, H., and Adams, S. (2000). Effects of a dissolved workplace romance and rater characteristics on responses to a sexual harassment accusation. *Academy of Management Journal* 43: 869–80.

Pierce, C. A., Bryne, D., and Aguinis, H. (1996). Attraction in organizations: a model of workplace romance. *Journal of Organizational Behavior* 17: 5–32.

Powell, G. N. (1986). What do tomorrow's managers think about sexual intimacy in the workplace? *Business Horizons* July–August: 30–6.

(2001). Workplace romances between senior-level executives and lower-level employees: an issue of work disruption and gender. *Human Relations* 54: 1519–44.

Quinn, R. E. (1977). Coping with Cupid: the formation, impact, and management of romantic relationships in organizations. *Administrative Science Quarterly* 22: 30–45.

Quinn, R. E. and Lees, P. L. (1984). Attraction and harassment: dynamics of sexual harassment in the workplace. *Organizational Dynamics* 13: 35–46.

Raver, J. L. and Gelfand, M. J. (2005). Beyond the individual victim: linking sexual harassment, team processes, and team performance. *Academy of Management Journal* 48: 387–400.

Riach, K. and Wilson, K. (2006). Don't screw the crew. *British Journal of Management* 17: 1–14.

Rosston, G. (2004). For whom the bridge tolls? Retrieved November 17, 2005. From *San Francisco Chronicle*. http://sfgate.com/cgi-bin/article.cgi?f=/c/a/2004/08/27/EDGMQ8EQ931.DTL.

Schaefer, C. M. and Tudor, T. R. (2001). Managing workplace romances. *SAM Advanced Management Journal* 66: 4–11.

Society for Human Resource Management (SHRM) (1998). *Workplace romance survey*. Alexandria, VA: SHRM Public Affairs Department.

Sternberg, R. J. (1986). A triangular theory of love. *Psychological Review* 93: 119–35.

Turner, N., Barling, J., and Zacharatos, A. (2002). Positive psychology at work. In C. R. Snyder and S. Lopez (eds.), *The handbook of positive psychology* (pp. 715–30). Oxford: Oxford University Press.

Twenge, J. M., Baumeister, R. F., Tice D. M., and Stucke, T. S. (2001). If you can't join them, beat them: effects of social exclusion on aggressive behavior. *Journal of Personality and Social Psychology* 81: 1058–69.

Zohar, D. (2000). A group-level model of safety climate: testing the effect of group climate on microaccidents in manufacturing jobs. *Journal of Applied Psychology* 85: 587–96.

(2002). The effects of leadership dimensions, safety climate and assigned priorities on minor injuries in work groups. *Journal of Organizational Behavior* 23: 75–92.

11 Ethnic diversity at work: an overview of theories and research

Wido G. M. Oerlemans, Maria C. W. Peeters, and Wilmar B. Schaufeli

Ethnic diversity in the workforce is a subject of growing interest for western organizations. In EU countries, continuous immigration flows of post-war guest workers and their family members, ex-colonial immigrants, political refugees, and highly educated workers have led to an increase of people with a foreign nationality (Organisation for Economic Co-operation and Development [OECD], 2003). However, foreign population percentages vary significantly between EU countries. For instance, Luxemburg (39.9%), Austria (10.3%), Germany (9.5%), and Belgium (9.1%) have relatively high rates, whereas the lowest rates, of about 2%, are found in Greece, Finland, Portugal, Spain, and Italy. Other EU countries fall somewhere in between these two extremes, such as the Netherlands, Denmark, Sweden, the UK, and France, with percentages ranging from 4.3 to 6% (OECD, 2003). In the future, ethnic diversity in many EU countries is likely to increase even further as demographic figures indicate that net-migration flows (immigration minus emigration) are larger than the natural growth of national populations (Ekamper and Wetters, 2005; OECD, 2003).

The increase in ethnic diversity, along with accompanying demographic developments, have had a significant impact on the composition of the workforce. About fifty years ago, the demographic features of most work organizations were fairly homogeneous (Williams and O'Reilly, 1998). Many employees shared a similar ethnic background, were male, and worked for the same employer throughout their working lives. Nowadays, managers are confronted with teams and departments that are more diverse in terms of gender, age, ethnicity, organizational tenure, functional background, educational background, and so on. Therefore, a growing number of companies (e.g. IBM, Siemens, Shell) have formulated diversity policies that are aimed at managing a diverse labor force. The reason for formulating diversity policies is often twofold: (1) it is considered to be a moral duty to have a labor force which mirrors the

211

demographic representation of a given society; and (2) having a labor force that is diverse in terms of demographics and personal characteristics may stimulate creativity which can give companies a competitive advantage. For example, in a policy paper on diversity published on the internet, Shell states, "We believe that by attracting and developing the best people of all backgrounds and experience we uphold our value of 'respect for people' and improve our ability to form relationships and compete in diverse cultures and markets" (Shell, 2006).

To date, almost no literature reviews are specifically aimed at describing the consequences of ethnic diversity in the workplace (for an exception, see Williams and O'Reilly, 1998). The aim of this chapter is to give an extensive overview of theory and research on the implications of the increasing ethnic diversity within organizations. First, the differences between the various definitions of ethnic diversity are briefly introduced. After this, several theories and models that may explain the consequences of ethnic diversity on work outcomes are discussed. Next, an overview of studies is presented, which focuses on the relationship between ethnic diversity on the one hand, and different work outcomes on the other, such as performance outcomes, behavioral outcomes, and affective outcomes. Finally, the chapter will conclude with a discussion of the challenges and opportunities for further research and practice that are at hand in this relatively young and promising area within occupational (health) psychology.

Definitions of ethnic diversity

Before addressing the consequences of ethnic diversity in the workforce, it is important to define it conceptually, since this can affect the manner in which the phenomenon itself is examined. Most studies still define "ethnicity" as a demographic characteristic that is on a personal level. However, from the 1980s onwards, authors of popular management literature as well as organizational researchers (e.g. Cox, 1993; Jackson, May, and Whitney, 1995; Jehn, Northcraft, and Neale, 1999) began to define certain demographic characteristics, such as ethnicity, as relational demographic characteristics (e.g. Jackson *et al.*, 1995; Tsui, Egan, and O'Reilly, 1992; Williams and O'Reilly, 1998). In short, relational demography involves comparing the demographic characteristics of an individual (e.g. ethnicity, age, or gender) to the demographic characteristics of a social group. For example, in terms of ethnicity, individuals may be very similar or dissimilar compared to the team in which they work. Following this rationale, Jackson *et al.* (1995: 217) define diversity as "the presence of differences among members of a social unit." Jackson *et al.* further refine the concept of diversity into surface-level and deep-level diversity. Surface-level diversity basically refers to characteristics of people that are readily observable, such as ethnicity, age, and gender. Deep-level diversity refers to characteristics that are more difficult to observe, such as one's personality, attitudes, skills, and competencies.

Other researchers claim that diversity is about the effective management of both demographic variation (e.g. age, gender, ethnicity) and personal variation (e.g. personal values, skills, and abilities) in the workforce (e.g. Rijsman, 1997). In this view, it is expected that diversity, when managed effectively, will entail economic benefits for organizations. In particular, diversity is expected to generate more creativity, multiple perspectives, and a broader access to informational networks that increase the quality of decision-making.

Still other diversity researchers argue that diversity is about the inclusion of socially disadvantaged groups in the workforce (e.g. Grossman, 2000; Linnehan and Konrad, 1999). Accordingly, ethnic minorities, together with other groups such as females, disabled people, gay men, and lesbians, are thought of as socially disadvantaged groups that actively need to be included and provided with equal opportunities in the workforce. Defined this way, "diversity" is closely related to the concept of affirmative action (e.g. Heilman, 1994). In sum, there is no uniform and generally accepted definition of ethnic diversity. Instead, different perspectives exist and some of the most used definitions are summarized in Table 11.1.

In this chapter, we distinguish between two major branches of definitions. First, we acknowledge that ethnic diversity can be a subtype of "surface-level diversity" or "social category diversity" as described in Table 11.1. Indeed, ethnicity is a readily detectable attribute (Jackson et al., 1995) which can be used to make distinctions between people based on the different ethnic groups to which they belong (Jehn et al., 1999). Second, we acknowledge that ethnic diversity can also be looked upon as cultural differences between members of ethnically diverse groups, which encompass differences in language, religion, values, norms, and beliefs. Etymologically speaking, ethnicity is derived from the Greek word "ethnos," which refers to a group of people or a nation. In its contemporary form, ethnicity still retains this basic meaning as it refers to a coherent group of people who are, at least latently, aware of having common origins, roots, and interests. Ethnicity can thus be used to define a self-conscious group of closely related people who, to some extent, share their customs, beliefs, values, institutions, language, religion, history, and land of origin, or to put it briefly, a group which has the same culture or roots (e.g. Cashmore, 1996; Smith, 1991). In this view, ethnic diversity thus also relates to cultural differences.

Table 11.1 *Definitions of diversity*

Diversity type	Definition
Readily detectable / Surface level diversity	"[differences in] readily detectable attributes [that] can be quickly and consensually determined with only brief exposure to a target person (e.g. sex, age, ethnicity, team tenure)." (Jackson *et al.*, 1995: 217)
Social category diversity	"explicit differences among group members in social category membership, such as race, gender and ethnicity." (Jehn *et al.*, 1999: 745)
Underlying / Deep-level diversity	"[differences in] underlying attributes that are more subject to construal and mutability (e.g. knowledge, skills, abilities, attitudes and values)." (Jackson *et al.*, 1995: 217)
Informational diversity	"differences in knowledge bases and perspectives that members bring to the group. Such differences are likely to arise as a function of differences among group members in education, experience and expertise." (Jehn *et al.*, 1999: 743)
Value diversity	"occurs when members of a workgroup differ in terms of what they think the group's real task, goal, target, or mission should be." (Jehn *et al.*, 1999: 745)

Theoretical approaches to ethnic diversity at work

Based on the two perspectives mentioned, we distinguish between two theoretical approaches that can be used to predict consequences of ethnic diversity in the workforce. First, the *social-psychological approach* refers to theories that are connected to ethnic diversity as a subtype of surface-level or social category diversity. This approach is concerned with the influence of a group's demographic composition on the behaviors and attitudes of its members. The second approach, the *cultural approach*, relates to ethnic diversity as cultural differences between group members and, above all, on how cultural differences can influence the interaction between members of different ethnic groups.

The social-psychological approach

Social identity theory (Tajfel, Billig, Bundy, and Flament, 1971) posits that people derive self-esteem and a sense of belonging from identifying themselves with social groups and from favorably comparing the group to which they belong with other groups. Tajfel and colleagues demonstrated in a series of laboratory studies that people are eager to identify themselves with a social group (called ingroup), even when group membership is based on trivial criteria such as the letter A or B. When people identify with a certain ingroup (e.g. group A), they tend to favor this ingroup over other (out)groups to which they do not belong (e.g. group B). These initial findings of Tajfel and his colleagues are confirmed in many other studies (for a meta-analysis on this topic, see Mullen, Brown, and Smith, 1992). According to this view, ethnicity is a surface-level characteristic (Jackson *et al.*, 1995) and as such it can be quickly used to divide a group of people into ethnic subgroups. Furthermore, people may frequently identify with their ethnic background because it provides them with a sense of belonging; it connects individuals to a group of closely related people who share a common culture (Cashmore, 1996; Smith, 1991). When people identify with an ethnic ingroup (e.g. Dutch, Turkish, Moroccan, Swedish, Kurdish, English) – and they usually do – social identity theory predicts that people will favor their own ethnic ingroup over other ethnic outgroups.

Social categorization theory (Turner, Hogg, and Oakes, 1987) further builds on the assumptions made in social identity theory by suggesting that the degree to which individuals identify with a social group depends on the specific context (Oakes, 1987; Turner, 1985). In this theory, "personal identity" is distinguished from "social identity." Personal identity emphasizes that an individual's identity should be distinguished from other members of the ingroup (Turner, 1982). Social identity, on the other hand, concerns what is shared with an ingroup, but not with members of an outgroup (Haslam, Powell, and Turner, 2000). In other words, there may be differences (e.g. in attitudes, beliefs, opinions) between members of the same social group. Social categorization theory emphasizes that individuals only identify with their ingroup when differences between members of the ingroup are smaller than the differences between the ingroup and other outgroups. Importantly, identification with a social group leads to behavior that is different from behavior originating from one's personal identity, as it is oriented toward the interests of the group as a whole instead of one's personal interests.

One situation in which individuals identify with their ingroup is when status differences between individuals of the ingroup are smaller than the status differences between the ingroup and the outgroups. Indicators of status differences are, for instance, power, socio-economic position, judicial status, numerical majority, and dominant culture. It is often the case that immigrant groups have a lower status (e.g. numerical minority, minority culture, lower functional levels, more unemployment) compared to the national group of a country. According to social categorization theory, status differences between ethnic groups will lead to a stronger identification of individuals with their ethnic ingroup and behavior that is in the interest of the ethnic ingroup. For example, both Kanter (1977) and Tajfel (1978) predict that high-status groups may exaggerate the differences between themselves and low-status groups, which leads to polarization. Also, under such circumstances, low-status group members are expected to adapt to the values and norms of the high-status group. However, for immigrant groups, it may not be easy to adapt to the values and norms of the majority, as individuals often feel closely connected to their ethnic ingroup and its culture (Cashmore, 1996; Taylor and Moghaddam, 1994).

Another theoretical paradigm which may explain consequences of ethnic diversity is the similarity-attraction paradigm of Byrne (1971). This paradigm states that a great variety of physical, social, or other attributes can be used as a basis for expecting similarity in attitudes, beliefs, or personality. It has been found that "The consequences of high interpersonal attraction may include frequent communication, high social integration and a desire to maintain group affiliation" (Tsui *et al.*, 1992: 551). According to this view, people may expect others with similar physical features to hold similar attitudes and beliefs. As such, ethnically similar people may be more attracted to each other than ethnically dissimilar people.

In conclusion, both social identity theory and social categorization theory as well as the similarity-attraction paradigm predict that ethnic diversity holds negative consequences for organizations. According to these three theories, ethnic diversity in work teams may lead to psychological processes such as ingroup liking, ingroup attraction, and ingroup favoritism. In turn, these psychological processes may affect the behavior of individuals in such a way that they will favor employees belonging to their own ethnic ingroup over employees belonging to ethnic outgroups. In ethnically diverse work units, this may lead to a number of negative outcomes such as less cooperation, less communication, more conflicts, and less cohesiveness. Additionally, differences in ethnic background between the individual and the team may not only affect team functioning, but also have negative personal outcomes. When an employee differs in ethnicity from the rest of a work unit, he or she may experience less organizational commitment, more turnover intention, and less job satisfaction than employees working in ethnically similar teams.

A perspective that predicts positive outcomes of diversity is known as the information and decision-making theory (Wittenbaum and Stasser, 1996). The quality of decision-making depends on the unique and useful information a person has, as well as on the openness of the group to discuss these new insights. Unfortunately, individuals are more likely to base their decisions on shared information, that is, information that is collectively held by other group members (Stasser, 1992). In this way, unique information is withheld, which lessens the probability of group members engaging in innovative debates that create unique and high-quality ideas or solutions. Decision-making theorists argue that diversity can have positive effects on group performance, because diversity increases variation in terms of information, abilities, and skills.

Most organizational psychologists (Jackson, Joshi, and Erhardt, 2003; Jehn *et al.*, 1999) argue that diversity in task-related characteristics, in particular, leads to better team performance. Task-related characteristics refer to those characteristics of individuals that are necessary for performing a certain task, such as particular skills, abilities, experience, and competencies. Whether or not information and decision-making processes are of higher quality when work units are ethnically diverse may thus depend on the task a team has to perform. For example, an ethnically diverse team of teachers may be better qualified to teach ethnically diverse students than an ethnically homogeneous team of teachers. In this instance, it is expected that ethnic diversity in a team of teachers would increase the information, knowledge, skills, and abilities that are available for increasing performance. In other cases, ethnic diversity may not be such a relevant characteristic for performance outcomes (for instance in production units on an operational level).

The cultural approach

A second approach to understanding the relationship between ethnic diversity and work outcomes focuses on cultural differences. The concept of "culture" has been defined in many different ways. To give some examples, Larkey (1996) emphasizes that a culture includes a particular communication style, specific rules, dress codes, a shared meaning, and a particular language. Cox (1993) states that cultural groups share certain norms, values, and goal priorities, and have a similar sociocultural heritage. According to this view, it is not controversial to assume that people with the same ethnic background share, at least to some extent, a common culture (Cashmore, 1996; Smith 1991). Up till now, there are no scientific theories that elaborate on issues such as the impact of cultural diversity on work outcomes. Nevertheless, we will introduce and discuss some processes and heuristic models that are useful for understanding the effects of ethnic diversity on work outcomes.

First, ethnically diverse groups may encounter communication problems. It is obvious that differences in language use, intonations, communication styles, and non-verbal aspects across cultures can complicate intercultural contact between ethnically diverse employees (Maznevski, 1994). Second, ethnically diverse groups differ systematically regarding the cultural values they adhere to. Hofstede (1980, 1991) distinguishes between four cultural value domains: masculinity–femininity, individualism–collectivism, power distance, and uncertainty avoidance. The individualism–collectivism dimension, in particular, is known to relate to the attitudes and behavior that are likely to influence work outcomes. This dimension refers to whether one's identity is defined by personal choices and achievements or by the character of the collective group(s) to which one belongs. In general, people from collectivistic (mostly non-western) cultures are more willing to sacrifice personal needs and to help their social group than people from individualistic (mostly western) countries. Thus, compared to people from individualistic cultures, people from collectivistic cultures may be more cooperative and more willing to perform duties in order to achieve group goals (Smith and Bond, 1998). Other cultural value domains are: (1) power distance, the amount of respect and deference between those in superior and subordinate positions; (2) uncertainty avoidance, a focus on planning and the creation of stability as a way of dealing with life's uncertainties; and (3) masculinity–femininity, the relative emphasis on achievement or on interpersonal harmony – a distinction that characterizes gender differences in values across many national cultures.

Third, differences between the organizational culture and the cultural background of employees may complicate adaptation to the organizational culture. Hofstede (1989: 391) refers to organizational culture as "collective habits, expressed in such visible things like dress, language and jargon, status symbols, promotion criteria, tea and coffee rituals, meeting rituals, communications styles, and a lot more." Although organizational cultures differ across companies, it is conceivable that many organizational cultures have some overlap with the national culture of a particular society. Thus, immigrant employees who are raised in a culture that is distinctly different from an organizational culture may have more problems adapting to the organizational culture than native employees who share a cultural background that is more similar to the organizational culture.

Finally, immigrant employees may differ from each other when comparing acculturation attitudes. The first definition of acculturation was offered by Redfield, Linton, and Herskovits (1936: 149): "Acculturation comprehends those phenomena, which result when groups of individuals having different cultures come into continuous first-hand contact, with subsequent changes in the original cultural patterns of either or both groups." Nowadays, Berry's two-dimensional acculturation model (Berry, Kim, Power, Young, and Bujaki, 1989; Berry, 1997) is the most frequently used model to conceptualize acculturation (Van de Vijver and Phalet, 2004). According to this model, immigrants may engage in any of four acculturation strategies that are based on two dimensions: culture adaptation and culture maintenance. Culture adaptation refers to the extent to which immigrants wish to establish good relations with members of the host society. Culture maintenance refers to the importance of maintaining relations with one's native culture. The combination of these two dimensions in a fourfold table yields the following four acculturation strategies. Assimilation refers to a complete adaptation of immigrants to the dominant culture in a society of settlement without retaining one's own native culture. Integration refers to adaptation to the dominant culture as well as maintaining one's own native culture. Separation is a term used for immigrants who maintain their own native culture without adapting to the dominant culture. Finally, marginalization is what occurs when immigrants do not maintain or adapt to any culture. The acculturation model of Berry and his colleagues may provide a fruitful avenue for examining whether or not differences in acculturation attitudes affect important work outcomes. For instance, Bourhis, Moise, Perreault, and Senécal (1997) posited that differences in acculturation attitudes between ethnic majority (high-status) and ethnic minority (low-status) groups would lead to problematic or even conflictual intergroup relations. Thus, within organizations, differences in acculturation attitudes could lead to problematic or even conflictual relations between ethnically dissimilar employees depending on the importance the different groups attach to their cultural background.

Empirical results of studies on ethnic diversity in the workplace

In accordance with Jackson *et al.* (2003) we distinguish four different types of outcome variables that are often studied in diversity research. First, most studies have examined ethnic diversity in the context of team performance, including evaluations of team tasks, ratings of perceived team effectiveness, and "objective" measures of team performance, such as sales revenue, customer satisfaction, and sales productivity. Second, a fair amount of ethnic diversity research has focused on examining behavioral outcomes, encompassing communications, the use of information, and conflict and cooperation in teams. Third, a small amount of ethnic diversity research has also looked at the association between diversity and affective outcomes, including organizational commitment, job satisfaction, and identification with the job, the team, or the organization as a whole. Fourth, in some studies, it was assumed that ethnic diversity had an indirect relationship with performance outcomes. That is, it was hypothesized that ethnic diversity would first have an impact on behavioral and attitudinal outcomes, which would, in turn, affect performance outcomes. Results from empirical studies on these four types of outcomes are discussed below.

Performance outcomes

Laboratory studies have shown that there is a positive relationship between ethnic diversity and performance. For example, Watson, Kumar, and Michaelsen (1993) performed a longitudinal laboratory study in which they compared the performance outcomes of ethnically homogeneous and heterogeneous groups composed of undergraduate and graduate students on several cognitive tasks. In the end, results showed that the ethnically heterogeneous groups outperformed the homogeneous groups on several cognitive tasks (identifying problem perspectives and generating solution alternatives). For the first thirteen weeks, however, the ethnically homogeneous groups outperformed the heterogeneous groups. The ethnically heterogeneous groups thus needed to spend more time together than the homogeneous groups in order to perform effectively. Another study carried out by Watson, Johnson, and Zgourides (2002) confirmed the positive results of the earlier study (Watson *et al.*, 1993). For the first fifteen weeks, the ethnically homogeneous and heterogeneous groups performed equally well on several cognitive tasks. However, in the end, the ethnically heterogeneous groups outperformed the homogeneous groups. In a similar vein, McLeod and Lobel (1992) showed that ethnically diverse groups produced ideas that were of higher quality compared to ethnically homogeneous groups.

When comparing field studies on the association between ethnic diversity and performance outcomes, the results are more mixed. One field study performed by O'Reilly, Williams, and Barsade (1998) showed that ethnic diversity related positively to creativity and implementation ability in teams. Teams composed of Asians and Anglo-Americans turned out to be more creative and better at implementing new ideas compared to teams that were composed solely of Anglo-Americans. Other field studies indicated a more mixed, a negative, or no relationship at all between ethnic diversity and performance outcomes. For instance, a study performed by Riordan and Shore (1997) showed that the level of perceived workgroup productivity depended on the proportion of ethnic minority (African-Americans and Hispanics) versus ethnic majority

(Anglo-Americans) members in a team, as well as on the particular ethnic group studied. Anglo-American employees perceived less work-group productivity when working in teams that were composed of mostly minority members. However, African-American participants reported the same level of workgroup productivity across different team compositions. Other studies indicated that ethnic diversity related negatively or not at all to performance evaluations (Lefkowitz, 1994; Sacket, DuBois, and Noe, 1991; Greenhaus, Parasuraman, and Wormley, 1990). Greenhaus et al. (1990), for example, found that African-Americans were rated lower than Anglo-Americans by Anglo-American supervisors on task and relationship dimensions of performance, while Ely (2004) reported finding no relationship between ethnic diversity and objective measures of performance such as sales revenue, customer satisfaction, and sales productivity.

Behavioral outcomes

Much of the research which has examined ethnic diversity on a team level has shown it to be negatively associated with behavioral outcomes. For instance, Pelled and colleagues (Pelled, 1993; Pelled et al., 1999) concluded in their studies that ethnic diversity was associated with higher levels of emotional conflict in teams. Also, a study performed by Hoffman (1985) indicated that an increase in African-American representation in Anglo-American teams was negatively associated with the frequency of interpersonal communication. In the same study, however, results also demonstrated that an increased African-American representation related positively to organizational-level communication.

Whereas some studies have shown negative relationships between ethnic diversity and behavioral outcomes, others have shown positive relationships. For instance, a study performed by O'Reilly, Williams, and Barsade (1999) indicated that Anglo-American workers were more cooperative when working in ethnically diverse groups composed of Asians and Anglo-Americans than in groups composed solely of Anglo-Americans. The authors explained this puzzling result by suggesting that Asians may have had more collectivistic values and that collectivism could be positively related to cooperation with colleagues in teams. Cox, Lobel, and McLeod (1991) found similar results while studying differences in cooperative behavior between African-American and Anglo-American undergraduate and graduate students on a Prisoner's Dilemma task. Results indicated that African-American groups as well as mixed groups of African-Americans and Anglo-Americans were more cooperative than groups composed solely of Anglo-Americans. The authors expressed the need to further explore the positive effects of non-western cultures on organizational behavior and effectiveness. However, expectations with regard to cultural value differences across ethnic groups should be interpreted with caution, as other studies do not confirm the above described results (Espinoza and Garza, 1985; Garza and Santos, 1991).

Depending on the behavioral outcomes examined, some studies reported nonsignificant results. For example, the study of Pelled *et al.* (1999) showed no relationship between ethnic diversity and task-related conflicts in teams. Also, Riordan and Shore (1997) did not find a significant association between the degree of ethnic (dis)similarity and the perceived level of cohesiveness in teams.

Affective outcomes

Some studies have indicated that ethnic diversity is negatively related to affective outcomes, especially for ethnic minority employees. Greenhaus *et al.* (1990) found that ethnic minority managers (in this case African-Americans) felt less accepted and experienced lower levels of job satisfaction compared to managers of the ethnic majority (in this case, Anglo-American). Likewise, results from a study among Dutch civil service workers (Verkuyten, de Jong, and Masson, 1993) showed that ethnic minority employees perceived less job satisfaction than ethnic majority (Dutch) employees. In addition, employees who frequently worked together with ethnically similar colleagues showed more job satisfaction.

Furthermore, Lugtenberg and Peeters (2004) examined acculturation attitudes among employees in a Dutch governmental organization and results showed that acculturation attitudes of ethnic minority employees related differently to aspects of job-related well-being. A marginalized attitude among ethnic minority employees related to feeling less competent, less committed, and less satisfied at work, whereas ethnic minority employees who were positive toward integration reported being more competent and committed toward work. Similarly, a study performed by Luijters, van der Zee, and Otten (2004) indicated that "dual identity" (integration) was the preferred acculturation attitude among ethnic minority employees in the Netherlands. Also, a "dual identity" was connected to intercultural traits such as flexibility and emotional stability. Finally, Amason, Allen, and Holmes (1999) studied the level of acculturative stress (i.e. the amount of stress caused by adaptation to another [majority] culture) among Hispanic workers in a North American company. Results indicated that the perceived level of acculturative stress among Hispanic employees depended on the amount and type of social support received from Anglo-American co-workers. In particular, respect for and help with personal problems proved to be types of social support that were negatively related to the perception of acculturative stress among Hispanic employees.

Mediating effects of behavioral and affective outcomes on performance

A small number of studies have investigated the mediating role of behavioral or affective outcomes in the relationship between ethnic diversity and performance. There is some support for this mediating role. For instance, Watson et al. (1993) showed that ethnically homogeneous groups reported more "process effectiveness" than heterogeneous groups during the first three task periods (up to thirteen weeks). For the same three task periods, ethnically homogeneous teams outperformed heterogeneous teams. In the last time period after thirteen weeks, however, no significant process differences were found between both groups, and heterogeneous groups outperformed homogeneous groups on two types of performance measures (range of perspectives and alternatives generated). Although mediation effects were not statistically examined in this study, the case might be that heterogeneous groups needed more time to overcome behavioral difficulties than homogeneous groups did in order to perform effectively. Furthermore, Greenhaus et al. (1990) found that the relationship between ethnically diverse managers (black versus white managers) and performance evaluations was partly mediated by the lack of organizational experience among black managers. In particular, black managers perceived less job discretion and less acceptance than white managers which subsequently led to worse performance evaluations by their supervisors.

Other studies have not found support for the assumed mediating effect of behavioral processes on performance outcomes. Results from a longitudinal laboratory study of Watson et al. (2002) showed that differences in the level of cohesiveness between homogeneous and heterogeneous groups did not exist during all time periods, and thus could not mediate the relationship between ethnic diversity and performance. Interestingly, the study of Watson et al. (2002) did find differences in leadership styles between ethnically heterogeneous and homogeneous groups. The leadership style of homogeneous groups was task-oriented, whereas heterogeneous groups had an interpersonal leadership style. It may be that interpersonal leadership is necessary for dealing with the behavioral or attitudinal differences in ethnically diverse groups, while homogeneous groups have more similarity in behaviors and attitudes so that task-related leadership is more effective. Finally, results from a study performed by Pelled *et al.* (1999) showed that ethnic diversity was related to more emotional conflicts in teams. However, the level of emotional conflicts had no significant effect on group performance. Also, no direct effect of ethnic diversity on performance outcomes was found. Hence, the study of Pelled *et al.* (1999) failed to confirm the mediating role of affective outcomes. Noteworthy, however, is the fact that group longevity and task routineness decreased the positive relationship between ethnic diversity and emotional conflict. In other words, the longer a group worked together and the more tasks that became routine, the less emotional conflicts in ethnically diverse groups were reported.

Conclusions

Altogether, we reviewed nineteen empirical studies on ethnic diversity. Of these studies, eight (42.1%) investigated the effect of ethnic diversity on performance outcomes, ten (52.6%) examined ethnic diversity effects on behavioral outcomes, six (31.6%) related ethnic diversity to affective outcomes, and six (31.6%) examined two or more outcomes simultaneously. When linking the outcomes of these studies to the theories discussed earlier, several main conclusions can be drawn.

First, the predictions derived from social identity theory, social categorization theory, and the similarity-attraction paradigm are supported in most studies. Studies showed that ethnic diversity related negatively to commitment (Riordan and Shore, 1997), organizational experiences, career satisfaction, advancement opportunities (Greenhaus *et al.*, 1990), emotional conflict (Pelled, 1993; Pelled *et al.*, 1999), interpersonal communication (Hoffman, 1985), and job satisfaction (Verkuyten *et al.*, 1993). However, this conclusion is not as straightforward as it may seem and it should be qualified. Ethnic diversity does not relate negatively to all behavioral or affective outcomes. For instance, ethnic diversity does not appear to relate to task conflict (Pelled *et al.*, 1999), and it has a positive effect on organizational communication (Hoffman, 1985). Also, the effect of ethnic diversity on behavioral or affective outcomes seems to depend on the specific ethnic group (Riordan and Shore, 1997). Furthermore, other variables may moderate the negative effects of ethnic diversity on behavioral and affective outcomes. For example, a study performed by Pelled and colleagues (1999) showed that group longevity (the time that a group works together) and performing routine tasks appear to diminish the negative effects of ethnic diversity on emotional conflict in teams.

Second, the predictions based on information and decision-making theory are supported in longitudinal laboratory studies, but not in field studies. One reason for this could be that ethnically diverse groups of students in laboratory studies are somehow different from ethnically diverse teams studied in organizations. Another reason may be that laboratory studies have a longitudinal design, while most field studies have a cross-sectional design. Interestingly, laboratory studies only find positive results of ethnic diversity on performance in the last time period, which indicates that ethnically diverse groups may need more time to overcome initial behavioral or cultural differences than homogeneous groups. Furthermore, the outcome variables studied in laboratory studies are often different from the outcomes studied in field studies. Laboratory studies typically examine cognitive tasks, whereas field studies typically examine more subjective performance outcomes, such as perceived work-group productivity or performance evaluations. Also, other variables (like economic developments) are likely to influence performances of teams in real organizations.

Third, some support is found for the assumption that cultural values (i.e. collectivism versus individualism) affect behavioral outcomes in ethnically diverse teams. In particular, it is assumed that people from non-western cultures are more collectivistic than people from western cultures, which has been found to relate positively to cooperation in teams. Two studies (Cox et al., 1991; O'Reilly et al., 1999) support this hypothesis while two other studies (Espinoza and Garza, 1985; Garza and Santos, 1991) do not. One reason for these contradictory findings may be that, although people are born in non-western cultures, they may have spent a lot of time in an individualistic culture and adapted to the values of that culture. Also, when people from non-western cultures constitute a numerical minority, the pressure to adapt to the (individualistic) values of the ethnic majority may undermine the expression of collectivistic behavior.

Fourth, a small number of studies indicate that acculturation attitudes have a significant impact on behavioral and attitudinal outcomes among immigrant employees. The degree to which immigrant employees identify with their own ethnic culture and also the dominant culture of a host society affects important affective outcomes such as competence, commitment, and satisfaction toward work. The initial results of the first studies on acculturation and work outcomes appear to be promising. Studies that examine how differences in acculturation attitudes relate to work outcomes should thus be continued in future research.

Recommendations for future research and practice

In this final section, some future avenues for ethnic diversity research are presented. Furthermore, a number of recommendations are made for HRM managers on how to develop a constructive diversity policy.

Opportunities for future research on ethnic diversity

Although ethnic diversity research has broadened our knowledge of the potential consequences of ethnic diversity in organizations to some degree, some recommendations can still be made for future studies. First, most of the ethnic diversity studies discussed in this chapter have ignored the potential impact of the organizational context on ethnic diversity outcomes. However, certain aspects of an organizational context, such as the presence of a diversity policy and having an organizational culture that promotes the inclusiveness of ethnically diverse employees, are also likely to affect organizational outcomes. Second, longitudinal laboratory studies demonstrated an interesting longitudinal effect of ethnic diversity on performance outcomes. Ethnically homogeneous groups seem to outperform heterogeneous groups in the first few weeks, while heterogeneous groups outperform homogeneous groups in the long run. However, most field studies are cross-sectional, which may explain the fact that a positive relationship between ethnic diversity and performance outcomes cannot often be demonstrated. Longitudinal designs in field research should shed more light on this issue. Third, many ethnic diversity studies are performed in the United States. However, ethnic cultures of minority groups in the United States may be very different from ethnic cultures of minority groups in other countries, for instance with respect to the command of the dominant language, religious practices, or other values and norms. This limits the possibility of generalizing the findings to other ethnic minority groups in other countries. Thus, more ethnic diversity studies need to be performed outside the United States. Fourth, many field studies on ethnic diversity have only included subjective outcomes. For organizations, it would be crucial to learn whether or not subjective outcomes such as perceived cohesiveness, job satisfaction, organizational commitment, and cooperative behavior relate to objective outcomes such as the level of absenteeism, turnover of employees, or better objective performances of teams (Schaufeli, 2005). Fifth, although some subpopulations of immigrants, such as refugees and first-generation non-western immigrants, appear to have a higher risk of ending up on social welfare because of psychosomatic complaints, only a small number of studies examine the link between ethnic diversity and occupational health outcomes.

Towards the successful management of diversity at work

Visions, goals, and initiatives that are developed in organizations with respect to ethnic diversity initiatives appear to differ from one organization to the other. Moreover, not many studies on diversity have considered the effects of organizational diversity initiatives on important organizational outcomes. However, some ideas on the differential impact of ethnic diversity initiatives on organizational outcomes are mentioned by Cox and Blake (1991). They distinguish between three types of organizations: monolithic, plural, and multicultural organizations. In monolithic organizations, ethnic diversity policies are limited to the inclusion of ethnic minority employees. Research shows that this type of "affirmative action" has negative side effects in terms of less acceptance, more stress reactions, and less self-esteem among the personnel recruited in this manner (Heilman, 1994; Heilman, Block, and Lucas, 1992; Heilman, Rivero, and Brett, 1991). Plural organizations are characterized by a more proactive recruitment and promotion of ethnic minority employees in the organization. However, ethnic minorities are ultimately expected to assimilate to the dominant organizational culture. In multicultural organizations, differences are appreciated and used for organizational and personal gain. Cox and Blake argue that managing cultural diversity (which reflects the multicultural option) may lead to several organizational benefits such as reduced turnover and absenteeism, recruiting the best personnel, more cultural insight and sensitivity while marketing products and services, and increasing creativity and innovation.

In a similar vein, Ely and Thomas (2001) have developed three perspectives based on which predictions can be made regarding how cultural diversity in workgroups relates to the realization of organizational benefits. These predictions mirror to some degree the organizational types defined by Cox and Blake (1991). The first perspective is named the integration-and-learning perspective and posits that the insights, skills, and experiences of employees that are derived from being a member of various cultural identity groups are "potentially valuable resources that work groups can use to rethink its primary tasks and redefine its markets, products, strategies, and business practices in ways that will advance its mission" (p. 240). The authors argue that the integration-and-learning perspective can help facilitate open discussion that is based on different points of view and explicitly linked to cultural experiences. It encourages employees to express themselves as members of their cultural identity groups, which enhances opportunities for cross-cultural learning and workgroup creativity.

The second perspective is called the access-and-legitimacy perspective and is based on "a recognition that the organization's markets and constituencies are culturally diverse. In this case, organizations are promoting diversity in parts of its own workforce as a way of gaining access to and legitimacy with those markets and constituent groups" (p. 243). The authors warn that race-based staffing patterns may lead to racial segregation along functional levels, with whites having higher functional levels than people of color. This may increase interracial and interfunctional tensions and inhibit productive learning, as described in the first perspective.

The third perspective is called the discrimination-and-fairness perspective and is characterized by "a belief in a culturally diverse workforce as a moral imperative to ensure justice and the fair treatment of all members of society. It emphasizes diversification efforts on providing equal opportunities in hiring and promotion, suppressing prejudicial attitudes, and eliminating discrimination" (p. 245). The authors argue that cultural diversity on a moral basis does not emphasize the possible benefits that cultural diversity can offer. Instead, this perspective would lead to discussions about fairness that may strain interracial relations and put an emphasis on equality instead of valuing cultural diversity.

In conclusion, the specific vision, goals, and actions that need to be developed with respect to ethnic diversity are unique for each organization and depend on the specific context of the organization. Ethnically homogeneous workgroups may first want to focus on diversity goals such as the recruitment and inclusion of ethnically diverse personnel, while organizations that already have an ethnically diverse workforce may want to identify the consequences of ethnic diversity on important organizational outcomes. Literature on diversity policies, management, and initiatives suggests that a multicultural approach and an integration-and-learning perspective on diversity may be most beneficial for organizations.

References

Amason, P., Allen, M. W., and Holmes, S. A. (1999). Social support and acculturative stress in the multicultural workplace. *Journal of Applied Communication Research* 27: 310–34.

Berry, J. W. (1997). Immigration, acculturation, and adaptation. *Applied Psychology* 46: 5–34.

Berry, J. W., Kim, U., Power, S., Young, M., and Bujaki, M. (1989). Acculturation attitudes in plural societies. *Applied Psychology: An International Review* 38: 185–206.

Bourhis, R. Y., Moise, L. C., Perreault, S., and Senécal, S. (1997). Towards an interactive acculturation model: a social psychological approach. *International Journal of Psychology* 32: 369–86.

Byrne, D. (1971). *The attraction paradigm*. New York: Academic Press.

Cashmore, E. (1996). *Dictionary of race and ethnic relations*. London and New York: Routledge.

Cox, T. H. (1993). *Cultural diversity in organizations: theory, research, and practice*. San Francisco: Berret-Koehler.

Cox, T. H. and Blake, S. (1991). Managing cultural diversity: implications for organizational competitiveness. *Academy of Management Executive* 5: 45–56.

Cox, T. H., Lobel, S., and McLeod, P. (1991). Effects of ethnic group cultural differences on cooperative and competitive behavior on group task. *Academy of Management Journal* 34: 827–47.

Ekamper, P. and Wetters, R. (2005). *First EU demographic estimates for 2004*. Retrieved October 1, 2005, from www.nidi.knaw.nl/en/publications/2004.

Ely, R. J. (2004). A field study of group diversity, participation in diversity education programs, and performance. *Journal of Organizational Behavior* 25: 755–80.

Ely, R. J. and Thomas, D. A. (2001). Cultural diversity at work: the effects of diversity perspectives on work group processes and outcomes. *Administrative Science Quarterly* 46: 229–73.

Espinoza, J. and Garza, R. (1985). Social group salience and inter-ethnic cooperation. *Journal of Experimental Social Psychology* 21: 380–92.

Garza, R. and Santos, S. (1991). Ingroup/outgroup balance and interdependent inter-ethnic behavior. *Journal of Experimental Social Psychology* 27: 124–37.

Greenhaus, J. H., Parasuraman, S., and Wormley, W. M. (1990). Effects of race on organizational experiences, job performance evaluation, and career outcomes. *Academy of Management Journal* 33: 64–86.

Grossman, R. J. (2000). Is diversity working? *HR Magazine* 45: 46–50.

Haslam, S. A., Powell, C., and Turner, J. C. (2000). Social identity, self-categorization and work motivation: rethinking the contribution of the group to positive and sustainable organizational outcomes. *Applied Psychology: An International Review* 49: 319–39.

Heilman, M. E. (1994). Affirmative action: some unintended consequences for working women. *Research in Organizational Behaviour* 16: 125–69.

Heilman, M. E., Block, C. J., and Lucas, J. A. (1992). Presumed incompetent? Stigmatization and affirmative action efforts. *Journal of Applied Psychology* 77: 436–544.

Heilman, M. E., Rivero, J. C., and Brett, J. F. (1991). Skirting the competence issue: effects of sex based preferential selection on task choices of women and men. *Journal of Applied Psychology* 76: 99–105.

Hoffman, E. (1985). The effect of race-ratio composition on the frequency of organizational communication. *Social Psychology Quarterly* 48: 17–26.

Hofstede, G. (1980). *Culture's consequences: international differences in work-related values*. Beverly Hills, CA: Sage.
—— (1989). Organising for cultural diversity. *European Management Journal* 7: 390–7.
—— (1991). *Cultures and organizations: software of the mind*. London: McGraw-Hill.
Jackson, S. E., Joshi A., and Erhardt, N. L. (2003). Recent research on team and organizational diversity: SWOT analysis and implications. *Journal of Management* 29: 801–30.
Jackson, S. E., May, K. E., and Whitney, K. (1995). Understanding the dynamics of diversity in decision-making teams. In R. A. Guzzo and E. Salas (eds.), *Team effectiveness and decision making in organizations* (pp. 204–61). San Francisco: Jossey-Bass.
Jehn, K. A., Northcraft G. B., and Neale, M. A. (1999). Why differences make a difference: a field study of diversity, conflict and performance in workgroups. *Administrative Science Quarterly* 44: 741–63.
Kanter, R. M. (1977). *Men and women of the corporation*. New York: Basic Books.
Larkey, L. K. (1996). Toward a theory of communicative interactions in culturally diverse workgroups. *Academy of Management Review* 21: 464–91.
Lefkowitz, J. (1994). Race as a factor in job placement: serendipitous findings of "ethnic drift." *Personnel Psychology* 47: 497–513.
Linnehan, F. and Konrad, A. M. (1999). Diluting diversity: implications for intergroup inequality in organizations. *Journal of Management Inquiry* 8: 399–414.
Lugtenberg, M. and Peeters, M. C. W. (2004). Acculturatievisies van allochtone en autochtone werknemers: is er een verband met welbevinden op het werk? *De Psycholoog* September: 417–24.
Luijters, K., van der Zee, K. I., and Otten, S. (2004). Acculturation in organizations: when a dual identity is evaluated most positively. Paper presented at the Werkgemeenschap van Onderzoekers in de Arbeid- en Organisatie Psychologie (WAOP) conference, Utrecht, 2004.
Maznevski, M. L. (1994). Understanding our differences: performance in decision-making groups with diverse members. *Human Relations* 47: 531–52.
McLeod, P. and Lobel, S. (1992). The effects of ethnic diversity on idea generation in small groups. Paper presented at the Annual Academy of Management Meeting, Las Vegas, Nevada.
Mullen, B., Brown, R. J., and Smith, C. (1992). Ingroup bias as a function of salience, relevance and status: an integration. *European Journal of Social Psychology* 22: 103–22.
Oakes, P. J. (1987). The salience of social categories. In J. C. Turner, M. A. Hogg, P. J. Oakes, S. D. Reicher, and M. S. Wetherell (eds.), *Rediscovering the social group: a self-categorization theory* (pp. 117–41). Oxford: Blackwell.
O'Reilly, C. A., Williams, K. Y., and Barsade, S. G. (1998). Group demography and innovation: does diversity help? In E. Mannix and M. Neale (eds.), *Research in the management of groups and teams* (vol. 1, pp. 183–207). Greenwich, CT: JAI Press.

(1999). *The impact of relational demography on teamwork: when majorities are in the minority.* Research paper no. 1551. Palo Alto, CA: Stanford University, Graduate School of Business.

Organisation for Economic Co-operation and Development (2003). *Trends in international migration: SOPEMI 2002 edition.* Paris: OECD Paris Centre.

Pelled, L. H. (1993). Team diversity and conflict: a multivariate analysis. Working paper, School of Business Administration, University of Southern California.

Pelled, L. H., Eisenhardt, K. M., and Xin, K. R. (1999). Exploring the black box: an analysis of work group diversity, conflict, and performance. *Administrative Science Quarterly* 44: 1–28.

Redfield, R., Linton, R., and Herkovits, M. (1936). Memorandum on the study of acculturation. *American Anthropologist* 38: 149–52.

Rijsman, J. B. (1997). Social diversity: a social psychological analysis and some implications for groups and organizations. *European Journal of Work and Organizational Psychology* 6: 139–52.

Riordan, C. M. and Shore, L. M. (1997). Demographic diversity and employee attitudes: an empirical examination of relational demography within work-units. *Journal of Applied Psychology* 82: 342–58.

Sackett, P., DuBois, C., and Noe, A. (1991). Tokenism in performance evaluation: the effects of work representation on male–female and black–white differences in performance ratings. *Journal of Applied Psychology* 76: 263–7.

Schaufeli, W. B. (2005). The future of occupational health psychology. *Applied Psychology: An International Review* 53: 502–17.

Shell (2006). *Shell and diversity.* Retrieved October 1, 2006, from www.shell.com/home/Framework?siteId=royal-en&FC2=&FC3=/royal-en/html/iwgen/who_we_are/shell_and_diversity/shell_and_diversity.html.

Smith, A. D. (1991). The ethnic basis of national identity. In A. D. Smith (ed.), *National identity* (pp. 19–42). London: Penguin Books.

Smith, P. B. and Bond, M. H. (1998). *Social psychology across cultures* (2nd edn). Bath: Prentice Hall.

Stasser, G. (1992). Pooling of unshared information during group discussions. In S. Worchel, W. Wood, and J. A. Simpson (eds.), *Group process and productivity* (pp. 48–67). Newbury Park, CA: Sage.

Tajfel, H. (1978). *Differentiation between social groups: studies in the social psychology of intergroup relations.* London: Academic Press.

Tajfel, H., Billig, M., Bundy, R. P., and Flament, C. (1971). Social categorisation and intergroup behaviour. *European Journal of Social Psychology* 27: 27–36.

Taylor, D. M. and Moghaddam, F. M. (1994). *Theories of intergroup relations: international and social psychological perspectives* (2nd edn). Westport, CT: Praeger.

Tsui, A. S., Egan, T. D., and O'Reilly, C. A. (1992). Being different: relational demography and organizational attachment. *Administrative Science Quarterly* 37: 549–79.

Turner, J. C. (1982). Towards a cognitive redefinition of the social group. In H. Tajfel (ed.), *Social identity and intergroup relations* (pp. 15–40). Cambridge: Cambridge University Press.

(1985). Social categorization and the self-concept: a social cognitive theory of group behavior. In E. J. Lawler (ed.), *Advances in group processes* (vol. 2, pp. 77–122). Greenwich, CT: JAI Press.

Turner, J. C., Hogg, M. A., and Oakes, P. (1987). *Rediscovering the social group: a self-categorization theory.* Oxford: Blackwell.

Van de Vijver, F. J. R. and Phalet, K. (2004). Assessment in multicultural groups: the role of acculturation. *Applied Psychology: An International Review* 53: 215–36.

Verkuyten, M., de Jong, W., and Masson, C. N. (1993). Job satisfaction among ethnic minorities in the Netherlands. *Applied Psychology: An International Review* 42: 171–89.

Watson, E., Johnson, L., and Zgourides, G. D. (2002). The influence of ethnic diversity on leadership, group process, and performance: an examination of learning teams. *International Journal of Intercultural Relations* 26: 1–16.

Watson, W. E., Kumar, K., and Michaelsen, L. K. (1993). Cultural diversity's impact on interaction process and performance: comparing homogeneous and diverse task groups. *Academy of Management Journal* 36: 590–602.

Williams, K. Y. and O'Reilly, C. A. (1998). Demography and diversity in organisations: a review of 40 years of research. In B. M. Staw and L. L. Cummings (eds.), *Research in Organizational Behavior* (vol. 20, pp. 77–140). Greenwich, CT: JAI Press.

Wittenbaum, G. and Stasser, G. (1996). Management and information in small groups. In J. Nye and M. Brower (eds.), *What's social about social cognition? Social cognition research in small groups* (pp. 3–28). Thousand Oaks, CA: Sage.

Part II

Individual attempts at restoring the balance

12   Skeleton key or siren song: is coping the answer to balancing work and well-being?

Jaco Pienaar

That workplace stress exists and impacts on individual, organizational, and societal health is a commonly known fact. Stress has a significant economic impact on individuals and organizations (Danna and Griffin, 1999). Yet, if people perceive themselves as having the resources they require to meet the challenges they experience, they may suffer fewer negative consequences following exposure to said challenges, be they physiological or psychological (see Ganster and Fusilier, 1989). Coping has been described as an individual's ability to deal with stressful organizational situations, and been considered the variable that, in relation to its effectiveness, determines the degree of negative physiological and psychological consequences experienced (Bhagat *et al.*, 2001; Lazarus and Folkman, 1984). The coping styles that individuals use in responding to experienced challenges are related to specific organizational aspects such as job satisfaction (Bhagat, Allie, and Ford, 1995), and general well-being (Greenglass, 1996). In every industry or profession, prescriptive regulatory systems and guidelines shape the meaning individuals attach to their work (Aneshensel, 1992; Lai, Chan, Ko, and Boey, 2000; Pearlin, 1999). In turn, this meaning may be expected to inform employees' perceptions of work, influencing how they approach experienced challenges and accept certain coping strategies.

Work represents a unique context regarding the study of stress and coping (Brief and George, 1991), when compared to, for example, coping as found among hospital patients or professional athletes. If coping is viewed as a transaction between individuals and the environment in which they find themselves, the success thereof can only be determined by also seriously considering the environment in which the transaction takes place (Forsythe and Compas, 1987). This environment may determine the type of coping that is most effective in resolving an experienced challenge. For example, Violanti, Marshall, and Howe (1985) suggested that alcohol use does not develop apart from occupational structure, in their investigation of a macho police environment where alcohol abuse was more acceptable than the expression of distressing emotions.

Of course, no single coping approach can always be adaptive across all situations. In fact, overrelying on any one strategy may be even further damaging. A range of coping strategies should be applied across a range of stressful situations, and individuals should also demonstrate flexibility in the application of their strategies (Cheng and Cheung, 2005). While we have gradually become better able to distinguish between the effects of acutely (e.g. being retrenched) and chronically (e.g. daily monotonous work tasks) stressful situations, we still lack an understanding of how individuals cope with these situations sequentially (Sulsky and Smith, 2005). With the nature of the modern working life often requiring individuals to adjust and cope continuously, some coping styles have been found to be more effective in dealing with specific stressors. A specific form of conflict may, for example, require a specific form of coping (Rotondo, Carlson, and Kincaid, 2003).

A good understanding of the coping process and the factors relevant to the process is therefore important for managing employee mental health and organizational performance. This chapter seeks to delineate the concept of coping by first looking at its constituent components, taking into consideration specific issues such as the role of social support, and then elucidating individual dispositions important to coping. The chapter ends off by highlighting some unresolved issues regarding coping research and organizational responses. The purpose of the chapter is therefore to provide a thorough theoretical overview, which traces the development of the construct and, furthermore, offers suggestions for addressing commonly experienced and continual problems in this area.

Occupational stress, coping, and appraisal

Occupational stress and coping

Dewe, Cox, and Ferguson (1993) have emphasized that there are cognitive and emotional components to stress and that reactions to it occur on these levels as well. The stress process can be seen as sequential and cyclical, whereby the presence and perception of demands is followed by an evaluative process of the recognized demands, and then a response which may imply a change to the individual's current physiological and/or psychological state (Dewe *et al.*, 1993). From early on, authors on the subject of coping have noted its transactional nature (Lazarus and Folkman, 1984), in which every step may loop back to previous steps and, in turn, be influenced by them. The initial realization that a challenging situation exists has been labeled the "coping trigger" (Sulsky and Smith, 2005: 181), and as such represents the first step in a sequence of coping events. Siu, Spector, Cooper, Lu, and Yu (2002) also attribute stress to the *perception* of pressure, and not just the *presence* of it. The perception that a stressor exists should be followed by the realization that a response to it is demanded, be it at the physiological, behavioral, or psychological/emotional level. Thus, the person is forced to deviate from otherwise normal functioning in responding to the perceived challenge (Bhagat *et al.*, 1994). Besides this, another important consideration in the stress sequence is the individual's failure to cope effectively, and what such a failure may imply (Lazarus and Folkman, 1984).

Coping is defined as the efforts an individual may exhibit cognitively or behaviorally to meet a challenge they deem themselves as not having the resources for meeting (Lazarus and Folkman, 1984), and these challenges may be at an internal or external level (Folkman and Lazarus, 1980). Evans, Coman, Stanley, and Burrows (1993: 238) define *effective* coping as "(a) the efficacy with which the individual deals with their emotional responses to stressors and acts to resolve the stressors, and (b) the cost of their effectiveness to the individual." These definitions share the following: at the individual level, there is a reaction to the stressor at the cognitive, emotional, or behavioral level, or any combination of these. The stressor is appraised as demanding a response, again, on any one level or a combination of levels, and the stressor comes from within the individual, the environment outside of the individual, or the effect the one has on the other.

Primary and secondary appraisal

The process of coping typically takes the following form. First, there must exist a situation which the individual deems as exceeding his or her existing or available resources and which, therefore, is seen as a threat to his or her well-being. This step in the process is termed *primary appraisal*. In primary appraisal, the individual assesses events as potentially irrelevant, beneficial, or stressful. An irrelevant appraisal implies exactly what the name suggests – it has no consequence for the individual, and passes without significantly interacting with that individual, while beneficial appraisals are those that hold the promise of a positive outcome. Appraisals considered stressful may be considered in terms of harm/loss, threat, or challenge (Lazarus and Folkman, 1984; Lazarus and Launier, 1978). With harm/loss, the individual has already suffered the loss, and needs to come to terms with the fact that it has happened, for example when losing a valued position in the organization or a strategic partnership with an influential colleague. Threat and challenge appraisals both consider the possible outcomes of the coping process, with the difference being that threat appraisals are made when individuals expect a negative outcome, while challenge appraisals are made when the individual expects a positive outcome (Lazarus and Folkman, 1984).

Stress is experienced in the realization that something needs to be done to address the experienced threat, albeit with a lack of resources, which may imply an uncertain (and by further implication possibly negative) outcome (Locke and Taylor, 1990; Lai *et al.*, 2000). *Secondary appraisal* entails the individual's estimation of the adequacy of his or her resources in meeting the perceived challenge. Secondary appraisal thus involves a weighing and consideration of possible responses, and the selection of a coping strategy deemed most appropriate (Sulsky and Smith, 2005).

In considering different possible responses, factors such as the perceived benefits and drawbacks of each strategy, individual readiness to engage in a particular strategy, availability of support, and individual differences may play a role in selection (Sulsky and Smith, 2005). Roth and Cohen (1986) suggest that individual perceptions of controllability and levels of confidence, knowledge of the source of stress, and the anticipated long-term effects of the stressor further affect the selection of a coping strategy. Lazarus and Folkman (1984) have proposed that individuals evaluate the options available, their own abilities to effectively implement a strategy, and the likelihood of success for a chosen strategy. Individuals also consider how the perceived challenge will impact on their values and needs, and their appraisal is a function of the importance of these values and needs (Schuler, 1985).

Of course, the distinction between primary and secondary appraisal is more easily made theoretically than practically. Even Lazarus and Folkman (1984: 35) acknowledge that primary and secondary appraisal "interact with each other in shaping the degree of stress and the strength and quality (or content) of the emotional reaction." Essentially, the process is instantaneous, continuous, circular, and most likely unperceived by the individual experiencing it.

It also needs to be acknowledged that the processes of primary and secondary appraisal are highly individualistic. Individuals may, for example, take notice of interpersonal, situational, and contextual cues to different extents. Also, different coping strategies may require different cognitive processes (Chen and Cheung, 2005).

Lazarus (1991) suggests that the benefit of coping lies in the influence it exerts in stress appraisal. It is through the process of primary and secondary appraisal that the individual's perception of the challenge is changed (Lazarus, 1991; Rotondo *et al.*, 2003). The latter authors are of the opinion that, at best, using the wrong coping strategy may slow down resolving the perceived challenge and experienced uncertainty. At the very worst, of course, a wrong choice of strategy may lead to a further aggravation of the stressful situation.

Understanding the qualitative nature of appraisals has also been theorized as relevant to understanding coping (Lazarus and Folkman, 1984; McCrae, 1984, 1989), and attributing qualitative valence to appraisals may serve to simplify the coping process (Bjorck and Cohen, 1993; Bjorck and Klewicki, 1997). For example, reappraisal at the loss of a valuable organizational position, as may happen during retrenchment, may be more effective than an active coping strategy. In the case of retrenchment, the individual may do better trying to see the situation as a positive opportunity for a change of job, instead of actively trying to get the old job back, when the latter action seems unlikely to result in any success. The use of reappraisal would imply that the individual no longer exerts personal effort (in vain) to change the situation. Specifically, qualitative appraisals "might adaptively serve to limit the range of potential coping options, thereby preventing the need to consider all such choices in any given situation" (Bjorck and Cohen, 1993: 57).

Appraisal and coping Personal and situational characteristics, as well as contextual cues, seemingly play less of a role in determining the use of coping strategies than the individual's own perception of the challenging situation (Fleishman, 1984; Folkman and Lazarus, 1980).

When individuals perceive that they have greater control over the challenges they are experiencing, they are also likely to feel that they are less stressed and facing less threat or loss (Bjorck and Klewicki, 1997; Vitaliano *et al.*, 1990). An individual's unique *expectancies* for success should also act to influence his or her appraisal (Bandura, 1982). Here, expectancies refer to individuals' beliefs in their own ability to success-fully produce a behavior they deem to be associated with a successful outcome. The more positive an individual's expectancy, the more likely the appraisal is to be positive.

It has been indicated that challenge appraisals are associated with problem-focused approaches (McCrae, 1989), that threats are associated with avoidance, and that losses are associated with emotion-focused coping (McCrae, 1984). The seeking of support is, in turn, associated with dealing with emotional reactions to stress (Bjorck and Cohen, 1993; Bjorck and Klewicki, 1997). The challenge therefore lies in helping the individual to appraise a stressor as a challenge, rather than as a threat, or even worse, as a potential loss, if possible. Let us now turn to a closer examination of the individual components of coping identified in pre-vious research.

Components of coping

Stress and coping research has yet to produce a consistent or universal conceptualization of the dimensions of coping (Brough, O'Driscoll, and Kalliath, 2005). A central outstanding issue in this relates to being able to properly describe all of the fundamental dimensions or strategies of coping. Although this inconsistency in conceptualization implies a diversity of theoretical frameworks and approaches, it also carries with it a number of difficulties when it comes to comparing coping results across studies that make use of different measuring instruments (Cook and Heppner, 1997).

The conceptualization of coping presented by Folkman and Lazarus (1980) has subsequently been crystallized into two broad approaches: problem-focused coping and emotion-focused coping. Avoidance has also been suggested as a third basic coping strategy (Endler and Parker, 1990), and refers to choosing not to do anything about the experienced challenge. A review of literature using a specific coping inventory (The Coping Orientations to Problems Experienced [COPE] Inventory; Carver, Scheier, and Weintraub, 1989) further supports these three dimensions (Kallasmaa and Pulver, 2000). Cox and Ferguson (1991) have also expressed support for the three dimensions, and have suggested reappraisal as a fourth. Support for the latter dimension also comes from Phelps and Jarvis (1994), who termed it "acceptance." Reappraisal (or acceptance) can be taken to imply seeing the event in a different (more positive) light, in order to acknowledge it (and perhaps its unchangeability), and move on. Results of a second-order factor analysis of the authors of the COPE are also strongly suggestive of the four factors here indicated (Carver *et al.*, 1989). In a review of the results of the factor analytic studies of the COPE questionnaire, it was found that four factors seem to underlie the COPE questionnaire, which might be termed *approach coping*, *social/emotional coping*, *avoidance coping*, and *reappraisal* (Pienaar and Rothmann, 2003). Oxlad, Miller-Lewis, and Wade (2004), in reevaluating the Billings and Moos (1981) inventory, have proposed a similar four-factor structure which includes positive reappraisal, seeking support, avoidance, and information seeking. The seeking of social support may be theorized to serve an emotional coping function, while seeking information may be considered an active strategy, should such information be useful in resolving the stressful situation.

Other research has consistently pointed out three, and often four, dimensions relevant to coping. In early work, Billings and Moos (1981) identified three categories of coping: (a) active-cognitive, (b) active-behavioral, and (c) avoidance strategies. This classification drew a basic distinction between doing something about the experienced stress and avoiding doing anything about it. When individuals do however decide to do something about it, they may take direct action to resolve the stress, or try to change their appraisal of the situation. Osipow and Spokane (1984) distinguish between four categories of coping, namely cognitive coping (which includes prioritizing, avoiding distractions, and clear identification of the problem), social support (which includes having someone to count on, feeling loved and valued), recreation (which includes participating in favorite activities and just enjoying relaxing), and self-care (which relates to avoiding harmful substances and adopting health behaviors such as exercise and good sleeping habits). Latack (1986) developed three categories of coping activities: (a) control strategies, (b) escape strategies, and (c) symptom management. She drew an important distinction regarding active (action-oriented) and cognitive reappraisal strategies. The symptom management dimension included a wide variety of activities, including spiritual (religious) activity, taking of drugs or the use of alcohol, and the seeking of the company of friends or family. Dewe and Guest (1990), actively avoiding any preconceived theory in their approach, identified the coping categories of (a) rational task-oriented behavior (which includes direct action, managing feelings associated with the stress, and preventing repercussions), (b) emotional release (including the immediate expression of feelings), (c) utilization of home resources (which alluded to taking work home or talking the problem through with a significant other), (d) recovery and preparation to deal with the problem (which included waiting and talking to the boss), (e) postponing action by distracting attention or avoiding the issue (which included leaving the office early or having a few drinks), and (f) passive attempts to tolerate the effect (which included not thinking about the problem and self-reassurance). Edwards and Baglioni (1993) conceptualized coping in terms of five dimensions, namely (a) changing the situation (where active effort is exerted in changing the situation to make it more acceptable), (b) accommodation (where the individual reconsiders his or her own standards and expectations), (c) devaluation (where the individual devalues the significance of the problem or the problem itself), (d) avoidance (where attention is directed away from the situation), and (e) symptom reduction (where a focus on relieving stress reactions is aimed at improving well-being).

Considering the reviewed literature in general, there appear to be four consistent coping dimensions, or functions, which are found over a large span of time and methodological approaches. The first clear dimensions are those of active/problem- and emotion-focused coping, as originally conceptualized by Folkman and Lazarus (1980). Subsequent studies and reviews have highlighted two other important dimensions, namely reappraisal and avoidance. Summarizing the above, one can conclude that coping to manage stress can be expressed in terms of four broad functions implied by this conceptualization: *activity* – to remove/attenuate stressors, by focusing directly on taking concrete action to resolve the problem; *expression* – to focus on emotions, manage relationships, or utilize social support; *reappraisal* – to modify perceptions about stressors, to see things in a different and usually more positive light; and, *avoidance* – simply to avoid doing anything about the problem, or deciding that it is not worth investing energy or time in. The following sections investigate these four broad functions, based on a review of previous research findings.

Active/problem-focused coping

Snow, Swan, Raghavan, Connell, and Klein (2003) define active coping (*problem-focused coping*) as one's active efforts to solve problems, rethink situations, and change the environment. Research has found active/problem-focused coping to be negatively associated with levels of illness, burnout (Bhagat *et al.*, 1995), and reported symptoms (Snow *et al.*, 2003), and positively associated with lowered psychological distress (Violanti, 1992) and better adjustment to organizational change (Terry, Callan, and Sartori, 1996). A "buffering effect" for problem-focused coping has also been demonstrated, where it acts to mitigate the effects of job stress on mental health (Parkes, 1990).

Besides having a buffering effect, active coping has also been shown to act directly in changing the negative consequences of stress (Snow *et al.*, 2003). These authors attribute the effectiveness of active coping to its temporal stability and individuals' efficacy beliefs.

Emotional coping

Generally, it is not believed to be helpful for individuals to focus on their emotional reactions to the stress they experience at work (Hart, Wearing, and Headey, 1995). Most research correspondingly finds emotion-focused coping to be associated with higher levels of psychological distress (Violanti, 1992; Zeidner and Ben-Zur, 1994). Given, however, the emphasis placed on the situational and contextual variables in which coping takes place, as noted earlier in this chapter, there may well be situations in which emotion-focused coping is appropriate and could be beneficial (Stanton, Parsa, and Austenfeld, 2002). Here, one has to consider the possible positive effects of emotion-focused strategies in regard to interpersonal functioning (Stanton, Danoff-Burg, Cameron, and Ellis, 1994; Stanton, Kirk, Cameron, and Danoff-Burg, 2000). Also, in cases where it has progressed to a point where no intervention by the individual would make any difference, the individual may do better to focus on their emotional reaction to the situation, and on coming to terms with its consequences (Berghuis and Stanton, 2002; Terry and Hynes, 1998). It should also be kept in mind that individual employees often have very little influence in changing their day-to-day job responsibilities. In such circumstances, emotion-focused coping could be more suitable (Aryee, Luk, Leung, and Lo, 1999).

Avoidance coping

Individuals who choose to follow an avoidant coping strategy effectively choose to remove themselves from the situation, while a problem- or emotion-focused strategy implies that they remain in the situation (Kowalski and Crocker, 2001). This removal may be conceptualized as physical or psychological. Since avoidance coping may remove the individual from the stressful experience, it may be adaptive, and help individuals to manage feelings of distress (Rotondo et al., 2003). Individuals' removal of themselves from the stressful situation may be characterized as temporary or permanent, and when avoidance coping is used in combination with active coping strategies, it may also carry adaptive potential (Koeske, Kirk, and Koeske, 1993).

It seems that the more stress individuals experience, the more likely they are to opt for avoidant coping strategies (Ingledew, Hardy, and Cooper, 1997; Koeske et al., 1993). Research results, however, suggest that in general avoidance coping is associated with poorer outcomes, especially over time, as demonstrated in longitudinal studies (Ingledew et al., 1997; Koeske et al., 1993; Snow et al., 2003). The situation or context in which avoidance coping is the preferred strategy is again of relevance (Anshel and Wells, 2000). If the situation does not immediately permit individuals to address the problem, it would be to their detriment to continue investing effort in solving it. As such, *temporary* avoidance may be conceptualized as an adaptive strategy, where the individual waits for a more appropriate time to deal with and possibly resolve the problem, if it does not require immediate attention.

Reappraisal

As the name suggests, reappraisal is merely *another* appraisal. This further appraisal may be based on information taken from the situation or context, or on individuals' own perception of their coping effort and interaction with the situation or context. "A reappraisal is simply an appraisal that follows an earlier appraisal in the same encounter, and modifies it. In essence, appraisal and reappraisal do not differ" (Lazarus and Folkman, 1984: 38).

What seems especially helpful is when individuals can reappraise the challenges they face as something positive. Individuals who report more positive reappraisals report greater levels of mental health (Oxlad *et al.*, 2004) and general well-being (Garnefski, Baan, and Kraaij, 2005).

The role of social support

Sometimes, social support is not conceptualized as a separate coping strategy at all, but rather as a facilitative resource that enables other coping behaviors (Endler and Parker, 1990). In other instances, social support is seen as a coping strategy that represents a mixture of problem- and emotion-focused strategies (Ben-Zur, 1999). In other words, individuals may make use of social support to alleviate the source of stress (asking someone to help you or give you needed information – *resource*), or utilize social support to get rid of the source of stress (asking someone to take care of the matter, or solve the problem for you – *strategy*).

Coping may also be directed as serving an interpersonal function (Coyne and Smith, 1991; DeLongis and O'Brien, 1990). This function refers to coping aimed at the maintenance and protection of valued relationships during stressful periods. The maintenance and protection of such relationships may be an important consideration during stressful periods, especially when this stress originates from interpersonal issues (O'Brien and DeLongis, 1996).

Regarding social support, it is both the perceived availability (Snow *et al.*, 2003), and perhaps more importantly, the mobilization of available support that should be considered (Rotondo *et al.*, 2003). If social support is available, it may facilitate an individual's use of more active coping strategies (Heaney, House, Israel, and Mero, 1997; Snow *et al.*, 2003). Thus, if individuals are under the impression that there is someone to ask for help, they may feel more comfortable and inclined to ask for help. Billings and Moos (1980) also suggest a negative spiral for those who do not perceive themselves as enjoying social support. They prefer avoidance as coping strategy and thereby isolate themselves further socially.

Dispositional versus situational approaches

The general consensus appears to be that coping is not a function innate to the individual, but rather the result of both the individual's and the situation's characteristics, and the interaction of these (Kahn and Byosiere, 1992; Lazarus, 1996; Parkes, 1986; Stanton *et al.*, 2000). Lazarus and Folkman (1984) also note the importance of *situational control appraisals*, which refers to the amount of control individuals perceives themselves to have within a particular situation. It has been shown that individuals cope differently with work-related stress when compared to family-related stress (Folkman and Lazarus, 1980), and that different coping strategies are mobilized depending on the perceived stressfulness of the situation (McCrae, 1984). Sulsky and Smith (2005) take the fact that coping has been studied in a diversity of occupations as an indication of the importance of situational factors in studying coping.

Keeping our focus on both the individual and the situation in which coping takes place, it must be acknowledged that both can also influence the coping responses individuals report (Patterson, 2000). Research has emphasized that individual differences are influential in coping responses (Coyne and Downey, 1991, Folkman and Lazarus, 1980), strategy choice, and their respective effectiveness (Suls, David, and Harvey, 1996). One commonly studied category of individual difference in coping, gender differences, is considered below.

Individual preferences and dispositions may make certain coping behaviors more attractive to certain individuals (Carver *et al.*, 1989; McCrae and Costa, 1986; Suls *et al.*, 1996; Watson and Hubbard, 1996). Individuals' preferred coping strategies could influence outcomes, and consequently, personality factors and coping dispositions should not be treated separately in the stress process (Ben-Zur, 1999; Ferguson, 2001). Below, dispositions such as optimism, locus of control, and self-efficacy are considered.

Gender

Results for studies examining gender as the basis of coping differences are inconsistent and contradictory (Greenglass, 1995). Females are often characterized as being higher in emotional reactivity, which may in turn influence their reactions to a challenging situation (Zeidner and Ben-Zur, 1994).

The general consensus seems to be that problem-focused coping is used to a similar extent by both genders, but that females additionally use more emotion-focused coping (Ingledew, Hardy, Cooper, and Jemal, 1996) and help-seeking (Oxlad *et al.*, 2004). A central gender difference relates to the ease with which individuals utilize social support, and it seems that females are more comfortable doing so (Hobfoll and Vaux, 1993). Yet, converse results have also indicated that men and women pursue workplace support to the same extent (Gianakos, 2000). The available results seem to suggest that females may more actively seek, and more effectively utilize, social support once they have secured it.

Optimism

Dispositional optimism refers to generally optimistic beliefs across situations, and it is generally linked to positive emotional outcomes (Carver and Scheier, 1992; Scheier *et al.*, 1989). For individuals with chronic and severe health problems, a strong positive relationship exists between optimism and emotional well-being (Carver and Gaines, 1987). This phenomenon is attributed to optimists' beliefs that they can actively cope with the threat of severe illness, which encourages problem-focused coping (Carver and Scheier, 1992; Scheier and Carver, 1985).

The beneficial effects of reappraisal have also been indicated for cardiac patients, and it has been shown that greater optimism translates to more positive reappraisals. Conversely, less optimistic patients also employ more avoidance-oriented coping strategies (Oxlad *et al.*, 2004). Also, individuals who appraise themselves as having greater optimism perform better than individuals with more pessimistic appraisals of themselves in problem-solving situations (Bandura and Wood, 1989; Wood and Bandura, 1989).

Work locus of control

Spector and O'Connell (1994: 2) defined work locus of control as

[A] personality variable that concerns people's generalized expectancies that they can or cannot control reinforcements in their lives. People who hold expectancies that they control reinforcements are considered to be internals, and people who hold expectancies that outside forces or luck control reinforcements are considered to be externals.

When an individual finds himself or herself in a new or unfamiliar situation, where information from the environment is also minimal, locus of control may exert its greatest influence (Rotter, 1966, 1975). Typically, a person with an internal locus of control may feel more in control of the new, unfamiliar, and poorly defined situation, while the individual with an external locus would perceive less such control (Lazarus and Folkman, 1984). An external locus of control is also associated with feelings of helplessness (Lazarus and Folkman, 1984), and as such is associated with lower job satisfaction and mental well-being (Ganster and Fusilier, 1989; Siu *et al.*, 2002).

Self-efficacy

Self-efficacy refers to individuals' own perceived ability or confidence in their ability to mobilize the energy and behavioral responses required in a given situation (Wood and Bandura, 1989). What is typically found is that individuals who have a greater confidence in their own abilities more successfully implement appropriate coping behavior (Schwarzer and Fuchs, 1996). Bandura (1997) clearly indicated that self-efficacy is a generalized belief and not narrowly associated with a specific facet of an individual's existence. However, experiences that enhance individuals' self-efficacy in one sphere may relate positively to generalized self-efficacy. For example, achieving promotion and status at work may enhance individuals' belief in their competitive ability on the sports field, and vice versa. An individual with strong self-efficacy may typically strive to achieve more, actively approach challenges, and be more perseverant in their coping efforts (Bandura, 1982).

For both males and females, having more self-efficacy is associated with more problem-focused (i.e. active) coping strategies (Thongsukmag, 2003). Other authors (Schaubroeck, Jones, and Xie, 2001) suggest that greater self-efficacy should also be associated with better management of stress and greater performance.

The role of religion and spirituality

Individuals themselves, and their primary and secondary appraisals, coping behaviors, resources, and how they attribute meaning may all be influenced by their spirituality (Gall et al., 2005). The whole of the stress and coping process is influenced by spirituality, which manifests on various levels, facilitates individuals' ability to find meaning in stressful situations, and helps them make sense of their world, themselves, and others (Emmons, 1999; Park and Folkman, 1997). In contrast, a lack of meaning is associated with an inhibition of effective coping behaviors (Emmons, 1999). In situations that may be described as unchangeable, such as terminal illness, prayer represents an effective coping strategy (see Ganzevoort, 1998; Oxman, Freeman, and Manheimer, 1995).

"Spiritual resources are presumed to help people cope with stress primarily through the appraisal process – by providing a nexus of traditions or perceptual framework that can help to establish the meaning of a stressor in a larger context and can also prescribe acceptable coping techniques" (Zeidner and Hammer, 1992: 740). "Acts of God" seemingly do not require reasonable or rational explanation (Pienaar and Rothmann, 2003). Reappraisal coping may be done within a person's religious or spiritual framework, but individuals seem less likely to rely on religious coping when they make harm or loss appraisals (Bjorck and Cohen, 1993). The positive role of spirituality and religiosity has been highlighted by its association with both better physical and better psychological health (Levin and Chatters, 1998).

The "brave new world" of coping

In answering the question posed in the title of this chapter (Skeleton key or siren song?), one has to conclude that the coping construct may be the skeleton key to understanding all interactions between individuals, their well-being, and their work. It presents us with a clear concept for understanding and managing individual, organizational, and societal health. It may also be argued that effective coping could ultimately lead to improved mental well-being, which may be quantified in monetary terms as indicated by decreases in absenteeism, sickness leave, and work-related disability.

One of the key features of coping research is that it focuses on the measurement of coping as a disposition, and rests on the assumption that dispositions are adequately measured in cross-sectional fashion. The shrewdness of this approach needs to be seriously reconsidered. The ideas of primary and secondary appraisal, as continuous and interrelated, lead one to suggest, at the peril of sounding like a thousand previous cross-sectional researchers, "that longitudinal data is necessary." However, new advances, such as the use of electronic diaries for instantaneous and momentary assessment, could bring us a lot closer to understanding how the coping process really plays out from one moment to the next.

Qualitative research could also provide greater insight into the process of coping. The idea of primary appraisals constituting threats, losses, or challenges, in particular, could be more elucidated with qualitative research. Preferences for certain strategies may play an important role in this regard, despite the outcome of primary appraisal. Conversely, certain strategies may be preferred for certain appraisals. A deep understanding of these relations seems to be lacking in the extant literature.

Considering the clear emphasis on individual *and* situational factors in describing coping, we continue to approach it as a stable individual disposition at our own peril. Too many variables between, and within, individuals are at play. We might do much better to measure coping as a situational factor when studying specific stressors at the individual level, for example in order to understand how a specific individual reacts to a specific stressor at a specific point in time, or, to give another example, to understand how many people in a specific population react to a certain stressor in a certain way and at a specific point in time, when doing cross-sectional research. Ideally, coping as a disposition should only be studied longitudinally through asking how many people in a specific population are experiencing a specific stressor (for example job insecurity) and observing if people react with a specific coping strategy (for example avoidance) at a given time, and whether the strategy for this stressor is still employed at a subsequent time point.

The important situational factors relevant to understanding coping also imply that more attention needs to be paid to the differences between the contexts in which coping takes place. Coping, whether conceptualized as dispositional or situational, should differ from one organizational context to the next. Focusing on emotions in a service delivery setting could be useful, while a production context could require quick and specific problem-focused coping. "Contexts" should also not be understood in a broad, generic way. "Coping" by employees in a fast-food restaurant might look very different from "coping" by employees in a different fast-food restaurant. One could go so far as to argue that the situational factors are so complex and vast in number that coping can only be described for a specific population at a specific time, and should not be attributed to professions in general (i.e. statements such as "The way that policemen usually cope ... " should definitely be avoided). This argument leaves one, however, with the problem that highly contextualized studies of coping add little to a broader understanding of coping as dispositional construct. Here, the consistency of coping strategies, such as would be evidenced in longitudinal research, could provide a clearer answer. Regarding individual-level interventions, the fostering of an individual coping *repertoire* is seemingly indicated. Individuals should have a clear understanding of their own coping preferences, but also of lesser-known methods of coping with problematic situations. A certain flexibility thus needs to be developed in dealing with stressful situations – intelligently coping individuals should be able to judge which approach is most appropriate for a given situation.

Specific to the modern working life, the imperative rests with organizations to provide their employees with the resources the employee deems necessary for meeting the requirements of his or her task. Official documentation, statements, and policies should send a clear message as to the way "we do things around here." Deserving employees rewarded with autonomy may react to problems in a creative and proactive fashion. A culture of learning could encourage employees to find meaning in mistakes and learn from them. Employees encouraged to rely on their colleagues and supervisors for pooled expertise may build a social support network to the benefit of themselves and their employer. Finally, the development of a culture in which problems are addressed as they arise is a measure that should help avoid later surprises.

An important consideration, which has seemingly received very little, or no attention, is coping *effectiveness*. How does it help if we know that a specific population prefers a specific coping strategy in dealing with a specific job stressor? The question which really beckons concerns the effectiveness of the chosen coping strategy. Again, the answer to this will remain elusive in cross-sectional data studies. The answer might not even lie in longitudinal data – people may cognitively consider various alternatives before implementing action, take remedial action, and adjust their responses as soon as feedback from the environment starts. While this whole process may be termed "coping," how does one go about separating, measuring, and describing the different facets? The answer seems to lie more at the philosophical than the pragmatic level.

One could go so far as to state that our entire evolution as a species is built on our ability to cope successfully and to adjust to every curveball nature has thrown at us over the last few thousand years. "Coping" indeed is what we are doing in addressing issues of balancing work and private well-being. However, in helping people cope, we may simply start at a level so simple as to ask: What would make this easier for you? In dealing with individuals in a larger organizational setting, facilitating coping and the management thereof could easily be seen as developing into a competitive advantage. The organization that makes resources available, in whatever form, which facilitate working should generally see a more balanced employee. These resources can vary from practical assistance such as daycare, to ego-enhancing activities such as leadership and management training and self-development. In any attempts to instruct organizations however, especially on how to address organizational problems of the twenty-first century, we will have to tread ever more carefully, as there are limitations in our own understanding that may be highlighted by further research.

References

Aneshensel, C. S. (1992). Social stress: theory and research. *Annual Review of Sociology* 18: 15–38.

Anshel, M. H. and Wells, B. (2000). Personal and situational variables that describe coping with acute stress in competitive sport. *Journal of Social Psychology* 140: 434–50.

Aryee, S., Luk, V., Leung, A., and Lo, S. (1999). Role stressors, inter-role conflict, and well-being: the moderating influence of spousal support and coping behaviors among employed parents in Hong Kong. *Journal of Vocational Behavior* 54: 259–78.

Bandura, A. (1982). Self-efficacy mechanisms in human agency. *American Psychologist* 37: 122–47.

(1997). *Self-efficacy: the exercise of control.* New York: W. H. Freeman.

Bandura, A. and Wood, R. E. (1989). Effect of perceived controllability and performance standards on self-regulation of complex decision making. *Journal of Personality and Social Psychology* 56: 805–14.

Ben-Zur, H. (1999). The effectiveness of coping meta-strategies: perceived efficiency, emotional correlates and cognitive performance. *Personality and Individual Differences* 26: 923–39.

Berghuis, J. P. and Stanton, A. L. (2002). Adjustment to a dyadic stressor: a longitudinal study of coping and depressive symptoms in infertile couples over an insemination attempt. *Journal of Consulting and Clinical Psychology* 70: 433–8.

Bhagat, R. S., Allie, S. M., and Ford, D. L., Jr. (1995). Coping with stressful life events: an empirical analysis. In R. Crandall and P. L. Perrewé (eds.), *Occupational stress: a handbook* (pp. 93–112). Washington, DC: Taylor and Francis.

Bhagat, R. S., Ford, D. L., O' Driscoll, M. P., Frey, L., Babakus, E., and Mahanyele, M. (2001). Do South African managers cope differently from American managers? A cross-cultural investigation. *International Journal of Intercultural Relations* 25: 301–13.

Bhagat, S. R., O'Driscoll, M. P., Babakus, E., Frey, L., Chokkar, J., Ninokumar, B. H., Pate, L. E., Ryder, P. A., Jesus Gonzalez Fernandez, M., Ford, D. L., Jr., and Mahanyele, M. (1994). Organizational stress and coping in seven national contexts: a cross-cultural investigation. In G. P. Keita and J. J. Hurrel Jr. (eds.), *Job stress in a changing workforce: investigating gender, diversity and family issues* (pp. 93–105). Washington, DC: American Psychological Association.

Billings, A. G. and Moos, R. H. (1981). The role of coping responses and social resources in attenuating the stress of life events. *Journal of Behavioral Medicine* 4: 139–57.

Bjorck, J. P. and Cohen, L. H. (1993). Coping with threats, losses and challenges. *Journal of Social and Clinical Psychology* 12: 56–72.

Bjorck, J. P. and Klewicki, L. I. (1997). The effects of stressor type on projected coping. *Journal of Traumatic Stress* 10: 481–97.

Brief, A. P. and George, J. M. (1991). Psychological stress and the workplace: a brief comment on Lazarus' outlook. *Journal of Social Behavior and Personality* 6: 15–20.

Brough, P., O'Driscoll, M. O., and Kalliath, T. (2005). Confirmatory factor analysis of the cybernetic coping scale. *Journal of Occupational and Organizational Psychology* 78: 53–61.

Carver, C. S. and Gaines, J. G. (1987). Optimism, pessimism and post-partum depression. *Cognitive Therapy and Research* 11: 449–62.

Carver, C. S. and Scheier, M. F. (1992). Effects of optimism on psychological and physical well-being: theoretical overview and empirical update. *Cognitive Therapy and Research* 16: 201–28.

Carver, C. S., Scheier, M. F., and Weintraub, J. K. (1989). Assessing coping strategies: a theoretically based approach. *Journal of Personality and Social Psychology* 56: 267–83.

Chen, C. and Cheung, M. W. L. (2005). Cognitive processes underlying coping flexibility: differentiation and integration. *Journal of Personality* 73: 859–86.

Cook, S. W. and Heppner, P. P. (1997). A psychometric study of three coping measures. *Educational and Psychological Measurement* 57: 906–23.

Cox, T. and Ferguson, E. (1991). Individual differences, stress and coping. In C. L. Cooper and R. Payne (eds.), *Personality and stress: individual differences in the stress process*. Chichester: Wiley.

Coyne, J. C. and Downey, G. (1991). Social factors and psychopathology: stress, social support and coping processes. *Annual Review of Psychology* 42: 401–25.

Coyne, J. C. and Smith, D. A. F. (1991). Couples coping with a myocardial infarction: a contextual perspective on wives' distress. *Journal of Personality and Social Psychology* 61: 404–12.

Danna, K. and Griffin, R. (1999). Health and well-being in the workplace: a review and synthesis of the literature. *Journal of Management* 25: 357–79.

Day, A. L. and Livingstone, H. A. (2001). Chronic and acute stressors among military personnel: do coping styles buffer their negative impact on health? *Journal of Occupational Health Psychology* 6: 348–60.

DeFrank, R. S. and Ivancevich, J. M. (1998). Stress on the job: an executive update. *Academy of Management Executives* 12: 55–66.

DeLongis, A. and O'Brien, T. (1990). An interpersonal framework for stress and coping: an application to the families of Alzheimer's patients. In M. A. P. Stephens, J. H. Crowther, S. E. Hobfoll, and D. L. Tennenbaum (eds.), *Stress and coping in later life families* (pp. 221–39). Washington, DC: Hemisphere.

Dewe, P., Cox, T., and Ferguson, E. (1993). Individual strategies for coping with stress and work: a review. *Work and Stress* 7: 5–15.

Dewe, P. and Guest, D. (1990). Methods of coping with stress at work: a conceptual analysis and empirical study of measurement issues. *Journal of Organizational Behavior* 11: 135–50.

Edwards, J. R. and Baglioni, A. J., Jr. (1993). Empirical versus theoretical approaches to the measurement of coping: a comparison using the ways of coping questionnaire and the cybernetic coping scale. In P. Dewe, T. Cox, and M. Leiter (eds.), *Coping and health in organizations* (pp. 29–50). London: Taylor and Francis.

Emmons, R. A. (1999). *The psychology of ultimate concerns: motivation and spirituality in personality*. New York: The Guilford Press.

Endler, N. S. and Parker, J. D. A. (1990). *Coping Inventory for Stressful Situations (CISS): manual*. Toronto: Multi-Health Systems.

Evans, B. J., Coman, G. J., Stanley, R. O., and Burrows, G. D. (1993). Police officers' coping strategies: an Australian police survey. *Stress Medicine* 9: 237–46.

Ferguson, E. (2001). Personality and coping traits: a joint factor analysis. *British Journal of Health Psychology* 6: 311–25.

Fleishman, J. A. (1984). Personality characteristics and coping patterns. *Journal of Health and Social Behavior* 25: 229–44.

Folkman, S. and Lazarus, R. S. (1980). An analysis of coping in a middle-aged community sample. *Journal of Health and Social Behavior* 21: 219–39.

(1988). Coping as a mediator of emotion. *Journal of Personality and Social Psychology* 54: 466–75.

Forsythe, C. J. and Compas, B. E. (1987). Interaction of cognitive appraisals of stressful events and coping: testing the goodness of fit hypothesis. *Cognitive Therapy and Research* 11: 473–85.

Gall, T. L., Charbonneau, C., Clarke, N. H., Grant, K., Joseph, A., and Shouldice, L. (2005). Understanding the nature and role of spirituality in relation to coping and health: a conceptual framework. *Canadian Psychology* 46: 88–104.

Ganster, D. C. and Fusilier, M. R. (1989). Control in the workplace. In C. L. Cooper and I. T. Robertson (eds.), *International review of industrial and organizational psychology* (pp. 235–80). Chichester: Wiley.

Ganzevoort, R. R. (1998). Religious coping reconsidered, part one: an integrated approach. *Journal of Psychology and Theology* 26: 260–75.

Garnefski, N., Baan, N., and Kraaij, V. (2005). Psychological distress and cognitive emotion regulation strategies among farmers who fell victim to the foot-and-mouth crisis. *Personality and Individual Differences* 38: 1317–27.

Gianakos, I. (2000). Gender roles and coping with work stress. *Sex Roles* 42: 1059–79.

Greenglass, E. R. (1993). The contribution of social support to coping strategies. *Applied Psychology: An International Review* 42: 323–40.

(1995). Gender, work stress, and coping: theoretical implications. *Journal of Social Behavior and Personality* 10: 121–34.

(1996). Anger suppression, cynical distrust, and hostility: Implications for coronary heart disease. In J. M. T. Brebner, E. Greenglass, P. Laungani, and A. M. O'Roark (eds.), *Stress and emotion* (vol. 16, pp. 205–25). Washington, DC: Taylor and Francis.

Hart, P. M., Wearing, A. J., and Headey, B. (1995). Police stress and well-being: integrating personality, coping and daily work experiences. *Journal of Occupational and Organizational Psychology* 68: 133–56.

Heaney, C. A., House, J. S., Israel, B. A., and Mero, R. P. (1997). The relationship of organizational and social coping resources to employee coping behaviour: a longitudinal analysis. *Work and Stress* 9: 416–31.

Hobfoll, S. E. and Vaux, A. (1993). Social support: resources and context. In L. Goldberger and S. Breznitz (eds.), *Handbook of stress: theoretical and clinical aspects* (pp. 685–705). New York: The Free Press.

Ingledew, D. K., Hardy, L., and Cooper, C. L. (1997). Do resources bolster coping and does coping buffer stress? An organizational study with longitudinal aspect and control for negative affectivity. *Journal of Occupational Health Psychology* 2: 118–33.

Ingledew, D. K., Hardy, L., Cooper, C. L., and Jemal, H. (1996). Health behaviours reported as coping strategies: a factor analytical study. *British Journal of Health Psychology* 1: 263–81.

Kahn, R. L. and Byosiere, P. H. (1992). Stress in organizations. In M. Dunette and L. M. Hough (eds.), *Handbook of industrial and organizational psychology* (vol. 3, pp. 571–650). Palo Alto: Consulting Psychologists Press.

Kallasmaa, T. and Pulver, A. (2000). The structure and properties of the Estonian COPE inventory. *Personality and Individual Differences* 29: 881–94.

Koeske, G. F., Kirk, S. A., and Koeske, R. D. (1993). Coping with job stress: which strategies work best? *Journal of Occupational and Organizational Psychology* 66: 1–17.

Kowalski, K. C. and Crocker, P. R. E. (2001). Development and validation of the Coping Function Questionnaire for adolescents in sport. *Journal of Sport and Exercise Psychology* 23: 136–55.

Lai, G., Chan, K. B., Ko, Y. C., and Boey, K. W. (2000). Institutional context and stress appraisal: the experience of life insurance agents in Singapore. *African and Asian Studies* 35: 209–28.

Latack, J. C. (1986). Coping with work stress: measures and future directions for scale development. *Journal of Applied Psychology* 71: 377–85.

Lazarus, R. S. (1991). Psychological stress in the workplace. *Journal of Social Behavior and Personality* 6: 1–13.

(1996). The role of coping in the emotions and how coping changes over the life course. In C. Magai and S. H. McFadden (eds.), *Handbook of emotion, adult development, and aging* (pp. 289–306). San Diego, CA: Academic Press.

Lazarus, R. S. and Folkman, S. (1984). *Stress, appraisal and coping.* New York: Springer.

Lazarus, R. S. and Launier, R. (1978). *Stress-related transactions between person and environment.* London: Plenum Press.

Levin, J. and Chatters, L. (1998). Research on religion and mental health: an overview of empirical findings and theoretical issues. In H. G. Koenig (ed.), *Handbook of religion and mental health* (pp. 33–50). San Diego, CA: Academic Press.

Locke, E. A. and Taylor, M. S. (1990). Stress, coping, and the meaning of work. In A. Brief and W. R. Nord (eds.), *Meanings of occupational work* (pp. 135–70). Lexington, MA: Lexington Books.

McCrae, R. R. (1984). Situational determinants of coping responses: loss, threat, and challenge. *Journal of Personality and Social Psychology* 46: 919–28.

(1989). Age differences and changes in the use of coping mechanisms. *Journal of Gerontology* 44: 161–9.

McCrae, R. R. and Costa, P. T. (1986). Personality, coping and coping effectiveness in an adult sample. *Journal of Personality* 84: 385–406.

O'Brien, T. B. and DeLongis, A. (1996). The interactional context of problem-, emotion-, and relationship-focused coping: the role of the big five personality factors. *Journal of Personality* 64: 775–813.

Osipow, S. H. and Spokane, A. R. (1984). Measuring occupational stress, strain and coping. *Applied Social Psychology Annual* 5: 67–86.

Oxlad, M., Miller-Lewis, L., and Wade, T. D. (2004). The measurement of coping responses: validity of the Billings and Moos Coping Checklist. *Journal of Psychosomatic Research* 57: 477–84.

Oxman, T. E., Freeman, D. H., and Manheimer, E. D. (1995). Lack of social participation or religious strength and comfort as risk factors for death after cardiac surgery in the elderly. *Psychosomatic Medicine* 57: 5–15.

Park, G. L. and Folkman, S. (1997). Meaning in the context of stress and coping. *Review of General Psychology* 1: 115–44.

Parkes, K. R. (1986). Coping in stressful episodes: the role of individual differences, environmental factors, and situational characteristics. *Journal of Personality and Social Psychology* 51: 1277–92.

(1990). Coping, negative affectivity and the work environment: additive and interactive predictors of mental health. *Journal of Applied Psychology* 75: 399–409.

Patterson, G. T. (2000). Demographic factors as predictors of coping strategies among police officers. *Psychological Reports* 87: 275–83.

Pearlin, L. I. (1999). Stress and mental health. A conceptual overview. In A. V. Horwitz and T. L. Scheid (eds.), *A handbook for the study of mental health* (pp. 161–75). New York: Cambridge University Press.

Phelps, S. B. and Jarvis, P. A. (1994). Coping in adolescence: empirical evidence for a theoretically based approach to coping. *Journal of Youth and Adolescence* 23: 359–71.

Pienaar, J. and Rothmann, S. (2003). Coping strategies in the South African Police Service. *South African Journal of Industrial Psychology* 29: 81–90.

Roth, S. and Cohen, L. J. (1986). Approach, avoidance, and coping with stress. *American Psychologist* 41: 813–19.

Rotondo, D. M., Carlson, D. S., and Kincaid, J. F. (2003). Coping with multiple dimensions of work–family conflict. *Personnel Review* 32: 275–96.

Rotter, J. B. (1966). Generalized expectancies for internal versus external control of reinforcement. *Psychological Monographs: General and Applied* 80: 1–28.

(1975). Some problems and misconceptions related to the construct of internal versus external control of reinforcement. *Journal of Consulting and Clinical Psychology* 43: 56–67.

Schaubroeck, J., Jones, J. R., and Xie, J. L. (2001). Individual differences in utilizing control to cope with job demands: effects of susceptibility to infection disease. *Journal of Applied Psychology* 86: 265–78.

Scheier, M. F. and Carver, C. S. (1985). Optimism, coping and health: assessment and implications of generalized outcome expectancies. *Health Psychology* 4: 219–47.

Scheier, M. F., Magovern, G. J., Abbott, R. A., Matthews, K. L., Owens, J. F., Lefebvre, R. C., and Carver, C. S. (1989). Dispositional optimism and recovery from coronary artery bypass surgery: the beneficial effects on physical and psychological well-being. *Journal of Personality and Social Psychology* 57: 1024–40.

Schuler, R. S. (1985). Integrative transactional process model of coping with stress in organizations. In T. Beehr and R. Bhagat (eds.), *Human stress and cognition in organizations: an integrated perspective* (pp. 347–74). New York: Wiley.

Schwarzer, R. and Fuchs, R. (1996). Self-efficacy and health behaviors. In M. Conner and P. Norman (eds.), *Predicting health behavior: research and practice with social cognition models* (pp. 163–96). Buckingham: Open University Press.

Siu, O., Spector, P. E., Cooper, C. L., Lu, L., and Yu, S. (2002). Managerial stress in Greater China: the direct and moderator effects of coping strategies and work locus of control. *Applied Psychology: An International Review* 51: 608–32.

Snow, D. L., Swan, S. C., Raghavan, C., Connell, C. M., and Klein, I. (2003). The relationship of work stressors, coping and social support to psychological symptoms among female secretarial employees. *Work and Stress* 17: 241–63.

Spector, P. E. and O'Connell, B. J. (1994). The contribution of personality traits, negative affectivity, locus of control and Type A to the subsequent reports of job stressors and strains. *Journal of Occupational and Organizational Psychology* 67: 1–11.

Stanton, A. L., Danoff-Burg, S., Cameron, C. L., and Ellis, A. P. (1994). Coping through emotional approach: problems of conceptualization and confounding. *Journal of Personality and Social Psychology* 66: 350–62.

Stanton, A. L., Kirk, S. B., Cameron, C. L., and Danoff-Burg, S. (2000). Coping through emotional approach: scale construction and validation. *Journal of Personality and Social Psychology* 78: 1150–69.

Stanton, A. L., Parsa, A., and Austenfeld, J. L. (2002). The adaptive potential of coping through emotional approach. In C. R. Snyder and S. J. Lopez (eds.), *Handbook of positive psychology* (pp. 148–58). New York: Oxford University Press.

Suls, J., David, J. P., and Harvey, J. H. (1996). Personality and coping: three generations of research. *Journal of Personality* 64: 711–35.

Sulsky, L. and Smith, C. (2005). *Workstress*. Belmont, CA: Wadsworth.

Terry, D. J., Callan, V. J., and Sartori, G. (1996). Employee adjustment to an organizational merger: stress, coping and inter-group differences. *Stress Medicine* 12: 105–22.

Terry, D. J. and Hynes, G. J. (1998). Adjustment to a low-control situation: re-examining the role of coping responses. *Journal of Personality and Social Psychology* 74: 1078–92.

Thongsukmag, J. (2003). Fear in the workplace: the relationship among sex, self-efficacy, and coping strategies. Unpublished doctoral dissertation, Virginia Polytechnic Institute and State University, Falls Church, VA.

Violanti, J. M. (1992). Coping strategies among police recruits in a high-stress training environment. *Journal of Social Psychology* 132: 717–29.

Violanti, J. M., Marshall, J. R., and Howe, B. (1985). Stress, coping, and alcohol use: the police connection. *Journal of Police Science and Administration* 13: 106–10.

Vitaliano, P., DeWolfe, D. J., Maiuro, R. D., Russo, J., and Katon, W. (1990). Appraised changeability of a stressor as a modifier of the relationship between coping and depression: a test of the hypothesis of fit. *Journal of Personality and Social Psychology* 59: 582–92.

Watson, D. and Hubbard, B. (1996). Adaptational style and dispositional structure: coping in the context of the Five-Factor model. *Journal of Personality* 64: 737–74.

Wood, R. E. and Bandura, A. (1989). Impact of conceptions of ability on self-regulatory mechanisms and complex decision-making. *Journal of Personality and Social Psychology* 56: 407–15.

Zeidner, M. and Ben-Zur, H. (1994). Individual differences in anxiety, coping, and post-traumatic stress in the aftermath of the Persian Gulf War. *Personality and Individual Differences* 16: 459–76.

Zeidner, M. and Hammer, A. L. (1992). Coping with missile attack: resources, strategies, and outcomes. *Journal of Personality* 60: 709–46.

The dynamic influence of individual
characteristics on employee well-being:
a review of the theory, research,
and future directions

*Christopher J. L. Cunningham, Gabriel M. De La Rosa,
and Steve M. Jex*

Continuing changes to the nature of work brought on by technological
leaps (e.g. Kurland and Bailey, 1999), increasingly diverse workforces,
changes to the traditional contractual nature of work (e.g. Barley and
Kunda, 2006), and shifting industry demands make it necessary for
researchers who study workers and their work environments to consider
dynamic relationships at multiple levels within people and work organizations. Employees are consistently being forced to adapt to meet these
changing work demands and a potential cost is personal well-being.

Much of this book focuses on how changing work environments and
roles can influence the well-being of employees. It is also critically important to attend to the role of individual characteristics in this process.
Throughout this chapter the terms "individual characteristics/differences"
represent dispositions and more malleable personal qualities. We will
provide a conceptual model that integrates many existing findings regarding these issues and offers a set of clear options for future exploration. We
encourage readers to think critically about relationships between individual
characteristics and well-being in their own research and practice.

This chapter begins with a discussion of the critically important, complex, and yet underdiscussed well-being criterion. Our conceptual framework is presented, followed by a selective review of research on individual
characteristics associated with well-being that we feel are particularly
relevant in a changing work environment. Finally, we provide a summary
and thoughts for future work in this area.

Well-being and the workplace

There is no single, widely applicable theory of well-being. Well-being
researchers (e.g. Ryff and Singer, 2003) advocate and seem to agree on

the idea that well-being involves multiple dimensions, but no such agreement exists regarding which dimensions are most important. Although well-being is arguably a more general construct than health, this does not prevent models of health from providing a structure to our conceptualization of well-being.

Early models of health were conceived rather narrowly and negatively. The *medical model* of health, for example, suggests that a person can be considered "healthy" only when no symptoms of illness or injury are present. Adherence to this view leads to a focus on signs/symptoms of negative consequences of exposure to noxious stimuli at work, at home, or in the community. In a similar fashion, the *environmental model* of health suggests that individuals are healthy if, and only if, they can successfully adapt to their environments and meet the basic criterion of survival (Hofmann and Tetrick, 2003; Larson, 1999).

A more recent, positive, and conceptually broad perspective, especially prevalent within occupational health psychology research, is the *wellness model*. This model reflects health's physical, psychological, and social components, all of which contribute to a person's ability to flourish and adapt to life's challenges (e.g. Hofmann and Tetrick, 2003; Warr, 2005). From this perspective, health represents more than the absence of negative emotional or physical symptoms (see also Jahoda, 1958; Kornhauser, 1965). Viewing health in terms of more general wellness moves the construct into an overlapping position with well-being. A wellness model also supports proactive, as opposed to reactive, efforts to study and improve occupational health issues (e.g. Hofmann and Tetrick, 2003).

Within work organizations, the wellness model of health can guide efforts to maintain and improve employee well-being. Specifically, well-being can be evaluated in terms of (a) positive employee engagement on and off the job, (b) positive job-related behaviors (cf. Warr, 2005), (c) heightened job involvement and performance (e.g. Keyes, Hysom, and Lupo, 2000), and (d) strong positive attitudes toward the organization. By leveraging physical, psychological, and social factors, employee well-being can be enhanced even in changing work environments where maintaining such well-being is critical, to prevent creating additional impediments to employee learning and adaptation (e.g. Cotton and Hart, 2003; Karasek and Theorell, 1990).

From our perspective, well-being is a natural result of a person's ability to adapt to changing demands, and to "deal with reality" smoothly and effectively (Semmer, 2003: 107). Factors contributing to well-being are clearly outlined in the wellness model of health. In a changing work environment, it will be important for researchers and practitioners to consider both subjective and objective indicators of well-being if they are truly interested in addressing the threats to and opportunities for achieving employee well-being.

Subjective well-being typically involves a consideration of both positive affect and positive attitudes toward the job or one's life in general. Objective well-being is an understudied criterion within the workplace, even though several forms of criteria have already been identified to help. Perhaps the best indicator of objective well-being is the presence of occupational disabilities, conditions that prevent a person from fully functioning in an occupational, social, or personal setting (e.g. somatic problems/injuries from occupational stressors and/or work-related negligence, hazardous exposures, and repetitive motions; American Medical Association, 2000). We suggest occupational disabilities may represent a critical indication of well-being in more objective terms than has been considered in the past.

In general, well-being is best maintained by people who effectively handle the challenges of living an engaged life (Ryff and Singer, 2003). For this to be true, well-being must be seen as dynamic (e.g. Ryan and Frederick, 1997; Warr, 2005), rather than as an unchanging individual characteristic or desired predetermined end-state. In such dynamic terms, it then becomes possible to focus on specific worker characteristics that may help or hinder people as they manage well-being while facing changing work demands.

No two people confronted with the same situational factors are likely to respond in exactly the same way. What is not well known or studied is which personal characteristics might be playing critical roles and how these characteristics are having influence. Existing research has shown that person and situation interact (e.g. Mischel and Shoda, 1995; Shoda and Mischel, 1996) to influence well-being and other personal states and behaviors. Our concern is that as the nature of work continues to change, the balance within this interaction is likely to shift.

More specifically, the strength of work situations is likely to decrease as formality is replaced with flexibility and as long-term, established workforces are replaced with short-term contracts and contingency employment. This in turn will leave more room for individual characteristics to influence employees in every way, increasing the importance of the *person* as the primary factor influencing work-related well-being. In the following section we attempt to offer a bit of context for this concern.

Worker characteristics and well-being

The relationship between the worker and his/her well-being received its first serious study beginning in the 1930s, involving researchers such as

Hersey (1932/1977), Mayo (1930), Münsterberg (1913), and Viteles (1953). For example, Hersey's (1932/1977) observational and anthropological research chronicles the work and nonwork lives and emotions of "real" working men over time. This work highlights the "importance and validity" of individual differences (1932/1977: 373), but also the universality of certain work-related experiences. Hersey's studies of workers and their natural, fluxing emotional states even led him to suggest an "ideal" set of personality qualities for work, which involves many elements associated today with high-functioning individuals with high levels of well-being (e.g. sense of humor, long-term life perspective, intelligence, and courage to face reality; Hersey 1932/1977: 390).

Arthur Kornhauser also advanced research and interest into worker characteristics and well-being by focusing on (among other things) employee morale and attitudes, use of labor unions as levers for enhancing well-being, and worker mental health as an important dependent variable (Zickar, 2003). Kornhauser's (1965) research with industrial workers in the automobile industry led him to view individual differences in terms of personality as the end result of "everything that has been part of his life history" (p. 12). He went on to suggest that a person can be meaningfully considered in terms of "those inner processes that direct behavior toward ends or goals ('motives') and those processes that provide the means or instrumentalities of action ('mechanisms' – perceptual and thought habits, knowledge, skills, etc.)" (p. 12).

As these and other early researchers noted, a person's emotional and physical states are dictated by both underlying personal characteristics and environmental influences (e.g. Warr, 1999). Acknowledging this, most research that studies individual characteristics and well-being does so by testing a version of the hypothesis that an individual characteristic Z influences the relationship between stressor X and strain Y. Many of these studies are based on the Demands–Control theory, in which the effect of job demands on strain is expected to be mitigated by an employee's ability to make decisions and take actions in response to such job demands (i.e. a form of actual control over the job demands) (Karasek, 1979).

As work environments continue to evolve, however, the complexities and demands that they impose on workers are likely to grow exponentially. In addition, the consistency of various elements of more traditional work environments is likely to disappear as more and more employees do their work from an expanded set of possible work sites (e.g. home office, coffee shop, temporary office). These increasingly complex and less stable work environments pose a new challenge for researchers focused on complex phenomena such as well-being.

The Demands–Control theoretical framework has guided a great deal of important stress–strain research, but it does not encourage researchers to consider important individual characteristics (e.g. Fernet *et al.*, 2004; Van der Doef and Maes, 1999). This is because it draws attention to features of the work environment rather than employee characteristics that might influence perceptions of capabilities or control. Given the scenario of a changing work environment, the Demands–Control framework cannot fully explain why some employees will react positively and others negatively to multiple sets of environmental cues and changes. For starters, social support and self-efficacy may influence the Demands–Control interaction (e.g. Schaubroeck and Fink, 1998), but other factors need additional consideration. The likely decreasing of situational consistency in the work environment makes it necessary to understand which individual characteristics may augment or diminish a person's well-being when confronted with these types of changes in work demands.

Proposing a new conceptual model

As Warr (2005: 560) suggests, "[a] change of emphasis is now required," away from the environment and toward the person. The nature of work is changing and will continue to change, and we can never expect to perfectly predict the effects of such change. Therefore, instead of listing past research findings pertaining to separate, specific individual characteristics, we have endeavored to offer four pathways or processes with which individual characteristics are likely to influence the relationships between changing work environments and employee well-being.

We have located these processes within the overarching framework of an individual's approach to cope successfully with potentially challenging characteristics of the work environment. In keeping with appraisal (e.g. Lazarus, 1999; Lazarus and Folkman, 1987) and resource protection/replenishment theories (e.g. Hobfoll, 1989, 2002), effective coping generally allows a person to maintain and possibly improve his/her well-being in the face of challenging (positive) or threatening (negative) situations.

Figure 13.1 illustrates our conceptual framework, developed in the following sections that discuss four main pathways (cf. Kasl and Rapp, 1991) by which individual characteristics may dynamically influence well-being in a changing work context: (a) *resilience* (i.e. general, physiological, and/or physical "fitness" for handling difficult demands/situations), (b) *fit* (between person and organization on multiple levels), (c) *cognitive and emotional processes* (i.e. perception, appraisal, emotion, attitudes), and (d) *behaviors* (related specifically to coping with challenges at work).

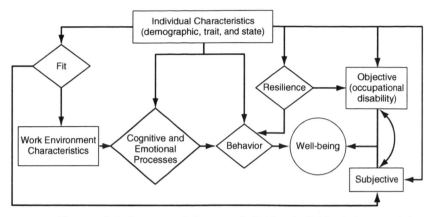

Figure 13.1 Conceptual framework linking individual characteristics and well-being

Resilience

There are many possible reasons why some people handle work demands and change better than other people. One distinct possibility is that their unique personal characteristics somehow relate to a better biological or physiological tolerance for stress. These individuals may also demonstrate a high stress threshold or a greater degree of resilience. Supporting this perspective, researchers are increasingly identifying linkages between various individual characteristics and differences in physiological functioning under stress that could influence well-being by improving or damaging a person's resilience within a work environment (e.g. Semmer, 2003).

Fit

It has long been recognized in industrial-organizational psychology that the fit between a person and his/her organization and job are critically important. This is especially true when the goal is to achieve a lasting work relationship with minimal negative personal or organizational outcomes (e.g. Kristof, 1996; Schneider, 1987; Verquer, Beehr, and Wagner, 2003). Multiple other forms of fit are also relevant to our present discussion (Kristof, 1996), including congruence between a person's needs and what the organization can supply (needs–supply fit) and the congruence between an organization's or job's demands and a person's abilities to meet those demands (demands–abilities fit).

From a stress perspective, as incongruence (i.e. lack of fit) increases for any of these forms of fit, an employee is likely to experience more stress and eventual strain (e.g. Edwards and Cooper, 1990). As competition within and between organizations for recruiting and retaining the best talent increases, issues of fit are likely to become increasingly pronounced. Because incongruence can result in more negative outcomes for employees and their organizations (e.g. Warr, 1999), it is easy to see how (mis)fit can function as an important pathway linking individual characteristics to well-being.

Cognitive and emotional processes

Even perfectly designed work environments and balanced work demands will not necessarily lead to improved well-being for every worker. The reasons for this are complex and beyond the scope of the present chapter, but in many ways the differences in well-being can stem from differences in individuals' underlying cognitive and emotional processes. These processes guide the experience of work for people and are strongly influenced by individual characteristics. Thus, individual characteristics can impact well-being via processes of perception and appraisal, and attitudes and emotions. Multiple examples of these pathways in operation are provided in the following sections.

Behavior

Behavioral response tendencies are generally expected to be consistent within a single person across different situations, but not across different individuals in a single situation. Multiple individual characteristics can influence well-being through an employee's general lifestyle and more constrained workplace behaviors (e.g. Warr, 1999). In the present discussion we focus on individual characteristics that might influence work-related coping behaviors that could influence well-being (acknowledging that general lifestyle behaviors will also play a role in peoples' maintenance of general health, which pervades work and non-work life domains).

Connecting the pieces

Our conceptual model is offered to facilitate consideration of the multiple ways in which individual characteristics may be involved with changing work environments in influencing well-being. The four main pathways in Figure 13.1 are expected to be critical elements connecting individual characteristics to well-being and it is important to consider a few of these relationships explicitly.

The first element, resilience, is likely to have a direct impact on a person's objective well-being given the psychological and physical components of resilience. It is also expected that resilience may influence a person's choice of behaviors in response to work environment characteristics. Second, with respect to the multiple forms of fit, it is easy to see how people would be motivated to avoid such misfit before even taking a work position or actively engaging in work demands or coming into contact with other work environment characteristics. For this reason, the establishment of fit perceptions is expected to influence the way in which a person navigates and addresses complex characteristics within a work environment. In addition perceptions of fit can be expected to influence subjective perceptions of well-being.

The remaining two pathways by which individual characteristics are likely to influence well-being are a person's cognitive and emotional processes and coping-related behaviors. These two elements are very closely interrelated as a person's coping behaviors are commonly dictated by the severity of his/her cognitive and emotional appraisals of environmental cues (e.g. Lazarus, 1999) and the strength and lability of his/her emotions (e.g. Hersey, 1955). Within the present model, both elements are expected to intervene between work demands and eventual perceptions of well-being. It is also likely that both elements could have an impact on both subjective and objective components of well-being.

Integrating individual characteristics into the model

Traditional trait characteristics

A great deal of research has focused on stable (i.e. unchanging) underlying personality traits as predictors of or intervening variables that contribute to a person's well-being. This approach to the study of individual characteristics assumes that people maintain a biologically predetermined threshold before which negative well-being is experienced, and beyond which positive well-being emerges. There is a great deal of additional empirical support linking dimensions of well-being with personality traits such as extraversion (e.g. van den Berg and Pitariu, 2005; Zellars, Hochwarter, Perrewé, Hoffman, and Ford, 2004), neuroticism (e.g. Langelaan, Bakker, van Doornen, and Schaufeli, 2006; van den Berg and Pitariu, 2005; Zellars et al., 2004), openness to experience (van den Berg and Pitariu, 2005), agreeableness, and emotional stability (e.g. Dijkstra, van Dierendonck, Evers, and De Dreu, 2005).

Collectively these traits represent the commonly utilized five-factor theory and model of personality (e.g. Costa and McCrae, 1980; McCrae and Costa, 1997), which posits that people's personalities can be adequately described in common language terms representing five traits. People with high levels of neuroticism tend to more frequently experience negative emotions (e.g. depression and anxiety), while highly extraverted individuals are able to socialize easily and tend to experience positive emotions frequently (e.g. Costa and McCrae, 1980; Headey and Wearing, 1992). Individuals high on openness to experience tend to be more flexible in responding to stimuli, more creative, and more imaginative (McCrae, 1993). People who are highly agreeable are generally good natured and amenable. Individuals high on conscientiousness tend to be well organized, diligent, and hard working (McCrae and Costa, 1997).

In a changing work environment there are likely to be several work environmental factors that could interact with traits to influence well-being. One possible factor is the expected increase in time pressures placed on employees (e.g. Landsbergis, 2003). An increase in this work environment characteristic may, for example, increase the chances that high levels of conscientiousness and neuroticism will have an increasingly positive and negative influence (respectively) on well-being.

Via a second path, that of cognitive and emotional processes, continuing globalization and multinational operations could create a second condition in which traits may influence well-being. More specifically, faced with new pressures from a broadening of an industry's or company's scope, high levels of traits such as neuroticism and extraversion may lead to higher or lower perceptions of interpersonal stress across ethnic groupings in mixed workforces. This in turn has the potential to contribute to a reduction in employees' well-being.

As another example, those with low agreeableness and emotional stability may have an especially difficult time engaging in effective cognitive and emotional processing of new forms of interpersonal stress (Dijkstra *et al.*, 2005), such as those likely to develop in a changing work environment. It is also likely that openness to experience will emerge as an important dimension to consider among employees working in cross-culturally diverse working environments (e.g. Flynn, 2005; Jordan and Cartwright, 1998). Traits may also influence cognitive and emotional processes of job attitude formation. For example, while conscientiousness and openness to experience are positively related to job satisfaction, the opposite is true for neuroticism (e.g. Judge, Bono, and Locke, 2000; Judge, Heller, and Mount, 2002; van den Berg and Pitariu, 2005).

Cognitive perceptions of job insecurity may also be closely aligned with underlying traits and well-being. Neuroticism has been positively associated with this strongly threatening work stressor (e.g. Roskies, Louis-Guerin, and Fournier, 1993; Slack and Jones, 2005). Unfortunately, it is likely that such insecurity will become a standard feature of many employment arrangements in the future (e.g. Barley and Kunda, 2006), making neuroticism an even more critical trait to study further.

It is also possible that traits may affect well-being through burnout, a strongly negative psychological and physical condition of reduced resilience in which the person feels emotionally exhausted, depersonalized in their work role, and diminished with respect to personal accomplishments (e.g. Lee and Ashforth, 1993; Leiter, 1990). For example, neuroticism has been linked to increased levels of emotional exhaustion and depersonalization, two main components of burnout (Zellars *et al.*, 2004), making this trait a significant distinguishing characteristic for employees with higher versus lower levels of burnout (e.g. Langelaan *et al.*, 2006).

Thus "positive" traits such as conscientiousness, extraversion, and openness to experience seem to be generally adaptive (leading to positive well-being; e.g. DeNeve and Cooper, 1998), while more "negative" traits such as neuroticism are generally deleterious to employee well-being. Although more research here is much needed, it can be expected based on these previous findings that employees with higher levels of positive traits are more likely to maintain a higher degree of well-being in a changing work environment than their more negatively traited co-workers.

Various other psychological traits have also been linked with objective well-being, including internal locus of control, which is positively related to return to work after experiencing significant back pain (Haldorsen, Indahl, and Ursin, 1998). In addition, negative affectivity has been identified as a significant risk factor for workplace injury, perhaps because individuals with high levels of negative affectivity tend to select more hazardous jobs (Frone, 1998) and/or tend to report more physical symptoms (e.g. headache pain; Trask, Iezzi, and Kreeft, 2001).

Many researchers feel important individual characteristics are ignored when focusing only on the "Big Five" (e.g. John, 1990; Paunonen and Jackson, 2000) or other static traits. Often, these traits do not help researchers understand the process underlying relationships between personality and complex outcomes such as well-being (cf. Diener and Lucas, 1999; Paunonen and Jackson, 2000; Pervin, 1994). Dispositional traits are of especially limited use when studying dynamic criteria such as well-being because they are rather deterministic – a person's standing on a set of traits is viewed as stable and unchangeable, limiting options for improving well-being.

For these and other reasons many researchers prefer to consider more cognitively or behaviorally oriented individual characteristics, especially when studying issues such as how people react to stress at work and in life. This approach to individual differences recognizes that personality can reflect an individual's underlying goals and unique way of viewing and adapting to the external environment. Aspects of personality can also apply to an individual's knowledge of and control over his or her internal environment; or knowledge and control of self (e.g. McAdams and Pals, 2006). At present the best prediction we can offer is that employee well-being within a changing work environment is likely to be influenced by both traditional and stable, as well as the alternative, more malleable, individual characteristics.

Alternative individual characteristics

Although trait approaches to the study of individual difference often converge on the simple five-factor model of personality, no such structure has been applied to other forms of individual characteristics. For the present discussion we focus on the main alternative individual character-istics that we expect to be increasingly influential to employees' well-being as work environments evolve.

Age As a demographic characteristic, age plays a central role in the functioning of a person's biological and physiological processes. As a large proportion of the workforce advances in age, it is likely that researchers of industrial gerontology will play an important role in help-ing organizations to address the well-being issues faced by aging workers. A critical issue to attend to is that just as age is an individual difference, its impacts are also differentially felt by people because of the fact that aging can take place on many different levels or dimensions of a person's life (e.g. chronologically, biologically, psychologically, and socially; e.g. Sterns and Miklos, 1995).

Much more research is needed to understand how age may influence well-being at work. Initial evidence suggests that very young (i.e. around 20 years old) and older workers may report higher job-specific well-being than workers in-between these age ranges, suggesting a possible curvi-linear relationship between age and well-being (e.g. Clark, Oswald, and Warr, 1996; Warr, 1999). There is some evidence that age may influence well-being via its effects on behaviors and possible perceptions of fit. For example, compared to adults, teenaged employees are more likely to be employed in lower-status positions (e.g. manual labor) and situations that place them at greater risk for occupational injury (Frone, 1998; Loughlin and Frone, 2004). In terms of physical resilience, however, workers over the age of 45 tend to require more time to recover from occupational injuries than their younger co-workers (Cheadle *et al.*, 1994).

Findings such as these call into question the outdated belief that psychological well-being and physical health should decrease with age. In all likelihood no such linear or consistent relationship will ever be identified between age and a criterion as complex as well-being. Nevertheless, much more research is needed to answer questions pertaining to how age affects resilience and cognitive and emotional processing of environmental information when facing changing work conditions. These and other issues relevant to the workplace are discussed by Sterns and Miklos (1995) and it is time for researchers to turn more attention in this direction.

Ethnicity A person's ethnic background may also represent a demographic individual characteristic that will need to be considered in future attempts to improve worker well-being. Although the findings are currently inconsistent (cf. Friedman-Jimenez, 1989; Murray, 2003; Robinson, 1989; Strong and Zimmerman, 2005; Wagner and Winn, 1991), there is some evidence that ethnicity may predict the likelihood of occupational disability. In part this may be due to simple response-style differences when completing research questionnaires (e.g. Wagner and Winn, 1991). It is also possible, however, that a high rate of occupational injuries among minorities is due to the hazardous work environments in which many of these individuals find themselves employed (Friedman-Jimenez, 1989; Murray, 2003; Robinson, 1989). From within the present conceptual framework, this possibility suggests that ethnicity may have linkages to well-being via fit perceptions and work-related behaviors.

Biological sex Few individual characteristics are as strongly differentiating as one's biological sex. Whether and how one's sex might influence well-being in a changing work environment is a tricky question requiring more empirical research. Recent research calls into question earlier conclusions that no differences existed between men and women in terms of perceived and/or experienced stress at work (e.g. Martocchio and O'Leary, 1989). Instead, it seems that sex-based differences may be present depending on the nature of the stress experience (i.e. whether it involves acute or chronic stressors; Krajewski and Goffin, 2005; Nelson and Burke, 2002). It is possible that one's sex could therefore influence one's psychological resilience and cognitive and emotional processing within a changing work environment.

The possibility that responses to organizational restructuring and change could differ between men and women is a major issue (e.g. Karambayya, 2002). Emotionally, women's well-being may be more at risk than men's when faced with stress (Jick and Mitz, 1985), owing to women's tendency to experience stronger and more frequent negative affect (Heinisch and Jex, 1997; Jex, Adams, and Ehler, 2002a) and affect in general (e.g. Jex *et al.*, 2002a; Wood, Rhodes, and Whelan, 1989). This latter tendency toward a higher degree of general emotionality may make women more susceptible to the full spectrum of emotional strains associated with occupational stress.

Differences in well-being may also be partially understood by considering biological sex as it interfaces with coping behaviors. Choice and implementation of coping behaviors may actually differ for men and women (e.g. Nelson and Burke, 2002), with men tending toward more problem-focused and/or avoidance efforts and women toward emotion-focused ones (including seeking social support and maintaining a healthy diet; e.g. Jex *et al.*, 2002a; Lindquist, Beilin, and Knuiman, 1997).

There is a separate behavioral link between biological sex and occupational disability, in that men are more likely than women to experience occupational injury, possibly because of the tendency to take more risks on the job. Alternatively, this inflated injury rate may be due to differences in perceptions of fit, leading men to select more physically demanding and risky jobs than women would feel comfortable occupying (e.g. Frone, 1998). Differences have also been shown with respect to the type of injuries and the length of recovery time needed for men and women (e.g. Abenhaim, Suissa, and Rossignol, 1988; Cheadle *et al.*, 1994; Thomas *et al.*, 1999). Adolescent men also consistently demonstrate a higher occupational injury risk than women (Brooks, Davis, and Gallagher, 1993; Layne, Castillo, Stout, and Cutlip, 1994; National Institute for Occupational Safety and Health, 1997). These findings suggest a possible sex-related difference in physical resilience that also needs more study within occupational settings.

Resilience, adaptability, hardiness Moving away from demographic individual characteristics, there is some evidence that certain individuals may simply possess a greater amount of general resilience, adaptability, and/or hardiness (e.g. Kobasa, Maddi, and Kahn, 1982) when facing stressful conditions. Within a changing work environment, these individuals can be expected to quickly and successfully adapt their perceptions and expectations to fit more realistically and positively with the current work environment. Unclear at this point is whether resilience is a hard-wired (e.g. Bonanno, 2005) or modifiable individual characteristic (cf. Ferris, Sinclair, and Kline, 2005).

The latter perspective is that resilience as an individual characteristic may result from a combination of individual characteristics. These characteristics include flexibility in emotional expression (e.g. Bonanno, Papa, Lalande, Westphal, and Coifman, 2004), accurate perception of when to persevere and when to disengage in the pursuit of a goal (e.g. Carver and Scheier, 2003), and a tendency to: (a) view the world optimistically, (b) accept setbacks/failures as normal, keeping them in perspective (maintaining a sense of purpose), (c) perceive themselves as in control over their own lives (viewing stress as challenging), and (d) demonstrate emotional stability that leans toward relatively stable positive affect (Semmer, 2003; Tugade and Fredrickson, 2004). Clearly there is room for more research in this area.

Type A behavior pattern Among the many non-demographic individual characteristics potentially associated with psychological and physiological strain, the Type A behavior pattern is perhaps the most well known. Evolving from its original form discussed by Friedman and Rosenman (1959), Type A is now most commonly treated as a multifaceted constellation of individual characteristics including hostility/irritability, job involvement, hard-driving/competitive nature, perceived time pressure, achievement orientation, and hyper-physiological reactance (e.g. Edwards and Baglioni, 1991; Jex, Adams, Elacqua, and Bachrach, 2002b).

At present the impact of Type A on physiological resilience appears to stem from specific Type A components. Of particular concern are the linkages that have been identified between Type A components such as ambition, drive, and competitiveness and increased risk of coronary heart disease (e.g. Edwards and Baglioni, 1991). It has also been demonstrated that different components of Type A may lead to separate consequences, and that the achievement striving component may actually reduce the relationships between stressors and strains, even when the other Type A components may have exacerbated this effect (Jex *et al.*, 2002b).

As employees face changes in increasingly complex work environments, these findings suggest that Type A will be an important individual characteristic to continue studying (e.g. Schaubroeck, Ganster, and Kemmerer, 1994). Paradoxically, those employees most likely to be high performers (i.e. those with high achievement strivings, a central component of Type A) in such situations may also be the hardest hit by increased work demands (e.g. Jex *et al.*, 2002b). In part this may be due to Type A influencing cognitive and emotional appraisals of job control.

For example, Lee, Ashford, and Bobko (1990) demonstrated that those with a strong Type A and high perceived control performed better and reported higher levels of job satisfaction than high Type A individuals with a low sense of control. Unfortunately the former group also reported more physical symptoms. There are many examples of this type of relationship, including work by Burke (1998), who found that high (as opposed to low) Type A police officers reported more active efforts at coping and less escapist coping, but also more work–family conflict and physical strain.

Self-efficacy Self-efficacy is another individual characteristic that may influence well-being via physiological resilience, perceptions of fit, cognitive and emotional processes, and work-related coping behaviors. Self-efficacy is a construct most strongly developed in work by Bandura (1986, 1997). It reflects an individual's belief that he/she has the skill and ability needed to successfully achieve a desired goal (i.e. the confident feeling of I *can* do this and here is how). In Bandura's work and the work of other researchers, self-efficacy has been linked with a person's motivation, emotions, thoughts, and actions, making it a critically important individual characteristic to consider when considering how changing work environments could influence worker well-being.

In the present context, self-efficacy may influence well-being via multiple pathways in our guiding framework. For instance, individuals with high self-efficacy and high perceptions of control have been shown to experience lower physiological arousal (i.e. lower blood pressure) than individuals with low self-efficacy (e.g. Schaubroeck and Merritt, 1997). Interestingly, perceived job control in the absence of self-efficacy has also been shown to negatively influence elements of well-being (e.g. Schaubroeck, Jones, and Xie, 2001).

A person's self-efficacy may also influence the types of jobs and work environments employees will seek (Grau, Salanova, and Peiró, 2001; Jex and Bliese, 1999; Matsui and Onglatco, 1992). Bandura (1997) has also suggested from a theoretical perspective that those with high self-efficacy would fit and function best in positions that involve high challenge and responsibility, two characteristics that are likely to be used when defining the work environments of the future. Indeed, high self-efficacy may be especially desirable in a workplace where autonomy and continuous learning are joined with high demands and role ambiguity.

Particularly relevant to the present chapter is the finding that self-efficacy may help workers cope with the stress brought on by large-scale technological changes in the workplace (e.g. Grau *et al.*, 2001). Evidence also suggests that self-efficacy may lead individuals to create more posi-tive cognitive and emotional appraisals of occupational stressors, thereby protecting well-being (e.g. Jex, Bliese, Buzzell, and Primeau, 2001). Self-efficacy may also operate through behavioral means to protect well-being among workers. For example, self-efficacy may improve workers' coping behaviors when faced with long work hours and work overload (e.g. Jex and Bliese, 1999; Jex *et al.*, 2001).

Controllability awareness Related to self-efficacy, a person's ability to accurately perceive his/her control over situational characteristics (i.e. controllability awareness) at work is likely to influence both cognitive and emotional processes and behaviors associated with well-being. By defi-nition, controllability awareness refers to a person's potential to distin-guish between controllable and uncontrollable aspects of situations, and then to enact the appropriate responses (Heth and Somer, 2002). Research has shown a clear and consistent positive relationship between perceived control and work-related attitudes (e.g. Spector, 1986), but control as a construct is very difficult to define and fully conceptualize (e.g. Terry and Jimmieson, 1999).

Most often control refers to a person's perceived ability to exert actions that then result in some desired response or change to a desired target (though it can be internally focused as well, cf. Troup and Dewe, 2002). An issue for future researchers to pay more attention to is that "personal control enables well-being, but it is neither a necessary nor a sufficient condition" to guarantee well-being is maintained (Peterson, 1999: 288). Thus, more control is not always better when it comes to an employee's well-being.

People with high controllability awareness can be expected to form more positive appraisals of work stressors because these individuals are capable of accurately perceiving the feasibility and futility of their response options. In other words, individuals with low controllability awareness are unable to make as accurate a distinction between control-lable and uncontrollable situational aspects, leading to a higher incidence of both negative stress appraisals (i.e. sense of being overwhelmed) and ineffective behavioral attempts at coping.

Self-monitoring The degree to which an individual actively man-ages and controls his/her self-expressive behaviors and person-to-person presentation (i.e. the degree to which a person *self-monitors*; e.g. Fox and Dwyer, 1995) may also prove to be important in maintaining well-being in changing work environments. Theoretically, high self-monitoring may allow an individual to adapt his/her behaviors more quickly to changing situational cues (e.g. Snyder, 1974). Alternatively, high self-monitors may also become more easily frustrated when their behaviors are constrained by work or environmental demands (Fox and Dwyer, 1995; Sparacino, Ronchi, Bigley, Flesch, and Kuhn, 1983). For example, high self-monitors may function more effectively in work situations where situational constraints are low, and where customer contact and/ or close teamwork relationships are required because these individuals are capable of maintaining positive interpersonal interactions better than low self-monitors (e.g. Fox and Dwyer, 1995).

Concluding thoughts

In this chapter we have provided a conceptual framework that serves to highlight the importance of both state and trait individual characteristics in the development and maintenance of worker well-being in a changing work environment. In this framework, four pathways were developed that serve to link individual characteristics. Employees' general resilience, perceptions of fit within the job and organization, cognitive and emotional processes at work, and response behaviors to these perceptions, appraisals, emotions, and attitudes are all expected to function in conjunction with individual characteristics in explaining changes in well-being within different individuals facing changing working environments. The present attention to both subjective and objective forms of well-being opens new doors for occupational health researchers interested in studying these issues.

From the research reviewed in this chapter it is evident that individuals with certain combinations of individual characteristics may be better able to handle changes in work environments. For researchers and practitioners who focus on well-being it will be increasingly important for future work to incorporate dispositional traits, demographic features, and malleable individual characteristics, as all of these types of individual characteristics have the potential to influence workers' well-being.

Implications and future directions

In concluding this chapter we would like to highlight a few important points. Research is in its initial stages on many of the individual characteristics we discussed and it is not yet entirely clear when low or high levels of particular characteristics will help or hurt a person's well-being. More research is needed to build our understanding in this area and to guide interventions that could improve employees' abilities to adapt and cope in changing work environments. The greatest positive effects in this area may be found by focusing on developing malleable cognitively and behaviorally oriented individual characteristics that can directly influence employees' cognitive, emotional, and behavioral processes in the work domain.

It is also time for occupational health researchers to fully acknowledge the importance of achieving congruence between people and their jobs and organizations. Incongruence (in terms of general fit, or a mismatch between needs–supplies and abilities–demands) is detrimental to both the person and the organization (cf. Chess and Thomas, 1991, for a similar perspective). Fortunately additional research and practice along these lines may make it possible to eventually avoid such person–organization incongruence.

Several additional future directions are raised by our discussion. First, there is a need to better understand how increasingly complex models (ours included) and theories of well-being and health can be translated into empirical research and actual practice within organizations. Schwarz and Strack (1999) provide an excellent discussion of similar issues related to the measurement of subjective well-being and personality and their discussion deserves review by any researcher considering work in this area.

Second, more research is needed to understand which individual characteristics influence human judgement and decision-making processes that could then influence a person's well-being (and how such influence occurs). Although we have touched on this issue with our discussion of individual characteristics affecting perception and appraisal processes (e.g. the dispositional appraisal bias; Warr, 2005), there are many other issues related to accurate and efficient judgements of self and others and work-related decisions and choice formation that need the attention of researchers who are also interested in enhancing employee well-being.

Third, it is unlikely the effects of separate individual characteristics can be realistically studied in isolation because of their necessary overlap in reality. Depending on features of the work situation and other individual characteristics, the effects may be completely different, making it imperative for researchers to consider the interaction among multiple individual characteristics when designing and testing hypotheses pertaining to employees in actual work environments.

Fourth, although not emphasized in the present chapter, the relationships we discussed were described at the level of the individual employee. Researchers need to explore the possible influences of workgroup- and organization-level aggregations of individual characteristics (i.e. a group profile) on group well-being. As one example, the question can be examined of how well-being within an organization changes as the average age of its workforce increases/decreases, or when other group-level characteristics are changed such as gender mix, or with saturation of other specific individual characteristics.

We hope that our presentation of these issues will inspire you to consider these and other variables of this sort when you study worker well-being in changing work environments. We know enough to understand that the situation will be complicated. It is imperative that we use this knowledge to guide future work that seeks to improve the interaction of worker and work environment to maximize well-being.

References

Abenhaim, L., Suissa, S., and Rossignol, M. (1988). Risk of recurrence of occupational back pain over three year follow up. *British Journal of Industrial Medicine* 45: 829–33.

American Medical Association (2000). *Mastering the AMA guides: a medical and legal transition to guides to the evaluation* (5th edn). Chicago: American Medical Association.

Bandura, A. (1986). *Social foundations of thought and action: a social cognitive theory*. Englewood Cliffs, NJ: Prentice Hall.

(1997). *Self-efficacy: the exercise of control*. New York: Freeman.

(1999). Social cognitive theory of personality. In L. Pervin and O. John (eds.), *Handbook of personality* (pp. 154–96). New York: Guilford Publications.

Barley, S. R. and Kunda, G. (2006). Contracting: a new form of professional practice. *Academy of Management Perspectives* 20: 45–66.

Bonanno, G. A. (2005). Resilience in the face of potential trauma. *Current Directions in Psychological Science* 14: 135–8.

Bonanno, G. A., Papa, A., Lalande, K., Westphal, M., and Coifman, K. (2004). The importance of being flexible: the ability to both enhance and suppress emotional expression predicts long-term adjustment. *Psychological Science* 15: 482–7.

Brooks, D. R., Davis, L. K., and Gallagher, S. S. (1993) Work-related injuries among Massachusetts children: a study based on emergency department data. *American Journal of Industrial Medicine* 24: 313–24.

Burke, R. J. (1998). Work and non-work stressors and well-being among police officers: the role of coping. *Anxiety, Stress and Coping* 11: 345.

Carver, C. S. and Scheier, M. F. (2003). Three human strengths. In L. G. Aspinwall and U. M. Staudinger (eds.), *A psychology of human strengths: fundamental questions and future directions for a positive psychology* (pp. 87–102). Washington, DC: American Psychological Association.

Cheadle, A., Franklin, G., Wolfhagen, C., Savarino, J., Liu, P. Y., Salley, C., *et al.* (1994). Factors influencing the duration of work-related disability: a population based study of Washington state workers' compensation. *American Journal of Public Health* 84: 190–6.

Chess, S. and Thomas, A. (1991). Temperament and the concept of goodness of fit. In J. Strelau and A. Angleitner (eds.), *Explorations in temperament: international perspectives on theory and measurement* (pp. 15–28). New York: Plenum Press.

Clark, A. E., Oswald, A. J., and Warr, P. B. (1996). Is job satisfaction U-shaped in age? *Journal of Occupational and Organizational Psychology* 69: 57–81.

Costa, P. T. and McCrae, R. R. (1980). Influence of extraversion and neuroticism on subjective well-being: happy and unhappy people. *Journal of Personality and Social Psychology* 38: 668–78.

Cotton, P. and Hart, P. M. (2003). Occupational wellbeing and performance: a review of organizational health research. *Australian Psychologist* 38: 118–27.

DeNeve, K. and Cooper, H. (1998). The happy personality: a meta-analysis of 137 personality traits and subjective well-being. *Psychological Bulletin* 124: 197–229.

Diener, E. and Lucas, R. E. (1999). Personality and subjective well-being. In D. Kahneman, E. Diener, and N. Schwarz (eds.), *Well-being: the foundations of hedonic psychology* (pp. 213–29). New York: Russell Sage Foundation.

Dijkstra, M. T. M., van Dierendonck, D., Evers, A., and De Dreu, C. K. W. (2005). Conflict and well-being at work: the moderating role of personality. *Journal of Managerial Psychology* 20: 87–104.

Edwards, J. R. and Baglioni, A. J., Jr. (1991). Relationship between Type A behavior pattern and mental and physical symptoms: a comparison of global and component measures. *Journal of Applied Psychology* 76: 276–90.

Edwards, J. R. and Cooper, C. L. (1990). The person–environment fit approach to stress: recurring problems and some suggested solutions. *Journal of Organizational behavior* 11: 293–307.

Fernet, C., Guay, F., and Senecal, C. (2004). Adjusting to job demands: the role of work self-determination and job control in predicting burnout. *Journal of Vocational Behavior* 65: 39–56.

Ferris, P. A., Sinclair, C., and Kline, T. J. (2005). It takes two to tango: personal and organizational resilience as predictors of strain and cardiovascular disease risk in a work sample. *Journal of Occupational Health Psychology* 10: 225–38.

Flynn, F. J. (2005). Having an open mind: the impact of openness to experience on interracial attitudes and attitude formation. *Journal of Personality and Social Psychology* 88: 816–26.

Fox, M. L. and Dwyer, D. L. (1995). Stressful job demands and worker health: an investigation of the effects of self-monitoring. *Journal of Applied Social Psychology* 25: 1973–95.

Friedman, M. and Rosenman, R. (1959). Association of specific overt behavior pattern with blood and cardiovascular findings. *Journal of the American Medical Association* 12: 1286–96.

Friedman-Jimenez, G. (1989). Occupational disease among minority workers: a common and preventable public health problem. *American Association of Occupational Health Nurses* 37: 64–70.

Frone, M. R. (1998). Predictors of work injuries among employed adolescents. *Journal of Applied Psychology* 83: 565–76.

Grau, R., Salanova, M., and Peiró, J. M. (2001). Moderator effects of self-efficacy on occupational stress. *Psychology in Spain* 5: 63–74.

Haldorsen, E. M. H., Indahl, A., and Ursin, H. (1998). Patients with low back pain not returning to work: a 12-month follow up study. *Spine* 23: 1202–8.

Headey, B. W. and Wearing, A. J. (1992). *Understanding happiness.* Melbourne: Longman Cheshire.

Heinisch, D. A. and Jex, S. M. (1997). Measurement of negative affectivity: a comparison of self-reports and observer ratings. *Work and Stress* 12: 145–60.

Hersey, R. B. (1932/1977). *Research studies XVIII: workers' emotions in shop and home.* New York: Arno Press.

(1955) *Zest for work: industry rediscovers the individual.* New York: Harper and Brothers.

Heth, J. T. and Somer, E. (2002). Characterizing stress tolerance: "controllability awareness" and its relationship to perceived stress and reported health. *Personality and Individual Differences* 33: 883–95.

Hobfoll, S. E. (1989). Conservation of resources: a new attempt at conceptualizing stress. *American Psychologist* 44: 513–24.

(2002). Social and psychological resources and adaptation. *Review of General Psychology* 6: 307–24.

Hofmann, D. A. and Tetrick, L. E. (2003). The etiology of the concept of health: implications for "organizing" individual and organizational health. In D. A. Hofmann and L. E. Tetrick (eds.), *Health and safety in organizations: a multilevel perspective* (pp. 1–28). San Francisco: Jossey-Bass.

Jahoda, M. (1958). *Current concepts of positive mental health.* New York: Basic Books.

Jex, S. M., Adams, G. A., and Ehler, M. L. (2002a). Assessing the role of negative affectivity in occupational stress research: does gender make a difference. In D. L. Nelson and R. J. Burke (eds.), *Gender, work stress, and health* (pp. 71–84). Washington, DC: American Psychological Association.

Jex, S. M., Adams, G. A., Elacqua, T. C., and Bachrach, D. G. (2002b). Type A as a moderator of stressors and job complexity: a comparison of achievement strivings and impatience-irritability. *Journal of Applied Social Psychology* 32: 977–96.

Jex, S. M. and Bliese, P. D. (1999). Efficacy beliefs as a moderator of the impact of work-related stressors: a multilevel study. *Journal of Applied Psychology* 84: 349–61.

Jex, S. M., Bliese, P. D., Buzzell, S., and Primeau, J. (2001). The impact of self-efficacy on stressor–strain relations: coping style as an explanatory mechanism. *Journal of Applied Psychology* 86: 401–9.

Jick, T. D. and Mitz, L. F. (1985). Sex differences in work stress. *Academy of Management Review* 10: 408–20.

John, O. P. (1990). The search for basic dimensions of personality: a review and critique. *Advances in Psychological Assessment* 7: 1–37.

Jordan, J. and Cartwright, S. (1998). Selecting expatriate managers: key traits and competencies. *Leadership and Organizational Journal* 19: 89–96.

Judge, T. A., Bono, J. E., and Locke, E. A. (2000). Personality and job satisfaction: the mediating role of job characteristics. *Journal of Applied Psychology* 85: 237–49.

Judge, T. A., Heller, D., and Mount, M. K. (2002). Five-factor model of personality and job satisfaction: a meta-analysis. *Journal of Applied Psychology* 87: 530–41.

Karambayya, R. (2002). Women and corporate restructuring: sources and consequences of stress. In D. L. Nelson and R. J. Burke (eds.), *Gender, work stress, and health* (pp. 55–69). Washington, DC: American Psychological Association.

Karasek, R. A. (1979). Job demands, job decision latitude, and mental strain: implications for job redesign. *Administrative Science Quarterly* 24: 285–308.

Karasek, R. A. and Theorell, T. (1990). *Healthy work: stress, productivity, and the reconstruction of working life*. New York: Basic Books.

Kasl, S. V. and Rapp, S. R. (1991). Stress, health, and well-being: the role of individual differences. In C. L. Cooper and R. Payne (eds.), *Personality and stress: individual differences in the stress process* (vol. 14, pp. 269–84). New York: John Wiley.

Keyes, C. L. M., Hysom, S. J., and Lupo, K. L. (2000). The positive organization: leadership legitimacy, employee well-being, and the bottom line. *The Psychologist-Manager Journal* 4: 143–53.

Kobasa, S., Maddi, S., and Kahn, S. (1982). Hardiness and health: a prospective study. *Journal of Personality and Social Psychology* 42: 168–77.

Kornhauser, A. (1965). *Mental health of the industrial worker: a Detroit study*. New York: John Wiley.

Krajewski, H. T. and Goffin, R. D. (2005). Predicting occupational coping responses: the interactive effect of gender and work stressor context. *Journal of Occupational Health Psychology* 10: 44–53.

Kristof, A. L. (1996). Person–organization fit: an integrative review of its conceptualizations, measurement, and implications. *Personnel Psychology* 49: 1–49.

Kurland, N. and Bailey, D. (1999). Telework: the advantages and challenges of working here, there, anywhere, and anytime. *Organizational Dynamics* 28: 53–67.

Landsbergis, P. A. (2003). The changing organization of work and the safety of working people: a commentary. *Journal of Occupational and Environmental Medicine* 45: 61–72.

Langelaan, S., Bakker, A. B., van Doornen, L. J. P., and Schaufeli, W. B. (2006). Burnout and work engagement: do individual differences make a difference? *Personality and Individual Differences* 40: 521–32.

Larson, J. S. (1999). The conceptualization of health. *Medical Care Research and Review* 56: 123–36.

Layne, L. A., Castillo, D. N., Stout, N., and Cutlip, P. (1994). Adolescent occupational injuries requiring hospital emergency department treatment: a nationally representative sample. *American Journal of Public Health* 84: 657–60.

Lazarus, R. S. (1999). *Stress and emotion: a new synthesis*. New York: Springer.

Lazarus, R. S. and Folkman, S. (1987). Transactional theory and research on emotions and coping. *European Journal of Personality* 1: 141–69.

Lee, R. T. and Ashforth, B. E. (1993). A further examination of managerial burnout: towards an integrated model. *Journal of Organizational Behavior* 1: 3–20.

Lee, C., Ashford, S. J., and Bobko, P. (1990). Interactive effects of "Type A" behavior and perceived control on worker performance, job satisfaction, and somatic complaints. *Academy of Management Journal* 33: 870–81.

Leiter, M. P. (1990). The impact of family resources, control coping, and skill utilization on the development of burnout: a longitudinal study. *Human Relations* 43: 1067–83.

Lindquist, T. L., Beilin, L. J., and Knuiman, M. W. (1997). Influence of lifestyle, coping and job stress on blood pressure in men and women. *Hypertension* 29: 1–7.

Loughlin, C. and Frone, M. R. (2004). Young workers' occupational safety. In J. Barling and M. R. Frone (eds.), *The psychology of workplace safety* (pp. 107–25). Washington, DC: American Psychological Association.

Martocchio, J. J. and O'Leary, A. M. (1989). Sex differences in occupational stress: a meta-analytic review. *Journal of Applied Psychology* 74: 495–501.

Matsui, T. and Onglatco, M. L. (1992). Career self-efficacy as a moderator of the relations between occupational stress and strain. *Journal of Vocational Behavior* 41: 79–88.

Mayo, E. (1930). The human effect of mechanization. *42nd Annual Meeting, American Economic Association, Papers and Proceedings* 20: 156–76.

McAdams, D. P. and Pals, J. L. (2006). A new big five: fundamental principles for an integrative science of personality. *American Psychologist* 61: 204–17.

McCrae, R. R. (1993). Openness to experience as a basic dimension of personality. *Imagination, Cognition and Personality* 13: 39–55.

McCrae, R. R. and Costa, P. T. (1997). Personality trait structure as a human universal. *American Psychologist* 52: 509–16.

Mischel, W. and Shoda, Y. (1995). A cognitive-affective system theory of personality: reconceptualizing situations, dispositions, dynamics, and invariance in personality structure. *Psychological Review* 102: 246–68.

Münsterberg, H. (1913). *Psychology and industrial efficiency.* Boston: Houghton Mifflin.

Murray, L. R. (2003). Sick and tired of being sick and tired: scientific evidence, methods, and research implications for racial and ethnic disparities in occupational health. *American Journal of Public Health* 93: 221–6.

National Institute for Occupational Safety and Health (1997). *Special Hazard Review: child labor research needs* (DHHA Publication NIOSH 1997–143). Washington, DC: Government Printing Office.

Nelson, D. L. and Burke, R. J. (2002). A framework for examining gender, work stress, and health. In D. L. Nelson and R. J. Burke (eds.), *Gender, work stress, and health* (pp. 3–14). Washington, DC: American Psychological Association.

Paunonen, S. V. and Jackson, D. N. (2000). What is beyond the Big Five? Plenty! *Journal of Personality* 68: 821–35.

Pervin, L. A. (1994). A critical analysis of current trait theory. *Psychological Inquiry* 5: 103–13.

Peterson, C. (1999). Personal control and well-being. In D. Kahneman, E. Diener, and N. Schwarz (eds.), *Well-being: the foundations of hedonic psychology* (pp. 288–301). New York: Russell Sage Foundation.

Robinson, J. C. (1989). Trends in racial inequality and exposure to work-related hazards. *American Association of Occupational Health Nurses* 37: 56–63.

Roskies, E., Louis-Guerin, C., and Fournier, C. (1993). Coping with job insecurity: how does personality make a difference? *Journal of Organizational Behavior* 14: 617–30.

Ryan, R. M. and Frederick, C. (1997). On energy, personality, and health: subjective vitality as a dynamic reflection of well-being. *Journal of Personality* 65: 529–65.

Ryff, C. D. and Singer, B. (2003). Ironies of the human condition: well-being and health on the way to mortality. In L. G. Aspinwall and U. M. Staudinger (eds.), *A psychology of human strengths: fundamental questions and future directions for a positive psychology* (pp. 271–87). Washington, DC: American Psychological Association.

Ryff, C. D., Singer, B., Wing, E. H., and Love, G. D. (2001). Elective affinities and uninvited agonies. Mapping emotion with significant others onto health. In C. D. Ryff and B. H. Singer (eds.), *Emotion, social relationships, and health* (pp. 133–75). New York: Oxford University Press.

Schaubroeck, J. and Fink, L. S. (1998). Facilitating and inhibiting effects of job control and social support on stress outcomes and role behavior: a contingency model. *Journal of Organizational Behavior* 19: 167–95.

Schaubroeck, J., Ganster, D. C., and Kemmerer, B. E. (1994). Job complexity, "Type A" behavior, and cardiovascular disorder: a prospective study. *Academy of Management Journal* 37: 426–39.

Schaubroeck, J., Jones, J. R., and Xie, J. L. (2001). Individual differences in utilizing control to cope with job demands: effects on susceptibility to infectious disease. *Journal of Applied Psychology* 86: 265–78.

Schaubroeck, J. and Merritt, D. E. (1997). Divergent effects of job control on coping with work stressors: the key role of self-efficacy. *Academy of Management Journal* 40: 738–54.

Schneider, B. (1987). E = f(P, B): the road to a radical approach to person–environment fit. *Journal of Vocational Behavior* 31: 353–61.

Schwarz, N. and Strack, F. (1999). Reports of subjective well-being: judgmental processes and their methodological implications. In D. Kahneman, E. Diener, and N. Schwarz (eds.), *Well-being: the foundations of hedonic psychology* (pp. 61–84). New York: Russell Sage Foundation.

Semmer, N. K. (2003). Individual differences, work stress and health. In M. J. Schabracq, J. A. M. Winnubst, and C. L. Cooper (eds.), *The handbook of work and health psychology* (2nd edn, pp. 83–120). New York: John Wiley.

Shoda, Y. and Mischel, W. (1996). Toward a unified, intra-individual dynamic conception of personality. *Journal of Research in Personality* 30: 414–28.

Slack, K. J. and Jones, A. P. (2005). Job insecurity and well-being in the context of employment. Paper presented at the annual meeting of the Society for Industrial and Organizational Psychology, Los Angeles, CA.

Snyder, M. (1974). Self-monitoring of expressive behavior. *Journal of Personality and Social Psychology* 30: 526–37.

Sparacino, J., Ronchi, D., Bigley, T. K., Flesch, A. L., and Khun, J. W. (1983). Self-monitoring and blood pressure. *Journal of Personality and Social Psychology* 44: 365–75.

Spector, P. E. (1986). Perceived control by employees: a meta-analysis of studies concerning autonomy and participation at work. *Human Relations* 39: 1005–16.

Sterns, H. L. and Miklos, S. M. (1995). The aging worker in a changing environment: organizational and individual issues. *Journal of Vocational Behavior* 47: 248–68.

Strong, L. L. and Zimmerman, F. J. (2005). Occupational injury and absence from work among African American, Hispanic, and non-Hispanic white workers in the national longitudinal survey of youth. *American Journal of Public Health* 95: 1226–32.

Terry, D. J. and Jimmieson, N. L. (1999). Work control and employee well-being: a decade review. In C. L. Cooper and I. T. Robertson (eds.), *International review of industrial and organizational psychology* (vol. 14, pp. 95–148). Chichester: John Wiley.

Thomas, E., Silman, A. J., Croft, P. R., Papageorgiou, A. C., Jayson, M. I. V., and Macfarlane, G. J. (1999). Predicting who develops chronic low back pain in primary care: a prospective study. *British Medical Journal* 381: 1662–7.

Trask, P. C., Iezzi, T., and Kreeft, J. (2001). Comparison of headache parameters using headache type and emotional status. *Journal of Psychosomatic Research* 51: 529–36.

Troup, C. and Dewe, P. (2002). Exploring the nature of control and its role in the appraisal of workplace stress. *Work and Stress* 16: 335–55.

Tugade, M. M. and Fredrickson, B. L. (2004). Resilient individuals use positive emotions to bounce back from negative emotional experiences. *Journal of Personality and Social Psychology* 86: 320–33.

van den Berg, P. T. and Pitariu, H. (2005). The relationships between personality and well-being during societal change. *Personality and Individual Difference* 39: 229–34.

Van Der Doef, M. and Maes, S. (1999). The Job Demand–Control(-Support) model and psychological well-being: a review of 20 years of empirical research. *Work and Stress* 13: 87–114.

Verquer, M. L., Beehr, T. A., and Wagner, S. H. (2003). A meta-analysis of relations between person–organization fit and work attitudes. *Journal of Vocational Behavior* 63: 473–89.

Viteles, M. S. (1953). *Motivation and morale in industry*. New York: Norton.

Wagner D. K. and Winn, D. W. (1991). Injuries in working populations: black–white differences. *American Journal of Public Health* 81: 1408–14.

Warr, P. (1999). Well-being and the workplace. In D. Kahneman, E. Diener, and N. Schwarz (eds.), *Well-being: the foundations of hedonic psychology* (pp. 392–412). New York: Russell Sage Foundation.

(2005). Work, well-being, and mental health. In J. Barling, E. K. Kelloway, and M. R. Frone (eds.), *Handbook of work stress* (pp. 547–73). Thousand Oaks, CA: Sage.

Wood, W., Rhodes, N., and Whelan, M. (1989). Sex differences in positive well-being: a consideration of emotional style and marital status. *Psychological Bulletin* 106: 249–64.

Zellars, K. L., Hochwarter, W. A., Perrewé, P. L., Hoffman, N., and Ford, E. W. (2004). Experiencing job burnout: the roles of positive and negative traits and states. *Journal of Applied Social Psychology* 34: 887–911.

Zickar, M. J. (2003). Remembering Arthur Kornhauser: industrial psychology's advocate for worker well-being. *Journal of Applied Psychology* 88: 363–9.

14   Stress and coping at work: new research trends and their implications for practice

José M. Peiró

Research on work stress and the ways individuals cope with it has a long tradition that has lasted for more than half a century and that has increased dramatically during the last few decades. Work stress is a phenomenon that has often been related to poor well-being at work and to psychosomatic complaints. Its relation to workers' physical and mental health has also been established (Sonnentag and Frese, 2003). Moreover, stress has negative outcomes for companies because of absence behaviors and low performance. In fact, several authors have reported work stress to be a significant source of labor costs for companies (Cooper, Liukkonen, and Cartwright, 1996; Goetzel *et al.*, 1998).

In recent times, labor markets, organizations, and the nature of work itself have experienced important transformations caused by globalization and social, economic, market, and technological changes. These changes have had an impact on work context, work activities, and workers' health and well-being. In many facets working conditions have improved, but new risks, most of them of a psychosocial nature, have appeared or intensified. This emerging reality poses new demands and threats for workers and professionals, but it also offers new opportunities for development and personal fulfillment. Stress experiences can hamper employees' well-being and health, but under certain conditions they can also have beneficial consequences. In fact, as pointed out by Selye (1956), an important distinction can be made between stress that is positive, labeled "eustress," and negative stress, which is sometimes known as "distress." Research has also pointed out that an individual's appraisal of stressors and coping strategies plays an important role in stress and its consequences, although the working conditions, and the available resources and social support, also play a role in the stress–strain relationship. Nevertheless, current research shows there are important limitations to coping strategies. The latter have been considered mainly from an individual point of view, putting too much emphasis on the competency of individuals to manage and cope with stress, and ignoring the fact that, in many instances, the individual has no control over the work stressors that depend on organizational arrangements. Moreover, coping has also commonly been conceptualized as reactive responses to stressors already taxing the individuals, which does not lend itself to the fact that anticipation and proactive behaviors are increasingly necessary in dynamic and complex work environments that present new psychosocial risks.

In this context, the prediction and understanding of stress and coping require new research and professional efforts, and the emerging research trends on stress and coping deserve more attention. This chapter aims to describe some of these trends and outline their implications for practice. In the next section, we will focus on the demands facing stress research in the European context, as they are derived from the policies on occupational risk prevention and health promotion. Afterwards, we will analyze the limitations of the inherited research paradigm on work stress and its insufficiency for meeting the demands of health promotion in the new work contexts and experiences. In the fourth section, we will review four emerging trends in research on work stress and coping, and examine their implications for practice. In so doing, we will take into consideration the implications of positive psychology for work stress research and practice, and look at the emphasis on broadening the conceptualization of the context in which work stress is experienced as a way of overcoming the limitations of the previous theoretical models. We will also review the proactive and anticipatory approach to the study of work stress and coping, and, finally, we will focus on a multilevel approach to stress and coping, which emphasizes that stress does not occur only at an individual level, as it can also be fruitfully analyzed at the collective level (team, work unit or department, organization, etc.) and at the cross-level between influences and interactions. The chapter will end with a summary and some important conclusions.

Stress prevention in Europe

During the past few decades, psychosocial risks at work have received attention in European work policies and laws. Their prevention has been clearly established as a "must" in the European Framework Directive 89/391 of the European Community. This directive compelled the member states to adapt their legislation in order to implement psychosocial risk analysis and prevention. It has become compulsory for every job, and the prevention of the risks identified needs to be guaranteed. This requirement has brought about a professional response, with these new demands promoting research in Europe as well as the development of assessment tools and intervention programs. In fact, several publications have presented the challenges and achievements connected with some of the recent research in the field (Cox, Griffiths, and Rial-González, 2000; EASHW, 2002). Some developments that occurred during the 1990s in Belgium, Finland, the Netherlands, the United Kingdom, Spain, and the USA were reported on in a special issue of the *Spanish Journal of Work and Organizational Psychology* (Peiró and Bravo, 1999). In 2000, the European Union published its *Guidance on work-related stress* (Levi, 2000), which clearly indicates that stress can be positive ("the spice of life") or negative ("a kiss of death"), depending on the context and individual variation.

A stronger emphasis has been placed on these issues in the EU policy on work health promotion presented in the communication *Adapting to change in work and society: a new Community strategy on health and safety at work 2002–2006* (Commission of the European Communities, 2002), and a Framework Agreement on work-related stress was signed by social agents in 2004 (Social Dialogue, 2004). This emphasis on psychosocial risk prevention has propelled the interest in and research on work stress in Europe (Kompier, De Gier, Smulders, and Draaisma, 1994). In fact, several authors (Cooper and Dewe, 2004; Cox and Griffiths, 1996; Cox and Rial-González, 2000; Levi, 2002; Peiró, 1999; Sverke, Gallagher, and Hellgren, 2000) have stressed that most emergent psychosocial risks can be better understood with the help of further research based on stress models. The theories and scientific knowledge that we have gained in this area are important ingredients for addressing the call for psychosocial risk analysis and prevention. Related assessment and intervention methodologies should also not be overlooked, as they can provide a rich set of resources for professionals working in this area. Nevertheless, a number of issues are still pending, and the development of new and more effective tools and strategies is required.

The above-mentioned documents from the Commission of the European Communities emphasize several aspects that require more attention (e.g. Commission of the European Communities, 2002). First, they point out the need for a positive approach to health, one which aims to promote a true sense of well-being at work – physically, morally, and socially – and whose efficacy is not measured only in terms of its lack of accidents or professional diseases. Second, they draw attention to the emergent stressors in their context, keeping in mind the changes produced in the world of work and the emergence of new risks, especially psychosocial ones. Third, they insist on taking an anticipatory approach that aims to strengthen the culture of risk prevention through information, education, and participation. Lastly, there is also an emphasis put on the role of social agents, with attention being paid not only to the individual but also to collective actions. The role of both good practices and collective strategies is underscored, along with the importance of social dialogue and corporate social responsibility. In our view, fulfilling these demands implies revising theoretical models of stress research and performing a critical analysis of the implicit assumptions that have inspired it for more than half a century.

Stress research: the inherited paradigm and its criticisms

For more than half a century, research on work stress has been carried out based on a number of assumptions that have inspired and oriented the issues addressed and the prevailing approaches. Among these assumptions, several are worth mentioning here. First, research has mainly focused on stress as a negative phenomenon (distress) that hampers health and well-being. Moreover, it has been considered as a naturalistic phenomenon taxing the person, and the predominant view of it has focused on the lack of fit between the person and the environment. Third, affects and emotions have been considered in a rather limited way, with the focus mostly being on the negative affects produced by distressful experiences (Lazarus, 1993). Fourth, stress has mainly been analyzed once it has occurred, and coping has been considered a reactive response. The person under stress has been considered in an individualized and decontextualized way and from an agentic point of view in which the ability to manage and control stress is seen as resting with the individual. This does not imply that social phenomena have not been considered in the research, but that they have mainly been considered as a source of stress or as moderators of stress–strain relations.

Criticism of the inherited paradigm

Critical voices have been raised since the 1990s, pointing out the limitations of such an approach. Most of these criticisms have originated from research traditions other than positivism. The cultural theory of stress emphasizes stress as a shared symbol within the culture of the organization, pointing out the collective nature of stress perceptions (Abbot, 1990). Also, analyses of the institutional, cultural, and political phenomena (or power balance) within organizations have proven very useful in understanding collective stress in organizations, viewing the differences among groups as a function of their structural and power status positions, and underscoring the limitations of an individualistic and agentic approach (Meyerson, 1994). From a critical perspective, Newton (1995) has presented a number of broad and in-depth criticisms of most of the assumptions of the mainstream research that has dominated the scene for more than half a century. He pointed out the agentic, individualistic, decontextualized, ahistorical, and apolitical approach of the dominant research paradigm. From a socioconstructionist and psychodynamic view of emotions in organizations, Fineman (1996) pointed out several limitations of the research on work stress, such as the use of naturalistic and objectivistic approaches that disregard the forces driving the dominant construction of the stress phenomena. Finally, from a psychoanalytic perspective, James (1999) has highlighted many of the biases of the mainstream research tradition. Within the positivistic tradition, several voices have asserted that new approaches are required. The methodological developments in multilevel and cross-level analyses have opened up new possibilities for the study of work stress, making it possible to analyze the collective phenomena at work and the multilevel relationship between stress and its consequences, as well as the contextual influences on the emergence and development of collective stress in work units and work organizations (Bliese and Jex, 1999).

In summary, we can note the following criticisms. First, most research has focused on individual stress experiences and, in doing so, imputes the individual, assuming that he or she should be able to cope effectively with stress. In many cases, work stressors exist apart from the individual's control and are embedded in the structure and organizational arrangements, serving the interests of the dominant party. Second, research has overemphasized individual differences and too often assumed that the individual is the main agent for managing stress. In this regard, stress is basically conceptualized as an individual phenomenon, which is a notion that undervalues the importance of the cultural, structural, and collective forces serving the dominant group. Third, it assumes an objective and naturalistic approach to stress rather than a socially constructed approach that draws the attention away from radical changes designed to help eliminate the root causes of it. With this approach, stress is considered a natural phenomenon, rather than a socially construed reality mainly influenced by those in power. Fourth, the analysis of stress and the strategies considered for controlling or reducing it are kept at an individual level, without questioning the contextual, political, and historical conditions that contributed to creating a stressed and alienated society. Many of these criticisms open up new issues and represent new opportunities for future research on this topic.

New research perspectives in stress and coping

The above-mentioned demands of the European agenda on psychosocial risk prevention, along with the criticisms of stress research described above, have stimulated the exploration of new perspectives on work stress. First, an approach from a positive psychology perspective aims to broaden the focus of research, while drawing attention to other relevant issues besides distress. It also aims to identify the conditions that enhance eustress as a way of promoting workers' well-being and development. Second, a more socially contextualized method of analysis is growing in use, enabling researchers to better understand work stress in its organizational, political, and cultural contexts. The identification of relevant variables and models that can account for these phenomena is essential for examining the new global context of today's working world. Third, an anticipatory and proactive approach to stress and coping points out that individuals, groups, and organizations should anticipate stress and proactively cope with it. Anticipation is essential in a dynamic world where changes are constant and require action in order both to avoid negative effects and to profit from new opportunities for enhancing positive effects. Finally, a multilevel and cross-level approach entails seeking a better understanding of the emergence and development of individual and collective phenomena, as well as of their consequences for individuals, groups, and organizations. To focus only on individual experiences of stress will produce an incomplete picture of the situation, and impede the consideration of other important features of stress and coping phenomena. It also narrows the range of interventions by focusing on those more directly related to the individual and leaving out those that could lead to a redesigning of organizational structure or work system arrangements, for example, or even change the power structure and political balance.

An approach to work stress from a Positive Psychology perspective

Positive Psychology has a long tradition within psychology. One clear exponent of it was Maslow in the 1960s, who emphasized the idea of peak human experiences (Maslow, 1962). Nonetheless, for decades, psychology has focused mainly on human deficits, dysfunctions, and pathologies, and its main efforts were directed toward repairing damage. Recently, a revitalization of the positive tradition has pointed out that psychology should not be considered mainly a remedial and corrective science. Its principle aim should be, rather, to promote positive experiences, the development of human beings, and flow experiences (Seligman and Csikszentmihalyi, 2000). Positive psychology concentrates on positive subjective experiences, positive individual traits, and positive institutions. It emphasizes strengths and virtues, rather than weakness and suffering, and its focus is on understanding and promoting the development of the qualities that allow individuals to flourish (Nelson and Cooper, 2005; Nelson and Simmons, 2003).

To see stress in a positive light is not new, as the distinction between "eustress" and "distress" was made decades ago (Selye, 1956). The problem is that the literature that often mentioned this distinction concentrated its attention on distress, and so the research has hardly considered the positive stress experiences. In the renewed approach, there are several questions that deserve attention, and clear definitions of eustress and distress are required. Selye (1987) indicated earlier that the distressful or eustressful nature of any particular stressor depends on how the individual interprets it and chooses to react to it. More recently, Nelson and Simmons (2003) have operationally defined eustress as "a positive psychological response to a stressor, as indicated by the presence of positive psychological states" (p. 104), and distress as "a negative psychological response to a stressor, as indicated by the presence of negative psychological states" (p. 104). Moreover, Le Fevre, Matheny, and Kot (2003) have pointed out that the difference between eustress and distress cannot be formulated on the basis of the intensity of the stress experience. Taking into account these issues, new questions arise in stress research. It would be interesting, for instance, to better understand the processes and mechanisms for enhancing eustress and converting distress into eustress. In fact, some recent literature has given attention to the processes that can contribute to deriving benefits from stressful events (Britt, Adler, and Bartone, 2001). It would also be worthwhile to identify the conditions that make it possible for eustress to happen, and how they contribute to the understanding of the way this positive experience could stimulate individual and group growth, in addition to reducing the negative consequences of distress.

Moreover, recent evidence has shown that positive and negative emotions co-occur throughout the stress process. This "prompted new research about the role of positive emotions in the stress process and the role of coping in generating and sustaining these emotions" (Folkman and Moskowitz, 2004: 747). It is important to better understand the combinations of different types of emotions, both positive and negative, and their sequences when individuals experience stress. A similar issue arises when considering the consequences of stress and the related question of coping effectiveness. This is a complex issue that has often been addressed in a simplified way, in which only the negative effects of stress are considered and assessed along with the effectiveness of coping in reducing these negative effects. However, as Folkman and Moskowitz (2004) suggest, in a stressful situation there is a multiplicity of goals, and some of them can produce positive outcomes, while others produce negative ones, such as negative well-being. Given this plurality of out-comes, individuals tend to establish priorities in order to obtain benefits from some goals, even while assuming costs from others, when they experience and cope with stress (e.g. accepting a foreign job that improves career opportunities may imply accepting some personal or family costs). Thus, stress does not only produce negative outcomes for health and well-being. It is also important to identify the positive out-comes and the priorities individuals and groups give to these different outcomes (McGowan, Gardner, and Fletcher, 2006). In this context, work stress research should concentrate more on the combination of positive and negative outcomes when examining individuals' stress expe-riences and how they use strategies to cope with it, taking both stress processes into consideration in a more holistic model. Nelson and Simmons (2003) provide a more comprehensive view of work stress, which should help us gain more insight into why individuals willingly commit themselves to stressful situations. In utilizing this more complete picture, it becomes necessary to consider the aspect of "savoring," that is, one's enjoying of the situation or the opportunity as a response to eustress, which parallels coping as the response to distress. Along with this, a closer examination of the mix between costs and benefits which influences whether stress is perceived to constitute a threat or an oppor-tunity would be worthwhile. To conceptualize stress mainly in terms of distress or eustress influences the type of emotions (positive and nega-tive), and their combinations, that can be applied to a stressful situation. Furthermore, it also affects the enactment of coping strategies (problem oriented or palliative) and savoring, as well as their combination and sequence. These issues are even more complex when we take into account that the outcomes of stress experiences and the effectiveness of coping can differ when considered in the short term or in the long run. Sometimes stressed individuals will assume costs in the short term in order to get benefits in the longer term, while under other circumstances (e.g. with no spare resources) they will accept missing opportunities in the long run just to prevent and avoid the threats and damages in the short term. More research is needed to understand under what conditions individuals give priority to obtaining short-term benefits (e.g. ventilation, distancing, etc.) and renounce positive and valuable results in the longer term, and in which circumstances the opposite occurs.

All of these issues show that a combination of positive and negative outcomes is often present in a stressful situation, and that the individual's (and the group's) interpretation and appraisal of such a situation is critical. These processes of appraisal will influence, and be influenced by, the emotions that emerge, and both the appraisal and the emotions will interact with coping behaviors that individuals and groups will utilize in order to achieve certain outcomes.

This picture becomes even more complex because the meaning of positive outcomes (e.g. well-being) is heavily influenced by beliefs and values. Current research on well-being is rooted in two general perspectives (Ryan and Deci, 2001). On the one hand, the *hedonic* approach defines well-being in terms of pleasure attainment and pain avoidance. On the other hand, the *eudaimonic* approach defines well-being in terms of the "degree to which a person is fully functioning" and achieves "actualization of his or her human potentials." These different beliefs about happiness also influence the appraisal of stress situations, their interpretations as threats or opportunities, and the emotions and their valence (e.g. religious beliefs can have an important influence on the emotions experienced by a person when a close relative dies). All these complex phenomena, in turn, will determine coping behaviors. Future research should aim to disentangle these complexities.

All these issues have clear implications for risk analysis and prevention. It is possible to identify opportunities as well as threats in order to achieve a more holistic view of the work situation and its risks and opportunities. It is also useful to assess the positive personal features and the way they can be enhanced to promote well-being among employees. Furthermore, the positive approach focuses on identifying preventive strategies that will promote opportunities and not only reduce the risks. Finally, it is helpful to use sources of eustress as resources to prevent or neutralize the negative effects of distress. A time perspective must be taken into account in the understanding of situational conditions of eustress and distress in a given context and in planning interventions to enhance the former and prevent or correct the latter.

A more contextualized approach to work stress

The relevant phenomena at work are changing. During the past few decades, important transformations, such as the globalization of society and the economy, and the development of new information and communication technologies, are having an important impact on work and organizations. In this context, *work activities* are becoming more cognitive and often imply emotional labor. Many jobs require performing under conditions of uncertainty, often with a lack of sufficient information, and their performance often requires extra-role behaviors, initiative, role innovation, self-regulation, and dedication. Furthermore, responsibility and risk assumption is often asked for even in low-level jobs. Teamwork is spread out and generalized, requiring new competences and new types of coordination because of task interdependence.

The *workforce* is also more diverse in the labor market and within the companies. This diversity occurs with regard to several important features, such as gender (more women are incorporated into the labor force), education (with a trend toward increasing the education of the labor force), ethnic groups (given the migration flows), and values and lifestyles that are also more differentiated than in traditional societies.

Organizations have been subjected to extensive transformations that are partly required because of changes in the environment (market competition, laws, deregulation, etc.). This has included strategies for increasing flexibility (such as mergers, restructuring, downsizing, etc.) and for utilizing technology to enhance the possibilities of virtual interactions. Organizational change has become more accelerated, now being the norm for many companies, while change management has become more complex and uncertain, not only in technical but also in social and political terms.

Industrial relations have undergone important changes as well. On the one hand, there has been a trend toward individualization. On the other hand, there have been changes in the ways companies look for labor flexibility, with many turning to externalization, franchising, subcontracting, flexible contracts, temporary workers, etc. (Silla, Gracia, and Peiró, 2005). Finally, the roles played by the unions at the company level, in private and public organizations, and at the societal level, are also changing.

Political policies also play a role in this context. It is interesting to analyze the regulations and policies formulated during the last few years by the European Commission. They are framed within the general goal formulated by the Lisbon Summit (European Council, 2000), which aims to achieve "the most competitive and dynamic knowledge-based economy in the world, capable of sustainable economic growth with more and better jobs and greater social cohesion." In this context, more specific policies have been formulated, tackling different facets of work, labor markets, and organizations. There is an aim to promote more and better jobs in organizations that enhance the quality of working life. Another objective is to promote the anticipation and management of changes in a way that avoids the negative effects of "industrial mutations." Health promotion and safety at work are addressed by the laws at the European level. The mobility of the labor force across Europe and social inclusion, integration, and participation in economic and social life are core topics of the European Social Agenda (Commission of the European Communities, 2000). Finally, it is expected that social dialogue will contribute to meeting these various challenges.

All these changes require enlarging and redefining the models and domains of work stress research. In fact, recent studies have drawn more attention to their role as stressors and/or as resources that carry with them opportunities regarding the following organizational phenomena: human resource policies and practices in organizations; structural changes (mergers, acquisitions, privatization, downsizing, relocation, etc.); flexibility (contractual, location, etc.) and insecurity (Silla *et al.*, 2005); new careers and their prospects and management; conciliation and balance between work and other life spheres; loss of status at work or in the occupation; and social demands and cross-cultural phenomena.

The full incorporation of the aforementioned topics into stress research implies a reformulation of the theoretical models and a revision of their assumptions. Since the seventies, the most outstanding and reputed models of stress have focused on an imbalance between the person and the environment as the basic phenomenon, and this was thought to occur when work demands were taxing, threatening, and noxious. In fact, the Demands–Control model formulated by Karasek (1979; see also Karasek and Theorell, 1990) and its followers (Johnson, Hall, and Theorell, 1989; Rodríguez, Bravo, Peiró, and Schaufeli, 2001) have proved to be useful for understanding under what conditions (low control, high demands, and low support) the lack of fit between the person and the job can have negative effects on the individual's health and well-being. Based on a similar rationale, the Demands–Resources model (Bakker, Demerouti, Taris, Schaufeli, and Schreurs, 2003) has also focused on similar mechanisms and emphasized the interaction between the individual and the environment based on a transactional view of stress. The vitamin model formulated by Warr (1987) was based on the same transactional and fit assumptions. In this case, it focused on the intensity of the job characteristics and distinguished two types of job features that operate differently in terms of the demands placed on the workers. Some features, when exceeding certain thresholds, become harmful for the individuals, while an excess of others has no negative effects.

In our view, these and similar models fall short in explaining a number of work and organizational phenomena that are becoming more and more relevant in work contexts. The focus on stress should not just be centered on job activities and their conditions anymore, but needs to extend to other organizational and environmental phenomena. The broader context of work extends to the company's policies and practices of human resource management, the industrial relations and the psychological contract established between the employee and the company, the changes in the structure of the company, ownership and mergers, the situation of the labor market, and the labor flexibility and career development policies, as well as the politics and power balance in organizations. All these phenomena can represent important sources of stress (eustress and distress) that require theoretical models to analyze them. They imply complex social relationships at different levels. On the one hand, the individual and collective exchanges between employer and employees require reciprocity, fairness, and justice perceptions, although they are hard to attain. On the other, the intensified social and interpersonal relations at work (with customers, team members, supervisors, etc.) have led to relational phenomena taking on a more predominant role in explaining positive and negative work effects. Psychosocial theories, such as exchange, fairness and justice, social comparison, or social cognition, are thus becoming more relevant to adequately understanding work stress.

Accordingly, in our opinion, the models that best inspire the research on work stress nowadays are those that deal with the intricate dynamics of exchange between the parts involved in the work situation and process. So it is important to understand the balance in the exchange between the employee and the company (e.g. Effort–Reward Imbalance; Siegrist, 1998) or between different actors in the work setting. In understanding this balance, several social mechanisms and processes become relevant, such as social comparison processes (Buunk, Zurriaga, Peiró, Nauta, and Gosalvez, 2005; Carmona, Buunk, Peiró, Rodríguez, and Bravo, 2006) and fairness and reciprocity processes. Justice models distinguishing distributive, procedural, interactional, informational, and retributive justice and their interactions provide an interesting theoretical framework for approaching the study of work stress, given both the positive and negative outcomes stemming from such experiences (Cropanzano, Goldman, and Benson, 2005; Moliner, Martínez-Tur, Peiró, and Ramos, 2005; Zohar, 1995). Thus, in addition to taking into account the abilities and demands at work, and the fit between the values and expectations of the individual and the company, future research will also have to analyze the intricate dynamic of exchange between parts. The rationale of psychological contract theory (focusing on promises, including their fulfillment or violation, as well as the fairness of the exchange, and trust in the relationships between parts) can contribute to more contextualized analyses of stress (Gakovic and Tetrick, 2003; Guest 2004; Rousseau, 1995; 2005). In this regard, research on power (Peiró and Meliá, 2003) and on conflict should be integrated into theoretical models that aim to better understand work stress in organizations. Power and conflict are complex phenomena that play multiple functions in social systems like organizations. They occur not only at an interpersonal level, but also at a societal level involving political maneuverings. These processes are permeated throughout organizations and play a significant role in the above-mentioned social processes involved in work stress, whose study deserves more attention.

Accordingly, psychosocial risk analysis and prevention have to take into account fairness, promises, and the fulfillment of expectations, as well as processes aimed at establishing reciprocity and justice, such as social comparison, influence, and conflict management. Moreover, the cultural, social, economic, and historical contexts need to be analyzed in risk diagnoses. They cannot only focus on objective features of the environment, but must also include relational phenomena whose meaning and potential harmful or beneficial effects are socially construed. Thus, interventions aimed at improving the work situation have to be aware that the target is not only the individual but also its context, including other individuals interacting in the same situation. Building mutual trust between employees and employer and among the employees themselves is an important asset in promoting effective interventions.

An anticipatory and proactive approach to the study of stress and coping

The historical nature of human beings brings them to shape their reality throughout their lives, as this process is influenced by a person's history. In other words, the present reality of a person can only be understood through his or her past (the personal history that made the present situation possible) and through his or her future outlook (in the form of projects, plans, intentions, and expectations), because both provide meaning for the present behavior. As the Spanish philosopher Ortega y Gasset (1958; Carpintero, 2000) forwarded, human beings are by their very nature "future oriented." So, only when paying attention to intentions, plans, goals, and expectations can their current behaviors be properly understood.

As the meaning of one's current behavior is strongly related to one's future orientation (projects), anticipation and proactivity are essential activities for human lives. In spite of this, most research on work stress has focused on reactive and past-oriented responses. In the current social and work contexts, it becomes even more important to anticipate changes because they are more frequent and in-depth, and they quite often have important consequences for individuals. Some of these changes have been characterized as industrial "mutations," where the emphasis is placed on the dramatic consequences they may have for individuals and companies if they are not anticipated and managed. For instance, the lack of anticipation involved in such mutations can strongly reduce the employability of individuals or the competitiveness of the company. In order to cope effectively with this mutation, individuals have to identify future training needs and engage in continuous professional development that will keep them prepared for new demands in the labor market. In a more general way, psychosocial risks other than the ones related to working conditions should be prevented at work and not only "corrected" once they have appeared. Thus, emergent risks for workers derived from globalization, technological innovation, and changes in work and labor markets need to be anticipated in order to assure their employability, jobs, and professional development. Also, social relations in work contexts are becoming more complex and frequent, and they require more developed social abilities that would contribute to preventing phenomena such as social and sexual harassment or other disputes to occur. Primary prevention requires a proactive approach to risk management.

In this context, stress research should place more emphasis on the aspect of time. But this does not only mean in terms of longitudinal designs, aimed at identifying causal relationships between stressors and consequences; it also implies paying more attention to the relevance of a future orientation in regard to stress and coping. Following this rationale, *stress appraisal* should not only be studied from a "presentist" point of view, but should also consider anticipatory and future-oriented phenomena. In many cases, it is the plans and intentions of the agent that give meaning to the situation. Whether something is appraised as being threatening, taxing, or beneficial, or even as an opportunity, is often influenced by what is aimed for and/or expected. Thus, research should not focus only on the current demands that can be seen as taxing or noxious and the effectiveness of related coping responses. It also has to study future stressors in the form of threats, challenges, and opportunities that may be anticipated by individuals in relation to their plans, intentions, and expectations. Research should also take a closer look at the way individuals can profit from the anticipation of future desired or feared events, preventing at the same time their negative effects and consequences and promoting their positive effects. An anticipatory and proactive approach to stress is necessary if development and growth are to be expected as common outcomes of stress, in addition to the negative outcomes that are now often exclusively considered in stress. To address this, theoretical models suitable to better understanding and explaining these phenomena are needed.

It is interesting to note that coping research has recently been focusing on proactive actions (Aspinwall and Taylor, 1997; Carver, Scheier, and Weintraub, 1989; Greenglass, 2002; Schwarzer and Knoll, 2003). In fact, several future-oriented coping types have been differentiated. *Anticipatory coping* refers to the efforts to deal with a critical event that is fairly certain to occur in the near future, *preventive coping* aims to foreshadow an uncertain threat potential in the distant future, and *proactive coping* focuses on upcoming challenges that are potentially self-promoting because they could create opportunities for growth. Greenglass, Schwarzer, and Tauber (1999) have described three main features of proactive coping: it integrates planning and preventive strategies with proactive self-regulatory goal attainment; it also involves proactive goal attainment with identification and use of social resources; and it utilizes proactive emotional coping for self-regulatory goal attainment.

Finally, research on anticipatory and proactive stress appraisal and coping has clear implications in the applied and professional contexts that have been promoted by the framework established by the aforementioned EU community strategy on health and safety at work (Commission of the European Communities, 2002). The anticipation and prevention of risks, including psychosocial risks, is one of the main tenets of the strategy. This approach provides new insights for analysis and interventions, both to enhance the opportunities for eustress and to prevent the risks of distress. Risk diagnosis has to pay attention to signs that help anticipate threats and opportunities; it also has to be more strategic and future oriented. In addition, interventions have to be designed to prevent the occurrence of the risks and to convert threats into opportunities. The theory of conservation of resources provides interesting insights for prospective and anticipatory prevention strategies (Hobfoll, 2001; Schwarzer, 2001).

A multilevel approach to work stress

Work and organizations are social realities that are embedded with phenomena with different levels of complexity. Some of those phenomena occur and can be understood at an individual level, involving individual behaviors and psychological processes, such as perception, motivation, learning, and decision-making. Others take place at a collective level (group or organizational level), and their research requires a macro approach. In addition, the phenomena at one level can, and often do, influence other phenomena at another level. In this framework, Klein and Kozlowski (2000) pointed out that a leveled approach combining micro and macro (collective) perspectives engenders a more integrated science of organizations. Recent progress in research methods has increased the possibilities for this type of research. For instance, Random Coefficient Modeling Programs (Bliese and Jex, 2002) make it possible to deal with multilevel phenomena more accurately than before. Multilevel research can be complemented by cross-level analysis, which encompasses both top-down and bottom-up processes. The focus on top-down processes aims to understand contextual influences. A given context often has

either direct or moderating effects on lower-level processes and outcomes. Attention to bottom-up processes looks for emergent phenomena. In fact, many psychosocial phenomena in collective units have
their foundations in cognition, affects, and behavior, which, through
social interaction, have emergent properties that manifest at higher levels
(González-Romá, Peiró, and Tordera, 2002). So, identifying the conditions, antecedents, and processes that produce emergent properties of
the collective reality is one important issue in psychosocial research.

In recent years, research has begun to examine collective stress in work
units and organizations (Peiró, 2001), but a more systematic approach is
still needed in order to understand the complex interrelationships between
work stress phenomena at different levels. When work stress is analyzed
from an individual perspective, a number of relevant phenomena become
salient, such as the misfit between demands and resources or control
available, the individual's appraisal of this situation, the emotions experienced, and the coping strategies enacted. However, other relevant phenomena, such as how this experience is shared among the members of the
same department or work unit, are not taken into account. Quite often,
stress is jointly experienced by members of the same work unit, and they
also present shared affective responses and may initiate collective actions
to cope with it. Thus, a collective and cross-level analysis of work stress is
needed to better understand work stress in social systems such as
organizations.

In our research unit (www.uv.es/uipot), a research program is in progress that aims to study the different components of work stress from a
multilevel and cross-level approach. The basic model states that the different components of stress (appraisal, emotions, and coping) must be considered not only as individual phenomena but also as collective ones.
Furthermore, the emergent processes and properties of these collective
realities deserve investigation because they play an important role in collective stress (see Figure 14.1). In the following section, we will provide
an overview of the conceptualization and of the new research issues concerning stress components considered from a collective perspective.

A multilevel approach to the study of stress appraisal Stress appraisal
is the first subjective stage of the stress experience. Under certain conditions, a group of people can develop shared perceptions of a given
situation, and they can interpret it as being threatening or as beneficial.
In this situation, a collective experience of stress can emerge. This was the
case in three independent divisions of a company where collective properties of stress experiences were identified using the qualitative methodology of grounded theory (Länsisalmi, Peiró, and Kivimäki, 2000, 2004).

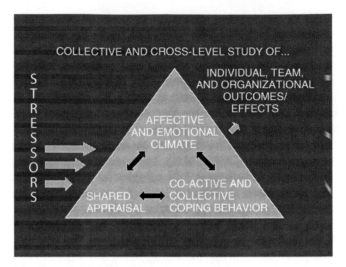

Figure 14.1 Multilevel research on work stress

It is interesting that when these stress experiences emerge, they become a holistic property that cannot be reduced to its lower-level elements and yet still has an influence on them. This collective experience of stress has important consequences for individuals, the group itself, and the organization. Shared appraisal can be produced through several processes. It can be the result of the exposure of group members to the same stressor. Even then, the shared interpretation of the stressor by the group members is influenced by their interactions, which shape individual perceptions in order to induce convergence and consensus. Thus, the common experience of stress is also the result of a culture and of shared "rules of appraisal" (Averill, 1986). Faced with a similar stressful situation, certain groups can perceive a threat, while others may perceive an opportunity to thrive. Leadership qualities such as sense-making and charisma also shape the perceptions of the group members. Leaders' perceptions of work stress could influence the stress experiences of the group members. Team selection processes based on the Attraction–Selection–Attrition model (Schneider, 1987) can also contribute to bringing together people who tend to perceive and interpret situations and events in a similar way. Finally, group socialization processes contribute to facilitating common interpretations of the situations, and thus increase the probabilities of shared appraisal of certain situations as stressful. Thus, the study of collective stress requires focusing on the processes through which the members of a group tend to share interpretations of a given situation or event and perceive it as stressful. When they do, a collective experience of stress emerges, and it gives rise to other emotional and behavioral processes that can also become collective. In a recent study carried out in a sample of 156 bank branches, Gamero, González-Romá, and Peiró (in press) found that work units that experienced higher task conflict presented more negative affective climate. Moreover, this relationship was mediated by relationship conflict.

A multilevel approach to the study of emotions induced by stress at work The way people appraise stressful situations and events influences their emotional experiences, which, in turn, influence appraisal (McGowan, Gardner, and Fletcher, 2006). This complex process has been researched at an individual level, and Lazarus (1993) has emphasized that research on stress should focus on emotions in order to better understand and predict behaviors related to it.

When groups share their stress experiences, their members will probably tend to experience and express similar emotions, and an emotional climate will emerge. Recently, several authors examined these phenomena. George (1990, 1996) has described it as "group affective tone"; Barsade, Ward, Turner, and Sonnenfeld (2000) referred to it as "shared emotions"; Bartel and Saavedra (2000) featured it as "group moods"; and De Rivera (1992) defined it as "emotional climate." This last author pointed out that emotional climate is conceived as an objective, although socially constructed, fact, and it can be considered as a subjective construct (emotions are in the minds of the individuals) as well as an objective one (they are shared and manifested in collective ways of behaving). González-Romá, Peiró, Subirats, and Mañas (2000) have provided empirical support for the validity of what they have called "affective work team climate." González-Morales, Peiró, Rodríguez, and Bliese (2005) found evidence, in a sample of 555 teachers from 100 schools, which supported the existence of shared burnout, both cynicism and emotional exhaustion, within schools. Moreover, a collective climate of burnout did predict change in individual teachers' job satisfaction over time, above and beyond the individual ratings of both core dimensions of burnout. The negative group-level relationship of collective cynicism was more related to teachers' job satisfaction than was individual-level cynicism level; and in the case of emotional exhaustion, only collective emotional exhaustion and teaching stressors significantly predicted the change in individual teachers' job satisfaction over time.

Thus, as in the case of appraisal, it is necessary to understand the mechanisms that may contribute to emotional climate formation. First, shared appraisal of stressful events may induce shared affects and emotions. Once the members perceive a stressful situation in a similar way, it is most probable that they will develop similar emotions and affects and that these states will also be shared by the group. Other mechanisms can also contribute to the emergence of collective emotional and affective experiences: leader behaviors and leader interaction with other members; group member interactions influencing deviant members to converge with the group emotional state; and group norms on the expression of emotions, establishing the accepted ways to do so. Moreover, affective social comparisons under conditions of uncertainty help the members of a group to interpret their experiences and to express the appropriate emotions that are more in agreement with other group members. There are also different processes of emotional contagion (both conscious and unconscious), which have been thought to explain the way individuals share their emotions and affects. Finally, several mechanisms of selection (such as those described in the Attraction–Selection–Attrition model) and socialization within groups contribute to the emerging processes (Barsade, 2002; Barsade *et al.*, 2000; Bartel and Saavedra, 2000). Future research will have to explore the relevance of these mechanisms in producing emotional climates induced by shared stress experiences.

A multilevel approach to the study of coping In the inherited paradigm of stress research, coping has been studied almost exclusively from an individualistic perspective, under the assumptions that individuals function rather independently, and decide themselves how to manage stressors. In recent times, the limitations of this approach have become evident and have led to a greater awareness of the social components of coping. Social support has been emphasized as an additional resource for individuals to use as a coping strategy. Nevertheless, this way of considering social dimensions is limited, especially in work settings, where effective coping is often beyond the control of the individual worker, since systems are designed and operate in a broader structure. Thus, individualistic approaches to coping can be ineffective or even counterproductive, leading to frustration, and leaving collective coping strategies as the only avenue for reducing job stress in these cases. Some authors have looked at these collective phenomena from several perspectives, such as the communal perspective (Dunahoo, Geller, and Hobfoll, 1996; Korczynski, 2003; Lyons, Mickelson, Sullivan, and Coyne, 1998) and one that concentrates on collective coping (Länsisalmi *et al.*, 2000; Torkelson, Muhonen, and Peiró, in press). For instance, Degoey (2000) has reviewed two forms of action that could be considered collective coping strategies: collective protests and group-based impression management. In this chapter, however, we distinguish between two different types of aggregate coping. First, *coactive coping* occurs when individuals in a group or work unit use similar individual ways of coping, owing to social pressure, shared perceptions or beliefs, or imitation strategies. This could occur, for example, in a situation where absenteeism norms lead individuals in the same group to use episodes of absence as a way of avoiding stressful experiences. Secondly, *collective coping* occurs when a group, faced with a common perceived threat or noxious situation, collectively initiates actions to prevent, eliminate, or reduce the stressful situation, to interpret the situation in a more positive way, or to alleviate its negative effects and consequences. Collective coping implies collective goals, and actions of group members and group members' activities are directed toward achieving these goals, even when there are individual costs. The study of these phenomena is especially important in work settings where the control of stressful events is often not in the hands of the individual. Sometimes, individuals imitate those individual coping strategies that appear to be more effective. However, under certain conditions, only collective action can result in the effective control of stress. In our research, we found evidence showing that, while individual and coactive coping of teachers in primary and secondary schools were ineffective in reducing collective stress during the academic year, the use of collective actions, such as discussing and developing a common plan to deal with student misbehavior, or seeking training to cope with the introduction of new information technologies, was effective for reducing individual and collective levels of stress from the beginning to the end of the academic year (Peiró, Rodriguez, and Bravo, 2003).

In summary, more research is needed in order to better understand the collective process of appraising stress, the emotional climates that emerge from these experiences, and the collective coping strategies that can help groups and work units to control stressful situations more effectively. Furthermore, cross-level analyses can contribute to the understanding of the intricate relationships between individual and collective psychosocial phenomena.

This multilevel approach to stress has important implications for psychosocial risk analysis and prevention. First, the priority should be given to understanding collective stress processes and not only individual ones. The analysis of shared stress appraisal in work units or organizations can help to identify new features of stressful situations useful for disentangling relevant processes for effective psychosocial risk prevention. Second, it is important to identify collective emotions related to stress and the way they emerge and are contagious for other members in the group. This knowledge may help us utilize these collective emotions in a positive way and influence their formation. Thirdly, it is especially useful to identify the collective actions and strategies often used in work settings by groups to prevent distress and promote health and human development. The assessment of the effectiveness of these collective strategies is also an important ingredient in improving professional interventions.

As Bliese and Halverson (1996: 1173) stated, "the nomothetic perspective may be particularly useful in designing interventions (Schwartz, 1994). For example, it may be more efficient to find ways to reduce the workload requirements for a group under a heavy work load than to attempt to teach members of the group how to cope with the heavy workload." However, a nomothetic approach, that is, an approach which looks for generalizable conclusions regarding these phenomena, should not necessarily lie in a realistic epistemology; it can also be useful within a socioconstructivistic approach. Identifying the "socially constructed" situation and shared emotional experiences, as well as collective ways of preventing and coping with these experiences at a team or organizational level, can provide new insight for diagnosis and for preventive and corrective interventions (Peiró and Bravo, 1999; Oeij and Morvan, 2004). In our research unit (the Research Unit of Organizational and Work Psychology; UIPOT), we have developed a model and a methodology to implement a general checklist of psychosocial risks in organizations, aiming for a multilevel diagnosis and a set of guidelines for intervention (Peiró, 2000, 2003, 2004, 2007).

Conclusions

Important changes have occurred in the world of work during the last few decades. At the onset of the twenty-first century, work activities and their contexts, regarding employment, industrial relations, the labor market, and work organization, have undergone, and continue to undergo, profound transformations. These changes are producing new psychosocial risks and new opportunities for personal development and flow experiences. In order to prevent or protect individuals from the risks and promote positive opportunities, new theoretical models need to be developed in stress research. In our search for innovative approaches that could shed light on this reality and contribute to fulfilling the social demands of promoting a healthy work place in accordance with current social aspirations, we have identified four relevant trends. These trends emphasize an approach to work stress that stems from positive psychology, and which turns to more socially contextualized theoretical models, puts an emphasis on the study of anticipatory and proactive coping, and utilizes a multilevel study of work stress phenomena.

The contributions coming from this reorientation have clear implications for professional interventions such as risk analysis and prevention, as well as the promotion of health and well-being at work. We expect that further developments in these research areas will contribute to developing better policies and strategies for achieving new advances in the quality of working life and in the humanization of work and companies in the twenty-first century, as an important part of their corporate social responsibility.

References

Abbot, A. D. (1990). Positivism and interpretation in sociology: lessons from sociologists from the history of stress research. *Sociological Forum* 5: 435–58.

Aspinwall, L. G. and Taylor, S. E. (1997). A stitch in time: self-regulation and proactive coping. *Psychological Bulletin* 121: 417–36.

Averill, J. R. (1986). The acquisition of emotions during adulthood. In R. Harré (ed.), *The social construction of emotions* (pp. 98–118). Oxford: Basil Blackwell.

Bakker, A. B., Demerouti, E., Taris, T., Schaufeli, W. B., and Schreurs, P. (2003). A multi-group analysis of the Job Demands–Resources model in four home care organizations. *International Journal of Stress Management* 10: 16–38.

Barsade, S. G. (2002). The ripple effect: emotional contagion and its influence on group behavior. *Administrative Science Quarterly* 47: 644–75.

Barsade, S. G., Ward, A. J., Turner, J. D., and Sonnenfeld, J. A. (2000). To your heart's content: a model of affective diversity in top management teams. *Administrative Science Quarterly* 45: 802–36.

Bartel, C. A. and Saavedra, R. (2000). The collective construction of work group moods. *Administrative Science Quarterly* 45: 197–231.

Bliese, P. D. and Halverson, R. R. (1996). Individual and nomothetic models of job stress: an examination of work hours, cohesion and well-being. *Journal of Applied Social Psychology* 26: 1171–89.

Bliese, P. D. and Jex, S. M. (1999). Incorporating multiple levels of analysis into occupational stress research. *Work and Stress* 13: 1–6.

(2002). Incorporating a multilevel perspective into occupational stress research: theoretical, methodological, and practical implications. *Journal of Occupational Health Psychology* 7: 265–76.

Britt, T. W., Adler, A. B., and Bartone, P. T. (2001). Deriving benefits from stressful events. The role of engagement in meaningful work and hardiness. *Journal of Occupational Health Psychology* 6: 53–63.

Buunk, B. P., Zurriaga, R., Peiró, J. M., Nauta, A., and Gosalvez, I. (2005). Social comparisons at work as related to a cooperative social climate and to individual differences in social comparison orientation. *Applied Psychology: An International Review* 54: 61–80.

Carmona, C., Buunk, B. P., Peiró, J. M., Rodríguez, I., and Bravo, M. J. (2006). Do social comparison and coping styles play a role in the development of burnout? Cross-sectional and longitudinal findings. *Journal of Occupational and Organizational Psychology* 79: 85–99.

Carpintero, H. (2000). *Esbozo de una psicología de la razón vital.* Madrid: Real Academia de Ciencias Morales y Políticas.

Carver, C. S., Scheier, M. F., and Weintraub, J. K. (1989). Assessing coping strategies: a theoretically based approach. *Journal of Personality and Social Psychology* 56: 267–83.

Commission of the European Communities (2000). *Social policy agenda* (COM 2000, 379 final). Brussels, 28.6.2000.

    (2002) *Adapting to change in work and society: a new Community strategy on health and safety at work 2002–2006* (COM 2002, 118 final). Brussels, 11.3.2002.

Cooper, C. L. and Dewe, P. (2004). *Stress: a brief history*. Oxford: Blackwell.

Cooper, C. L., Liukkonen, P., and Cartwright, S. (1996). *Stress prevention in the work place: assessing the costs and benefits to organizations*. Dublin: European Foundation for the Improvement of Living and Working Conditions.

Cox, T. and Griffiths, A. J. (1996). The assessment of psychosocial hazards at work. In M. J. Schabracq, J. A. M. Winnubst, and C. L. Cooper (eds.), *Handbook of work and health psychology* (pp. 127–46). Chichester: John Wiley.

Cox, T., Griffiths, A., and Rial-González, E. (2000). *Research on work-related stress*. Brussels: European Agency for Safety and Health at Work.

Cox, T. and Rial-González, E. (2000). Risk management, psychosocial hazards and work stress. In J. Rantanen and S. Lehtinen (eds.), *Psychological stress at work*. Helsinki: Finnish Institute of Occupational Health.

Cropanzano, R., Goldman, B., and Benson, L., III (2005). Organizational justice. In J. Barling, K. Kelloway, and M. Frone (eds.), *Handbook of work stress* (pp. 63–87). Beverly Hills, CA: Sage.

Degoey, P. (2000). Contagious justice: exploring the social construction of justice in organizations. In B. M. Staw and R. I. Sutton (eds.), *Research in organizational behavior* (vol. 22, pp. 51–102). Amsterdam: JAI Elsevier.

De Rivera, J. H. (1992). Emotional climate: social structure and emotional dynamics. In K. T. Strongman (ed.), *International review of studies on emotion* (vol. 2, pp. 197–218). Chichester: John Wiley.

Dunahoo, C. L., Geller, P. A., and Hobfoll, S. E. (1996). Women's coping: communal versus individualistic. In M. J. Schabracq, J. A. M. Winnubst, and C. L. Cooper (eds.), *Handbook of work and health psychology* (pp. 183–204). Chichester: John Wiley.

EASHW (2002). *Prevention of psychosocial risks and stress at work in practice*. Bilbao: European Agency for Safety and Health at Work.

European Council (2000). *Presidency conclusions*. Lisbon European council. 23 and 24 March 2000. http://ue.eu.int/ueDocs/cms_Data/docs/pressData/en/ec/00100-r1.en0.htm.

Fineman, S. (1996). Emotion and organizing. In S. R. Clegg, C. Hardy, and W. R. Nord (eds.), *Handbook of organization studies* (pp. 543–64). London: Sage.

Folkman, S. and Moskowitz, J. T. (2004). Coping: pitfalls and promise. *Annual Review of Psychology* 55: 745–74.

Gakovic, A. and Tetrick, L. E. (2003). Psychological contract breach as a source of strain for employees. *Journal of Business and Psychology* 18: 235–46.

Gamero, N., González-Romá, V., and Peiró, J. M. (in press). The influence of intra-team conflict on work teams' affective climate: a longitudinal study. *Journal of Occupational and Organizational Psychology*.

George, J. M. (1990). Personality, affect and behavior in groups. *Journal of Applied Psychology* 75: 107–16.

(1996). Group affective tone. In M. A. West (ed.), *Handbook of work group psychology* (pp. 77–94). Chichester: John Wiley.

Goetzel, R. Z., Anderson, D. R., Whitmer, R. W., Ozminkowski, R. J., Dunn, R. L., and Wasserman, J. (1998). The relationships between modifiable health risks and health care expenditures. *Journal of Occupational and Environmental Medicine* 40: 843–54.

González-Morales, M. G., Peiró, J. M., Rodríguez, I., and Bliese, P. D. (2005). A longitudinal multilevel analysis of burnout consequences on teachers' job satisfaction from a gender perspective. Paper presented at the Xth European Congress of Psychology, Granada, 7–12 July.

González-Romá, V., Peiró, J. M., Subirats, M., and Mañas, M. A. (2000). The validity of affective work team climates. In M. Vartiainen, F. Avallone, and N. Anderson (eds.), *Innovative theories, tools, and practices in work and organizational psychology* (pp. 97–109). Göttingen: Hogrefe and Huber.

González-Romá, V., Peiró, J. M., and Tordera, N. (2002). An examination of the antecedents and moderator influences of climate strength. *Journal of Applied Psychology* 87: 465–73.

Greenglass, E. R. (2002). Work stress, coping, and social support: implications for women's occupational well-being. In D. L. Nelson and R. J. Burke (eds.), *Gender, work stress and health* (pp. 85–96). Washington, DC: American Psychological Association.

Greenglass, E. R., Schwarzer, R., and Taubert, S. (1999). *The Proactive Coping Inventory (PCI): a multidimensional research instrument.* On-line publication. Available at www.psych.yorku.ca/greenglass/.

Guest, D. (2004). Flexible employment contracts, the psychological contract and employee outcomes: an analysis and review of the evidence. *International Journal of Management Reviews* 5: 1–19.

Hobfoll, S. E. (2001). The influence of culture, community, and the nested-self in the stress process: advancing Conservation of Resources theory. *Applied Psychology: An International Review* 50: 337–70.

James, K. (1999). Re-thinking organisational stress: the transition to the new employment age. *Journal of Managerial Psychology* 14: 545–57.

Johnson, J. V., Hall, E. M., and Theorell, T. (1989). Combined effects of job strain and social isolation on cardiovascular disease morbidity and mortality in a random sample of the Swedish male working population. *Scandinavian Journal of Work, Environment and Health* 15: 271–9.

Karasek, R. A. (1979). Job demands, job control and mental strain: implications for job redesign. *Administrative Science Quarterly* 24: 285–308.

Karasek, R. A. and Theorell, T. (1990). *Healthy work stress, productivity and the reconstruction of working life.* New York: Free Press.

Klein, K. J. and Kozlowski, S. W. J. (2000). *Multilevel theory, research and methods in organizations: foundations, extensions and new directions.* San Francisco: Jossey-Bass.

Kompier, M., De Gier, E., Smulders, P., and Draaisma, D. (1994). Regulations, policies and practices concerning work stress in five European countries. *Work and Stress* 8: 296–318.

308   Peiró

Korczynski, M. (2003). Communities of coping: collective emotional labour in service work. *Organization* 10: 55–79.

Länsisalmi, H., Peiró, J. M., and Kivimäki, M. (2000). Collective stress and coping in the context of organizational culture. *European Journal of Work and Organizational Psychology* 9: 527–59.

(2004). Grounded theory in organizational research. In C. Cassell and G. Symon (eds.), *Essential guide to qualitative methods in organizational research* (pp. 242–55). London: Sage.

Lazarus, R. S. (1993). From psychological stress to the emotions: a history of changing outlooks. *Annual Review of Psychology* 44: 1–21.

Le Fevre, M., Matheny, J., and Kot, G. S. (2003). Eustress, distress, and interpretation in occupational stress. *Journal of Managerial Psychology* 18: 726–44.

Levi, L. (2000). *Guidance on work-related stress: spice of life, or kiss of death?* http://ec.europa.eu/employment_social/publications/2002/ke4502361_en.html. Luxemburg: Office for Official Publications of the European Communities.

(2002). The European Commission's guidance on work-related stress: from words to action. *TUTB Newsletter* 19–20: 12–17.

Lyons, R. F., Mickelson, K. D., Sullivan, M. J. L., and Coyne, J. C. (1998). Coping as a communal process. *Journal of Social and Personality Relationships* 15: 579–605.

Maslow, A. H. (1962). *Toward a psychology of being*. Princeton, NJ: D. Van Nostrand.

McGowan, J., Gardner, D., and Fletcher, R. (2006). Positive and negative affective outcomes of occupational stress. *New Zealand Journal of Psychology* 35: 92–8.

Meyerson, D. E. (1994). Interpretations of stress in institutions: the cultural production of ambiguity and burnout. *Administrative Science Quarterly* 39: 628–53.

Moliner, C., Martínez-Tur, V., Peiró, J. M., and Ramos, J. (2005). Linking organizational justice to burnout: are men and women different? *Psychological Reports* 96: 805–16.

Nelson, D. L. and Cooper, C. (2005). Stress and health: a positive direction. *Stress and Health* 21: 73–5.

Nelson, D. L. and Simmons, B. L. (2003). Health psychology and work stress: a more positive approach. In J. C. Quick and L. Tetrick (eds.), *Handbook of occupational health psychology* (pp. 97–119). Washington, DC: American Psychological Association.

Newton, T. (1995). *Managing stress: emotions and power at work*. London: Sage.

Oeij, P. R. A. and Morvan, E. (eds.) (2004). *European ways to combat psychosocial risks related to work organisation: towards organisational interventions?* Hoofdorp, NL: TNO Work and Employment, in association with PEROSH, Partnership for European Research in Occupational Safety and Health, Barcelona.

Ortega y Gasset, J. (1958). *Obras completas I–XI. Volumen VII*. Madrid: Revista de Occidente.

Peiró, J. M. (1999). *Desencadenantes del estrés laboral* [Work stressors] (2nd edn). Madrid: Pirámide.

(2000). Assessment of psychosocial risks and prevention strategies: the AMIGO model as the basis of the PREVENLAB/PSYCHOSOCIAL methodology. *Psychology in Spain* 4: 139–66.

(2001). Stressed teams in organizations: a multilevel approach to the study of stress in work units. In J. Pryce, C. Weilkert, and E. Torkelson (eds.), *Occupational health psychology: Europe 2001* (pp. 9–13). Nottingham: European Academy of Occupational Health.

(2003). Metodología Prevenlab para el análisis y prevención de riesgos psicosociales [Prevenlab methodology for the analysis and prevention of psychosocial risks at work]. *Capital Humano* 167: 82–90.

(2004). Análisis de los riesgos psicosociales, diagnóstico e intervención. Metodología Prevenlab [Psychosocial risk analysis: diagnosis and intervention. Prevenlab methodology]. In *I simposium sobre riesgos laborales en las administraciones públicas* (pp. 185–97). Oviedo: Narcea.

(2007). La metodología "Prevenlab-Psicosocial" para la evaluación de riesgos psicosociales en la empresa [The methodology "Prevenlab-Psychosocial" for psychosocial risk assessment in the companies]. In J. L. Meliá *et al.* (eds.), *Manual de análisis e intervención en riesgos psicosociales en la empresa* (pp. 105–30). Barcelona: Foment.

Peiró, J. M. and Bravo, M. J. (1999). Factores psicosociales en la prevención de riesgos laborales: oportunidades y retos para la psicología del trabajo y de las organizaciones [Psychosocial factors in work risk prevention. Opportunities and challenges for work and organizational psychology]. *Revista de Psicología del Trabajo y de las Organizaciones* 15: 137–46.

Peiró, J. M. and Meliá, J. L. (2003). Formal and informal interpersonal power in organisations: testing a bifactorial model of power in role-sets. *Applied Psychology: An International Review* 52: 14–35.

Peiró, J. M., Rodriguez, I., and Bravo, M. J. (2003). Individual, coactive and collective coping effects on occupational stress: a longitudinal study. Paper presented at the Conference Work Stress and Health: New Challenges in a Changing Workplace, Toronto, 20–22 March.

Rodríguez, I., Bravo, M. J., Peiró, J. M., and Schaufeli, W. (2001). The Demands-Control-Support model, locus of control and job dissatisfaction: a longitudinal study. *Work and Stress* 15: 97–114.

Rousseau, D. M. (1995). *Psychological contract in organizations: understanding written and unwritten agreements*. Thousand Oaks, CA: Sage.

(2005). *I-DEALS: Idiosyncratic Deals employees bargain for themselves*. Armonk, NY: M.E. Sharpes.

Ryan, R. M. and Deci, E. L. (2001). On happiness and human potentials: a review of research on hedonic and eudaimonic well-being. *Annual Review of Psychology* 52: 141–66.

Salanova, M., Agut, S., and Peiró, J. M. (2005). Linking organizational resources and work engagement to employee performance and customer loyalty: the mediation of service climate. *Journal of Applied Psychology* 90: 1217–27.

Schneider, B. (1987). The people make the place. *Personnel Psychology* 40: 437–53.

Schwarzer, R. (2001). Stress, resources and proactive coping. *Applied Psychology: An International Review* 50: 400–7.

Schwarzer, R. and Knoll, N. (2003). Positive coping: mastering demands and searching meaning. In A. M. Nezu, C. M. Nezu, and P. A. Geller (eds.), *Comprehensive handbook of psychology* (vol. 9, pp. 393–409). New York: Wiley.

Seligman, M. E. P. and Csikszentmihalyi, M. (2000). Positive psychology. An introduction. *American Psychologist* 55: 5–14.

Selye, H. (1956). *The stress of life*. New York: McGraw Hill.

(1987). Stress without distress. In L. Levi (ed.), *Society, stress, and disease, vol. 5: Old age* (pp. 257–62). New York: Oxford University Press.

Shore, L. M., Tetrick, L. E., Taylor, M. S., Shapiro, J. A., Liden, R. C., Parks, J. M., Morrison, E. W., Porter, L. W., Robinson, S. L., Roehling, M. V., Rousseau, D. M., Schalk, R., Tsui, A. S., and Van Dyne, L. (2004). The employee–organization relationship: a timely concept in a period of transition. In J. J. Martocchio (ed.), *Research in personnel and human resources management* (vol. 22, pp. 291–370). Amsterdam: Elsevier, Science/JAI Press.

Siegrist, J. (1998). Adverse health effects of effort–reward imbalance at work: theory, empirical support, and implications for prevention. In C. L. Cooper (ed.), *Theories of organizational stress* (pp. 190–204). Oxford: Oxford University Press.

Silla, I., Gracia, F., and Peiró, J. M. (2005). Job insecurity and health-related outcomes among different types of temporary workers. *Economic and Industrial Democracy* 26: 89–118.

Social Dialogue (2004). *Framework Agreement on Work-related Stress*. Brussels: ETUC (www.etuc.org/a/529).

Sonnentag, S. and Frese, M. (2003). Stress in organizations. In W. C. Borman, D. R. Ilgen, and R. J. Klimoski (eds.), *Handbook of psychology: industrial and organizational psychology* (vol. 12, pp. 453–91). Hoboken, NJ: John Wiley.

Sverke, M., Gallagher, D. G., and Hellgren, J. (2000). Alternative work arrangements: job stress, well-being and pro-organizational attitudes among employees with different employment contracts. In K. Isaksson, C. Hogstedt, C. Eriksson, and T. Theorell (eds.), *Health effects of the new labour market* (pp. 145–67). New York: Plenum.

Torkelson, E., Muhonen, T., and Peiró, J. M. (in press). Constructions of work stress and coping in a female- and a male-dominated department. *Scandinavian Journal of Psychology*.

Warr, P. B. (1987). *Work, unemployment, and mental health*. Oxford: Clarendon Press.

Zohar, D. (1995). The justice perspective on job stress. *Journal of Organizational Behavior* 15: 487–95.

15 Work stress, coping, and gender: implications for health and well-being

Eva Torkelson and Tuija Muhonen

Stressful working conditions and their implications for health are important topics in occupational health psychology today (Paoli and Merllié, 2001; Spielberger and Reheiser, 2005). Studies show that increasing demands in the workplace have induced negative stress among employees (Lidwall and Skogman-Thoursie, 2001), and especially among women (Lundberg, 2002; Lundberg and Gonäs, 1998; Matuszek, Nelson, and Quick, 1995). Although both women and men report work-related stressors, such as role ambiguity, downsizing, and time pressure, women are confronted with additional stressors (Nelson and Burke, 2002). Jobs dominated by women have lower status, are less well paid, and have limited opportunities for personal and career development (Alexanderson and Östlin, 2001; Greenglass, 2002; Lundberg and Gonäs, 1998; Nelson and Burke, 2002). Women are often exposed to role conflicts and conflicts between work and family responsibilities (Burke and Greenglass, 1999; Greenglass, 2002; Lundberg, 1998), as well as sex discrimination and underutilization of skills (Greenglass, 2002). Women also experience more psychological and physical symptoms (Alexanderson and Östlin, 2001; Matuszek *et al.*, 1995; Väänänen, Toppinen-Tanner, Kalimo, Mutanen, Vahtera, and Peiró, 2003). In a longitudinal study, Bildt and Michélsen (2002) identified more occupational risk factors predicting poor mental health for women than for men, suggesting that these findings mirror the gender-segregated labor market. Bildt (2001) concluded that several aspects at today's workplaces are harmful for many female employees' mental health.

Women's participation in the workforce has grown in recent years and, in western societies, is nearly as high as male labor force participation (Bäckman and Edling, 2001; Vinnicombe, 2000). However, several authors (Banyard and Graham-Bermann, 1993; Long and Cox, 2000; Pugliesi, 1999) have noted that studies on occupational health, stress, and coping have previously involved mainly male populations and that the issue of gender needs to be investigated further. Even though the amount of research including women has increased during the last decade

(Pugliesi, 1999), this work has been focused on women in professional and managerial positions, while women in lower positions have been neglected (Long and Cox, 2000).

This chapter starts with a brief review of research concerning work stress, coping, gender, and health. We also present results from a study which is part of a larger ongoing project: *Collective stress and coping at work from a gender perspective.* The study puts forth a complementary approach to the individualistic perspective by viewing coping as both an individual and a collective phenomenon. The aim of the study was to investigate the link between health problems and the collective and individualistic coping strategies among women and men in managerial and non-managerial positions in the organization.

Coping with stress at work

Considerable attention has been paid to how people cope with workplace stress (see Latack and Havlovic, 1992; Tamres, Janicki, and Helgeson, 2002). Coping has been defined in different ways (Dewe, 2000), but a common theme that emerges in various approaches is to view coping as part of a transaction between the person and the environment. In this respect coping is seen as a process concerned both with the appraisal of threats of various kinds and with the mobilization of strategies to manage the problems and emotions involved. Lazarus and Folkman (1984: 141) have defined coping as "constantly changing cognitive and behavioral efforts to manage specific external and/or internal demands that are appraised as taxing or exceeding the resources of the person." Coping refers here to efforts aimed at dealing with different demands that are placed on the individual, regardless of the efficacy of such efforts.

According to Lazarus and Folkman (1984), the appraisal of a stressful situation is central for how people cope with a variety of difficulties that can be detrimental to the individual's well-being. In terms of their model, two types of cognitive appraisals are involved in assessing a situation. First, a primary appraisal is carried out to evaluate the situation with regard to the person's well-being, and this is followed by a secondary appraisal evaluating the resources the individual has available for dealing with the situation.

Typically, research in the area of occupational stress has differentiated between problem- and emotion-focused coping as suggested by Folkman and Lazarus (1980). Other distinctions have also been made (Kenny and McIntyre, 2005), but the division into problem- and emotion-focused coping is the one most commonly used when comparisons are made between women and men (Tamres *et al.*, 2002). Problem-focused coping strategies involve efforts to solve a problem or change a difficult situation in an active way. Emotion-focused coping strategies, in contrast, do not change the problem or situation directly, but help to assign new meaning to the situation or to regulate the emotions that are aroused.

Although there is no clear consensus concerning which coping strategies are most beneficial, investigators generally expect problem-focused coping to be more adaptive than emotion-focused coping (Thoits, 1995). Problem-focused strategies have been found to be more beneficial for well-being (Bhagat, Allie, and Ford, 1991) and to be negatively related to distress symptoms (Billings and Moos, 1984). Emotion-focused strategies, on the other hand, are often considered to be positively associated with psychological distress (Coyne and Racioppo, 2000). However, Torkelson and Muhonen (2003, 2004) found no relationship between problem-focused strategies and health, and in a series of meta-analyses Penley, Tomaka, and Wiebe (2002) found that problem-focused coping was positively correlated with overall health outcomes. Furthermore, Thoits (1995) argued that no coping strategy is efficacious across all situations.

Coping and gender

A number of studies report that women differ from men in the coping strategies they employ, even though the results of these studies have been contradictory. Some studies have shown men to be more inclined to use active, problem-focused coping strategies (Folkman and Lazarus, 1980; Hurst and Hurst, 1997; Ptacek, Smith, and Dodge, 1994; Tamres et al., 2002), and women to make greater use of emotion-focused coping strategies (Carver, Scheier, and Weintraub, 1989; Hurst and Hurst, 1997; Muhonen and Torkelson, 2001; Torkelson and Muhonen, 2003). Furthermore, men have been found more often to report using alcohol or drugs as a means of coping (Carver et al., 1989; Muhonen and Torkelson, 2001). Other studies, in contrast, have not shown gender differences in regard to coping (Bhagat et al., 1991; Parkes, 1990) or been able to find that the strategies are at least partly related to the level in the organization (McDonald and Korabik, 1991; Torkelson and Muhonen, 2004). Greenglass (2002) pointed out that when education, occupation, and position in the organization are controlled for, few gender differences in coping appear.

Several researchers maintain that there has not been enough emphasis on the issue of power when gender differences in stress and coping have been studied in previous research (Banyard and Graham-Bermann, 1993; Long and Cox, 2000). The majority of women have jobs that are characterized by limited autonomy and limited resources, e.g. low pay, inflexibility, low status, and lack of career development opportunities (Alexanderson and Östlin, 2001; Long and Cox, 2000; Lundberg and Gonäs, 1998; Nelson and Burke, 2002), which in turn can restrict women's possibilities to cope (Long and Cox, 2000; Matud, 2004). Narayanan, Menon, and Spector (1999) suggested that the manner of coping differs across the organizational hierarchy, being more problem-focused in higher positions and more emotion-focused in lower-level jobs. Owing to women's subordinate position in the labor market, as well as in society as a whole, it can be argued that so-called gender differences in coping behavior can be accounted for by differences in access to power between women and men.

Toward a collective approach in studying work stress and coping

There is a growing body of criticism against the individualistic perspective that has dominated previous stress and coping research (Banyard and Graham-Bermann, 1993; Hobfoll, Dunahoo, Ben-Porath, and Monnier, 1994; Long and Cox, 2000; Mickelson, Lyons, Sullivan, and Coyne, 2001; Länsisalmi, Peiró, and Kivimäki, 2000; Newton, 1995). The individualistic perspective has focused on the individual's appraisal of stress isolated from its social context (Länsisalmi *et al.*, 2000; Newton, 1995). Handy (1995), Mickelson *et al.* (2001), and Peiró (2001) have discussed the need for other approaches to the study of stress and to move beyond simplistic models which isolate the individual worker from the rest of the workplace. Graumann and Kruse (1990) stated that it is evident that both stress and coping are socially mediated processes that take place through interactions between individuals. Social context has a strong influence on the appraisal of a stressful situation, as well as on the appraisal of available coping strategies (Graumann and Kruse, 1990). The efforts made in conjunction with others to influence adverse situations is regarded by Banyard and Graham-Bermann (1993) as collective coping.

One approach to capturing the collective nature of stress and coping has been suggested by Hobfoll *et al.* (1994), Mickelson *et al.* (2001), and Hobfoll, Geller, and Dunahoo (2003) at Kent State University. Hobfoll *et al.* (2003) have developed the multiaxial model of coping and a questionnaire (SACS – Strategic Approach to Coping Scale) to assess the different dimensions of the model, i.e. social–antisocial, active–passive, and direct–indirect strategies. In a two-dimensional framework of coping, Mickelson *et al.* (2001: 187) described what they called communal coping as "a shared appraisal of stress and a shared action orientation to managing the stressor." The stressor is then conceptualized as "ours" instead of "mine" and it is "our" instead of "my" responsibility to take action.

Coping can be interpreted by focusing on the social processes in the organization. Different roles and attitudes may then be seen as socially constructed (Nelson and Burke, 2002), and behaviors generally labeled as female or male are produced and reproduced through social interaction (Riger, 1992; Hare-Mustin and Marecek, 1988). Ptacek *et al.* (1994) claimed that gender differences in coping reflect gender-role stereotypes in which men are seen as independent and rational, and women as emotional, supportive, and dependent. Hobfoll *et al.* (2003) pointed out that, traditionally, organizations are dominated by a male culture characterized by individualism and dominance, not by team work. As the underlying models of coping are based on individualism and ignore social and communal aspects of coping, the coping activities that women more likely engage in, such as considering others' needs, may never be measured (Hobfoll *et al.*, 2003).

The study

The study presented below aimed to analyze whether collective and individualistic coping strategies were associated with fewer health problems for women and men in managerial and non-managerial positions in the organization. By including both collective and individualistic strategies in the study, the aim was to avoid the potential problem of not being able to measure beneficial coping strategies, those more likely to be used by women (Hobfoll *et al.*, 2003). In addition, we consider organizational level in the analyses, as the manner of coping differs across the organization hierarchy (Narayanan *et al.*, 1999), and there has not been enough emphasis on the issue of power in studies of coping and gender in previous research (Banyard and Graham-Bermann, 1993; Long and Cox, 2000).

Method

Procedure and participants

An internet-based questionnaire was sent to 1,345 female and male employees at both managerial and non-managerial levels working in a Swedish telecom company. The company develops internet-based services and products, and provides individual solutions for communications needs for both small and large organizations. The departments where the participants work are comparable to call centers. Customers, both inside and outside the company, order products or call to obtain help with different kinds of problems concerning the telecom system and network. Like many telecom companies in recent years, the one in the study has gone through several organizational changes and restructurings. These have resulted, amongst other things, in a reduction of staff. The organizational restructurings were still in progress at the time of the study.

A total of 950 completed surveys were received, a response rate of 71%. Of the respondents, 502 were women (82 managers, 407 non-managers, and 13 who had not specified their position) and 448 were men (89 managers, 357 non-managers, and two who had not specified their position). The mean age of the participants was 47, and most of them were married (76%) and worked full time (91%). The participants had been working in the company for about twenty-four years on average, only 28% had children under 12 living at home, and a minority (15%) had university education. Men were university educated and worked full-time to a somewhat greater extent than women. No other gender differences concerning the demographic variables were found.

Measures

Demographics. The demographic items included age, gender, marital status, number of children living at home (and under 12), years of employment, working hours (full-time/part-time), and educational and occupational level.

Control at work was measured by three items from the COPSOQ – Copenhagen Psychosocial Questionnaire (Kristensen, 2001). A sample question was "Do you have a large degree of influence concerning your work?" Response alternatives ranged from 1 (never/hardly ever) to 4 (always). The reliability coefficient for the control scale was $\alpha = .73$.

Individualistic coping was assessed by means of four different scales from the Swedish version (Muhonen and Torkelson, 2001) of the COPE inventory (Carver *et al.*, 1989). Two scales – active coping, and positive reinterpretation and growth – were considered to measure different aspects of problem-focused coping. Active coping included taking direct action in order to deal with the problem. A sample item was "I take additional action to try to get rid of the problem." Positive reinterpretation and growth consisted of items such as "I try to grow as a person as a result of the experience," e.g. assessing efforts to construe the stressful situation in a positive way. Another two scales – acceptance, and focus on and venting of emotions – assessed dimensions of emotion-focused coping. Acceptance implied simply accepting the situation, e.g. "I learn to live with it." Focus on and venting of emotions denoted attempts to focus on the distress caused by the situation and ventilate feelings evoked by it. A sample item is "I get upset and let my emotions out." Participants were asked to indicate what they usually did when they were under considerable stress at work. Response alternatives ranged from 1 "I usually don't do this at all" to 4 "I usually do this a lot". The reliability coefficients for the individualistic coping scales ranged from $\alpha = .68$ to $\alpha = .72$.

Collective coping was assessed by two scales from the COPE inventory (seeking social support for instrumental reasons and seeking social support for emotional reasons) and one scale (social joining) from SACS – Strategic Approach to Coping Scale (Hobfoll *et al.*, 1994). Seeking social support for instrumental reasons included seeking advice, assistance, or information. A sample item was "I ask people who had similar experiences what they did." Seeking emotional social support implied getting sympathy and understanding. A sample item was "I talk to someone about how I feel." Social joining stood for joining with others and considering others' feelings and wishes before taking action. A sample item was "Think carefully about how others feel before deciding what to do." The collective coping scales consisted of four items each, except for social joining which contained five items. Participants were asked to indicate what they usually did when they were under considerable stress at work. Response alternatives ranged from 1 ("I usually don't do this at all") to 4 ("I usually do this a lot"). The reliability coefficients for the collective coping scales ranged from $\alpha = .68$ to $\alpha = .73$.

Health problems were assessed by the Hopkins Symptom Checklist-25 (HSCL-25) (Derogatis, Lipman, Rickels, Uhlenhuth, and Covi, 1974). HSCL-25 consists of twenty-five items that measure such health problems as headaches, difficulties in falling asleep or in staying asleep, feelings of hopelessness regarding the future, feeling nervous and worried, faintness or dizziness, and pounding or racing of the heart. The respondents indicated the intensity of different health problems on a four-point scale ranging from 1 (not bothered) to 4 (extremely bothered). The scale measuring health problems showed an internal consistency of $\alpha = .95$.

Results

Initial analysis

Table 15.1 shows the means, standard deviations, and intercorrelations of all the study variables. The results show that age, full-time/part-time work, and occupational level were negatively correlated to health problems, indicating that participants who were older, worked full-time and/ or had a managerial position experienced fewer problems. Furthermore,

Table 15.1 Means, standard deviations, and correlations for the study variables

Variables	M	SD	1	2	3	4	5	6	7	8	9	10	11	12	13	14	15	16	17
1. Age	46.9	9.7	—																
2. Gender	.5	.5	-.02	—															
3. Marital status	.8	.4	.03	.06	—														
4. Number of children at home	.5	.9	-.38**	.00	.18**	—													
5. Years of employment	24.2	11.3	.84**	.05	.05	-.37**	—												
6. Full-time work	.9	.3	.13**	-.20**	-.06	-.29**	.13**	—											
7. Educational level	.2	.4	-.16**	-.10**	.00	.16**	-.29**	.01	—										
8. Occupational level	.2	.4	-.10**	-.04	.01	.08*	-.12**	.12**	.16**	—									
9. Control	7.2	2.0	.01	-.14**	.03	.07*	.02	.07*	.06	.30**	—								
10. Active coping	12.6	1.8	-.11**	.02	-.04	.05	-.10**	.06	.06	.17**	.16**	—							
11. Positive reinterpretation	11.7	2.0	-.14**	.12**	-.01	.04	-.13**	.05	.10**	.27**	.26**	.52**	—						
12. Acceptance	10.5	2.2	-.02	.03	-.03	.00	-.01	.01	-.02	-.10**	-.17**	.05	.12**	—					
13. Focus on emotions	8.6	2.2	-.04	.23**	-.01	.00	.00	-.06	-.06	-.07*	-.15**	.00	.02	.06	—				
14. Seeking instrumental support	11.0	2.1	-.08*	.23**	-.02	.01	-.06	-.02	-.02	.13**	.16**	.32**	.34**	-.08*	.24**	—			
15. Seeking emotional support	9.4	2.5	-.16**	.38**	-.02	.02	-.11**	-.09**	.01	.05	.03	.08*	.25**	.06	.47**	.54**	—		
16. Social joining	13.9	2.2	-.09**	.24**	.01	.02	-.04	.01	-.01	.16**	.11**	.46**	.50**	.08*	.20**	.56**	.47**	—	
17. Health problems	39.9	12.2	-.07*	.08*	-.04	.00	-.04	-.13**	-.02	-.13**	-.33**	-.12**	-.20**	.15**	.31**	-.13**	.09**	-.03	—

$N = 836—951$. Gender (0 = male; 1 = female); marital status (0 = single; 1 = married or cohabitant); full-time work (0 = part-time; 1 = full-time); educational level (0 = below university level; 1 = university level); occupational level (0 = non-manager; 1 = manager).

* $p < .05$,

** $p < .01$.

participants who perceived having control in their work reported significantly fewer health problems. Gender, on the other hand, was positively
related to health problems, which means that the women reported more
health problems than men did.

Among the individualistic strategies, active coping and positive reinterpretation correlated negatively with health problems, as acceptance
and focus on emotions correlated positively. The collective strategy of
seeking instrumental social support was negatively related to reported
health problems, while seeking emotional social support was found to be
positively related. There was no significant relationship between the
collective coping strategy of social joining and reported health problems.
The intercorrelations between several of the coping strategies were high,
suggesting that there was an overlap between the different coping
concepts.

Predicting health problems

Separate regression analyses were run on the data to predict health problems for women and men at managerial and non-managerial levels. The
results of the regression analyses are presented in Table 15.2.

In the first step, the two demographic variables of age and full-time
employment were controlled for since they were related to health problems as discussed above (see Table 15.1). The variable control was also
included in the first step, given its relationship to health in the present
study, as well as in earlier studies (Karasek and Theorell, 1990). The
results show that control was a significant predictor of fewer health
problems for both women and men at the non-managerial level. Full-
time work was also shown to be a beneficial variable for the female non-
managers. For men at a managerial level, perceived control was linked to
better health. However, step one did not contribute significantly to predicting health problems for the female managers.

In the second step of the analysis, four individualistic coping strategies,
active, positive reinterpretation and growth, and acceptance and focus on
and venting of emotions, were entered. Among those at a non-managerial
level, a clear gender difference was found in how health problems could
be predicted by the individualistic coping strategies. The individualistic
strategies accounted for a significantly higher proportion of variance in
health problems among men (18%) than among women (6%) ($z = 2.73$,
$p < .01$). For both women and men, the strategy of positive reinterpretation and growth was linked to fewer health problems, whereas the strategy
of focus on and venting of emotions was associated with more health
problems. In addition, acceptance was a maladaptive coping strategy for

Table 15.2 *Summary of hierarchical regression analyses predicting health problems for female and male managers and non-managers*

Variable	Female non-managers (n = 387) β	Male non-managers (n = 347) β	Female managers (n = 79) β	Male managers (n = 83) β
Step 1 Control variables				
Age	−.09	−.01	−.06	−.19
Full-time employment	−.11*	−.08	.05	−.08
Control	−.20***	−.24***	−.08	−.31**
ΔR^2	.09***	.16***	.03	.18**
Step 2 Individualistic coping				
Active coping	.06	−.10	.11	.11
Positive reinterpretation	−.14*	−.19***	−.04	−.13
Acceptance	.05	.13**	.03	.02
Focus on emotions	.23***	.35***	.31**	.24*
ΔR^2	.06***	.18***	.15*	.11*
Step 3 Collective coping				
Seeking instrumental support	−.26***	−.06	−.32*	−.23*
Seeking emotional support	.03	.00	.07	.27*
Social joining	.16*	.01	.38**	−.05
ΔR^2	.04***	.00	.15**	.06
R^2	.19	.35	.33	.35

*$p < .05$,
**$p < .01$,
***$p < .001$.

the men at a non-managerial level in the organization. For managers, just as for non-managers, focus on and venting of emotion was the main predictor of health problems for both genders in step two. None of the individualistic strategies were linked to fewer health problems, neither for female nor for male managers.

In the third step, the collective coping strategies were entered. The collective strategies explained further variance in health for the female employees at both non-managerial and managerial levels. Whereas seeking instrumental social support was linked to fewer health problems, social joining could be regarded as an adverse aspect of collective coping, associated with more health problems. Social joining predicted health problems to a higher extent for the female managers ($\beta = .38$, $p < .01$)

than for the female non-managers ($\beta = .16, p < .05$). However, the difference was not significant ($z = 1.90$, $p = .056$). For males, the collective coping strategies entered in step three did not explain any further variance in the model. The lack of significant increment in explained variance for the male managers when the collective strategies were entered may be due to the small number of managers in the study.

The full regression models accounted for significantly less variance in reported health problems for female non-managers (19%) compared to the male non-managers (35%) ($z = 2.88, p < .01$). For the managers, the model accounted for 33% of the variance for women and 35% for men ($z = .17$, *ns*).

Discussion

Nowadays, work-related stress is regarded as one of the major challenges to working people's health (e.g. Leka, Griffiths, and Cox, 2005). At the beginning of this chapter, we presented a brief review of earlier research concerning work stress, coping, gender, and health. One conclusion of the review was that previous studies have mainly focused upon individual coping strategies and their relationship to health, while little attention has been paid to different collective strategies and their covariance with health. We then introduced a study that adopts a complementary approach to the individualistic perspective. Coping is viewed here as both an individual and a collective phenomenon; i.e. employees are seen as using a combination of strategies, both individually or together with their colleagues, in order to handle problems at work.

The aim of the study was to analyze whether the collective and individual coping strategies were associated with fewer health problems for women and men at managerial and non-managerial positions in the organization. The results concerning individualistic strategies and their association with health problems were somewhat different for managers and non-managers, a finding that supports the idea that coping differs depending on hierarchical level in the organization (Narayanan *et al.*, 1999). Among those at the managerial level, none of the individualistic strategies were related to fewer health problems, neither for women nor for men. However, at a non-managerial level, the strategy of positive reinterpretation and growth was adaptive and contributed to fewer problems for both female and male employees. One explanation for this result could be embedded in the non-managerial positions per se – that it is beneficial to engage in reinterpretation when active changes are not able to be made at an individualistic level.

The individualistic strategy of focus on and venting of emotions was maladaptive for all categories of employees in the study, supporting earlier research by, for example, Day and Livingstone (2001) and Torkelson and Muhonen (2004). The causal chain behind this result, however, is unclear. Rather than regarding the venting of emotions as an underlying cause of health problems, it could be the other way around. The venting of emotions might follow upon distress, rather than cause distress as suggested by Coyne and Racioppo (2000).

The collective strategies of seeking instrumental support and social joining were linked to health problems only for the female employees in the study. Collective coping strategies, such as considering other people's needs, have previously been suggested to be beneficial for female workers (Hobfoll *et al.*, 2003). However, the results of our study showed that one collective strategy was beneficial and one was maladaptive. Seeking instrumental social support was related to fewer health problems, whereas social joining was associated with more health problems. The two collective strategies differ in the way that seeking instrumental support implies asking other people for help while social joining is directed toward considering others' feelings and wishes when coping with the situation. One explanation for why social joining was related to health problems for the female managers in the study could have to do with the fact that the organization has recently gone through several restructurings. To make decisions and cope with difficulties in a turbulent environment can be problematic, particularly when other employees' feelings and wishes are to be considered at the same time, as is the case in social joining. These results may be interpreted in relation to the socialization into gender roles. In western cultures the roles of women are characterized by supportive behaviors and interpersonal interactions (Karambayya, 2002; Nelson and Burke, 2002). To consider other people's wishes and feelings when taking action during periods of restructuring in the organization seems to be a problematic coping strategy, especially for the female managers. Maddock (1999) claimed that during organizational restructuring, competitive behaviors often increase at the expense of cooperation. The stereotyped expectation that women should be supportive may pose a dilemma in the hostile and competitive context that can emerge during organizational changes and reconstructions (Karambayya, 2002). The tensions that arise when trying to cope and at the same time balance the dualistic positions as women and as competent managers have also been discussed by Fournier and Kelemen (2001).

For the men in the study, at both organizational levels, the collective strategies did not account for any significant explained variance in health problems. It seems therefore that collective strategies may have greater importance for women's than for men's health. On the other hand, the fact that there were only a small number of male managers in the study may have affected the results, and a different pattern might have emerged if there had been more participants in this group. The regression model was more applicable for the male non-managers ($R^2 = .35$) than for the female non-managers ($R^2 = .19$). It appears that there could have been additional factors, either at work or outside of work, that may have had a greater importance for female non-managers' health than those investigated in this study.

There are some limitations in the study that may have affected the generalizability of the results. First, there is an overlap between the different coping strategies. The categorization into individualistic and collective strategies is not clear-cut. Another limitation is the small number of managers compared to non-managers. Furthermore, the moderating effect of coping between stressors and their outcome was not tested. The need for research that examines the moderating role of different coping strategies is addressed by Fortes-Ferreira, Peiró, González-Morales, and Martín (2006). In addition, the cross-sectional design does not allow causal conclusions to be drawn on the basis of the results.

Conclusion

The results showed that the individualistic coping strategies were not beneficial for either women's or men's health at the managerial level. Among the non-managers, one individualistic strategy, positive reinterpretation and growth, was linked to fewer health problems for both women and men. The collective strategies were associated with perceived health problems only among the females, both managers and non-managers. One strategy, seeking instrumental social support, was beneficial and one strategy, social joining, was maladaptive.

It can be concluded that collective and individual coping are important components in the process of coping with occupational stress and health. Moreover, coping appears to be related to both gender and occupational level. In particular, the collective strategy of social joining during organizational change and its relationship to health for female managers should be further investigated. There is a need for studies that include an examination of the social forces of coping with stress at work, with gender being taken into account at the different occupational levels as well. In addition, the changing nature of the organizations of today (Sverke, Hellgren, and Näswall, 2002) should be considered when studying how people individually and collectively try to cope with stress at work.

Acknowledgements

The project was funded by the Swedish Council for Working Life and Social Research.

References

Alexanderson, K. and Östlin, P. (2001). Work and ill-health among women and men in Sweden. In S. Marklund (ed.), *Worklife and health in Sweden 2000* (pp. 119–34). Stockholm: National Institute for Working Life.

Bäckman, O. and Edling, C. (2001). Work environment and work-related health problems in the 1990s. In S. Marklund (ed.), *Worklife and health in Sweden 2000* (pp. 101–17). Stockholm: National Institute for Working Life.

Banyard, V. L. and Graham-Bermann, S. A. (1993). Can women cope? *Psychology of Women Quarterly* 17: 303–18.

Bhagat, R. S., Allie, S. M., and Ford, D. L., Jr. (1991). Organizational stress, personal life stress and symptoms of life strain: an inquiry into the moderating role of styles of coping. *Journal of Social Behavior and Personality* 6: 163–84.

Bildt, C. (2001). Working conditions and mental health among women. In C. Bildt and L. Karlquist (eds.), *Women's conditions in working life* (pp. 73–82). Stockholm: National Institute for Working Life.

Bildt, C. and Michélsen, H. (2002). Gender differences in the effects from working conditions on mental health: a 4-year follow-up. *International Archives of Occupational and Environmental Health* 75: 252–8.

Billings, A. G. and Moos, R. H. (1984). Coping, stress, and social resources among adults with unipolar depression. *Journal of Personality and Social Psychology* 4: 877–91.

Burke, R. J. and Greenglass, E. R. (1999). Work–family conflict, spouse support, and nursing staff well-being during organizational restructuring. *Journal of Occupational and Organizational Psychology* 4: 327–36.

Carver, C. S., Scheier, M. F., and Weintraub, J. K. (1989). Assessing coping strategies: a theoretically based approach. *Journal of Personality and Social Psychology* 56: 267–83.

Coyne, J. C. and Racioppo, M. W. (2000). Never the twain shall meet? Closing the gap between coping research and clinical intervention research. *American Psychologist* 55: 655–64.

Day, A. L. and Livingstone, H. A. (2001). Chronic and acute stressors among military personnel: do coping styles buffer their negative impact on health? *Journal of Occupational Health Psychology* 6: 348–60.

Derogatis, L. R., Lipman, R. S., Rickels, K., Uhlenhuth, E. H., and Covi, L. (1974). The Hopkins symptom checklist (HSCL): a self-report symptom inventory. *Behavioral Science* 19: 1–15.

Dewe, P. (2000). Measures of coping with stress at work: a review and a critique. In P. Dewe, M. Leiter, and T. Cox (eds.), *Coping, health and organizations* (pp. 3–28). London: Taylor and Francis.

Folkman, S. and Lazarus, R. S. (1980). An analysis of coping in middle-aged community sample. *Journal of Health and Social Behavior* 21: 219–39.

Fortes-Ferreira, L., Peiró, J. M., González-Morales, G., and Martín, I. (2006). Work-related stress and well-being: the role of direct action coping and palliative coping. *Scandinavian Journal of Psychology* 47: 293–302.

Fournier, V. and Kelemen, M. (2001). The crafting of community: recoupling discourses of management and womanhood. *Gender, Work and Organization* 8: 267–90.

Graumann, C. F. and Kruse, L. (1990). The environment: social construction and psychological problems. In H. T. Himmelweit and G. Gaskell (eds.), *Societal psychology* (pp. 212–29). London: Sage.

Greenglass, E. R. (2002). Work stress, coping, and social support: implications for women's occupational well-being. In D. L. Nelson, and R. J. Burke (eds.), *Gender, work stress, and health* (pp. 85–96). Washington, DC: American Psychological Association.

Handy, J. (1995). Rethinking stress: seeing the collective. In T. Newton, J. Handy, and S. Fineman (eds.), *Managing stress: emotion and power at work* (pp. 85–96). London: Sage.

Hare-Mustin, R. T. and Marecek, J. (1988). The meaning of difference. Gender theory, postmodernism, and psychology. *American Psychologist* 43: 455–64.

Hobfoll, S. E., Dunahoo, C., Ben-Porath, Y., and Monnier, J. (1994). Gender and coping: the dual axis model of coping. *American Journal of Community Psychology* 22: 49–82.

Hobfoll, S. E., Geller, P., and Dunahoo, C. (2003). Women's coping: communal versus individualistic orientation. In M. J. Schabracq, J. A. M. Winnubst, and C. L. Cooper (eds.), *Handbook of work and health psychology* (pp. 239–57). Chichester: John Wiley.

Hurst, T. E. and Hurst, M. H. (1997). Gender differences in mediation of severe occupational stress among correctional officers. *American Journal of Criminal Justice* 22: 121–37.

Karambayya, R. (2002). Women and corporate restructuring: sources and consequences of stress. In D. L. Nelson and R. J. Burke (eds.), *Gender, work stress, and health* (pp. 55–69). Washington, DC: American Psychological Association.

Karasek, R. and Theorell, T. (1990). *Healthy work: stress, productivity, and the reconstruction of working life.* New York: Basic Books.

Kenny, D. and McIntyre, D. (2005). Constructions of occupational stress: nuisances, nuances or novelties? In A.-S. G. Antoniou and C. L. Cooper (eds.), *Research companion to organizational health psychology* (pp. 20–58). Northampton, MA: Edward Elgar.

Kristensen, T. S. (2001). A new tool for assessing psychosocial work environment factors: the Copenhagen Psychosocial Questionnaire. In M. Hagberg, B. Knave, L. Lillienberg, and H. Westberg (eds.), *X2001 exposure assessment in epidemiology and practice: arbete och hälsa* (vol. 10, pp. 210–13). Stockholm: Arbetslivsinstitutet.

Länsisalmi, H., Peiró, J. M., and Kivimäki, M. (2000). Collective stress and coping in the context of organizational culture. *European Journal of Work and Organizational Psychology* 9: 527–59.

Latack, J. C. and Havlovic, S. J. (1992). Coping with job stress: a conceptual evaluation framework for coping measures. *Journal of Organizational Behavior* 13: 479–508.

Lazarus, R. S. and Folkman, S. (1984). *Stress, appraisal, and coping.* New York: Springer.

Leka, S., Griffiths, A., and Cox, T. (2005). Work-related stress: the risk management paradigm. In A.-S. G. Antoniou and C. L. Cooper (eds.), *Research companion to organizational health psychology* (pp. 174–87). Northampton, MA: Edward Elgar.

Lidwall, U. and Skogman-Thoursie, P. (2001). Sickness absence during the last decades. In S. Marklund (ed.), *Worklife and health in Sweden 2000* (pp. 81–100). Stockholm: National Institute for Working Life.

Long, B. C. and Cox, R. C. (2000). Women's way of coping with employment stress: a feminist contextual analysis. In P. Dewe, M. Leiter, and T. Cox (eds.), *Coping, health and organizations* (pp. 109–23). London: Taylor and Francis.

Lundberg, O. and Gonäs, L. (1998). Trends in women's psychosocial work environment and health, and structural changes on the labor market. In K. Orth-Gomér, M. Chesney, and N. K. Wenger (eds.), *Women, stress, and heart disease* (pp. 57–72). New York: Lawrence Erlbaum.

Lundberg, U. (1998). Work and stress in women. In K. Orth-Gomér, M. Chesney, and N. K. Wenger (eds.), *Women, stress, and heart disease* (pp. 41–56). New York: Lawrence Erlbaum.

(2002). Gender, multiple roles and physiological reactions. In S. P. Wamala and J. Lynch (eds.), *Gender and social inequities in health* (pp. 123–57). Lund: Studentlitteratur.

Maddock, S. (1999). *Challenging women: gender, culture and organization.* Thousand Oaks, CA: Sage.

Matud, M. P. (2004). Gender differences in stress and coping styles. *Personality and Individual Differences* 37: 1401–15.

Matuszek, P. A., Nelson, D. L., and Quick, J. C. (1995). Gender differences in distress. Are we asking the right questions? *Journal of Social Behavior and Personality* 10: 99–120.

McDonald, L. M. and Korabik, K. (1991). Sources of stress and ways of coping among male and female managers. *Journal of Social Behavior and Personality* 6: 185–98.

Mickelson, K., Lyons, R. F., Sullivan, M. J. L., and Coyne, J. C. (2001). Yours, mine, ours: the relational context of communal coping. In B. R. Sarason and S. Duck (eds.), *Personal relationships: implications for clinical and community psychology* (pp. 181–200). Chichester: John Wiley.

Muhonen, T. and Torkelson, E. (2001). A Swedish version of the COPE inventory. *Lund Psychological Reports* 2.

Narayanan, L., Menon, S., and Spector, P. E. (1999). Stress in the workplace: a comparison of gender and occupations. *Journal of Organizational Behavior* 20: 63–73.

Nelson, D. L. and Burke, R. J. (2002). A framework for examining gender, work-stress, and health. In D. L. Nelson and R. J. Burke (eds.), *Gender, work stress, and health* (pp. 3–14). Washington, DC: American Psychological Association.

Newton, T. (1995). Introduction: agency, subjectivity and the stress discourse. In
T. Newton, J. Handy, and S. Fineman (eds.), *Managing stress: emotion and
power at work* (pp. 1–17). London: Sage.

Paoli, P. and Merllié, D. (2001). *Third European Survey on Working Conditions
2000*. Luxemburg: Office for Official Publications of the European
Communities. www.eurofound.eu.int/publications/files/EF0121EN.pdf.

Parkes, K. P. (1990). Coping, negative affectivity, and the work environment:
additive and interactive predictors of mental health. *Journal of Applied
Psychology* 75: 399–409.

Peiró, J. (2001). *Stressed teams in organizations: a multilevel approach to the study of
stress in work units*. Proceedings of the Third European Conference of the
European Academy of Occupational Health Psychology, Barcelona, Spain,
24–27 October 2001.

Penley, J. A., Tomaka, J., and Wiebe, J. S. (2002). The association of coping to
physical and psychological health outcomes: a meta-analytic review. *Journal
of Behavioral Medicine* 25: 551–601.

Ptacek, J. T., Smith, R. E., and Dodge, K. L. (1994). Gender differences in
coping with stress: when stressors and appraisals do not differ. *Personality
and Social Psychology Bulletin* 20: 421–30.

Pugliesi, K. (1999). Gender and work stress: differential exposure and vulnerability. *Journal of Gender, Culture and Health* 4: 97–117.

Riger, S. (1992). Epistemological debates, feminist voices: science, social values,
and the study of women. *American Psychologist* 47: 730–40.

Spielberger, C. D. and Reheiser, E. C. (2005). Occupational stress and health. In
A.-S. G. Antoniou and C. L. Cooper (eds.), *Research companion to organizational health psychology* (pp. 441–54). Northampton, MA: Edward Elgar.

Sverke, M., Hellgren, J., and Näswall, K. (2002). No security: a meta-analysis
and review of job insecurity and its consequences. *Journal of Occupational
Health Psychology* 7: 242–64.

Tamres, L. K., Janicki, D., and Helgeson, V. S. (2002). Sex differences in coping
behavior: a meta-analytic review and an examination of relative coping.
Journal of Personality and Social Psychology Review 6: 2–30.

Thoits, P. A. (1995). Stress, coping, and social support processes: where are we?
What next? *Journal of Health and Social Behavior* 35: 53–79.

Torkelson, E. and Muhonen, T. (2003). Coping strategies and health symptoms
among women and men in a downsizing organisation. *Psychological Reports*
92: 899–907.

  (2004). The role of gender and level in coping with occupational stress. *Work
and Stress* 18: 267–74.

Väänänen, A., Toppinen-Tanner, S., Kalimo, R., Mutanen, P., Vahtera, J., and
Peiró, J. M. (2003). Job characteristics, physical and psychological symptoms,
and social support as antecedents of sickness absence among men and women
in the private industrial sector. *Social Science and Medicine* 57: 807–24.

Vinnicombe, S. (2000). The position of women in management in Europe. In
M. J. Davidson and R. J. Burke (eds.), *Women in management: current research
issues* (vol. II, pp. 9–25). London: Sage.

16 The role of protean career attitude during unemployment and re-employment: a literature review and conceptual model

Lea Waters

The current business environment is one of volatility and uncertainty and, as a consequence, the modern career is characterized by multiple job changes and, increasingly, repeated episodes of job loss (Kanfer, Wanberg, and Kantrowitz, 2001; Winefield, Montgomery, Gault, Muller, O'Gorman, Reser, and Roland, 2002). According to Mirvis and Hall (1994: 366), these occupational transitions often "seem abrupt, frenzied, and fractious" to the individual. Such insecure employment conditions have increased the need for today's worker to develop effective job-search skills (Wanberg, Glomb, Song, and Sorenson, 2005; Wanberg, Kanfer, and Rotundo, 1999). The new "jobless economy" (Butts, 1997: 111) means that many are now faced with the challenge of maintaining psychological health during the stressful situation of unemployment (Mantler, Matejicek, Matheson, and Anisman, 2005; Vansteenkiste, Lens, De Witte, and Feather, 2005; Waters, 2007).

Under these insecure employment conditions, the concept of "protean career attitude" has emerged as a potential enabler of career success (MacDermid, Lee, Buck, and Williams, 2001; McDonald, Brown, and Bradley, 2005). Hall (2004: 4) defines a protean career as "one in which the person, not the organization, is in charge," where "the core values are freedom and growth."

Whilst the role of protean career attitude has not yet been considered by job loss researchers, a protean career attitude may be extremely useful during unemployment. It will be argued in this chapter that the adoption of a protean career attitude allows one to use unemployment as a time to reappraise the way in which one defines notions of self and, thus, positively reshape one's own career. As such, the adoption of a protean attitude toward one's career may lead people from unemployment to re-employment in a way that promotes career growth (Eby and Buch, 1995). This is in stark contrast to the typical experience of unemployment as a psychologically damaging event which leads to low-quality re-employment (Butts, 1997; Rifkin, 1995; Romeyn, 1992; Wanberg, Hough, and Song, 2002).

Protean career attitude is a construct that warrants empirical investigation within the job loss area. However, before the role of protean career attitude can be empirically studied, a clear and detailed conceptual framework is required. This chapter will present a conceptual framework which outlines the potential interrelationships between protean career attitude, psychological health, job search behavior, re-employment quality, and job growth. The framework has been developed following a review of both the job loss and the careers literature. It must be noted that this chapter marries together selected aspects of job loss and careers literature and it is not intended to be an exhaustive review of these two bodies of research. For a recent review of job loss research, see McKee-Ryan, Song, Wanberg, and Kinicki (2005). For recent reviews of careers literature see Hall (2004) and Guichard (2001).

This chapter reviews previous theory and research and suggests eight propositions that outline the way in which protean career attitude may be related to psychological health, job search intensity, re-employment quality, and job growth. The chapter begins by arguing that unemployment needs to be redefined (both by researchers and by today's workers) as a career *event*, rather than a career *break*. The job loss and careers literature are then reviewed to make a case for the way in which protean career attitude may be related to psychological health and job search during unemployment. The role that protean career attitude may play upon re-employment in terms of re-employment quality and career growth is then discussed. Next, the role that financial strain is likely to play in influencing protean career attitude, psychological health, job search intensity, re-employment quality, and job growth is discussed. The chapter then presents some implications of the role that protean career attitude can play to assist people during unemployment and ends by suggesting ways in which future researchers could test the conceptual model.

This chapter aims to extend the literature in four major ways. First, by demonstrating how unemployment can be viewed as a career event, rather than a career break, it opens the door for future researchers to empirically study unemployment within the context of a long-term career rather than as a one-off episode. Second, this chapter is the first to consider the theory of protean career attitude in an unemployment context and, therefore, to discuss the role that being self-directed and values-driven plays in relation to psychological health, job search, obtaining re-employment of a high quality, and achieving career growth. Third, it provides practical implications for careers counselors and personal development training. Finally, it provides suggestions for future researchers to test the model depicted in Figure 16.1.

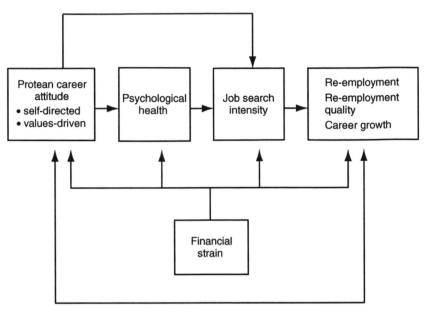

Figure 16.1 Conceptual model depicting the interrelationship between protean career attitude, psychological health, job search intensity, re-employment, re-employment quality, career growth, and financial strain

Unemployment as a career event

According to authors such as Burnes (2000) and Arthur, Khapova, and Wilderom (2005), rapid change, job insecurity, and lack of career structure are likely to be permanent and pervasive features of the new employment environment. As a consequence, researchers have suggested that individuals need to realign their career approach to match these insecure and unpredictable business conditions (Arthur, Inkson, and Pringle, 1999).

To date, only a relatively small amount of published literature has considered the way in which a person's career approach, career attitude, career exploration, and/or career needs influence psychological reactions to unemployment (Donohue and Patton, 1998). Perhaps the reason why these career constructs have not been adequately explored in the job loss literature is because unemployment has commonly been viewed as an event that occurs outside of one's career, or as an unwanted interruption to one's career (Cassidy, 2001; Eby and Buch, 1995). The unspoken assumption is that whilst a person is without paid employment they are without a career path. This assumption pervades much of the literature.

For instance, Super, Osborne, Walsh, Brown, and Niles (2001) cite unemployment as an example of a career interruption. A more targeted review of the unemployment literature shows that unemployment has been described variously as "career withdrawal" (Latack and Dozier, 1986: 376), "loss of career progress" (Pearson, 1988: 251), "loss of the career role" (Latack and Dozier, 1986: 377), a "disruption to one's career" (Zikic and Klehe, in press), and "dying professionally" (Latack and Dozier 1986: 377).

However, unemployment needs to be reconceptualized as an event that occurs *within* a person's career, rather than as an event that places the person *outside* of his/her career path. This shift in thinking is necessary if we are to develop knowledge that can be used to help people successfully manage their career during episodes of unemployment. Such knowledge will be helpful to people in countries such as Australia, United States, Canada, England, Sweden, Taiwan, and Japan for which the statistics suggest that unemployment is likely to be a common (albeit unwanted) career experience (Australian Bureau of Statistics, 2004; Campbell and Webber, 1996; Crespo, Boisjoly, and Bernard, 1998; Huang, 2003; Weir, 2003).

According to Mirvis and Hall (1994: 365), "Definitions of work, non-work, and careers are surely changing." There are two major ways in which recent changes to definitions of career accommodate the experience of unemployment. First, the modern notion of a career as "a lifelong series of work-related experiences and personal learning" (Hall, 1996: 9) allows people to be without paid work and yet still have a career. Certainly, Super *et al.* (2001) suggest that a temporary break from the "worker role" does not stop the life-long career from unfolding. Although, traditionally speaking, unemployment is an "out-of-work" experience, research by Leana and Feldman (1992) and Patton and Donohue (1998) shows that job loss leads people to spend considerable time asking themselves career-related questions, considering career issues, making career plans, attending job interviews, exploring retraining options, and so forth – all of which could be viewed as "work-related experiences" and, thus, still retained within Mirvis and Hall's (1994) definition of career. Furthermore, the "personal learning" component of the above career definition is certainly present within an individual who is experiencing an absence of paid employment. Indeed, for participants in Fryer and Payne's (1984) classic qualitative study, it was the onset of unemployment itself that triggered personal learning and new discoveries about identity and capabilities. Fryer and Payne's (1984) research provides strong evidence that people can still see themselves as contributing to their career and personal development despite job loss.

Second, modern notions of a career as a series of short cycles of employment that span numerous workplaces, rather than a single, linear career with one employer (Super *et al.*, 2001), means that job loss simply signifies the end of, or a disengagement from, one career cycle rather than the end of the entire career. Hall and Mirvis (1996: 81) conceptualize careers as consisting of "peaks and valleys, left turns, moves from one line of work to another." Under such a conceptualization, unemployment can be viewed as a "valley" or a "left turn" that forms part of the network of life-long experiences which make up a person's career. In further support of this argument, Super (1990) and his colleagues (Super, Savickas, and Super, 1996) also suggest that careers are no longer viewed as one "life-long event" but rather as a series of unfolding choices that people cycle (and recycle) through. Thus, the modern career is characterized by many transitions, including changing jobs and changing occupations, as well as leaving and re-entering the labor market. Finally, Arnold, Cooper, and Robertson (1998) propose that modern careers include both different employment forms (such as self-employment and short-term contracts) and non-work experiences (such as training, voluntary work, and unemployment). All of these new career descriptions allow for unemployment to be reconceptualized as an event that occurs *within* a person's career, rather than as an event that puts the person *outside* of the career path.

Protean career attitude and psychological health during unemployment

Given the premise that unemployment is an event occurring within one's career rather than a "break" that puts one outside of this career, job loss researchers need to look for suitable career constructs that can be used to build on the current understanding of factors that affect psychological health during unemployment. One such construct is Hall's protean career attitude. Hall and his colleagues contend that the current career landscape is particularly well suited to a "protean" conceptualization of career (Hall, Briscoe, and Kram, 1997; Hall and Moss, 1998; Mirvis and Hall, 1994).

Hall (2004) argues that the two most important features of a protean approach to one's career are self-direction and being values-driven. Self-direction expresses the degree to which an individual takes control of, and is in charge of, his/her own career (Mirvis and Hall, 1994). Under this aspect of proteanism, career attitude is characterized by a self-reliance in making career plans and decisions, a proactive attitude, a willingness to seek out change, and a willingness to take action (Briscoe and Hall, 2003). The protean notion of self-direction is highly salient during the experience of unemployment. Indeed, given that the individual can no longer rely on the organization to guide a career, the need for self-direction becomes essential. Furthermore, self-direction is likely to be positively associated with psychological health during unemployment. This argument is presented following Fryer's Agency Theory (1986, 1992). Fryer characterized agency as the initiation of, intervention in, or reperception of a situation that allows the person (i.e. agent) to act on his or her own behalf in times of change. Fryer argued that people who are able to display high levels of agency (or in the protean vernacular, high levels of self-direction) during unemployment will be those who also display positive psychological health.

The second key characteristic of a protean career attitude is that of being values-driven. Being values-driven reflects the extent to which people make career decisions that are closely aligned with their own personal values, rather than being driven by objective rewards or the values of others (Briscoe, Hall, and DeMuth, 2006). Although values themselves are seen as enduring beliefs (Rokeach, 1973), research has shown that the degree to which we choose to express our values through our words, actions, and behaviors can alter over time and situation (Katz and Kahn, 1978). Indeed, Kram, Yeager, and Reed (1989) found in their sample of managers that values were selectively concealed, suppressed, or withheld in various aspects of workplace behavior. Argyris (1990) has also documented that values espoused by managers were not necessarily reflected in their "theories in use." According to Briscoe *et al.* (2006), people who hold a protean career attitude are highly values-driven, and thus choose to reveal and disclose their values actively and regularly through their actions, behaviors, and career choices.

Whilst the role of being values-driven during unemployment has not been tested, indirect evidence for the link between being values-driven and psychological health can be seen in the finding that the ability to hold on to one's core identity during unemployment is positively associated with psychological health (Cassidy, 2001). Katz and Kahn (1978) suggest that values are essential for building and clarifying identity. In a similar way, theorists such as Rogers (1951), Bandura (1991), and Carver and Scheier (1982) posit that expressing values consistent with one's identity is critical to maintaining psychological health. Hence, it is likely that expressing personal values during unemployment is one way to retain a strong sense of identity, thus facilitating psychological health (see Figure 16.1). The literature review above has been used to develop proposition one. In all the propositions presented in this chapter, protean career attitude is comprised of self-direction and being values-driven.

Proposition one: Protean career attitude will be positively associated with psychological health during unemployment.

Protean career attitude and job search during unemployment

The many career transitions, including unemployment, that today's workers are likely to experience have increased the importance of job search skills in a person's career (Vinokur and Schul, 1997; Wanberg, Watt, and Rumsey, 1996). Kanfer, Wanberg, and Kantrowitz (2001: 838) depict job search as a "purposive, volitional pattern of action that begins with the identification and commitment to pursuing an employment goal." The same authors suggest that job search is "a product of the self-regulatory, management process by which individuals identify, initiate and pursue actions for the purpose of obtaining new employment and re-employment" (2001: 849). These descriptions tie in strongly with both dimensions of a protean career attitude. The self-regulatory nature of job search may be facilitated by the protean person's high levels of self-direction. In addition, the identification of goals and actions during the job search process is likely to be assisted by the protean person's values and a need to express these values through actions. For example, people who place a high value on social relationships may be likely to engage in face-to-face interaction with potential employers rather than sending their curriculum vitae to a range of unknown employers via the internet. As another example, a high value placed on creativity may be manifested through novel job search techniques and creative CVs.

The protean dimensions of self-direction and being values-driven have not been explicitly tested in relation to job search. However, there is indirect evidence that self-direction may play a significant role when the related constructs of perceived control and mastery with job search are examined. Perceived control and mastery have been found to be important antecedents to job search during unemployment (Vinokur and Schul, 1997, 2002; Wanberg, 1997). Job seekers who see their career as being within their own control and being directed by their own values will have strong "effort–outcome link" (Seligman, 1991), and hence believe that the time and energy they put into job search will pay off by assisting them to find work.

In contrast to the above scenario, the majority of unemployed people report low levels of control and mastery (Cvetanovski and Jex, 1994; Price, Choi, and Vinokur, 2002; Shams and Jackson, 1994). This may be because they, like many other people (Gratton, Zaleska, and De

Menezes, 2002; McDonald, Brown, and Bradley, 2005), are still holding on to a traditional view of career. In this traditional view, the organization has responsibility for and control over the individual's career path. As such, the organization, rather than the individual, provides career development opportunities, career guidance, training, and opportunities for promotion. For people who hold this traditional notion of career, losing one's job also brings the loss of the supporting structure (i.e. the organization) that directs or controls one's career. Many unemployed people report that they have low perceived control (Cvetanovski and Jex, 1994; Price et al., 2002; Shams and Jackson, 1994) which may stem from holding on to a traditional career attitude. It could be postulated that if they were to adopt a protean attitude, this would bring about a greater sense of control over the job search process. There is research evidence which demonstrates that an internal locus of control can be heightened via therapeutic techniques (Parks, Becker, Chamberlain, and Crandell, 1975), use of verbal conditioning tasks (Eisenman, 1972), camp experience (Nowicki and Barnes, 1973), and encounter groups (Diamond and Shapiro, 1973). Perhaps, an intervention that increases a person's protean career attitude (see implications section later in this chapter) may serve to increase a person's sense of self-direction over the job search process.

It is likely that job seekers who are highly self-directed are more able to generate a wide variety of job search techniques of their own accord. This is in comparison with those who are less self-directed who may only use the job search techniques that have been predetermined by a welfare agency or a job search case-manager. Personally chosen job search techniques used by self-directed individuals are likely to be positively associated with job search intensity, as individuals are engaging in activities they have chosen to do and have, presumably, tailored to suit their own strengths and values.

As with self-direction, the second element of a protean attitude, that of being values-driven, has not been directly empirically tested in relation to job search behavior. However, as depicted in Figure 16.1, a positive relationship between being values-driven and job search is proposed in this chapter. Values may act as a compass to aid job search. Certainly, Wanberg et al.'s (2005) research shows that one of the reasons people do *not* search for work is a feeling of uncertainty about what to do in the next job. Presumably, people who have strong values can use these as an anchor to develop clarity about the type of work they hope to achieve and the type of job search techniques they feel comfortable engaging in. This clarity may facilitate high job search intensity. The arguments presented above have been used to develop proposition two.

Proposition two: Protean career attitude will be positively associated with job search intensity during unemployment.

Protean career attitude may also be indirectly related to job search intensity via its positive effect upon psychological health. In a protean approach, it is the person rather than the organization that is in charge of the career. As such, the career can still move forward even when the person is divorced from an organization/employer. Given that a protean attitude means that identity is not directly tied to the organization, a disconnection with the organization via unemployment is not likely to lead to the feelings of failure and loss of identity that are so typically reported by unemployed people (Creed, Bloxsome, and Johnston, 2001; McKee *et al.*, 2005; Waters and Moore, 2002b). By facilitating the maintenance of psychological health, a protean attitude is likely to have a positive effect on job search intensity (see Figure 16.1). Certainly, psychological health and self-confidence have been positively associated with job search intensity and re-employment in other unemployment studies (Creed *et al.*, 2001; Wanberg *et al.*, 1999; Waters and Moore, 2002a). Protean career attitude theory, together with previous empirical evidence, has been used to develop proposition three.

Proposition three: Protean career attitude will have a positive, indirect relationship with job search intensity during unemployment via its positive effect on psychological health.

Protean career attitude, re-employment quality, and career growth

As well as considering the effect that protean career attitude may have on psychological health and job search during unemployment, this chapter will also outline the role that protean career attitude potentially plays in re-employment outcomes. Wanberg *et al.* (2002: 1101) suggest that subjective assessments of the quality of re-employment can be made by asking participants to assess job/organization–person fit, which can then be "used to portray the extent to which the new job and organization measure up to the type of job and organization the job seeker had hoped to find."

Research has established that many unemployed people re-entering the workforce take a job of lower quality (Butts, 1997; Romeyn, 1992; Wanberg *et al.*, 2002). Holding a protean career attitude may serve to buck this trend. Given that the protean career attitude has been linked with higher levels of self-awareness and career exploration (Hall and Mirvis, 1996), individuals with a protean attitude are likely to be highly adept at exploring the labor market and securing a job which enables them to express their own values. In the context of unemployment, a high need for being values-driven means that one is unlikely to take a job of lower quality, as operationalized through poor person–environment fit. The association between having a protean attitude and learning from experience (Hall *et al.*, 1997) may also foster a transition into high-quality employment. Hall and Mirvis (1996: 32) state that, "If a person has the ability to self-reflect, to continue assessing and learning about her- or himself, and to change behaviors and attitudes, the chances are much greater of making a successful mid-career transition and achieving a good fit with new environment."

It could also be that the personal qualities associated with a protean attitude (e.g. proactivity, openness to change, self-efficacy, and adaptability) make these people highly attractive to potential employers, thus leading to numerous job offers from which the protean person can choose the highest-quality offer. In support of this idea, Fugate, Kinicki, and Ashforth (2004) have suggested that the personal characteristic of adaptability would be an attractive quality for employers in the current business environment. Kanfer *et al.* (2001) found that openness to experience was associated with a shorter unemployment period and that self-efficacy was associated with a greater likelihood of obtaining re-employment and receiving more job offers. The evidence above leads to proposition four.

Proposition four: Protean career attitude will be positively associated with re-employment quality as operationalized via person–environment fit in the new job.

Protean career attitude and career growth

Although unemployment is typically a negative experience, researchers have shown that positive outcomes can arise from unemployment (Eby and Buch, 1995; Payne and Jones, 1987; Zikic and Klehe, in press). Latack and Dozier (1986) examined unemployment as a career transition that, given certain conditions, can lead to career growth. They defined career growth as the situation where the transition from job loss to re-employment provides new, and sometimes more, opportunities for psychological success. Additionally, they saw career growth occurring when career gains of the job loss outweighed the career losses. They suggested that if people are able to use unemployment as a time to reappraise their career goals, gain greater self-insight, and develop new competences, they may find that this leads to career growth.

Latack and Dozier's "career growth from job loss model" outlines three categories of factors which moderate the job loss to career growth conversion, namely: (1) individual characteristics (pre-job loss work attitudes, career stage, activity level); (2) environmental characteristics (financial resources, social support, flexible family structure); and (3) characteristics of the transition process (professional approach to the termination decision on the part of the organization, resolution of grief and anger, avoidance of prolonged unemployment). Whilst Eby and Buch (1995) found empirical support for the "career growth from job loss model" (25% explained variance for involuntarily displaced professional men and 45% explained variance for involuntarily displaced professional women) they also suggested that a number of individual characteristics need to be added to the model in order to increase its predictive ability. Protean career attitude may be an individual-difference variable to be added to the Latack and Dozier (1986) model.

The contemporary definitions of career presented earlier in this chapter allow people who have a protean career attitude to regard unemployment as just one of many work-related events over the course of a career. Such an attitude may mean that people are able to view their unemployment within a long-term framework, and are thus able to examine whether they can use their unemployment as a career episode through which to make career and life changes that facilitate growth. The positive association between protean career attitude and receptiveness to learning from experience (Hall and Mirvis, 1996) means that unemployment may be used as a time to learn more about one's values and career goals. It may even be that unemployment is used as a time to question one's existing career path and set a new career direction (Zikic and Klehe, in press). If this is the case, a person who adopts a protean attitude and sees job loss as a time when the personal learning and discoveries outweigh the stresses of being without work will experience career growth. Hence, rather than unemployment being experienced as an "identity-threatening event" it could be experienced as an "identity-enhancing event" (Thoits, 1991). Gaining greater self-insight and being more self-directed is likely to mean that the individual places him/herself into a new employment environment that allows for career growth (Zikic and Klehe, in press) (see Figure 16.1). With this in mind, proposition five has been developed.

Proposition five: Protean career attitude will be positively associated with career growth.

Can unemployment and re-employment lead to a stronger protean career attitude?

There are some interesting feedback loops to explore in this chapter. Just as protean career attitude can influence the way in which people respond during unemployment and upon re-employment, it may also be that the experiences of unemployment and re-employment alter a person's career attitude. The work of Hall (1986, 2002) and Zikic and Klehe (in press) shows that people can use their joblessness as a time to reflect on, and alter, their views of career. Hall (1986) proposes that experiences which disrupt (or "bust") career routines may be necessary triggers for career change. Hall (2002) also suggests that a failure experience in the work role would be one such trigger. Job loss is arguably one of the most extreme forms of work role failure. In fact, Latack and Dozier (1986: 377) describe job loss as "the antithesis of psychological success."

One of the most dominant psychological responses to unemployment is a rupture, or at its extreme a loss, of self-identity (Amundson, 1994). In western societies, employment and the social relationships attached to an organization are powerful forces in shaping one's identity (Fineman, 1983; O'Callaghan and Pickard, 1995). Unemployment brings about losses to external signposts (e.g. the company one works for), established roles (e.g. bread winner), and traditional ways of judging success (e.g. salary and organizational seniority) that are associated with identity. It is no wonder then that O'Callaghan and Pickard (1995: 20) argue that "being unemployed can dislocate the ways in which we make sense of ourselves and our lives."

The loss of traditional, employment-related ways in which to judge ourselves during unemployment requires people to find new anchors around which to build their identity. In order to establish new identity anchors, the process of self-exploration is ignited (Blustein, 1997; Savickas, 1997). According to the cyclical view of careers, exploration is the first activity that people engage in when a new career cycle begins and, as argued above, job loss can be considered as placing people (albeit an unwanted placement for many) into a new career cycle. Amundson (1994) suggests that unemployment is a critical time for identity exploration and that, during unemployment, people need to renegotiate who they are and how they can best approach their future career. Mirvis and Hall (1994) suggest that whilst job loss is generally not a welcome event, it may offer people an opportunity to engage in necessary self-exploration that was not present during the previous period of employment where there were many competing demands and little time for self-reflection and exploration.

Gordon and Whelan (1998: 14) found that self-exploration leads to "new perspectives ... new models for thinking about success, and career progression." One new perspective that may emerge as a result of self-exploration during unemployment is a shift toward the adoption of a protean career attitude. Mirvis and Hall (1994: 377) argue that people who are laid off feel "betrayed, jilted and abandoned" by their employers.

It may be that these feelings lead people to discard their traditional reliance on the organization as the governing body that steers their career, and instead take on greater responsibility for, and direction over, their own career direction. Even if the employee and the organization part on good terms, the person no longer has the organization as a governing body to rely on and thus is compelled to become more self-directed. One advantage of adopting a protean career attitude during unemployment is that it offers a "more flexible way to see careers unfold over time and space" (Mirvis and Hall, 1994: 370), which is particularly useful when people are reviewing their future options. Choosing to approach one's career using a protean attitude may also assist people to find re-employment options that align more closely with their own values than perhaps they had been able to do in their previous job – considering Kram *et al.*'s (1989) research showing that organizations can constrain a person's ability to express his/her values. The above reasoning leads to proposition six below.

Proposition six: Unemployment will be a career event that triggers a change in career attitude toward the adoption of a more protean attitude.

As well as potentially altering a person's career attitude from traditional to protean, unemployment and re-employment experiences may reinforce and strengthen existing protean career attitudes. If adopting a protean career attitude was found to be a useful factor in helping a person maintain psychological health and job search during unemployment, as well as fostering high-quality re-employment and career growth, the individual may see the benefit of continuing to utilize a protean career attitude in future career events.

This positive spiral of proteanism may be explained via the reinforcement processes outlined in Bandura's (1977, 1986) Social Cognition theory. The basic premise of his theory is that "past experiences create expectations that certain actions will bring valued results" (Bandura, 1977: 18). Applying this here, it may be that the internal processes attached to a protean attitude (being self-directed and values-driven) help to determine particular behaviors (for example, high levels of job search and choosing a new job based upon values fit). These behaviors then influence the situations surrounding the person – in this case gaining re-employment and obtaining job growth. These positive situational outcomes in turn serve to reinforce, and possibly heighten, the original protean career attitude. The literature review above has been used to develop proposition seven.

Proposition seven: In people who already have a protean career attitude, the experiences of quality re-employment and career growth will serve to further heighten a protean attitude.

The role of financial strain in protean career attitude, psychological health, job search, re-employment quality, and career growth

Financial strain is one of the most difficult and consistent problems experienced during unemployment (Viinamaki, Koskela, Niskanen, and Arnkill, 1993; Waters and Moore, 2001) and it has been negatively associated with psychological health (Feather, 1997; Jones, 1991; Liem and Liem, 1988; Vinokur, Price, and Caplan, 1996), and positively associated with job search intensity and re-employment (Kinicki, Prussia, and McKee-Ryan, 2000; Leana and Feldman, 1995). Financial strain is, therefore, an important variable to build into Figure 16.1, given the strong research evidence that exists to link it with three major aspects of the proposed model (i.e. psychological health, job search intensity, and re-employment).

It is also possible that financial strain may determine, in part, the adoption of a protean career attitude during unemployment. For instance, a person who is under extreme financial pressure may have to accept the first job that comes along, regardless of whether it is compatible with his or her own values. In addition, adequate financial resources may be required to allow the person to operate in an independent and self-directed manner because money provides people with a greater capacity to conduct a job search that goes beyond the official assistance received from government and welfare agencies. Cappelli (1999, 2002) and Briscoe and Hall (2003) have recognized that financial pressures may negatively influence a person's ability to make self-initiated job and career moves. To date, there has been no empirical test of this proposition. However, work by Hall and Briscoe (2003) can be used to argue that the financial situation of the unemployed job seeker may influence the likelihood of following a protean approach. The evidence and arguments above lead to proposition eight.

Proposition eight: Financial strain will be negatively related to protean career attitude, psychological health, and re-employment quality, and it will be positively associated with job search intensity.

Implications

This chapter suggests that the protean career attitude is a useful construct through which to study unemployment from a careers perspective. More specifically, protean career attitude may assist researchers and practitioners to gain a greater understanding of psychological health during unemployment, levels of job search intensity, and re-employment quality as well as the ways in which people construct opportunities from unemployment that lead to career growth.

If the propositions of this chapter receive support, once empirically tested, researchers may choose to design interventions that encourage unemployed people to adopt a protean career attitude. Authors such as Amundson (1994), Muller (1995), and Waters and Moore (2002b) have suggested that current unemployment assistance programs need to go beyond typical skill-based vocational training programs to include elements of personal development. One area of personal development that could be targeted is the attitude people hold toward their career. Given that protean career attitude *is* an attitude, it is amenable to change.

Interventions focused upon encouraging a protean career attitude may start with an attempt to help people understand the relationship between their own identity and the broader labor market as a way to help them let go of a traditional career orientation, namely that their career must be moored to an employer, and move toward a self-directed relationship with the labor market. Building a protean career attitude may be achieved by engaging in a process of identity examination that encourages unemployed people to clarify their guiding values and to consider non-work achievements and capacities in how they define themselves and their career. This broader view will assist them to maintain a positive sense of identity despite being out of work. Careers counselors can, therefore, encourage unemployed people to use their unemployment experience as a time to engage in "identity negotiation" (Amundson, 1994) that allows them to redefine the self independently of the job, to clarify their own values, and to look for ways to become more self-directed.

Examination and clarification of core values and life goals could be facilitated through self-assessment surveys, analysis of critical career incidents, and feedback from others. The narrative approach to career counseling may also be helpful and has already been shown by Gibson (2004) to work successfully in the context of the boundaryless career. Training to enhance self-direction could be improved using the application of Seligman's (1991) learned optimism model. This model teaches people to identify their adversities, beliefs, and consequences with the aim of assisting them to cognitively reframe their situation to one over which they have direction/control. Counseling techniques such as distraction, evidence seeking, alternative generation, and disputation may encourage people to break that pattern of psychological distress that is typically associated with unemployment.

Along similar lines, Hollenbeck and Hall's (2004) self-confidence formula may be highly applicable during unemployment. This self-confidence formula encourages people to appraise a situation (for example, job search) by considering their perceived capabilities minus the perceived requirements of the task. Career and outplacement counselors can help unemployed people to break down the job search task into manageable parts (e.g. career exploration, updating the curriculum vitae, interview preparation) and then to assess these tasks against their own capabilities (e.g. research skills, written and oral communication). Career counselors may find the self-confidence formula to be a helpful tool in creating higher levels of self-direction.

Future research

In order to test the conceptual model presented in Figure 16.1 and/or to maximize empirical investigation of the role that protean career attitude plays during unemployment, future researchers could adopt an "ipsative–normative" design (Marceil, 1977). Ipsative pertains to intraindividual comparison while normative refers to interindividual comparison. The combination of a longitudinal and a cross-sectional approach allows for repeated observations of individuals in comparison groups. Such a design would capture the interplay between protean career attitude, psychological health, job search intensity, and various re-employment outcomes over time by making repeated observations of the same person. In addition to these repeated intraindividual comparisons, the interindividual approach would allow an examination of patterns of normative vulnerability in unemployed people who are classified as low on protean career attitude compared to those classified as high. This design also allows researchers to test for feedback loops in order to examine whether protean career attitude itself changes over time and/or changes with variations in employment status (e.g. move from unemployment to re-employment or vice versa).

Such a design would be strengthened by the use of analytical techniques that allow for a test of the reciprocal relationships contained in the Figure 16.1. In particular, the use of Structural Equation Modeling (SEM) is recommended because it examines a series of dependence relationships simultaneously (Jöreskog and Sörbom, 1982). In addition, because SEM allows the same variable to act as an independent and dependent variable (Hair, Anderson, Tatham, and Black, 1995) it is able to capture the interrelationships that may occur between protean career attitude, psychological health, job search intensity, and re-employment. Moreover, because the paths can be interpreted as standardized regression coefficients, SEM allows researchers to compare the relative contribution of each variable within the model. In this way, researchers may, for example, compare the degree to which job search is influenced by protean career attitude versus financial strain – as well as seeing how these two factors combine to predict job search. A further advantage of SEM derives from its ability to correct for attenuation in random measurement error of manifest variables, and from the maximum likelihood method, which produces both a statistical measure of goodness-of-fit and an explained variance (R^2) of the model (Tabachnick and Fidell, 1995).

However, the use of this quantitative technique need not be at the exclusion of qualitative assessments. Fryer (1992), Pernice (1996), and Waters (2000) have called for a reintegration of qualitative methods in unemployment research. Given that protean career attitude is subjective, and is perhaps even context specific, future researchers will benefit from using qualitative methods that allow them to "inquire from the inside."

Concluding statement

This chapter has reviewed previous theory and research in the job loss and careers areas to make the argument that a protean career attitude is likely to be beneficial during unemployment. Eight propositions and a conceptual model were presented to outline the possible ways in which a protean career attitude can assist people to cope with unemployment and obtain high-quality re-employment. More specifically, this chapter discussed the roles that being self-directed and values-driven may play in relation to psychological health, job search, obtaining re-employment of a high quality, and achieving career growth. The chapter provided practical implications for the way in which a protean career attitude can be enhanced by careers counselors used by unemployed people as well as suggestions for future researchers.

New organizational, economic, and career realities indicate that many people will be required to operate in a protean fashion if they are to succeed in their future career endeavors. As a career concept, the protean attitude gives high levels of flexibility – to researchers, career practitioners, and workers alike – that allow careers to be defined in broad terms and to unfold in many different ways. The adoption of protean career theory allows researchers to study unemployment as an event that occurs within a career, rather than a situation that leads to a rupture of that career. This critical shift in mind-set means that empirical studies can investigate unemployment within the context of a long-term career rather than as a one-off episode. For unemployed people, a protean view allows them to proceed with their career in a proactive and continuous way, despite the temporary absence of paid employment.

References

Amundson, N. (1994). Negotiating identity during unemployment. *Journal of Employment Counseling* 31: 98–105.

Argyris, C. (1990). *Overcoming organizational defenses: facilitating professional effectiveness*. Boston: Allyn and Bacon.

Arnold, J., Cooper, C., and Robertson, I. (1998) *Work psychology: understanding human behavior in the workplace* (4th edn). Harlow: Prentice Hall.

Arthur, M. B., Inkson, K., and Pringle, J. K. (1999). *The new careers: individual action and economic change*. Thousand Oaks, CA: Sage.

Arthur, M., Khapova, S., and Wilderom, C. (2005). Career success in a boundaryless career world. *Journal of Organizational Behavior* 26: 177–202.

Australian Bureau of Statistics (2004). *Labour Force Australia* (Catalogue No. 6202.0). Canberra: Australian Bureau of Statistics.

Bandura, A. (1977). *Social learning theory*. Englewood Cliffs, NJ: Prentice Hall.
  (1986). *Social foundations of thought and action: a social cognitive theory*. Englewood Cliffs, NJ: Prentice Hall.
  (1991). Social cognitive theory of moral thought and action. In W. M. Kurtines and J. L. Gewirtz (Eds.), *Handbook of moral behavior and development* (pp. 45–103). Hillsdale, NJ: Lawrence Erlbaum.

Blustein, D. L. (1997). A context-rich perspective of career exploration across the life roles. *Career Development Quarterly* 45: 260–74.

Briscoe, J. P. and Hall, D. T. (2003). Being and becoming protean: individual and experiential frameworks in adapting to the new career. Unpublished technical report. DeKalb, IL: Department of Management, Northern Illinois University, DeKalb.

Briscoe, J. P., Hall, D. T., and DeMuth, R. (2006). Protean and boundaryless careers: an empirical exploration. *Journal of Vocational Behavior* 69: 30–47.

Burnes, B. (2000). *Managing change: a strategic approach to organisational development*. Harlow: Pearson Education.

Butts, D. (1997). Joblessness, pain, power pathology and promise. *Journal of Organizational Change Management* 10: 111–29.

Campbell, I. and Webber, M. (1996). Retrenchment and labour market flows in Australia. *Economic and Labour Relations Review* 7: 88–119.

Cappelli, P. (1999). *The new deal at work: managing the market-driven workforce*. Boston: Harvard Business School Press.
  (2002). The path to the top: the changing model of career advancement. Paper presented at the Harvard Business School Conference on Career Evolution, London, 13–15 June.

Carver, C. S. and Scheier, M. F. (1982). *Attention and self-regulation: a control theory approach*. New York: Springer Verlag.

Cassidy, T. (2001). Self-categorization, coping and psychological health among unemployed mid-career executives. *Counselling Psychology Quarterly* 14: 303–15.

Creed, P. A., Bloxsome, T. D., and Johnston, K. (2001). Self-esteem and self-efficacy outcomes for unemployed individuals attending occupational skills training programs. *Community, Work and Family* 4: 285–303.

Crespo, S., Boisjoly, J., and Bernard, P. (1998). *What do people do when they are laid off?* Income and labour dynamics working chapter, Catalogue 98–08. Ottawa: Statistics Canada Product No. 75F0002M.

Cvetanovski, J. and Jex, S. (1994). Locus of control of unemployed people and its relationship to psychological and physical well-being. *Work and Stress* 8: 60–7.

Diamond, M. and Shapiro, J. (1973). Changes in locus of control as a function of encounter group experiences. *Journal of Abnormal Psychology* 88: 297–8.

Donohue, R. and Patton, W. (1998). The effectiveness of a career guidance program with long term unemployed individuals. *Journal of Employment Counseling* 35: 179–84.

Eby, L. T. and Buch, K. (1995). Job loss as career growth: response to involuntary career transitions. *Career Development Quarterly* 44: 26–42.

Eisenman, R. (1972). Experience in experiments and change in internal–external control scores. *Journal of Consulting and Clinical Psychology* 39: 434–5.

Feather, N. T. (1997). Economic deprivation and the psychological impact of unemployment. *Australian Psychologist* 32: 37–45.

Fineman, S. (1983). Counselling the unemployed: help and helplessness. *British Journal of Guidance and Counselling* 11: 1–9.

Fryer, D. (1986). Employment deprivation and personal agency during unemployment: a critical discussion of Jahoda's explanation of the psychological effects of unemployment. *Social Behaviour* 1: 3–23.

(1992). Poverty stricken? A plea for a greater emphasis on the role of poverty in psychological research on unemployment and mental health in the social context. In C. Verhaar and L. Jansam (eds.), *On the mysteries of unemployment: causes, consequences and policy*. Boston: Kluwer Academic.

Fryer, D. and Payne, R. (1984). Proactive behaviour in unemployment: findings and implications. *Leisure Studies* 3: 273–95.

Fugate, M., Kinicki, A. J., and Ashforth, B. E. (2004). Employability: a psychosocial construct, its dimensions and applications. *Journal of Vocational Behavior* 65: 14–38.

Gibson, P. (2004). Where to from here? A narrative approach to career counseling. *Career Development International* 9: 176–89.

Gordon, J. H. and Whelan, K. S. (1998). Successful professional women in midlife: how organizations can more effectively understand and respond to the challenges. *Academy of Management Executive* 12: 8–27.

Gratton, L., Zaleska, K. J., and De Menezes, L. (2002). The rhetoric and reality of the "new careers." Paper presented at the Harvard Business School Conference on Career Evolution, London, 13–15 June.

Guichard, J. (2001). A century of career education: review and perspectives. *International Journal for Educational and Vocational Guidance* 1: 155–76.

Hair, J., Anderson, R., Tatham, R., and Black, W. (1995). *Multivariate data analysis* (4th edn). Englewood Cliffs, NJ: Prentice Hall.

Hall, D. T. (1986). Breaking career routines: mid-career choice and identity development. In D. T. Hall and associates (eds.), *Career development in organizations* (pp. 120–59). San Francisco: Jossey-Bass.

(1996). Protean careers of the 21st century. *Academy of Management Executive* 10: 8–16.

(2002). *Careers in and out of the organization*. Thousand Oaks, CA: Sage.

(2004). The protean career: a quarter-century journey. *Journal of Vocational Behavior* 65: 1–13.

Hall, D. T. and Briscoe, J. P. (2003). Protean and bounded careers: an empirical exploration. Paper presented at annual meeting of the Academy of Management, Seattle, WA, 4 August.

Hall, D. T., Briscoe, J. P., and Kram, K. E. (1997). Identity, values and learning in the protean career. In C. L. Cooper and S. E. Jackson (eds.), *Creating tomorrow's organizations* (pp. 321–35). London: John Wiley.

Hall, D. T. and Mirvis, P. H. (1996). The new protean career: psychological success and the path with a heart. In D. T. Hall and associates (eds.), *The career is dead – long live the career: a relational approach to careers* (pp. 14–45). San Francisco: Jossey-Bass.

Hall, D. T. and Moss, J. E. (1998). The new protean career contract: helping organizations and employees adapt. *Organizational Dynamics*, 26: 22–37.

Hollenbeck, G. and Hall, D. (2004). Self-confidence and leader performance. *Organizational Dynamics* 33: 254–69.

Huang, T. (2003).Unemployment and family behavior in Taiwan. *Journal of Family and Economic Issues* 24: 27–48.

Jones, L. (1991). The health consequences of economic recessions. *Journal of Health and Social Policy* 3: 1–14.

Jöreskog, K. and Sörbom, D. (1982). Recent developments in structural equation modeling. *Journal of Marketing Research* 19: 404–16.

Kanfer, R., Wanberg, C., and Kantrowitz, T. (2001). Job search and employment: a personality-motivational analysis and meta-analytic review. *Journal of Applied Psychology* 86: 837–55.

Katz, D. and Kahn, R. L. (1978). *The social psychology of organizations* (2nd edn). New York: Wiley.

Kinicki, A., Prussia, G., and McKee-Ryan, F. (2000). A panel study of coping with involuntary job loss. *Academy of Management Journal* 43: 90–100.

Kram, K. E., Yeager, P. C., and Reed, G. E. (1989). Decisions and dilemmas: the ethical dimension in the corporate context. In J. E. Post (ed.), *Research in corporate performance and policy* (vol. 11, pp. 21–53). Greenwich, CT: JAI Press.

Latack, J. C. and Dozier, J. (1986). After the ax falls: job loss as a career transition. *Academy of Management Review* 11: 377–85.

Leana, C. R. and Feldman, D. C. (1992). *Individual responses to job loss: how individuals, organizations and communities respond to layoffs*. New York: Lexington.

(1995). Finding new jobs after a plant closing: antecedents and outcomes of the occurrence and quality of reemployment. *Human Relations* 48: 1381–1401.

Liem, R. and Liem, J. H. (1988). Psychological effects of unemployment on workers and their families. *Journal of Social Issues* 44: 87–105.

MacDermid, S., Lee, M., Buck, M., and Williams, M. (2001). Alternative work arrangements among professionals and managers: rethinking career development and success. *Journal of Management Development* 20: 305–17.

Mantler, J., Matejicek, A., Matheson, K., and Anisman, H. (2005). Coping with employment uncertainty: a comparison of employed and unemployed workers. *Journal of Occupational Health Psychology* 10: 200–9.

Marceil, J. (1977). Implicit dimensions of idiography and nomothesis: a reformulation. *American Psychologist* 32: 1046–55.

McDonald, P., Brown, K., and Bradley, L. (2005). Have traditional career paths given way to protean ones? Evidence from senior managers in the Australian sector. *Career Development International* 10: 109–29.

McKee-Ryan, F., Song, Z., Wanberg, C., and Kinicki, A. (2005). Psychological and physical well-being during unemployment: a meta-analytic study. *Journal of Applied Psychology* 90: 53–76.

Mirvis, P. H. and Hall, D. T. (1994). Psychological success and the boundaryless career. *Journal of Organizational Behavior* 15: 365–80.

Muller, J. (1995). Women in unemployment research: findings and future issues. In R. Hicks, P. Creed, W. Patton, and J. Tomlinson (eds.), *Unemployment developments and transitions* (pp. 104–14). Brisbane: Australian Academic Press.

Nowicki, S. and Barnes, J. (1973). Effects of a structured camp experience on locus of control orientation. *Journal of Genetic Psychology* 122: 247–52.

O'Callaghan, J. and Pickard, E. (1995). Reconstruction for re-engagement: stress management for transition. *Employee Counselling Today* 7: 20–4.

Parks, C., Becker, M., Chamberlain, J., and Crandell, J. (1975). Eliminating self-defeating behaviors and change in locus of control. *Journal of Psychology* 91: 115–20.

Patton, W. and Donohue, R. (1998). Coping with long term unemployment. *Journal of Community and Applied Social Psychology* 8: 331–43.

Payne, R. L. and Jones, J. G. (1987). The effects of long-term unemployment on attitudes to employment. *Journal of Occupational Behaviour* 8: 351–8.

Pearson, R. W. (1988). Creating flexible careers: some observations on a "bridge" programme for unemployed professionals. *British Journal of Guidance and Counselling* 16: 250–67.

Pernice, R. (1996). Methodological issues in unemployment research: quantitative and/or qualitative approaches? *Journal of Occupational and Organizational Psychology* 69: 339–49.

Price, R., Choi, J., and Vinokur, A. (2002). Links in the chain of adversity following job loss: how financial strain and loss of personal control lead to depression, impaired functioning, and poor health. *Journal of Occupational Health Psychology* 7: 302–12.

Rifkin, J. (1995). *The end of work: the decline of the global labour force and the dawn of the post-market era*. New York: G. P. Putnam's Sons.

Rogers, C. R. (1951). *Client-centered therapy: its current practice, implications, and theory*. Boston: Houghton.

Rokeach, M. (1973). *The nature of human values*. New York: Free Press.

Romeyn, J. (1992). *Flexible working time: part time and casual employment*. Canberra: Australian Government Publishing Service.

Savickas, M. L. (1997). Career adaptability: an integrative construct for life-span, life-space theory. *Career Development Quarterly* 45: 247–59.

Seligman, M. (1991). *Learned optimism*. New York: Pocket Books.

Shams, M. and Jackson, P. R. (1994). The impact of unemployment on the psychological well-being of British Asians. *Psychological Medicine* 24: 347–55.

Super, D. (1990). A life-span, life-space approach to career development. In D. Brown and L. Brooks (eds.), *Career choice and development* (pp. 167–261). San Francisco: Jossey-Bass.

Super, D., Osborne, L., Walsh, D., Brown, S., and Niles, S. (2001). Developmental career assessment and counseling: the C-DAC model. *Journal of Counseling and Development* 71: 74–80.

Super, D. E., Savickas, M. L., and Super, C. M. (1996). The life-span, life-space approaches to careers. In D. Brown, L. Brooks, and associates (eds.), *Career choice and development* (3rd edn, pp. 121–78). San Francisco: Jossey-Bass.

Tabachnick, B. and Fidell, L. (1995). *Using multivariate statistics* (3rd edn). New York: HarperCollins.

Thoits, P. (1991). On merging identity theory and stress research. *Social Psychology Quarterly* 54: 101–12.

Vansteenkiste, M., Lens, W., De Witte, H., and Feather, N. T. (2005). Understanding unemployed people's job search behaviour, unemployment experience and well-being: a comparison of expectancy-value theory and self-determination theory. *British Journal of Social Psychology* 44: 269–87.

Viinamaki, H., Koskela, K., Niskanen, L., and Arnkill, R. (1993). Unemployment, financial stress and mental well-being: a factory closure study. *European Journal of Psychiatry* 7: 95–102.

Vinokur, A. and Schul, Y. (1997). Mastery and inoculation against setbacks as active ingredients in the jobs intervention for the unemployed. *Journal of Consulting and Clinical Psychology* 65: 876–7.

  (2002). The web of coping resources and pathways to re-employment following a job loss. *Journal of Occupational Health Psychology* 7: 68–83.

Vinokur, A., Price, R., and Caplan, R. (1996). Hard times and hurtful partners: how financial strain affects depression and relationship satisfaction of unemployed persons and their spouses. *Journal of Personality and Social Psychology* 71: 166–79.

Wanberg, C. (1997). Antecedents and outcomes of coping behaviors among unemployed and re-employed individuals. *Journal of Applied Psychology* 82: 731–44.

Wanberg, C., Glomb, T., Song, Z., and Sorenson, S. (2005). Job search persistence during unemployment: a 10-wave longitudinal study. *Journal of Applied Psychology* 90: 411–30.

Wanberg, C., Hough, L., and Song, Z. (2002). Predictive validity of a multidisciplinary model of re-employment success. *Journal of Applied Psychology* 87: 1100–20.

Wanberg, C., Kanfer, R., and Rotundo, M. (1999). Unemployed individuals: motives, job search competencies, and job search constraints as predictors of job seeking and re-employment. *Journal of Applied Psychology* 84: 897–920.

Wanberg, C., Watt, J. D., and Rumsey, D. J. (1996). Individuals without jobs: an empirical study of job-seeking behavior and re-employment. *Journal of Applied Psychology* 81: 76–87.

Waters, L. (2000). Coping with unemployment: a literature review and presentation of a new model. *International Journal of Management Review* 2: 169–82.

(2007). Experiential differences between voluntary and involuntary job redundancy on depression, job-search activity, affective employee outcomes, and re-employment quality. *Journal of Occupational and Organizational Psychology* 80: 279–99.

Waters, L. and Moore, K. (2001). Coping with economic deprivation during unemployment. *Journal of Economic Psychology* 22: 461–82.

(2002a). Psychological health and coping: a comparison of unemployed and re-employed people. *Journal of Organizational Behavior* 23: 593–604.

(2002b). Psychological adjustment to unemployment: interactions between gender and employment status on self-esteem. *Journal of Employment Counseling* 39: 171–89.

Weir, G. (2003). Job separations. *Labour Market Trends* 111: 121–32.

Winefield, A. H., Montgomery, B., Gault, U., Muller, J., O'Gorman, J., Reser, J., and Roland, D. (2002). The psychology of work and unemployment in Australia today: an Australian Psychological Society discussion paper. *Australian Psychologist* 37: 1–9.

Zikic, J. and Klehe, U.-C. (in press). Job loss as a blessing in disguise: the role of career exploration and career planning in predicting reemployment quality. *Journal of Vocational Behavior*.

Part III

Intervention and promotion on the
organizational level

17 Participatory action research as work stress intervention

Maureen F. Dollard, Pascale M. Le Blanc, and Sarah J. Cotton

Work stress is a major concern in all developing and industrialized countries, affecting not only employees but also organizations and society as a whole. Over the past decades, the workplace has changed substantially owing to globalization of economic activities, increased utilization of information and communication technology, growing diversity in the workplace (e.g. more women, and older and more highly educated people, as well as increased migration, particularly between the EU member states), flexible work arrangements, and changed organizational work patterns (e.g. Just in Time management) (European Foundation for the Improvement of Living and Working Conditions [EFILWC], 2005; Landsbergis, 2003; Le Blanc, de Jonge, and Schaufeli, in press). The impact of the global economy has also led to an increase in knowledge- and service-based organizations. One of the most striking developments, however, is the changing nature of work itself and increased workloads. Nowadays, for many employees, work poses primarily mental and emotional demands instead of physical ones (de Jonge and Dormann, 2003; de Jonge, Mulder, and Nijhuis, 1999).

These recent developments in working life are reflected by a marked increase in (scientific) research on work stress, its causes, and its consequences. Moreover, researchers, managers, and policy makers seek gold standards in the evidence base for policy and practice. Increasingly, cost-benefit analyses of work stress interventions are sought and there is a growing recognition that health and well-being measures are a quintessential component of organizational performance analysis. While such developments have provided valuable impetus for the understanding of work stress and interventions, there remain limitations and unknowns in the scientific method and theories employed. Specifically, researchers and the researched have come to question the capacity of conventional research approaches – such as outsider survey research – to understand and stimulate action on complex stress issues encountered within the context of organizational settings. At the same time, governments are seeking research that starts from a user focus, that is not just aimed at esoteric journals (David, 2002). Increasingly therefore, researchers are using Participatory Action Research (PAR) approaches, taking the users' local context as a starting point for the research and sharing control over the research and knowledge generation process with them (Mikkelsen and Gunderson, 2003). PAR can be seen as a methodology that promotes control and active learning through direct participation of workers (e.g. Karasek, 1992; Parkes and Sparkes, 1998). In fact, the philosophy behind PAR is that organizational interventions designed to promote employee health cannot take place without the participation and experience of the subjects under study (Griffiths, 1999). As such, PAR as a philosophy and method holds promise for the reduction of psychosocial hazards in the workplace, particularly when hazards arise from conflict between management and workers (Pasmore and Friedlander, 1982; Susman and Evered, 1978).

The aim of this chapter is to argue in favor of participatory approaches to work stress intervention (research). We will discuss why PAR is suitable for the problem, describe PAR characteristics and processes, and explore links between PAR, Risk Assessment (Cox, 1993), and "best practice" in work stress intervention (Kompier and Cooper, 1999). However, despite the attractive ideological aspects of PAR (e.g. participation, collaboration, empowerment), implementation is often fraught with difficulty. We will illustrate some key *applied* issues derived from four case studies: (1) developing a participatory organizational structure; (2) developing local participatory structures; (3) feedback, validation, and refinement of findings and actions; and (4) continuity and evaluation. Finally, we will discuss the transdomain potential for PAR. We hope that this chapter will assist researchers as well as organizational members to embark on PAR projects that have mutual benefits for organizational and academic goals alike.

Why PAR?

Limitations of grand theory, evolution of local theory

Since the early 1960s, research in the work stress area has burgeoned, leading to different understandings about what stress is or means. As Baker (1985: 368) argues, "since stress certainly has a multifactorial etiology, investigators have been able to formulate, and at least partially validate, substantially different models of the causes of stress." The feasibility of one overarching theoretical framework of work stress can be seriously questioned, because of the rapidly changing nature of work(ing conditions) described in the introduction to this chapter. This has had important implications for the nature of work stress and thus for the theoretical models describing it. Theories should be considered complementary rather than mutually exclusive (Le Blanc *et al.*, in press), implying also that there are problems in starting research on work stress (intervention) from (only) a single theoretical viewpoint (Dollard, 2003).

Moreover, there are still many unknowns about work stress, which require researchers and practitioners to look closely at the local context – including local economic, social, and political ideologies – in trying to understand work stress situations. For this reason, a growing body of research is beginning at the "site of the struggle," using PAR approaches and evolving local theory (e.g. Dollard, Heffernan, Winefield, and Winefield, 1997; Landsbergis and Vivona-Vaughan, 1995).

We do not suggest that approaches to work stress (intervention) should be atheoretical, but rather that scope should be provided for the development of local theory in order to develop a wider understanding of work stress in a local context. We still have only limited knowledge about the relevance and usefulness of the work stress concept in other settings, for example in western versus eastern cultures; in developed versus emerging economies; transculturally and across regions; in dominant versus indigenous cultures; in metropolitan versus rural locations; in large versus small to medium enterprises; in corporations versus owner operator arrangements, and so on (Laungani, 1996). And we see that, even in western societies, different sociopolitical contexts give rise to different emphases in work stress theories (Calnan, Wainwright, and Almond, 2000).

Unique opportunities exist for the application of PAR in these varied settings to uncover local theories as well as to look for systematic singular regularity ("grand theory") in employees' behaviors, in interpretations, and in organizational processes and cultures (Lee, 1999). Limitations in grand theory to fully account for local experiences and in traditional methodologies to produce knowledge that would lead to effective interventions and their implementation have stimulated a rethink of philosophy and approach. Using PAR, a dialectic occurs so that theories spawned in dominant cultures are not merely transposed to new settings unproblematically. Such participatory approaches attempt to uncover emic elements (i.e. culture bound or culture specific), by treating the organization under study as its own unique culture, at least to some degree. At the same time, etic elements (i.e. more general or universal aspects from known theories) may be relevant. Together emic and etic elements are incorporated into an emerging tailored model of stress in the organization under study (e.g. Narayanan, Menon, and Spector, 1999).

Politics and values

Another complicating factor in work stress (intervention) research is that the politics of work stress is ever apparent at the worksite. Work stress research and intervention inevitably become political, first because of conflicting beliefs and values of interested stakeholders and ultimately because there may be resource implications (and resources in organizations are always finite).

For example, work stress theories have emphasized broader structural factors relating to management and its control over the work process (i.e. the way work is organized) and their links with work stress. This approach draws on the early work of Karl Marx, who suggested that management control over work inevitably leads to alienation of workers. As a result of the scientific management principles referred to as Taylorism, management gained control over the planning and other discretionary elements of work. Peterson (1999: 154) notes, "as management attitudes are based on exercising control that does not appreciate and value the work of its employees, this reflects a basic alienating characteristic of capitalist work experience." His study in an Australian manufacturing organization (Peterson, 1999) showed that alienating conditions on the job (lack of control and lack of skill utilization and variety) were related to stress and ill health. These structural notions are somewhat embodied in two contemporary models of work stress: Karasek's (1979) Job Demand–Control (DC) model and Siegrist's (1996) Effort–Reward Imbalance (ERI) model. The former emphasizes a lack of control over the job and the utilization of skills, and the latter emphasizes the imbalance of rewards (money, esteem, security, valuing) in relation to efforts. These formulations predict that those most at risk for work stress occupy low-level positions (e.g. women, migrants) in organizations and are in low socio-economic jobs. Significant support for the central ideas of the DC and ERI model can be found in the literature (e.g. de Jonge, Bosma, Peter, and Siegrist, 2000; de Lange, Taris, Kompier, Houtman, and Bongers, 2003; Tsutsumi and Kawakami, 2004; van Vegchel, de Jonge, Bosma, and Schaufeli, 2005). In addition, the above-mentioned study by Peterson (1999) showed that the effects of structural control by management (role conflict and poor relationships) were even more important, especially the effects of a negative climate of attitudes by management. Further, conflict at work, undoubtedly a consequence of unsatisfactory work arrangements, anecdotally is claimed to underlie up to 60% of recent workers' compensation stress claims in a large Australian public sector workforce.

The alienation and conflict employees can experience at work is redoubled when researchers study the work stress phenomenon to inform organizational change using the scientific model or so-called investigator driven prevention research (Hughes, 2003). Knowledge leads to power and the front-line role of university researchers in this complicity, operating as experts and constructing knowledge without regard to the expertise of workers, reinforces these alienating structures (see also David, 2002). The participative/collaborative approach embodied in PAR reflects devolution of control over decision-making to workers and can be an effective way to help organizations switch from highly formalized power structures to more equalized ones (Pasmore and Friedlander, 1982). According to Pasmore and Friedlander, benefits can accrue to both organizations and the social sciences by explicitly recognizing the need to create an atmosphere in which inquiry itself leads to significant changes in labor–management relations. They argue that we should "abandon methods of inquiry that reinforce existing problems created by organizational structure and develop a new paradigm of action research" (1982: 361).

Moreover, they noted that the problems encountered by the organization could not have been understood or affected by traditional research methods that place emphasis on the maintenance of rigor rather than on using data to help influence organizational behavior in desired ways. Further they argue that we should recognize our power to influence both individual and organizational behavior in beneficial ways through our study methods.

Understanding the meaning of stress is further confounded by the fact that the concept of stress is not value free. Indeed, occupational stress is a social and political issue as much as a health problem (Levi, 1990). PAR involves the participation of key stakeholders in all phases of the project, and as such is an especially suitable method to overcome/incorporate political issues through ongoing dialogue.

In sum, the politics, competing perspectives, values, alienation, and conflict that certain groups experience in dealing with workplace stress require an engaging process where all affected parties are involved. The questioning of conventional research approaches in understanding and stimulating research on these – often complex and long-term – factors related to work stress has led to the new research paradigm called Action Research, which aims to contribute both to the practical concerns of people in an immediate problematic situation (*action*) and to the goals of social science (*research*) by joint collaboration within a mutually acceptable ethical framework (Rapaport, 1970).

What is it?

PAR is a "continual reflective dialectic between theory application and application of knowledge gained as a continuous research cycle. This reflective dialectic involves 'outsiders', professional university-based researchers working collaboratively with insiders, i.e. organization-based researchers" (May *et al.*, 2002, in Hughes, 2003: 6). In seeking to define PAR in more detail, we will explore its five key principles that set it apart from both traditional research methods and other modes of Action Research.

First of all, *active participation* is evident in PAR by the involvement of various stakeholders throughout all phases of the project (e.g. Israel, Schurman, and Hugentobler, 1992; Schurman, 1996). Wadsworth (1998) states that the reason why many researchers have felt compelled to add the "P" for participation to the "AR" for Action Research has been because of how the existing levels of conventional participation have been taken for granted. It is this significant level of participant involvement that is therefore the most fundamental principle of PAR (Kronenburg, 1986; Selener, 1997). According to Whyte (1989, 1991), PAR means that people in the community *participate actively* with the professional researcher throughout the entire research process. Traditionally, a place might have been seen for participation by the various parties at the outset (e.g. on a committee) or at the end as recipients of a report. Increasingly, instead, the researched might become contributors to all stages of the research cycle (e.g. as designers, selectors of methods, contributors of data, analyzers, concluders) and actors in the action stage (e.g. interventions) (Balcazar *et al.*, in press; Wadsworth, 1998). Such increased levels of participation are seen as a key factor for establishing lasting improvements in democracy and in reducing alienation and stress (e.g. Mikkelsen, Saksvik, and Landsbergis, 2000).

Second, consistent with its participatory nature, PAR involves *collaboration* between researchers and clients (Gronhaug and Olson, 1999; Parkes and Sparkes, 1998). In order for the researchers to be effective in influencing the creation of collaboration, they must be sufficiently involved in the life of the organization, have some idea of which topics are of interest, and understand which individuals might be called together to discuss these topics (Schensul, 1994). Researchers cannot be familiar with all aspects of the organization that must be considered in a project. Collaboration can therefore lead to a more comprehensive and relevant understanding of the organizational setting in which the research and related change or development strategies are to take place (Schensul, 1994). In fact, Selener (1997) highlights that a direct involvement of organizational members in the research process facilitates a more accurate and authentic analysis of their social reality. Experienced workers who perform job tasks on a daily basis often have (their own) ideas on how to make these jobs less strenuous and more efficient (Rosecrance and

Cook, 2000). So, PAR approaches with union/worker involvement have significant advantages over expert-dominated or management-dominated intervention programs (Dollard and Metzer, 1999; Landsbergis et al., 1993) because all voices are heard.

As already indicated above, the aim of the collaborative relationship is that those in the organization under study become fully involved in the research process as co-researchers (equals) (e.g. Aimers, 1999; Israel, Schurman, and Hugentobler, 1992) rather than in the traditional role of research subject or even as respondent (Pasmore and Friedlander, 1982). The employees (inside experts) are the problem owners and contribute their local theories and practical knowledge (both objective and subjective aspects) of the workplace, while the researchers (outside experts) contribute their theoretical knowledge and methodological expertise (e.g. Argyris, 1983; Hughes, 2003; Rosecrance and Cook, 2000; Selener, 1997). The development of interventions is therefore both contextually grounded and rooted in accumulated organizational and theoretical knowledge (Schurman, 1996). While neither type of expertise has primacy (Hughes, 2003), meaning and the context for the research should come from within the group rather than being imposed by the researcher(s) (Fals-Borda and Rahman, 1991; Swantz, 1996). The research is therefore "undertaken as if from inside the culture, from the premises of the people and their situation" (Swantz, 1996: 124). It is the long-term goal of employee participation and continued collaboration to transfer complete control and ownership over (1) input (whether the study will be done, who will influence the process), (2) process (what methods will be used, how the knowledge will be produced), and (3) outcome (how the knowledge will be used) (Hughes, 2003) to the employees themselves (Imada, 1991).

A third distinctive feature of PAR is *employee empowerment*. If the research can satisfy a climate of participation and collaboration (shared control/ownership) then PAR should provide a valuable tool to encourage organizational involvement (give people a "voice"), which is productive and empowering to employees (e.g. Aimers, 1999; Fals-Borda and Rahman, 1991; Martin, 1996; Park, 1993; Selener, 1997). PAR empowers previously subjugated and passive groups by giving them a sense of control (Rosecrance and Cook, 2000), increased ownership of ideas, responsibility, and legitimacy to their enlarged role (Pasmore and Friedlander, 1982). PAR empowers employees throughout the life of the study and enhances likelihood of successful intervention implementation, and potentially affects the overall perception of the intervention process (Rosecrance and Cook, 2000). Further increased awareness about employees' own resources and strengths (Selener, 1997) also builds an organization's capacity to solve self-identified problems (see also Hughes, 2003) as the cycle continues and the "outsider experts" leave the scene.

Fourth, PAR leads to *increased local knowledge*, which can be used by workers to change the organization (find effective and viable solutions; *action*) and by researchers to refine work stress theory (*research*) (Balcazar *et al.*, in press; Park, 1993; Susman and Evered, 1978). Thus, PAR results in co-learning where researchers involve organizations in developing local theory that explains their own situation, and theory may be criticized from the perspective of practice (Gronhaug and Olson, 1999).

Finally, what drives PAR, like any other research, is the need to "know" in order to bring about desired *change* (Wadsworth, 1998) in both the organization and the social sciences (Pasmore and Friedlander, 1982). Susman and Evered (1978) described Action Research as an enabling science. In their view, it creates trust, openness, and a willingness to inquire into and reach joint solutions to tough but inescapable organizational problems. According to Pasmore and Friedlander (1982), Action Research creates a new setting in which employees and managers can jointly inquire into issues concerning their *relationship*, thereby reducing feelings of mistrust. Through the development of co-appreciative relationships, they are more able to examine the organization in which they are embedded, so that their shared interest in the survival of the organization is realized and supported in organizational actions. It should be noted, however, that often it takes time for those involved to acquire new knowledge, or more precisely to change their cognitive structures in such a way that their reality constructions change too. The emphasis in Action Research on what Argyris and Schon (1974) have termed double-looped learning relates to this point, that is, the actors' worldview must be altered if they are going to initiate change for improvements (Gronhaug and Olson, 1999). Furthermore, having correct knowledge does not of itself lead to change. Attention also needs to be paid to the matrix of cultural and social perceptions and the system of which the individuals are a part (Lewin and Grabbe, 1945). When change is a desired outcome, it is more easily achieved if people are committed to the change. It must involve not only active participation and ownership of ideas by stakeholders; these factors must also be valued and utilized by them (Dick, 1993). Involvement in all aspects of the research guarantees use of the results in change efforts (Schensul, 1994). At the same time, top management support is a prerequisite if interventions are going to be implemented and the required resources made available.

In summary, the key principles of PAR, namely active participation, collaboration (perceived control and ownership), and empowerment of employees, seek to enhance the development of local knowledge and the likelihood of stronger consensus for change (Elden, 1986; Graves, 1991; Imada, 1991). PAR also provides an especially suitable method for dealing equitably with power problems and political issues that occur in applied research (Dollard and Metzer, 1999; Landsbergis *et al.*, 1993).

The process

PAR involves workers in a *cyclic process*, participating in Step 1, defining the issues or problems (if they exist); Step 2, developing the methodology and data collection to inform of the problem; Step 3, making sense of the data; Step 4, defining interventions; Step 5, helping to implement them; and Step 6, evaluating the results (Wadsworth, 1998). There are various ways of describing the elements of the cycles; however, the common stages outlined by Kemmis and McTaggart (1988) – plan, act, observe, and reflect – provide a useful overview of the process. In line with the key principles discussed previously, the process is participatory in that the problem, the research, and the action are generated by the organization in collaboration with the researchers, rather than driven by the theoretical interests of the researchers (Susman and Evered, 1978).

In PAR, not only are the effects of all participants' actions of interest, but it is proposed that it is not possible for the researcher to avoid influencing what is going on. So, whereas conventional research methods attempt to minimize researcher influence, PAR seeks to make a virtue of it (Argyris, 1967). However, the power invested in the role of the academic researcher should reduce over time as a transfer of learning occurs and participants become more expert in process and analysis: "workers as researchers" (Israel, Schurman, and House, 1989). For organizations to be "learning" environments, this process needs to be ongoing, and also iterative so that continuous improvements can be made in the work environment conducive to good health in workers as well as to improved productivity. Key stakeholders must be closely involved at every stage to ensure shared understanding of issues and interventions.

Links between PAR, risk assessment, and best practice in work stress intervention

Obvious overlaps can be seen between the PAR methodology outlined above and risk assessment approaches to work stress. Whereas "stress surveys" tend to measure (psychosocial) hazards or outcomes, risk assessment "intends to establish an association between hazards and health outcomes, and to evaluate the risk to health from exposure to a hazard"

(Cox, Griffiths, and Rial-Gonzalez, 2000: 8). Risk assessment is being used increasingly in the European Union and Australia (Victorian WorkCover Authority, 2006) and is supported by legislative frameworks. Originally proposed by Cox (1993), it is an evidence-based, problem-solving approach consisting of six stages: (1) preparation and introduction of the project; (2) problem identification and risk-assessment; (3) choice of measures and planning of interventions (control strategies); (4) implementation of interventions; (5) evaluation of interventions and reassessment of risks (similar to those of the control cycle; Cox and Cox, 1993); and (6) review of information needs and training needs of employees exposed to hazards (Cox and Griffiths, 1996; Janssen, Nijhuis, Lourijsen, and Schaufeli, 1996). The risk assessment approach is elegantly illustrated by Griffiths, Randall, Santos, and Cox (2003) with senior nurses and is especially relevant for PAR in stress management. Risk assessment is clearly a form of Action Research, contributing to the practical concerns of a workgroup, in which additional *participation* of key stakeholders theoretically promises more accurate problem definition and sustainable workable interventions. Further, like PAR, it intends to draw lessons from the organizational research/risk assessment process, and develop knowledge and theory.

Moreover, there are also many parallels between PAR principles and the "best practice" recommendations in work stress intervention made by Kompier and Cooper (1999) on the basis of eleven European case studies. For example, both approaches emphasize the importance of a *stepwise method* to reduce work stress, both consider the involvement and *participation of workers* in the process of stress management as crucial to its success, and both argue that interventions need to be *context-specific* and based on an accurate assessment of both individual and organizational factors rather than relying on prepackaged, context-independent programs (see also Israel *et al.*, 1996; Ivancevich, Matteson, Fredman, and Phillips, 1990; Karasek, 1994; Murphy, Hurrell, and Quick, 1992; Sauter, Murphy, and Hurrell, 1990). Finally, both approaches consider *(top) management support* as a critical success factor.

In line with the above, it may not come as a surprise that the effectiveness of PAR approaches to stress management intervention has also been demonstrated empirically. In a study among human-service workers for developmentally disabled or mentally ill adults, Heaney *et al.* (1995) evaluated the effects of a training program designed to increase individual and group psychosocial coping resources and individuals' abilities to use these resources when coping with job demands. Results showed that the program enhanced workteam climate, increased the amount of supervisor support received on the job, strengthened employees' perceptions of coping abilities, and reduced depressive symptoms and somatization. In a study by Munz, Kohler, and Greenberg (2001) among customer/sales representatives from a large telecommunications company, it was found that the combination of a PAR approach to stressor reduction and self-management training improved participants' emotional well-being (perceived stress, depression, and affect), increased their work units' productivity (sales revenue per order), and decreased registered absenteeism. Van Gorp and Schaufeli (1996) carried out a PAR program to reduce burnout in three large Dutch community mental health centers. After one and a half years employees were satisfied with the way most work-related problems were tackled, but levels of burnout had not decreased markedly. However, in one center registered absenteeism had dropped significantly, whereas in the two remaining centers psychosomatic complaints decreased substantively. Finally, Mikkelsen *et al.* (2000) investigated the effect of a short-term participatory intervention among employees of two community health care institutions in Norway. Results showed that the intervention had a positive but limited effect on job characteristics (job demands, decision authority, social support, and role harmony), work related stress, learning climate, and management style (consideration for individuals), and seemed to have started a beneficial change process.

Actions required and lessons learned

Despite the attractive ideological aspects of PAR and the increasing empirical support, implementation is fraught with difficulty. Indeed, Wadsworth (1998) and McNicoll (1999) warn that it can be very hard to achieve the ideal conditions for such a participatory process. Ladkin (2004) goes one step further and suggests that

Perfect Action Research cannot exist. At its root is the unpredictability and confounding nature of human beings and our systems. Taking authentic action itself is risky and has unpredictable consequences. The success of the Action Researcher must in some way be measured by his or her willingness to grapple with messiness and imperfections and the impossibility of ever getting it "right" while still holding onto the notion of the possibility of a research method which contributes, as Reason and Bradbury (2001) suggest, to the flourishing of the human spirit. (p. 547)

In an attempt to continue to improve the utilization of PAR within the organizational context, we will now address four important *actions* (and difficulties) for PAR approaches to worksite stress management using illustrative material from four different case studies, and outline lessons learned for each action.

Case 17.1 Occupational strain and efficacy in human service workers (Dollard, Winefield, and Winefield, 2001)

A research reference group (RRG) was established to represent all the possible demographic variations of human service workers in the organization: older and younger workers, all workgroups, union and management, stress injured and non-injured workers, dominant and minority groups, men and women, and key organizational units. Also, a representative of the external funding body was a member of the committee. Recommendations for membership of the reference group were made in joint meetings with a union representative, and a manager from the Occupational Health and Safety Unit. Through regular meetings with the RRG, in-depth interviews with all members of the RRG, and focus groups with Occupational Health and Safety representatives, we attempted to gain participation in all research steps. We built a theoretical model of stress in the organization through interviews with stress-injured workers, interviews with managers, analysis of organizational data (sick leave, policies, and injury statistics) and an organization-wide survey, and developed an intervention strategy that was participatory, involving management, workers, and the research reference group (fully involved in the study process).

Action 1. Development of a participatory organizational structure

A common approach to enable participation in organizational PAR research is to establish a research reference group (RRG) with broad participation from a range of stakeholders.

Lesson 1a The *reference group* is very important in representing multiple stakeholder perspectives and plays a valuable role in the outcome/acceptance/credibility of the project within the organization (Case Study 17.1 and 17.2).

Lesson 1b In organizations, which experience particularly high levels of mistrust, the *process* by which the reference group is selected and its potential impact on the entire research process should not be underestimated. For instance, we found perceptions of fairness can vary even when a full ballot was used (Case Study 17.2). Whilst a full-ballot process was perceived by most as a fair way to establish the RRG, the downside was that it was a very costly (time and money) exercise.

Case 17.2 **Trust in a correctional work setting (Knott, Hietmann, Dollard, and Winefield, in press)**

In the study, levels of trust between management and the workers was an issue. A full ballot used to elect staff members to the committee was seen as the way forward to prevent the workers from perceiving the RRG as a management tool. In an evaluation of the ballot process by those who voted for nominees we asked: "Do you trust the process for selecting staff representatives to the Research Reference Group?" 78% said that they trusted the process by which the selection for participation in the RRG occurred. The main themes elaborated by those who agreed were:

Yes comments
- Open, fair, democratic, everyone given a chance to nominate/ vote, selection by staff gives credibility
- Anonymous, confidential
- Independent, outside body
- Balanced, broad spectrum of staff (age, gender, roles)

No comments
- Voting system – numbered envelopes – not anonymous or confidential
- Manipulation of results to ensure female, etc., representatives
- Undemocratic, manipulative, politically correct
- Favors metropolitan workers
- Nominees ("Don't know them," or "Don't trust some")
- Cynicism ("Can't see anything changing")
- No information on the process

Action 2. Developing local participatory structures

Participation can be at various levels. Case 17.3 demonstrates the implementation of a PAR approach using locally based (i.e. workteam) approaches to burnout prevention training which also evaluated outcomes (Le Blanc and Schaufeli, 2003; Le Blanc, Hox, Schaufeli, Taris, and Peeters, 2007).

Lesson 2 Local participatory structures (problem-solving teams) are important so as to identify the most important stressors. Cases 17.3 and 17.1 highlight the importance of using grounded approaches to uncover the unique dimensions of specific professions and organizations (e.g. violent exposures to clients in Case 17.1). Exploration of local variables

---

Case 17.3 **Take care! Intervention program in Dutch oncology care providers (radiation assistants, physicians and nurses; Le Blanc and Schaufeli, 2003; Le Blanc *et al.*, 2007)**

As team functioning was of crucial importance for people working in this field, a team-based approach was chosen. Before the intervention program started, the team counselors (psychologists employed at a consultancy firm) held extensive intakes with the management (e.g. head nurses, physicians, coordinators, and team leaders) of each of the wards where the program was to be implemented. During these conversations, the protocol of the intervention was clarified, and potential intervention effects ("gains") were discussed. The counselors also inquired after the ward management's reasons to participate in the intervention program, their main objectives, and their "criteria" for successfulness of the intervention. Moreover, they also gathered information on the structure and policies of the larger organization. Finally, the ward management's perception of the working situation, including the main sources of job stress, was discussed. By means of these intakes, the team counselors tried to increase the ward management's motivation for the implementation of organizational change processes.

Next, a "kick-off" meeting for the entire team of each of these wards was organized. During this meeting, the team counselors presented the protocol of the intervention program, whereas the researcher once more explained the study design. Staff were encouraged to ask questions about the intervention protocol and/or the study design. By means of these meetings, we tried to increase staff's commitment to participate and to promote positive anticipatory attitudes toward the intervention program.

The information that was gathered during the intakes and the kick-off meetings was written down in a so-called "take-off" document, which was the first in a series of reports about the progress and results of the program. These reports formed a sort of "log-book," to keep all participants informed during the periods in between the program sessions.

The intervention program itself consisted of six monthly sessions of three hours each, which were supervised by both team counselors. During the sessions, participants formed problem-solving teams that collectively designed, implemented, evaluated, and reformulated plans of action to cope with the most important stressors in their working situation. During the first session, the results of the first questionnaire measurement on participants' work situation and well-being were fed back to the participants (survey feedback method). This was done to help the participants to structure their subjective feelings by providing them with relevant topics for discussion and for their plans to reduce work stress. However, participants were only informed about the ward's scores on (perceptions of) aspects of the working situation, because these formed the starting point for later actions. We deliberately informed neither the team counselors nor the participants about the team's burnout and motivation scores, because we wanted to avoid potential effects of "labeling" (low- versus high-risk profile). The study showed that the intervention program had stabilizing effects on oncology care providers' burnout levels.

provides a better understanding of stress/strain rather than using the key variables specified in the dominant models alone.

Action 3. Feedback to participants and validation of findings

An essential component of PAR is empowerment, which can be achieved through providing feedback to participants and seeking their advice to refine meanings and shoehorn actions. Case 17.4 incorporated focus group feedback to all participants in a longitudinal study of Australian clergy well-being throughout five states/territories of Australia (Cotton, Dollard, and de Jonge, 2003), which also provided the opportunity to assess the face validity of the findings, and shows its importance for ownership of information, validation of findings, grounding of results, and development of actions.

Lesson 3 We believe that the PAR process enabled an unprecedented level of commitment and openness in an organization hitherto shrouded in secrecy and resistant to change (Case 17.4). By engaging different stakeholders (leadership, the steering committee, experts in the field and officers through the feedback/focus groups) of the system throughout the research process *greater ownership* of the issues was engendered. It was clear that by including stakeholders in the collaborative partnership, the most productive process outcomes were achieved (high response rates and high levels of participation at focus groups). Mikkelsen and Gunderson (2003: 108) also highlight the importance of *process* and participation of key stakeholders as a key success factor in a number of PAR studies they have undertaken: "when a proper and meaningful dialogue existed between the supervisors, employees, and

Case 17.4 **The Salvation Army officers' well-being feedback/ focus group sessions (Cotton, Dollard, and de Jonge, 2003)**

It was essential to the success of the study that officers were well informed of the Time 1 findings. An effective medium to communicate results to members of an organization is through feedback/focus group sessions (Griffiths, 1999). The feedback/focus groups included each of the five divisions in the Southern Territory. Given the uniqueness of some divisions, more than one focus group was conducted. In total, eleven focus groups were run between January and June (2002), six months after the completion of the Time 1 questionnaire. Approximately 59% (327) of active officers participated in a feedback/focus group.

Instead of the standard size (10–12 people) and procedure of a traditional focus group, the structure of the groups was tailored to the organizational need in consultation with the steering committee and the individual divisional management. Although each session was uniquely different, the procedure was standardized as much as practically possible. The aims of the half-day feedback/focus groups were to provide feedback and to validate findings "How well do the results fit with their experience as an officer?" as well as to elicit recommendations for intervention from the participants themselves.

The feedback/focus groups conducted throughout the territory were very effective in achieving the goals they set out to achieve. The benefits of running such sessions throughout the territory far exceeded the researchers' expectations. It was clear from the researchers' observations and later officer feedback (through the Time 2 questionnaire) that the majority (85%) of officers found the session to be very helpful. Although this was not the first organizational study to be conducted, many officers commented that it had been the first time that they had ever received any feedback about the results. Although an air of skepticism was clearly present in each focus group, officers were in general positive about the study and hoped that significant changes toward the improvement of officer well-being would be achieved: "We believe for once that The Salvation Army is looking at the personal needs of officers which have been over-looked for many years. Thanks for what is happening at the present time, looking forward to the future reports and findings" (officer comment).

The presentation of the key findings enabled officers to actively interpret the results from their own experience. It was clear that the majority (64%) of officers found the results to be highly accurate in

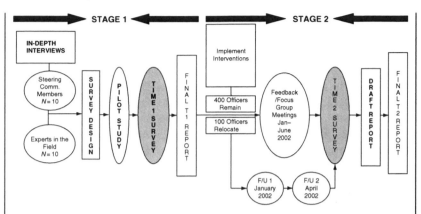

Figure 17.1 Overview of the study (stage one and stage two)
Note: T1 – Time 1; F/U – Follow-up; T2 – Time 2

reflecting their experience of officership. A further 33% felt that the results were accurate in most cases. From a researcher's point of view, such confirming results provided a level of confidence in the accuracy of the findings and the opportunity for clarification.

The concerns and questions raised from officers throughout the discussion provided the research team and steering committee members with a more complete picture regarding the findings, and valuable information to fine-tune the conclusions drawn from data. It also provided officers with an opportunity to work with the research team and steering committee in proposing recommendations, and enabled questionnaire refinement for the Time 2 study. The recommendations put forward by officers as a whole provided a wealth of practical suggestions for improving officer well-being.

instructor, the improvement methodology and improvement activities that were proposed were followed up and acted upon ... the results were positive."

Action 4. Continuity and evaluation

Despite the best intentions, it is very difficult to implement a full-phase PAR project. Often, organizations seek arms-length expert research, there are time and resource limitations, and the cycle embraces only steps one to four (see previous section on "The process"). Moreover, problems with respect to the sustainability of a project in terms of continuity of the process as well as evaluation may emerge after the (academic) researchers have left.

Lesson 4a Local knowledge is important in planning the interventions and research methodology: to understand the context, such as organizational history, as well as to show sensitivity to the organizational calendar. In Case 17.4 clear evaluation of the impact of relocation and associated support interventions was hampered by the coincidence of the highly demanding Red Shield Appeal (an annual nationwide appeal to meet the budget needs for the Salvation Army's community service programs).

Lesson 4b Stakeholder committee members often see value in continuing within the organization as a committee (e.g. Occupational Health and Safety committee with a mandate to monitor and continuously improve the social and emotional well-being of organizational members). As recently outlined by Halbesleben, Osburn, and Mumford (2006: 23) "they serve as change agents in implementing [and evaluating] the recommendations derived from the project ... [the committee essentially adopts] the pattern of action and reflection that was started with the project for the continued improvement of the [organization] using the collaborative principles that guided the original project." Given the possibility of management turnover and organizational change, *engagement of key stakeholders in a decision-making committee* provides a sense of consistency and strength/ownership (the development of a culture) within the organization that is hard to simply dismiss with the arrival of new management, or when the researchers withdraw. Further, their role is essential to the ongoing implementation and evaluation of interventions.

Lesson 5 One of the common threads of the case studies is the importance of *providing feedback* to both the organizational management and its workers. Providing feedback to participants is a challenge for modern researchers. People are tired of filling out endless questionnaires, never really knowing why and rarely receiving feedback. Researchers could inform participants via posting readable summaries of the research on the World Wide Web so that participants can have access to the results. If research is conducted in organizations, then focus groups, newsletters, and other media could provide a means of fairly distributing information obtained in the research. The case studies have illustrated some creative and effective ways of ensuring that workers are well informed as well as given the opportunity to comment/add to the recommendations, have an active role, and be given a voice.

Lesson 6 The strength of all of these studies was the utilization of the employee resource in understanding and managing organizational problems. As highlighted by Pasmore and Friedlander (1982), these studies have (with the assistance of management and researchers) enabled the true potential of employees to be realized. After all, who best to ask about the stressors of the work environment than the workers (those at the coalface) themselves?

Transdomain potential for PAR

All PAR stress interventions that we have described in our case studies have been organizationally based, yet they could also be based in other domains, for example in the community. As discussed earlier, the issue of worker stress has been linked to issues of power and control in the workplace, to socio-economic status and to the imperatives of a flexible labor market (the oppressive labor market leading to precarious employment). As such, the issue of stress is as much a public health issue as a work specific issue.

Workplace issues, especially those linked to mental and emotional ill health, cannot be explored freely in many worksites. Management is often resistant to intervention research or to utilization of results and can be obstructive in all of these areas. Some argue "corporations have no capacity for empathy with those damaged in the drive to maximize profits" (Albee and Fryer, 2003: 74). Community-based research is another way to develop knowledge about work issues not easily developed within an organization context. There are some good examples in the literature of participatory community approaches to health issues that appear to emanate from industry (e.g. Community Action Against Asthma [in children] project in Detroit; Keeler *et al.*, 2002). Further, some proponents of PAR call upon the power of researchers to "initiate projects and promote participant involvement" (Fenge, 2002; Healy, 2001) and this seems especially relevant when community health is affected by stressful experiences at work. For example, Smith, Roman, Dollard, Winefield, and Siegrist (2005) have recently shown that anger in a community sample was linked to effort–reward imbalance at work, and was in turn linked to cardiovascular risk.

Community-based research has potentially powerful outcomes when communities/families become informed or recognize that their members experience poor health or work–life imbalance because of stressful work conditions. Community members can become empowered through new information, and can ask new questions and/or stimulate research and/or utilize information in action (e.g. use local media to name risky industries). Utilization of the media in itself is interesting and of course not balanced. Earlier research of Australian newsprint media representations of work stress showed that work stress was represented as a public sector phenomenon of epidemic proportions overshadowing the problem in the private sector (Lewig and Dollard, 2001; Macklin, Smith, and Dollard, 2006). Community research and action could highlight issues difficult to explore in organizational research. Indeed the apparent underrepresentation of research in private sector organizations could be redressed in this way. Albee and Fryer (2003: 74) argue for the development of a critical public health psychology: "if decent mental health for all is to be achieved, perhaps it is now time to bring together a coalition of national and international groups to expose the role of pathogenic corporations and religions in the causation of mental and emotional ill-health, and to develop prevention strategies and recommendations for action." From this perspective a reduction in stressful work structures and practices could also be achieved through community participation and action on the issue.

Conclusion

In conclusion, this chapter has argued for participatory approaches to work stress intervention (research). Over the past decades, participatory research methodologies that use multiple theories and methods, and intend to develop new local theory, new understandings, and new opportunities involving those most aggrieved, as well as management, have increasingly emerged. Indeed, theoretical pluralism, multi-methods and participative approaches are increasingly advocated in organizational stress research (Theorell, 1998). This (r)evolution has emerged as a result of difficulties in grand theory testing, identified (contextual-local) organizational problems, and "the researched" taking a stand, as well as researcher values about empowering workers to gain knowledge of their own situation. Limitations in the scientific method have led to more active, participatory designs utilizing multiple testing points, with continuous feedback from participants, that are problem driven rather than merely theoretically driven. PAR as a philosophy and method embodies core ingredients of successful stress management interventions, and therefore holds promise for the reduction of stress hazards in contemporary working life. It also has the added potential of contributing to organizational sustainability, as organizations learn to continuously problem solve as new issues emerge.

However, there still remain some theoretical and practical issues to be solved. As regards future research, more systematic investigation of the merits and issues in the PAR *process* is needed to gain (theoretical) insight into *how* beneficial outcomes are brought about. Further, an interesting research angle would be to interview the researchers themselves, as the stories and insights that unfold will likely not be as they appear in the scientific media. Indeed, the qualities of the researchers themselves are quintessential to the process and need to be made explicit, as "the nature of action research requires certain characteristics of action researchers that are not always discussed in the literature" (Greenwood, 1994: 84).

From a practical point of view, in implementing PAR approaches, touchy issues such as who will influence the process, and the potential undue influence of funders (David, 2002), have to be dealt with. Work psychologists could turn their skills to finding practical solutions to these difficulties, as well as to the (further) development of sustainable learning methodologies, such as participatory learning and action (PLA) techniques (see Mayoux, 2003).

Despite these issues, we are of the opinion that the results of empirical studies as well as the case studies that were presented and discussed in this chapter convincingly demonstrate the surplus value of PAR interventions to reduce (problems related to) work stress as compared to more "traditional" approaches.

Acknowledgements

This research is supported by an Australian Research Council International Linkage Grant: "The Australian–Netherlands Project on Work and Stress Research."

Case 17.2 supported by an ARC SPIRT Grant: "The role of trust in the correctional work environment and implications for intervention"; Case 17.3 supported by a grant of the Dutch Cancer Society / Koningin Wilhelmina Fonds: "Burnout in cancer care: incidence, etiology, and intervention"; Case 17.4 supported by an ARC Linkage Grant: "Flashpoint in the third sector: a longitudinal study of clergy care and well-being in Salvation Army."

Thanks to Phil Heffernan for ideas on the etic/emic aspects of cross-cultural research.

References

Aimers, J. (1999). Using participatory action research in a local government setting. In I. Hughes (ed.), *Action research electronic reader* (online). The

University of Sydney. Retrieved March 2004 from www.scu.edu.au/schools/gcm/ar/arr/arow/aimers.html.

Albee, G. W. and Fryer, D. M. (2003). Praxis: towards a public health psychology. *Journal of Community and Applied Social Psychology* 13: 71–5.

Argyris, C. (1967). On the future of laboratory education. *Journal of Applied Behavioral Science* 3: 153–83.

——— (1983). Action science and intervention. *Journal of Applied Behavioral Science* 19: 115–40.

Argyris, C. and Schon, D. (1974). *Theory in practice: increasing professional effectiveness.* San Francisco: Jossey-Bass.

Baker, D. B. (1985). The study of stress at work. *Annual Review of Public Health* 6: 367–81.

Balcazar, F. E., Keys, C. B., Kaplan, D. L., and Suarez-Balcazar, Y. (in press). Participatory Action Research and people with disabilities: principles and challenges. *Condition: Journal of Rehabilitation.*

Calnan, M., Wainwright, D., and Almond, S. (2000). Job strain, effort–reward imbalance and mental distress: a study of occupations in general medical practice. *Work and Stress* 14: 297–311.

Cotton, S. J., Dollard, M. F., and de Jonge, J. (2003). *The Salvation Army Officer Well-Being Study: final report Time 2.* Work and Stress Research Group, Adelaide, Salvation Army Southern Territory (Internal Report).

Cox, T. (1993). *Stress research and stress management: putting theory to work.* Sudbury: HSE Books.

Cox, T. and Cox, S. (1993). *Psychosocial and organizational hazards at work: control and monitoring.* Copenhagen: WHO Regional Office.

Cox, T. and Griffiths, A. (1996). The assessment of psychosocial hazards at work. In M. J. Schabracq, J. A. M. Winnubst, and C. Cooper (eds.), *Handbook of work health psychology* (pp. 127–43). Chichester: Wiley.

Cox, T., Griffiths, A., and Rial-Gonzalez, E. (2000). *Research on work-related stress.* European Agency for Safety and Health at Work. http://agency.osha.eu.int/publications/reports/stress/full.php3.

David, M. (2002). Problems of participation: the limits of action research. *International Journal of Social Research Methodology* 1: 11–17.

de Jonge, J., Bosma, H., Peter, R., and Siegrist, J. (2000). Job strain, effort–reward imbalance and employee well-being: a large scale cross-sectional study. *Social Science and Medicine* 50: 1317–27.

de Jonge, J. and Dormann, C. (2003). The DISC model: demand-induced strain compensation mechanisms in job stress. In M. F. Dollard, A. H. Winefield, and H. R. Winefield (eds.), *Occupational stress in the service professions* (pp. 43–75). London: Taylor and Francis.

de Jonge, J., Mulder, M. J. G. P., and Nijhuis, F. J. N. (1999). The incorporation of different demand concepts in the Job Demand–Control model: effects on health care professionals. *Social Science and Medicine* 48: 1149–60.

de Lange, A., Taris, T. W., Kompier, M. A. J., Houtman, I. L. D., and Bongers, P. M. (2003). The very best of the millennium: longitudinal research and the Demand–Control–(Support) model. *Journal of Occupational Health Psychology* 8: 282–305.

Dick, B. (1993). *You want to do an action research thesis? How to conduct and report action research.* Old Chapel Hill. Retrieved 19 December 2003 from www.scu.edu.au/schools/gcm/ar/arthesis.html.

Dollard, M. F. (2003). Introduction: costs, theoretical approaches, research designs. In M. F. Dollard, A. H. Winefield, and H. R. Winefield (eds.), *Occupational stress in the service professions* (pp. 1–42). London: Taylor and Francis.

Dollard, M. F., Heffernan, P., Winefield, A. H., and Winefield, H. R. (1997). Conducive production: how to produce a PAR worksite proposal. *New Solutions: A Journal of Environmental and Occupational Health Policy* 7: 58–70.

Dollard, M. F. and Metzer, J. C. (1999). Psychological research, practice and production: the occupational stress problem. *International Journal of Stress Management* 6: 241–54.

Dollard, M. F., Winefield, H. R., and Winefield, A. H. (2001). *Occupational strain and efficacy in human service workers.* Dordrecht: Kluwer Academic.

Elden, M. (1986). Sociotechnical systems ideas as public policy in Norway: empowering participation through worker-managed change. *Journal of Applied Behavioral Science* 22: 239–55.

European Foundation for the Improvement of Living and Working Conditions (EFILWC). (2005). *Work-related stress.* Dublin: European Foundation for the Improvement of Living and Working Conditions (available in electronic format only).

Fals-Borda, O. and Rahman, M. (eds.) (1991). *Action and knowledge: breaking the monopoly with participatory action research.* New York: Intermediate Technology/Apex.

Fenge, L. (2002). Practicing partnership-participative enquiry with older people. *Social Work Education* 21: 171–81.

Graves, W. (1991). *Participatory action research.* Address to the National Association of Research and Training Centers. Washington, DC, May.

Greenwood, J. (1994). Action research and action researchers: some introductory considerations. *Contemporary Nursing* 3: 84–92.

Griffiths, A. (1999). Organisational interventions. Facing the limits of the natural science paradigm. *Scandinavian Journal on Work Environment and Health* 25: 589–96.

Griffiths, Q., Randall, R., Santos, A., and Cox, T. (2003). Senior nurses: interventions to reduce work stress. In M. F. Dollard, A. H. Winefield, and H. R. Winefield (eds.), *Occupational stress in the service professions* (pp. 169–91). London: Taylor and Francis.

Gronhaug, K. and Olson, O. (1999). Action research and knowledge creation: merits and challenges. *Qualitative Market Research: An International Journal* 2: 6–14.

Halbesleben, J. R. B., Osburn, H. K., and Mumford, M. D. (2006). Action research as a burnout intervention: reducing burnout in the Federal Fire Service. *Journal of Applied Behavioral Science* 42: 244–66.

Healy, K. (2001). Participatory action research and social work: a critical appraisal. *International Social Work* 44: 93–105.

Heaney, C. A., Price, R. H., and Rafferty, J. (1995). Increasing coping resources at work: a field experiment to increase social support, improve work team functioning, and enhance employee mental health. *Journal of Organizational Behavior* 16: 335–53.

Hughes, J. (2003). Commentary: participatory action research leads to sustainable school and community improvement. *School Psychology Review* 32: 38–43.

Imada, A. S. (1991). The rationale and tools of participatory ergonomics. In K. Noro and A. S. Imada (eds.), *Participatory ergonomics* (pp. 30–51). London: Taylor & Francis.

Israel, B. A., Baker, E. A., Goldenhar, L. M., Heany, C. A., and Schurman, S. J. (1996).Occupational stress, safety, and health: conceptual framework and principles for effective prevention interventions. *Journal of Occupational Health Psychology* 1: 261–86.

Israel, B. A., Schurman, S. J., and House, J. S. (1989). Action research on occupational stress: involving workers as researchers. *International Journal of Health Services* 19: 135–55.

Israel, B. A., Schurman, S. J., and Hugentobler, M. K. (1992). Conducting action research: relationships between organization members and researchers. *Journal of Applied Behavioral Science* 28: 75–101.

Ivancevich, J. M., Matteson, M. T., Freedman, S. M., and Phillips, J. S. (1990). Worksite stress management interventions. *American Psychologist* 45: 252–61.

Janssen, P. P. M., Nijhuis, F. J. N., Lourijsen, E. C. M. P., and Schaufeli, W. B. (1996). *Healthy work; less absenteeism! A manual for work-site health promotion.* Amsterdam: NIA.

Karasek, R. A. (1979). Job demands, job decision latitude, and mental strain: implications for job redesign. *Administrative Science Quarterly* 24: 285–308.

(1992). Stress prevention through work reorganization: a summary of 19 international case studies. In ILO, *Conditions of work digest on preventing stress at work* 11: 23–41.

(1994). Stress at work: an integrative approach. *New Solutions* 4: 28–35.

Keeler, G. J., Dvonch, J. T., Yip, F. Y., Parker, E. A., Israel, B. A., Marsik, F. J., Morishita, M., Barres, J. A., Robins, T. G., Brakefield-Caldwell, W., and Sam, M. (2002). Assessment of personal and community-level exposures to particulate matter among children with asthma in Detroit, Michigan, as part of Community Action Against Asthma (CAAA). *Environmental Health Perspective Supplements* 110: 173–91.

Kemmis, S. and McTaggart, R. (eds.) (1988). *The action research plannet* (3rd edn). Victoria: Deakin University.

Knott, V., Hietmann, M., Dollard, M. F., and Winefield, A. H. (in press). Trust in the correctional work environment. *International Journal of Forensic Psychology*.

Kompier, M. and Cooper, C. (1999). *Preventing stress, improving productivity*. London: Routledge.

Kronenburg, J. B. M. (1986). *Empowerment of the poor: a comparative analysis of two development endeavours in Kenya.* Amsterdam: Koninklijk Instituut voor de Tropen.

Ladkin, D. (2004). Action research. In C. F. Seale, G. Gobo, J. F. Gubrium, and D. Silverman (eds.), *Research practice* (pp. 563–78). London: Sage.

Landsbergis, P. A. (2003). The changing organisation of work and the safety and health of working people: a commentary. *Journal of Occupational Environmental Medicine* 45: 61–72.

Landsbergis, P. A., Schurman, S. J., Israel, B. A., Schnall, P. L., Hugentobler, M. K., Cahill. J., and Baker, D. (1993). Job stress and heart disease. *New Solutions* 3: 42–58.

Landsbergis, P. A. and Vivona-Vaughan, E. (1995). Evaluation of an occupational stress intervention in a public sector agency. *Journal of Organizational Behavior* 16: 29–48.

Laungani, P. (1996). Cross-cultural investigation of stress: conceptual and methodological consideration. *International Journal of Stress Management* 3: 25–35.

Le Blanc, P. M., de Jonge, J., and Schaufeli, W. B. (in press). Job stress and occupational health. In N. Chmiel (ed.), *Introduction to work and organizational psychology* (2nd edn). Oxford: Blackwell.

Le Blanc, P. M., Hox, J. J., Schaufeli, W. B., Taris, T. W., and Peeters, M. C. W. (2007). Take care! A team based burnout intervention program for oncology care providers. *Journal of Applied Psychology* 72: 213–27.

Le Blanc, P. and Schaufeli, W. B. (2003). Burnout among oncology care providers: radiation assistants, physicians and nurses. In M. F. Dollard, A. H. Winefield, and H. R. Winefield (eds.), *Occupational stress in the service professions* (pp. 143–69). London: Taylor & Francis.

Lee, T. W. (1999). *Using qualitative methods in organizational research*. Thousand Oaks, CA: Sage.

Levi, L. (1990). Occupational stress: spice of life or kiss of death? *American Psychologist* 45: 1142–5.

Lewig, K. A. and Dollard, M. F. (2001). Social construction of work stress: Australian news-print media portrayal of work stress 1997–98. *Work and Stress* 15: 179–90.

Lewin, K. and Grabbe, P. (1945). Conduct, knowledge and acceptance of new values. *Journal of Social Issues* 1: 53–64.

Macklin, D., Smith, L., and Dollard, M. F. (2006). Public and private sector work stress: workers compensation, levels of distress and the demand–control–support model. *Australian Journal of Psychology* 58: 130–43.

Martin, M. (1996). Issues of power in the participatory research process. In K. De Koning and M. Martin (eds.), *Participatory research in health: issues and experiences* (pp. 82–93). London: Zed Books.

Mayoux, L. (2003). *Sustainable learning for women's empowerment: ways forward for micro-finance*. New Dehli: Samskriti.

McNicoll, P. (1999). Issues in teaching participatory action research. *Journal of Social Work Education* 35: 51–63.

Mikkelsen, A. and Gunderson, M. (2003). The effect of a participatory organizational intervention on work environment, job stress, and subjective health complaints. *International Journal of Stress Management* 10: 91–110.

Mikkelsen, A., Saksvik, P. Ø., and Landsbergis, P. (2000). The impact of a participatory organizational intervention on job stress in community health institutions. *Work and Stress* 14: 156–70.

Munz, D. C., Kohler, J. M., and Greenberg, C. I. (2001). Effectiveness of a comprehensive worksite stress management program: combining organizational and individual interventions. *International Journal of Stress Management* 8: 49–62.

Murphy, L. R., Hurrell, J. J., and Quick, J. C. (1992). Work and well-being: where do we go from here? In J. C. Quick, L. R. Murphy, and J. J. Hurrell Jr. (eds.), *Stress and well-being at work: assessment and interventions for occupational mental health* (pp. 331–47). Washington, DC: American Psychological Association.

Narayanan, L., Menon, S., and Spector, P. (1999). A cross-cultural comparison of job stressors and reactions among employees holding comparable jobs in two countries. *International Journal of Stress Management* 6: 197–212.

Park, P. (1993). What is participatory research? A theoretical and methodological perspective. In P. Park, M. Bryden-Miller, B. Hall, and T. Jackson (eds.), *Voices of change: participatory research in the United States and Canada* (pp. 1–19). Westport, CT: Bergin and Garvey.

Parkes, K. R. and Sparkes, T. J. (1998). *Organisational interventions to reduce work stress. Are they effective? A review of the literature.* Oxford: Department of Experimental Psychology.

Pasmore, W. and Friedlander, F. (1982). An action-research program for increasing employee participation in problem solving. *Administrative Science Quarterly* 27: 343–62.

Peterson, C. L. (1999). *Stress at work: a sociological perspective.* New York: Baywood.

Rapaport, R. (1970). Three dilemmas in action research. *Human Relations* 23: 499–513.

Reason, P. and Bradbury, H. (2001). Action Research looking forward: an interleaving of special issues and open issues. *Action Research* 3: 237–8.

Rosecrance, J. C. and Cook, T. M. (2000). The use of participatory action research and ergonomics in the prevention of work-related musculoskeletal disorders in the newspaper industry. *Applied Occupational and Environmental Health* 15: 255–62.

Sauter, S. L., Murphy, L. R., and Hurrell, J. J., Jr. (1990). Prevention of work-related psychological disorders. *American Psychologist* 45: 1146–58.

Schensul, J. J. (1994). *The development and maintenance of community research partnerships.* Occasional Paper in Applied Research Methods. Retrieved 23 February 2004 from www.mapcruzin.com/community-research/schensul1.htm.

Schurman, S. J. (1996). Making the "New American Workplace" safe and healthy: a joint labor–management–researcher approach. *American Journal of Industrial Medicine* 29: 373–7.

Selener, D. (1997). *Participatory action research and social change.* Ithaca, NY: Cornell Participatory Action Research Network, Cornell University.

Siegrist, J. (1996). Adverse health effects of high-effort/low-reward conditions. *Journal of Occupational Health Psychology* 1: 27–41.

Smith, L. A., Roman, A., Dollard. M. F., Winefield, A. H., and Siegrist, J. (2005). Effort reward imbalance at work: the effects of work stress on anger and cardiovascular disease symptoms in a community sample. *Stress and Health* 21: 113–28.

Spector, P. E., Cooper, C. L., and Aguilar-Vafaie, M. E. (2002). A comparative study of perceived job stressor sources and job strain in American and Iranian managers. *Applied Psychology: An International Review* 51: 446–57.

Spector, P. E., Cooper, C. L., Poelmans, S., Allen, T. D., *et al.* (2004). A cross-national comparative study of work–family stressors, working hours, and well being: China and Latin-America versus the Anglo world. *Personnel Psychology* 57: 119–42.

Susman, G. I. and Evered, R. D. (1978). An assessment of the scientific merit of action research. *Administrative Science Quarterly* 23: 582–603.

Swantz, M. (1996). A personal position paper on participatory research: personal quest for living knowledge. *Qualitative Inquiry* 2: 120–37.

Theorell, T. (1998). Job characteristics in theoretical and practical health context. In C. Cooper (ed.), *Theories of organizational stress* (pp. 205–19). Oxford: Oxford University Press.

Tsutsumi, A. and Kawakami, N. (2004). A review of empirical studies on the model of effort–reward imbalance at work: reducing occupational stress by implementing a new theory. *Social Science and Medicine* 59: 2335–59.

Van Gorp, K. and Schaufeli, W. B. (1996). *Een gezonde geest in een gezond lichaam* [A healthy mind in a healthy organization]. The Hague: VUGA.

van Vegchel, N., de Jonge, J., Bosma, H., and Schaufeli, W. (2005). Reviewing the effort–reward imbalance model: drawing up the balance of 45 empirical studies. *Social Science and Medicine* 60: 1117–31.

Victorian WorkCover Authority (2006). 2004–05 Stress Prevention Study in the Victorian Budget sector, Melbourne.

Wadsworth, Y. (1998). *What is participatory action research?* Action Research: International, Paper 2. Available www.scu.edu.au/schools/sawd/ari/ari-wadsworth.html.

Whyte, W. F. (1989). Advancing scientific knowledge through participatory action research. *Sociological Forum* 4: 367–85.

(1991). *Participatory action research*. Newbury Park, CA: Sage.

Wilmar B. Schaufeli and Marisa Salanova

This chapter introduces a recently emerged psychological concept – work engagement – and seeks to apply this notion to the management of human resources in organizations. Our point of departure is that in order to prosper and survive in today's continuously changing environment, rather than merely "healthy" employees, organizations need engaged employees. What we exactly mean by work engagement and how this term is used throughout the literature is explained next. Because we strongly feel that recommendations for using HRM strategies to increase levels of employee engagement should be based on sound empirical research, we present an overview thereof. More specifically, we focus on the relationship of work engagement with related concepts and on the antecedents and consequences of work engagement. The assessment of work engagement is addressed in a separate section. In addition, we discuss how employees' work engagement may be optimized by using HRM strategies. The chapter closes with some conclusions about work engagement research and about the usefulness of work engagement in the context of HRM. Our aim is to demonstrate the viability of the concept of work engagement for human resources practices in organizations.

The need for engaged workers in modern organizations

Table 18.1 illustrates what kinds of changes force today's organizations to rely more and more on the psychological knowledge and experience of their employees.

Essentially, the changes summarized in Table 18.1 boil down to a "psychologization" of organizations. Instead of traditional organizational structures (i.e. control mechanism, chain of command) and a strong emphasis on economic principles (i.e. cost reduction, efficiency, cash flow), the focus in modern organizations is on the management of human capital. Currently, organizations expect their employees to be proactive and show initiative, collaborate smoothly with others in teams, take responsibility for their own professional development, and

Table 18.1 *Changes in modern organizations*

From	To
Cost reduction	Customer satisfaction
Efficiency	Effectiveness
Employee satisfaction	Employee motivation
Control	Empowerment
Short-term focus on cash flow	Long-term focus on vision, planning, and growth
Vertical structure (chain of command)	Horizontal networks (collaboration in interdependent chains)
Dependence on company (e.g. company training)	Personal responsibility (e.g. employability)

be committed to high-quality performance. This means that – in the words of Dave Ulrich (1997: 125), a leading HRM expert – "Employee contribution becomes a critical business issue because in trying to produce more output with less employee input, companies have no choice but to try to engage not only the body but the mind and soul of every employee." Clearly, producing more output with less employee input cannot be achieved with a workforce that is "healthy" in the traditional sense, that is, with employees who are merely symptom free. Instead of just "doing one's job," employees are expected "to go the extra mile." Thus, employees are needed who feel energetic and dedicated, and who are absorbed by their work. In other words, organizations need engaged workers. Besides, as Wright (2003) has argued, instead of just considering employees as a means to the desired end of organizational productivity, the pursuit of employee happiness, health, and engagement creates valuable goals and ends in themselves. But what exactly is work engagement, and how can it be conceptualized?

Work engagement: an emerging concept

We defined work engagement as "a positive, fulfilling, work-related state of mind that is characterized by vigor, dedication, and absorption" (Schaufeli, Salanova, González-Romá, and Bakker, 2002b: 74). Rather than a momentary and specific state, engagement refers to a more persistent and pervasive affective-cognitive state that is not focused on any particular object, event, individual, or behavior. *Vigor* is characterized by high levels of energy and mental resilience while working, the willingness to invest effort in one's work, and persistence even in the face of difficulties. *Dedication* refers to being strongly involved in one's work, and experiencing a sense of significance, enthusiasm, inspiration, pride, and challenge. *Absorption* is characterized by being fully concentrated and happily engrossed in one's work, whereby time passes quickly and one has difficulties with detaching oneself from work. Being fully absorbed in one's work comes close to what has been called "flow," a state of optimal experience that is characterized by focused attention, clear mind, mind and body unison, effortless concentration, complete control, loss of self-consciousness, distortion of time, and intrinsic enjoyment (Csikszentmihalyi, 1990). However, typically, flow is a more complex concept that includes many aspects and refers to rather particular, short-term "peak" experiences instead of a more pervasive and persistent state of mind, as is the case with engagement. The three dimensions of engagement can be assessed using the Utrecht Work Engagement Scale (UWES), which is discussed below.

Our conceptualization of engagement closely matches the one described by May, Gilson, and Harter (2004), who introduced a similar three-dimensional concept of engagement. Although they use slightly different labels, their operationalization is strikingly similar to our UWES. More specifically, May *et al.* (2004) distinguish between a physical component (e.g. "I exert a lot of energy performing my job"), an emotional component (e.g. "I really put my heart into my job"), and a cognitive component (e.g. "Performing my job is so absorbing that I forget about everything else"). It is easy to see that these dimensions correspond with vigor, dedication, and absorption, respectively. Shirom (2003) introduced a conceptualization of vigor that is defined as the employees' physical strength, emotional energy, and cognitive liveliness. The three-dimensional Shirom-Malemed Vigor Measure (SMVM) is used to assess the construct, whereby the physical fatigue scale (e.g. "I feel energetic," "I feel vigorous") is quite similar to the physical component of May *et al.* (2004) and to the vigor scale of the UWES, which is discussed in greater detail below. Recently, Peterson, Park, and Seligman (2005) considered engagement – which in their conceptualization is similar to absorption as assessed with the UWES (e.g. "I am always very absorbed in what I do") – together with meaning and pleasure as one of the basic orientations to happiness. Indeed, they showed that those who were most happy and satisfied with their lives scored high on each of these three orientations, with engagement being the strongest predictor. Finally, Harter, Schmidt, and Hayes (2002: 269) describe engaged employees in terms of cognitive vigilance and emotional connectedness; according to them engaged workers "know what is expected of them, have what they need to do their work, have opportunities to feel an impact and fulfillment in their work, perceive that they are part of something significant with co-workers they trust, and have chances to improve and develop." Harter *et al.*'s (2002) concept of engagement is assessed with a twelve-item questionnaire. It is concluded that work engagement, as conceptualized in this chapter, closely resembles the way in which other authors have defined and operationalized the construct, although Harter *et al.* (2002) use a somewhat broader concept, while Shirom (2003) and Peterson *et al.* (2005) each focus on particular aspects: i.e. vigor and absorption, respectively.

How is work engagement experienced by employees? Structured qualitative interviews with a heterogeneous group of Dutch employees who scored high on the UWES showed that engaged employees were active agents, who took initiative at work, and generated their own positive feedback loops (Schaufeli, Taris, Le Blanc, Peeters, Bakker, and de Jonge, 2001). For instance, engaged employees kept looking for new challenges, and when they no longer felt challenged, they took action in order to enforce the desired changes. Eventually, they even changed their jobs. Also, because of their involvement, they were committed to performing on a high-quality level, which usually generated positive feedback from their supervisors (e.g. praise, promotion, salary raise, fringe benefits) as well as from their customers (e.g. appreciation, gratitude, satisfaction). Furthermore, the values of engaged employees seemed to match quite well with those of the organization they work for, and they also seemed to be engaged in other activities outside their work. Finally, the interviewed engaged employees did not seem to be addicted to their work, as they enjoyed other things outside work and, unlike workaholics, they did not work hard because of a strong and irresistible inner drive, but because of the fun of it. As we will see below, many of these qualitative results are confirmed by quantitative studies, using a psychometrically validated questionnaire to assess work engagement.

A brief overview of research findings

In this section, a summary is presented of the most important research findings on engagement that have been obtained so far. Most studies used the UWES, and only occasionally were other measures of work engagement employed. We start by examining the relationship of engagement to related concepts such as burnout, personality, workaholism, job involvement, and organizational commitment, and then we consider the antecedents and consequences of work engagement.

Work engagement and related concepts

Because work engagement is supposed to be the positive antithesis of burnout (Maslach, Schaufeli, and Leiter, 2001), negative correlations are expected between both constructs. Indeed, the three aspects of burnout – exhaustion, cynicism, and reduced professional efficacy, as measured with the Maslach Burnout Inventory (MBI; Maslach, Jackson, and Leiter, 1996) – have been found to be negatively related to the three aspects of work engagement – vigor, dedication, and absorption (Demerouti, Bakker, Janssen, and Schaufeli, 2001; De Vries, Peters, and Hoogstraten, 2004; Durán, Extremera, and Rey, 2004; Llorens, Salanova, Bakker, and Schaufeli, in press; Montgomery, Peeters, Schaufeli, and den Ouden, 2003; Salanova, Grau, Cifre, and Llorens, 2000; Salanova, Schaufeli, Llorens, Peiró, and Grau, 2000; Schaufeli and Bakker, 2003, 2004a, 2004b; Schaufeli, Salanova, González-Romá, and Bakker, 2002b; Schaufeli, Martínez, Marques Pinto, Salanova, and Bakker, 2002b; Xanthopoulou, Bakker, Kantas, and Demerouti, in press). However, the pattern of relationships slightly differs from what was expected; instead of positively relating to the MBI burnout factor, lack of professional efficacy related negatively to the UWES engagement factor. A possible explanation for the unexpected findings obtained by the just mentioned studies may be that lack of professional efficacy was measured with items that were positively formulated and then subsequently reversed in order to constitute a "negative" score that was supposed to be indicative of a *lack* of professional efficacy (Bresó, Salanova, and Schaufeli, 2007). Consistent with our theoretical expectations, vigor and exhaustion – as well as dedication and cynicism – appear to be each other's direct opposites. Using a non-parametric scaling technique, González-Romá, Schaufeli, Bakker, and Lloret (2006) showed that two sets of items, exhaustion–vigor and cynicism–dedication, were scalable on two distinct underlying bipolar dimensions, labeled energy and identification, respectively. This indicates that burnout is characterized by low levels of energy and identification, whereas engagement is characterized by high levels of energy and identification.

One of the most popular views on personality assumes that people differ systematically on two basic personality factors: neuroticism and extraversion (Costa and McCrae, 1980). The former refers to the general tendency to experience distressing emotions such as fear, depression, and frustration, whereas the latter refers to the disposition toward cheerfulness, sociability, and assertiveness. Using discriminant analysis, engaged and burned-out employees could be distinguished from their non-engaged and non-burned-out counterparts based on their personality profiles (Langelaan, Bakker, Van Doornen, and Schaufeli, 2006). Burned-out employees were characterized by high levels of neuroticism, whereas engaged employees were characterized by low levels of neuroticism in combination with high levels of extraversion. In addition, a high level of mobility (i.e. the ability to respond adequately to changes in stimulus conditions, adapt quickly to new surroundings, and switch easily between activities) was typical for engaged employees but not for burned-out employees. Thus, it appeared that the personality profile of engaged and burned-out employees differed while neuroticism showed an opposite pattern: those who were engaged were low in neuroticism, whereas those who felt burned-out where high in neuroticism.

Work addiction or workaholism is the irresistible inner drive to work very hard; that is, workaholics work excessively and compulsively (Schaufeli, Taris, and Van Rhenen, in press). Engagement and workaholism seem to be hardly related to each other, with the exception of absorption, which correlates moderately positively with the workaholism scale that assessed excess work (Schaufeli *et al.*, in press). Although work engagement and workaholism seem to share the element of absorption, the underlying motivation to be completely engrossed in one's work is different: engaged employees are absorbed because their work is intrinsically motivating, whereas workaholics are absorbed because of an inner drive they cannot resist.

For work engagement to be considered a valid contribution, its ability to discriminate not only against personality and employee well-being (burnout and workaholism), but also against other adjacent constructs, such as work involvement and organizational commitment, must be established. Work involvement refers to the psychological identification with work, including the notion that work may satisfy salient needs, whereas organizational commitment refers to the emotional attachment that employees form with their organization. Indeed, it was demonstrated that work engagement, job involvement, and organization commitment were empirically distinct constructs (Hallberg and Schaufeli, 2006). Not only did these three constructs constitute three different factors, they were also differentially related to health complaints, job and personal characteristics, and turnover intention. Work engagement was particularly related to good health, while job involvement and organizational commitment were particularly related to intrinsic motivation and low turnover intention, respectively.

Antecedents of work engagement

Work engagement is found to be positively associated with job resources; that is, to those aspects of the job that have the capacity to reduce job demands, are functional in achieving work goals, and may stimulate personal growth, learning, and development. For instance, work engagement tends to be positively related to social support from co-workers and from one's superior, as well as to performance feedback, coaching, job control, task variety, and training facilities (Demerouti *et al.*, 2001; Salanova, Grau, Llorens, and Schaufeli, 2001; Salanova, Llorens, Cifre, Martínez, and Schaufeli, 2003; Schaufeli and Bakker, 2004b; Hakanen, Bakker, and Schaufeli, 2006). Hence, the more job resources are available, the more likely it is that employees feel engaged. This is in line with the Job Characteristics Theory (Hackman and Oldham, 1980), which assumes that particular job characteristics, such as skill variety, autonomy, and feedback, have motivating potential and predict positive outcomes, including intrinsic motivation, which is close to our concept of work engagement. Sonnentag (2003) showed that the level of experienced work engagement was positively associated with the extent to which employees recovered from their previous working day. Employees who felt that they sufficiently recovered during leisure time experienced higher levels of work engagement during the subsequent workday. Moreover, in this study, work engagement mediated the effects of recovery on proactive behavior, indicating not only that recovered employees felt more engaged the next day, but also that they showed more personal initiative at work. Recently, Salanova and Schaufeli (in press) found, in a Dutch and a Spanish employee sample, a similar mediating role of work engagement but, in this case, with respect to the relationship between job resources (i.e. control, feedback, and variety) and proactive behavior. It appeared that the availability of resources increased work engagement, which, in turn, seemed to foster proactive organizational behavior.

Work engagement has also been found to be positively related to self-efficacy (Salanova *et al.*, 2001), which according to Social Cognitive Theory (SCT) is the "belief in one's capabilities to organize and execute the courses of action required to produce given attainments" (Bandura, 1997: 3). Quite interestingly, it seems that self-efficacy may precede *as well as* follow engagement (Llorens, Schaufeli, Bakker, and Salanova, 2007; Salanova, Bresó, and Schaufeli, 2005b; Salanova *et al.*, 2000). This may point to the existence of an upward spiral: self-efficacy fuels engagement, which, in turn, increases efficacy beliefs, and so on. This is in line with SCT (Bandura, 2001), which holds that there are reciprocal relationships between self-efficacy and positive affective-cognitive outcomes such as work engagement. This reciprocal relationship is also compatible with the notion of so-called "gain spirals" as described by the Conservation of Resources (COR) theory (Hobfoll and Shirom, 2000). According to COR theory, people strive to obtain, retain, and protect their resources, including personal resources such as self-efficacy. Such resources are likely to be accumulated across time, in that self-efficacy may breed self-efficacy, with engagement potentially playing an intermediate role.

In addition, it was observed that self-efficacy beliefs mediated the relationship between positive emotions (i.e. enthusiasm, satisfaction, and comfort) and work engagement (Salanova et al., 2005b). This is compatible with the Broaden-and-Build theory of Frederickson (2001), which posits that experiencing positive emotions broadens people's momentary thought-action repertoires, which, in turn, fosters the accumulation of resources, such as levels of self-efficacy. Since the accumulation of these resources is associated with positive emotions, the broaden-and-build spiral is completed.

The possible causes of work engagement do not lie only in the work situation. For instance, it appeared that employees who took positive experiences home from work (or vice versa) exhibited higher levels of engagement compared to those for whom there was no positive transmission between the two different life domains (Montgomery et al., 2003). In other words, a positive interplay between work and home seems to be associated with engagement. In a somewhat similar vein, in a study among working couples, it was shown that the wives' levels of vigor and dedication uniquely contributed to the husbands' levels of vigor and dedication, respectively, even when several work and home demands were controlled for (Bakker, Demerouti, and Schaufeli, 2005). The husbands' levels of engagement were likewise influenced by their wives' levels of engagement. This could indicate that engagement is "contagious," as it crosses over from one partner to the other, and vice versa. The transmission of engagement in this manner suggests that a process akin to that of emotional contagion is taking place (Hatfield, Cacioppo, and Rapson, 1994).

Taken together, these results suggest that there is a complex interplay amongst job resources, efficacy beliefs, positive outcomes, and engagement. It seems that these are all elements of a self-perpetuating motivational process in which work engagement plays a crucial role; it may act as both an antecedent (of proactivity and self-efficacy) and an outcome (of self-efficacy and positive emotions). From a slightly different perspective, this also means that efficacy beliefs play a role in boosting work engagement, thereby perpetuating a positive gain spiral. In addition, it seems that work engagement spills over from one domain (work) to another domain (home), and that it is passed from husband to wife, and vice versa.

Consequences of work engagement

The possible consequences of work engagement pertain to positive job-related attitudes, individual health, extra-role behaviors, and performance. Compared to those who do not feel engaged, those who feel engaged seem to be more satisfied with their jobs, feel more committed to the organization, and do not intend to leave the organization (Demerouti *et al.*, 2001; Schaufeli and Bakker, 2003, 2004b). Also, engaged workers seem to enjoy good mental (Schaufeli *et al.*, in press) and psychosomatic health (Demerouti *et al.*, 2001). Furthermore, they exhibit personal initiative, proactive behavior, and learning motivation (Salanova and Schaufeli, in press; Sonnentag, 2003), and engagement seems to play a mediating role between the availability of job resources and these positive organizational behaviors. Taken together, the results concerning positive organizational behavior suggest that engaged workers seem to be able and willing to "go the extra mile." This is also illustrated by the finding in a representative Dutch sample where, compared to non-engaged employees, engaged employees worked more overtime (Beckers, Van der Linden, Smulders, Kompier, Van Veldhoven, and Van Yperen, 2004).

Most importantly for organizations, those who are engaged seem to perform better. Recently, Salanova, Agut, and Peiró (2005a) showed that the levels of work engagement of contact employees from hotels and restaurants were related to service quality, as perceived by customers. More specifically, it was found that the more engaged the employees were, the better the service climate was, and the more loyal the customers were. In another study, it was similarly shown that the more engaged students were, the more exams they had passed during the previous semester. This retrospective result was found in Spain, Portugal, and the Netherlands (Schaufeli *et al.*, 2002a). But what is more, levels of engagement also *predicted* future academic performance; the more engaged the students felt, the higher their next year's grade point average (Salanova *et al.*, 2005b). In addition, it seemed that past success increased students' efficacy beliefs and levels of engagement, which, in turn, increased future academic success – yet another illustration of a gain spiral. Finally, Harter *et al.* (2002) showed that levels of employee engagement were positively related to business-unit performance (i.e. customer satisfaction and loyalty, profitability, productivity, turnover, and safety) across almost 8,000 business units of thirty-six companies. The observed correlation of engagement with a composite performance measure was .22, and increased to .38 when corrected for measurement error and restriction of range. The authors concluded that engagement is "related to meaningful business outcomes at a magnitude that is important to many organizations" (2002: 276).

In sum, work engagement can be discriminated from job involvement, organizational commitment, burnout, and workaholism based on, amongst other factors, the employee's personality profile. Moreover, it is not only the possible antecedents (i.e. job resources and positive home experiences) and possible consequences (i.e. positive attitudes, extra-role behaviors, health, and performance) of engagement that have been identified, but research has also found indications of underlying motivational processes. Results point to a complex reciprocal relationship existing between resources, engagement, and positive outcomes that may result in an upward gain spiral. More specifically, it seems that job resources and personal resources (efficacy beliefs) increase positive outcomes via work engagement, *and* that these positive outcomes and high levels of engagement have a positive impact on both types of resources.

Measuring work engagement with the Utrecht Work Engagement Scale (UWES)

Based on our previous definition of work engagement, a self-report questionnaire has been developed that includes the three constituting aspects of work engagement: vigor, dedication, and absorption (Schaufeli *et al.*, 2002b). The instrument was dubbed the Utrecht Work Engagement Scale (UWES: see appendix) and is now available in seventeen languages.[1] Meanwhile an international database exists that includes engagement records of about 30,000 employees. In addition to the original UWES that contains seventeen items, a shortened version of nine items is available that shows similar encouraging psychometric features (Schaufeli, Bakker, and Salanova, 2006).

The psychometric features of the UWES are encouraging. For instance, confirmatory factor analyses showed convincingly that the hypothesized three-factor structure of the UWES was (slightly) superior to the one-factor model (assuming an undifferentiated engagement factor) and that it fitted well to the data of various samples in different countries such as Greece (Xanthopoulou *et al.*, in press), Japan (Shimazu *et al.*, 2006), the Netherlands (Schaufeli *et al.*, 2002a, 2002b; Schaufeli and Bakker, 2003), Spain (Salanova *et al.*, 2000), Sweden (Hallberg and Schaufeli, 2006), and South Africa (Storm and Rothmann, 2003). However, it appears that the three dimensions of engagement are closely related. Usually correlations between the observed factors exceed .65, whereas correlations between the latent factors range from about .80 to about .90 (Hallberg and Schaufeli, 2006; Salanova *et al.*, 2000; Schaufeli

---

[1] Afrikaans, Chinese, Czech, Dutch, English, Finnish, French, German, Greek, Italian, Japanese, Norwegian, Polish, Portuguese, Russian, Spanish, and Swedish. These language versions, as well as the test manual may be downloaded from www.schaufeli.com.

et al., 2002b; Schaufeli and Bakker, 2003, 2004a, 2004b). So it is not very surprising that Sonnentag (2003), using explorative factor analyses, did *not* find a clear three-factor structure and decided to use the total, composite score of the UWES as a measure for work engagement. Furthermore, the internal consistency of the three scales of the UWES is good with values of Cronbach's α for the UWES scales ranging between .80 and .90 (e.g. Demerouti *et al.*, 2001; Durán *et al.*, 2004; Salanova *et al.*, 2000; Salanova *et al.*, 2001; Schaufeli and Bakker, 2004a; 2004b; Xanthopoulou *et al.*, in press). Two longitudinal studies carried out in Australia and Norway showed one-year test-retest stability coefficients ranging between .50 and .60 for the UWES scales (Schaufeli and Bakker, 2003).

Work engagement as measured with the UWES correlates weakly and positively with age, indicating that older employees feel slightly more engaged than younger employees. Perhaps this reflects the so-called "healthy worker effect," when only those who are healthy "survive" and remain in their jobs, and unhealthy (i.e. not engaged) employees drop out. However, the strength of the relationship between engagement and age is very weak and usually does not exceed .15 (Schaufeli and Bakker, 2003, 2004a). Men score slightly higher on engagement than women, but again the differences are very small and hardly bear any practical significance (Schaufeli and Bakker, 2003, 2004a). As far as professional groups are concerned, managers, executives, entrepreneurs, and farmers score relatively high on engagement, whereas blue-collar workers, police officers, and homecare staff score relatively low (Schaufeli and Bakker, 2003, 2004a). Most likely, the jobs of managers, executives, entrepreneurs, and farmers are more challenging, complex, and resourceful as compared to those of blue-collar workers, police officers, and home care staff. Moreover, selection bias cannot be excluded, because, for instance, in order to be a successful executive or entrepreneur, a certain level of engagement is required.

In conclusion, the empirical results confirm the factorial validity, internal consistency, and stability of the UWES. Although, psychometrically speaking, three factors of engagement (i.e. vigor, dedication, and absorption) can be distinguished, for practical purposes the total score of the UWES can be used since the three aspects are highly interrelated. Hardly any systematic differences in work engagement were observed between men and women, or across age groups. In some occupational groups, engagement levels were found to be higher than in other groups (e.g. executives versus blue-collar workers). The fact that similar psychometric results were observed among different samples from various countries confirms the robustness of the findings.

How can work engagement be optimized using HRM strategies?

By building engagement, synergy is created between individual employees and the organization as a whole, leading to optimal outcomes for them both. As we have seen above, for engaged employees, these outcomes might include: (1) positive job-related attitudes and a strong identification with one's work; (2) good mental health, including positive emotions and a lower risk of burning out; (3) good performance; (4) increased intrinsic motivation; and (5) the acquisition of job resources and personal resources, particularly self-efficacy. Most of these individual outcomes are – directly or indirectly – beneficial for the organization as well. In addition, for organizations, high levels of employee engagement may result in: (1) the retention of valued and talented employees; (2) a positive corporate image (see www.eu100best.org); (3) a healthy, competitive, and effective organization; and (4) positive business-unit performance.

In order to increase engagement, it is essential to initiate and maintain so-called gain spirals. As we have seen above, these are upward spirals that are set into motion by job resources and personal resources (self-efficacy beliefs), and may result in various positive outcomes via work engagement. In turn, these positive outcomes may increase resources and foster high levels of engagement, and so on. Following the logic of these gain spirals, work engagement may be increased by stimulating either link of the spiral, be it resources or positive outcomes. Below it is outlined how this can be achieved using various HRM strategies.

Assessment and evaluation of employees

Personnel assessment and evaluation is about increasing identification, motivation, and commitment – from the perspective of the organization – as well as about personal and professional development – from the perspective of the employee. Work engagement may play a crucial role because it fosters employee identification, motivation, and commitment, but it also increases levels of self-efficacy, which is an important prerequisite for learning and development (Bandura, 1997). The following three strategies can be distinguished that may enhance work engagement.

The Employee Development Agreement An optimal fit between employee and organization may be achieved by following three steps: (1) assessing the employee's values, preferences, and personal and professional goals; (2) negotiating and drafting a written contract ("Employee Development Agreement") that acknowledges (some of) these goals and provides the necessary resources to be supplemented by the organization (e.g. training, coaching, equipment, budget); and (3) monitoring this written agreement periodically in terms of goal achievement, including the readjustment of goals and the provision of additional resources. Essentially, we propose that a goal-setting system (Locke, 1968) be implemented that could be integrated into existing systems of performance appraisal and evaluation. However, instead of addressing organizational goals (e.g. productivity, quality, efficiency) our Employee Development Agreement is to entail *personal* goals (e.g. development of skills and competences, promotion, mastery of particular tasks or duties) as well as the necessary *resources* to achieve these personal goals. This Employee Development Agreement is expected to be successful because it is job resources that drive the motivational process that increases work engagement and eventually leads to positive outcomes. By providing the necessary resources to meet valued individual goals, an upward gain cycle is set in motion, where high levels of engagement and success tend to accumulate resources, and so on.

Wellness audit The aim of wellness audits is to inform employees as well as the organizations they work for about the levels of employee wellness, including engagement. This information is important for making decisions about what improvement measures should be taken, either by the employee or by the organization. Such wellness audits are currently being used in Spain and in the Netherlands,[2] and they examine job stressors (e.g. work overload, conflicts, role problems, emotional demands, work–home interference), job resources (e.g. variety, feedback, social support, job control, career development), burnout, engagament, negative personal and organizational outcomes (e.g. depression, distress, absenteeism, turnover intention), and positive personal and organizational outcomes (e.g. job satisfaction, organizational commitment, extra-role performance). In addition, personal and job information is included as well as personal resources such as self-efficacy, and mental and emotional competences.

Workshops The aim of the workshops is to promote work engagement by augmenting personal resources. Traditionally, workshops have been used to prevent or reduce job stress (Van der Klink, Blonk, Schene, and Van Dijk, 2001), but, in order to build engagement, a shift in focus from decreasing stress symptoms toward optimizing the quality of work

[2] Online Spanish and English versions are available at www.wont.uji.es/

and the level of employee functioning is needed. In that sense, workshops that aim at increasing engagement are similar to so-called Quality Circles, except that they focus on the enhancement of *personal* resources, such as cognitive, behavioral, and social skills (e.g. positive thinking, goal setting, time management, and lifestyle improvement).

Job (re)design and work changes

As we have seen above, in order to increase engagement, the motivating potential of job resources should be exploited. Resources not only are necessary in order to deal with job demands and "get things done," but also are important in their own right because they stimulate the personal growth, learning, and development of employees. Moreover, job resources may set in motion gain spirals that increase work engagement. Job Characteristics Theory (Hackman and Oldham, 1980) acknowledges the motivating potential of job resources and predicts that particular job redesigning strategies, such as job enrichment, job enlargement, and job rotation, have positive effects on employee well-being, motivation, and performance. Which resources are most important for increasing engagement depends not only on the nature of the job, but also on the values, preferences, and goals of the individual employee. With the use of a wellness audit, it is possible to pinpoint which resources are lacking and, if feasible, to incorporate them into an Employee Development Agreement.

Another related strategy is to implement *work changes*. In doing so, job resources are not additionally provided or increased, but are merely changed, as, for example, when jobs are rotated, or employees are temporarily assigned to carry out special projects, or are reassigned to completely different jobs. As argued by Schabracq (2003), work changes challenge employees, increase their motivation, flexibility, and employability, and stimulate learning and professional development. Based on qualitative research on engagement (Schaufeli *et al.*, 2001), we may add that, most likely, changing work also increases work engagement. This is particularly the case when employees are highly challenged in their new jobs and at the same time possess the necessary competences to meet these challenges (Salanova *et al.*, 2001). However, the positive effects of changing work are only to be expected when the change is carefully planned and in accordance with the preferences, goals, and personal resources (knowledge, skills, competences) of the employee. If this is not the case and work changes are exclusively used as a means to solve organizational problems, it will do employees more harm than good. Ideally, work changes should be agreed upon in the Employee Development Agreement.

Leadership

An important task of leaders is to optimize the emotional climate within their team. A good leader is able to enhance motivation and engagement. Results from research suggest that engagement is "contagious," and its tendency to spread should apply well to workteams. Team members feel engaged as they converge emotionally with the engagement of other members in the workteam. Moreover, it appears that engagement is a collective phenomenon, as teams may feel "engaged" when their members closely collaborate to accomplish particular tasks (Salanova *et al.*, 2003). This implies that team leaders are in a position where they can have a positive impact on the levels of individual and collective engagement, depending on the way they manage the social-psychological processes involved. For example, Aguilar and Salanova (2005) found that "selling" leaders (who are high in task behavior and support behavior) were particularly effective at increasing individual work engagement compared to those displaying other patterns of leadership behavior. Generally speaking, transformational leadership (Bass, 1985) is particularly suitable for fostering engagement since transformational leaders are inspiring and visionary. They display conviction, take stands, challenge group members with high standards, communicate optimism about future goal attainment, stimulate and encourage creativity and innovation, and listen to the members' concerns and needs. Not surprisingly, transformational leadership has a positive impact on members' health and well-being (Howell and Hall-Merenda, 1999) as well as on job satisfaction, performance, and motivation (Judge and Piccolo, 2004).

Training and career development

The objective of work training is to modify those behaviors that are relevant for job performance via changes in attitudes, beliefs, and values. A powerful method of achieving this is to increase employees' efficacy beliefs, or "the power to believe that you can." According to Social Cognitive Theory (SCT), self-efficacy lies at the core of human agency, influencing employees' behavior, thinking, motivation, and feelings (Bandura, 2001). Research on engagement has shown that an upward gain spiral seems to exist in which self-efficacy boosts engagement, which, in turn, increases efficacy beliefs, and so on (e.g. Llorens *et al.*, 2007; Salanova *et al.*, 2005b). But how may self-efficacy – and therefore work engagement – be enhanced? According to SCT, efficacy beliefs may be enhanced by mastery experiences, vicarious experience, verbal persuasion, and positive emotional states (Bandura, 1997, 2001). Training programs should therefore include these elements, which can take the form of, for instance, practical exercises to provide experiences of vocational success (mastery experiences), and the use of role models of good performance (vicarious experiences), as well as methods of coaching and encouragement (verbal persuasion) and reducing fear of rejection or failure (managing emotional states).

Finally, we would like to address the relevance of *career development* as a strategy to optimize employee engagement. Although most employees favor life-long job stability and vertical, upward mobility, this perspective is no longer self-evident in current organizational life. For instance, organizations are now frequently assigning employees to projects rather than jobs. In such cases, regular working hours may not exist, and employees are accountable to their project team, which is, in turn, accountable to the larger project. When the project ends, employees move on to another project. In this type of environment, individual employees need to continuously develop their knowledge, competences, and skills in order to remain competitive in the labor market. In other words, they have to increase their employability (see Table 18.1), and, more than before, employees have to rely on their own initiative if they are to continuously develop themselves professionally and personally. In our view, employability also includes a high level of engagement since it makes employees better fit and more successful at their jobs. However, with the upward gain spiral of engagement, the reverse may also be true: by carefully planning one's career, that is, by successively selecting those jobs that provide many opportunities for professional and personal development, it is likely that engagement levels will remain high. In order to monitor levels of engagement, an online career monitor for the members of the Dutch Medical Association has been developed (Bakker, Schaufeli, Bulters, Van Rooijen, and Ten Broek, 2002). Based on the feedback, measures can be taken when levels of engagement drop markedly. The key issue for employees to remain engaged in their jobs is to keep developing themselves throughout their careers.

Summary and conclusions

In order to survive and prosper in a continuously changing environment, modern organizations do not merely need "healthy" employees – that is, employees who are free of symptoms – but employees who are vigorous, dedicated, and absorbed in their work. In short: they need *engaged* employees. After introducing the recently emerged concept of work engagement and discussing its empirical underpinnings, six conclusions can be drawn from the brief overview of empirical studies presented in this area.

1. Work engagement is positively associated with various job resources, such as social support, performance feedback, job autonomy, coaching, and task variety. Also, a positive interplay between work and home is associated with work engagement (and vice versa).
2. Work engagement is associated with positive organizational outcomes at the attitudinal and behavioral level, including job satisfaction, organizational commitment, extra-role behavior, and high performance. In addition, work engagement is associated with good mental health.
3. As hypothesized, work engagement is negatively related to burnout. Although engagement and workaholism seem to share the element of absorption, the underlying motivation to be completely engrossed in one's work differs between these two psychological states.
4. A process of emotional contagion seems to be responsible for transmitting work engagement among spouses and co-workers.
5. A positive upward spiral seems to exist involving resources, self-efficacy, work engagement, and success. The availability of resources and high levels of self-efficacy increase employee engagement and boost performance. Because of the successes, resources are accumulated, and self-efficacy and engagement are further enhanced.
6. Work engagement can be reliably and validly assessed by a self-report instrument – the Utrecht Work Engagement Scale (UWES).

In the second part of this chapter, we considered the practical implications of work engagement for current organizations. The main objective was to explore what organizations could do to increase work engagement among their employees, using particular HRM strategies. Based on this overview, the following five conclusions can be drawn.

1. Wellness audits inform employees (online) about their current levels of engagement and other associated factors so that they can take action when necessary. By drafting and monitoring a so-called Employee Development Agreement, that states personal goals for future development as well as what organizational resources are necessary to accomplish these goals, employee engagement is likely to be increased. Also, participative workshops may be helpful in increasing engagement and organizational effectiveness.
2. Job (re)designing may enhance work engagement by making use of the motivating potential of job resources. (Re)designing in order to promote engagement boils down to increasing job resources. Also, job rotation and the changing of jobs can result in higher engagement levels as this challenges employees, increases their motivation, and stimulates learning and professional development.
3. Since engagement seems to be contagious and may spread across members of workteams, leaders play a special role when it comes to

fostering work engagement. It is to be expected that transformational leadership, in particular, can be successful in accomplishing this. Moreover, research suggests that leaders are key social resources for the development of employee engagement, for instance in their role as coach.

4. Training programs in organizations that aim to increase work engagement should focus on enhancing efficacy beliefs. High levels of self-efficacy set in motion an upward gain spiral that increases engagement and subsequent performance, which, in turn, increases efficacy beliefs, and so on.

5. Career planning and development in modern organizations basically boils down to increasing employability. This is achieved by ensuring continuous personal and professional development, with employees having to rely more and more on their own initiative. To the extent that employees are able to keep developing themselves throughout their careers, their levels of engagement are likely to remain high.

We believe that the emerging concept of work engagement, which has resulted from a recent shift in occupational health psychology from a negative disease-oriented approach to a positive wellness approach, is a viable construct that is firmly rooted in empirical research. What is more, it may play a crucial role in the development of organizations' human capital. As an essential, positive element of employee health and well-being, work engagement may help to create synergy between positive outcomes for individual employees and for the organization as a whole.

Appendix: Utrecht Work Engagement Scale (UWES)©

The following 17 statements are about how you feel at work. Please read each statement carefully and decide if you ever feel this way about your job. If you have never had this feeling, cross the "0" (zero) in the space after the statement. If you have had this feeling, indicate how often you feel it by crossing the number (from 1 to 6) that best describes how frequently you feel that way

	Almost never	Rarely	Sometimes	Often	Very often	Always
0	1	2	3	4	5	6
Never	A few times a year or less	Once a month or less	A few times a month	Once a week	A few times a week	Every day

1. ____ At my work, I feel bursting with energy*(VI1)
2. ____ I find the work that I do full of meaning and purpose (DE1)
3. ____ Time flies when I'm working (AB1)
4. ____ At my job, I feel strong and vigorous (VI2)*
5. ____ I am enthusiastic about my job (DE2)*

6. ____ When I am working, I forget everything else around me *(AB2)*
7. ____ My job inspires me *(DE3)* *
8. ____ When I get up in the morning, I feel like going to work *(VI3)* *
9. ____ I feel happy when I am working intensely *(AB3)* *
10. ____ I am proud of the work that I do *(DE4)* *
11. ____ I am immersed in my work *(AB4)* *
12. ____ I can continue working for very long periods at a time *(VI4)*
13. ____ To me, my job is challenging *(DE5)*
14. ____ I get carried away when I'm working *(AB5)* *
15. ____ At my job, I am very resilient, mentally *(VI5)*
16. ____ It is difficult to detach myself from my job *(AB6)*
17. ____ At my work I always persevere, even when things do not go well *(VI6)*

---

* Shortened version (UBES-9); *VI* = Vigor; *DE* = Dedication; *AB* = Absorption
© Schaufeli and Bakker (2003) The Utrecht Work Engagement Scale is free for use for non-commercial scientific research. Commercial and/or non-scientific use is prohibited, unless previous written permission is granted by the authors.

References

Aguilar, A. and Salanova, M. (2005). Leadership style and its relationship with subordinate well-being (manuscript submitted for publication).

Bakker, A. B., Demerouti, E., and Schaufeli, W. B. (2005). The cross-over of burnout and work engagement among working couples. *Human Relations* 58: 661–89.

Bakker, A. B., Schaufeli, W. B., Bulters, A. J., Van Rooijen, A., and Ten Broek, E. (2002). Carrière-counseling voor artsen via internet [Career counseling for physicians using the internet]. *Medisch Contact* 57: 454–6.

Bandura, A. (1997). *Self-efficacy: the exercise of control*. New York: Freeman.

(2001). Social cognitive theory: an agentic perspective. *Annual Review of Psychology* 52: 1–26.

Bass, B. M. (1985). *Leadership and performance beyond expectations*. New York: Free Press.

Beckers, D. G. J., Van der Linden, D., Smulders, P. G. W., Kompier, M. A. J., Van Veldhoven, M. J. P. M., and Van Yperen, N. W. (2004). Working over-time hours: relations with fatigue, work motivation, and the quality of work. *Journal of Occupational and Environmental Medicine* 46: 1282–9.

Bresó, E., Salanova, M., and Schaufeli, W. (2007). In search of the "third dimension" of burnout: a cross-national study among university students. *Applied Psychology: An International Review* 56: 460–78.

Costa, P. T., Jr. and McCrae, R. R. (1980). Influence of extraversion and neuroticism on subjective well-being: happy and unhappy people. *Journal of Personality and Social Psychology* 38: 668–78.

Csikszentmihalyi, M. (1990). *Flow: the psychology of optimal experience*. New York: Harper and Row.

Demerouti, E., Bakker, A. B., Janssen, P. P. M., and Schaufeli, W. B. (2001). Burnout and engagement at work as a function of demands and control. *Scandinavian Journal of Work, Environment & Health* 27: 279–86.

De Vries, T. A., Peters, L., and Hoogstraten, J. (2004). Burnout en bevlogenheid bij fysiotherapeuten [Burnout and work engagement among physiotherapists]. *Gedrag & Gezondheid* 32: 241–50.

Durán, A., Extremera, N., and Rey, L. (2004). Engagement and burnout: analyzing their association patterns. *Psychological Reports* 94: 1048–50.

Frederickson, B. L. (2001). The role of positive emotions in positive psychology: the broaden-and-build theory of positive emotions. *American Psychologist* 56: 218–26.

González-Romá, V., Schaufeli, W. B., Bakker, A., and Lloret, S. (2006). Burnout and engagement: independent factors or opposite poles? *Journal of Vocational Behavior* 68: 165–74.

Hackman, J. R. and Oldham, G. R. (1980). *Work redesign*. Reading, MA: Addison Wesley.

Hakanen, J. J., Bakker, A. B., and Schaufeli, W. B. (2006). Burnout and work engagement among teachers. *Journal of School Psychology* 43: 495–513.

Hallberg, U. and Schaufeli, W. B. (2006). "Same same" but different: can work engagement be discriminated from job involvement and organizational commitment? *European Psychologist* 11: 119–27.

Harter, J. K., Schmidt, F. L., and Hayes, T. L. (2002). Business-unit-level relationship between employee satisfaction, employee engagement, and business outcomes: a meta-analysis. *Journal of Applied Psychology* 87: 268–79.

Hatfield, E., Cacioppo, J. T., and Rapson, R. L. (1994). *Emotional contagion*. New York: Cambridge University Press.

Hobfoll, S. E. and Shirom, A. (2000). Conservation of resources theory: applications to stress and management in the workplace. In R. T. Golembiewski (ed.), *Handbook of organizational behavior* (2nd edn, pp. 57–81). New York: Marcel Dekker.

Howell, J. M. and Hall-Merenda, K. E. (1999). The ties that bind: the impact of leader–member exchange, transformational and transactional leadership, and distance on predicting follower performance. *Journal of Applied Psychology* 84: 680–94.

Judge, T. A. and Piccolo, R. F. (2004). Transformational and transactional leadership: a meta-analytic test of their relative validity. *Journal of Applied Psychology* 89: 755–86.

Langelaan, S., Bakker, A. B., Van Doornen, L. J. P., and Schaufeli, W. B. (2006). Burnout and work engagement: do individual differences make a difference? *Personality and Individual Differences* 40: 521–32.

Llorens, S., Schaufeli, W. B., Bakker, A., and Salanova, M. (2007). Does a positive gain spiral of resources, efficacy beliefs and engagement exist? *Computers in Human Behavior* 23: 825–41.

Llorens, S., Salanova, M., Bakker, A., and Schaufeli, W. B. (in press). Burnout and engagement among information technology workers: a cross-cultural study. *Anxiety, Stress & Coping*.

Locke, E. A. (1968). Towards a theory of task performance and incentives. *Organizational Behavior and Human Performance* 3: 157–89.

Maslach, C., Jackson, S. E., and Leiter, M. P. (1996). *Maslach Burnout Inventory: manual* (3rd revised edn). Palo Alto, CA: Consulting Psychologists Press.

Maslach, C., Schaufeli, W. B., and Leiter, M. P. (2001). Job burnout. *Annual Review of Psychology* 52: 397–422.

May, D. R., Gilson, R. L., and Harter, L. M. (2004). The psychological conditions of meaningfulness, safety and availability and the engagement of the human spirit at work. *Journal of Occupational and Organizational Psychology* 77: 11–37.

Montgomery, A., Peeters, M. C. W., Schaufeli, W. B., and Den Ouden, M. (2003). Work–home interference among newspaper managers: its relationship with burnout and engagement. *Anxiety, Stress & Coping* 16: 195–211.

Peterson, C., Park, N., and Seligman, M. E. P. (2005). Orientations to happiness and life satisfaction: the full life versus the empty life. *Journal of Happiness Studies* 6: 25–41.

Salanova, M., Agut, S., and Peiró, J. M. (2005a). Linking organizational resources and work engagement to employee performance and customer loyalty: the mediating role of service climate. *Journal of Applied Psychology* 90: 1217–27.

Salanova, M., Bresó, E., and Schaufeli, W. B. (2005b). Hacia un modelo espiral de la autoeficacia en el estudio del burnout y engagement [Towards a spiral model of self-efficacy in burnout and engagement research]. *Ansiedad y Estrés* 11: 215–31.

Salanova, M., Grau, R., Cifre, E., and Llorens, S. (2000). Computer training, frequency of use and burnout: the moderating role of computer self-efficacy. *Computers in Human Behavior* 16: 575–90.

Salanova, M., Grau, R., Llorens, S., and Schaufeli, W. B. (2001). Exposición a las tecnologías de la información, burnout y engagement: el rol modulador de la autoeficacia profesional [Exposure to information and communication technology, burnout and engagement: the moderating role of professional self-efficacy]. *Revista de Psicología Social Aplicada* 11: 69–89.

Salanova, M., Llorens, S., Cifre, E., Martinez, I., and Schaufeli, W. B. (2003). Perceived collective efficacy, subjective well-being and task performance among electronic work groups: an experimental study. *Small Groups Research* 34: 43–73.

Salanova, M. and Schaufeli, W. (in press). Work engagement as a mediator between job resources and proactive behaviour: a cross-national study. *International Journal of Human Resources Management*.

Salanova, M., Schaufeli, W. B., Llorens, S., Peiró, J. M., and Grau, R. (2000). Desde el "burnout" al "engagement": una nueva perspectiva [From burnout to engagement: a new perspective]. *Revista de Psicología del Trabajo y de las Organizaciones* 16: 117–34.

Schabracq, M. J. (2003). Organisational culture, stress and change. In M. J. Schabracq, J. A. M. Winnubst and C. L. Cooper (eds.), *Handbook of work and health psychology* (pp. 37–62). Chichester: Wiley.

Schabracq, M. J. and Cooper, C. L. (2000). The changing nature of work and stress. *Journal of Management Psychology* 15: 227–41.

Schaufeli, W. B. (2005). The future of occupational health psychology. *Applied Psychology: An International Review* 53: 502–17.

Schaufeli, W. B. and Bakker, A. B. (2001). Werk en welbevinden: naar een positieve benadering in de arbeids- en gezondheidspsychologie [Work and well-being: towards a positive approach in occupational health psychology]. *Gedrag & Organisatie* 14: 229–53.

—— (2003). UWES – Utrecht Work Engagement Scale: test manual. Unpublished manuscript, Department of Psychology, Utrecht University (www.schaufeli.com).

—— (2004a). Bevlogenheid: een begrip gemeten [Work engagement: the measurement of a concept]. *Gedrag & Organisatie* 17: 89–112.

—— (2004b). Job demands, job resources and their relationship with burnout and engagement: a multi-sample study. *Journal of Organizational Behavior* 25: 293–315.

Schaufeli, W. B., Bakker, A. B., and Salanova, M. (2006). The measurement of work engagement with a short questionnaire: a cross-national study. *Educational and Psychological Measurement* 66: 701–16.

Schaufeli, W. B., Martínez, I., Marques Pinto, A., Salanova, M., and Bakker, A. B. (2002a). Burnout and engagement in university students: a cross national study. *Journal of Cross-Cultural Psychology* 33: 464–81.

Schaufeli, W. B., Salanova, M., González-Romá, V., and Bakker, A. B. (2002b). The measurement of engagement and burnout: a confirmative analytic approach. *Journal of Happiness Studies* 3: 71–92.

Schaufeli, W. B., Taris, T. W., Le Blanc, P., Peeters, M., Bakker, A., and de Jonge, J. (2001). Maakt arbeid gezond? Op zoek naar de bevlogen werknemer [Does work make happy? In search of the engaged worker]. *De Psycholoog* 36: 422–8.

Schaufeli, W. B., Taris, T. W., and Van Rhenen, W. (in press). Workaholism, burnout and engagement: three of a kind or three different kinds of employee well-being? *Applied Psychology: An International Review.*

Shimazu, A., Schaufeli, W. B., Kosugi, S., Suzuki, A., Nashiwa, H., Kato, A., Sakamoto, M., Irimajiri, H., Amano, S., Hirohata, K., Goto, R., and Kitaoka-Higashiguchi, K. (2006). Work engagement in Japan: development and validation of the Japanese version of the Utrecht Work Engagement Scale (manuscript submitted for publication).

Shirom, A. (2003). Feeling vigorous at work? The construct of vigor and the study of positive affect in organizations. In D. Ganster and P. L. Perrewé (eds.), *Research in organizational stress and well-being* (vol. 3, pp. 135–65). Greenwich, CT: JAI Press.

Sonnentag, S. (2003). Recovery, work engagement, and proactive behavior: a new look at the interface between non-work and work. *Journal of Applied Psychology* 88: 518–28.

Storm, K. and Rothmann, I. (2003). A psychometric analysis of the Utrecht Work Engagement Scale in the South African police service. *South African Journal of Industrial Psychology* 29: 62–70.

Ulrich, D. (1997). *Human resource champions.* Boston, MA: Harvard Business School Press.

Van der Klink, J., Blonk, R., Schene, A., and Van Dijk, F. (2001). The benefits of interventions for work-related stress. *American Journal of Public Health* 91: 270–6.

Verhoff, J., Douvan, E., and Kulka, R. A. (1981). *The inner American*. New York: Basic Books.

Wright, T. A. (2003). Positive organizational behavior: an idea whose time has truly come. *Journal of Organizational Behavior* 24: 437–42.

Xanthopoulou, D., Bakker, A. B., Kantas, A., and Demerouti, E. (in press). The measurement of burnout and work engagement: a comparison of Greece and the Netherlands. *New Review of Social Psychology*.

19 Prevention: integrating health protection and health promotion perspectives

Lois E. Tetrick

Health protection and health promotion activities in organizations have been approached from different disciplines and perspectives, and the work environment has become safer and healthier. However, today's organizations continue to struggle with threats to both the safety and the health of workers and their families. Health protection has taken a preventive approach to eliminating and reducing accidents and occupational injuries in the workplace, as has health promotion. But health promotion has taken more of a public health perspective, using the workplace as a "convenient" location for contacting adults (Rantanen, 2003). Both perspectives have provided valuable insights into risk factors in the workplace and for workers' lives outside of work. However, it is apparent that these different perspectives and streams of knowledge need to be integrated to reflect the system in which workers and their families exist. If we are to have a full understanding of the health and safety of the workforce, then we need to understand the facilitators and barriers to the integration of health protection and health promotion. The purpose of this chapter is to review and integrate the health protection and health promotion literature in developing a framework for understanding prevention activities and needs in the workplace.

Health protection

Health protection has historically focused on providing workers with a safe and healthy work environment. The primary focus of health protection has been on preventing occupational injuries and diseases arising from risks that are involuntary and outside the scope of individual employees' control and that may be undetectable by individual workers (Sorensen, Stoddard, Ockene, Hunt, and Youngstrom, 1996). Prevention is accomplished by removing the hazard, such as substituting a hazardous chemical with a non-hazardous chemical in the production process, providing engineering controls to reduce exposure to the hazard, such as cover guards to prevent access to cutting edges, and providing personal protective equipment (Sorensen *et al.*, 1996). The latter option is generally considered to be the least effective, as it does not remove the risk of exposure and places primary responsibility for occupational health and safety on the worker. The fundamental philosophy and expressed values of health protection have been that employers are responsible for providing a safe and healthy work environment (Rantanen, 2003), although there is a long history of participation by labor through joint health and safety committees (Chen, 2003; Mbakaya, Onyoyo, and Lwaki, 1999; Milgate, Innes, and O'Loughlin, 2002; Peltomäki, Johansson, and Ahrens, 2003). The disciplines traditionally involved in health protection have been industrial hygiene, safety engineering, occupational medicine, occupational nursing, and, more recently, occupational health psychology, ergonomics, organizational behavior, and management science.

Health protection was enacted by legislation and implemented through governmental agencies such as the Health Protection Agency in the United Kingdom and the Centers for Disease Control and Prevention in the United States (Nicoll and Murray, 2002), and collective bargaining agreements have traditionally included health protection language. It has been suggested that conflicting values between management, whose focus is on production, and workers who are exposed to the production processes may have necessitated the use of legislation and pressure from workers for management to invest resources in occupational health and safety (Chen, 2003; Ratajczak, 1993).

Health promotion

Health promotion also has taken a prevention approach, using a public health perspective to improve the health of the population, with the workplace being a "convenient" location for contacting adults. The goal of health promotion has been to improve the health of employees in general and it has focused less on the specific workplace factors that may put workers at risk of ill health. Typical health promotion activities have included smoking cessation, weight loss, and fitness programs. The fundamental philosophy and expressed values in health promotion have been that employees are responsible for maintaining and enhancing their health (Rantanen, 2003). The disciplines typically involved include behavioral medicine, health psychology, public health, medicine, and nursing.

In contrast to the legislative impetus of health protection, the orientation of health promotion has been to improve individuals' health through reducing their negative health behaviors and increasing their positive health behaviors. Worksite health promotion programs are often justified by management, based on the argument that they will reduce health care costs and time lost because of ill health. Workers have been somewhat resistant to management's efforts in this arena. It may be that some activities are viewed as being outside the purview of management rights. For example, lifestyle behaviors such as smoking and eating, which are done outside of working hours and not on company property, may be considered to be personal, private matters, which are not appropriate for management actions. Despite this privacy issue, there have been instances where disciplinary actions by employers have been upheld for employees' health risk behaviors, such as smoking behavior outside of work, at least in the United States.

In addition to privacy issues, there has been some resistance to health promotion activities in organizations by workers, as they may be seen as a reduction in management's commitment to the responsibility for providing a safe and healthy work environment (Sorensen et al., 1996). Health promotion activities focus on individuals' behaviors that put them at risk for poor health – they do not address occupational exposures. There is not a focus on work-related behaviors. Also, participation in employer-sponsored health promotion activities frequently happens during the employee's own time, sending a clear message that the organization has placed the responsibility for health on the individual employee.

One notable exception to this separation between health protection and health promotion programs is the WellWorks project (see Sorensen et al., 1996). This takes an integrative approach by developing an intervention that combines health protection components with health promotion components. Specifically, programs focused on tobacco control, reduction in exposure to occupational carcinogens, and decreased dietary fat and increased dietary fiber consumption among workers. The interventions included employee advisory boards, which were similar to health and safety committees but focused on the actual intervention and its implementation. They also included consultation with the organization on worksite changes, following the hierarchy of controls recommended by safety engineers – substitution of safer substances for potential carcinogens, implementation of engineering controls to reduce exposures, and, lastly, the use of personal protective equipment. The third component of the interventions was aimed at changes in individual workers' behaviors through coordinated educational programs targeting smoking, exposure to occupational carcinogens, and dietary fat and fiber consumption as risk factors for cancer.

The results of this intervention study found that the incorporation of health protection factors (with the inclusion of environmental changes) was related to participation in the health promotion activities. Sorensen *et al.* (1996) suggested that the inclusion of the environmental change component was effective in communicating management's commitment to the provision of a safe and healthy work environment, which is a major component of safety and health climate (Zohar, 2003). This involvement in worksite changes also signaled management's acceptance of responsibility for occupational health and safety.

These results are also consistent with social exchange theory. Social exchange theory posits that if employees feel that management is concerned about their individual well-being and is willing to invest in making the work environment safer, then they will reciprocate with positive organizational behaviors (Cropanzano and Mitchell, 2005; Hofmann, Morgeson, and Gerras, 2003; Lee and Bruvold, 2003). These positive organizational behaviors may take the form of higher levels of performance, organizational citizenship behaviors, organizational commitment, and loyalty to the organization. In this instance, the greater the extent to which the organization signals that workers' health and safety is important and the organization is willing to invest in employees' health and well-being, the more likely it is that employees will respond by increasing their own positive health behaviors with respect to both their work behaviors and their lifestyle behaviors. Therefore, the WellWorks project supports the potential gains in health and safety of integrating health protection and health promotion activities.

The integration of health protection and health promotion is not a new recommendation. In 1984, for example, Pelletier suggested that health promotion should incorporate both organizational and environmental factors by attending to working conditions that might put employees at risk and by considering risky lifestyle behaviors (see also Bennett, Cook, and Pelletier, 2003). This would clearly integrate health protection into health promotion activities.

Health promotion has typically focused on improving individuals' health. Recently, DeJoy and Wilson (2003) have conceptualized and expanded health promotion to the organizational level. They expanded traditional, individual-focused health promotion approaches by making the observation that just as there are controllable risk factors for individuals' health, there are also controllable risk factors for organizations' health. In their model, they suggest that organizations can build *health promotive capacity*, which is the ability to maintain and improve organizational health. This health promotive capacity is similar to the concept of absorptive capacity used in the organizational change literature (see below). Dejoy and Wilson posited that health promotive capacity facilitates organizational change and innovation, resulting in enhanced individual and organizational health. Therefore, DeJoy and Wilson clearly are calling for multilevel models of health promotion – one at the individual level wherein individual behaviors and the perceptions of environmental, organizational, and working conditions affect the health of employees, one at the organizational level wherein factors such as organizational structure, policies, and practices affect organizational health, and a cross-level model in which organizational factors affect the health of employees, which in turn affects organizational health. The remainder of this chapter discusses the facilitators and barriers to integrating health protection and promotion within this multilevel framework.

Facilitators and barriers to health protection and promotion

Health protection and health promotion activities in work organizations frequently are housed in different departments within the organization. Safety is often housed in Safety departments while concern for the physical and psychological health of workers is frequently handled by Human Resources departments (Tetrick and Ellis, 2002). The assignment of these various functions in organizations reflects the different etiologies of these functions, their associated disciplines, and top management's values and beliefs relative to health protection and promotion. Research has not examined, to my knowledge, whether there is one best placement for these functions. But organizational theory would suggest that the integration of health protection and health promotion functions may be hampered by organizational structure. For example, dispersion of the health protection and health promotion functions may weaken communication and coordination among activities (Tetrick and Camburn, 2004). Also, an organizational structure that maintains separation between health protection and health promotion functions might reinforce the notion that they are competing for the same resources and undermine either or both health protection and health promotion programs. This could result in a diminished organizational climate for safety and health.

Climate for safety

The past two decades have seen considerable research demonstrating that safety climate has a direct relation to safety behavior and performance (Hofmann and Stezer, 1996; Zohar, 2003). Climate has been defined in multiple ways, ranging from climate reflecting the shared perceptions of employees within an organization, to psychological climate reflecting individual perceptions of the organization or unit. Oftentimes, climate at the organizational level is operationalized as the aggregation of individual perceptions, providing there is sufficient agreement among employees within an organization. Organizational-level climate for safety is a surface level of culture (see Ostroff, Kinicki, and Tamkins, 2003), which is posited to result from the shared values and norms of behavior espoused by senior management. These values are transmitted through the levels in the organization into effective work practices (Gaba, Singer, Sinaiko, Bowen, and Ciavarelli, 2003; Schein, 1990).

Interestingly, there is no clear agreement in the literature on the dimensions of the safety climate. Mueller, DaSilva, Townsend, and Tetrick (1999) found that among the existing safety climate measures at the time, which were frequently developed for specific populations (manufacturing, construction, etc.), there did appear to be support for four common dimensions: (a) rewards for working safely, (b) effect of safe behavior on social status, (c) effect of required work pace on safety, and (d) management's attitude toward safety. These four dimensions were similar to Zohar's (1980) initial conceptualization of safety climate. More recently, Griffin and Neal (2000) identified the dimensions as management values, safety inspections, personnel training, and safety communication, in their first study, and as management values, safety communication, safety practices, safety training, and safety equipment, in their second study. Across contexts and industry, the one aspect of safety climate that has been consistently found is management support for safety.

Little empirical research has actually addressed the antecedents of safety climate. Drawing on organizational culture and climate literature and research (see, for example, Ashkanasy, Wilderom, and Peterson, 2000), it is anticipated that there would be a number of organizational-level and departmental/workgroup-level antecedents of safety climate. The objective safety climate would in turn affect individuals' perceptions of safety climate, and individuals' perceptions of safety climate subsequently would predict safety behaviors, as shown in Figure 19.1.

Among the organizational-level antecedents suggested in the literature are top management values, top management leadership style, human resources policies (espoused policies relative to safety), human resource practices (enacted policies relative to safety), occupational health and safety policies (espoused), occupational health and safety practices (enacted), engineering policies and practices, and organizational structure, including where the safety function is housed and what the reporting channels are within the organization (see Ashkanasy *et al.*, 2000). At the

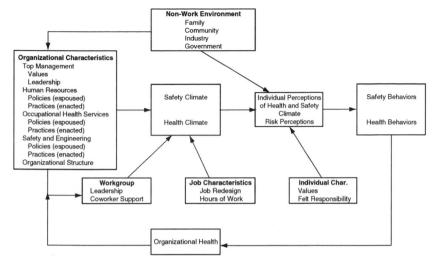

Figure 19.1 Relation between safety climate and safety behaviors

more proximal departmental or workgroup level, the literature suggests that supervision and leadership, teamwork, interdependence, supervisory support, and co-worker support would be antecedents of safety climate. Many of these factors have been examined in the general organizational culture and climate literature. But no studies, to my knowledge, have examined all of these aspects concurrently, or specifically with respect to safety climate.

One antecedent that has been found to affect safety climate and safety behaviors is leadership (Hofmann and Morgeson, 2003; Zohar, 2000, 2002). While it has been theorized that top management values create the safety climate, most studies have actually focused on the more proximal, group supervisor leadership rather than top management leadership. This leaves open questions as to whether more distal aspects of the organization affect safety climate and whether safety climate mediates the effects of these organizational characteristics on safety behavior, or whether the organizational characteristics affect the more proximal aspects of the work environment such as workgroup and job characteristics subsequently resulting in safety climate.

It is noted that much of the literature on safety climate has not actually examined safety climate per se in that studies have not included organizational-level or even group-level accounts of climate. Instead many studies have examined psychological climate based on individuals' perceptions of the safety climate (but see Hofmann and Stetzer, 1996).

Repetti (1987), in one of the first multilevel analyses reported in a psychological journal, found that there were organizational climate effects as well as individual perceptions of climate effects of the work environment on employees' mental health. Therefore, although safety climate affects safety behaviors, it would appear that it may do so through individual perceptions of safety climate, as shown in Figure 19.1.

Climate for health

It has been suggested that organizations have a climate for health in the same vein as they have a climate for safety. However, there has been little research examining health climate. Health climate has been found to be related to employees' involvement in health promotion activities, management support, and the enactment of health promotion programs (Basen-Engquist, Hudmon, Tripp, and Chamberlain, 1998). Also, Mearns, Hope, Cheyne, Ford, and Tetrick (forthcoming) found that organizational investment in occupational health was related both to health and safety climate at the organizational level and to risk-taking at the individual level. It appears that, consistent with Repetti (1987), there are organizational and individual components of health climate that influence the effectiveness of health promotion activities.

In the health promotion literature, environmental factors other than health climate have been suggested to affect whether employees participate in health promotion activities and which health promotion activities organizations may offer. These include management style, industry type, organization rank, worksite size, organizational structure, degree of support from top management, inclusion of incentives or recognition for healthy behaviors or participation in a health promotion program, modeling of health behaviors by the CEO, policies reinforcing health behaviors, job design including employee autonomy and control over work activities, and subcultures within the organization (Basen-Engquist *et al.*, 1998). The health promotion literature thus suggests that the antecedents of health climate mirror, at least to an extent, the antecedents of safety climate, although this literature is not as well developed as the safety climate literature. Further, with the exception of Mearns *et al.* (forthcoming), it appears that research on health climate has not considered multilevel factors but has primarily examined individuals' perceptions of the health climate. Therefore, the health climate literature suffers from many of the same gaps as the safety climate literature. The health climate literature generally has not explicitly examined the potential antecedents of health climate, has not differentiated between organizational-level and more proximal departmental or workgroup levels of health climate, and has not examined the role of worker values and perceptions of responsibility for health.

It may be that there are parallel processes in the development of a health climate, as for safety climate relative to organizational characteristics, departmental/workgroup characteristics, and individual characteristics. In a parallel process mode, it would be expected that health climate would predict healthy behaviors and safety climate would predict safety behaviors. The literature really has not explicitly addressed the link between safety and health. Clearly, if one were harmed in an unsafe work environment, then one's health would be impaired, at least temporarily. It might also be argued that concern over the lack of safety in the work environment might contribute to a decline in one's health and well-being, much as a lack of psychological safety can impair one's functioning (Edmondson, 1999). There is a clear need for theory development and empirical research on the relation between health and safety as well as health climate and safety climate.

Figure 19.1 reflects a hypothesized direct relation from safety behavior and healthy behavior to organizational health, which can result in subsequent changes in organizational characteristics. This impact of individual safety and health on organizational health has been a fundamental assumption in occupational health psychology research (DeJoy and Wilson, 2003; Hofmann and Tetrick, 2003; Tetrick and Quick, 2003); however, it has not been empirically established in the literature (Tetrick, 2002). This is a critical linkage, as health protection and promotion activities have to compete with other performance-enhancing strategies in organizations (DeJoy and Wilson, 2003). Further, the conflicting values as described above and in Bennett et al. (2003) may weaken the case for investment in health protection and promotion unless it can be demonstrated to be a value-added activity or, alternatively, organizations are required to engage in these activities through legislation or collective bargaining, which may be less effective in the long run.

Change and innovation

Improvement of the safety and health of workers as well as organizations is believed to require organizational-level change and individual behavioral change. One of the most influential models of individual change used in the health promotion literature is the TransTheoretical Model of Change (Prochaska and Norcross, 2001). According to this model, individuals progress through five stages of change. The first stage is precontemplation, which is characterized by not recognizing that there is a problem and hence having no intent to change. The second stage is called the contemplation stage and reflects an awareness of the problem and involves the weighing of the pros and cons of the problem behavior. The third stage, preparation, involves a decision to change in the near future and may actually involve some small behavioral changes. The fourth stage is the action stage where one changes the behavior or environment to overcome the problem, and, lastly, the maintenance stage is characterized as working to prevent reverting to one's prior behavior and sustaining the desired change. The TransTheoretical Model of Change has been used frequently to develop interventions and is probably the most influential model of individual behavior change, conceptually; however, the empirical evidence has been mixed (Blanchard, Morgenstern, Morgan, Labouvie, and Bux, 2003).

The TransTheoretical Model of Change also has been extended to address organizational change. For example, Levesque, Prochaska, Prochaska, Dewart, Hamby, and Weeks (2001) extended this model to examine the adoption of continuous quality improvement processes in health care. They found support for a stage-matching intervention for physicians by tailoring the intervention to the stage of change (readiness to take action) of individual physicians. For example, if a person is in the precontemplation stage, it is most important to provide information that would help him/her recognize the need to change, whereas if the individual is in the contemplation stage, it would be most appropriate to provide information on the advantages and disadvantages of changing.

Simpson (2002) and Lehman, Greener, and Simpson (2002) took a slightly different approach for conceptualizing organizational readiness for change. Incorporating the technology transfer literature, they suggested focusing on the motivational readiness of leaders and staff, including the perceived need and pressure for change, efficacy, professional growth, influence, and adaptability. They also incorporated organizational climate, which consisted specifically of clarity of mission and goals, staff cohesion, autonomy, openness of communication, stress, and openness to change; and institutional resources, including staffing levels, physical resources, training levels, and technology accessibility and availability. Simpson (2002), citing Backer, suggested that there are four conditions for effective implementation of new programs in organizations. These four conditions are (1) people in the organization need to know the research upon which effective interventions can be developed, (2) data are needed which indicate that the program is feasible and effective, (3) resources are sufficient for the program, and (4) incentives are provided for individuals and organizations to change. This model has been used to develop diagnostic tools for planning interventions to facilitate organizational change, primarily change efforts in human services organizations, such as drug treatment facilities aimed at transferring research to practice.

There is a larger body of literature on organizational change and innovation, which has focused on manufacturing and other for-profit organizations, that have taken a somewhat different perspective from the previous two models discussed above. A common thread running through the organizational science literature on individual and organizational change is the notion of absorptive capacity. Cohen and Levinthal (1990) introduced the term absorptive capacity to provide a new perspective on organizational learning and innovation. Drawing on the learning and problem-solving literature, they suggested that cognitive structures are necessary for individual learning and that an individual's learning is based on the prior related knowledge and diversity of these cognitive structures. Moving to the organizational level, Cohen and Levinthal indicated there are three abilities that organizations (and individuals) must develop in order to learn. These are the ability to recognize the value of new information, the ability to assimilate this new information, and the ability to apply this new knowledge. These abilities are a function of prior related knowledge and diversity of background. Zahra and George (2002) reviewed the literature on absorptive capacity and extended the notion of absorptive capacity. They defined absorptive capacity as "a set of organizational routines and processes by which firms acquire, assimilate, transform, and exploit (that is, use) knowledge to produce dynamic organizational capability" (p. 186). The acquisition and assimilation of knowledge reflects the organization's potential capacity, and the transformation and exploitation of the knowledge reflects the realized capacity. This reconceptualization of absorptive capacity parallels the literature on organizational culture and climate as discussed earlier (see Ashkanasy et al., 2000).

It seems that the absorptive capacity of individual and organizational change and innovation is consistent with the TransTheoretical Model of Change as reflected in Figure 19.2. In order for organizations (and individuals) to leave the precontemplation stage of change according to the TransTheoretical Model of Change, there must be recognition of a need for change. This knowledge can be obtained from within the organization or from outside of the organization, according to the literature on absorptive capacity. Outside sources may be other firms in the industry, governmental agencies, community organizations, especially the public health and the educational communities, and family. In other words, relevant information may be obtained from multiple sources, and some of these knowledge acquisition functions may be formalized within specific units and individuals' boundary spanning and information gathering

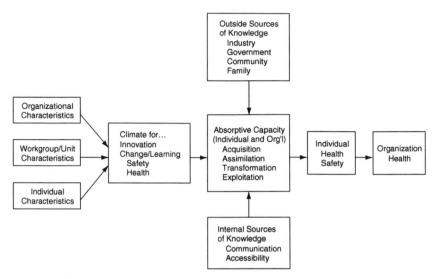

Figure 19.2 TransTheoretical Model of Change

responsibilities. However, it is important that informal sources are not overlooked. Communication channels and the sharing of expertise among organizational units and workers are also important sources in the acquisition of knowledge.

Once the organization (or individual) has recognized the need to change then it is important for the knowledge to be assimilated within the organization. This may be through formal or informal communication channels and may be facilitated or impaired by organizational characteristics, culture, and climate. Worker participation in health promotion and protection programs and activities would be expected to facilitate the assimilation of knowledge relevant to occupational safety and health as employees have first-hand knowledge of the production processes and potential exposures to risk factors. Therefore, the process of assimilation of knowledge is critical to the contemplation stage of change in the TransTheoretical Model of Change, where the positives and negatives of the information concerning change are weighed and the positives need to outweigh the negatives for individuals to transition to the preparation and subsequent action stages of change.

The dynamic interplay of organizational members with knowledge sources both within and outside of the organization results in the potential absorptive capacity of the organization. These processes build the prior related knowledge upon which the organization must rely to realize its absorptive capacity (Zahra and George, 2002). To realize its absorptive capacity, the organization (and its members) must transform the knowledge obtained to fit the specific situation and then prepare a means for exploiting this knowledge. In the absorptive capacity literature, exploiting the knowledge refers to using the knowledge for commercial ends. However, within the occupational health and safety arena, I suggest that exploitation involves the successful implementation of effective health protection and promotion programs in an integrated and coordinated manner.

Conclusion

This chapter has proposed an integrative model of health protection and health promotion in the workplace. Consistent with organizational theory, an integration of these functions within organizations is argued to result in enhanced individual and organizational safety and health. In addition, one of the challenges for organizations today is the need for continuous improvement through the transfer of knowledge about safety and health into successful organizational practices. The literature on individual and organizational change identifies several factors for the successful integration of the health protection and health promotion literatures. Communication and education among all members of the organization are important, as are the development and maintenance of a positive organizational climate for innovation, change/learning, safety, and health. These factors appear to be critical in the integration of health protection and promotion and in the effective design and implementation of programs to enhance the safety and health of the work environment.

References

Ashkanasy, N., Wilderom, C. P. M., and Peterson, M. F. (eds.) (2000). *Handbook of organizational culture and climate*. Thousand Oaks, CA: Sage.

Basen-Engquist, K., Hudmon, K. S., Tripp, M., and Chamberlain, R. (1998). Worksite health and safety climate: scale development and effects of a health promotion intervention. *Preventive Medicine* 27: 111–19.

Bennett, J. B., Cook, R. F., and Pelletier, K. R. (2003). Toward an integrated framework for comprehensive organizational wellness: concepts, practices, and research in workplace health promotion. In J. C. Quick and L. E. Tetrick (eds.), *Handbook of occupational health psychology* (pp. 69–95). Washington, DC: American Psychological Association.

Blanchard, K. A., Morgenstern, J., Morgan, T. J., Labouvie, E., and Bux, D. A. (2003). Motivational subtypes and continuous measures of readiness for change: current and predictive validity. *Psychology of Addictive Behaviors* 17: 56–65.

Chen, M. (2003). Workers' participation and their health and safety protection in China's transitional industrial economy. *International Journal of Occupational and Environmental Health* 9: 368–77.

Cohen, W. M. and Levinthal, D. A. (1990). Absorptive capacity: a new perspective on learning and innovation. *Administrative Science Quarterly* 36: 128–52.

Cropanzano, R. and Mitchell, M. S. (2005). Social exchange theory: an interdisciplinary review. *Journal of Management* 31: 874–900.

DeJoy, D. M. and Wilson, M. G. (2003). Organizational health promotion: broadening the horizon of workplace health promotion. *American Journal of Health Promotion* 17: 337–41.

Edmondson, A. C. (1999). Psychological safety and learning behavior in work teams. *Administrative Science Quarterly* 44: 350–83.

Gaba, D. M., Singer, S. J., Sinaiko, A. D., Bowen, J. D., and Ciavarelli, A. P. (2003). Differences in safety climate between hospital personnel and naval aviators. *Human Factors* 45: 173–85.

Griffin, M. A. and Neal, A. (2000). Perceptions of safety at work: a framework for linking safety climate to safety performance, knowledge, and motivation. *Journal of Occupational Health Psychology* 5: 347–58.

Hofmann, D. A. and Morgeson, F. P. (2003). The role of leadership in safety performance. In J. Barling and M. Frone (eds.), *The psychology of workplace safety* (pp. 159–80). Washington, DC: American Psychological Association.

Hofmann, D. A., Morgeson, F. P., and Gerras, S. J. (2003). Climate as a moderator of the relationship between leader–member exchange and content specific citizenship: safety climate as an exemplar. *Journal of Applied Psychology* 88: 170–8.

Hofmann, D.A. and Stetzer, A. (1996). A cross-level investigation of factors influencing unsafe behaviors and accidents. *Personnel Psychology* 49: 307–39.

Hofmann, D. A. and Tetrick, L. E. (2003). The etiology of health: implications for "organizing" individual and organizational health. In D. A. Hofmann and L. E. Tetrick (eds.), *Health and safety in organizations: a multilevel perspective* (pp. 1–27). Organizational Frontier Series, Society for Industrial and Organizational Psychology. San Francisco: Jossey-Bass.

Lee, C. H. and Bruvold, N. T. (2003). Creating value for employees: investment in employee development. *International Journal of Human Resource Management* 14: 981–1000.

Lehman, W. E. K., Greener, J. M., and Simpson, D. D. (2002). Assessing organizational readiness for change. *Journal of Substance Abuse Treatment* 22: 197–209.

Levesque, D. A., Prochaska, J. M., Prochaska, J. O., Dewart, S. R., Hamby, L. S., and Weeks, W. P. (2001). Organizational stages and processes of change for continuous quality improvement in healthcare. *Counseling Psychology Journal: Practice and Research* 53: 139–53.

Mbakaya, C. F. L., Onyoyo, H. A., and Lwaki, S. A. (1999). A survey on management perspectives of the state of workplace health and safety practices in Kenya. *Accident Analysis and Prevention* 31: 305–12.

Mearns, K., Hope, L., Cheyne, A., Ford, M., and Tetrick, L. E. (forthcoming). Investment in workforce health: exploring the implications for workforce safety and commitment. Unpublished manuscript, University of Aberdeen.

Milgate, N., Innes, E., and O'Loughlin, K. (2002). Examining the effectiveness of health and safety committees and representatives: a review. *Work: Journal of Prevention, Assessment and Rehabilitation* 19: 281–90.

Mueller, L. (2005). Organizational level referenced climate items: implications for organizational surveys. Paper presented at the Academy of Management Meetings, Honolulu, August.

Mueller, L., Da Silva, N., Townsend, J. C., and Tetrick, L. E. (1999). An empirical evaluation of competing safety climate measurement models. Paper presented at the annual meeting for Society of Industrial and Organizational Psychology, Atlanta, May.

Nicoll, A. and Murray, V. (2002). Health protection – a strategy and a national agency. *Public Health* 116: 129–37.

Ostroff, C., Kinicki, A. J., and Tamkins, M. M. (2003). Organizational culture and climate. In W. C. Borman, D. R. Ilgen, and R. J. Klimoski (eds.), *Handbook of psychology*, vol. 12. *Industrial and organizational psychology* (pp. 565–93). Hoboken, NJ: Wiley.

Pelletier, K. E. (1983). *Healthy people in unhealthy places: stress and fitness at work.* New York: Delacorte Press.

Peltomäki, P., Johansson, M., and Ahrens, W. (2003). Social context for workplace health promotion: feasibility considerations in Costa Rica, Finland, Germany, Spain and Sweden. *Health Promotion International* 18: 115–26.

Prochaska, J. O. and Norcross, J. C. (2001). Stages of change. *Psychotherapy* 38: 443–8.

Rantanen, J. (2003). International perspective: integrating health promotion and protection. Paper presented at Steps to a Healthier US Workforce Linking Workplace Protection and Workplace Promotion: Synergy in Action, NIOSH, Cincinnati, OH.

Ratajczak, Z. (1993). Conflicting perspective on health promotion in the workplace. *Polish Psychological Bulletin* 24: 75–81.

Repetti, R. L. (1987). Individual and common components of the social environment at work and psychological well-being. *Journal of Personality and Social Psychology* 52: 710–20.

Robbins, L. (1992). Health and safety committees as a means of relieving psychological stress. In J. C. Quick, L. R. Murphy, and J. J. Hurrell Jr. (eds.), *Stress and well-being at work: assessments and interventions for occupational mental health* (pp. 193–206). Washington, DC: American Psychological Association.

Schein, E. H. (1990). Organizational culture. *American Psychologist* 45: 109–19.

Seashore, S. E., Lawler, E. E., Mirvis, P. H., and Cammann, C. (eds.) (1983). *Assessing organizational change: a guide to methods, measures, and practices.* New York: Wiley.

Simpson, D. D. (2002). A conceptual framework for transferring research to practice. *Journal of Substance Abuse Treatment* 22: 171–82.

Sorensen, G., Stoddard, A., Ockene, J. K., Hunt, M. K., and Youngstrom, R. (1996). Worker participation in an integrated health promotion/health protection program: results from the WellWorks project. *Health Education Quarterly* 23: 191–203.

Tetrick, L. E. (2002). Individual and organizational health. In P. Perrewé and D. Ganster (eds.), *Research in occupational stress and well-being* (vol. 2, pp. 3–17). Stamford, CT: JAI Press.

Tetrick, L. E. and Camburn, M. K. (2004). Organizational structure. In S. Zedeck (ed.), *Encyclopedia of applied psychology* (vol. 2, pp. 747–53). Oxford: Elsevier Academic.

Tetrick, L. E. and Ellis, B. B. (2002). Developing an OHP curriculum that addresses the needs of organizations and labor unions in the USA. Paper presented at the European Academy of Occupational Health Psychology, Vienna.

Tetrick, L. E. and Quick, J. C. (2003). Prevention at work: public health in occupational settings. In J. C. Quick and L. E. Tetrick (eds.), *Handbook of occupational health psychology* (pp. 3–17). Washington, DC: American Psychological Association.

Zahra, S. A. and George, G. (2002). Absorptive capacity: a review, reconceptualization, and extension. *Academy of Management Review* 27: 185–203.

Zohar, D. (1980). Safety climate in industrial organizations: theoretical and applied implications. *Journal of Applied Psychology* 65: 96–102.

(2000). A group-level model of safety climate: testing the effect of group climate on microaccidents in manufacturing jobs. *Journal of Applied Psychology* 85: 587–96.

(2002). Modifying supervisory practices to improve subunit safety: a leadership-based intervention model. *Journal of Applied Psychology* 87: 156–63.

(2003). Safety climate: conceptual and measurement issues. In J. C. Quick and L. E. Tetrick (eds.), *Handbook of occupational health psychology* (pp. 123–42). Washington, DC: American Psychological Association.

20 Workplace interventions for occupational stress

*E. Kevin Kelloway, Joseph J. Hurrell Jr.,
and Arla Day*

Research consistently has documented the same phenomenon across the developed world: as the pace of competition increases and we enter a truly global marketplace, stress and its consequences are becoming epidemic (Sauter, Murphy, and Hurrell, 1990). Increased work hours, increased pressure, increased insecurity (e.g. Bond, Galinsky, and Swanberg, 1997), and myriad other organizational stressors have immediate and long-term consequences for both individuals and organizations. Consequently, it is not surprising that research on work stress has proliferated. However, the question of what organizations can do to avert or mitigate the negative consequences of stress – arguably the single most important question in the field – remains largely unaddressed and, therefore, unanswered. In this chapter, we summarize what is known about how organizations can deal with the proliferation of organizational stressors. In doing so, we also attempt to identify what is not known – thereby establishing agendas for both practice and research.

A model of job stress

A variety of "models" of job stress exist, varying in both their breadth and the complexity of the processes underlying the model predictions (Kelloway and Day, 2005a). Despite diverse theoretical approaches, we suggest that most work stress researchers would agree with a basic model postulating that a set of organizational stressors (i.e. events that occur in the work environment outside the individual; Pratt and Barling, 1988) may be perceived as stressful by the individual, and consequently can result in a variety of strain reactions (see, for example, Hurrell and Kelloway, in press). Strain reactions have been further characterized as comprising psychological, physiological, behavioral, and organizational reactions (Kelloway and Day, 2005a) that often impact individual and/or organizational health.

Work-related stressors

In proposing their national strategy for the prevention of work-related stress disorders, Sauter *et al.* (1990) identified six major categories of stressors that have been consistently identified in the empirical literature: (1) work load and pace; (2) role stressors; (3) career concerns; (4) work schedules; (5) interpersonal relationships; and (6) job content and job control.

Work load and pace reflect how much work one has to do and the time in which the work is expected to be completed. Data consistently support associations between work overload and measures of health (e.g. Jex and Beehr, 1991; Kelloway and Barling, 1991). *Role stressors* include role conflict, role ambiguity, and interrole conflict; a vast array of literature supports associations between these stressors and strain outcomes (for reviews, see Beehr and Glazer, 2005; Bellavia and Frone, 2005; Mullen, Kelley, and Kelloway, in press). *Career concerns* include issues such as job insecurity (e.g. Probst, 2005) and job safety (e.g. Barlow and Iverson, 2005). *Work schedules* (Totterdell, 2005), including both shift work and the length of the work day, are frequently identified as stressors, as is the quality of *interpersonal relationships* in the organization. In recent years, researchers have focused on issues of workplace violence/aggression (Kelloway, Barling, and Hurrell, 2006; Schat and Kelloway, 2005) and leadership (Kelloway, Sivanathan, Francis, and Barling, 2005b) as key interpersonal issues in the workplace. In their review, Sauter *et al.* (1990: 1153) summarized *job content and job control*, noting that jobs that are "narrow, fragmented, invariant and short-cycle tasks that provide little stimulation, allow little use of skills or expression of creativity and have little intrinsic meaning for workers" are stressful.

Strain reactions

As noted earlier, strain reactions comprise a diverse array of responses to organizational stressors. *Psychological strain* is typically manifested as disturbances in either affect or cognition (Kelloway and Day, 2005a). The most studied forms of *physiological strain* include hypertension, coronary heart disease, musculoskeletal disorders, increased risk of infectious disease, and minor psychosomatic symptoms (see Hurrell and Kelloway, in press, and Kelloway and Day, 2005a for overviews). *Behavioral strain* includes both nervous habits (tics and fidgeting) and substance abuse or behavioral disorders such as alcoholism, smoking, and the use of illicit drugs (Kelloway and Day, 2005a). Not surprisingly, stress can also manifest in the workplace. *Organizational strain* includes absenteeism, turnover, and decreased performance (for reviews, see Jex, 1998; Jex and Cossley, 2005).

Taken together these strains exact substantial individual, organizational, and societal costs. For example, Matteson and Ivancevich (1982) estimated that businesses in the US lose at least $60 billion per year because of stress related illness. By 1990, the estimate had risen to $150 billion per year (Karasek and Theorell, 1990), and just over a decade later the American Institute of Stress (2002) estimated the societal cost of stress to be $300 billion annually.

Although we should recognize that these estimates involve considerable "guesswork," it is clear that workplace stress is a large and growing problem with considerable consequences for individuals and organizations. For example, claims for stress related illnesses in California increased by approximately 560% over a six-year period (Quick, Quick, Nelson, and Hurrell, 1997), inflating costs for both organizations and society. Although claims have since declined in that state, stress related compensation claims remain a major cost. The National Institute for Occupational Health and Safety in the United States noted that although the median time lost that is attributable to non-fatal illness is about six days per incident, stress related claims are associated with a median of twenty-five lost days, and over 40% of all stress related claims entail more than thirty days of missed time. Although the magnitude of these estimates of the societal and organizational cost of stress is frequently cited as the rationale for being concerned with job stress, Cartwright and Cooper (1997) appropriately noted that we also should not forget the substantial individual costs in human suffering associated with workplace stress.

Workplace interventions

This model of work stress, wherein stressors may lead to strains, has resulted in the popularization of a unifying framework for classifying interventions. Drawing on public health terminology, Hurrell and Murphy (1996; see also Hurrell, 2005) delineated primary, secondary, and tertiary modes of intervention. *Primary* interventions are focused on reducing or eliminating the stressors (Hurrell, 2005; Quick *et al.*, 1997). *Secondary* interventions focus on changing the individual's reactions to being exposed to work stressors. Finally, *tertiary* interventions represent a "heal the wounded" approach in which the focus is to treat individuals who have developed strain reactions (Quick *et al.*, 1997). Embedded in this framework, which differentiates intervention programs on the basis of their "focus," is a related typology that examines the "level" at which interventions are implemented. In their review of work stress interventions,

DeFrank and Cooper (1987) conceptualized different "levels" of interventions, in terms of strategies aimed at: individuals; the interaction between individual and organization (e.g. person–environment fit; interpersonal relationships); and organization and social contexts (e.g. job redesign, organizational restructuring). Therefore, as we review these primary, secondary, and tertiary modes of intervention, we take these different levels of intervention (i.e. individual level, individual–organizational interaction, and organizational level) into consideration as well.

Primary intervention

Although generally thought to be the most effective approach to dealing with work stress (Kelloway and Day, 2005b), primary interventions are one of the least studied areas of work stress. Nonetheless, data do exist suggesting the effectiveness of this approach. In their comprehensive review, Parkes and Sparkes (1998) described two types of primary intervention: psychosocial interventions and sociotechnical interventions. As noted by Hurrell (2005: 624), psychosocial interventions "focus *primarily* on human processes and psychosocial aspects of the work setting and aim to reduce stress by changing employee perceptions of the work environment." In contrast, sociotechnical interventions "focus *primarily* on changes to objective work conditions" (Hurrell, 2005: 625). As indicated by his emphasis, these distinctions can be difficult to make in practice because some interventions involve both objective and subjective changes; often, the distinction between a psychosocial and sociotechnical intervention may be a matter of degree rather than of kind. Nonetheless, the Parkes and Sparkes (1998) framework provides a starting point for our review of primary interventions.

Psychosocial interventions Most of the psychosocial interventions are based on a model of participatory action research in which employees and "experts" engage in a joint process of identifying problems, developing and implementing solutions, and evaluating outcomes (Hurrell, 2005). Interventions based on this model are necessarily ambitious and frequently run into "real world" constraints, such as the inability to implement the programs as planned (e.g. Campbell, 1973), the co-occurrence of confounding organizational events (Heaney, Israel, Schurman, Baker, House, and Hugentobler, 1993), and the necessity for short, small-scale implementations (e.g. Landsbergis and Vivona-Vaughan, 1995). These practical constraints have limited researchers' ability to draw conclusions about the effectiveness, or ineffectiveness, of such interventions.

However, some promising results have emerged from this psychosocial intervention research. Mikkelsen, Saksvik, and Landsbergis (2000) examined the impact of a short-term intervention that was conducted at two different Norwegian community mental health care institutions. Sixty-four participants (including managers and supervisors) were randomly assigned to either an experimental or a control group, each of which involved completion of intervention assessments at baseline, one-week, and one-year follow-ups. Experimental group participants identified job stressors and developed plans for their reduction. Analysis at post-test showed a reduction in work-related stress and perceived psychological demands. Unfortunately, pragmatic constraints prohibited a longer-term follow-up.

Research has examined the effectiveness of developing autonomous teams and using participatory job redesign. Wall and Clegg (1981) conducted a thirty-three-month study of job redesign and showed that the implementation of two leaderless teams with responsibility for the complete production process resulted in improvements in job attitudes, motivation, and mental health. Using a similar intervention by implementing autonomous work groups, Wall, Kemp, Jackson, and Clegg (1986) found positive effects of the creation of these groups on job satisfaction, although there were no significant changes in mental health, commitment, and performance. The introduction of twenty self-managed workteams in a Dutch manufacturing company also resulted in striking results: they experienced a 50% decrease in absenteeism and a corresponding 66% increase in productivity (Terra, 1995). Similarly, Wahlstedt and Edling (1997) reported on the development of workgroups and other aspects of work design among postal workers. They found that perceptions of skill discretion and decision authority were higher twelve months following intervention, but that these positive perceptions did not translate into beneficial health outcomes. Bond and Bunce (2001) found that a participatory action research project involving job redesign resulted in enhanced perceptions of job control, which, in turn, led to improved mental health, reduced absence, and enhanced (self-rated) performance one year after implementation. Finally, job satisfaction was increased following a participatory job redesign in a study reported by Griffeth (1985). The use of a 2 (participation) × 2 (redesign) experimental design revealed evidence that the primary effect appeared to be derived from the redesign itself, rather than from the participatory aspect of the design (Griffeth, 1985).

Other forms of psychosocial interventions have focused on training, rather than on group development and work redesign. For example, Schaubroeck, Ganster, Sime, and Ditman (1993) conducted a field experiment in which training over a two-year period was provided in order to clarify the supervisory role. The results provided some evidence that supervisory role clarification resulted in reduced role ambiguity, but did not necessarily enhance mental health outcomes, for subordinates. Beaton, Johnson, Infield, Ollis, and Bond (2001) also focused on organizational leaders in their study of urban firefighters. Leaders reported significant improvements on a number of stress related symptom indices at both the three- and nine-month follow-ups. Similarly, Theorell, Emdad, Arnetz, and Weingarten (2001) trained forty-two managers in a Swedish insurance company. A control group consisted of employees in another department of the company that was unaffected by the intervention. The intervention resulted in both lowered serum cortisol levels and improved self-reported decision authority among employees.

Finally, Schweiger and DeNisi (1991) examined the impact of an intervention carried out in two plants (i.e. which acted as the experimental and control groups) of a manufacturing company that was undergoing a merger. The intervention involved a communications program designed to provide the 126 experimental plant employees with frequent information regarding the situation, to treat employees fairly, and to address questions and concerns. The results of the study indicated a positive effect of the intervention on perceptions of uncertainty, job satisfaction, organizational commitment, and belief in the company's trustworthiness.

PSYCHOSOCIAL INTERVENTIONS SUMMARY Although the results of many of these studies have been encouraging, we reiterate Parkes and Sparkes' (1998) conclusion that clear evidence for the effectiveness of psychosocial interventions is not yet available. Indeed, many of the studies in this area tend to be methodologically lacking, causally ambiguous, and difficult to interpret (Parkes and Sparkes, 1998). We do not suggest that this lack of conclusive evidence reflects an inherent weakness in the ability of stress researchers. Rather, the studies reviewed above consistently point to the almost insurmountable difficulties inherent in designing high-quality and unambiguous field studies. Moreover, Murphy and Sauter (2003) suggested that these "stressor-reduction interventions" may be perceived as not being successful because the studies examining the impact of these interventions need to be of a longer duration. That is, "interventions that focus on job redesign might increase worker stress in the short-term" (2003: 153), and therefore they may be perceived as ineffective. However, because they may have beneficial effects in the long term, studies need to assess outcomes across a longer time span.

Sociotechnical interventions In contrast to the focus on individual perceptions and attitudes that are inherent in the psychosocial interventions, the goal of a sociotechnical intervention is to change objective working conditions. As Hurrell (2005) noted, much of the work in this area has focused on changing workload, work schedules, or work processes. For example, "family friendly" or "work–life balance" organizational policies and practices can be viewed in this context. The basic intent of such policies is to help employees balance their personal or family life with job responsibilities. Work–life programs and policies can include: maternity and paternity leave benefits; allowances for personal and sick time; work schedule flexibility; telecommuting policies; breastfeeding arrangements; and employer-supported child and elder care. These interventions appear to have a beneficial impact on various employee factors, such as increased job satisfaction and employee motivation and reduced job stress (see for example, Saltzstein, Ting, and Saltzstein, 2001).

One of the first studies to examine the effectiveness of workload reduction was initiated in 1985 (Parkes, 1995; Parkes, Broadbent, Johnston, Rendall, Matthews, and Smith, 1986). The intervention investigated the effects of reducing objective workload for a large sample of driving examiners in the United Kingdom. Reducing the number of tests conducted each day resulted in decreased anxiety and perceived demands as well as increasing job satisfaction, improving cognitive performance, and enhancing cardio-vascular functioning (Parkes, 1995; Parkes *et al.*, 1986). Meijman, Mulder, van Dormolen, and Cremer (1992) also conducted a workload intervention with driving examiners. Reducing the workload of these examiners resulted in lower tension and improved mental efficiency, but no effects were found for either their blood pressure or their adrenalin levels.

The introduction of alternate work schedules, often associated with work–family interventions (Gottlieb, Kelloway, and Barham, 1998), has been frequently investigated. Baltes, Briggs, Huff, Wright, and Neuman (1999) conducted a meta-analysis of the effects of flexible and com-pressed workweek schedules on outcomes such as productivity/performance, job satisfaction, absenteeism, and satisfaction with work schedule, and found generally positive effects. Intervention studies largely support this finding. For example, Ivancevich and Lyon (1977) conducted a field experiment on the introduction of a compressed workweek. Thirteen months following the intervention, workers on the compressed workweek were more satisfied with autonomy, personal worth, job security, and pay than were workers in the control group. They also reported less anxiety-stress and showed greater productivity than workers in the control group. No significant differences emerged at follow-up twenty-five months after the intervention.

When comparing absenteeism and performance between an experimental group who had a flextime program and a control group who did not, Kim and Campagna (1981) found that flextime was associated with higher performance and lower unpaid absence, although there were no differences between the groups in paid absence. Other studies of flextime have found improved employee flexibility, workgroup relationships, and superior–subordinate relationships as well as decreased absenteeism as a result of the more flexible schedule (Narayanan and Nath, 1982), although these effects seem to be moderated by group cohesion (Narayanan and Nath, 1984). Dunham, Pierce, and Castaneda (1987) described two quasi-experimental field studies that examined the effects of both a compressed workweek and the introduction of flextime. The most powerful effect of both schedules was on measures directly related to the schedules (e.g. worker attitudes toward the specific work schedule), with the least robust effect on measures of family and social life.

More micro-interventions focus on the "within day" work schedule rather than the workweek per se. That is, rather than focusing on the schedule of shifts within a workweek or pay period, micro-interventions examine the scheduling of tasks or breaks within the workday. Galinsky, Swanson, Sauter, Hurrell, and Schleifer (2000) conducted a field study that examined the effects of providing supplementary rest breaks on mood, musculoskeletal discomfort, eyestrain, and performance in forty-two data-entry workers. Results indicated that adding twenty minutes of additional break time each day resulted in lowered discomfort and eyestrain, without reductions in data-entry performance.

In addition to work schedule changes, the processes of work have been redesigned in efforts to reduce job stress. Using an experimental design, Jackson (1983) examined the effects of increased participation in decision-making. Participation was associated with decreased role conflict and role ambiguity, and increased perceived influence six months after the introduction of the intervention. Both conflict and ambiguity were found to be associated with emotional strain and job dissatisfaction. Job influence was found to have beneficial effects on job satisfaction and turnover intentions. Wall, Corbett, Martin, Clegg, and Jackson (1990) examined the impact of having increased control over work processes by assembly machine operators. Providing operators with more control resulted in reduced downtime, and was associated with greater intrinsic job satisfaction and less perceived time pressure. However, there were no effects on extrinsic job satisfaction, general strain, or job-related strain. A more complex intervention focused on changing work processes and procedures: relative to organizational controls, depression scores were found to decrease for the intervention group (Kawakami, Araki,

Kawashima, Masumoto, and Hayashi, 1997). Correspondingly, sick leave decreased in the last follow-up only in the intervention group.

Evans, Johansson, and Rydstedt (1999) examined the effects of physical changes in bus route design and technological innovations (designed to decrease traffic congestion, lessen passenger demands on bus operators, and generally ease bus operations) on driver health. The bus drivers in the experimental group experienced significant pre–post decreases in systolic blood pressure, heart rate, perceived stress, and perceived job hassles. Conversely, the control group drivers experienced a decrease of systolic blood pressure, but they experienced little or no changes on the other measured outcomes.

Participative employee health circles have evolved as a result of legislation requiring organizations in Germany to focus on preventative measures to improve employee health (Aust and Ducki, 2004). These health circles consist of groups of employees who identify and recommend (and, in some cases, help implement) organizational changes (e.g. ergonomic changes, improved communication strategies, job redesign) to help improve employee health (Aust and Ducki, 2004). In their review of eleven studies that critiqued eighty-one health circles in Germany, Aust and Ducki (2004) reported some preliminary positive outcomes of these circles, such as improved working conditions, reduced absenteeism, and improved psychosocial and physiological health indicators. It is not clear the extent to which some of the improvements were due to the increased communication and decision-making allowed by the circles (i.e. psychosocial interventions), or to the organizational changes that were implemented as a result of the health circles (i.e. sociotechnical interventions). These circles are not widely used elsewhere; more research examining the effectiveness of these types of intervention is necessary before firm conclusions can be made about their effectiveness.

SOCIOTECHNICAL INTERVENTIONS SUMMARY When compared to the psychosocial interventions reviewed earlier, the literature on the sociotechnical interventions provides more unambiguous support for their effectiveness. Although these studies also are impacted by the pragmatics of organizational research, it has generally been more feasible to use rigorous experimental and quasi-experimental designs and to examine effects across an array of strain outcomes (Hurrell, 2005).

Secondary intervention

Secondary interventions generally focus on altering the relationship between stressors and strains either by increasing individual resilience to stress (e.g. through health promotion) or by teaching specific techniques to address the symptoms of strain (e.g. stress management training). Perhaps ironically, secondary interventions are often thought to be less effective, but are implemented more frequently in organizations, than are primary interventions. Secondary interventions may be less effective because they are either too general (i.e. not targeted toward a particular experience) or are invoked only after the stress has occurred (Kelloway, Francis, and Montgomery, 2005a). Moreover, these types of individual-level interventions do not tend to have long-term organizational or individual health benefits, perhaps because they have "limited ability ... to stimulate long-term behaviour changes" (Giga, Noblet, and Cooper, 2003: 163). Despite these criticisms, Giga *et al.* (2003) found that most of the research on stress interventions in the UK has focused on the individual (in terms of cognitive behavioral therapy and relaxation training). These secondary interventions may be preferred over primary interventions by organizational decision-makers because the costs and logistics of primary preventions are presumed to be excessive (Hepburn, Loughlin, and Barling, 1997).

Health promotion Health promotion and corporate "wellness" programs have become increasingly common. In the United States, for example, health related programs are implemented in as many as 90% of mid-sized companies (Aldana, 2001; Riedel *et al.*, 2001). Many of these programs are implemented in an attempt to reduce health care costs. However, even in Canada, where the presence of a government-funded health care system substantially reduces those costs, 64% of companies have implemented some form of wellness programming (Lowe, 2003). About half of the European companies surveyed by Kompier and Cooper (1999) had some form of health screening and 40% had "lifestyle" policies. Although the content of such programs varies widely, the typical focus of such programs includes the attempt to promote a healthier lifestyle and/or identify the early symptoms of disease (Ganster, 1995; Murphy and Cooper, 2000).

In general, wellness or health promotion programs can be incorporated with at least one of three goals (Gebhardt and Crump, 1990). First, programs can focus on *increasing awareness*, rather than effecting behavioral change. Such programs typically comprise newsletters, health fairs, screening sessions (e.g. blood pressure screening), posters, and brochures. Second, short-term (e.g. 8–12 weeks) health programs often aim for long-term benefit by focusing on *behavioral changes*, such as losing weight, increasing physical fitness, or improving diet. Finally, programs and policies can focus on creating a workplace that *promotes a healthy lifestyle*. Ensuring that cafeterias offer healthy foods, providing bike racks or locker facilities in the workplace, having on-site fitness facilities, or removing cigarette or candy machines from the workplace are all examples of a supportive organizational environment (Kelloway *et al.*, 2005a).

Evidence for the effectiveness of these interventions is mixed. Although many companies claim to have achieved substantial reductions in costs or absenteeism through the use of these types of interventions (Cooper and Cartwright, 1994), several reviewers have suggested that there is little evidence for the effectiveness of health promotion programs (e.g. Everly, 1986). Based on their review, Ivancevich and Matteson (1986) suggested that programs may enhance health but that any improvements in health attributable to such programs are short lived. In contrast, in their study of the effects of a lifestyle education program, Lindquist and Cooper (1999) found significant improvements in employees' levels of stress.

At least part of the debate over the effectiveness of such interventions is attributable to critiques of the use of weak evaluation designs and flaws in implementation. With regard to the latter, Lowe (2003) noted that health promotion programs are often divorced from other human resources practices in the firm. Moreover, the exclusive focus on individual attitudes and behavior, to the exclusion of organizational or even societal influences, may substantially limit the effectiveness of such programs. Everly (1986) noted that prepackaged, canned intervention programs that are not tailored to the specific needs and context of the organization are likely to fail.

HEALTH PROMOTION SUMMARY Health promotion programs are popular and appear to be gaining in acceptance in industry. Although there is mixed evidence for the success of such interventions, there is little doubt that they are popular among employees (Cartwright and Cooper, 2005).

Stress management A wide variety of interventions fall under the rubric of stress management, including relaxation/meditation techniques, exercise, educational programs, cognitive behavioral approaches, biofeedback, lifestyle programming, and interpersonal skills training (Cartwright and Cooper, 2005).

Incorporating some form of relaxation training is probably one of the most popular of all stress management techniques (Giga, Faragher, and Cooper, 2002). Empirical evaluation studies have generally supported the effectiveness of a variety of relaxation techniques, at least in the short term. For example, meditation tends to be successful in reducing stress levels (Winzelberg and Luskin, 1999), and relaxation and Tai-Chi may be effective at reducing some symptoms of stress (Wiholm, Arnetz, and

Berg, 2000). Massage therapy is another workplace intervention (e.g. Hodge, Robinson, Boehmer, and Klein, 2000) that is based on relaxation, and has been shown to be effective in reducing strain symptoms, including blood pressure (e.g. Moyer, Rounds, and Hannum, 2004). Even single applications of massage therapy appear to be effective (Moyer *et al.*, 2004).

In addition to relaxation, general physical exercise has been demonstrated to help people cope with stress. Even a single session of aerobic exercise is able to reduce state anxiety levels (Atchiler and Motta, 1994). Moreover, exercise tends to be the most effective means of stress reduction over stress awareness and rational emotive behavior therapy (Whatmore, Cooper, and Cartwright, 1999).

Cognitive behavioral therapy is also a popular element of stress management programs (Cooper and Cartwright, 2005), and there is evidence of its effectiveness (Kushnir and Malkinson, 1993). Perhaps the most common approach to stress management training in organizations, however, is the implementation of a multimode program that incorporates both the elements described above in addition to other programs (e.g. education on the nature of stressors, stress, and strain).

Bekker, Nijssen, and Hens (2001) conducted an evaluation of such a multimode intervention and found significant reductions in stress and symptoms of stress in employees both immediately after the training and three months later. Thomason and Pond (1995) found more equivocal evidence: a stress management training program had no effect on participants' blood pressure, somatic data, anxiety, or job satisfaction in comparison to a control group. However, incorporating a self-management module into the training (i.e. goal setting, self-reinforcement) resulted in significant effects on all criteria except job satisfaction. Keyes (1995) also reported significant effects of stress management training.

STRESS MANAGEMENT SUMMARY A wide variety of techniques have been incorporated into stress management programs. There is evidence for the effectiveness of such programs, although some of these effects may be only short-term (see Giga *et al.*, 2003). In contrast to research on health promotion activities, in which the evidence may be more equivocal, the data generally support the implementation of stress management programs for the reduction of employee stress.

Tertiary intervention

In contrast to the secondary focus on treating the short-term symptoms of stress, tertiary interventions are focused on treating the consequences of exposure to job stressors (i.e. strain reactions). The implementation of an Employee Assistance Program (EAP) is by far the most frequently occurring form of tertiary intervention (Kelloway et al., 2005a). Growing out of the earliest forms of industrial social work, EAPs date back to the nineteenth century with the social betterment movement (Kelloway et al., 2005a). By 1920, one in three of the largest companies in the United States had a full-time welfare secretary to counsel employees having personal problems (Popple, 1981). By the 1940s, programs that focused almost exclusively on employee alcoholism emerged (Matteson and Ivancevich, 1988). Modern EAP programs address a wide range of personal problems, including financial, legal, family, and substance use problems (Mio and Goishi, 1988).

EAPs most commonly provide educational services (e.g. awareness) around potential problems or health issues, emergency referrals, and individual counseling and psychotherapy. In some sense, the basic service of EAPs is to provide access to individual counseling. There is little doubt that counseling and psychotherapy can result in symptom reduction (e.g. Bower, Rowland, and Hardy 2003; Lambert and Bergin, 1994). Although some researchers have questioned the organizational impact of these programs (e.g. Reynolds, 1997), other researchers have reported substantial organizational benefits for EAP "graduates" (Landy, Quick, and Kasl, 1994).

In addition to EAPs, some organizations, particularly emergency service organizations, routinely provide access to services designed to assist individuals with the consequences of traumatic stress. In their review of Canadian emergency services, Kelloway, Francis, Catano, Cameron, and Day (2004) found that every emergency service surveyed across Canada provided some form of stress debriefing following exposure to traumatic stressors. Recent reviews of the traumatic stress literature have been critical of this practice, concluding that single sessions of individual psychological debriefing after trauma are not effective in reducing symptoms or subsequent posttraumatic stress disorder (e.g. Ehlers and Clark, 2003; Hurrell, 2006). Indeed, there are data suggesting that participation in such sessions may in fact impede recovery (McNally, Bryant, and Ehlers, 2003). These reviewers do not argue that intervention is impossible in these cases. In fact the same reviewers point to the effectiveness of interventions based on principles of cognitive behavioral therapy. Their main criticism is that short (single-session) debriefing is ineffective and may have negative consequences for the affected employee.

The provision of social support is also an important tertiary intervention that has been shown to have beneficial consequences. For example, Chisholm, Kasl, and Mueller (1986) found that social support had a direct effect on well-being and buffered the stress of a crisis among employees at the Three Mile Island nuclear facility. In their study of more than 800 firefighters in Canada and the United States, Corneil, Beaton, Murphy, Johnson, and Pike (1999) found that exposure to traumatic events does not necessarily predict posttraumatic stress disorder and that the exposure–outcome relationship may be mediated by both social support and chronic stress levels. Finally, studies of workplace violence have emphasized the moderating role of social support, suggesting that provision of such support may mitigate the stressful consequences of exposure to workplace violence (e.g. Schat and Kelloway, 2002).

TERTIARY INTERVENTIONS SUMMARY It is not always possible to eliminate stressors from the lives of individuals; therefore, a comprehensive approach to workplace stress should include tertiary interventions (Kelloway and Day, 2005b). Empirical data support the general effectiveness of both individual counseling and the provision of counseling through EAPs. Social support also appears to be effective in reducing the adverse consequences experienced as a result of traumatic exposure; however, the data on single session debriefings are more equivocal.

Summary and conclusion: workplace interventions for job stress

The extant literature supports the general effectiveness of primary, secondary, and tertiary stress interventions as means of reducing job stress and the negative consequences of exposure to job stressors. Given that each intervention may not always be possible, or effective, for all stressors, it is clear that a comprehensive approach to the issue of job stress should include all three forms of intervention. Pragmatically, the only way that organizations can reduce their risk exposure and resulting organizational costs is to implement effective programs aimed at prevention (i.e. primary intervention), buffering or remediation (i.e. secondary intervention), and treatment (i.e. tertiary intervention). A comprehensive approach to stress management involves multiple activities at multiple levels of intervention.

One interesting sidelight emerged from our review. Previous reviews have generally expressed a preference for primary as opposed to secondary or tertiary interventions (e.g. Kelloway and Day, 2005b; Sauter *et al.*, 1990). Kelloway and Day (2005b: 296) expressed a common view by stating:

Few would debate the necessity for effective treatment of mental disorders and mental diseases. To do so would be simply irresponsible because there always will be an ongoing need in organizations for the services of employee assistance programs, stress management programs, lifestyle programs, and the full range of interventions designed to enhance individual well-being. A sole focus on treatment, however, will limit us to continually "healing the wounded." A complementary initiative should focus on primary intervention, in which organizations focus on reducing workplace stressors.

Ideologically, we continue to support this statement. Morally, we believe that the elimination and reduction of stressors must remain a primary focus because it is simply wrong to do otherwise. Sufficient data have accumulated to conclude that job stressors are risk factors for individual health (Sauter *et al.*, 1990), and the reduction or elimination of preventable risk is a cornerstone of modern occupational health and safety programming. Despite these beliefs, we are struck by the paucity of empirical evidence supporting the effectiveness of primary intervention. More specifically, we are chagrined to find little empirical support for our preference for primary prevention over secondary and tertiary interventions.

Beyond the triad: the role of countervailing interventions

For the most part, work stress interventions have been classifiable according to the schema of primary, secondary, and tertiary interventions outlined in this chapter. The focus, therefore, has been on the reduction of stressors, mitigating the impact of stressors, or ameliorating the outcome of stressors (i.e. strain). We suggest that this focus is limited and that researchers should consider the need and effectiveness of what we term "countervailing interventions."

We define countervailing interventions as interventions that are focused on increasing the positive experience of work rather than decreasing the negative aspects. This approach is important and viable to improving well-being at work for several reasons. First, enhancing the positive experience of work is consistent with an emergent body of literature on organizational behavior showing that the work environment can substantially enhance well-being (Luthans, 2002). Based on the principles of positive psychology, Luthans (2002) identified characteristics such as hope, self-efficacy, and optimism as qualities that can be influenced by the workplace and that are essential to well-being. Interventions that enhance these aspects of well-being may provide a powerful countervailing force that counteracts the effect of workplace stressors. Second, some research has suggested that mental health is a function of the ratio of positive to negative experiences (Fredrickson and Losada, 2005), and, by extension, interventions that enhance positive work experiences would change the ratio in favor of enhanced mental health. Third, our proposal that researchers consider countervailing interventions is consistent with empirical observations that positive experiences in the workplace, such as trust in management (Harvey, Kelloway, and Duncan-Leiper, 2003) and being exposed to positive leadership styles (Arnold, Barling, Turner, Kelloway, and McKee, in press), predict well-being.

The range of what might be considered a countervailing intervention may be quite broad, and we can look at both the applied and empirical literatures for suggestions. However, more research must thoroughly evaluate the effectiveness of such policies.

There also are programs that focus on promoting positive attitudes and "fun" at work (e.g. Lundin, Paul, and Christensen, 2000), although there has been little or no research that empirically evaluates specific programs. However, research on the positive effects of social support on health and productivity (e.g. Baruch-Feldman, Brondolo, Ben-Dayan, and Schwartz, 2002) may inform future research on developing supportive environments as a countervailing intervention. Moreover, although the evidence surrounding humor and laughter with health has been inconclusive (see Martin, 2001, for a review), future research on their health benefits (using more rigorous research methods and designs) is worth pursuing (Martin, 2001). Techniques are also emerging from both the literature on positive psychology (Seligman, Steen, Park, and Peterson, 2005) and the psychotherapy literature (e.g. Wong, 2006) that may inform the development of countervailing interventions in organizations.

Final thoughts

To call for more field experimentation and rigorous evaluation of interventions is hardly novel (cf. Giga *et al.*, 2003; Murphy and Sauter, 2003). It is doubtful whether any review of the stress literature in the past twenty years has not made at least passing reference to the predominance of passive observational research designs. As researchers, we are well aware of the trials and tribulations of attempting intervention studies in real organizations and in real time. Our experience in conducting organizational research suggests that it will rarely be possible to evaluate real interventions without lingering doubts due to other organizational changes, the temporal duration of effects, or the potential influence of any one of a host of threats to internal validity. Nonetheless, our experience both as researchers and as employees suggests that this research is vital to the promotion of well-being and the prevention of stress related disorders in the workplace.

Acknowledgements

All three authors are affiliated with the CN Centre for Occupational Health and Safety. Preparation of this chapter was supported by grants from the Nova Scotia Health Research Fund and the Social Sciences and Humanities Research Council of Canada.

References

Aldana, S. G. (2001). Financial impact of health promotion programs: a comprehensive review of the literature. *American Journal of Health Promotion* 15: 296–320.

American Institute of Stress (2002). *Job stress*. New York: American Institute of Stress.

Arnold, K., Barling, J., Turner, N., Kelloway, E. K., and McKee, M. (in press). Transformational leadership and well-being: the mediating role of meaningful work. *Journal of Occupational Health Psychology*.

Aust, B. and Ducki, A. (2004). Comprehensive health promotion interventions at the workplace: experiences with health circles in Germany. *Journal of Occupational Health Psychology* 9: 258–70.

Baltes, B. B., Briggs, T. E., Huff, J. W., Wright, J. A., and Neuman, G. A. (1999). Flexible and compressed workweek schedules: a meta-analysis of their effects on work-related criteria. *Journal of Applied Psychology* 84: 496–513.

Barlow, L. and Iverson, R. D. (2005). Workplace safety. In J. Barling, E. K. Kelloway, and M. R. Frone (eds.), *Handbook of work stress* (pp. 247–65). Thousand Oaks, CA: Sage.

Baruch-Feldman, C., Brondolo, E., Ben-Dayan, D., and Schwartz, J. (2002). Sources of social support and burnout, job satisfaction, and productivity. *Journal of Occupational Health Psychology* 7: 84–93.

Beaton, R., Johnson, L. C., Infield, S., Ollis, T., and Bond, G. (2001). Outcomes of a leadership intervention for a metropolitan fire department. *Psychological Reports* 88: 1049–66.

Beehr, T. A. and Glazer, S. (2005). Organizational role stress. In J. Barling, E. K. Kelloway, and M. R. Frone (eds.), *Handbook of work stress* (pp. 7–34). Thousand Oaks, CA: Sage.

Bekker, M. H. J., Nijssen, A., and Hens, G. (2001). Stress prevention training: sex differences in types of stressors, coping and training effects. *Stress and Health* 17: 207–19.

Bellavia, G. M. and Frone, M. R. (2005). Work–family conflict. In J. Barling, E. K. Kelloway, and M. R. Frone (eds.), *Handbook of work stress* (pp. 113–47). Thousand Oaks, CA: Sage.

Bond, F. W. and Bunce, D. (2001). Job control mediates changes in a work reorganization intervention for stress reduction. *Journal of Occupational Health Psychology* 6: 290–302.

Bond, J. T., Galinsky, E., and Swanberg, J. E. (1997). *The 1997 national study of the changing workforce*. New York: Families and Work Institute.

Bower, P., Rowland, N., and Hardy, R. (2003). The clinical effectiveness of counseling in primary care: a systematic review and meta-analysis. *Psychological Medicine* 33: 203–15.

Campbell, D. (1973). A program to reduce coronary heart disease risk by altering job stresses. Unpublished doctoral dissertation, University of Michigan, Ann Arbor.

Cartwright, S. and Cooper, C. L. (1997). *Managing workplace stress.* Thousand Oaks, CA: Sage.

(2005). Individually targeted interventions. In J. Barling, E. K. Kelloway, and M. R. Frone (eds.), *Handbook of work stress* (pp. 607–21). Thousand Oaks, CA: Sage.

Chisholm, R. F., Kasl, S. V., and Muller, L. (1986). The effects of social support on nuclear worker responses to the Three Mile Island incident. *Journal of Occupational Behavior* 7: 179–93.

Cooper, C. L. and Cartwright, S. (1994). Stress-management interventions in the workplace: stress counselling and stress audits. *British Journal of Guidance and Counselling* 22: 65–73.

Corneil, W., Beaton, R., Murphy, S., Johnson, C., and Pike, K. (1999). Exposure to traumatic incidents and prevalence of posttraumatic stress symptomology in urban firefighters in two countries. *Journal of Occupational Health Psychology* 4: 131–41.

DeFrank, R. S. and Cooper, C. L. (1987). Worksite stress management interventions: their effectiveness and conceptualization. *Journal of Managerial Psychology* 2: 4–10.

Dunham, R. B., Pierce, J. L., and Castaneda, M. B. (1987). Alternative work schedules: two field quasi-experiments. *Personnel Psychology* 40: 215–42.

Ehlers, A. and Clark, D. M. (2003). Early psychological interventions for adult survivors of trauma: a review. *Biological Psychiatry* 53: 817–26.

Evans, G. W., Johansson, G., and Rydstedt, L. (1999). Hassles on the job: a study of a job intervention with urban bus drivers. *Journal of Organizational Behavior* 20: 199–208.

Everly, G. S., Jr. (1986). An introduction to occupational health psychology. In P. A. Keller and L. G. Ritt (eds.), *Innovations in clinical practice: a source book* (vol. 5, pp. 331–8). Sarasota, FL: Professional Resource Exchange.

Fredrickson, B. L. and Losada, B. F. (2005). Positive affect and the complex dynamics of human flourishing. *American Psychologist* 60: 678–86.

Galinsky, T. L., Swanson, N. G., Sauter, S. L., Hurrell, J. J. Jr., and Schleifer, L. M. (2000). A field study of supplementary rest breaks for data-entry operators. *Ergonomics* 43: 622–38.

Ganster, D. C. (1995). Interventions for building healthy organizations. In L. R. Murphy, J. R. Hurrell, S. L. Sauter and G. P. Keita (eds.), *Job stress interventions* (pp. 323–36). Washington, DC: American Psychological Association.

Gebhardt, D. L. and Crump, C. E. (1990). Employee fitness and wellness programs in the workplace. *American Psychologist* 45: 262–72.

Giga, S., Faragher, B., and Cooper, C. L. (2002). *Identification of good practice in stress prevention /management: a state of the art review.* University of Manchester

Institute of Science and Technology, Report commissioned by the UK Health and Safety Executive, Report 4301/R54.082.

Giga, S. I., Noblet, A. J., and Cooper, C. L. (2003). The UK perspective: a review of research on organisational stress management interventions. *Australian Psychologist* 38: 158–64.

Gottlieb, B., Kelloway, E. K., and Barham, E. J. (1998). *Flexible work arrangements: managing the work–family boundary*. Chichester: John Wiley and Sons.

Griffeth, R. W. (1985). Moderation of the effects of job enrichment by participation: a longitudinal field experiment. *Organizational Behavior and Human Decision Making Processes* 35: 73–93.

Harvey, S., Kelloway, E. K., and Duncan-Leiper, L. (2003). Trust in management as a buffer of the relationships between overload and strain. *Journal of Occupational Health Psychology* 8: 306–15.

Heaney, C. A., Israel, B. A., Schurman, S. J., Baker, E. A., House, J. S., and Hugentobler, M. (1993). Industrial relations, worksite stress reduction, and employee well-being: a participatory action research investigation. *Journal of Organizational Behavior* 14: 495–510.

Hepburn, C. G., Loughlin, C. A., and Barling, J. (1997). Coping with chronic work stress. In B. H. Gottlieb (ed.), *Coping with chronic work stress* (pp. 343–66). New York: Plenum Press.

Hodge, M., Robinson, C., Boehmer, J., and Klein, S. (2000). Employee outcomes following work-site acupressure and massage. *Massage Therapy Journal* 39: 48–64.

Hurrell, J. J. (2005) Organizational stress interventions. In J. Barling, E. K. Kelloway, and M. R. Frone (eds.), *Handbook of work stress* (pp. 623–46). Thousand Oaks, CA: Sage.

(2006). Critical incident stress debriefing and workplace violence. In E. K. Kelloway, J. Barling, and J. J. Hurrell (eds.), *Handbook of workplace violence* (pp. 535–48). Thousand Oaks, CA: Sage.

Hurrell, J. J., Jr. and Kelloway, E. K. (in press). Psychological job stress. In W. N. Rom (ed.), *Environmental and occupational medicine* (4th edn). New York: Lippincott-Raven.

Hurrell, J. J., Jr. and Murphy, L. R. (1996). Occupational stress intervention. *American Journal of Industrial Medicine* 29: 338–41.

Ivancevich, J. M. and Lyon, H. L. (1977). The shortened workweek: a field experiment. *Journal of Applied Psychology* 62: 34–7.

Ivancevich, J. and Matteson, M. T. (1986). Organizational level stress management interventions: a review of recommendations. *Journal of Organizational Behavior Management* 8: 229–48.

Jackson, S. E. (1983). Participation in decision making as a strategy for reducing job-related strain. *Journal of Applied Psychology* 68: 3–19.

Jex, S. M. (1998). *Stress and job performance: theory research and implications for managerial practice*. Thousand Oaks, CA: Sage.

Jex, S. M. and Beehr, T. A. (1991). Emerging theoretical and methodological issues in the study of work-related stress. In K. M. Rowland and G. R. Ferris (eds.), *Research in personnel and human resources management* (vol. 9, pp. 311–65). Greenwich, CT: JAI Press.

Jex, S. M. and Crossley, C. D. (2005). Organizational consequences. In J. Barling, E. K. Kelloway, and M. R. Frone (eds.), *Handbook of work stress* (pp. 575–600). Thousand Oaks, CA: Sage.

Karasek, R. A. and Theorell, T. (1990). *Healthy work: stress productivity and the reconstruction of working life.* New York: Basic Books.

Kawakami, N., Araki, S., Kawashima, M., Masumoto, T., and Hayashi, T. (1997). Effects of work-related stress reduction on depressive symptoms among Japanese blue collar workers. *Scandinavian Journal of Work, Environment and Health* 23: 54–9.

Kelloway, E. K. and Barling, J. (1991). Job characteristics, role stress and mental health. *Journal of Occupational Psychology* 64: 291–304.

Kelloway, E. K., Barling, J., and Hurrell, J. J. (2006). *Handbook of workplace violence.* Thousand Oaks, CA: Sage.

Kelloway, E. K. and Day, A. L. (2005a). Building healthy organizations: what we know so far. *Canadian Journal of Behavioural Science* 37: 223–36.

    (2005b). Building healthy organizations: where we need to be. *Canadian Journal of Behavioural Science* 37: 309–12.

Kelloway, E. K., Francis, L., Catano, V. M., Cameron, J., and Day, A. (2004). *Psychological disorders in the Canadian Forces: legal and social issues.* Contractor's Report. National Defence Headquarters. Ottawa, ON: Director Human Resources Research and Evaluation.

Kelloway, E. K., Francis, L., and Montgomery, J. (2005a). *Management of occupational health and safety* (3rd edn). Toronto: Nelson.

Kelloway, E. K., Sivanathan, N., Francis, L., and Barling, J. (2005b). Poor leadership. In J. Barling, E. K. Kelloway, and M. R. Frone (eds.), *Handbook of work stress* (pp. 89–112). Thousand Oaks, CA: Sage.

Keyes, J. B. (1995). Stress inoculation training for staff working with persons with mental retardation: a model program. In L. R. Murphy, J. J. Hurrell, Jr., S. L. Sauter, and G. P. Keita (eds.), *Job stress interventions* (pp. 45–56). Washington, DC: American Psychological Association.

Kim, J. S. and Campagna, A. F. (1981). Effects of flextime on employee attendance and performance. *Academy of Management Journal* 24: 729–41.

Kompier, M. and Cooper, C. L. (1999). *Preventing stress, improving productivity: European case studies in the workplace.* London: Routledge.

Kushnir, T. and Malkinson, R. (1993). A rational-emotive group intervention for preventing and coping with stress amongst safety officers. *Journal of Rational-Emotive Cognitive-Behavior Therapy* 11: 195–206.

Lambert, M. J. and Bergin, A. E. (1994). The effectiveness of psychotherapy. In A. E. Bergin and S. L. Garfield (eds.), *Handbook of psychotherapy and behavior change* (pp. 143–89). New York: John Wiley & Sons.

Landsbergis, P. A. and Vivona-Vaughan, E. (1995). Evaluation of an occupational stress intervention in a public health agency. *Journal of Organizational Behavior* 16: 29–49.

Landy, F., Quick, J. C., and Kasl, S. (1994). Work, stress, and well-being. *International Journal of Stress Management* 1: 33–73.

Lindquist, T. L. and Cooper, C. L. (1999). Using lifestyle and coping to reduce job stress and improve health in "at risk" office workers. *Stress Medicine* 15: 143–52.

Lowe, G. S. (2003). *Healthy workplaces and productivity: a discussion paper.* Ottawa: Minister of Public Works and Government Services.

Lundin, S. C., Paul, H., and Christensen, J. (2000) *FISH: a remarkable way to boost morale and improve results.* New York: Hyperion.

Luthans, F. (2002). The need for and meaning of positive organization behavior. *Journal of Organizational Behavior* 23: 695–706.

Martin, R. A. (2001). Humor, laughter, and physical health: methodological issues and research findings. *Psychological Bulletin* 127: 504–19.

Matteson, M. T. and Ivancevich, J. M. (1982). *Managing job stress and health: the intelligent person's guide.* New York: Free Press.

(1988). Health promotion at work. In C. L. Cooper and I. Robertson (eds.), *International review of industrial and organizational psychology* (pp. 279–306). Oxford: John Wiley & Sons.

McNally, R. J., Bryant, R. A., and Ehlers, A. (2003). Does psychological intervention promote recovery from post traumatic stress? *Psychological Science in the Public Interest* 4: 45–79.

Meijman, T. F., Mulder, G., vanDormolen, M., and Cremer, R. (1992). Workload of driving examiners: a psychosocial field study. In H. Kragt (ed.), *Enhancing industrial performance: experiences of integrating human factors* (pp. 245–58). London: Taylor and Francis.

Mikkelsen, A., Saksvik, P. O., and Landsbergis, P. (2000). The impact of a participatory organizational intervention on job stress in a community health care institution. *Work and Stress* 14: 156–70.

Mio, J. S. and Goishi, C. K. (1988). The employee assistance program: raising productivity by lifting constraints. In P. Whitney and R. B. Ochsman (eds.), *Psychology and productivity* (pp. 105–25). New York: Plenum Press.

Moyer, C. A., Rounds, J., and Hannum, J. W. (2004). A meta-analysis of massage therapy research. *Psychological Bulletin* 130: 3–18.

Mullen, J., Kelley, E., and Kelloway, E. K. (in press). Health and well-being outcomes of the work family interface. In K. Korabik, D. Lero, and D. Whitehead (eds.), *Handbook of work and family.* New York: Elsevier.

Murphy, L. R. and Cooper, C. L. (2000). *Healthy and productive work: an international perspective.* London: Taylor & Francis.

Murphy, L. R. and Sauter, S. L. (2003). The USA perspective: current issues and trends in the management of work stress. *Australian Psychologist* 38: 151–7.

Narayanan, V. K. and Nath, R. (1982). A field test of some attitudinal and behavioral consequences of flextime. *Journal of Applied Psychology* 67: 214–18.

(1984). The influence of group cohesiveness on some changes induced by flextime: a quasi-experiment. *Journal of Applied Behavioral Science* 20: 265–72.

National Institute for Occupational Safety and Health (2004). *Worker health chartbook.* Cincinnati, OH: NIOSH.

Parkes, K. R. (1995). The effects of objective workload on cognitive performance in a field setting: a two-period cross-over trial. *Applied Cognitive Psychology* 9: 153–7.

Parkes, K. R., Broadbent, D. E., Johnston, D., Rendall, D., Matthews, J., and Smith, A. P. (1986). *Occupational stress among driving examiners: a study of the*

440   *Kelloway, Hurrell, and Day*

effects of workload reduction. Final report and recommendations. Prepared under HSE commission, 1/MS/126/158/79. Department of Experimental Psychology, University of Oxford.

Parkes, K. R. and Sparkes, T. J. (1998). *Organizational interventions to reduce work stress: are they effective? A review of the literature.* Oxford: University of Oxford, Health and Safety Executive, Contract Report No. 193/198.

Popple, P. R. (1981). Social work in business and industry. *Social Services Review* 6: 257–69.

Pratt, L. I. and Barling, J. (1988). Differentiating between daily events, acute and chronic stressors: a framework and its implications. In J. J. Hurrell, L. R. Murphy, S. L. Sauter, and C. L. Cooper (eds.), *Occupational stress: issues and development in research* (pp. 41–53). London: Taylor & Francis.

Probst, T. M. (2005). Economic stressors. In J. Barling, E. K. Kelloway, and M. R. Frone (eds.), *Handbook of work stress* (pp. 267–98). Thousand Oaks, CA: Sage.

Quick, J. C., Quick, J. D., Nelson, D. L., and Hurrell, J. J., Jr. (1997). *Preventive stress management in organizations.* Washington, DC: American Psychological Association.

Reynolds, S. (1997). Psychological well-being at work: is prevention better than cure? *Journal of Psychosomatic Research* 1: 93–102.

Riedel, J. E., Baase, C., Hymel, P., Lynch, W., McCabe, M., Mercer, W. R., and Peterson, K. (2001). The effect of disease prevention and health promotion on workplace productivity: a literature review. *American Journal of Health Promotion* 15: 167–90.

Saltzstein, A. L., Ting, Y., and Saltzstein, G. H. (2001). Work–family balance and job satisfaction: the impact of family-friendly policies on attitudes of Federal Government employees. *Public Administration Review* 61: 452–63.

Sauter, S. L., Murphy, L. R., and Hurrell, J. J., Jr. (1990). Prevention of work-related psychological disorders: a national strategy proposed by the National Institute for Occupational Safety and Health (NIOSH). *American Psychologist* 45: 1146–58.

Schat, A. C. H. and Kelloway, E. K. (2002). Reducing the adverse consequences of workplace aggression and violence: the buffering effects of organizational support. *Journal of Occupational Health Psychology* 8: 110–22.

(2005). Workplace aggression. In J. Barling, E. K. Kelloway, and M. R. Frone (eds.), *Handbook of work stress* (pp. 189–218). Thousand Oaks, CA: Sage.

Schaubroeck, J., Ganster D. C., Sime, W. E., and Ditman, D. (1993). A field experiment testing supervisory role clarification. *Personnel Psychology* 46: 1–25.

Schweiger, D. M. and DeNisi, A. S. (1991). Communications with employees following a merger: a longitudinal field experiment. *Academy of Management Journal* 34: 110–35.

Seligman, M. E. P., Steen, T. A., Park, N., and Peterson, C. (2005) Positive psychology progress: empirical validation of interventions. *American Psychologist* 60: 410–21.

Terra, N. (1995). The prevention of job stress by redesigning jobs and implementing self-regulating teams. In L. R. Murphy, J. J. Hurrell Jr., S. L. Sauter, and G. P. Keita (eds.), *Job stress interventions* (pp. 265–81). Washington, DC: American Psychological Association.

Theorell, T., Emdad, R., Arnetz, B., and Weingarten, A. (2001). Employee effects of an educational program for managers at an insurance company. *Psychosomatic Medicine* 63: 724–33.

Thomason, J. A., and Pond, S. B. (1995). Effects of instruction on stress management skills and self-management skills among blue-collar employees. In L. R. Murphy, J. J. Hurrell Jr., S. L. Sauter, and G. P. Keita (eds.), *Job stress interventions* (pp. 7–20). Washington, DC: American Psychological Association.

Totterdell, P. (2005). Work schedules. In J. Barling, E. K. Kelloway, and M. R. Frone (eds.), *Handbook of workstress* (pp. 35–62). Thousand Oaks, CA: Sage.

Wahlstedt, K. G. I. and Edling, C. (1997). Organizational changes at a postal sorting terminal: their effects upon work satisfaction, psychosomatic complaints, and sick leave. *Work and Stress* 11: 279–91.

Wall, T. D. and Clegg, C. W. (1981). A longitudinal study of group work redesign. *Journal of Occupational Behavior* 2: 31–49.

Wall, T. D., Corbett, J. M., Martin, R., Clegg, C. W., and Jackson, P. R. (1990). Advanced manufacturing technology, work design, and performance: a change study. *Journal of Applied Psychology* 75: 691–7.

Wall, T. D., Kemp, N. J., Jackson, P. R., and Clegg, C. W. (1986). Outcomes of autonomous workgroups: a long-term field experiment. *Academy of Management Journal* 29: 280–304.

Whatmore, L., Cartwright, S. and Cooper, C. L. (1999). United Kingdom: an evaluation of a stress management programme in the public sector. In M. Kompier and C. Cooper (eds.), *Preventing stress, improving productivity: European case studies in the workplace*. London: Routledge.

Wiholm, C., Arnetz, B., and Berg, M. (2000). The impact of stress management on computer related skin problems. *Stress Medicine* 16: 279–85.

Winzelberg, A. J. and Luskin, F. M. (1999). The effect of meditation on stress levels in secondary school teachers. *Stress Medicine* 15: 69–79.

Wong, Y. J. (2006). Strength-centered therapy: a social constructionist, virtues-based psychotherapy. *Psychotherapy: Theory, Research, Practice, Training* 43: 133–46.

Index

Lightning Source UK Ltd.
Milton Keynes UK
15 January 2011

165784UK00001B/39/P